Ideas and Mechanism

Ideas and Mechanism

ESSAYS ON

EARLY MODERN PHILOSOPHY

• *MARGARET DAULER WILSON* •

PRINCETON UNIVERSITY PRESS

PRINCETON, NEW JERSEY

Portions of this book have been previously published in slightly different versions.
A list of sources and acknowledgments appears at the back of the book.

Library of Congress Cataloging-in-Publication Data

Wilson, Margaret Dauler.
Ideas and mechanism : essays on early modern philosophy / by
Margaret Dauler Wilson.
p.   cm.
Includes bibliographical references and index.
ISBN 0-691-00470-6 (cloth : alk. paper). — ISBN 0-691-00471-4
(pbk. : alk. paper)
1. Philosophy, Modern.   2. Descartes, René, 1596–1650.
3. Berkeley, George, 1685–1753.   4. Leibniz, Gottfried Wilhelm,
Freiherr von, 1646–1716.   I. Title.
B791.W53   1999   190'.9'032—dc21   98-35153   CIP

This book has been composed in Times Roman

The paper used in this publication meets the minimum requirements
of ANSI/NISO Z39.48-1992 (R 1997) (Permanence of Paper)

http://pup.princeton.edu

Printed in the United States of America

1   3   5   7   9   10   8   6   4   2

1   3   5   7   9   10   8   6   4   2
(pbk.)

· *FOR EMMETT* ·

• C O N T E N T S •

THE ESSAYS in this collection were written over a period of about thirty years. Nearly all have been separately published. "The Issue of 'Common Sensibles' in Berkeley's *New Theory of Vision*" is the main exception: it is published here for the first time. "True and Immutable Natures" appears here for the first time in English, although it was previously published in Portuguese translation. I haven't made any effort to update or otherwise alter the content of the papers (except for one note in one paper correcting a misstatement of a particular interpretation of Locke).

There has, of course, been an enormous accumulation of valuable work on early modern philosophy of science in the period spanned by these essays. None of the less recent papers (at least) could be written today just as it is presented here. I have no doubt that some papers show their age in ways that will actually be uncomfortable to knowledgeable readers. Some have been the subject of searching critical commentary. However, all the essays I have included do seem to me still viable to a reasonable degree, from one point of view or another.

I hope that the arrangement of the essays in this book will help to bring out certain interesting linking issues about the interpretation and understanding of major early modern philosophers, especially on topics in metaphysics and philosophy of mind. At one time I had thought of trying to explain in some kind of systematic way a few long-term preoccupations of mine that underlie many of the papers. But I found I was unable to do that effectively, without detracting from the specific inquiries and arguments of the individual papers; so in the end I put the idea of striving for generalities aside. It should be obvious, however, that a principal focus—evident from the first chapter, and reflected in the title of the volume—is the relation of mental representation or contents to a physical world conceived mechanistically.[1] It has long seemed to me that the many difficulties presented by this relationship are far more important to most of the major systems of the period—even including Berkeley's—than any obsession with epistemological "foundationalism," or questions generated from within "ordinary experience" (which at least at one time tended to receive interpretive emphasis). A few chapters deal with the closely related but distinct topic of the status of "the mind" in relation to "the (human) body." Two recent essays are concerned with early modern views about the mental capacities of "brutes." Several chapters have to do with problems about necessity, causality, and contingency, or with a priori knowledge (interests that go back to my doctoral thesis on Leibniz).

Although the collection contains a lot of papers—more, perhaps than the Press originally envisaged—I would like to take this chance to mention a few of the omitted ones (for different reasons). One of the readers for the Press regret-

ted—or at least wondered about—the omission of "Cartesian Dualism," originally published in *Descartes: A Collection of Critical Essays*, edited by Michael Hooker (Baltimore: Johns Hopkins University Press, 1978). Although I
appreciated the reader's expression of continuing interest in that article, I still
think it is sufficiently available both in its original publication, and as section 2
of chapter 6 of my book *Descartes* (London: Routledge and Kegan Paul, 1978),
that another separate publication is not really needed. "Spinoza's Theory of
Knowledge," my contribution to the *Cambridge Companion to Spinoza*, edited
by Don Garrett (Cambridge: Cambridge University Press, 1996), seemed for
various reasons (including length) unsuitable to be reproduced here; yet it does
represent a fairly extensive development of ideas implicit in two or three of the
Spinoza papers that I include. Finally, I left out with some regret a paper I
presented several times as a general lecture, "Pascal and Spinoza on Salvation:
Two Views of the Thinking Reed," because of its impressionistic nature. I remain interested in the topic of the paper, though, especially the interrelations
and contrasts between Pascal and Spinoza on the subjects of finitude and death.
An edited version was published in the *Harvard Graduate Society Newsletter*,
Fall 1992, pp. 8–13).[2]

Neither Princeton University Press nor I thought it necessary or really useful
to recast the innumerable citations in order to render the format consistent
across all the papers. However, minor changes have been made here and there
to try to reduce distracting anomalies in abbreviations from paper to paper. A
list of abbreviations for major or frequently cited works is provided below.
Perhaps the most awkward remaining anomalies are found in the various forms
of citations of Propositions, Corollaries, and so on from Spinoza's *Ethics*.
Again, the effort needed to homogenize these seemed prohibitive, given the
limited improvement in intuitive comprehension that I might expect to achieve.
A fuller explanation can be found in the abbreviations list. Naturally, some of
the earlier papers cite editions of works of the major philosophers that have
since been superseded. I hope these references are adequately covered by internal references and the initial list of abbreviations.

In a few cases up-to-date publication data have replaced references to "forthcoming" papers, which may have appeared in print after the publication of the
essays in which they are cited. I'm afraid there remain many minor stylistic
anomalies—which, again, could have been corrected only at the cost of too
much time and effort for the little gain in elegance to be achieved. Among these
is the form of possessives. For instance, the possessive of "Descartes" is sometimes written here with an extra "s" and sometimes not. I am personally convinced that "Descartes's" is the only defensible form in an English language
essay, but I have frequently been overridden by editors and others.

Although the general idea of publishing a collection like this has been floating
around for a few years, it took the timely, energetic, and selfless intervention of
my friend Anne Jaap Jacobson in the winter of 1997–1998 to start to move the
project toward reality. Anne has continued to provide many kinds of assistance
and support through the intervening period, despite her own very extensive

academic responsibilities. There is no way I can adequately express my grati-
tude. I only hope that the result will seem to her reasonably worth all her time
and efforts.

Ann Wald, editor-in-chief of Princeton University Press, has also provided
extraordinary help and support. The quick and friendly responsiveness of Ann,
and her assistant Kristin Gager, to every kind of question and worry helped
bring the project together much more expeditiously than I would have thought
possible. Molan Chun Goldstein oversaw the production of the volume; and the
copy-editing assignment fell to Margaret Case, whose work was a lesson in
precision. I cordially thank them both. I'm also grateful to Carol Roberts for
preparing the index.

Princeton University, particularly its Philosophy Department, has supported
this project, along with all my other work since 1970, in many generous ways.
During a large part of the period from then till now Paul Benacerraf has served
as Chair of the department. I want to take this opportunity to thank Paul for his
many kindnesses toward me. John Cooper also served as Chair at a time when
support was needed for particular arrangements conducive to my work, and I
thank him, too, for his help and savvy.

John Carriero and Kenneth Winkler provided detailed, valuable comments
that significantly affected the content and structure of the volume. Catherine
Wilson quite inadvertently and unknowingly caused the inclusion of a Leibniz
paper that would otherwise have been left out.

Shawn Travis helped in some major ways with the final preparation of the
manuscript, including (among other things) the effort to reduce confusion of
abbreviations, and notice of mistakes and missing information that would otherwise have been overlooked. He also helped to keep me in good cheer. Steve
Todd, under the supervision of Anne Jacobson, took care of the initial task of
writing for permissions to republish thirty papers. Marie Leiggi helped in many
ways, ranging from copying, to locating books and papers, to delivering material to the Press. Ann Getson, of the Princeton Philosophy Department staff, has
provided superb secretarial help for many years, and above all has been a won-
derful friend.

The period during which this volume was produced has been exceptionally
difficult for reasons of ill health. Besides the individuals mentioned above,
many others have provided all kinds of moral support, which have made it
possible to complete the project. I want especially to mention my colleague
Beatrice Longuenesse—for the peanut butter cookies, among many other
things. And finally, my husband Emmett, who helped make what could have
been a dismal time one of the most engaging of my life. I dedicate the book to
him, with love.[3]

NOTES

1. The mechanism characteristic of the new science of the seventeeth century may be
briefly characterized as follows: Mechanists held that all macroscopic bodily phenomena

result from the motions and impacts of submicroscopic particles, or corpuscles, each of which can be fully characterized in terms of a strictly limited range of (primary) properties: size, shape, motion, and, perhaps, solidity or impenetrability.

2. The published version is marred by the accidental omission of a crucial piece of the quotation from Pascal in the middle of the far right column on page 10 (the famous "thinking reed" passage). The correct reading of the affected part is as follows: "But even if the universe were to crush him, man would still be nobler than his slayer, because he knows that he is dying, and the advantage the universe has over him. The universe knows none of this. Thus all our dignity. . . ."

3. Margeret Wilson was unable to see this book through the final stages of its production. In addition to those thanked above, Laurence Carlin, who greatly helped with proofreading, and Lisa Downing, who provided the content of note 1 above as Margeret requested, deserve thanks for their contributions to the completion of this important project.—AJJ

THE FOLLOWING list includes abbreviations of editions and individual works of major philosophers that are used in this collection, as well as a small number of secondary works. Abbreviations are listed under the names of the major figures, presented in alphabetical order.

BERKELEY

The following abbreviations are used to refer to particular works of Berkeley:

Dialogues	*Three Dialogues between Hylas and Philonous*
NTV	*New Theory of Vision*
PC	*Philosophical Commentaries*
PHK	*A Treatise Concerning the Principles of Human Knowledge*
TVV	*Theory of Vision Vindicated*

Most citations are for the following standard edition of Berkeley's texts:

Works   *The Works of George Berkeley, Bishop of Cloyne*, edited by A. Luce and T. Jessop, 9 vols. (London: Thomas Nelson, 1948–1957).

Some *PC* citations are from the following edition:

Philosophical Commentaries by George Berkeley, edited by G. H. Thomas (New York: Garland, 1989; reprint of 1976 edition).

The following abbreviation is also used:

BRV   *Berkeley's Revolution in Vision*, by M. Atherton (Ithaca: Cornell University Press, 1990).

DESCARTES

Standard edition of Descartes's texts:

AT   *Oeuvres de Descartes*, edited by C. Adam and P. Tannery, 12 vols. (Paris: Cerf, 1897–1913; reprinted Paris: J. Vrin, 1964–1976).

Standard English edition:

CSM   *The Philosophical Writings of Descartes*, translated by J. Cottingham, R. Stoothoff, and D. Murdoch, 2 vols. (Cambridge: Cambridge University Press, 1984).

Standard English edition of Descartes's letters:

CSM-K   Volume 3 of the preceding, by the same translators and A. Kenney (Cambridge: Cambridge University Press, 1991).

Former standard English edition of Descartes's texts:

HR   *The Philosophical Works of Descartes*, translated by E. Haldane and G. Ross, 2 vols. (Cambridge: Cambridge University Press, 1911; reprinted with corrections 1931).

Former standard English edition of Descartes's letters:

PL   *Descartes: Philosophical Letters*, translated by A. Kenny (Oxford: Clarendon Press, 1970).

The following abbreviations are used to refer to particular works of Descartes:

CB	*Conversation with Burman*
Diop	*Dioptrics*
Med	*Meditations*
NiP	*Notae in Programma* (formerly known as *Notes against a Program*, but translated by CSM as *Comments on a Certain Broadsheet*)
O	*Discourse on Method, Optics, Geometry, and Meteorology*, translated by P. Olscamp (Indianapolis: Bobbs-Merrill, 1965).
PP	*Principles of Philosophy*
PS	*Passions of the Soul*
RO	*Replies to Objections* (to the *Meditations*)
Rules	*Rules for the Direction of the Mind*
TL	*Treatise on Light*
TM	*Treatise on Man*

For citations from *CB* that are followed by page numbers not preceded by either "AT" or "CSM," references are to:

Descartes' Conversation with Burman, translated by J. Cottingham (Oxford: Clarendon Press, 1976).

For citations from *O* that are followed by page numbers not preceded by either "AT" or "CSM," references are to:

> *Discourse on Method, Optics, Geometry, and Meteorology*, translated by P. Olscamp (Indianapolis: Bobbs-Merrill, 1965).

For citations from *TM* that are followed by "H," references are to:

H   *Treatise of Man*, translated by T. S. Hall (Cambridge: Harvard University Press, 1972).

Some references include the following abbreviations:

LV   Latin version
FV   French version

HUME

Citations use the following abbreviation and refer to the following edition:

Treatise   *Treatise of Human Nature*, edited by L. Selby-Bigge (Oxford: Clarendon Press, 1888).

KANT

Standard critical edition of Kant's works:

> *Kant's gesammelte Schriften*, edited by the Deutsche Akademie der Wissenschaften, 29 vols. (Berlin: George Reimer, subsequently Walter de Gruyter, 1900–).

The following English language editions are cited:

> *Critique of Pure Reason*, translated by N. K. Smith, 2nd edition (London: Macmillan, 1933).
> *Prolegomena to Any Future Metaphysics*, translated by L. Beck (Indianapolis: Bobbs-Merrill, 1950).

The following abbreviations are used to refer to particular works of Kant:

Prolegomena   *Prolegomena to Any Future Metaphysics*
Critique   *Critique of Pure Reason*

Citations to the *Critique* include references to page numbers in Kant's first ("A") and second ("B") editions. If both A and B page numbers are cited, then the passage appears in both editions; otherwise, the passage appears in just the edition cited.

LEIBNIZ

Abbreviations for editions of Leibniz's texts include:

DA
G. W. Leibniz: Sämtliche Schriften und Briefe, edited by Deutsche Akademie der Wissenschaften zu Berlin (Berlin: Akademie Verlag, 1923–).
References are to series and volume.

Ger
Die Philosophischen Schriften von Leibniz, edited by C. Gerhardt, 7 vols. (Berlin: Weidmann, 1875–90; reprinted Hildesheim: Olms, 1965).

GM
Leibnizens Mathematische Schriften, edited by C. Gerhardt, 7 vols. (Berlin and Halle: Schmidt, 1848–63; reprinted Hildesheim: Olms, 1962).

Grua
Leibniz: Textes inédits, edited by Gaston Grua, 2 vols. (Paris: Presses Universitaires de France, 1948).

LA
The Leibniz-Arnauld Correspondence, translated by H. Mason (Manchester: Manchester University Press, 1967).

Langley
New Essays on Human Understanding, edited by A. Langley, 2nd edition (New York: Open Court, 1916).

Loemker
G. W. Leibniz: Philosophical Papers and Letters, translated and edited by L. Loemker, 2nd edition (Dordrecht: Reidel, 1969).

Lucas & Grint
Discourse on Metaphysics, translated by P. Lucas and L. Grint (Manchester: Manchester University Press, 1953).

Wiener
Leibniz: Selections, edited by P. Wiener (New York: Scribner's, 1951).

Additional abbreviations:

DM; Discourse
Discourse on Metaphysics

Naert
Memoire et conscience de soi selon Leibniz, E. Naert (Paris: Vrin, 1961).

NE
Nouveaux essais sur l'entendement humain (New Essays on Human Understanding)

References to the NE are by chapter and section, followed by the edition (DA or Langley) and page number.

LOCKE

The following abbreviations are used to refer to particular works of Locke:

CS	*Correspondence with the Bishop of Worcester* (i.e., Stillingfleet)
EM	*Examination of P. Malebranche's Opinion of Seeing All Things in God*
Essay	*An Essay Concerning Human Understanding*
TE	*Thoughts Concerning Education*

References to the *Essay* usually cite the Nidditch edition, though some cite *The Works of John Locke* edition. References to *CS, EM*, and *TE* cite *The Works of John Locke* edition, volumes IV, IX, and IX, respectively.

> *The Works of John Locke* (London: Otridge, 1812; reprinted 1964).
>
> *An Essay Concerning Human Understanding*, edited by P. Nidditch (Oxford: Clarendon Press, 1960; reprinted 1975).

An occasional reference to the *Essay* cites an edition edited by Fraser. These references are marked as follows:

Essay (F)	*Essay Concerning Human Understanding*, edited by A.C. Fraser (New York: Dover, 1959).

MALEBRANCHE

Editions principally consulted for these essays:

> *Oeuvres*, edited by G. Rodis-Lewis (Paris: Gallimard, 1979–   ).
>
> *Oeuvres complètes*, edited by A. Robinet (Paris: J. Vrin, 1958–1970).

The following abbreviation is used:

Search	*Search for Truth*

SPINOZA

Standard edition of Spinoza's texts:

Geb	*Spinoza Opera*, edited by C. Gebhardt, 4 vols. (Heidelberg: Carl Winter, 1925).

References to Geb are made by volume, page, and line(s). For example, Geb II/308/26 (or a variant, such as Geb II, 308, 26) refers to volume two, page 308, line 26 of Geb.

Current standard English edition of Spinoza's texts:

> *The Collected Works of Spinoza*, translated by E. Curley, 2 vols. (Princeton: Princeton University Press, 1985 [vol. 1] and forthcoming [vol. 2]).

Former standard English edition of Spinoza's letters:

Wolf   *The Correspondence of Spinoza*, translated by A. Wolf (London: Frank Cass, 1966).

The following abbreviations are used to refer to particular works of Spinoza:

E	*Ethica*
	(*Ethics*)
TTP	*Tractatus Theologico-Politicus*
	(*Theologico-Political Treatise*)

The following abbreviations are used to refer to particular elements of *E*:

Ax; A	Axiom
C	Corollary
Def; D	Definition
Dm; D	Demonstration
P	Proposition
S	Scholium

References to *E* are of the following form: *E* IVP42S (or a close variant, such as *E* IV, P42, S), which refers to the Scholium to Proposition 42 of Part IV of *E* (less close variants may occasionally occur; it is hoped that they will still be sufficiently perspicuous). If the abbreviation "D" is preceded by a number and the abbreviation "P", then it refers to the demonstration for the numbered proposition; otherwise, it refers to a definition. For example, *E* IIP7D (or *E* IIP7Dm) refers to the Demonstration of Proposition 7 of Part II of *E*, whereas *E* IID1 (or *E* IIDef1) refers to Definition 1 of Part II of *E*.

Ideas and Mechanism

Skepticism without Indubitability

IN *Philosophy and the Mirror of Nature* Richard Rorty traces the emergence of "foundationalist epistemology . . . as the paradigm of philosophy."[1] According to Rorty, a key step in this development was Descartes's un-Aristotelian construal of "sensory grasp of particulars" as "mental" (54). The resulting conception of the mind as "an inner arena with its inner observer" "permitted" the seventeenth century "to pose the problem of the veil of ideas, the problem which made epistemology central to philosophy" (51). Thus Descartes, by "carving out inner space," "simultaneously made possible veil-of-ideas skepticism and a discipline devoted to circumventing such skepticism" (140).

In seeking to account for Descartes's fateful introduction of an account of sense perception focused on ideas of sense, Rorty tentatively appeals to an apparently idiosyncratic Cartesian preoccupation with "indubitability" (55). Although Descartes himself sought the foundations of knowledge in distinct ideas of reason rather than in sensory particulars, the move to empiricistic foundationalism was readily accomplished by Locke, on Rorty's account. On the Cartesian model, adapted by Locke, the Eye of the Mind is restricted to surveying the ideas or representations in inner space, "hoping to find some mark which will testify to their fidelity" to extra-mental reality (45).

Rorty is surely right that a strong distinction or contrast between sensations or "ideas of sense," on the one hand, and external physical things on the other hand, emerges as central doctrine in seventeenth-century philosophy. Further, the distinction is, as he indicates, closely connected with both the modern mind-body problem and certain sorts of skeptical reasoning. It is also true that both Descartes and Locke speak of knowledge as requiring a "foundation" in indubitable ideas. Nevertheless, there is a crucial element missing from Rorty's account of seventeenth-century concerns: an element that is also omitted or slighted by many other critics who either look back on the period from the dubious vantage of twentieth-century sense-data theories, or look forward (so to speak) from the standpoint of ancient skepticism. I have in mind the fact that the seventeenth-century contrast between ideas of sense and physical things at least partly derives from the conception of material reality provided by mechanistic science, and the disparity between this conception of reality and the seeming givens of ordinary perceptual experience.[2]

I

Underlying seventeenth-century accounts of perception is the metaphysical view that "real and physical" qualities include just extension, figure, motion, and (for some) impenetrability or solidity (together with structural qualities such as texture, which result from combining extended particles in various ways). Proceeding from this conception of material reality, philosophers of the period espouse a broad theory of perception that includes the following basic tenets:

1. In ordinary sense experience certain entities arise "in us" or "in the mind." These entities are variously referred to as "ideas of sense," "sensations," "images," "phantasms," or (rarely) "species."

2. These sensory ideas (as I shall call them) are formed in the mind as the result of mechanistic processes, involving (characteristically) material things external to our bodies, and the sensory-systems of our bodies themselves.

3. Sensory ideas correlate with discrete sensible qualities, like blue, soft, putrid. In Locke's words, they "enter by the senses simple and unmixed," even though the qualities that produce them are "united and blended" in the things themselves.

4. Whole classes of the sensory ideas formed in our minds—ideas of colors and tastes, for instance—are completely "unlike" the material things we are ordinarily said to perceive, or any qualities really in the things. This tenet is universally regarded as contrary to common sense.

5. We do apprehend real qualities of material things, through our representations of size, shape, and motion. Not all philosophers clearly indicate whether our representations of the latter qualities are always sensory ideas, and there is not much unanimity among those who do take positions on this point.

The theory constituted by these five tenets is vigorously propounded by Hobbes, Malebranche, and Boyle, as well as Descartes and Locke. They commonly ascribe to the conception of physical reality that underlies this view of perception an a priori or essentialist grounding in "the concept of body." Descartes, Boyle, and others also stress the *explanatory success* of strictly mechanistic concepts in accounting for perception, as well as the other phenomena of nature.

The relations between this general account of perception and skeptical concerns are complex. Here I wish to distinguish two separate connections. In the next section I focus on the notion, implicit in tenet 4, that human beings in general are systematically and literally constantly deceived in ordinary sense experience. Seventeenth-century philosophers employ skeptical arguments in aid of this conviction: to this extent the arguments function instrumentally, and depend on a confident background conception of the true nature of material things. In the third section I consider more closely some relations among the characteristic seventeenth-century account of sense perception, the "veil-of-perception" position (which has its proponents today), and non-instrumental skepticism.

Approached from the perspective of theory of nature and the resulting conception of perceptual experience, the problem of sensory contact with the external world that arises in seventeenth-century thought appears both more readily intelligible and less tightly dependent on preoccupations with justification and

certainty than is often supposed. Accordingly, the problem does not automatically vanish if we follow Rorty in rejecting, as anachronistic or artificial,
attempts to "ground" empirical knowledge claims in an indubitable sensory
given.

II

A typical statement of the distinction between ideas of sense and physical quality occurs in the following passage from Malebranche:

> In order . . . to judge soundly about light and colors, as well as all the other sensible
> qualities, one must distinguish with care the sensation [*sentiment*] of color from the
> movement of the optic nerve, and recognize by reason, that movements and impul-
> sions are the properties of bodies, and that hence they can be encountered in the
> objects, and in the organs of our senses; but light, and the colors that we see, are
> modifications of the soul quite different from the others, and of which we also have
> quite different ideas.[3]

Of course seventeenth-century writers often acknowledge interpretations of a
statement like "the violet is blue" on which this statement comes out literally
true: in saying that the violet is blue we may be predicating of it a certain
superficial microstructure, or a "power" deriving from such a surface structure
to affect sentient beings with a particular sort of sensation. Nevertheless they
steadfastly maintain that such qualities in objects are utterly different from—
fail to "resemble"—sensory appearances. Thus, they *do* deny that colors and so
forth are in objects in the way that we normally take them to be—as real,
discrete, irreducible qualities, manifest in sense experiences, and on a footing
with size and shape. Contrary to Malebranche's admonition, we do not normally judge soundly about colors, smells, tastes, sounds, and the like, but (as
Locke says) "by mistake attribute" reality to them. Indeed we are peculiarly
obstinate in our error: "Men are hardly to be brought to think, that *Sweetness
and Whiteness are not really in Manna*."[4] The same point is expressed, in quite
similar terms, by Descartes, Malebranche, Hobbes, and Boyle.

   This sort of universal "deception" is of much more than passing concern. The
widespread human error about the objectivity of sensible qualities is generally
felt to require some kind of explanation, and even to raise problems of theodicy.
Descartes elaborately traces such errors to habits arising in infancy, and to a
tendency simply to conflate mere sensations—intended to alert us to things
good or bad in the environment—with our "clear" perceptions of physically
real qualities.[5] Malebranche, who develops a quite complex analysis of perceptual judgment and error, locates a source of the basic problem in the fall of
Adam.[6] Hobbes offers a *physical* explanation of our tendency to project sensations on things in terms of the "endeavor outward" that he takes to be characteristic of sensory processes.[7] (Some of these philosophers also discuss ways of
overcoming such "error.")

The claim that the senses constantly—not just episodically—lead us into error about physical reality provides an important perspective for understanding the stress on skeptical arguments in seventeenth-century work. In Descartes and Malebranche, in particular, such arguments are overtly used to shake our faith in the senses, as purveyors of objective truth. "Detachment from sense" is of course not a professed aim of empiricists like Hobbes or Locke. Still Locke and other writers draw on the relativity considerations associated with traditional skepticism to underscore the subjectivity of certain broad classes of sensory states, to which their theory of reality independently commits them.

From this perspective, relativity arguments, Descartes's dreaming argument, and other attacks on the senses, appear to be propounded for a decent dogmatic purpose. Their role is neither to convert us to an equinanimous agnosticism, nor to focus our attention on our indubitable "inner sensory representations" with the aim of building from them to well-founded objective knowledge claims. They are intended to prepare us to accept the austere "new" truths about what the world around us is really like in the face of our natural resistance.

III

The tenets of the view of sense perception I outlined above do not explicitly include either the claim that sensory ideas are states of "mental substances" or the claim that the mind perceives (or immediately perceives) only its own ideas. In fact, historically, this conception of sense perception is not invariably accompanied by the latter claims. Hobbes, for example, definitely maintains that we perceive physical objects, not the sensory "phantasms" they produce in us.[8] Further, he holds that all substances are bodies, and explicitly identifies phantasms with motions in the sensory system. Despite this fact, the account of perception that arises from the mechanistic picture of nature does help illuminate—more, I think, than any preoccupation with indubitability or epistemological foundations—the systematic origins of the veil-of-perception position.

It *is*, as we've seen, an explicit feature of the widely shared seventeenth-century view that we err in thinking of colors-as-experienced (for example) as real qualities of bodies. What are they then? Hobbes's bold identification of sensory experiences with material states of the sentient organism was a far from unproblematic move—as recent decades of debate of the materialist identity thesis have surely made clear. It seems understandable enough that Descartes and some of his successors should conclude that colors and other "mere sensations" are no more to be identified with states of the nervous system than with "external" physical qualities—and see no alternative to construing them as merely mental entities. Further, while Descartes does connect this interpretation of the status of sensations with indubitability in the *Meditations*, consideration of the early parts of the *Treatise on Light* and the *Dioptrics* (for instance) shows that he by no means invariably does so. (Malebranche is merely restating Cartesian assumptions when he remarks that the true understanding of the difference between mind and body was achieved only "in the last few years," when it came to be appreciated that "sensible qualities" *are not contained in the idea of matter.)*[9]

The view that we do not perceive—or immediately perceive—physical objects is sometimes said to be a "presupposition" or a logical consequence of the seventeenth-century distinction between sensory ideas of color and the like, on the one hand, and the real qualities of bodies on the other hand.[10] I believe that this is an overstatement: one can consistently give a Hobbesian account of perceptual experience in terms of phantasms, without taking the step of holding that we *perceive* phantasms. But there *is* a fairly simple path to the view that what the Eye of the Mind perceives are its own ideas, from the account of perception summarized above. The key notion is that when we think we are looking at, listening to, touching (etc.) the world we after all do perceive colors, sounds, warmth, and cold, etc. But colors, sounds, warmth, and cold, etc. are merely ideas or sensations in the mind. Therefore, what we perceive in these cases, at least, are (properly) ideas. This, I take it, is the viewpoint behind the following classic Cartesian statement of the veil-of-perception position:

> . . . [B]esides the extension, figures, and motion of bodies, I also sensed in them hardness, and heat, and other tactile qualities; and further light, and colors, and odors, and tastes, and sounds, from the variety of which I distinguished heaven, earth, sea, and other bodies from each other. And surely it was not without reason, on account of the ideas of all these qualities which offered themselves to my thought, and which alone I properly and immediately sensed, I thought I sensed certain things completely different from my thought, namely bodies from which these ideas proceeded.[11]

Admittedly, the reasoning sketched so far does not explicitly cover figure, motion, and other qualities that (on the mechanistic hypothesis) "are not otherwise sensed or understood by us than they are, or at least can be in objects."[12] There are various considerations that would tend to support the inclusion of perceptions of such qualities in the "veil" theory: the consideration, for instance, that sensibly experienced shapes and so on are pervaded by the qualities regarded s thoroughly subjective, like color. As mentioned under tenet 5, however, this is a textually complex issue; and I cannot fully deal with it here.

The account so far offered indicates why—apart from preoccupation with indubitability or foundationalism—Descartes and his successors would tend to treat sensory grasp of particulars as falling within the realm of the mental; why they might tend to consider our immediate perceptions as failing to provide *direct* cognitive contact with physical reality; and why they would seek to instill doubt of the senses. The question that remains to be considered is whether this perspective on the veil-of-perception position suggests any connection with skepticism of a noninstrumental sort.

Now, I think in fact concern with "circumventing" veil-of-perception skepticism—or seeking internal marks of "fidelity" in inner representations of sense—is far from rampant in seventeenth-century philosophy. (Incidentally, such concern is arguably more noticeable in Descartes and Malebranche than in Locke.) This observation fits with the tendencies to untroubled perceptual realism which have often been discerned in the period and with the notion that the veil-of-perception position is correlative to a positive theory of nature. Nevertheless, it seems to me that the position does permit—even, ultimately, support—a very perplexed attitude toward our sensory contact with the world, whether or not seventeenth-century theorists themselves exhibit serious perplexity about this problem. Berkeley put his finger on the crucial point when he objected that the materialists, for all their emphasis upon explanatory success, in fact could offer no intelligible explanation of how sensory ideas are produced by matter.[13]

Suppose that someone who accepts the proposition that the immediate objects of perception are mental, requests an account of how exactly the sensory particulars that he immediately perceives are connected with, serve to relate him cognitively to, real things out there. The cheerful Boylean or Lockean answer—heard again in recent years[14]—is that the things *produce* the ideas via our sensory systems; Descartes, in his more searching moments, holds that changes in the brain serve as signs to the mind, giving it "occasion" to generate sensations.[15] The latter view leaves unilluminated the central step of the mind's receiving signs from the brain, and to this extent seems dismissible as a vague metaphor. The simpler language of causal production seems more plausible, more commonsensical, even scientific. However, I am inclined to think that this appearance is deceptive.

According to proponents of the veil-of-perception view our sensations are remotely caused or explained by the physical objects that we indirectly perceive; proximately they are caused or explained by material changes in our brains. Against the objection that the position leads to skepticism because of a problem in principle about postulating "unobserved causes," recent advocates have argued (with some reference to scientific procedure) that such postulation is fully justified when it is explanatorily effective.[16] But this brings us back to the question whether an intelligible explanation of sensation in terms of (say) brain states is in fact available or (at least) imaginable. In the seventeenth century the question took the form of consternation about how body acts on mind, as well as indications that inference from sensory ideas to their putative explanatory causes is peculiarly problematic. Today we find objections to the notion of psychophysical laws. Although these objections are not usually related specifically to perception, they do serve to raise doubts about the ultimate intelligibility of the veil-of-perception position. (Can we, for instance, tolerate the possibility that *all our immediate objects of perception* are "nomological danglers"?[17]) There are also more specific problems. For instance, considered from the physical side, the causal chain said to result in ideas of sense seems literally to go nowhere. The qualia we perceive (ideas of sense) by hypothesis are not qualities of physical things; one may presumably infer that they are not locatable in physical space. If so, it follows at least that a Humean conception of causal relations including a contiguity condition cannot be fulfilled.

Such reasons for questioning the intelligibility of the relation between our immediate objects of perception and material things, as portrayed by the veil-of-perception theory, are no more tied to preoccupation with foundationalist epistemology than the position itself is strictly the offspring of a chimerical quest for certainty. And I think they are sufficient for skepticism of a sort.

Notes

Presented in an APA symposium on Skepticism, December 28, 1984. Barry Stroud was co-symposiast, and Robert Fogelin commented; see *Journal of Philosophy*, LXXXI, 10 (October 1984), 545–551 and 552, respectively, for their contributions.

1. Princeton, N.J.: University Press, 1979, p. 59. Subsequent page references are given in the text.

2. Of course numerous historians have stressed this point, but its importance continues to be overlooked, particularly by epistemologically oriented commentators.

3. *Search for Truth*, I, xii, 5.

4. *Essay*, II, viii, 14, 18.

5. *PP*, I, 67/8.

6. *Search*, I, v, 1 and 2; I, xii, 2.

7. Cf. *Leviathan*, I, i.

8. *Concerning Body*, xxv, 3, 10. Hobbes does sometimes speak of phantasms as "proper objects of the senses."

9. *Search*, Preface [N. Malebranche, *Oeuvres*, I. ed. G. Rodis-Lewis (Paris: Gallimard, 1979)], p. 13.

10. Cf. J. L. Mackie, *Problems from Locke* (New York: Oxford, 1976), p. 7.

11. Meditation VI, AT, vol. VII, pp. 74/5.

12. Decartes, *PP* I, 70.

13. See, e.g., *PHK*, I, 50.

14. Cf. Frank Jackson, *Perception* (New York: Cambridge, 1977), p. 126 and *passim*.

15. Cf. *NiP*, AT VIII-2, 358/9.

16. Cf. Mackie, *op. cit.*, ch. 2, and 7; *op. cit.*, ch. 6.

17. J. J. C. Smart argues for this conception of "irreducibly psychic" sensations in "Sensations and Brain Processes," *Philosophical Review*, LXVIII, 2 (April 1959): 141–156.

Descartes on Sense and "Resemblance"

DESCARTES begins the *Meditations* with the stated purpose of overthrowing those of his 'former beliefs' that allow of doubt, in the hope of erecting in their place a 'firm and permanent' scientific structure. His first step is to withdraw his 'trust' from the senses, on the grounds that they have sometimes 'deceived' him. 'Whatever I have up to now accepted as most true, I have received either from the senses or through the senses; however, I have sometimes found these to deceive; and it is prudent never to trust completely those who have deceived us even once' (AT VII 18).[1] In the Sixth Meditation, tracing his progress from naïve 'faith' in the senses to scepticism concerning their deliverances, he writes:

> afterwards many experiences gradually destroyed all the faith that I had in my senses; for I from time to time observed that towers which from a distance looked round, appeared square from close up, and that enormous statues standing on their pediments did not seem large when viewed from the ground; and in these and countless other such cases I found that judgements of the external senses were mistaken. (AT VII 76)

Readers of the *Meditations*, focusing on passages such as these, have often concluded that Descartes's basic 'sceptical' point concerning the senses' inadequacy is grounded on ordinary daily experience: discrepancies that arise among our 'perceptions' when we perceive the same thing under different circumstances—at small and at great distances, for example—show that we cannot regard a judgement as certain beyond any doubt, merely because we take it to express what we have seen or otherwise perceived by sense. According to this point of view, Descartes introduces 'sensory ideas' as the indubitable residue that remains when judgements about external objects are called into question. In fact, though (as is now widely recognized), Descartes is aiming at a broader and more radical form of 'detachment from sense'—one that seems to carry with it the postulation of sensory ideas quite apart from any issues about 'certainty'. He wants to establish that sense experiences actually work *against* a true or reliable conception of what there is: that we cannot *in general* rely on our senses to reveal to us the nature of things.

One reason Descartes regards sense experience as an inadequate means for achieving knowledge of reality is that he holds that the real does not reduce to the physical or corporeal, but includes incorporeal and hence absolutely non-sensible entities: God and the thinking self. More to the point here, though, is his contention that the senses generally fail to provide us with an accurate or reliable conception of the nature or qualities of *physical things themselves*, of the bodies around us. True, our knowledge that such things *exist* ultimately depends on their having some effect on our sense organs and brain—and through the latter some effect on our minds. Also he takes it that variations in our sense experience correspond with *some kind* of differences in external things. Beyond that, however, the ordinary sense-based conception of the physical world (which, Descartes implies, gains its hold on us in unwary childhood) is inherently and broadly mistaken and confused: it amounts to a constant and pervasive 'deception of sense'.

Descartes asserts this position particularly insistently and directly in the *Principles of Philosophy*. The following passage is representative:

> the perceptions of sense . . . do not, except occasionally and accidentally, teach us what external bodies are like in themselves. Thus . . . we may easily set aside the prejudices of the senses, and in this matter rely on the intellect alone, attending carefully to the ideas with which it is endowed by nature. (*PP*, pt. II, art. 3: AT VIIIA 41–2).

Many familiar passages in the *Meditations* convey a similar message. Apart from providing the basis of our knowledge of the *existence* of a physical world, and of the legitimate claim that this world includes a variety of material states, the senses seem to be limited to the role of preserving the mind-body union, by alerting us to what is good or bad for us—considered as embodied beings—in the environment. In the Sixth Meditation Descartes particularly insists that one must not rely on the senses beyond this appointed role, 'as though they were certain rules for immediately discerning the essence of bodies located outside us'; for about this 'they only indicate what is most obscure and confused' (AT VII 83). Knowledge of the truth about bodies pertains to 'mind alone', and not mind and body in conjunction (AT VII 82–3).

Of course the supposed deliverance of 'the mind' concerning the nature of matter and bodies coincides with the basic concepts of Descartes's mechanistic science. To understand and explain what goes on in the physical world, Descartes holds, we must clearly realize that bodies are merely bits of extension, with their particular figures, and particular motions relative to each other. This insight requires firmly grasping the distinction between manifest perceptual experience and the scientific reality: between mere sensory ideas in the mind, on the one hand, and the quantities in bodies, on the other hand. (But the global contrast between perceptual phenomenology and 'real' physical things is not necessarily dependent on the more naïve and obsolete features of the Cartesian theory of matter.)

Descartes characteristically expresses this distinction by denying that his sensory ideas—which, he says, are present to his mind, and 'immediately sensed'—'resemble' bodies, or are 'similar' to them. For example, he notes in the Third Meditation that the 'principal and most common error' that is found in his judgements consists in 'the fact that I judge that the ideas [of sense] which are in me are similar or conformable to certain things located outside me' (AT VII 37). The following passage (which occurs a little earlier in the Third Meditation) presents this view a bit more expansively:

I have before received and admitted many things to be very certain and manifest, which yet afterwards I found to be doubtful. What then were these things? They were the earth, sky, stars and all other things which I apprehended by the senses. But what did I clearly perceive of them? Just that the ideas or thoughts of such things appeared before my mind. [*Nempe ipsas talium rerum ideas, sive cogitationes, menti meae obversari.*] But even now I do not deny that these ideas are in me. But there was something else which I used to affirm, and which, because of the habit of believing, I judged that I perceived clearly, which nevertheless I did not perceive, that there were certain things outside of me from which these ideas proceeded, and to which they were entirely similar. (AT VII 35).

Here Descartes ascribes to himself (and by implication to others) *the views that*, first, sense experience involves the presence of such 'ideas' to the mind; and, secondly, that the ideas 'resemble' external objects from which they also 'proceed'. The former view is said to be genuinely 'clearly perceived'—i.e. (one may here gloss) evidently and reliably apprehended to be so. The latter view, however, is only speciously 'clear', is not genuinely evident, or reliably apprehended. A few pages later Descartes suggests that the unfortunate habit of belief in the 'resemblance' of our ideas to external objects that produce them arises from nothing more than 'blind impulse' (AT VII 40). A slightly more rationalized view of the origin of this erroneous assumption about perceptual experience emerges in the Sixth Meditation, where Descartes comments:

Outside me, besides the extension, figure, and movements of bodies, I also sensed in them hardness, heat, and other tactile qualities, and further, light, and colours, and odours, and tastes and sounds, from the variety of which I distinguished the sky, the earth, the sea, and generally all the other bodies from each other. And surely it was not without reason that, from the ideas of all these qualities which offered themselves to thought, and which alone I properly and immediately sensed, I believed that I sensed certain things completely different from my thought, namely bodies from which these ideas proceeded . . . [*Nec sane absque ratione, ob ideas istarum omnium qualitatum quae cogitationi meae se offerebant, & quas solas proprie & immediate sentiebam, putabam me sentire res quasdam a mea cogitatione plane diversas, nempe corpora a quibus ideae istae procederent . . .*] (AT VII 74–5)

The first 'reason' Descartes mentions here is that he is not able to bring about or prevent the occurrence of such ideas. He continues:

And since the ideas perceived by sense were much more vivid and lively, and even in their own way more distinct than any of those which I formed by knowing meditation . . . it did not seem possible that they proceeded from myself; and thus it had to be the case that they came from some other things. And since I had no other knowledge of such things except from these very ideas, nothing else could come to my mind than that the things were similar to the ideas. (AT VII 75).

But even if the belief in 'resemblance' is to this extent natural and understandable, further critical reflection will establish that it is simply not rationally tenable: there is simply *no good* reason to suppose that there is in a white or green body 'the same whiteness or greenness that I sense'; or that there exists in fire 'anything resembling heat' (any more than there is reason to suppose that there exists in fire something similar to the pain that I experience if I approach too closely) (AT VII 82–3). With respect to the fire all I have *reason* to believe is that 'there is something in it, whatever it may be', which excites the sensations of heat (or pain) in me. Closely parallel passages occur in the *Principles*. For example, in pt. I, art. 66, Descartes remarks that, 'when we saw a certain colour, we thought we saw some thing which was located outside of us and completely similar to the idea of colour that we were then experiencing in ourselves . . .' (AT VIIIA 32).

Jonathan Bennett has popularized the expression 'veil-of-perception theory' as a characterization of conceptions of sense perception which turn on the notion that (mental) 'ideas', and not bodies or their qualities, are the immediate or direct objects of awareness in sense experience.[2] Statements such as those I have just quoted from Descartes certainly appear to put him in the veil-of-perception camp. It is only ideas or thoughts that are present to his mind in sense experience. In so far as he relies on sense, these ideas seem to provide all the information he has to go on in trying to size up (what he assumes to be) the things around him. And while the ideas are taken to give him some contact with an independent physical world, they do not enable him to apprehend the actual qualities (or 'essence') of bodies.

In fact these passages, and others found almost up to the end of the *Meditations*, seem to convey a largely *negative and purgative* approach to sense experience: only when we have accepted the view of the senses as thoroughly and systematically 'deceptive' are we in a position to make advances in physics, by replacing theories cast in terms of the old sensory, qualitative, 'confused' ideas of body with explanations formulated entirely in terms of the 'distinct', intellectual, Cartesian geometrical ones. For this reason I once suggested that the *Meditations* seems hardly to present a theory of sense perception at all, 'in the ordinary philosophical sense'.[3] (I observed in a note that of course Descartes does develop a scientific theory of perception, in the *Dioptrics* and elsewhere). I particularly mentioned that it would be misleading to label the position sketched in the Sixth Meditation a form of representative or causal realism. Certainly this observation was in no way based on a denial that Descartes's mind, in the *Meditations*, is ensconced behind a veil of (mental) ideas. I took it as obvious that passages such as those just quoted established that this was in fact his position. My point, on the contrary, was that Descartes allowed too little range for our *piercing* the veil, on the purely empirical level, to count as a 'realist' about sense perception ('representational' or otherwise).

Today, 'veil-of-perception' theories are widely regarded as absurd. (And indeed Bennett intended his designation as derogatory: it was meant, as he says, to 'express what is wrong with the theory'.[4]) Perhaps partly for this reason, there has developed a certain following for the notion that Descartes is not, after all, accurately interpreted as postulating (mental) ideas as intermediates between the mind and physical objects in sense perception. In 1983 both

Ronald Arbini and Michael J. Costa published articles opposing the interpretation of Descartes as postulating mental intermediates in our perception of
bodies.[5] Arbini focuses on Descartes's accounts of perception of size, shape,
distance, and position in the *Dioptrics* and the Sixth Replies. He suggests that
in these works Descartes explains '*how* the understanding operates together
with the senses to dispel scepticism concerning the observed properties of matter'.[6] Thus, he says, they show us how to fill out Descartes's sketchy indication,
at the end of the *Meditations*, that we can reliably determine the particular
sizes, shapes, and so on of bodies, by utilizing all the resources of memory and
intellect, joined to sense (AT VII 89). Mental 'ideas', Arbini points out, do not
significantly figure in these accounts. Costa holds that, when Descartes talks of
ideas being immediately present to the mind, he means corporeal ideas in the
brain—not some kind of mental 'image-like entity' or 'phenomenal object'.
(This may still count as a *physical* veil of ideas account—an issue I will not
further pursue.) John Yolton, in a 1975 paper (cited by Costa as supporting his
interpretive position) and in his later book, *Perceptual Acquaintance*, maintains
that for Descartes to have an idea is just *to perceive*—and I take it he means to
perceive *a physical object, directly*.[7] More recently, Ann Wilbur MacKenzie has
suggested that (for cases *other than* sensations of colour and so forth) Descartes's conception of representation provides 'the raw materials for an interesting conception of direct sensory access to the world, according to which nothing sensed or cognized in the sensory process mediates sensory awareness of
the physical object'.[8]

All of these treatments of Descartes's position on sense perception are quite
complex, and cover a wide range of Cartesian material. I am not going to
attempt a point-by-point discussion of them here.[9] I only want to reconsider, in
the light of some of the points made in this debate, the claim that Descartes's
conception of 'ideas of sense' carries with it the assumption that we do not
perceive physical entities 'directly' in ordinary sense experience. I have to confess in advance that my motivation for this effort is not so much that I find that
the works cited above have ultimately caused very much change in my views
about sense perception in the *Meditations*. But they have caused me to reexamine them, with the result that I can attempt to offer a few observations that
may be helpful in further clarifying some of the issues.

Of course it would be nice, in undertaking a discussion of this interpretive
problem, to have before us a precise statement of what is being disputed.
Shortly I will suggest that the question whether mental ideas function as 'intermediaries' in Descartes's conception of sense perception admits of varying interpretations. But for a start I will simply invoke Yolton's formulations. He
denies that mental ideas are 'entities' that intervene between the mind and perceived bodies. He holds, on the contrary, that ideas are simply 'acts' of perception.[10]

I used to think that the Sixth Meditation passage, in which Descartes says
that only ideas of colours and so forth are 'properly and immediately sensed',

counted conclusively in favour of a veil-of-perception interpretation. And, indeed, the translations both of Haldane and Rose and of Cottingham tend to enforce this impression. The former have Descartes saying 'considering the ideas of all these qualities which presented themselves to my mind, and *which alone I perceived properly or immediately* . . .'; and the latter can be read as going even further in the direction of commitment: 'Considering the ideas of all these qualities which presented themselves to my thought, although the ideas were, strictly speaking, *the only immediate objects* of my sensory awareness . . .' (emphases added).[11] (I should add, though, that, if Cottingham's insertion of 'object' seems peculiarly tendentious, he at least keeps the term 'sense' in the picture. In this respect his translation is not only closer to the text, but preserves a feature that may be crucial, for a reason I am about to mention.) I now realize, however, that I was probably misunderstanding an aspect of this passage. Descartes's account of the 'levels of sense' in the Sixth Replies gives reason to think that behind this passage from the Sixth Meditation may lie a distinction between what 'properly' belongs to *sense* (basically, the old 'special sensibles') and *perceptual states that involve intellectual or computational processes* (as do determinations of size and situation, for example, according to both the *Dioptrics* and the Sixth Replies). In the Sixth Replies, the latter forms of perception are said not strictly to belong to *sense*—even though, in deference to common ways of speaking, Descartes there classifies them as belonging to 'the third level of sense' (AT VII 437). Thus (I now think) Descartes may *not* be explicitly making the point, in the Sixth Meditation passage, that we *directly perceive ideas of sense, as opposed to physical things*. Rather, he may just be isolating what is 'properly and immediately sensed', according to terminological assumptions which distinguish what is 'proper to sense' from perception involving active intellectual processes. This reading would help to leave open the question of whether or not *physical objects or bodies* actually are (immediately or directly) 'perceived', in circumstances that *we* would count as sense perception.

Further, I think Arbini is right in asserting that Descartes's accounts of our perception of bodies' size, shape, and distance in the *Dioptrics* and the Sixth Replies to a considerable degree avoid the veil-of-perception view of external world perception as mediated by sensory ideas. In the *Dioptrics*, it is true, Descartes appeals to various 'sensations' (such as those involved in awareness of the position of the head or eyes) in explaining our ability to 'judge' such physical features as position and distance. But such sensations are treated as subliminal informational inputs, rather than as providing an intermediate, strictly 'mental' set of perceptual *objects* which our minds use as stepping stones in working outward to the actual *physical* things.[12]

Descartes's rejection of 'replica' accounts of perception in the *Dioptrics* and elsewhere may provide additional ammunition for the view that he *rejects* accounts of perception of external objects that appeal to awareness of intermediate entities. As he writes in the *Dioptrics*:

one must be careful not to suppose that, in order to sense, the mind needs to contemplate certain images which are sent by the objects to the brain, as our Philosophers commonly do; or, at least, one must conceive the nature of these images quite
differently than they do. For, besides the fact that they do not consider anything
about [the images] except that they ought to resemble the objects they represent, it
is impossible for [the Philosophers] to show us how [the images] can be formed by
these objects, received by the external sense organs, and transmitted by the nerves
to the brain. (AT VI 112)

According to Descartes, the only reason philosophers have for assuming that
sense perception of objects requires resembling images in the brain is the assumption that vision must be modelled on the bringing to mind of originals by
means of their pictorial representations: 'seeing that our thought can easily be
excited by a picture to conceive the object painted there, it seemed to them that
it must be excited in the same way to conceive those objects that touch our
senses by some little pictures that are formed in our head . . .' (AT VI 112).
'The Philosophers' suppose that perception of external objects can and must be
explained by postulating images or pictures, transmitted from the objects to the
brain, which resemble the objects, and are then perceived, 'as if there were yet
other eyes in our brain with which we could perceive them' (AT VI 130).[13] In
his ridicule of this type of theory Descartes seems to suggest both (*a*) that it is
futile to try to explain the perception of objects by postulating the perception of
some stand-ins for the objects; and (*b*) that processes invoked in the explanation
of perception need not be interpreted as being themselves *perceived*. Although
he does not deny that images formed in the brain play a role in the causal
explanation of perception, he says that the only question to be raised with
respect to such images is 'how they can give the mind the means to sense all
the different qualities of the objects to which they relate, and not at all how they
carry resemblance to them' (AT VI 113).[14] And—according to at least one line
of thought which he advocates—the fact that brain-states of whatever type regularly excite a certain type of 'thought' or sensation in the mind is due merely
to a divinely ordained concomitance or 'natural institution' (AT VI 130).[15]

Of course, Descartes's objections to the replica theory have to do with the
physical conditions of sense perception, not with the issue of whether some
kind of *mental* entities serve as intermediaries between the mind and the 'objects'. But one can see the temptation to generalize this point to the view that
he would reject *any* stand-ins, within the human being, for the external things in
theorizing about perception. If not, would he not say so? But, in fact, he does
not—in the *Dioptrics, The Treatise on Light*, the Sixth Replies, and other works
concerned with theoretical accounts of sense experience—treat perception as
involving the problematic inferences from mental to physical entities that are
characteristic of veil-of-perception views.

I think it is important to insist, though, that Descartes's objectives in the
Dioptrics and related works are really quite different, for the most part, from
the concerns of the *Meditations*. Arbini seems to scoff at the distinction, im-

plied in my earlier remarks, between 'philosophical' and 'scientific' theories of perception.[16] I agree that the distinction between 'philosophical' and 'scientific' concerns is often made too glibly—and that I took it too much for granted in my earlier remarks on Descartes's views on perception. I am certainly a great believer in the importance of Descartes's commitments as a mechanistic scientist for the interpretation of the *Meditations* in general; and I think the increased interest in the whole range of Descartes's writings—including, particularly, the 'scientific' ones—is one of the greatest improvements in Cartesian scholarship in recent decades. I even agree with Arbini that consideration of the *Dioptrics* and the Sixth Replies helps to shed a little light on Descartes's comments, towards the end of the Sixth Meditation, about the possibilities of arriving at truth concerning 'things that are particular only', such as that the sun is of a certain size (AT VII 80).

All that said, it seems to me that the sceptical issues that pervade the *Meditations* really are correctly distinguished as specifically 'philosophical'. Today, people attempting to explain the physical and physiological basis of our perceptual experience generally do not have much time for such issues as whether there really is anything 'out there' for us *to* perceive (even though one does often find more-or-less casual mention of the appearance/reality distinction at the beginning of psychological texts on perception). I see no good reason for denying to Descartes, the scientist, a similar kind of abstraction from the sceptical and scientific realist commitments addressed in the *Meditations* and certain parts of the *Principles*.

This line of thought, I suggest, leads to a delineation of grounds for a veil-of-perception reading of the Meditations which, as far as I can see, are wholly untouched by both considerations drawn from Descartes's treatment of perception in works such as the *Dioptrics* and by Yolton's discussion in *Perceptual Acquaintance* (which ultimately centres more on the *Meditations*). I do not see how there can be any legitimate question that in the *Meditations* Descartes treats knowledge of physical existence as secondary to, and inferentially derivative from, knowledge of mental ideas. Thus, in the Second Meditation he asserts (however problematically) that the indubitability of the existence of ideas is established through the indubitability of the meditator's existence as a thinking thing—while the existence of *any* physical entity is still in doubt (AT VII 27–9). Of course Descartes eventually affirms that sensory ideas depend on the mind-body union, but knowledge of their 'presence in me' is prior to any well-grounded knowledge of that union. These familiar considerations, it seems to me, establish a clear sense in which Descartes does hold a veil-of-ideas theory with respect to the perception of bodies—i.e. our knowledge that we actually perceive any bodies is dependent upon, and derived from, the epistemologically prior affirmation that we have in our minds ideas 'of them'.

A similar point can be made with respect to Descartes's conception of the 'objective reality' of ideas (prominent in the Third Meditation), on which Yolton places particular stress. Yolton holds, with some textual basis, that the objective reality of an idea for Descartes is just the (immediate) presence to the mind of an object: thus, he interprets, 'to have an idea is just to perceive'.[17] In one sense this may be true, and it may well provide a basis (as Yolton holds) for distinguishing Descartes's conception of the idea-object relation from Malebranche's, helping to give one legitimate sense to the claim that awareness of objects is 'immediate' for Descartes. Nevertheless, in whatever sense Descartes wishes to maintain that the objective reality of his ideas involves the presence of objects to his mind, it *has* to be compatible with another sense in which it does not. That is, Descartes can know all about the objective as well as the formal aspects of his ideas, *without yet knowing whether any extra-mental entities exist.*

Perhaps another sense can be given to the claim that Descartes holds a veil-of-perception theory, apart from issues of epistemic priority and inference. The proposal I have in mind depends on how we answer the question whether or not he takes colour sensations (and the others on the list quoted above) in any way to *represent* physical qualities (in the sense of presenting them, or having objective content). Some have held that he does *not*: Ann MacKenzie, for instance, who regards as decisive Descartes's remark in the *Principles* that such sensations 'represent nothing outside thought'.[18] Now Descartes seems to indicate in a passage I have quoted from the Sixth Meditation (AT VII 74–5) that such sensations are necessary for our perceptually distinguishing physical things from each other. Well, one may reason, if colour sensations, and the others, do not even represent anything outside the mind, yet are essential to our distinguishing of bodies in sense perception, then here is *another* sense, apparently distinct from issues about the order of certainty, in which perception of physical things is strictly mediated by purely mental entities. That is, our ability to perceive the diversity of bodies around us is mediated (on this view) by our awareness of mere mental modes with a strictly external, causal relation to the bodies they somehow help us discriminate. In still other words, because of the nature and role of sensations, Cartesian ideas of bodies cannot after all be fully understood merely as acts of perception in which bodies are immediately grasped, or 'present to the mind'.

(Yolton summarizes the role of sensation in discrimination at the end of his chapter on Descartes in the following way:

> Perceptual discriminations (*a*) do not require any entities (particles or images) to be transmitted from object to perceiver; (*b*) do not require any similarities between idea and object; (*c*) are made on the basis of sensations felt by the perceiver; and (*d*) those sensations are a response to or an interpretation of natural signs, i.e. motions in the environment that are duplicated in nerves and brain.[19]

This is an accurate, concise statement of Descartes's general position in the *Dioptrics* and elsewhere. But the observation that, for Descartes, discrimination of bodies depends on 'sensations felt by the perceiver' seems to raise serious questions for Yolton's interpretive claim that perception of physical things is not supposed to involve intermediate mental entities.)

I am not sure how much emphasis I want to put on this argument. For one thing, Descartes's conception of the role of mere sensation in perceptual discrimination of bodies is not very clearly developed.[20] For another, I myself have come to doubt whether Descartes ever intends strictly to deny that sensations do in some limited sense represent (in the sense of 'present') the physical qualities that are their external causes (spinning of particles, in the case of colour). My main reason for this reservation (which involves a change in view from what I say in my book) is that even in the *Principles* he continues to talk of sensations as 'confused images'; and to me this terminology strongly suggests some kind of objective presentation.[21] Even so, I think the argument helps to articulate somewhat precisely the intuition—expressed, for instance, by John Mackie in *Problems from Locke*—that the mechanists' insistence on a pervasive difference and contrast between sensory ideas and bodies as they really are implies a denial that sensory awareness of bodies is 'direct'.[22] To put the point briefly, the contrast between sensory experience and real qualities drives the mechanists to an understanding of sensations ('ideas of secondary qualities') as purely mental entities, without objective content. To the extent that sensations are still ascribed an important role in the discrimination of bodies, however, we are left indeed with mental intermediaries between our perceiving minds and the external physical things.

Finally, I want to turn briefly to the question how, exactly, Descartes's denial that sensory ideas 'resemble' qualities in bodies should be understood. As we have partly seen, Descartes, in analysing the perceptual process, emphatically denies 'resemblance' at more than one point: in fact, he denies it at three. Sensory ideas do not resemble either their 'objects', or the brain states that are the immediate causes of the ideas in thought; and the brain states do not resemble the bodies that are their (more-or-less) remote causes.

Today it may seem odd enough even to enquire whether a *brain state*—physical entity though it may be—'resembles' an external physical object such as a tree. But we know that Descartes took himself to be opposing the view that when we see trees there are fairly exact pictorial duplications of trees in our brains (to which the mind somehow has access). In any case, I am not particularly concerned here with the question whether physical things as diverse as trees and brain states can be meaningfully affirmed or denied to 'resemble' each other. Rather, I want to ask what sense can be made of the sober denial that certain mental entities or 'thoughts' 'resemble' physical qualities or states. And for the sake of brevity I will deal only with the denial that sensory ideas resemble the *objects* to which they are normally 'referred'.

As early as the *Treatise on Light* Descartes emphasizes that it is a common error to suppose that sensations 'resemble' the objects that are their (distal) physical causes: 'For although everyone is commonly persuaded that the ideas that we have in our thought are entirely similar to the objects from which they proceed, I do not at all see any reason that assures us that this is so . . .' (AT XI 3). He goes on to mention several examples of ordinary phenomena—beginning with the fact that words, while 'having no resemblance to the things that they signify do not fail to make us conceive them' (AT XI 4). Similar examples occur in the *Dioptrics* and the *Principles*, again in support of the point that what 'makes us conceive' certain objects need not resemble the objects conceived (*PP*, pt. IV, art. 197: AT VI 112–13; VIIIA 320–1). In both the *Treatise on Light* and the *Principles* Descartes notes that the reader might object that the analogy is imperfect: when we understand the meaning of words, the mind or understanding interprets the purely sensuous apprehension (but does not contribute in the same way to sense itself). In the *Treatise on Light* Descartes says this objection is not really sound: 'in just the same way it is our mind which represents to us the idea of light each time the action that signifies it touches our eye' (AT XI 4). In all three works, Descartes moves on to other examples, which I will not consider here. The observation I want to make with respect to the remarks in the *Treatise* is just that Descartes suggests that the denial of resemblance between mental and physical entities is illuminated by considering alleged non-resemblance between cause and effect *within* the realm of the mental: the thought of a tree is not at all like the experience of hearing the word 'tree', which brings it to mind. The implicit contrast, I take it, is between hearing the word, and actually seeing a picture of a tree.

Consider, then, the contrast Descartes goes on to draw in the *Treatise* between the sensation of sound and the 'true image' of the 'object' of that sensation:

> most Philosophers maintain that sound is nothing but a certain trembling (vibration) of air which comes to strike our ears; so that if the sense of hearing conveyed to our thought the true image of its object, it would have to be the case that, instead of making us conceive sound, it made us conceive the movement of the parts of air which tremble against our ears at the time. (AT XI 5).

Similarly, a gendarme whose buckle or strap is pressing him under his armour may think he has suffered a wound. No such error would be possible if 'his touch, in making him sense [*sentir*] this strap, had imprinted its image on his thought' (AT XI 6). Again, Descartes writes in the *Principles*:

> such is the nature of our mind that from the fact alone that certain motions occur in the body, it can be stimulated to have all sorts of thoughts, *carrying no image of these motions* . . . and especially those confused thoughts called sensings or sensations. (*PP*, pt. IV, art. 197: AT VIIIA 320; emphasis added)[23]

What I want to propose is, first, that Descartes's denial of 'resemblance' between his sensory ideas and the qualities of bodies after all relies to some extent on comparing mental awarenesses. Against the experience of the sensation of sound, we place the (mental) 'image' of motions of air particles. The two, phenomenally, do not 'resemble' each other. Thus, strictly, the denial of resemblance between mental and physical entities is mediated by the denial of resemblance between two *mental* entities: the *sensation*, and the mechanistic imaging of such physical qualities as light and sound. Yet of course, Descartes, in denying that sensations resemble their objects, is not principally maintaining that they fail to resemble other mental states. He is implicitly making the further point that sensations are not 'true' to their objects, in the way that mechanistic images of bodies in motion may be.

Underlying this way of understanding the resemblance issue is the assumption that physical reality *is imageable*: that it can be presented to us as it is by our imagination. Descartes does clearly to some degree maintain this view: for instance, he stresses his ability distinctly to imagine *res extensa* at the beginning of the Fifth Meditation (AT VII 63). Yet a number of passages—particularly in the *Meditations*—indicate that not all aspects even of *physical* reality can be grasped by imagination: the *understanding* is required in order for us to grasp the indefinite variability of the single piece of wax (Second Meditation); and the imagination is unable to present even specific determinate shapes if they are quite complex (in which case they can only be *understood*) (Sixth Meditation: AT VII 72–3).

Again, though Descartes does speak of distinctly *imagining*, he most commonly associates distinct (as opposed to confused) ideas or perception with the *understanding*. Thus sensations are accounted 'confused' not merely because they fail to present or exhibit to us 'true images' of external occurrences; but also because they fail to present *anything intelligible*. This view lies behind Descartes's remark in the Third Meditation, in the context of a discussion of the 'objective reality' of his various ideas, that his sensations 'exhibit so little reality' to him that he 'can scarcely distinguish it from non-being' (AT VII 44). But he particularly stresses this point in the *Principles*:

> in order that we may here distinguish that which is clear from that which is obscure we must very carefully note that we have a clear or distinct knowledge of pain, colour, and other things of the sort when we view them simply as sensations or thought. But when we judge these to be some sort of things existing outside of our minds, in no way are we able at all to understand what sort of things they are, but it is just the same, when someone says that he sees a colour in some body, or feels a pain in some limb, as if he said that he there saw or felt something but was completely ignorant of what it was, that is, that he did not know what he saw or felt. (*PP*, pt. I, art. 68: AT VIIIA 33)

This point is quickly combined with the usual observations about erroneous beliefs in 'resemblance':

> For even though, when he is less attentive, he may easily persuade himself that he has some notion of it, because he supposes that it is something similar to this sensation of colour or pain which he experiences in himself, yet if he examines what it is, that is presented by this sensation of colour or pain, as if existing in a coloured body or suffering part, he will notice that he is totally ignorant of it. (ibid.)

In the next Principle (art. 69) he observes that 'we know [*cognoscere*] in a very different way' 'what size, or shape, or motion . . . or position, or duration, or number and the like are in a body that we see' (qualities that he says are 'clearly perceived'), than we know what may be, in the same body, 'colour, or pain, or odour, or taste, or any of the other things that I have said should be referred to sense'. In article 70 he reiterates the point that our sensations do not enable us to *understand* anything about bodies:

> It is therefore evident that it is really the same, when we say that we perceive colours in objects, as if we said that we perceived something in the objects of which we are ignorant what it is, but by which is caused [*a quo efficitur*] in us this particular (*ipsis . . . quidam*) very manifest and perspicuous sensation, which is called the sensation of colour. (AT VIIIA 34)

As long as we restrict ourselves to noncommittal causal judgment, we will not go astray:

> But when we think we perceive colours in objects, although we do not know what this might be, that we are calling by the name of 'colour', and we are not able *to understand* any similarity between the colour which we suppose to be in objects and what we experience to be in sense: because we nevertheless do not notice this, and [because] there are many other [things] such as magnitude, figure, number, etc., which we clearly perceive are not otherwise sensed or *understood* by us, than they are or at least can be in objects: it is easy for us to fall into the error of judging that that, which we call colour in the objects, is something entirely similar to the colour we sense, and thus to judge that that, which we in no way perceive, is clearly perceived by us. (AT VII 34–5; emphasis added)

To say that sensations are 'confused' or 'obscure' is to say that they fail to provide a distinct *understanding* of real qualities of bodies, not merely that they fail to provide *images* of the right sort. We cannot tell by having them, or by inspecting them, what sort of configurations of parts of extension, transferring motion, give rise to them—or even that they have such a cause. Our ideas of figure, size, etc., by contrast, do afford distinct understanding of qualities as they may exist in nature.

Given the close association, in Descartes's writings, between saying sensations are 'confused' or 'obscure', and insisting that they fail to 'resemble' external things, it seems reasonable to assume that the concept of 'resemblance' should be understood partly metaphorically, and not merely pictorially. A 'nonresembling' idea, that is, should be construed as one that fails to yield intelligibility—and this may not be entirely a matter of failing to present a 'true image' of a physical cause. Conversely, on this reading, a geometer's idea of a chiliagon may 'resemble' external reality, even though (according to Descartes) we are unable to provide ourselves through imagination with a clear mental picture of a chiliagon.

And, indeed, Descartes's one *positive* statement (that I know of) about an idea resembling something physical appears to concern an *intellectual* idea: 'We clearly understand this [matter] as a thing entirely different from ourselves, or from our mind; and we also seem to see clearly that the idea of it comes to us from things located outside ourselves, to which it is entirely similar' (*PP*, pt. II, art. 1: AT VIIIA 41).[24]

Still, it would be a mistake to *under*estimate the importance of imagination and images in Descartes's conception of nature: and, correspondingly, in his conception of distinct and resembling, as opposed to confused and non-resembling ideas. Both the prominence of imagistic thinking, and the tendency to insist also on the understanding as a different and superior factor in our grasp of the world, are evident in the following revealing remark from the end of the *Principles*:

> who has ever doubted that bodies move and have various sizes and shapes, according to which diversity their motions also vary; or that from intercollision larger bodies are divided into many smaller ones and change their shapes? We find this out not just by one sense but several—sight, touch and hearing; *and we also distinctly imagine and understand it*. But the same cannot be said of the rest, such as colour, sound and so forth, which are perceived not by several senses but by one alone; *for their images in our thought are always confused, nor do we know what they are.* (*PP*, pt. IV, art. 200: AT VIIIA 323–4; emphasis added)[25]

I conclude, then, that Descartes's talk of (non-)resemblance between ideas and bodies can *partly* be interpreted in terms of the issue of a comparison between *mental* entities (sensations, images of motion); and can *partly* be interpreted metaphorically, in terms of the question whether sensations afford an *intelligible* conception of the physical objects or qualities that give rise to them. An intelligible conception of something physical may not necessarily involve a 'true image'; and, even when there is such an image, its 'truth' may involve an intellectual element that does not reduce to phenomenal presentation. I do not say that these observations are fully sufficient to counter Berkeley's riposte to the 'resemblance' terminology of his scientific realist opponents: that an idea can be 'like' nothing but an idea. But I do think that they help to place the talk of resemblance in a philosophically serious context.

In summary, I have tried here to defend the attribution of a 'veil-of-perception' theory to Descartes. In part this defence has involved distinguishing the objectives and concerns of the Meditations from those of the more 'scientifically' oriented writings on perception; in part on emphasizing the role of colour and other sensations in discriminating bodies. And, finally, I have tried to help make some sense of the talk of (non-)resemblance between ideas and bodies, which is so prominent a feature of the classic scientific realist veil-of-perception views.

NOTES

1. I take responsibility for the translations in this paper; but at the same time I wish to acknowledge that my readings have to some degree been influenced by both CSM and HR.

2. See J. Bennett, *Locke, Berkeley, Hume: Central Themes* (Oxford: Oxford University Press, 1971), 68 ff. (Bennett had already introduced this terminology in an earlier paper.)

3. M. Wilson, *Descartes* (London: Routledge and Kegan Paul, 1978), 203.

4. Bennett, *Locke, Berkeley, Hume*, 69.

5. R. Arbini, 'Did Descartes have a Philosophical Theory of Sense Perception?' *Journal of the History of Philosophy* 21 (1983), 317–37, and M. J. Costa, 'What Cartesian Ideas are not', *Journal of the History of Philosophy* 21 (1983), 537–49.

6. Arbini, 'Did Descartes have a Philosophical Theory of Sense Perception?', 319.

7. J. Yolton, 'Ideas and Knowledge in Seventeenth-Century Philosophy', in *Perceptual Acquaintance from Descartes to Reid* (Minneapolis: University of Minnesota Press, 1984) (see e.g. p. 15).

8. A. W. MacKenzie, 'Descartes on Life and Sense', 178. MacKenzie cites Yolton's 'more sweeping interpretation', in his article and his book, as an encouraging example for her own. See also B. O'Neil, *Epistemological Direct Realism in Descartes' Philosophy*, (Albuquerque: University of New Mexico Press, 1974), which Yolton discusses at some length, though critically.

9. For more detailed discussion, see my reviews of Yolton and O'Neil in, respectively, *Philosophical Review*, July 1980, 408–10; and *TLS*, August 16, 1985.

10. Yolton, *Perceptual Acquaintance*, 34–9. Yolton notes (p. 36) that in the Preface to the Reader (of the *Meditations*) Descartes indicates that 'idea' can be used in two senses: as an operation of understanding, or 'for the thing represented by that operation of the understanding'. It appears to be Yolton's position that, except in the case of God, for a thing to 'be in the understanding' is just for it to be understood: i.e. that the second sense of 'idea' involves, in general, no 'ontic' commitment. I do not find his position on this point very clearly explained or defended (see my review cited in the previous note). For a fuller discussion of the concept of 'idea' in Descartes see V. Chappell, 'The Theory of Ideas', in *Essays on Descartes' "Meditations"*, edited by A. O. Rorty (Berkeley and Los Angeles, University of California Press, 1986), 177–98.

11. HR, i 187–8; CSM II 52.

12. See especially the Sixth Discourse.

13. Descartes's satirical characterization of his predecessor's views is historically questionable. See G. Hatfield, 'Descartes' Physiology and its Relation to his Psychology', in *Cambridge Companion to Descartes*, edited by J. Cottingham (New York: Cambridge University Press, 1992), 335–70.

14. He notes that the mind can be stimulated to think of an object by words or signs that do not at all resemble it, as well as by resembling pictures (AT VI 112). See also the *Treatise on Light* (AT XI 3–6), and below, pp. 222–3.

15. See also the Sixth Meditation (AT VII 87–8). For additional references and more detailed, critical discussion of Descartes's views about the causation of sensation, see M. Wilson, 'Descartes on the Origin of Sensation' (Chapter 4 in this volume). In 'Descartes on Life and Sense' (*Canadian Journal of Philosophy* 19 (1980), 178–92), Ann MacKenzie discusses in detail, from a somewhat different point of view, the quoted passages from the *Dioptrics*, and many related texts concerned with perception.

16. Arbini, 'Did Descartes have a Philosophical Theory of Sense Perception?', 330.

17. Yolton, *Perceptual Acquaintance*, 38.

18. See MacKenzie, 'Descartes on Life and Sense', 180. MacKenzie also offers other texts, and some detailed argument, in support of this interpretive position.

19. Yolton, *Perceptual Acquaintance*, 39.

20. One of the most detailed discussions of this issue, in the Sixth Replies, presents plenty of problems of its own. (See M. Wilson, 'Descartes on the Perception of Primary Qualities' (Chapter 3 in this volume), and C. Wolf-Devine, *Descartes on Seeing* (Carbondale and Edwardsville: Southern Illinois University Press, 1993), 84–8).

21. See M. Wilson, 'Descartes on the Representationality of Sensation' (Chapter 5 in this volume).

22. J. L. Mackie, *Problems from Locke* (Oxford: Clarendon Press, 1976), 7, 16, 28; ch. 2. Mackie does not deny that ideas of secondary qualities are 'representative' for Locke (p. 16), but I think he means only that the idea-types are (as Locke says) correlated in some causal way with types of mechanical states of objects.

23. Cf. the Sixth Meditation (AT VII 88) 'when the nerves in the foot are moved in a strong and unusual manner, this motion, reaching through the spinal cord to the inner parts of the brain, there gives the mind a signal to sense something, namely pain as if existing in the foot. . . . It is true that the nature of man could have been so constituted by God that this same motion in the brain would exhibit something else to the mind: either itself [the motion] as it is in the brain, or as it is in the foot, or in any of the intermediate locations . . .'

24. This remark contrasts, though, with the remark quoted above from the beginning of the Fifth Meditation in which Descartes seems to stress the distinct *imaginability* of *res extensa* (AT VII 63). Descartes observes in the Third Meditation that he finds in himself 'two different ideas of the sun' which (respectively) present it as small or large. He says that the former is acquired 'as if' from the senses, while the latter is derived from 'certain motions innate in me, or made by me in some other manner'. These remarks perhaps suggest by implication that the favoured idea (the second) resembles the sun: 'certainly both cannot be similar to the same sun existing outside me'. But what he mainly stresses is, again, that the idea derived 'as if' from sense does *not* resemble the sun (see AT VII 39–40).

Note that Descartes hedges in this passage with regard to the origin of both ideas: he does not say straightforwardly that the former comes from sense, nor that the latter is derived from innate ideas. Thus the passage does not really tell against the suggestion I made earlier that Descartes may understand 'ideas of sense' in a quite peculiar and restricted way, relating to the 'special sensibles'; further it is compatible with his suggestion towards the end of the *Meditations* that the true determination of the sun's size requires the resources of sense and memory as well as intellect. I want to thank John Nelson for a comment that caused me to look at the passage again, with a question about its implications for some of what I have said here.

25. The emphasis in this passage on the tradition between 'special' and 'common sensibles' is atypical for Descartes. But it occurs in a context where he is expressly concerned to argue that he has not employed any principle not accepted by Aristotle and 'other philosophers of every age'.

Descartes on the Perception of Primary Qualities

THROUGHOUT his writings Descartes contrasts "sensations" of color, sound, taste, and so on with ideas of size, shape, position, and motion. The former are merely "confused" ideas, which fail to "resemble" any quality existing in physical reality: they must be "attributed to sense." In the *Principles of Philosophy*, for instance, he remarks of color:

> . . . when we think we perceive colors in objects although we do not know what this might be, that we call by the name of color, and we cannot understand any similarity between the color which we suppose to be in objects and what we experience to be in sense, yet, because we do not notice this . . . , it is easy to allow ourselves to fall into the error of judging that that which we call color in objects is something entirely similar to the color we sense, and thus supposing what we in no way perceived is clearly perceived by us. (I, a. 70: AT VIII-1, 34; CSM I, 218)[1]

When Descartes denies that confused ideas or sensations "resemble" or are similar to qualities in physical objects, part of what he has in mind is that sensations (of sound, color, and so on) do not present to us "images" of variations of motion and figure; but such variations are all that is really present in the external world, are what account for the different confused sensations in us.[2]

Ideas of size, shape, motion, and position, however, "are not otherwise understood or sensed by us than they are or at least can be in bodies." Thus, he writes in *Principles* I, a. 69:

> We know [*cognoscere*] in a quite different way what size, or shape, or motion . . . , or position, or duration, or number, and the like are in a body that we see, which [qualities] I have already said are clearly perceived, than we know what color, or pain, or odor, or taste, or any other of those things are, which I've said must be attributed to the senses. (AT VIII-I, 33–34; CSM I, 217–218)

And at the end of the *Principles* he defends his mechanistic explanatory framework in the following terms:

> . . . who has ever doubted that bodies move and have various sizes and shapes, and that their various different motions correspond to these differences in size and shape; or who doubts that when bodies collide bigger bodies are divided into many smaller ones and change their shapes? We detect these facts not just with one sense but several—sight, touch and hearing; and they can also be distinctly imagined and understood by us. But the same cannot be said of the other characteristics like color, sound and the rest, each of which is perceived not by several senses but by one alone; for the images of them which we have in our thought are always confused,

and we do not know what they really are. (IV, a. 200: AT VIII-1, 323–324; CSM I, 286)[3]

Ideas of size, shape, position, and motion, which apply exclusively to body, together with a small number of other ideas (such as number and duration) that apply equally to mental and corporeal substance, thus constitute the total repertoire of "clear and distinct" knowledge of bodies. As Descartes explains in the Third Meditation, in discounting the "objective reality" of sensation, there is very little in the ideas of corporeal objects which he perceives clearly and distinctly:

> [I do clearly and distinctly perceive in corporeal things] size or extension in length, breadth, or depth; shape which results from the boundary of this extension; position, which the different figured things [*figurata*] maintain with respect to each other; and motion, or the change of these positions; to which can be added substance, duration and number. . . . (AT VII, 43; CSM II, 30)

We know that Locke, in his famous account of the "primary/secondary quality distinction" in chapter 8 of Book II of the *Essay*, combines the *denial* that ideas of colors, sounds, tastes, and the like "resemble" qualities in objects, with the affirmation that ideas of such "primary qualities" as size, shape, and motion "*are Resemblances* of them, and their patterns do really exist in the objects themselves. . . ." His discussion makes clear that he intends to maintain that *particular sense ideas of primary qualities* "resemble" the concretely realized qualities of particular objects that are sensed:

> A piece of *Manna* of a sensible Bulk, is able to produce in us the *Idea* of a round or square Figure; and, by being removed from one place to another, the *Idea* of Motion. This *Idea* of Motion represents it, as it really is in the *Manna* moving: A Circle or Square are the same, whether in *Idea* or Existence; in the Mind, or in the *Manna*. . . .[5]

Occasional remarks of Descartes's suggest that he holds a somewhat similar, simplistic view about sensory perception of primary qualities of bodies: for example, the statement about detecting differences of size and shape, and so on by "more than one sense."[6] I believe, however, that systematic consideration of the Cartesian texts establishes that he in fact holds a far more complex and qualified view about our perception of bodily shapes, sizes, locations, and motions.

Briefly, my claims will be these. First, when Descartes writes (in the *Meditations* and *Principles*) of our ability to apprehend such qualities clearly and/or distinctly, he normally has in mind qualities understood *generally or abstractly*—as opposed to the specific, fully determinate qualities of actual bodies around us. Although it may be "stimulated" by sense, such apprehension is *intellectual* (possibly with assistance from imagination). Second, insofar as Descartes does acknowledge that we are able to apprehend reliably the size, position, shape, motion, and distance (from us) of actual bodies, he insists that we do not do so strictly *by sense*. (Although *this* kind of primary quality perception is also "intellectual," there are reasons to doubt that it can broadly be characterized as "distinct.") *Both* aspects of his position on primary quality perception bear on the interpretation of certain passages that suggest an extreme antiempiricism, a virtual nihilism about sense perception, such as the following from *Principles* II, a. 3:

> Perceptions of the senses do not teach [us] what really is in things. . . . Perceptions of the senses . . . do not teach us, except occasionally and by accident [*nisi interdum & ex accidenti*] what exists in (external bodies) themselves [*qualia in seipsis existant*]. (AT VIII-1, 42; CSM I, 224)

Certain expressions in passages already quoted should make us wary of attributing to Descartes the claim that, with regard at least to "primary qualities," we do perceive by sense particular qualities as they exist in bodies around us (say the size and shape of a chair across the room). Consider the cautious formulation from *Principles* I, a. 70: "are not otherwise sensed or understood by us than they are or at least can be in bodies." Descartes is surely not asserting that shapes and sizes and motions are in bodies *as* we (concretely and determinately) sense them; he is rather indicating that we apprehend these qualities as real in the sense that we understand clearly what extension, shape, and so on *are* (and perhaps what triangularity and so on are), and see that they are qualities that bodies can really have. The same point applies to the proof of the existence of bodies in the Sixth Meditation. This argument concludes with the observation that while corporeal things

> do not all perhaps exist just as I comprehend them by sense, . . . at least all those things are in them which I clearly and distinctly understand, that is to say, all things which, viewed generally [*generaliter spectata*], are comprehended in the object of pure Mathematics. (AT VII, 80; CSM II, 55)

The phrase "speaking generally" quite evidently excludes the apprehension of particular qualities as realized in actual things; for Descartes goes on to remark,

> So far as concerns the rest, however, which are either only particulars [*tantu, particularia sunt*], as for example, that the sun is of such a size and shape, &c., or which are less clearly understood, such as light, sound, pain and the like, it is certain that although they are very doubtful and uncertain, nevertheless this same fact, that God is not deceptive, and that consequently he has not brought about that any falsity occurs in my opinions unless there also is in me some other faculty deriving from God for correcting it, presents to me a sure hope of attaining the truth even in these matters. (AT VII, 80; CSM II, 55–56)

I will consider later what "truth" Descartes has in mind in the last clause. The point I am concerned with at the moment is just this: it is as qualities considered generally or abstractly, not as particular qualities of actual things at a particular time, that the ideas in question are accepted as "distinct."

Even passages in which Descartes seems at first to be saying, precisely, that we perceive the particular figures of actual bodies affecting our senses much more distinctly than their colors, and so on, tend not to sustain such a reading very well on close inspection. For example, the following passage from *Principles* I, a. 69, which appears first to be conveying such a position, takes on a more ambiguous aspect when reconsidered in light of the possibility that Descartes only has in mind qualities understood generally or abstractly:

> . . . we know in a very different way what size is in a body which is seen, or figure or movement . . . , or situation, or duration, or number, and the like, which as already said are clearly perceived, than what color is in the same body, or pain [*sic*], odor, taste, or any other of those things which I have said are to be attributed to the senses. For although in seeing any body we are not more certain that it exists in that it appears figured than from its appearance of being colored: nevertheless we much more evidently know what being figured is in it, than what being colored is. (AT VIII-1, 33–34; CSM I, 217–218)

At first sight Descartes may seem to be saying here that we do have a clear knowledge, through sense perception, of the particular shapes and so on of the things around us. But what he actually says we know clearly with respect to a given body is just "what being figured is in it." Even the existence of a body is said to be apprehended just "from the fact that it appears figured [*quatenus apparet figuratum*]"—or colored for that matter; there is no commitment whatsoever to the view that a particular body's shape is reliably presented to us in a particular sense perception.[7]

The curious phrasing of the passage in the *Principles* concerned with establishing the existence of a physical world conveys even more clearly an emphasis on grasp of the general features of matter, a downplaying of the significance of any particular sensory given:

> . . . inasmuch as we perceive, or rather stimulated by sense we apprehend clearly and distinctly a matter which is extended in length, breadth, and depth, the various parts of which have various shapes and motions, and give rise to the sensations we have of colors, odors, pains etc. (II, a. 1: AT VIII-1, 40; CSM I, 223)

And it is with respect to this matter in general that Descartes here introduces a very rare *positive* use of the notion of resemblance between idea and physical reality:

> . . . we clearly apprehend this matter as different from God, or ourselves, or our mind, and appear to discern very plainly that the idea of it is due to objects outside of ourselves to which it is altogether similar. (AT VIII-1, 41; CSM I, 223)[8]

The phrase "stimulated by sense, we apprehend . . ." suggests, it seems me, that Descartes is consciously avoiding committing himself to the view that we perceive by sense the true qualities of the physical world; it thus fits in with the claim previously cited that the senses do not tell us, "except occasionally and accidentally," what things are like in themselves.

What then, are the "truths" about particularities of sense that Descartes has in mind in the passage recently quoted from the Sixth Meditation? The claims that he goes on to make in the following paragraphs of this Meditation are closely similar to those he endorses in other works; and they allow to the senses an *extremely* minimal role in conveying information to us. Besides testifying to the fact of our own embodiment, the senses "teach" us (1) that there are bodies around ours; (2) that some of these are beneficial to us, and others harmful; and finally (3):

> . . . from the fact that I sense very different colors, sounds, odors, tastes, heat, hardness and the like, I rightly infer that there are in the bodies from which these various sensory perceptions come, certain variations corresponding to them [i.e., to the different sensations], though perhaps not similar to them. (AT VII, 81; CSM II, 56)

The beliefs that I have *mistakenly* supposed that my senses reliably taught me include not only the views that there are empty spaces; or that there are in bodies the heat, colors, and tastes that I perceive through my senses (or exact resemblances of these "ideas"); but also "that stars and towers and other distant bodies have the same size and shape which they present to my senses" (AT VII, 82; CSM II, 57). In short, the nature God has given us, as a composite of mind and body,

> . . . does not appear to teach us . . . to draw any conclusions from these perceptions of the senses about things located outside us without a prior examination by the understanding. For to know the truth about such matters seems to pertain to the mind alone, not to the composite. (AT VII, 82–83; CSM II, 57)

Thus the internal qualitative differences within our sensory manifold inform us reliably *only* about corresponding "variations" in the physical world (a theme of the *Dioptrics* and *Principles* also). Beyond this, and their pragmatic role in preserving the mind-body union, the senses provide *stimulation* to distinct perception of those *general or abstract* features of physical reality which are also presented in imagination and understanding.

The final sentence of the last passage raises a question, however. Does "the truth about such matters" encompass also truths about the particular (primary) qualities of actual bodies which Descartes has mentioned a little earlier: that the sun is of such and such a size and shape, for instance? Does Descartes really mean to hold that "the mind alone" can apprehend such qualities? In a way, I think he does. But to explain the meaning of this suggestion I need to introduce additional texts.

There are important parts of Descartes's treatments of "primary quality" perception that are not at all covered by the reading I have so far developed. These include, particularly, the impressive discussion of distance perception and related issues in the Sixth Discourse of the *Dioptrics*, and a fairly well-known but rather anomalous discussion of "levels of sense" that occurs in Descartes's Replies to the Sixth Objections to the *Meditations*. In both of these passages Descartes evidently takes for granted that human beings routinely determine with reasonable accuracy the size, shape, and location (at least) of particular objects presented to them by the senses.

At the beginning of the Sixth Discourse of the *Dioptrics*—"Of Vision"— Descartes observes that "all the qualities that we apprehend in the objects of sight can be reduced to six principal ones, which are: light, color, position, distance, size, and shape" (AT VI, 130; CSM I, 167). His purpose in the chapter is to explain "what enables our mind to know," or be "informed of" or to "perceive" these qualities: He comments that light and color "alone properly belong to the sense of sight": our perception of light depends on the "force" of the movements at the base of the optic nerves in the brain; whereas the perception of color depends on the nature of the movements (AT VI, 130–131; CSM I, 167). He further discusses the physiology of these perceptions—noting, for instance, how aspects of the structure of the optic nerves inevitably limit the range of colors, and distinctness of outline, that can be perceived under certain circumstances. All of these comments accord well enough with the view that we have very limited powers to apprehend the particular qualities of bodies, for the perceptions of brightness and color he is discussing may easily be understood as essentially *mere* discriminations of variations or differences among external stimuli.

The case is a bit different with respect to his discussion of position, distance, size, and shape, however. He does emphasize quite strongly that it is "easy to be mistaken" in distance perception (AT VI, 147; CSM I, 175; cf. AT VI, 144; CSM I, 173). And (anticipating several comments in the *Meditations*), he particularly stresses the illusions characteristic of our perception of extremely distant objects. But it certainly *appears* that throughout this discussion Descartes is assuming that we do with some reliability (and not merely "accidentally," as the *Principles* has it) visually determine the actual qualities of specific bodies— at least insofar as we are concerned with position, distance, size, and shape— when the conditions of observation are not unfavorable. His point, it seems, is not that we cannot do this, but rather that understanding *how* we do it will make plain why there are such definite limitations on the reliability of vision, and also show that "images" do not play the central and literal role that one might tend to ascribe to them. I will give some indication of the character of his treatment.

Descartes notes that neither the perception of distance nor the perception of position can be fully explained by postulating images emitted from objects.[9] The perception of an object's position, for instance, depends on the position of our own eyes or head, as registered in the inmost parts of the brain: the appropriate "movements" in the brain, by virtue of an "institution of nature," in effect notify the mind of where we are looking, and hence where the different parts of the object are situated in relation to us. Thus we must not be surprised "that the objects can be seen in their true position, even though the picture that they imprint on the eye has a quite opposite one," or that only one object is seen despite there being two retinal images (AT VI, 135–137; CSM I, 169–170).

Size perception, he says, is determined in part by our beliefs about how far away the objects are "compared with the size of the images that they imprint on the back of the eye; and not absolutely by the size of these images . . . ," as the phenomenon of size constancy demonstrates (AT VI, 140; CSM I, 172). Finally,

> . . . it is also obvious that shape is judged by the knowledge, or opinion, that we have of the position of various parts of the objects, and not by the resemblance of the pictures in the eye; for these pictures usually contain only ovals and diamond-shapes, yet they cause us to see circles and squares. (AT VI, 140–141; CSM I, 172)

I said that it *appears* clear that Descartes is assuming that at least in favored cases we apprehend by vision the qualities of actual bodies. The reason for this qualification is not that the text leaves much room for doubt that we do apprehend such qualities in favorable cases: it is rather that there is room for arguing about whether he means to imply that we apprehend them by the *sense* of sight. Throughout the discussion of our perception of these qualities—particularly distance, size, and shape—Descartes makes frequent references to "judgment," and some references to "implicit reasoning." For example, we "judge" the distance of an object in part by distinctness of outline and strength of light, in part by its known size, in part by the fact that some other objects may be seen as interposed between it and ourselves, and in part by comparison of shapes and colors, among other factors (AT VI, 138–140; CSM I, 172). In a particularly famous passage he even holds that convergence of our eyes helps us determine distance, by virtue of an implicit reasoning "quite similar to that used by surveyors" (AT VI, 138; CSM I, 170).[10] Is it possible that when Descartes, in other works, rejects the senses as a source of knowledge of the actual qualities of bodies, in contrast to the legitimate claims of intellect, he is using "sense" in a peculiar and restricted way, that abstracts from much of what we would normally consider sense perception? If so, his dismissal of sense perception as a source of knowledge of particular qualities of things would not, after all, rule out the reliable apprehension of the determinate (primary) qualities of objects before us in *what we normally think of as sense perception*. Perhaps, in insisting on the extreme limitations of "the senses," Descartes only means to indicate that the normal ways of acquiring knowledge of particular bodies and their qualities, traditionally considered "sensory," ought to be reclassified as largely "intellectual"—not that they should be broadly dismissed.

This hypothesis derives strong support from a passage in the Sixth Replies. Descartes is responding to a suggestion that sensory errors are corrected by other sensory data, not by "the understanding." (For example, the sense of touch corrects the erroneous belief derived from vision that a stick placed in water becomes bent.) In rejecting this suggestion he finds it necessary to distinguish "three degrees" [*gradus*] of sense. One is the strictly physiological, shared by humans and brutes: "and this can be nothing but the motion of the particles of the [sense] organs, and the change of figure and position resulting from this motion" (AT VII, 436–437; CSM II, 294). In human beings, however, such motions in the body "immediately result" in changes in the mind that is united to it; the second level comprises "all" of these:

The second [level] includes all that immediately results in the mind because it is united to a corporeal organ affected in this way, and such are the perceptions of pain, pleasure, thirst, hunger, color, sound, taste, odor, heat, cold and the like, which arise from the union and as it were the intermingling of mind and body, as I have explained in the Sixth Meditation. (Sixth Replies: AT VII, 437; CSM II, 294–295)

A little later Descartes makes the observation that I am most concerned to emphasize here, namely: *"Nothing else should be ascribed to sense, if we want to distinguish it accurately from the intellect* [. . . *nihil aliud ad sensum esset referendum, si accurate illum ab intellectu distinguere vellemus*]" (AT VII, 437; CSM II, 295). He eventually concludes this passage with the remark that,

we have to have some reason to believe the judgment based on touch concerning this matter, rather than that based on vision; which reason, since it was not in us from infancy, must be attributed not to sense, but only to the understanding. (AT VII, 439; CSM II, 296)

But this suggestion that a learned preference for the testimony of touch—*not* formed "from early infancy and without any consideration" (AT VII, 438; CSM II, 295)—must be ascribed to a supersensory faculty, obscures the point Descartes first makes in drawing the distinction between the second and third "levels of sense." For he draws this distinction in a way that ascribes the perception of certain qualities *within* one sense (vision) to the understanding, *even when the perception does date from early infancy.*

The third grade of sense, he begins, "includes all those judgments which, on the occasion of motions in the organs of the body, we have been accustomed to make since our earliest youth about things outside us" (AT VII, 437; CSM II, 295). In considering an example of visual perception—seeing a stick—he distinguishes the elements of sense, properly so called, from the third level of sense, which is the level at which judgment occurs. In seeing the stick, I perceive light or color reflected from it: these sensations alone belong to the second level.

For although from this sensation of color that affects me, I judge that the stick located outside me is colored, and also from the extension of this color [*ex istius coloris extensione*], its boundary, and its position in relation to the parts of the brain, I reason out [*ratiociner*] the size, figure, and distance of this stick: although this is commonly attributed to the senses, and for this reason I have here referred it to the third grade of sensing, nevertheless it manifestly depends on the understanding alone. But I have demonstrated in the *Dioptrics* that size, distance and figure can only be perceived by reasoning out [*ratiocinationem*] one from the others. (AT VII, 437–438; CSM II, 295)

This passage may help to explain Descartes's cagey references to "sense or understanding" in his discussion of the distinct ideas of bodies. It further suggests that his extremely derogatory comments elsewhere about the cognitive role of "sense" or "sense perception" need to be interpreted with care. For it opens the possibility that in such passages he is restricting his reference to what he here calls the "second level" of sense, rather than employing the broad common usage. If so, the antiempiricistic implications of such passages may be considerably less drastic, in relation to ordinary beliefs, than at first appears.

I will not attempt to pursue this possibility further here. Rather, I will close with some further observations relating to the interpretation of the Sixth Replies passage, and its relation to the *Dioptrics* and other works.

One thing that quickly emerges from Descartes's further remarks in the Sixth Replies is that he does not intend to equate the intellectuality of the judgments here at issue with *reliability*. (Here as elsewhere in Descartes an association with earliest infancy connotes unreliability or prejudice.)

> . . . when we say *the certainty of the understanding is much greater than the certainty of the senses*, this means only that now that we are adults the judgments we make as the result of any new observations are more certain than those which we made from earliest infancy and without any consideration; which is true without doubt. (AT VII, 438; CSM II, 295)

From this comment it seems quite clear that whatever the significance of the intellectual aspects of the "third level of sense," and whatever Descartes's reasons may be for distinguishing the second and third levels in this way at this place, the "distinctness" elsewhere attributed to ideas of size, shape, and position is not directly a function of their intellectuality understood in *this* way.[11]

There are a number of other things that seem to me quite confusing about this passage, considered in conjunction with the part of *Dioptrics* to which Descartes here alludes. Let me briefly indicate the most important.

First, the neat distinction between sense and judgment put forward in the Replies just does not square that well with the discussion of our perception of position, distance, size, and shape in the *Dioptrics*. For instance, in the latter work (as we saw) the head's or the eyes' position is said to figure in the perception of position by virtue of the "natural institution" of a relation between body state and mind; "natural institution" is also appealed to in explaining the effect of the shape of the eye on the perception to distance. In other words, the direct results of embodiment are not restricted to sensations like color and light (AT VI, 134–137; CSM I, 169–170).[12]

Second, there is certainly room for confusion about what exactly Descartes thinks is directly and prejudgmentally given in sense, even if one restricts one's consideration to the Sixth Replies, and does not worry too much for the moment about the issue of conscious awareness. He seems to want to say that only color and light are available on the "second level of sense," yet he simultaneously clearly implies that *in some sense* shape, size, and position are too ("the extension of the color, the boundary, the position"). And of course the picture is further muddled when one notes that in the *Dioptrics* there seems to be no particular distinction drawn, with respect to aids for judging something's distance, between "knowing its size," "the distinctness of its shape and color," and "changes in the shape of the body of the eye."

The issue of conscious awareness complicates these problems further. In the *Dioptrics* Descartes does not take a definite position on the extent to which we are conscious of the various physical and mental states that he thinks underlie our perception of distance, and the other qualities under discussion.[13] But he does tend to write as if all these perceptions rested on something quite like ordinary discursive reasoning, presumably accessible to consciousness:

> [A]s to the manner in which we see the size and shape of objects, I need not say anything in particular, inasmuch as it is all included in the manner in which we see the distance and the position of their parts. That is, their size is estimated according to the knowledge, or the opinion, that we have of their distance, compared with the size of the images that they imprint on the back of the eye. . . . And it is also obvious that shape is judged by the knowledge, or opinion that we have of the position of various parts of the objects. . . . (*Diop* Discourse 6: AT VI, 140; CSM I, 172)

And, in any case, it seems obvious that in Descartes's metaphysical scheme the "surveyor-like" reasoning said to be involved in distance perception *must* be ascribed to the realm of mind, not body. Yet Descartes's official doctrine concerning the mind is that we must be "in some manner conscious" of everything that is in it. But is it even remotely plausible to suppose that we are conscious, even potentially, of the effect of the eyes' convergence on normal distance judgments—let alone of the retinal images that we are said to "compare" with our "knowledge or opinion" of the relative distances of things?

It must be acknowledged that Descartes confronts this issue with some directness in the Sixth Replies. "I demonstrated in the *Dioptrics*," he writes,

> that size, distance, and shape can be perceived only by reasoning out one from the others. The only difference is that those things which we now judge for the first time because of some new observation, we attribute to the intellect; but those which we have judged, or even inferred by reasoning, from our earliest years, in exactly the same way as now, concerning the things that affect our senses, we attribute to sense. This is because we carry out the reasoning and judging [*ratiocinamur & judicamus*] concerning the latter at great speed on account of habit, or rather we remember the judgments we have long made about similar things; and so we do not distinguish these operations from simple sense perception. (AT VII, 438; CSM II, 295)

So apparently Descartes does mean to hold that most of the factors that go into our judgments of distance are in principle accessible to consciousness: we are not aware of them most of the time simply because of a lack of attention born of familiarity.[14]

This position is open to various obvious challenges. It seems perfectly in order to argue against it that we are not in fact able to become conscious of many of the "reasonings" or "judgments" that Descartes claims underlie our outer "perceptions." Further, there is the painfully obvious question of how the human ability to home in on a distant object relates, on the one hand, to distance perception as Descartes interprets it, and, on the other hand, to the ability of *animals* to do the same thing. Without making an issue about "consciousness," it's still hard to deny that in some sense my dog "knows" where the ball fell as well as I do: after all, he runs directly to it, just as I do. Now according to Descartes subhuman animals have no reasoning ability at all. It would seem to follow that, on Cartesian theory, either I do not rely for such physical acts on distance and position perceptions as Descartes explains them or that the explanation of my dog's ability is *totally* disanalogous to the explanation of mine. Both positions are, it seem to me, extremely implausible.[15]

As I have noted, Descartes does in the *Dioptrics* connect perception of position and distance with the natural institution of brute correlations between body and mind, as well as with imagination, judgment, and reasoning. And although the former aspect of his discussion there may be (as I've said) somewhat in conflict with the Sixth Replies passage, one may still feel that it is on the right track, in so far as it at least mutes an otherwise overly intellectualistic conception of perceptual processes. But it should be noted that even this aspect of his treatment is of no help in connection with the problem of animal abilities: for animals no more have mind-body unions than they have the ability to reason, on the Cartesian view.

It is perhaps also worth observing in this context (though obvious, from the point of view of contemporary psychology) that Descartes's attempt to drive the sense/intellect wedge at the point that he does in the Sixth Replies runs afoul of the fact that perceptions of colors and sounds are themselves not really reducible to the passive reception of atomistic sensations. Descartes, as I've mentioned, appeals to the phenomenon now known as size constancy in arguing that perceived size is not a direct function of the size of the retinal image. Color constancy, however, is an equally powerful and pervasive phenomenon; and color perception also depends on many factors like background, juxtaposition, and so on (as well as on one's conceptual repertoire).[16]

It would be childish, of course, to belabor the observational and theoretical limitations of a perceptual theorist working at the dawn of modern science. The nature and limitations of Descartes's claims about sense perception are nevertheless worth taking seriously in view of their close interconnections with interpretive and critical problems that arise with respect to his broader philosophical position. In conclusion I want particularly to stress the following points.

First, Descartes does, in the *Dioptrics* and Sixth Replies passages, construe the perception of position, distance, size, and shape as involving strong intellectual elements (if not as *wholly* intellectual, as the Replies passage almost suggests); and he holds that they differ in this fundamental respect from ordinary perceptions of color, sound, heat and cold, taste, and the like, which are said to consist just in having "sensations" that "arise from the mind-body union."[17]

Second, this position leaves room for uncertainty about what he means when he speaks elsewhere of the near-uselessness of sense perceptions in informing us of particular qualities of bodies, in so far as it opens the possibility of a quite restricted understanding of 'sense perception' in these contexts.

Third, Descartes (unlike Locke) *pervasively* distinguishes the ideas of size, shape, position, and motion from simple ideas of sense—though (as I have argued) there are two different ways of understanding Descartes's position on this point. The ideas in question are either, it seems, distinct abstract or general ideas with their source in the intellect, or (if one has in mind the shapes and so on of particular bodies "presented to sense") complicated constructs based to some degree on a rather opaquely specified sensory given. In the *Meditations* and the *Principles* Descartes for the most part has in mind the former when he discusses the contract between the confused and the distinct "ideas of body."[18]

Fourth, the intellectual constructions of the "third degree of sense" are not in any direct way connected with certainty or (presumably) *distinctness* of perception. *All* distance perception, for instance, involves intellectuality in this sense, but *such* intellectuality is consistent with judgments about the distance of things being at least as liable to error as judgments of other sorts.

Finally, the treatments of perception in the *Dioptrics* and the Sixth Replies, impressive as they may be in some respects, are far from presenting a coherent and consistent position, that can settle difficulties found in Descartes's remarks on the subject elsewhere.[19] If anything, they make it *harder* to be sure how Descartes thinks of the relation between sense experience on the one hand, and the intellect, certainty, the mind-body union and so forth on the other hand. In particular, they raise additional complications for already difficult interpretive questions concerning Descartes's view of the cognitive role of the senses.[20]

NOTES

1. I use the standard abbreviations for the Adam and Tannery edition (AT) and the Cottingham, Stoothoff, Murdoch translation (CSM). Translations are substantially my own, however.

2. This point is clear from passages such as the following:

> . . . if the sense of hearing brought to our thought the true image of its object, it would have to be the case that, instead of making us conceive sound, it made us conceive the movement of the parts of Air which tremble against our ears at the time. (*TL*, AT X1, 5; CSM I, 82)

> . . . colors are nothing else, in bodies we call colored, than the diverse ways in which these bodies receive light and reflect it against our eyes. (*Diop*, Discourse 1: AT VI, 85; CSM I, 153)

3. The emphasis placed here on the distinction between the common and special sensibles is unusual in Descartes's writings. Presumably it is at least partly explained by the fact that the passage is concerned to establish that Descartes has not employed any principle not accepted by Aristotle and "other philosophers of every age."

4. John Locke, *Essay*, bk. II, ch. 8, sec. 15, p. 137.

5. Ibid., sec. 18, p. 138.

6. The term 'primary quality' is not used by Descartes, so far as I know. It is not used always the same way by those seventeenth-century writers in whose works it does occur—e.g., Galileo, Boyle, and Locke. Locke himself does not maintain one constant view of what the primary qualities are (i.e., which qualities are primary qualities). In this essay I use the term to designate what Descartes takes to be the qualities that are "really in" body uniquely: that is, size, shape, distance, position, motion. (I do not, however, discuss in detail his treatments of our perception of each of these qualities individually.)

7. Compare *Principles* IV, a. 198, where the caption seems to indicate that the message will be that we know only size, shape, and motion in bodies through the senses; but where the text does not endorse any view about apprehending particular quality-instances by sense (AT VIII-1, 321–322; CSM I, 284–285).

8. Comparing different passages from the *Principles*, the *Meditations* (V and VI), the Replies, the *Notae in Programma*, and so on gives rise to a lot of questions about just how, and to what extent, Descartes conceives of our ideas of bodies as "due to" bodies. I discuss some of these issues in detail in "Descartes on the Origin of Sensation," *Philosophical Topics* 19 (1991): 293–323 (Chapter 4 of this volume).

9. Position ("*situation*") Descartes defines as "the direction towards which each part of an object is placed in relation to our body . . ." (AT VI, 134; CSM I, 169).

10. "As if by a natural geometry" is the famous phrase—although Descartes does not in fact use it directly of visual perception in this passage. Rather it is embedded in the ongoing analogy of the blind man discriminating the qualities—in this case the location—of a thing by the use of sticks in his hands.

In my opinion the "natural geometry" phrase has been widely overemphasized and overread. (On this point see Celia Rose Curtis Wolf, *The Retreat from Realism: Philosophical Theories of Vision from Descartes to Berkeley* [Ann Arbor: University Microfilms International, 1987], 223–226. A revised version of this dissertation appears in the *Journal of the History of Philosophy* monograph series under the title *Descartes on Seeing: Epistemology and Visual Perception* [Carbondale: Southern Illinois University Press, 1993].)

11. See Gary Hatfield, "The Senses and the Fleshless Eye: the *Meditations* as Cognitive Exercises," in *Essays on Descartes' Meditations*, ed. Amélie Rorty (Berkeley: University of California Press, 1986), 59. Hatfield indicates that the "third level" is really constituted just by the judgments of our early years, with those of mature adulthood counting as a "fourth level." Relative certitude is limited to the latter. It is important to note, though, that Descartes goes on to stress that the judgments of childhood involve "exactly the same" processes as those we make now. Also, it seems to me open to question whether even the maturest judgments about particular features of things around us are meant to count as "distinct."

12. Wolf, *Retreat from Realism* (212–213), points out that one should not take at face value Descartes's indication in the Sixth Replies that he is there only reiterating what he said in the *Dioptrics*. Wolf discusses in detail changes in Descartes's accounts of position, distance, and so forth through various works.

13. He does indicate that we ordinarily change the shape of our eyes without reflecting on it (AT VI, 137; CSM I, 170).

14. Ronald Arbini seems to take it as self-evident that the processes in question could not be conscious, and to use this point in challenging a representationalist interpretation of Descartes that in effect makes mental sense data or ideas the basis of all knowledge of external things; see his "Did Descartes have a Philosophical Theory of Sense Percep-

tion?," *Journal of the History of Philosophy* 21 (1983): 321. He is too hasty, I think, in asssuming Descartes would accept his premises—evident as they may seem today.

In "The Sensory Core and the Medieval Foundations of Early Modern Perceptual Theory" (*Isis* 70 [1979]: 377) Gary Hatfield and William Epstein stress that, in virtue of Descartes's equation of the mental and the conscious, events at the "second level of sense" must be regarded as conscious. They are inexplicit, though, about whether the judgments based on these sensory items must themselves be accessible to consciousness.

15. A similar point is raised by Wolf, *Retreat from Realism*, 231. My present phrasing of the worry owes something to an objection by Jean-Marie Beyssade to an earlier version, though I am by no means sure I have fully met this objection.

16. I have talked with people who think that the phenomenon of color constancy (that something that looks a certain color under normal lighting will continue more or less to look that color under radically different lighting) is sufficient to suggest that colors, like shape are "objective." I am not sure, however, why they consider this fact more impressive, in this connection, than the simple fact that things retain "their" colors from time to time under *normal* lighting. Perhaps there is a tendency to conflate the idea that a perception may involve complex cognitive processes—and hence is not a "mere sensation"—with the idea that it is not "just in the mind."

In "The Case of the Colorblind Painter" Oliver Sacks and Robert Wasserman discuss the problem of understanding color "judgments," comparing it in passing with "a *much simpler*" form of visual "judgment—the judgment or perception of depth (stereopsis) . . ." (emphasis added) (*New York Review of Books* 34, no. 18 [19 November 1987]: 31).

17. As Peter Markie has pointed out (see n. 20), the distinction between the second and third levels of sense does not correspond well with the *Meditations* distinction between what the senses "teach us" and the determinations of intellect. That we are embodied, that there are bodies around ours, and so on, though "taught by sense," are still *judgments*. I believe that this observation invites a further distinction between mere inferences to external causes of an idea, and the reasoning or judgment involved in the actual construction of a specific quality perception—say, of the distance of a thing.

18. In his discussion of the "Molyneux Problem" (*Essay*, bk. II, ch. 9. secs. 8–10, 145–146) Locke himself acknowledges that the "*ideas we receive by sensation, are often* in grown People *alter'd by the Judgment*, without our taking notice of it" (p. 145). Thus, upon receiving the "idea" of a variously colored or shaded plane circle, we come habitually to form by judgment the "perception of a convex Figure, and an uniform Colour. . . ." Like Descartes before him, Locke explains that the judgment is unnoticed because formed so quickly and so habitually: the result, he says, is that "we take that for the Perception of our Sensation, which is an *Idea* formed by our Judgment . . ." (p. 146). The implications of this concession for the doctrine of simple ideas developed through bk II, ch. 8 are severe; but my interest in Locke is here restricted to the statements of these early sections.

19. Although I believe that Descartes's writings on perception have important interconnections with his more properly "philosophical" views, I am unable to agree with Arbini's claim (in "Did Descartes have a Philosophical Theory of Sense Perception?") that the *Dioptrics* and related texts provide "a clear coherent account of sense perception" which can be shown to provide solutions for problems set forth in the *Meditations* (pp. 317–318; 328ff.).

Incidentally, Arbini is mistaken in taking me to have held in my book *Descartes* (London: Routledge and Kegan Paul, 1978) that Descartes "was somehow committed to one or another form of perceptual representationalism" (p. 317). The passage he cites (without quoting the relevant part) in fact has more or less the opposite significance: After raising the question whether the Sixth Meditation provides grounds for ascribing to Descartes any "theory of sense perception at all, in the ordinary philosophical sense," I comment, "It would certainly be misleading to call him either a causal realist or a representative realist, as far as the evidence of the Sixth Meditation goes . . ." (*Descartes*, 203). My reasons for raising the question there were similar to those developed in greater detail in this essay, having to do with the highly depreciatory cast of many of Descartes's remarks about the cognitive role of the senses.

20. Earlier versions of this paper were presented at colloquia at the University of California at San Diego, the University of Cincinnati, the Instituto de Investigaciones Filosóficas of the Autonomous University of Mexico, and St. Mary's College, Maryland, as well as at the San José Conference. Of the many helpful comments made on these occasions I would like to single out for special thanks some remarks by Philip Kitcher and written criticisms by Peter Markie, both of which have substantially influenced the present version.

Descartes on the Origin of Sensation

DESCARTES holds that it is "the mind that senses, not the body,"[1] but he clearly believes that certain motions in the brain play a crucial role in all episodes of sense perception. Most readers of Descartes, from the seventeenth century to the present, have taken the role in question to be that of efficient causality: states of the brain are supposed to *produce* sensations in the mind. Beginning with Descartes's contemporaries, however, many critics have objected that there is something peculiarly suspect, unintelligible, or even inconsistent in the notion that an extended unthinking thing (body) interacts causally with an unextended thinking thing (mind or soul). Often the objection to body-mind interaction takes the form of a straightforward claim that interact between substances of such "different natures" is inconceivable and impossible: Robert Richardson has dubbed this claim the "heterogeneity objection."[2] Sometimes the critic focuses on issues of internal consistency: alleging, for instance, that body-mind causation violates restrictions on causality espoused by Descartes himself.[3] It is not even uncommon to find writers attributing to *Descartes* the view that mind-body interaction is peculiarly problematic, or even "impossible."[4] A few have held that Descartes in fact did not mean to maintain that states of the brain actually cause sensations in the mind.[5] Recently, however, several scholars have impressively defended the claims that (a) Descartes does think of the relation as one of efficient causality; (b) he forthrightly rejects the notion that there is anything particularly problematic about body-mind interaction; and (c) he has not been shown wrong on this point.[6]

Recent apologists have made important contributions to our understanding of Descartes; I find their positions persuasive, up to a point. It seems to me, though, that both Descartes's critics and his defenders have oversimplified the problem of attributing to him a coherent and univocal position of the role of bodily states in the origin of sensation. In this essay, I want, first to assess and reinforce the progress that has recently been made in understanding Cartesian interactionism with respect specifically to the origin of sensation; and, second, to call attention to complexities, difficulties, and apparent contradictions that remain to be confronted in the Cartesian position.[7]

To appraise the problem accurately, it is necessary to consider a much wider range of Cartesian texts than one usually finds cited in this connection. Also, one needs often to take note of the original language terms. I begin by providing, in the first section, an overview of representative passages concerned with sensation, from both the scientific and philosophical writings. In the second section, I draw on these and other passages to evaluate some prominent interpretations and criticisms, with particular emphasis on the merits of recent defenses of the coherence and consistency of Descartes's position. In the remaining sections, I focus on problematic aspects of Descartes's statements about sensation that have not been adequately addressed by his defenders.

In section three, I discuss an apparent conflict in Descartes's statements about where ideas of sense "come from" and a related problem about the alleged "passivity" of the mind in sensation. Although I suggest some ways to mitigate the problems, I think that the texts may be genuinely inconsistent. (That is, the difficulties spring from a real conflict between ways in which Descartes thinks about the origin of sensory ideas in different contexts, rather than superficial incongruities.)

In the fourth section, I document the prominence in Descartes's work of the notion that the brain-mind relation in sensation involves the brain "presenting" something (a pattern of motions) to the mind. This conception, besides being intrinsically bizarre, is evidently at odds with other familiar Cartesian doctrine. I argue that attempts to dismiss it as merely metaphorical are inconclusive.

In section five, I briefly discuss the more nearly associationist picture of the brain-mind relation presented in other passages. I agree with some recent apologists at least to the extent of regarding this as Descartes's *best* account of the body-mind relation in sensation, though I cannot accept the view that it is his *standard* account. In section six, I argue, however, that efforts to interpret this account through respected modern positions about causality aren't fully borne out by the texts and involve some conceptual loose ends as well.

I

How, then, does Descartes describe the relation between bodily state and mental "idea" in sensation? Often he says simply that motions in the brain (following upon motions in the sensory nerves) "excite" (*excitare*) or "bring about" (*inferre*) sensory ideas or sensations of pain, warmth, color, sound, etc. in the mind; or "affect" (*afficere*) or "act on" (*agir contre*) the mind so that sensations "follow" in it; or "make" (*faire*) the mind sense or perceive; or "stimulate" (*impellere*) it to have sensations. The following passages are representative:

> But the motions which are thus excited in the brain by the nerves affect (*afficiunt*) the soul or mind, which is intimately conjoined with the brain, in different ways, according to their own diversity. And the different affections of our mind, or thoughts, immediately following upon (*consequentes*) these motions, are called perceptions of the senses, or in common speech, sensations. (*PP* IV, 189: AT VIII–I, 316; CSM I, 280.)[8]

> . . . such is the nature of our mind that from the fact alone that certain motions occur in the body, it can be stimulated (*possit-impelli*) to have all sorts of thoughts, carrying no image of these motions . . . ; and especially those confused thoughts called sensings or sensations (*sensus, sive sensationes*). (*PP* IV, 197: AT VIII–I, 320; CSM I, 284)

. . . if this motion [in the nerve filaments] is augmented or diminished by some unusual cause, its augmentation will make (*fera*) the soul have the sensation of heat, its diminution, the sensation of cold. And finally, according to the different other ways in which they are moved, they will make [the soul] sense all the other qualities which belong to touch in general, such as *humidity*, *dryness*, *weight*, and the like. (*TM*: AT XI, 144–45; H 39–40)

. . . any one of the motions which are in that part of the brain which immediately affects (*afficit*) the mind brings about (*infert*) one particular sensation in it . . . (*Med* VI: AT VII, 87; CSM II, 60)

It is notable that in these and many similar passages in which Descartes alludes to the body-mind relation in sensation he uses terms other than French or Latin cognates of the word 'cause'. This fact might seem to lend credence to the position of those who deny that Descartes did think of the relation as a "causal" one. Yet the terms he does commonly use—such as *faire*, *afficere*, and *inferre* surely carry causal connotations. In the *Meditations*, he uses *producendi* and *efficiendi* in the context of an argument for the material origin of sensory ideas (AT VII, 79; CSM II, 55). And in fact the term *causer* is itself used occasionally: for instance, in a passage from the *Meteors* and in a letter to Elizabeth.[9]

But the complexity of Descartes's comments on the body-mind relation in sensation goes beyond the terminological diversity so far surveyed. Frequently, for example, Descartes indicates that the effects that brain motions have on the mind depend on connections "instituted by nature" (or by God):

it is the motions [in the brain] . . . which, acting immediately on (*agissans contre*) our soul in as much as it is united to our body, are instituted by Nature to make it have such sensations (*luy fait avoir de tels sentiments*). (*Diop* VI: AT VI, 130; CSM I, 167)[10]

A conception of the body-mind relation as a "sign" relation is often introduced in conjunction with this notion of "natural institution":

But if words, which signify nothing except by the institution of men, are sufficient to make us conceive of things which they have no resemblance, why is Nature not able to have also established a certain sign which makes us have the sensation of light (*qui nous fasse avoir le sentiment de la Lumiere*), even though this sign has no feature which is similar to that sensation. (*TL* I: AT XI, 4; CSM I, 81)

Descartes used the word or sign analogy to help establish the point, essential to his mechanistic approach to physical phenomena, that the state of the brain that leads up to perceptual experience need not "resemble" the perceptual experience itself: for instance, our experiences of colors do not follow on the instantiation in the brain of colors as we experience them, and even experiences of particular shapes are not generally traceable to an instantiation in the brain of *those particular* shapes.[11] When developing this vein of thought, Descartes may stress that it is an entirely arbitrary matter which brain state is connected with which sensory idea:

Of course the nature of man could have been so constituted by God that the same motion in the brain [as in fact gives rise to the sensation of pain in the foot] would exhibit something else to the mind: namely, either itself [i.e. the motion], in so far as it is in the brain, or in so far as it is in the foot, or in some intermediate location, or finally anything else at all . . . (*Med* VI: AT VII, 88; CSM II, 60–61)[12]

Sometimes the sign the brain gives the soul is said to "make" the soul have a certain sensation, as in the passage quoted just above from the *Treatise on Light*. Rather often, though, Descartes speaks of the brain motions as "giving occasion to" the mind "to form" or "to conceive" ideas of sense:

For [in hearing] it will be these little blows [of air against the ear membrane] which, passing to the brain through the intermediation of these nerves, will give occasion to the soul to conceive the idea of sound (*donneront occasion à l'âme de concevoir l'idée des sons*). (*TM*: AT XI, 149; H 46)[13]

. . . not because these things [outside us] transmitted the ideas themselves to our mind through the organs of sense, but rather because they transmitted something which gave [the mind] occasion to form them (*ei dedit occasionem ad ipsas . . . efformandas*), through a faculty innate to itself, at this time rather than another. (*NiP*: AT VIII–2, 359; CSM I, 304)[14]

He also sometimes speaks of the transaction between brain and mind that occurs when we sense in terms of the mind "considering" images (or *corporeal ideas*) in the brain:

. . . it is only those [figures] traced . . . on the surface of gland *H*, where the seat of imagination, and of the common sense is, that should be taken to be ideas, that is to say, to be the forms or images that the rational soul will consider immediately when, being united to this machine, it will imagine or will sense any object. (*TM*: AT XI, 176–77; H 86).[15]

Elsewhere he speaks of the mind as having sensations "impressed" or "imprinted" on it by brain movements.[16] He also sometimes says (in apparent contradiction with a passage just quoted from the *Comments*) that ideas of corporeal things are "transmitted to" or "come to" the mind from the physical world, from bodies.[17]

II

I have already pointed out that many of the terms which figure prominently in Descartes's accounts of the brain state-sensation relation—including cognates of 'cause' itself—are hardly compatible with the thesis that Descartes did not think of the relation as *causal*. Further, though, even the passages that are most often taken to support this thesis—those which say that the brain "gives a sign" to the mind or gives the mind "occasion to form" a sensation—do not clearly count against a causal interpretation, for "giving A occasion to F" or "giving a sign to A to F" are not antithetical to "having an effect on A." Indeed, it's hard to see how something could give a sign to A without in some way having an effect on A or causing some change of state in A.[18] (As I will explain below, these locutions do raise a question about whether Descartes consistently holds that the mind *passively receives* its ideas of sense *from outside*; but this is a different issue.) In any case, it is very far from clear that trying to substitute "occasion" or "sign" accounts of the relation of the brain to mind in sensation for the postulation of causal efficacy will bring about a net improvement in intelligibility. If it's hard to understand how the brain can cause ideas in the mind, it's at least equally hard to understand how the brain can, non-causally, "give the mind signs."[19]

Much more promising are the several recent attempts to meet the heterogeneity objection head-on by denying that it constitutes a genuine problem: in Descartes's mind, or as an inadvertent internal problem for his system, or with respect to what is philosophically tenable. Of particular importance to this position is Descartes's own emphatic statement that critics who advance the heterogeneity objection are just confused. The key statement occurs in a letter to Clerselier, originally published with the French version of the *Replies to Objections*. (The letter concerns a summary of Gassendian objections which had been submitted to Descartes.) Descartes writes:

> As for the two questions added at the end, namely: *how the soul moves the body, if it is not at all material? & how it can receive the species of corporeal objects?* . . . I will tell you privately, that all the difficulty they contain only proceeds from a supposition which is false, and which cannot at all be proved, namely, that if the soul and the body are two substances of different nature, that prevents them from being able to act the one upon (*countre*) the other. . . . (AT IX–I, 213; CSM II, 275)[20]

It does seem that this clear rebuttal puts the burden of proof on those who want to make the heterogeneity objection stick. I also think that the recent repudiators of the objection are quite right in claiming that critics of Descartes—from Elizabeth, Gassendi, Simon Foucher, and Leibniz to the present—have failed to make clear why exactly "heterogeneity" is supposed to preclude interaction.[21] As some of the recent defenders have observed, critics of Descartes's position may be assuming that "intelligible" causal relations are just those that conform to mechanistic "impact" models, but twentieth-century critics, at least, should know better than to make such an assumption.[22] And they have rightly remarked that Descartes himself sometimes seems to indicate that body-mind causation is none the worse for not being a case of causation by impact.[23]

Besides making these general points, recent defenders of Descartes have discussed aspects of the body-mind interaction issue in some detail. One question which has received considerable attention in the apologetic as well as the critical literature is how Descartes's "causal principles" bear on the postulation of body-mind causation. I basically agree with the apologists that we have yet to see demonstrated any insurmountable inconsistency in principle between Descartes's restrictions on causality and the assumption of body-mind interaction. I want to review the issue briefly, however, for only when one sees why the causal restrictions do *not* in principle rule out body-mind causation is one in a position to understand where the consistency problems in Descartes's position *really* lie.

There can be no doubt that Descartes sometimes endorses conceptual restrictions on what can be supposed to cause what. Such restrictions figure prominently in his "causal" arguments for the existence of God in Meditation III and the proof of the existence of body in Meditation VI. There has been a great deal of controversy, however, over precisely what causal restrictions Descartes wishes to propound.[24] Disagreements over whether his "causal principles" create problems for the postulation of body-mind causation to a large extent hinge on the identification of these principles. Those who see a consistency problem of this nature tend to ascribe to Descartes a principle that the cause must be "like" the effect.[25] Others argue that Descartes holds only that the cause must contain "at least as much reality as" the effect. They point out that *this* principle seems to present no problem for body-mind causation.[26] Descartes's rankings of things by "degrees of reality" are not complex, they basically reduce to the two assertions that infinite substances have more reality than finite substances, and finite substances have more reality than modes. Hence what the "reality" principle rules out is just that a mode could "cause" a substance, or a finite substance an infinite one. Some commentators, however, find in Descartes's works a further restriction on causation—distinct from a "likeness" principle"—that renders body-mind causation at least prima facie problematic: namely the principle that the (total efficient) cause must *contain the effect*, formally or eminently.[27]

Descartes's defenders have adequately established both that there is no basis for ascribing to him a "causal likeness" principle and that the "degrees of reality" principle is consistent with body-mind causation on his three-tiered ranking of "reality."[28] It is true, though, that Descartes also claims that the cause must "contain the effect, formally or eminently."[29] (He stresses in response to objections that he means the "efficient and total cause.")[30] And there is reason to suggest that this principle does present a problem for the postulation of body-mind causality which does not emerge from the "degrees of reality" constraint alone.

Basically the difficulty is this. Body clearly does not contain mental modes ("thoughts") "formally" for to contain a state formally is literally to have that state, as when a moving body causes motion in another body or the sun causes heat in a stone.[31] (And surely anything that has a thought in this sense *is a mind*.) But it does not seem that body can contain mental modes "eminently" either, for Descartes holds that eminent containment requires that the cause contain "more excellent perfections" than those found in the effect or that it be "more noble" than what can contain the perfections of the effect.[32] (So God contains bodies eminently.) It seems highly implausible to ascribe to him the view that body contains "perfections more excellent than" mental modes; and he explicitly says that the human mind is "much nobler than" the body.[33] So (it would seem to follow) the causal containment principle rules out body-mind causation.

There are two, mutually compatible, ways of replying to this objection. In order to explain them, it will be helpful first to take note of Descartes's distinction between two senses of 'idea' in the *Meditations'* "Preface to the Reader" (AT VII, 8; CSM II, 7). By 'idea', he says, one can mean either an "operation of the understanding" or "the thing represented by this operation." In Meditation III, Descartes remarks that *he* (as mind) is the source of all his ideas in the first sense: if his ideas are considered simply as modes of thought, disregarding their different representative contents, they "all seem to proceed from me (*a me procedere*) in the same manner" (AT VII, 40; CSM II, 27–28); each of them is a "work of the mind" (AT IX, 32, FV).[34] Presumably such locutions imply that the mind at least contributes to the efficient causality of its ideas, viewed in one way. Bodily modes might then be admitted as *partial* causes of ideas (considered in this way) without being required, under the containment principle, to contain the ideas caused. (The containment principles applies only to *total* causes, and could be satisfied in the case envisaged as long as the cause constituted of mind plus bodily states may be said to "contain" ideas formally or eminently.)[35]

Secondly, and perhaps less tenuously, it appears that body is a perfectly legitimate candidate under the containment principle to serve as cause of ideas considered in the second sense—in other words, as what is represented in the mind.[36] According to Descartes's conclusion about the existence of bodies in Meditation VI, all the properties that I "clearly and distinctly understand" in bodies are formally contained in actual bodies (AT VII, 83; CSM II, 57). He further explains that these properties are all those which, generally considered, are comprehended in the object of pure mathematics. This "object" has previously been characterized (at the beginning of Meditation V) as continuous quantity in which are numbered various parts with their respective sizes, shapes, positions, and motions. It seems, then, that body is eligible to cause the presentation in the mind of these qualities while satisfying the constraint of *formal* containment. It further seems quite plausible to suppose that Descartes might think the contents (such as they are) of mere sensations or confused ideas of sense—such as color, taste, etc., which on his principles fail to "exhibit" any properties formally contained in body—are *eminently* contained in body, for after all he has said in Meditation III that such ideas "exhibit so little reality," he can hardly distinguish it from non-being (AT VII, 44; CSM II, 30). Although his conclusion there was that he himself (as mind) could be their cause, it seems that by parity of reasoning he could just as well conclude that virtually *anything* with "perfections" could be their cause under the condition of eminent containment.[37]

For these reasons, I believe that Descartes's apologists are correct in denying that even the "containment" restriction on causality is straightforwardly inconsistent with body-mind causation.[38] Now, however, we are in a position to see that Descartes's treatments of the causation of sensory ideas do present other problems of consistency and coherence. In the next section, I will try to establish this point with respect to two closely related questions. First, does Descartes wish to maintain that sensory ideas of bodies (considered as representative contents) actually are caused in the mind by bodies in which they are antecendently contained? Second, is the fact that we do not voluntarily produce the sensory contents in our mind sufficient to establish that we are merely passive recipients of them?

III

The source of our sensory ideas of bodies is the ostensible focus of the proof of the existence of body in Meditation VI. Descartes notes that he has a "certain passive faculty of sensing, or of receiving and recognizing the ideas of sensible things" and that this faculty would be useless unless there were also, in himself or something else, an active faculty "for producing or bringing about these ideas" (AT VII, 79; CSM II, 55). He first eliminates himself as the cause of such ideas (considered as *representing* physical things) on the grounds that they are produced in him "without my cooperation, and even also against my will (*invito*)." He then concludes that such ideas *are sent forth from* corporeal things (*a rebus corporeis emitti*), on the grounds that he has a strong disposition to believe that they are send forth from bodies, so any other hypothesis about their origin would entail that God is a deceiver (AT VII, 79–80; CSM II, 55). Similarly, in *Principles* II.1, he holds that such ideas come from *advenire*, that they are "exhibited to" us by corporeal objects—or by "extended matter"—on the grounds that it is not in our power to bring about particular sensations.[39] So far it looks as if Descartes thinks that bodies cause sensory contents in us by sending them into our minds; and it looks as if he holds that bodies are able to do this in virtue of actually exemplifying the very qualities represented in the ideas—at least with respect to perceptions of shapes, sizes, positions, and motions.

I will now try to show, first, that close inspection of both the *Meditations* and the *Principles* passages reveals a tendency of thought contrary to this conception of the production of sensory ideas; and, second, that other texts—especially *Comments on a Broadsheet*—appear flatly to contradict it.

We have seen that Descartes begins by talking about *sensory* ideas of bodies in both the *Meditations* and *Principles* arguments for the existence of matter: it is these which come to him "without my cooperation" (Meditation VI), which "are not in our power" (*PP* II.1). He does *not* conclude, though, that the specific, determinate qualities represented by particular sensory ideas are exemplified in particular external physical objects which actually cause the ideas: not even specific sizes, shapes, and motions. It is the idea of *matter in general* which, according to both passages, we must suppose to have "formal" existence outside the mind if we are to avoid the conclusion that God is a deceiver. According to the *Principles*, "we sense, or rather stimulated by sense we clearly

and distinctly perceive" this matter. According to the *Meditations*, we can ultimately conclude only that corporeal things possess all the properties which
considered generally are, in *res extensa*, considered as mathematical objects. He
specifically goes on to indicate that such "particular aspects" of body as that the
sun is of such and such a size or shape, as well as obscure ideas of light or
sound or pain, do not fall within the scope of this argument. What he actually
seems to be saying, then, is that (a) sensory ideas are "produced" by matter;
that (b) matter formally possesses, in some *general* sense, those mathematical
properties that are clearly and distinctly apprehended; but (c) not even the size,
shape, and motion represented in a particular sensory idea need be actually
exemplified in a particular external body that constitutes the cause of the idea.[40]

A later work, *Comments on a Broadsheet*, not only draws back from but
directly repudiates the notion—suggested by much of the *Meditations* passage
especially—that ideas of external qualities are simply received into the mind
from particular external bodies which exemplify them. As already mentioned,
Descartes there holds that external things transmit to our mind, through the
organs of sense, something which "gives [the mind] occasion to form [the
ideas]." In this work, he also says that "we form in [or by] thought" the ideas of
external things when bodily motions provide the occasion to the mind; and that,
on the occasion of appropriate motions in the brain, the mind "exhibits to itself"
ideas of pain, color, sound, and the like.[41] To some extent this language accords
with the view, discussed above, that the mind itself is the cause of its ideas
considered as modes of thought, as "operations of the understanding"; but Descartes here goes much further. He holds also that sensory ideas *as contents* are
innate in, or within the productive power of, our "faculty of thought":

> . . . there is *nothing in our ideas*, which is not innate in the mind, or the faculty of
> thought, except for those circumstances, which have regard to experience: i.e., that
> we judge that these or those ideas, which we now have present to our thought, are
> to be attributed to certain things outside us: not because these things transmit (*immi-
> serunt*) the ideas themselves to our minds through the organs of sense, but because
> they nevertheless transmit something, which gives the mind occasion to form the
> ideas, by a faculty innate in it, at this time rather than another. (AT VIII–2, 358–9;
> CSM I, 304, emphasis added)[42]

On this picture the division of labor between brain and mind seems to be as
follows: a motion in the brain "excites" the mind to "form" as an actual conscious state a sensation which previously existed in it, but only potentially, or as
a capacity of thought.

Cartesian texts, then, fail to give a single consistent answer to the question
whether ideas considered as sensory contents have their origin in bodies—even
when the favored "mathematical" qualities are at issue. Further, the reason Descartes offers when he advances a negative answer to this question is not at all
bound up with the containment restriction or any other general causal principle.

When, in the *Comments*, Descartes claims that sensory ideas are innate and
that the mind simply "exhibits them to itself" under appropriate stimulation, he

grounds these claims on the mechanistic account of sensation he has previously presented in the *Dioptrics* and *Principles*.[43] He writes:

> . . . whoever correctly observes how far our senses extend, and what it is precisely that can come (*pervenire*) from them to our faculty of thought, must admit that in no case do they exhibit to us the ideas of things, such as we form them in thought. So much so that there is nothing in our ideas, that is not innate in the mind, or faculty of thinking, except only those circumstances which have regard to experience . . . (AT VIII–2, 358; CSM I, 304).

That the sensory ideas we have of bodies cannot come from bodies through the senses, or be "exhibited" by our physical sensory system to our mind, is evident, Descartes here holds, from the facts about the perceptual process established in his earlier works. All that "approaches (*accedit*) our mind from external things through the sense organs" are certain corporeal motions; and even these, "and the figures which arise from them [in the nerves], are not conceived by us such as they occur in the organs of sense." It follows from all this, Descartes concludes,

> . . . that the ideas of the motions and figures are themselves innate in us. So much the more must the ideas of pain, color, sound and the like be innate, that our mind may, on occasion of certain corporeal motions, exhibit them to itself; for they have no likeness (*similtudinem*) to the corporeal motions. (AT VIII–2, 359; CSM I, 304).

The position presented here clearly rests on the assumption that the lack of "likeness" between ideas of sense and actual brain states is sufficient to establish that the former must "come from" the mind. Descartes seems to be assuming, that is, that ideas in the mind could "come from" the brain only if the brain movements provided the mind with *exact models or images* for what is represented in idea. Because they present to the mind much less than that, they must be regarded only as "occasions" of the mind's representational activity. *This* is the reason for Descartes's claim that the senses, rather than transmitting ideas of corporeal things to the mind, merely "transmit something which . . . gives the mind occasion to form these ideas, by a faculty innate in it."[44]

Note that the lack of "likeness" between idea and brain state with which Descartes is here concerned is different from that at issue in the heterogeneity objection. The issue here is not heterogeneity of mental *qua* mental from physical *qua* physical, otherwise Descartes could not indicate that certain mental states are more like the exciting brain state than others ("so much the more . . ."). The point is rather that, while the exciting brain state will be, say, an instance of circular motion, the resulting sensory idea will be a color or perhaps an oval (the latter having claim to *limited* resemblance to its actual physical cause). By the same token, Descartes's *reason* for thinking the lack of resemblance in question establishes that ideas of sense are innate is not directly connected with the containment restriction on causality.

This passage suggests implicitly a view that is more overt in other passages—including one or two already cited: that the brain's causal role in the origin of sensation consists in (so to speak) forcing something on the mind's attention (even if not a full-fledged model for the subsequent mental idea). I will discuss the implications of this "presentational" model of the body-mind relation in sensation in the next section. But, setting this issue aside for the moment, I want to contrast the *Comments'* conception of the mind as actively forming ideas of sense, which it in some sense already possesses as dispositions, with the position stated elsewhere in Descartes's works, that the mind passively receives its ideas of sense from without.[45]

Descartes very often characterizes sensations as "passions" of the mind; this characterization rests on the commonsensical, phenomenological observation that the *will* plays no role in their origin, together with the further stipulation that for "only [the mind's] volitions are actions."[46] As we have seen, this doctrine indeed provides an important part of the basis for Descartes's arguments in the *Meditations* and the *Principles* that his (sensory) ideas of bodies are caused by bodies. When Descartes argues in the *Comments* that his ideas of sense are innate, he does not deal with the issue of involuntariness at all. Since it is not believable that he changed his mind—even temporarily—about whether ideas of sense are voluntary, one must suppose that he did relinquish—at least temporarily—the view that involuntariness is sufficient to establish an extra-mental origin.[47]

There are, then, two levels to the conflict between the implications Descartes draws from his mechanistic theory of perception in the *Comments* and the treatment of the origin of ideas of sense in his proofs of the existence of body. Not only are opposed conclusions offered concerning the source of sensory ideas of body, but also the account in the *Comments* raises problems of consistency with respect to what can be concluded from the fact that sensations arise in our minds independently of our will. In fact, by suggesting that the mind *does* something in sensation—"forms" its ideas—the *Comments* account seem generally at odds with Descartes's emphasis elsewhere on the mind's passivity in sensing.

Some progress may be made in resolving these conflicts if we allow that Descartes is simply expressing himself very loosely in passages concerned with proving the existence of body. For example, we may suppose that when he speaks of sensory ideas of body "coming from" body itself, he is expressing in misleading terms the notion that bodily motions do play the role of *exciting* our minds to form these sensory ideas (and nothing more).[48] In behalf of this reading we may appeal to the fact that even in the midst of the argument for the existence of body in the *Principles* he employs the phrase, "we perceive, or rather stimulated (*impulsi*) by sense we apprehend [matter] . . ."[49] Alternatively, we might suggest a qualification on Descartes's claims that ideas of *res extensa* and its modes come from the mind. Perhaps, after all, some sensory ideas of body really do "come to the mind from the body," in that the brain does exhibit *some* potential idea contents to the mind. Shapes, for example, really are present in the brain when we sense, and hence can be "exhibited to the mind" if any brain state can be, even though our specific sensible ideas of shape on a given occasion may not precisely "resemble" any shapes present in the brain at that time.[50] (This reading requires treating the *Comments* passage as a partial overstatement, while *also* reading the Meditation VI argument in a qualified way.)

These observations may help to reduce the impression of a hopelessly sharp conflict among certain of Descartes's statements about the source of ideas of sense. To me, though, they have a rather "cooked" feel. The most credible hypothesis is that when Descartes was primarily concerned with arguing for the existence of bodies, he drew on phenomenological observations to conclude that ideas of sense come from without the mind. In these circumstances, he found it convenient to interpret involuntariness as signifying causation from outside the mind. When he focused on the implications of his scientific account of perception, however, he concluded that ideas of bodies—even of shape or size—*could not* strictly come from bodies.[51] In these contexts, involuntariness is simply not allowed to count against a conclusion presented as evident on independent grounds.

In any case, I trust it is clear that the "reconciliations" I have tentatively proposed do not fully accommodate Descartes's actual statements. Further, they do not at all resolve the problem about how the mind, if truly "passive" in sensation, can help to bring about sensory ideas—as both the text of the *Comments* and the "containment" principle seem to require.[52]

IV

According the Descartes's account of sense perception in the *Comments*, the brain "exhibits" certain patterns of motion to the mind, which then, in response, brings to consciousness or actualizes appropriate innate ideas. This account provides an instance of what I have called the "presentation" model of the brain-mind relation in sensation. Such a conception is still more explicit in the passage from Descartes's much earlier work, *Treatise on Man*, cited at the end of section II. Recent Cartesian apologists have scarcely taken note of this model; those who have have not addressed its oddity.[53] In this section, I will first indicate more fully the range of texts in which versions of the presentation conception figure prominently, then sketch some of the problems that it involves (which are, it seems to me, all too obvious). Finally, I consider the relation of the presentation account to other models of sensation that occur in Descartes's works, particularly with respect to the question whether the presentation model needs to be taken seriously and "literally."[54]

It is important to notice, first, that Descartes freely employs the presentation model in discussing the brain-mind relation in imagination, memory, and the origin of emotion, as well as in sensation. Imagination, as well as sensation, is at issue in the *Treatise on Man* passage already cited. The account of imagination offered at the beginning of the Meditation VI is entirely cast in presentational terminology. The best explanation of the faculty of imagination, Descartes says, lies in the assumption that the mind is joined to a body "in such a way that it can apply itself at will to, as it were, inspect" that body (*ut ad illud veluti inspiciendum pro arbitro se applicet*) (AT VII, 73; CSM II, 51). As he further explains,

> . . . when [the mind] imagines, it turns to (*se convertat ad*) the body, and views (*intueatur*) in it something which conforms to an idea understood by itself [i.e., by the mind] or perceived by sense. (Ibid.)

In a latter to Arnauld, he says that for memory to occur it is not sufficient that traces be left in the brain by earlier thoughts; rather, it is necessary that there be traces such that "the mind recognizes that they were not always present in us but at some time entered de novo," traces that "when impressed are recognized by pure understanding to be new" (AT V, 220; *PL* 234). In the *Rules*, Descartes says that sense, imagination, and memory are distinguished by the manner in which the mind, a purely spiritual power distinct from the body, "applies itself" to parts of the brain (AT X, 415–16). The presentation model also figures in Descartes's work on the passions. Thus—to cite a passage of exceptional oddity—he distinguishes the *passion* of joy from the corresponding active affect by noting that in the case of the passion, *impressions in the brain* represent a good to the soul (*luy representent*) as its own; whereas in the active affect—"purely intellectual joy"—the *understanding* represents a good to the soul as its own (*PS* II.91: AT XI, 396–97; CSM I, 360–61).

Second, the presentation model is at least strongly suggested by Descartes's various accounts of sensation—in *Treatise on Light, Meditations,* and other works—in terms of the motions in the brain giving the mind a sign to sense something (. . . *ibi menti signum dat ad aliquid sentiendum*, as he puts it in Meditation VI).[55] Perhaps such language does not strictly involve a picture of the mind's *noticing* something in the brain; but "receiving a sign" surely does normally suggest intelligent recognition, and it is difficult to think of a more natural reading.

Texts in which the presentation model of sensation occurs independently of the "sign" terminology include *Passions of the Soul* and *Conversation with Burman,* as well as *Treatise on Man.* In *Passions,* Descartes argues that the double sensory (e.g., visual) images from a given object must be united at some place in the brain, so that only one object is "represented" to the soul (*PS* I, 32; AT XI, 352–53; CSM I, 340). But perhaps most impressive is a comment quoted by Burman (though of course Burman's reports cannot be taken as absolutely authoritative). When Burman asked Descartes about his use of the term '*inspicere*' in the discussion of imagination at the beginning of Meditation VI, Descartes's clarification (according to Burman's report) began as follows:

> It is a certain special mode of thinking, which is like this. When external objects act on my senses, and paint on them the idea, or rather figure of themselves, then the mind, when it turns to (*advertit*) these images which are thus painted on the gland, is said to *sense* . . . (AT V, 162; *CB* 27)

Descartes's main purpose in most of the passages concerned with perception may be to get across the idea that mental perceptions *aren't pictures* somehow transferred up from the brain into the mind. Nevertheless, his use of the presentational model suggests that he does retain to some extent an element of the view that the mind *apprehends a physical intermediary* in the process of perception, *not just* the distant object normally said to be perceived and *not just* the *mental* idea that is, as he says in the *Meditations*, the only thing we "properly and immediately sense" (AT VII, 75; CSM II, 52).

The oddities of the presentational model are obvious. The model suggests that the mind perceives external bodies by virtue of perceiving, or otherwise recognizing, something *else*: traces or motions in the brain. But it neither explains how it is possible for the mind to do *this*, nor tells us why the question of how the mind does this is not as legitimate as the original question about how perception of external things takes place.

Apart from its intrinsic strangeness, the presentation conception seems to conflict with fundamental Cartesian doctrine about the mind. The Cartesian mind is, after all, supposed to be conscious of its perceptions.[56] Yet it seems that we, as minds, are not conscious of these brain state perceptions or of receiving "signs" from the brain, but only of cups and saucers, tables and chairs, other human bodies, and the like.[57]

Cartesian apologists might suggest, in response to this criticism, that the presentation model is merely "metaphorical"—a harmless *façon de parler*.[58] In support of this view, Descartes's defenders could point to passages which suggest a less objectionable associationist conception and even to at least one passage that seems almost directly to ridicule the presentation conception.[59]

I don't at all deny the importance of such passages. (I will discuss some of them shortly.) Nor do I deny that some of Descartes's descriptions of the body-mind relation in sensation have to be taken less than literally. At the same time, however, I consider highly dubious the notion that the "presentational" passages can reasonably be shrugged off as innocently figurative. On balance, it seems more reasonable to believe that Descartes did not sharply or consistently distinguish a "literal" associationist view of the body-mind relation in sensation from a "metaphorical" presentation conception. Rather, the two conceptions existed more or less on a par in his thought, dominating different texts at different times. I will briefly indicate some reasons for taking the difficult presentational model more seriously than the "merely metaphorical" reading will allow before I focus on what I see as the alternative associationist conception.

As noted in Section II, Descartes occasionally says that the brain "impresses" or "imprints" sensory ideas on the mind. We have conclusive reason to interpret *these* passages as "merely metaphorical": not only does Descartes himself explicitly characterize one of them in this way, but the reason he offers for rejecting a literal reading is conclusive (within his dualistic framework).

In the *Rules*, he first says that talk of the brain taking on impressions from external objects as wax takes on impressions from a seal is *no* mere analogy. We can also say, he adds, that in receiving figures from external sense the mind resembles a seal, but in this case we *are* merely speaking analogically for "nothing at all like this [mental] power is to be found in corporeal things" (AT X, 415; CSM I, 42). In other words, conscious "reception" of ideas is not literally ascribable to a material thing like a seal. (Further, of course, we know that anything that *literally* receives "impressions" must be extended.)

We cannot argue along similar lines, however, that the power to perceive or notice or attend cannot literally be ascribed to the mind, for this is just the sort of thing that the mind does. Thus Descartes's own way of explaining why the "imprint" model has to be interpreted metaphorically cannot readily be adapted to the presentation model.

A further relevant difference between the imprint and presentation accounts of sensation lies in the fact that, while Descartes only *occasionally* uses the imprint or impact technology with respect to the brain-mind relation, the presentation model is extremely pervasive. As we have seen, it is prominent in Cartesian texts from the very early (the *Rules* and *Treatise on Man*) to the very late (*Comments* and *Passions*). In some of these texts it is quite elaborately developed with virtually no hint that a mere *façon de parler* is intended. Also significant, in my view, is the fact that the fairly detailed discussion of imagination in Meditation VI really requires that the presentation model of brain-mind relation be taken *quite* literally with respect to *that* mental power at least.

Finally, one must not overlook the fact that (if we can trust Burman's report) Descartes actually reinforces the presentation conception when given the opportunity to explain that he did not intend it to be taken literally.

Altogether, then, the Cartesian apologist who proposes to shrug off the presentation model as an incidental figure of speech has quite a bit of explaining away to do. It would be too rash to say in advance of the attempt that such a salvage enterprise will necessarily prove futile, but I hope to have established at least a presumption that it will be difficult. I now turn to the texts which present a more austere and, I think, clearly more palatable conception of the body-mind relation in sensation—texts which avoid both the imprint (or impact) and the presentational conceptions.

V

There surely are numerous passages in Descartes's scientific and philosophic works which suggest something approaching an associationist conception of the relation between brain states and sensory ideas. And there is one such passage which at least verges on direct ridicule of the presentation view. The latter passage occurs in the *Dioptrics*. In this important text, Descartes himself makes fun of the idea that there are "other eyes in our brain" with which we perceive the images that form there. In this passage, the rejection of the conception of perception in terms of the transmission of pictures or replicas extends, it seems, to a general rejection of the presentation model. Here Descartes explains that it is not by means of resemblance to external things that a picture in the brain "makes us perceive the object, as if there were yet other eyes in the brain with which we could perceive (*appercevoir*) it." Rather, he says,

> . . . it is the motions of which the picture is composed which, acting immediately on (*agissans contre*) the mind in as much as it is united to our body, are so established by nature as to make it have such perceptions . . . (AT VI, 130; CSM I, 167)[60]

Certain other passages similarly describe the brain-mind relation in sensation in terms which suggest a mere brute conjunction. Consider, for example, the following statement from Descartes's correspondence:

> It is not surprising that certain movements of the heart are thus naturally joined to certain thoughts, to which they have no resemblance; for, from the fact that our soul is of such a nature that it could be united to a body, it has also this property, that each of its thoughts can be so associated with certain motions as dispositions of the body that when the same dispositions recur in the body they induce (*induisent*) the soul to the same thought. (To Chanut, Feb. 1, 1647: AT IV, 604; *PL* 210)

Finally, one might point to one of Descartes's well-known letters to Princess Elizabeth in which he asserts that the notion of body-mind interaction derives from the "primitive" notion of mind-body union, which must not be confused either with notions applicable to mind only, like thought, or notions applicable to body only, like extension:

> . . . there are in us certain primitive notions, which are like originals on the pattern of which we form all our other knowledge. And there are very few such notions; for, after the most general, of being, number, duration, etc., which apply to all that we can conceive, we have only, for body in particular, the notion of extension. From which follow those of figure and motion; and for the soul alone, we have only that of thought, in which are included the perceptions of the understanding and the inclinations of the will; finally, for the soul and the body together, we have only that of their union, on which depends that of the force which the soul has to move the body, and the body to act on the soul, in causing its sensations and passions (*& le corps d'agir sur l'ame, en causant ses sentiments et ses passions*). (May 21, 1643: AT III, 665; *PL* 138)

Descartes goes on to say that error arises if one doesn't carefully distinguish these notions according to their appropriate sphere of application, or if "we want to explain one of these notions by another; for being primitives, each of them cannot be understood except by itself" (AT III, 666; *PL* 138). We get into this sort of trouble, he suggests, if we try to understand the mind's action on the body in terms of one body's moving another (as Elizabeth may have been doing).

Some critics sympathetic to Descartes have taken such passages as these as grounds for interpreting the relation of body-mind causation in the Cartesian system as a "primitive" relation that creates no peculiar intelligibility problems. Robert Richardson has claimed (primarily on the basis of the remarks to Elizabeth) that this relation between body and mind is analogous to that expressed in explanations in terms of basic physical forces.[61] And Louis Loeb seems to suggest obliquely that Cartesian interaction could beneficially be viewed in Humean terms of mere constant association of brain states and sensory ideas.[62] In support of this suggestion, one may adduce Descartes's talk of the brain state-idea connection as a relation of "association" (in the passage from a letter quoted above) together with his frequent stress on the *arbitrary* and *contingent* nature of the connection between particular brain states and the sensory ideas consequent upon them.[63] Thus we may perhaps say, giving weight to these texts, that Descartes is at least within reach of a conception of body-mind causation that is neither more nor less "intelligible" than body-body causation turns out to be on certain reasonably respected analyses.

On the basis of the arguments and exposition presented in Sections II–IV, I would of course deny that we can ascribe to Descartes consistent adherence to conceptions of causality in general, and of mind-body interaction in particular, that are easily aligned with views in fashion since Hume. Besides acknowledging Descartes's endorsement of restrictions on the causal possibilities (as represented, particularly, by his "containment" principle), one must also take note of his argument that ideas of sense have to be innate, since they don't "resemble" any purported physical causes. In addition, one must come to terms with his non-associationist "presentation" characterization of the brain-mind relation.

I agree with Loeb and Richardson, however, to the extent of granting that Descartes comes closest to advancing a *tenable* conception of body-mind causality when he steers clear of both the "imprinting" and the "presentation" models in favor of more nearly "associationist" conceptions suggested by certain statements. Still, I think they are too optimistic in their interpretations of even the favored passages. In the last section, I will argue that their interpretations require certain adjustments which move Descartes's "best" statements about body-mind causation in sensation further from a modern or a Humean viewpoint than they allow. I will also summarize the conclusions I hope to have established in the paper as a whole, concerning the strengths and limitations of recent defenses of Descartes, as they relate to his position on the origin of sensation.

VI

Promising as Descartes's talk of the "primitive" nature of the body-mind relation may appear, his elaboration of this concept in a later letter to Elizabeth shows that his conception is not the sophisticated one attributed to him by Richardson, but something far more specious. In this later letter, after noting that the soul is conceived by pure understanding, and the body by understanding aided by imagination, he explains that the body-mind relation can't be clearly understood at all but is simply "sensed":

> . . . I observe a large difference between these three sorts of notions, in that the soul
> is only conceived by pure understanding; the body, that is extension, figures, and

motions, can also be conceived by understanding alone, but much better by understanding aided by imagination; and finally, things which pertain to the union of the soul and the body, are only known obscurely by understanding alone, or understanding aided by imagination; but they are known very clearly by the senses. (June 28, 1643: AT III, 691–92; *PL* 141)

Descartes fails to explain, however, how this indistinct (if "clear") sensory "knowledge" can be admissible in a legitimate theory (especially one that tends to insist on the inferential nature of our knowledge of the existence of body). And he certainly fails to explain how it ties in with the account of sensation he elsewhere insists on, according to which movements in the brain cause or excite the mind to have ideas of sense. (Surely *that* account is not itself based on sense; the senses could hardly be supposed to tell us—"in the ordinary course of life", as Descartes adds—that brain states give rise to mind states according to correlations instituted by nature.) Descartes, in short, does not assert to Elizabeth the sophisticated view that Richardson's analogy with "basic forces" might suggest: that body-mind (or mind-body) causation is an irreducible *theoretical* primitive. Rather, in his discussion with her, he departs from the level of theory altogether, implying that the notion of mind-body interaction is irreducible in the sense that you just *feel* it. For these reasons I believe that Richardson's sympathetic interpretation is less well grounded in the texts than he supposes.

The same may be said of Loeb's reading of Descartes's statement quoted above from the Feb. 1, 1647, letter to Chanut as a "foreshadowing of a Humean, constant conjunction, or regularity analysis of causation."[64] Despite Descartes's use here of the term "association" for the relation between physical and mental states, several phrases in the passage indicate that he is still thinking of the relation as consisting in more than *mere* association:

There is no reason to be surprised that certain motions of the heart should be *naturally connected in this way* with certain thoughts, which they in no way resemble. The soul's *natural capacity for union with a body brings with it the possibility of* an association between thoughts and bodily motions or conditions so that when the same conditions recur they *induce* the soul to the same thought; and conversely when the same thought recurs, it *disposes* the body to return to the same condition.[65]

Although I think Loeb is wrong in suggesting that Descartes comes close to espousing pure Humean associationism in the passages he cites, I still agree with him that Descartes does, in these passages, express a certain nonchalance about which classes of entities or states can be linked by the causal relation (whatever exactly the latter may be). The passages, in other words, do conform to Descartes's direct denial of the heterogeneity problem in the polemical statements that Loeb and other apologists particularly stress.

One final problem needs to be mentioned in connection with attempts to assimilate Descartes's position on body-mind interaction either with causal relations at the level of basic forces, or with traditional Humean doctrine. At *Treatise* I, iii, 14, Hume specifies that causes and effects must be spatially, as well as temporally, contiguous.[66] Basic forces, even if not appropriately described as "contiguous," presumably do operate within an encompassing spatial framework. Whether body-mind interactions satisfy any spatial constraints is a perplexing question, however.[67] Some would say that the spatial condition can harmlessly be dropped in the case of body-mind causality.[68] Others might prefer to defend the view that a spatial contiguity condition intelligibly applies, even in this case.[69] I do not deny that an acceptable resolution of the issue may be possible, one way or another. My point is just that published defenses of Cartesian interactionism that interpret this position in terms of relatively sophisticated modern views have so far failed adequately to address the spatiality issue—or even to take note of it.[70]

VII. Conclusion

I have argued that recent defenders of Descartes are correct in maintaining that he conceived of the body-mind relation in sensation as one of efficient causation and in denying that the "heterogeneity objection" has received compelling defense. Although they have raised reasonable objections to claims that Descartes's causal principles rule out body-mind causation, some room remains to question the compatibility of Descartes's causal principles with his accounts of body-mind causality in sensation. I have pointed out problems in reconciling texts in which Descartes holds that all ideas of sense—particularly the most "confused" ideas of the qualities of bodies—are innate with texts that indicate that our ideas of bodies have to come from without. I have tried to establish the prominence of the presentation model of sensation in Descartes's works and have questioned the view that this model—with all its difficulties—can be dismissed as a mere figure of speech. Finally, I have acknowledged the strong presence in many texts of a conception of the relation of brain states to mental sensory ideas which seems to avoid the problems of the presentation model. I have argued, however, that certain attempts to construe this nonpresentation conception as foreshadowing respected modern views about causal connections neglect significant features of Descartes's actual statements; they neglect other peculiarities of the interactionist doctrine as well.

Notes

I am grateful to many people—too many, I regret, to mention individually—for comments in discussion and in writing on earlier versions of this paper. But I do want particularly to thank John Cottingham for incisive suggestions which have influenced the present version at several points. I also thank Princeton University for support of a year of leave during which much of the work on the paper was completed.

1. *Diop* iv: AT VI, 109; CSM I, 164. Although I cite standard English editions, translations in the paper are my own.

2. See R. C Richardson, "The 'Scandal' of Cartesian Interactionism," *Mind* 91 (1982): 20–37.

3. See Daisie Radner, "Descartes' Notion of the Union of Mind and Body," *Journal of the History of Philosophy* 9 (1971): 159–70; and Radner, "Is There a Problem of Cartesian Interaction?" *Journal of the History of Philosophy* 23: 35–49. In "Adequate Causes and Natural Change in Descartes' Philosophy", *Human Nature and Natural Knowledge*, ed. A. Donagan, et al. (Festschrift for Marjorie Grene) 107–22, Janet Broughton argues that body-mind causation is incompatible with Descartes's restrictions on causation on the assumption (which she endorses) that eminent containment is not a relevant possibility in this case.

4. Cf. S. V. Keeling, *Descartes*, 2nd ed. (Oxford: Oxford UP, 1968) 153: "The defining attributes of body and of mind being wholly different and mutually exclusive, direct causal interaction between them, [Descartes] maintains, is necessarily impossible." (Keeling supplies no references in support of this attribution.) Compare Martial Gueroult, *Descartes selon l'ordre des Raisons*, vol. 2 (Paris: Aubier-Montaigne, 1968) 84. Gueroult interprets Descartes as holding that the action of body on mind, *despite being inconceivable and contradictory*, is nevertheless actual. (He cites in this connection Descartes's doctrine that God is not bound by the limits of our understanding.)

5. Keeling, in the work cited above, is one example. A more recent proponent of this type of view is John Yolton, in *Perceptual Acquaintance from Descartes to Reid* (Minneapolis: U of Minnesota P, 1984). Like Keeling, Yolton seems to attribute to Descartes himself the view that it is unintelligible to assume causal relations between substances of diverse natures, and hence such causality is impossible—although Yolton's attribution is less definite than Keeling's: ". . . Descartes was confronted with the difficulty of how causation could work across categories, between body and mind, from physiology to psychology. There can in fact be no causal relation between such diverse substances, but the relation is nonetheless intimate." Like Keeling, Yolton provides no direct textual support for the suggestion that Descartes recognized this "difficulty."

In the paper cited in note 3, Broughton argues the Descartes *came* to reject body-mind causation, specifically in *NiP*.

6. Besides Richardson's paper cited in note 2, the following works defend these claims or closely similar ones: Louis E. Loeb, *From Descartes to Hume* (Ithaca, NY: Cornell UP, 1981) 134–56; Eileen O'Neill, *Mind and Mechanism: An Examination of Some Mind-Body Problems in Descartes' Philosophy*, diss. Princeton U, 1983; and O'Neill, "Mind-Body Interaction and Metaphysical Consistency: A Defense of Descartes," *Journal of the History of Philosophy* 25 (April, 1987): 227–45; Mark Bedau, "Cartesian Interaction," *Midwest Studies in Philosophy* 10 (1986): 483–502. See also Richardson's and Loeb's "Replies to Daisie Radner's 'Is There a Problem of Cartesian Interaction?'" *Journal of the History of Philosophy* 23 (1985): 221–31.

Issues raised by these writers, and discussed here particularly in Section II, have recently also been discussed by Nicholas Jolley in "Descartes and the Action of Body on Mind," *Studia Leibnitiana* 19 (1987): 41–53; and Tad M. Schmaltz, "Sensation, Occasionalism, and Descartes' Causal Principles," in *Minds, Ideas, and Objects*, ed. P. D. Cummins and G. Zoeller (Ascadero, CA: Ridgeview, 1992), in *North American Kant Society Studies in Philosophy* 20. Another paper of Schmaltz's, "Descartes on Innate Ideas, Sensation, and Scholasticism: The Response to Regius," in *Oxford Studies in the History of Philosophy*, vol. 2, ed. M. A. Stewart (Oxford: Oxford UP, 1997), also deals with certain issues concerning the origin of sensation in Descartes that I take up particularly in Sections III and IV. I obtained these papers too late to reflect their positions fully in this text, though I mention some points of convergence in the notes. Schmaltz had access to an earlier draft of this paper in preparing his work, and I had seen some of his in much earlier form; but (as he notes) we largely arrived at our views independently.

7. I will be directly concerned here only with the issue of effects of body on mind (specifically, in sensation), not with the effects of mind on body in voluntary action. For a good, sympathetic treatment of Descartes's position on causation in the mind-body "direction," see Daniel Garber, "Understanding Interaction: What Descartes Should Have Told Elizabeth," *Southern Journal of Philosophy* 21, Supplement (1983): 15–32.

8. See also *PP* IV. 191: AT VIII–I, 318; CSM I, 282:

> . . . [the nerves in the skin] excite (*excitant*) as many different sensations in the mind as there are different ways in which they are moved, or their ordinary motion prevented . . .

9. *Meteors*, viii: AT VI, 334; *O*, 338; To Elizabeth, May 21, 1643: AT III, 665; *PL* 138. In the *Meteors* passage, Descartes talks of motions impinging on the eyes as causes of sensation; in the letter to Elizabeth (further discussed in section V) of the (human) body as cause. See also AT VII, 165; CSM II, 117 (*RO* II), and AT XI, 346; CSM I, 337 (*PS* I.23), where Descartes speaks of our perceptions as "caused by" the objects we take ourselves to perceive. In the letter to Newcastle (October, 1645: AT IV, 326–27; *PL* 182), Descartes in two consecutive sentences talks of movements in the brain "exciting" sensation in the soul, "making" it sense colors and light, and "causing" sensations of thirst and hunger.

It should be stressed that English translations of Descartes—even the best ones—are of no help whatsoever as guides to his use of these terms.

10. See also, e.g., AT VII, 87; CSM II, 60 (*Med* VI) and AT IV, 604; *PL* 210 (to Chanut, Feb. 1, 1647).

11. See *Diop* vi: AT VI, 140; *O* 107.

12. From another point of view the associations between particular brain movements and particular sensations are not arbitrary: rather they reflect the goodness and wisdom of God. Descartes stresses this point both before and after the statement just quoted. He explains that any particular movement "occurring in the part of the brain that immediately affects the mind produces just one corresponding sensation." Experience shows, he goes on to say, "that the sensations which nature has given us" are just the ones most conducive to the preservation of the body in the face of the particular sensory stimulation producing them; this arrangement clearly bears witness "to the power and goodness of God" (AT VII, 87–88; CSM II, 60–61). The "pain as if existing in the foot" example is an illustration of this general claim. This quasi-teleological feature of Descartes's position will not further concern me here, however.

13. Descartes speaks of sensations of smell in similar terms in the preceding paragraph and of the soul being given occasion to feel pain and tingling a few pages earlier (AT XI, 144–45; H 37–38). In between he talks of the motion in the nerves "making the soul have" feelings of heat and cold and of small particles of food "making the soul sense" agreeable (or other) tastes (AT CI, 145, 146; H 39, 41). Such causal alternation of locutions (which one could never divine from Hall's translations) strongly suggests that Descartes did not intend any major opposition between "giving occasion to" and "making."

14. Other passages in which Descartes employs the "occasion" terminology include AT VI, 144; CSM 166 (*Diop* IV); and AT IX–2, 64 (*PP* II.1, FV). See also AT XI, 4;

CSM I, 81 (*TL* I): "our mind represents to us the idea of light each time our eye is affected by the action which signifies it."

15. See also AT X 415–16; CSM I, 42 (*Rules* XII); AT VII, 73; CSM II, 51 (*Med* VI); AT V, 162–63; *CB*, 27. This type of description is used particularly in connection with Descartes's theory of imagination, but also (as the quoted passage shows) sometimes in connection with sensation. I regard it as exemplifying a "presentation" model of the brain-mind relation in sensation; I discuss the significance of this type of description in section IV.

16. Cf. e.g., AT VIII–1, 320, 1.22 (*PP* IV, 196).

17. ". . . *non video qua ratione posset intelligi ipsum [Deum] non esse fallacem, si aliunde quam a rebus corporeis emitterentur*" (AT VII, 80; CSM II, 55 [*Med* VI]; cf. AT VII, 135; CSM II, 97 [*RO* II] and AT VIII-1, 40–41; CSM I, 223 [*PP* II.1]).

18. Yolton, in *Perceptual Acquaintance*, appears to assume that there is some kind of evident opposition between describing the body-mind relation as causal and describing it in terms of "sign-giving." Unfortunately, he gives no defense of his assumption, which seems strongly at odds with Descartes's persistent use of causal terms like '*faire*' and '*inferre*' in passages cited by Yolton himself. Broughton, in "Adequate Causes," does give reasons for thinking the occasionalist terminology in *NiP* signals that Descartes has abandoned the view that body acts on mind. Her arguments seem to me rather tenuous, however, and she does not take into account the fact that (a) Descartes mixes causal talk with occasionalist talk in other works—including the very early *Treatise on Man* and *Dioptrics*; and (b) the later *Passions* seems unblushingly interactionist. For reasons presented in section III, I do agree that the particular concept of the body-mind relation in sensation that Descartes expresses in *Comments on a Broadsheet* is not fully consistent with that presented in the *Meditations* and *Principles*; but this is not to say that the relation is no longer one of efficient causality.

Against what I say here someone may want to argue that when *Malebranche* later talks of bodily states giving occasion *to God* to cause sensations, he is particularly trying to avoid the implication that God is just an extra link in the causal chain. (In fact Malebranche holds that finite entities or states are never causally efficacious, inasmuch as they do not truly necessitate any sequal.) Whether Malebranche's conception of "providing occasion to God" is really intelligible is another matter, however; and there seems no particular reason to saddle Descartes with its murkier elements of his successor's philosophy, just because he used the same term (in a non-theocentric context).

19. In fact, it's hard to understand how the brain can "give the mind signs" even if a an underlying causal relation is *not* ruled out. I return to this issue in Section IV.

20. See also Descartes's letter to Hyperaspistes, August 1641, AT III, 424; *PL* 112. In the Clerselier letter, Descartes indicates that people who accept "real accidents" suppose that they can act on body, even though there is "more difference" between such (supposed) accidents and corporeal substance than between two substances; in the Hyperaspistes letter, he remarks that real accidents are supposed to be "completely different in kind" from substance. John Cottingham has suggested (in correspondence) that Descartes is offering an *ad hominem* or *tu quoque* response to the objection, which does not necessarily indicate that he really sees no difficulty in it. It seems to me, however, that this denial of the heterogeneity objection is quite categorical—even though he does stress that certain of his contemporaries are at least as committed to denying it as he is. (I do not know whether Cottingham meant to suggest that Descartes supposed that the people to whom he was actually replying accepted the "real accident" metaphysics. It seems clear to me that Descartes was not making any such assumption.)

In "Cartesian Interaction," Mark Bedau characterizes the form of Descartes's response as "dialectical." Bedau sees Descartes as indicating that his (scholastic) objectors are not in a position to object to mind-body interaction. (But Bedau does not take this line of response as a sign that Descartes himself is wavering on the issue of the possibility of substances of different natures interacting.) Bedau also does not explain whether he takes Descartes to believe that the critics to whom he is actually replying accept the "scholastic" doctrine in question.

21. They fairly cite past writings of my own as exemplifying this fault.

22. There is a passage from the *Principles*, promoting mechanistic explanations of natural phenomena against scholastic ones, which Radner (in "Descartes' Notion") and Broughton (in "Adequate Causes") present as evidence that Descartes regarded causation between substances of different natures as inconceivable:

> . . . we very well understand in what manner (*pacto*) various local motions in one body are excited by the various size, figure, and motion of the parts of another body; but in no way can we understand in what manner from these same things (i.e., magnitude, figure, and motion) something else would be produced, of an entirely different nature from them, such as are those substantial forms and real qualities, which many suppose to be in things. (*PP* IV.198: AT VIII–1, 322; CSM I, 285).

O'Neill ("Mind-Body Interaction," 242ff.) and Bedau ("Cartesian Interaction", 485ff.) offer interpretations of the passage which render it compatible with the assumption that (it is conceivable that) substances of different natures do interact. Bedau tellingly observes that in the very next sentence Descartes goes on to insist that local motions are sufficient to excite all sensations in the soul (*diversi motus locales sufficiant ad omnes sensus in ea excitare*)! In fact Descartes adds that we "experience" that motions excite sensations in the soul (but we don't apprehend that anything other than motions go from the external organs to the brain). Descartes presumably could agree that mechanistic explanations are more thoroughly intelligible than the "how" of body-mind interaction, while maintaining that scholastic accounts of natural phenomena, unlike postulations of body-mind causation, (a) are eliminable in favor of more transparent mechanistic ones; and (b) postulate entities of which we have no direct awareness.

23. As shown in Section I, Descartes does occasionally use mechanistic-sounding terms like 'impress' to characterize the body's mode of action on the mind. It seems only fair, however, to assume that he does not intend such terms to be understood literally in such contexts. (I will return to this point in Section IV.)

24. Besides works previously cited by Loeb, O'Neill, Richardson, Bedau, and Broughton, see Kenneth Clatterbaugh, "Descartes' Casual Likeness Principle," *Philosophical Review*, Vol. LXXXIX, 1980.

25. See Clatterbaugh's paper, cited above.

26. See Loeb, *Frome Descartes to Hume*, 140–41 and Bedau, "Cartesian Interaction", 484–85.

27. Broughton, "Adequate Causes," and O'Neill, "Mind-Body Interaction."

28. Clatterbaugh's most direct support for attributing to Descartes the principle that the cause must be "like" the effect is a passage from the *Conversation with Burman*— which of course is not a work of Descartes himself (AT LV, 156; *CB*, 17). (In any case, in the passage in question Descartes goes on to say that the "remote" likeness between God and a stone is sufficient to satisfy the principle.)

The strongest grounds for attributing to Descartes a likeness principle are perhaps found in his argument in *NiP*, discussed below, that the ideas (qualities) of external things must be innate in the mind, since they don't resemble anything actually found in the brain. But I argue that the motivation for this position is independent of a general cause likeness principle.

29. See for instance *Med* III: AT VII, 41; CSM II, 28. It is by no means clear from Descartes's presentation here that he himself sees any significant distinction between the "reality" principle and the "containment" principle. If the latter reduces to the former, then bodily states presumably can unproblematically cause ideas, as explained above in the text. The "worst case" for Descartes's defenders depends on the assumption that the containment principle amounts to a *stronger* condition, by virtue of implying that either the cause must literally "have" the effect to start with, or it must possess something *superior* to the effect (not just something *equal* in reality to the effect). Because the latter, non-reductionist interpretation is at least arguable, it is worth seeing whether it is compatible with body-mind causation.

One interesting reason for thinking that the containment principle must imply a stronger constraint than the reality principle has to do with the substance-mode relation. By general consensus, substances are supposed to be higher in the reality hierarchy than modes, so it would seem that, under the reality constraint alone, any substance would be up to producing any mode. But Descartes does not seem to entertain the possibility that *res extensa* can cause motion in itself (See his Letter to Henry More, August 1649: AT V, 404; *PL* 258). Further, in Meditation III, considering explicitly whether he, as substance, contains the distinctly perceived modes of body eminently, he allows only that "it seems possible that" this is so (AT VII, 45; CSM II, 31).

30. Letter to Mersenne, December 31, 1640: AT III, 274; *PL* 91.

31. In fact there is room for some debate about the precise conditions of "formal containment": see O'Neill, "Mind-Body Interaction," 235ff; and compare Gueroult, *Descartes selon l'Ordre*, II, 77, n. 3. But the subtleties of this issue aren't really essential to the argument here.

32. *Med* III (FV): AT IX–1, 32; CSM II, 28 (see n.2); *Med* VI: AT VII, 79; CSM II, 55. See also O'Neill, "Mind-Body Interaction" for a defense of this conception of eminent containment.

33. O'Neill holds that eminent containment requires that the cause does not formally contain the effect, and that it is more perfect than anything that can contain the effect formally. This interpretation does seem to conform to the examples of eminent containment she cites from Descartes and also fits well with Descartes's insistence that *res extensa* (a substance) cannot cause motion (a mode) in itself. (See note 28.) But, as she recognizes, it is not easy to establish exactly what 'eminent containment' meant to Descartes, given his rather loose and vague explications of the term.

O'Neill, incidentally, holds that Descartes claims explicitly that mind is more perfect than body. Her references do not precisely substantiate that claim, however. In her main citation—a letter to Elizabeth—Descartes says that the mind is "much more noble" than the body. She also cites Principles I.23 where Descartes concludes that God is not extended, on the ground that extension implies divisibility, an imperfection. But this passages does not tell us that *finite* minds are more perfect than body or bodies. (Jolley, in "Descartes on the Action of Body on Mind," 45, draws the same conclusion from a passage in the Second Replies; but this passage, too, is concerned with the issue of absolute perfection, rather than finite substances.)

34. "*un ouvrage de l'esprit.*" Although no corresponding phrase occurs in the Latin original, the basic intent is constant: the formal reality of an idea ('idea' in the first

sense) derives from the mind, but its representative content ('idea' in the second sense) may require an external cause.

35. One who uses this line of reasoning to reconcile body-mind causation with the containment principle must actually hold that every mental mode with a physical cause has a partial mental cause as well. In a discussion of an earlier version of this paper, Richard Foley persuaded me that this assumption is viable.

In "Descartes on the Action," Jolley takes a similar approach to the same problem, but he concludes that the formal reality of ideas is caused by *God*.

36. I ignore the following question, which does come to mind in connection with the mind's alleged causality of its ideas: in what sense can the mind be said to contain its ideas (as operations of the understanding) *prior to their occurrence*?

(It should be noted, though, that in "Descartes on Innate Ideas," Tad Schmaltz argues that Descartes's position in *Comments on a Broadsheet* requires that the "content" of ideas of sense also be derived from the mind, though not from its intellectual faculty.)

37. My proposal for partial reconciliation of the containment principle with body-mind causation owes a good deal to O'Neill's discussion in *Mind and Mechanism* and to Broughton's in "Adequate Causes." My suggestion, however, requires rejecting Broughton's view that the Meditation VI proof of the existence of body must be taken to rule out the relevence of eminent containment altogether with respect to the causation of ideas of sense. It is true that Descartes seems to say there that if matter is the cause of ideas of sense, then the cause will contain formally all that is in the ideas objectively. But he also quickly goes on to indicate that only what is clearly and distinctly conceived of body is really in external matter. Either he has implicitly qualified the initial broad stance in the course of his argument, or he is implicitly denying that mere sensations (confused ideas) have objective reality. (On the latter notion, see M. D. Wilson, *Descartes*, New York: Routledge and Kegan Paul, 1978, 101ff.)

I differ from both O'Neill and Broughton in putting no weight, in the present context, on Descartes's statements that "the nature of the mind is such" that motions in the brain are sufficient to excite in it all sorts of sensations. While such statements do indicate some kind of contribution of the mind in the occurrence of sensation, they less clearly suggest *efficient* causality than the remarks I cite from Meditation III. And (as Paul Hoffman has stressed, in correspondence) Descartes does construe the containment principle as concerned specifically with efficient causation.

38. The same conclusion is reached in a slightly different way by William E. Seager, "Descartes on the Union of Mind and Body," *History of Philosophy Quarterly*, 5.2 (April, 1988): 126. (Seager's paper touches on several of the same issues that I take up here, but focuses on one that I largely set aside for reasons of space: the nature of mind-body union in Descartes and the relevance of this notion to the intelligibility of Interaction.)

39. . . . whatever we sense without doubt comes to us from some thing, which is different from our mind. For it is not in our power to bring it about that we sense one thing rather than another; but this clearly depends on that thing which affects (*afficit*) our senses. One can indeed ask whether that thing is God, or something different from God. But because we sense, or rather stimulated by sense we clearly and distinctly perceive, a certain matter extended in length, breadth, and depth, various parts of which have various figures and are moved with various motions, and also bring about that we have various sensations of colors, odors, pains, etc: if God immediately by himself exhibited (*exhiberet*) this idea of extended matter to our mind, or even if he brought it about that is

was exhibited by some other thing, in which there was no extension, or figure, or motion: no reason could be found why he should not be regarded as a deceiver. For we clearly understand it as a thing completely different from God and from us, or from our mind; and also we seem clearly to see that the idea of it comes (*advenire*) from things placed outside us, to which it is entirely similar . . . (AT VIII–1, 40–41; CSM I 223).

See also *Second Replies*, AT VII, 135; CSM II, 97; *Fifth Replies*, AT VII, 367; CSM II. 253; and *Passions of the Soul* xvii, AT XI, 342; CSM I 335.

40. One might assume that if the cause of an idea-content doesn't exactly exemplify that content, it doesn't formally contain it either. If this is so, then to the extent that Descartes backs off from holding that bodies acting on our minds exactly exemplify the qualities we "perceive" by sense, he loses one way of reconciling body-mind causation with the containment principle. The issue is a complicated one though. It is not clear, for instance, whether or not a body moving at velocity m + n "formally contains" velocity m; nor whether a body 300 miles wide "formally contains" a width of one mile, etc.

41. See also the comments on "workmen" in the next article of *Comments*.

42. For another brief expression of essentially the same claim, see Descartes's letter to Mersenne, July 22, 1641; AT III, 418; *PL* 108.

43. See also *PL* 108, to Mersenne, 7/41.

44. Again, this terminology need not be construed as an implicit denial of causality. Employing terminology favored by Gueroult (*op.cit.*, II, 102–03), we may say that—in passages such as this—Descartes construes physical states as *occasional* causes of ideas, but denies that they can be *exemplary* causes. (As noted already, it is not Descartes's position that ideas are actually, occurrently in the mind at all times, independent of any external causal influence. Rather, he says in the *Comments*, "innate ideas" are "in" the mind merely as dispositions until an appropriate stimulus activates the mind's capacity for forming them.)

45. There are certain passages—for example, at the beginning of Meditation V—where Descartes appears to be suggesting that the ideas of *res extensa* and its parts are derived from the mind itself, on the grounds that that the intelligibility of these indicates they are natural to reason, this is obviously a line of reasoning at cross purposes with that of the *Comments*, according to which *confused* ideas of sense have the strongest claim to innateness. It may not be at cross purposes, however, with the argument of Meditation VI that the sensory ideas of bodies come from bodies. One might speculate that Descartes's position about the origin of the idea of matter ultimately combines two elements: while the intelligibility of the idea of matter indicates it is "natural" to reason, one's disposition under circumstances of sense perception to believe that this idea, and/or the ideas of particular bodies, come from without is also to be relied on. In the latter circumstances, that is, the idea or ideas do "come from without" even though adequate resources to think them up are also independently present in the mind. (Schmaltz, in "Descartes on Innate Ideas," discusses at length the problem of reconciling Descartes's various statements about where ideas of sense "come from.")

46. To Mesland, May 2, 1646: AT IV, 113; *PL* 148. As Descartes indicates in *The Passions of the Soul* and related correspondence, a state of the soul is a passion if it arises through bodily causation, independently of volitional action. See, e.g. AT IV, 310; *PL* 178 (to Elizabeth, Oct. 6, 1645); and Loeb, *Descartes to Hume*, 152.

47. One may also wonder about how the equation of what is involuntary with what "comes from without" is to be reconciled with Descartes's indication in the *Meditations* that all ideas can, from one point of view, be regarded as mental "operations." (This

distinction between voluntariness and mental causation is also discussed by Schmaltz in "Descartes on Innate Ideas.")

48. Cf. Geuroult, *Descartes selon l'ordre*, Vol. II, 101–02. It is worth noting that when Descartes talks of ideas of bodies "coming from" bodies, he appears mainly to have in mind their origins in the *objects* of perception, rather than the brain states that proximately (so to speak) stimulate the mind.

I assume, incidentally, that passages which stress the *sufficiency* of cerebral motions to excite, or bring about, sensory ideas in the mind *need* not be read as conflicting with the position presented in the *Comments*. For presumably the former passages may be taken to mean only that motions in the brain are the only *bodily* cause of sensation (ruling out, in particular, scholastic "species"). Of course, to the extent that the passages in question suggest that, given certain bodily motions, sensory ideas result *inevitably*, and to the extent that such inevitability is inconsistent with mental activity (because incompatible with volitional control), they do suggest a problem which ties in closely with the one discussed in the text.

49. See the passage from *Principles* II.1 quoted above. In the French version (AT IX–2, 64), we find the following phrasing: "*l'idée [de la matiere] se forme en nous a l'occasion des corps de dehors . . .*"

50. Cf. *Diop*, Discourse IV, AT VI, 113; CSM I, 165–66.

51. In the *Dioptrics*, Descartes holds that perceptions of such qualities as size and distance require reasoning and judgment. It follows (again) that such ideas cannot come from without—and it even seems to follow that they somehow depend on the will (since, on Cartesian theory, judgment depends on the will)!

52. My conception of the problem of reconciling Descartes's position in the comments with the "passivity" claims has been influenced by correspondence with Paul Hoffman—though I believe our views of the matter may still be rather different.

53. Yolton, in so far as he stresses the natural "sign" conception of the body-mind relation in Descartes's writings, may be said to take note of it. (For, as explained below, the suggestion that the brain gives the mind signs appears to be a version of the presentation conception.) But he certainly fails to consider intelligibility problems inherent in the conception. Loeb, in correspondence, has expressed the view that the presentation model is merely metaphorical. I consider this suggestion at the end of the section.

54. I do not mean to imply that the use of presentation terminology to describe the body-mind relation in sensation (and imagination) is a novelty with Descartes. (It has been pointed out to me that it occurs in various works of Augustine, for instance.)

55. AT VII, 88; CSM II, 60.

56. For a perception is a thought, and thought is just "that which is in us in such a way that we are immediately conscious of it" (*RO* II: AT VII, 160; CSM II, 113). For a discussion of this issue and more references, see M. D. Wilson, *Descartes*, 152 ff.

57. One might propose that for Descartes the sensation just is the consciousness of the brain state that excites it—a *confused* consciousness, to be sure. It seems to me, however, that Descartes talks of sensations arising in the mind *in response to* the mind's receiving a sign from the brain; in other words, having the sensation is treated as a *sequel* to the mind's "noting" the brain motions, or receiving a sign, not as the *same* event.

58. As Louis Loeb has maintained in correspondence.

59. The latter is found in the *Dioptrics* (Discourse VI); I discuss it below.

60. It might be questioned whether Descartes's ridicule of the idea that there are *other*

eyes in the brain really amounts to the direct ridicule of the presentation model, which suggests only that *the mind* somehow apprehends brain states. It does seem fairly clear, though, that *something* about the notion of perceiving brain states struck Descartes as bizarre at the time he was writing this passage.

61. "The 'Scandal' of Cartesian Interactionism," 25–26.

62. *From Descartes to Hume*, 137.

63. See, for instance, Meditation VI: AT VII, 88; CSM II, 60–61; cf. Wilson, *Descartes*, 208–09.

64. *Descartes to Hume*, 137.

65. Here I give the passage in Kenny's translation (*PL* 210), which Loeb uses—except that I translate *induissent* as "induce" (as I did above) rather than "impel." The latter translation makes the passage look even less Humean than the former!

"The nature of the mind" figures in Descartes's account of body-mind interaction elsewhere as well: cf. AT VIII–1, 320; CSM I 184 (*PP* IV 197); AT XI, 143; H. 36–37.

66. *Treatise of Human Nature*, ed. L. A. Selby-Bigge (Oxford: Clarendon Press, 1888) 155; 170.

67. Notoriously, Descartes says that the mind operates primarily at the pineal gland: thus, he does seem to ascribe to the mind as a whole the capacity for location in ordinary physical space. But the mind is not supposed to be, strictly, extended; so it seems that if the modes of mind—such as sensations—themselves have location, they must all have precisely the *same* location. This is, to say the least, a difficult notion to grasp.

68. This is, roughly, the move made by Hume himself in a little noted section of the *Treatise* (I, iv, 5: 235–39; 246–50).

Loeb calls attention to Hume's use, in this section, of his view that "any thing may produce anything" to deny that there is any particular conceptual problem about mind-body causation (cf. *Descartes to Hume*, 361–62). Hume's dropping of the spatial contiguity condition in this discussion does, however, appear to be an *ad hoc* move that requires some reconciling with his earlier account of causal relations. (In this later section, Hume indeed writes as if causation and *temporal* "contiguity" are wholly distinct relations [p. 237].)

69. Loeb has ingeniously developed this notion in correspondence.

70. Some scholars have argued that Descartes did not really think of bodies or physical events as causes *at all*. See, for instance, Gary C. Hatfield, "Force (God) in Descartes' Physics," *Studies in the History and Philosophy of Science* 10 (1979): 113–40; and Daniel Garber, "Understanding Interaction: What Descartes Should Have Told Elisabeth," *Southern Journal of Philosophy* 21 (Supplement, 1983): 15–32. Garber particularly (if parenthetically) connects this position to the problem of body-mind causation (ibid., p. 26). The evaluation of their claims depends to a large degree on how, exactly, one understands the term 'cause', and on whether *causal efficacy* requires either physical *dynamism* or mental *action* (as opposed, say, to mere transfer of motion). My own view is that there is plenty of evidence—some of it cited in this paper—that Descartes did regard physical states as causally efficacious, despite his assumption that God's concurrence is necessary for the continuation of being presupposed by causality. In any case, my concern here has been only with the question whether, and in what ways, Descartes encounters *special* problems in postulating *body-mind* causation.

Descartes on the Representationality of Sensation

THROUGHOUT his writings Descartes identifies our ordinary experiences of color, odor, heat and cold, and other so-called sensible qualities as mere sensations which have a purely mental status. He consistently and emphatically denies that they "resemble" any quality that does or can exist in physical reality. Yet in the Third Meditation he seems to construe such sensations as "ideas of" cold and the like, which *misrepresent* "what cold is" to the mind. Their "falsity" consists in representing what is not a real physical quality as if it were. He presents this view as a corollary of the assumption that *all* "thoughts" are "as if of things."

In the Fourth set of Objections to the *Meditations* Antoine Arnauld strongly challenges the cogency of Descartes's position on sensation. Descartes's reply to Arnauld is both fairly detailed and extremely bewildering. In fact, on the surface it seems to involve a clumsy retraction of the view that sensations are in some way misrepresentations of cold, heat, etc.[1]

In later writings—the *Principles of Philosophy, Passions of the Soul*, and certain letters—Descartes provides further comments on the status of sensations, in relation to extra-mental reality, that bear on the issue of whether or not he continues to regard sensations as "representative" (or misrepresentative) "of things." This later material appears to suggest some alteration in Descartes's doctrine on the subject.

Descartes's position on the representationality of sensation (including the "passions") is important to a number of interpretive issues. Within the Cartesian system, sensations and passions are included among our "thoughts" (*cogitationes*); and the various Latin and French terms for 'sensation' are used more or less interchangeably with 'ideas of sense'. So, claims about Descartes's general position on the relation of thought and representation (or "intensionality"), and on the nature of ideas, really need to take account of his treatment of the sensations and passions, as a sort of problem-posing test case. Further, the issue is obviously relevant to the recently disputed question of whether or not Descartes regards the passive emotions as "cognitive." It is central, as well, to his position on the "primary-secondary quality distinction," on the mind-body union, and on the relation of mind to matter generally. Unfortunately, Descartes's various statements on this subject are exceptionally difficult to understand clearly, even considered individually; and the interpretation problem becomes even harder when one tries to figure out what is going on from one work to another.

In the first three parts of this paper I will (a) present the Third Meditation position more fully; (b) examine Arnauld's objection; and (c) try to make sense of Descartes's reply. I will propose a distinction between senses of 'represent' (or 'idea of') which, I suggest, helps to clarify the difference between Arnauld's and Descartes's positions, while making it easier to interpret the Cartesian texts as intelligible and consistent. In the fourth section I will use the same distinction to help reconcile with these texts seemingly conflicting statements from the *Principles of Philosophy* about whether sensations represent. The final section is concerned with Descartes's position on the representationality of the passive emotions.[2]

I

In an often-cited passage from the Third Meditation Descartes ties the concept of 'idea' in the strict sense to some notion of representation, or apprehending a "thing as subject of my thought."

> Of my thoughts some are as if images of things (*tanquam rerum imagines*), to which alone the term 'idea' is strictly appropriate: as when I think of man, or Chimaera, or Heaven, or Angel, or God. Others, though, have certain other forms besides: as when I will, when I fear, when I affirm, when I deny, I always indeed apprehend some thing (*aliquam rem apprehendo*) as the subject of my thought, but I also comprehend by thought something more than the similitude of this thing; and of these some are called volitions, or affects, but others judgments. (AT VII, 37)[3]

The point that ideas are necessarily "of things" is underscored in later stages of his discussion. For instance, Descartes observes that, although all ideas, considered just as modes of thought, are equal, nevertheless "some are very different from others" insofar as "one represents one thing, another another."[4]

He further relies on the notion that all ideas are "as if of things" in developing the concept of *material falsity*, specifically in relation to sensation. He asserts that "confused and obscure" ideas, notably his sensations of "light and colors, sounds, odors, tastes, heat and cold, and the other tactile qualities," fail to allow him to determine whether they "are the ideas of certain things or not of things" (*sint rerum quarundam ideae, an non rerum*): possibly they are in fact "of" non-things, of "privations" (AT VII, 43–44). But since all ideas are "as if of things" (*tanquam rerum*), even these "confused" ideas seem to represent things: thus they provide "material for error":

> For although . . . falsity properly so-called, or formal falsity, can only be found in judgements, there is nevertheless a certain other material falsity in ideas, when they represent what is not a thing as if a thing (*non rem tanquam rem repraesentant*). Thus, for example, the ideas that I have of heat and cold are so little clear and distinct, that from them I cannot tell whether cold is only the privation of heat, or heat the privation of cold, or each is a real quality, or neither. And because there can be no ideas that are not as if of things (*nisi tanquam rerum*), if indeed it is true that cold is nothing else than the privation of heat, the idea which represents it to me as

something real and positive (*idea quae mihi illud tanquam reale quid & positivum repraesentat*) will not improperly be called false, and so of the others. (AT VII, 43–44)

These statements clearly imply that our sensations are representative in two respects. First they are *ideas of* cold, heat and so forth (whatever these may be, and whether or not they are "real qualities"). Second, they present heat, cold, etc. to us *in a certain way, as being such-and-such*; specifically (since all ideas are "as if of things") they represent them to us as "real and positive qualities." But it may not in fact be true that both cold and heat are real and positive properties—or for that matter that either one is. In that case the relevant sensory idea tends to mislead us, or provide "material" for erroneous judgment.

It is important to remember that the issue whether certain putative qualities are "real" is distinct, in Descartes's writings, from the issue about whether anything possessing the qualities in question actually exists. Thus, Burman records that Descartes elaborated on the "material falsity" passage as follows:

There is . . . material for error, even if I refer [my ideas] to no things outside me, since I can err with respect to their nature itself. For instance, if I consider the idea of color, and say that it is a thing, a quality, or rather that the color itself, which is represented by this idea, is such (*tale quid esse*); or if I say that white is a quality, even if I refer that idea to no thing outside myself, and say or suppose that nothing is white, I can nevertheless err in the abstract, and about whiteness itself and its nature or idea. (AT V, 152)

Descartes also emphasizes the distinction between reality and existence at least twice in the *Meditations*.[5]

At this point one might well want to know more about the notion of "non-thing," insofar as it is distinguished from "non-existent thing." Can a non-thing really be an "it"? Is it intelligible to speculate about what this "it" is? ("If cold is nothing else than the privation of heat, then the idea which represents it to me. . . .") What exactly is the relation between the notion of "non-thing" and that of "privation," anyway?[6] And (most important in the present context), in what sense does a non-thing qualify to be *represented* at all—whether as a "thing" or, for that matter, as a non-thing?

As it happens, none of these questions (except possibly the last) figures in Arnauld's attack on the notion of material falsity. He appears to accept, for instance, that cold could be a non-thing (or anyway, a privation), and that we can intelligibly discuss what an idea "of it" could or could not be. What he particularly objects to is the notion of *misrepresentation* on which Descartes relies in characterizing the ideas of sensible qualities. In the following discussion I will focus on questions Arnauld does raise (to which Descartes replies), setting aside problems specifically concerned with the notion of a "non-thing" and its role in the material falsity passage.[7]

II

According to Arnauld, "if cold is merely a privation, then there cannot be an idea of cold which represents it to me as a positive thing (*quae illud mihi tanquam rem positivam repraesentet*). . . ." He elaborates:

> For what is the idea of cold? Cold itself in so far as it exists objectively in the intellect. But if cold is a privation, it cannot be objectively in the intellect by means of an idea whose objective being is a positive entity. Therefore, if cold is only a privation, there can never be a positive idea of it, and hence no (idea) which is materially false. (AT VII, 206)

Arnauld's claim is that a positive idea cannot in any sense represent a privation. To say that the idea is positive is to say that it represents something "real and positive." For what it "represents" is just the "objective being which it contains" (207). (Note that Arnauld is not denying that we can falsely *judge* that cold is something positive; his objection is partly directed toward establishing that Descartes has confused what is possible on the level of judgement with what is possible on the level of ideas alone. In this case our error would consist in judging that the positive idea "is the idea of cold" (206–07).) "Finally," Arnauld concludes:

> What does the idea of cold, which you say is materially false, exhibit to your mind? A privation? Then it is true. A positive entity? Then it is not the idea of cold. (207)[8]

There is some room for doubt about what Arnauld's main point is, exactly. Is he maintaining just that a positive idea cannot represent (or "exhibit") a privation? Or does he mean to endorse either or both of the following stronger claims:

(a) A privation cannot be represented by any idea at all (since for an idea to represent is just for it to exhibit some reality to the mind, or contain some reality objectively);

(b) For anything **n**, of which it is true that **n** is **P**, then any idea which exhibits something to the mind *as* **not-P** cannot be an idea of **n**?

It may seem at first that Arnauld does implicitly endorse (a). For he does suggest that for an idea to represent *is* for it to exhibit some reality to the mind. If so, the non-real could hardly be represented by any idea at all; and there is no indication that Arnauld means to distinguish the non-real and the privative (any more than Descartes himself does).[9] At the same time, however, Arnauld is prepared to advance the hypothesis that the idea of cold "exhibits a privation to the mind"—a possibility incompatible with (a).

It does appear fairly unproblematic, at any rate (and this is the important point here), that Arnauld is committed to (b), on some interpretation or other. For he rests his claim that a positive idea cannot represent a privation on the notion that a privation *is not* something positive. And there is nothing to indicate that privations are somehow special cases in this regard. In other words, he seems to take it that (in some sense) nothing can count as a representation of **n** that represents **n** *as other than* **n** in fact *is*.

It is hard to guess how broad an interpretation of (b) Arnauld would be prepared to endorse. Take Descartes's example, in Meditation III, of the "two different ideas of the sun" which he finds in himself. One of these, he says, is "as if acquired from the senses": through it the sun appears very small. The other is derived from astronomical reasoning: through it the sun is exhibited as larger than the earth. Surely, he concludes, "both cannot be similar to the same sun existing outside me"; and "reason persuades that that idea is utterly dissimilar to it which seems to emanate most directly from the sun itself" (AT VII, 39). Would Arnauld go so far as to hold that, if the sun is in fact larger than the earth, there can be no idea "of it" through which it appears very small?

Although Arnauld's comments provide no basis for a sure answer to such questions, I do want to suggest that his objection appears to rest on an assumption about representation which divides him from Descartes to greater or lesser degree (depending how exactly we interpret his implicit endorsement of (b)). Insofar as Arnauld assumes (with whatever qualification) that for an idea to be an idea of **n**, or to represent **n**, it cannot *present* **n** as other than **n** in fact is, he seems to rely on what we might call a purely presentational notion of representation. Descartes, as I will now try to bring out further, in examining the Fourth Replies, has what we may call a hybrid notion. For him the representationality of ideas does consist *partly* in presentational content. However, an idea's being an idea of **n**—its representing **n**—does *not* preclude that the idea presents n as other than it is. I will speak of Descartes's notion of representation as partially "referential," as a way of expressing the non-presentational element. (Later on, though, I will argue that the "referential" component of Cartesian representation is hard to explain clearly.) Recognizing this distinction between Arnauld's and Descartes's assumptions helps quite a bit, I will try to show, in making sense of Descartes's reply to Arnauld's criticisms. (One must also, however, be prepared to be very flexible in interpreting his words.) In addition (as I will explain later) it helps to reconcile (with each other and with the Third Meditation) two passages from the *Principles of Philosophy* (I.68 and I.71) in which Descartes appears both to affirm and to deny that sensations "represent" something "outside thought."

Before I move on to the Fourth Replies, let me try to clarify just a bit more the distinction with respect to aspects of representation that I intend to attribute to Descartes. I'm going to hold that (in Descartes's writings) the expressions, 'I have an idea of **n**', and 'my idea **i** represents something **P**' are both ambiguous, in similar ways, reflecting the "hybrid" nature of his conception of representation. Suppose that my mind is in fact an immaterial substance, though (at my present stage of philosophical development) I can only conceive of my mind as an attribute of my body. Then my idea of my mind is in one sense the idea of, and represents, an immaterial substance; in another sense it is not the idea of, and does not represent (to me) an immaterial substance. I introduce the following terms to distinguish the "senses" in question: in the example just given my

idea *referentially represents* an immaterial substance; it *presents* a bodily attribute. (Again, I am not going to claim that the notion of referential representation is ultimately a clear one; only that the distinction in question helps to
explain the texts.)[10]

III

Descartes's initial response to Arnauld's rejection of the notion of material falsity (specifically with respect to the "idea of cold") basically conforms to his
Third Meditation statement:

> . . . whether cold is a positive thing, or a privation, doesn't make any difference to
> the idea I have of it, but it remains in me the same that I have always had; and I say
> that this [idea] provides me with material for error, if cold truly is a privation and
> does not have as much reality as heat; because, considering the ideas respectively of
> cold and of heat just as I receive them both from the senses, I cannot see (*non
> possum advertere*) that more reality is exhibited to me by one than by the other. (AT
> VII, 232–33)

On the reading I propose, Descartes's point should be that neither idea *presents*
more reality than the other, though one may well referentially represent more
reality than the other, i.e., may referentially represent a real quality rather than a
privation.

Descartes goes on to reject Arnauld's claim that "the idea of cold is cold
itself insofar as it is objectively in the understanding" (233). We need, he says,
to make a distinction:

> for it often happens in obscure and confused ideas, among which those of heat and
> cold are included, that they are referred to something other than that of which they
> are truly the ideas (*ut ad aliud quid referantur quam ad id cujus revera ideae sunt*).

"Thus," he continues,

> if cold is only a privation, the idea of cold is not cold itself, insofar as it is objec-
> tively in the understanding, but something else which I wrongly take for this priva-
> tion (*sed aliud quid quod perperam pro ista privatione sumitur*); that is, a certain
> sensation which has no being outside the understanding. (233)

The idea is, referentially, the idea *of cold*; it *presents*, however, something else:
a mere, if "positive", sensation. It thus "provides the material" for my error of
judging that what is (positively if obscurely) presented to me is what the idea
refers to, namely cold (which is in fact, in the real world, a privation).[11] What
the idea referentially represents is not what it presentationally represents: that is
why Descartes can say that the idea of cold is referred to something other than
that of which it is in fact the idea. He is not, in other words, *categorically*
accepting Arnauld's claim that if cold is a privation, a positive idea is not the
idea of cold. He is merely agreeing that the idea would not be *presentationally*

the idea of cold as it "is" in nature, or *quam res* (namely, a privation). A similar point is at issue in the next paragraph, when Descartes implies that the source of error in our judgements about sensible qualities is that ideas of sense are "referred to something to which [they do] not conform." (233)[12]

A few lines later Descartes comes back to the original objection:

> But [he] asks what that idea of cold represents to me, which I say is materially false: "For if," he says, "it exhibits a privation, then it is true; if a positive being, then it is not the idea of cold."

Descartes now rather startlingly *agrees* with the objection: "*Recte*," he says. But, he continues,

> . . . I call that idea materially false only for this reason, that, since it is obscure and confused, I cannot decide whether what it exhibits to me as outside my sense is positive, or not; and thus I have occasion to judge that it is something positive, although perhaps it is only a privation. (234)

Although Descartes seems to give away the store here, I think he has merely expressed himself ineptly. He does not really intend to retract his position that a particular "positive" sensation counts as the "idea of cold," even if cold is in fact a privation. Despite apparent verbal indications to the contrary, he is really continuing on his original track: the sensation of cold referentially represents cold (let's suppose, a privation)—but fails to *present* cold as it is (namely, as a privation). In the latter respect only it is not the idea of cold, "but something else, which I wrongly take for this privation."

On my proposed reading of the Fourth Replies, Descartes continues to assume that an idea of **n** might represent (present) **n** as other than **n** is. One of course then wants to ask, what *is* it for an idea to be an idea of (say) cold, if it is *not* to present cold as it is (say, as a privation)?[13]

In view of some recent theories of reference and perception, one might hope for a *causal* account of "referential" or non-presentational representation: an idea, that is, referentially represents its cause (or cause under normal conditions), whatever that might be. Thus, for my idea of cold referentially to represent a certain physical state is just for that idea to be caused—in the "right" way—by that state, whatever it might be. On the hypothesis we have been following out—that cold is a privation—this approach would presumably require accepting the notion of privative causes. This sounds odd, but might in the end be tolerable. (Certainly Descartes does often seem to assume that the external reality "represented" by a sensation may just be the cause of that sensation; and who's to say that negative or inhibitory factors can't reasonably be ascribed causative significance?)

There is a more serious problem with this proposal, however. For Descartes (as I mentioned earlier) thinks that *non-existents* can be referentially represented. My (materially false) ideas of cold and white are ideas of cold and white, it seems, even if no physical things exist, and hence even if there are no instantiations of these qualities as they really are. I am pessimistic that such "entities" can be cast as "causes."[14]

A similar objection would apply as well if we tried to construe referential representation as *demonstrative*. For according to Descartes I can refer a sensation to "a part of the physical world" which in a quite ordinary sense fails to exist. To mention one of his favorite examples, I can point to where an amputated limb should be, in indicating the "location" of a pain. (So "what is going on *there*" will not always "pick out" the real state of the world which my sensation represents referentially.)[15]

On the whole I suspect that the causal account was influential in Descartes's thought, even if he was unable to develop it fully, to create a theory immune to counter-examples. Beyond this observation, I'm unable further to clarify the hybrid conception of representation I've attributed to Descartes. I can only claim that it, or something like it, does seem necessary to make good sense of his response to Arnauld's objection. Further, as I'll now try to show, this understanding helps to bring what he says about sensation in the *Principles* into some kind of alignment with his earlier remarks.

IV

Although Descartes does not say directly, in the Third Meditation, that all "*thoughts*" (as opposed to ideas properly so called) are "as if of things," his wording does suggest this position. Some thoughts are *just* "as if images of things"; others have other "forms" *besides*. So, it might seem to follow, Descartes does not wish to admit that there are "thoughts" that don't have the "of-a-thing" character *at least*. And he has indeed been interpreted in this way.[16] Works later than the *Meditations*, however, provide some reason to question whether this interpretation is correct. I have in mind his treatment of sensations (again, experiences of pain, color, odor and sound, etc.) in the *Principles of Philosophy*, and his account of passive emotions in *Principles* and in the *Passions of the Soul*. At one time I thought that the discussion of *Principles* I.68–71 indeed suggested a deep change in Descartes's position on the representationality of sensation.[17] However, I now think that the change is not so great after all. If we read the *Principles* passages in light of the distinction I have just proposed, they come out saying something at least fairly close to the position on sensation in the Third Meditation and Fourth Replies. I will try to establish this point first, then move on (in the next section) to murkier question of whether—or in what sense—Descartes construes the passive emotions, too, as "representational."

The following statement from I.71 provides the strongest apparent evidence that Descartes has come to deny that sensations do represent (are as if of things):

> . . . In early childhood our mind was so tightly bound to the body that it had no leisure for any other thoughts, except only those by which it sensed what affected the body: and it did not yet refer these to anything located outside itself, but only

sensed pain where something occurred harmful to the body; where something beneficial occurred, it felt pleasure; and where something affected the body without
much harm or benefit, for the different parts in which and ways in which the body
was affected, it had certain different sensations, namely those which we call the
sensations of taste, odor, sound, heat, cold, light, color and the like, *which represent
nothing located outside thought.* (*PP* I.71; emphasis added)

Later on, Descartes explains, the mind realized that its sensations were caused
by external objects, and mistakenly attributed heat, color, odor, etc. to the objects. In doing so it failed to recognize the different natures of the mere sensations on the one hand, and sizes, shapes, motions and the like on the other
hand: the latter only "were exhibited to it not as sensations, but as certain
things, or modes of things, existing, or at least capable of existing, outside
thought."

Yet a little earlier he has indicated, more visibly in keeping with the Third
Meditation, that sensations might be said to "represent" external states in some
very limited sense. The problem with sensations (he seems to say here) is just
that we "cannot tell" *what* they represent. An inattentive person, he remarks,
may persuade himself that sensations of color or pain give him some notion of
external physical qualities, because he may suppose that there is in the object
something similar to what he experiences;

but if he examines what it might be, which this sensation of color or pain represents, as if existing in the colored body or painful part, he will notice that he is
wholly ignorant of it. (*PP* I.68)

In line with what I have just proposed about the Fourth Replies, I suggest that
we read these passages as expressing the following view. First, nothing is *intelligibly presented* to the mind in ordinary sense experience "of" colors, odors,
and so on. Second, we nevertheless tend to take the presentational content of
sense experience to be something real, to refer *it* to external reality. (The story
of how we happen to do this is different from that found in the *Meditations*,
though, since it does not rely on the claim that "all ideas are as if of things," or
the notion of material falsity.) Third, the sensations may correctly be said to
have some *referential* representativeness, though what they represent in this
sense is wholly indeterminate from their presentational content. They are, in
other words, "as if images of things," but wholly *confused* images. This reading
is borne out by a remark towards the end of the *Principles*, when Descartes
remarks that color, sound, and the like are not distinctly imagined or understood; rather, "their images in our thought are always confused, and we do not
know what they are (*semper . . . eorum imagines in cogitatione nostra sunt
confusae, nec quidnam illa sint scimus*)" (*PP* IV.200).[18]

V

Descartes's treatment of the passive emotions provides another interesting set of
problems for the interpreter of his position on the representationality of thought.

In particular, it provides an even harder case than his treatment of sensation in the *Principles* for anyone who would hold that for Descartes any thought is necessarily representative, or involves a representative element.[19]

These days it has become common to hold that emotions are always, or nearly always, partially or even wholly cognitive states, essentially involving representation (presentation) of an object. For example, *fear* can only be understood as a state of the fearing being that essentially involves a judgement that something is dangerous to that being. Descartes is sometimes cited as a proponent of the opposed, erroneous view that emotions are mere feelings (perhaps "contingently" connected with an object which causes them).[20]

This interpretation may well seem to conflict directly with the statement from the Third Meditation that I quoted at the outset, in which Descartes mentions fear in particular, and the "affects" in general, as examples of "thoughts" which "always" include the apprehension of some "subject" of the thought, but also have "other forms besides."[21] But of course we cannot immediately exclude the possibility that Descartes changed his view about the affects, when he came to consider these states of mind more systematically in later works.

In the *Passions*, too, however, Descartes very often phrases his accounts of the various different passive emotions in terms of the soul's responses to objects it thinks of (responses caused and "fortified" by particular physiological changes). Here are a few examples:

WONDER

When the first encounter with some object surprises us, and we judge it to be novel, or very different from that which we knew before . . . , that causes us to wonder at it and be astonished by it. (II.53)

LOVE AND HATRED

. . . [W]hen a thing is represented to us as good for us, that is, as beneficial to us, that makes us have Love for it; and when it is represented as bad or harmful, that excites Hatred in us. (II.56)

CONCERNING PITY

Pity is a type of Sadness, mixed with Love or good will toward those whom we see suffer something bad, which we consider them not to deserve. Thus it is contrary to Envy, because of its object, and to Mockery, because it considers [the object] in another way. (III.185)

I will not try to settle here the question, just how far such passages go towards establishing that Descartes does think of passive emotions as *typically* tied, in a definitional or "non-contingent" way with mental presentations of (putative) external objects. (Clearly they do go *some* way to supporting such a reading.) What must be noted is that, first, Descartes explicitly acknowledges in both the *Passions* and *Principles* the existence of emotions that *lack*, so to speak, objective content. For instance, thick and sluggish blood produces a feeling of sadness, "although [the soul] perhaps does not know why it should be sad" (*PP* IV.190; cf. *PS* II.51). Further, in both works, Descartes does characterize passive emotions as feelings or "sensations" (*sensus, sentiments*), regardless of whether or not they include the thought of an object. Unlike the sensations of color, taste, etc., and even hunger and thirst, they are not "referred" to material reality: rather they are referred only, or particularly, to the soul (*PSI*.23–25; 27; cf. *PP* IV.189–90). And here I take that expression to mean that they are *attributed* to that in which, as thoughts, they occur; in this respect they do not refer beyond themselves. Does the fact that the passions actually present themselves as *internal states of the soul*—are not *referred to objects*, combined with the fact that some of them do not even require the conscious *presentation of objects*, show that this category of "thoughts," at least, includes some that have no representative aspect at all? Is there any use in invoking here the distinction between presentation and reference?

The objectless internal sensations probably do provide the best basis for questioning whether Descartes conceives thought as necessarily, or invariably, representational.[22] I doubt, though, that they provide a conclusive counter-example. My main reservation has to do with the fact that Descartes characterizes the internal sensations, like the external ones, as "confused thoughts" or "confused and obscure perceptions" (*PP* IV.190; *PS* I.27–8). If to call "external" sensations "confused" is to suggest (as Descartes does in the *Principles*) that they referentially represent something, but do not intelligibly present it, perhaps we should understand the term in the same sense, when it's used of the sensations that he calls "internal" in the *Passions*. Perhaps, for instance, an "objectless" sadness referentially represents and confusedly presents a bad condition of our own blood, even though the presentation is *so* confused that even the *sense* of external reference is lost. (This sort of sadness must be distinguished, of course, from the sadness we feel when it occurs to us *that* our blood may be diseased).[23]

As far as I know, there is no passage that directly confirms such a reading— and none that refutes it, either.[24] However, a remark from a late (February, 1647) letter to Chanut tells, I think, somewhat in favor of the view I am suggesting—that even the "objectless" affects are in some degenerate sense representations of physiological conditions. (It also provides an interesting insight into Descartes's conception of the relation between the sensational and "cognitive" components of emotion where both are in fact present.) Descartes is discussing the relation between rational love (such as love of God or of knowledge), which can occur wholly independently of any embodiment, and sensuous love. He writes:

> [Sensual love] is nothing but a confused thought, excited in the soul by some motion of the nerves, which disposes it to the other, clearer thought which constitutes rational love. Just as in thirst the sensation of dryness in the throat is a confused thought which disposes us to the desire for drink, but is not that desire itself; so, in love a mysterious heat is felt around the heart, and a great abundance of blood in the lungs, which make us open our arms as if to embrace something, and this makes the soul inclined to join itself voluntarily to the object which is present. But *the thought by which the soul feels the heat* is different from the thought which joins it

to this object; and it even sometimes happens that this sensation of love occurs in us without our will being impelled to love anything, because we do not discover any object we think worthy of it. (To Chanut, February, 1647; AT IV, 602–3; emphasis added.)

My conclusion, then, is that it is possible to defend attributing to Descartes a thoroughgoing conception of "thought" as representational, even down to the hardest case, the objectless passions. But the case gets more and more tenuous—and doubtless changes character—as one progresses from ordinary thoughts about this or that, to the treatment of sensation in Meditation III, to the treatment of sensation in later works, and finally to the treatment of the sensuous component in emotion—particularly the objectless affects.

NOTES

1. In my book, *Descartes* (London: Routledge & Kegan Paul, 1978), I uncharitably dismissed Descartes's response as "a model of confusion confounded." (I discuss the Arnauld-Descartes exchange on representation, and related issues, at pp. 100–119.) The present account is intended to supplement, and on some points correct, that earlier one. See also Anthony Kenny, "Descartes on Ideas," in Doney, *Descartes: A Collection of Critical Essays* (Garden City, NY: Doubleday, 1967), for a detailed, highly critical treatment of aspects of Descartes's position dealt with in the present paper. (Kenny's discussion also forms a part of his book, *Descartes* (New York: Random House, 1968).)

Some of the same ground is covered by Alan Gewirth in his well-known paper "Clearness and Distinctness in Descartes," also in Doney (but originally published in 1943). My approach resembles Gewirth's in being primarily constructive, rather than critical, but I try out different distinctions and terminology. For another related discussion see Vere Chappell, "The Theory of Ideas" in A. Rorty, *Essays on Descartes' "Meditations"* (Berkeley: University of California Press, 1986). (Chappell focuses on a passage from the Preface to the *Meditations* in which Descartes says that an 'idea' in one sense is a representing entity; in another sense 'idea' is what is represented—i.e. a represented content. I focus on other passages, in which (as Chappell grants) Descartes appears straightforwardly to assume that *what* ideas normally represent are simply things, states, etc.)

2. Much of what I will say corresponds quite closely to views expressed by Jean-Marie Beyssade in "Descartes on Material Falsity"—a paper read to the April, 1989 conference on "Ideas" in early modern philosophy, the University of Iowa, Iowa City. What I see as a convergence in our viewpoints is, however, coincidental: we did not know of each other's recent work on this subject in advance of preparing our respective essays.

3. I translate '*tanquam*' awkwardly as 'as if' in order to be able to translate it the same way in all contexts. ('Like', for instance, wouldn't work under this condition: Descartes's claim that "all ideas are *tanquam rerum*" (see below) can be translated "all ideas are as if of things," but (obviously) not "all ideas are like things.")

4. The "difference" in question here is not individuation of one idea from another, but rather difference of status on a three-tiered scale of "degree of (objective) reality": ideas which represent—or "exhibit"—substances stand higher than those which represent

modes, and one that represents God, or infinite substance, above those representing only finite substances.

5. AT VII, 46, 64. In *Descartes* (*op. cit.*, pp. 107–8) I suggest that a "real thing" in the sense relevant here is a possible existent, noting Descartes's claim (AT VII, 116) that possible existence is contained in the "concept or idea" of whatever is clearly and distinctly conceived. Unfortunately this suggestion doesn't help with the problem, touched on briefly below, of how a "non-thing" can be *represented*.

6. For what it's worth, Descartes does remark later in the Third Meditation that he "perceives" rest and darkness by the "negation" of motion and light (respectively) (AT VII, 45). Presumably, then, rest and darkness are privations, and are perceived by Descartes as privations. Either this does not count as having an idea of a non-thing that represents it as a non-thing, or Descartes is here violating the principle that all ideas are "as if of things." My own view is that Descartes *should* allow that the *content* of a distinct idea can be a privation, but not a non-thing. (I believe the underlying conception of reality is—or is tied to—distinct conceivability, and I take it that Descartes needs to be able to say that (relative) rest as well as motion is a distinctly conceivable physical state.) In other words, he should not conflate the two terms. There can be no doubt that he does, however.

7. I will not be able to discuss all of Arnauld's objections, however. Among the points that I will not touch on here is his claim that allowing positive content to an idea which Descartes allows might "arise from nothing" (as he says in passing about ideas of sensible qualities) violates Descartes's principle that an idea's "objective reality" requires a cause of at least equal "formal reality." I have discussed this issue at length in my book *Descartes* (*op. cit.*, ch. 3).

8. In the course of his exposition Arnauld draws some relevant morals from Descartes's argument, later in the Third Meditation, that the idea of God, as an infinitely perfect being, cannot but be true. I omit consideration of these remarks in the interest of keeping the discussion reasonably focused.

9. See note 5, above.

10. I don't claim either that the notion of presentational representation is free of problems. Roughly, though, it coincides with what the mind takes itself to be aware of. (If I think I see a tanager, then I can be ascribed a presentational representation of a tanager, regardless of what may actually be going on in the world or (otherwise) in me.) As Peter Markie has suggested to me, the notion may be close to that of "narrow content" in the jargon of contemporary philosophy of mind.

11. In the First Replies Descartes accepts that the idea of the sun "is the sun itself existing in the understanding." He makes clear, however, that the content existing in the understanding has "existing in the understanding" as an intrinsic denomination, whereas the sun in the heavens is only extrinsically related to the mind. He does not there address the question whether (or under what circumstances) a *misrepresentation* of the sun can count as "the sun itself existing in the understanding."

12. Later in the paragraph (AT VII, 234) Descartes says that "confused ideas coming from the senses," such as the ideas of color and of cold, "exhibit nothing real." I take him to mean that what is exhibited—namely the sensation itself—is not, as presented or exhibited, something real. This is the same position he takes in the *Principles*, which I discuss in the next section.

13. Cf. Kenny, "Descartes on Ideas," *op. cit.*, p. 245.

14. At the beginning of Meditation VI Descartes defends the claim that he can't form in imagination the idea of a chiliagon, by noting that,

If I . . . want to think of a chiliagon, . . . I well understand this to be a figure consisting of a thousand sides, as I understand a triangle to be a figure consisting of three; but I do not in the same way imagine those thousand sides, or intuit them as if present. And although, because I am in the habit of always imagining something, when I think of a corporeal thing, I perhaps represent some figure confusedly to myself, it is nevertheless obvious that this is not a chiliagon, because it is in no respect different from what I also represent to myself, if I should think of a myriagon or some other figure with more sides. (AT VII, 72)

What interests me in this passage is the suggestion that an "idea" (sc. in imagination) of a chiliagon, to be an idea of a chiliagon, has to be distinguishable (so to speak by inspection) from an idea of a myriagon. This suggests that such an idea's referentially representing **a** *does* depend on the idea's somehow *presentationally* exhibiting **a**. At present I regard this passage as presenting a problem for the interpretation of Descartes that I'm trying to support.

15. Calvin Normore stressed the phantom limb case as a problem for my proposed reading, in commenting on an earlier version of the paper. I'm not at all sure that the issue I deal with here captures the full force of his objection.

16. Norman Malcolm, "Thoughtless Brutes," Presidential Address delivered before the Sixty-ninth Annual Eastern meeting of the American Philosophical Association, December 28, 1972; Alan Donagan, *Spinoza* (Chicago: University of Chicago Press, 1988), pp. 37–38.

17. See *Descartes, op. cit.*, pp. 116–19.

18. Sometimes Descartes talks of external qualities that give rise to sensations as the "objects" of the sensations: cf. *PP* II.194 (FV); *Le Monde* (AT XI, 5): ". . . if the sense of hearing brought (*rapportoit*) to our thought the true image of its object, it would have to be the case that it made us conceive the movement of the parts of the air which tremble against our ears at the time, rather than making us conceive sound."

19. I take it to be clear that Descartes does regard the active or "interior" emotions—those caused in the soul by the soul itself—as always having an "object."

20. See, for instance, the editors' introduction to *What is an Emotion*, edited by Cheshire Calhoun and Robert C. Solomon (New York: Oxford University Press, 1984), pp. 10–11.

My discussion of the *Passions* has benefitted from, and in places follows rather closely, a paper by Ronald A. Nash, which as far as I know is not yet published. Because I haven't seen a final version of his paper, I won't try to comment in more detail on the relation of our views at this time.

21. I am assuming that, as traditional interpretation holds, "subject" here means "object" which a thought is "of," rather than subject to which it belongs. See, though, Third Replies, AT VII, 175, where "subject of a thought" has to be understood in the latter sense.

22. In the language of the Third Meditation, we could say that they are *mere* forms, detached from ideas.

23. Does this reading imply that the objectless affects are, after all, themselves *ideas*? I think I have to say yes to this question (which was brought to my attention by Nydia Lara), though I acknowledge that Descartes himself does not (as far as I know) call them ideas; and also that construing them as such creates problems for the Third Meditation distinction between ideas and "other forms" that merely attach (so to speak) to ideas.

24. William Lyons, while identifying Descartes as a proponent of "the feeling theory"

of the emotions, evidently takes *Passions* I.36 to show that Descartes regarded the passions as *perceptions of* physiological states (*Emotion* (Cambridge: Cambridge University Press, 1980), pp. 2–4). I think that construing emotions as "perceptions" of anything at all is at odds with construing them as simply "feelings," but (more to the point in the present context) I think Lyons' reading of *Passions* I.36 is untenable. *There* Descartes says only that certain physiological conditions are "ordained by nature to make" the soul experience certain passions.

Descartes: The Epistemological Argument for Mind-Body Distinctness

DESCARTES'S mind-body dualism is the aspect of his philosophy that has been most often cited and discussed in recent philosophical writing. Yet there has been, it seems to me, surprisingly little serious effort to gain an accurate understanding of his position. In another paper ([6]) I have tried to show that Cartesian dualism, as Descartes himself understood it, differs in both content and motivation from the view sometimes called "Cartesian dualism" in recent discussions of the mind-body problem. The differences derive, especially, from Descartes's conception of the possibilities and limitations of mechanistic physical explanation, and his peculiar contention that "the brain can be no use to pure understanding"—as opposed to the faculties of imagination and sense, which are more dependent on body (see [1] : Vol. VII, 358). It is true, on the other hand, that in trying to establish his dualism, Descartes himself places greatest stress on an argument for the immateriality of mind or self which does not seem to depend on these differences. This argument, which I call the "epistemological argument" for the distinctness of mind from body, is presented in the Sixth Meditation—and, in somewhat different versions, in various other works. Descartes's epistemological argument constitutes the principal bridge between historical Cartesianism and contemporary (i.e. twentieth century) discussions of the mind-body relation. I believe that even this argument, taken by itself, has not been correctly represented or criticized in the recent literature.

The epistemological argument of the Sixth Meditation has its roots in arguments developed in the Second Meditation concerning knowledge of the self as a thinking thing, and knowledge of body as something "extended, flexible, movable". Having used the demon hypothesis in the First Meditation to bring into "doubt" the existence of body, Descartes argues in the Second Meditation that this "doubt" does not extend to his own existence ("if he deceives me I exist"). He then considers what attributes can be ascribed with certainty to himself at this stage of his reasoning. He concludes that even certain properties traditionally associated with the soul or vital principle—for example, nutrition—must be presently excluded as part of the doubt of body. There is only one, he finds, that is not called into question on this basis:

> To think? Here I find it: thought [it] is; this alone cannot be separated from me. . . .
> I do not now admit anything except what necessarily is true. I am therefore strictly only a thinking thing, that is mind, or soul, or understanding or reason. . . . I am however a true and truly existing thing; but what sort of thing? I have answered, a thing which thinks. ([1] : VII, 27.)

This passage may seem to imply that Descartes thinks he has *already estab-lished* the conclusion of the epistemological argument: that he is nothing essen-tially but a thinking thing, and as such is distinct from anything physical: "thought alone cannot be separated from me". However, he is careful to cancel any such implication in the immediate sequel of the passage:

> But possibly it happens that these very [corporeal] things [such as the human body] which I supposed were nothing because they are unknown to me, are in the real state of things [*in rei veritate*] not different from this me which I know. I do not know, I do not dispute about this matter now, I can only give judgment on things that are known to me. ([1] : VII, 27.)

Descartes does not, then, wish to claim on the basis of the Second Meditation reasoning alone that he knows that only thought and nothing corporeal pertains to his nature. On the other hand, he is *not* at this point of the argument restrict-ing himself to an epistemically provisional conclusion like "as far as I now know I am a thinking thing and only a thinking thing". For instance, he is implicitly claiming to know, not merely that he thinks, but that thought pertains to his nature or essence: it "cannot be separated from me".[1] Also, he explicitly maintains that reasoning concerning the indubitability of his own existence (the "*cogito* reasoning") has brought him to the conclusion that he is a *true and truly existing thing* (*res vera et vere existens*). The importance of this statement should become clear later.

The Second Meditation contains at least one other assertion that is important to the epistemological argument: that Descartes has a *clear and distinct* idea of himself as a thinking thing (apart from any concept of the corporeal). He begins to hint at this point immediately after the statements already cited. And at the end of the Second Meditation, after arguing that his best knowledge of a typical physical object—a piece of wax—is derived from reason rather than sense, he concludes:

> What however shall I say of this same mind, or of myself? For so far I do not admit that there is in me anything except mind. What, I ask, [of] I who seem to perceive this wax so distinctly? Do I not then know myself not only much more truly, much more certainly, but even much more distinctly and evidently? ([1] : VII, 33.)

Additionally (as this passage also suggests) Descartes claims in the Second Meditation that he has a distinct conception of body as an extended thing— which conception is separate from that of thought. These claims about distinct perception are important because of Descartes's very consciously held position that *only* clear and distinct perceptions or conceptions will suffice as the basis for positive affirmations about the nature of a thing (see especially *NiP* [1]: Vol. VIII-2:337–69 and [2] : 80).

I won't try to elucidate in any detail the distinction between clear and distinct conception and "mere" conception. The distinction can, however, be partly brought out by the example of a geometrical proof. Call the conclusion of a given proof *T. After* one has examined (or constructed) the proof, one *distinctly* conceives or perceives that *T. Before* one has examined (or constructed) the proof one will, very likely, have been able to conceive that T : that is, one will have been in the state of thinking that it might be the case that T. Being able (merely) to conceive that T does not in any way preclude also being able (merely) to conceive that not-T. Clearly and distinctly conceiving that T, on the other hand, does preclude being able clearly and distinctly to conceive that not-T.

Between the Second and Sixth Meditations Descartes "validates" his distinct perceptions by setting forth "proofs" of the existence of an omnipotent and benevolent creator who would not permit him to be deceived in what is most evident. Descartes is, then, so far from concluding rashly from what he can conceive to what is the case, that he even finds it necessary to present God as a bridge from what he can *distinctly* conceive to what is the case.

I

We may now turn to the epistemological argument itself. The Sixth Meditation begins with the observation that God is capable of bringing about or making the case whatever I am capable of clearly and distinctly perceiving: ". . . And I never judged that anything could not be brought about by him, except for the reason that it was impossible for me to perceive it distinctly" ([1] : VII, 71). The first application of this principle is to establish the possible existence of "physical things conceived as the object of pure mathematics"—since previous Meditations have held these to be distinctly conceivable. The second application is in the epistemological argument.

> . . . Because I know that all that I clearly and distinctly understand can be brought about by God as I understand it, it is enough that I can clearly and distinctly understand one thing apart from another [*unam rem absque altera*], for me to be certain that one is different from another, because they can be placed apart [*seorsim poni*] at least by God; and it doesn't matter by which power this is done, in order for us to judge them to be different; and thus, from this very fact, that I know I exist, and that meanwhile I notice nothing else to pertain to my nature or essence, except this alone that I am a thinking thing, I rightly conclude that my essence consists in this one [thing] that I am a thinking thing. And although probably (or rather, as I will afterward say, certainly) I have a body, which is very closely conjoined to me, because nevertheless on the one hand I have a clear and distinct idea of myself, in so far as I am only a thinking thing, not extended, and on the other hand I have a distinct idea of body, in so far as it is only an extended thing, not thinking, it is certain that I am really distinct from my body, and can exist apart from it. ([1] : VII, 78.)

In lieu of detailed analysis of this passage—for which there is no space here—I will merely propose a provisional reading of Descartes's argument which seems to me natural:

1. If A can exist apart from B, and vice versa, A is really distinct from B, and B from A.

2. Whatever I can clearly and distinctly understand can be brought about by God (as I understand it).

3. If I can clearly and distinctly understand A apart from B, and B apart from A, then God can bring it about that A and B are apart (separate).

4. If God can bring it about that A and B are apart, then A and B can exist apart (and hence, by (1), are distinct).

5. I am able clearly and distinctly to understand A apart from B, and B apart from A, if there are attributes Φ and Ψ, such that I clearly and distinctly understand that Φ belongs to the nature of A, and Ψ belongs to the nature of B, and I have a clear and distinct conception of A which doesn't include Ψ, and a clear and distinct conception of B which doesn't include Φ.

6. Where A is myself, and B is body, thought and extension satisfy the above conditions on Φ and Ψ, respectively.

7. Hence, by 5, 6, 3, and 4, I am really distinct from body (and can exist apart from it).

What, if anything, is, wrong with this argument? Let me first mention some commonly-heard objections to Descartes's position on the distinctness of mind that are not in fact effective against it.[2]

Sometimes Descartes's mind-body dualism is taken to rest on (or partly on) the so-called "argument from doubt"—which is universally recognized to be fallacious. The argument from doubt is supposed to go something like this:

> My mind (or self) is distinct from all body. For something true of all body (that I can doubt it exists) is not true of myself (mind). But A and B are the same only if everything true of the one is true of the other.

We need not dwell here on the problems with this argument, for (I trust) it is, perfectly obvious that the argument we have quoted from the Sixth Meditation is not a version of it. Whatever may be the connection in Descartes's mind between his inability to doubt his own existence while doubting the existence of body, it is not successfully captured by this unsound reasoning.

According to another objection, Descartes's argument can show at best that mind and body are possibly or potentially distinct (would be distinct if God should choose to separate them)—not that they *are* distinct. This objection fundamentally misses Descartes's point. Descartes holds that "two" things *are* really distinct if it is *possible* for them to exist in separation. On this view actual *distinctness* does not entail actual *separateness*.

A third common criticism of Descartes's treatment of the distinctness of mind derives from the claim that, under sufficient conditions of ignorance, one can conceive almost anything. Thus, the fact that we can conceive that p does not entail that p is even possible: all that follows (at best) is that we have not yet noticed any contradiction in p. But, as our previous discussion indicates, Descartes would turn this objection aside by pointing out that his argument is not based on mere conceivability, but on clear and distinct conceivability. One cannot ignore this crucial distinction without radically misunderstanding his position.

I do not wish to claim that the appeal to the distinction between clear and distinct perception and mere perception raises no problems of its own. It raises, of course, the important question of how one recognizes clear and distinct perceptions. I will not attempt to evaluate this problem here. Instead I will turn to a criticism of Descartes's use of the notion of distinct perception in the epistemological argument that is, unquestionably, more directly relevant than the objections mentioned above.

II

The author of the first set of *Objections* to the *Meditations*, whose name was Caterus, found fault with Descartes's attempt to reason from the fact that *A* and *B* are distinctly and separately conceived to the conclusion that *A* and *B* can exist apart. He writes:

> Here I match the learned man against Scotus, who says that for it to be the case that one [thing] is conceived distinctly and separately from another, a distinction of the sort called formal and objective—intermediate between a real [distinction] and one of reason—is sufficient. And thus he distinguishes God's justice from His mercy; for, he says, they have concepts [*rationes*] formally diverse before all operation of the understanding, thus that even then the one is not the other; and nevertheless it does not follow: justice can be conceived separately from mercy, therefore can also exist separately. ([1]: VII, 100.)

Caterus here does not exactly follow Descartes's "clear and distinct conception" terminology; nevertheless he has put his finger on a problem that Descartes must come to terms with. For Descartes himself holds that such "simple natures" as extension, figure, and motion can each be clearly and distinctly conceived in itself; yet at the same time they are *not* really distinct; figure cannot exist apart from extended body, and so forth. (See especially *Rules for the Direction of the Mind*, Rules xii and xiv, in [1]: X, 410ff.) In his doctrine of simple natures Descartes appears to be squarely committed to the negation of the principle that what can be clearly and distinctly conceived in separation can *exist separately*.

Descartes replies to Caterus by stressing a distinction between *complete* and *incomplete* beings.

> As to the matter of formal distinction . . . I briefly say that it does not differ from a modal one, and extends only to incomplete beings, which I have accurately distinguished from complete [beings], for which [distinction] it indeed suffices that one [being] is conceived distinctly and separately from another by intellectual abstraction from a thing inadequately conceived, not however so distinctly and separately

that we understand one or the other [being] as if an entity in itself [*ens per se*] and distinct from all others. But for the latter to be the case a real distinction is always required. ([1] : VII, 120.)

Descartes goes on to give precisely the sort of example we would expect, in view of the doctrine of simple natures. Thus, he says,

The distinction between the motion and the figure of the same body is a formal one; and I can quite well understand the motion apart from the figure, and the figure apart from the motion; and I abstract both from the body: but nevertheless I cannot understand motion completely apart from a thing in which the motion is, nor the figure apart from a thing in which the figure is, nor motion in a thing in which figure cannot be, or figure in a thing incapable of motion. (*Ibid.*)

The same point, Descartes says, applies to the example brought forward by Caterus. With these cases Descartes contrasts the mind-body case:

But I completely understand what body is [French version: that is to say I conceive of a body as a complete thing] merely by thinking that it is extended, figured, mobile, etc., and denying of it all those things which pertain to the nature of the mind; and vice versa I understand the mind to be a complete thing, that doubts, understands, wills, and so forth, although I deny that any of those things contained in the idea of body are in it.

The gist of this passage seems to be that we can conceive body and mind not only *distinctly*, but *as complete things*, while denying of each whatever pertains to the nature of the other. Justice and motion, on the other hand, while perhaps capable of being understood distinctly "in separation", are not thereby capable of being understood "completely"—i.e., as complete beings.

I do not know what passage or passages Descartes may have in mind when he says he has "accurately distinguished" complete from incomplete beings. Certainly this distinction does not seem to be made explicit in the *Meditations*.[3] Further, we have seen that the argument as Descartes states it begins with the unrestricted claim that: "It is enough that I understand one thing clearly and distinctly apart from another, to know that one is different from another, for they can be placed apart, at least by God . . .". This statement must now be rephrased. In order to be able to conclude that *A* is different from *B* in the relevant way—i.e., *really* distinct—one must be able to conceive *A* clearly and distinctly and *completely* (as a complete being) apart from *B*. Also, we can now see that Descartes's further statement in the argument, that he has a clear and distinct conception of himself in so far as he is "only a thinking thing, not extended", must be given a different reading than that reflected in premiss (5), above. He must be saying *both* that the concept of himself as a thinking thing comprises no notion of extension, *and* that in thus conceiving himself as a thinking thing he clearly and distinctly conceives of himself as a complete being.

III

In the Fourth Objection, Antoine Arnauld picks up on Descartes's remarks to Caterus about the need for "complete knowledge" as a basis for the mind-body distinctness argument. Arnauld reads this as an acknowledgement that the argument will go through only if our knowledge of ourselves as thinking things is, demonstrably, complete in the sense of being exhaustive. He further observes that nothing in the *Meditations* seem to bear at all on this problem except the argument in the Second Meditation that one can be certain of one's own existence as a thinking thing while doubting or denying the existence of body. But, he concludes,

> . . . all I can see to follow from this, is that a certain notion of myself can be obtained apart from [the] notion of body. But it is not yet quite clear to me that this notion is complete and adequate, so that I am certain that I am not in error when I exclude body from my essence. ([1] : VII, 201.)

According to Arnauld, then, Descartes is not entitled to conclude that extension does not belong to his essence, merely from the observation that he clearly and distinctly perceives that thought is essential to him while he "notice[s] nothing else to pertain to [his] nature". For perhaps in perceiving himself as a thinking thing, he is perceiving, so to speak, only *part* of his essence. Arnauld is in effect taking issue, specifically, with the following statement from the epistemological argument—which signals the transition from the conclusions of the Second Meditation to those of the Sixth: "From this very fact, that I know I exist, and that meanwhile I notice nothing else to pertain to my nature or essence, except this alone that I am a thinking thing, I rightly conclude that my essence consists in this one [thing] that I am a thinking thing". Here Arnauld adduces the case of a man who clearly and distinctly conceives that a given triangle is right-angled, yet lacks a perception of the proportion of sides to hypoteneuse. Because his knowledge of the triangle is in this respect incomplete, the man is able to doubt, and even deny, that the sum of squares on the sides is equal to the square on the hypoteneuse. According to Arnauld, this man would be in a position to reason, in a way parallel to Descartes, that since the clear and distinct idea of a right triangle does not include the notion of Pythagorean proportion, God can make a right triangle with some other proportion among the squares. This conclusion, however, is false.[35] So the epistemological argument must be invalid.

Arnauld has misunderstood Descartes's use of the distinction between complete and incomplete knowledge in his reply to Caterus. However, as Descartes seems to recognize, clearing up this misunderstanding is not all that is necessary in order to answer Arnauld.

Descartes rightly takes Arnauld's main question to be: "Where did I begin to demonstrate how it follows from the fact that I know nothing else to belong to my essence . . . except that I am a thinking being, it follows that nothing else does truly belong to it?" ([1] : VII, 219.) And he answers:

> Surely where I have proved that God exists . . . who can do all that I clearly and distinctly know to be possible.
>
> For although much exists in me which I do not yet [at this stage of the *Meditations*] notice . . . yet *since that which I do notice is enough for me to subsist with this alone*, I am certain that I could have been created by God without other [attributes] which I do not notice. (*Ibid.*, emphasis added.)

Hence, these other attributes may be judged not to belong to my essence since "none of those [properties] without which a thing can exist is comprised in its essence". (There is a suspicion of 'could-can' sloppiness in the Latin, which I won't try to evaluate here.) Descartes further explains that when he spoke, in the First Replies, of the need for "complete knowledge", he did *not* mean exhaustive knowledge of the subject—as Arnauld seems to have assumed. Rather, he meant "knowledge of a thing sufficient to know it is complete", i.e. "endowed with those forms or attributes, which are sufficient that from them recognize that it is a substance." He concludes:

> . . . Mind can be perceived clearly and distinctly, or sufficiently so for it to be considered a complete thing, without any of those forms or attributes by which we recognize that body is a substance, *as I think I have sufficiently shown in the Second Meditation*; and body is understood distinctly and as a complete thing without those which pertain to mind. ([1] : VII, 223; emphasis added.)

He goes on to observe that Arnauld's triangle example is not effective against him, since it "differs from the case at hand" in making no use of the notion of "complete knowledge" in the sense that Descartes originally intended.

Arnauld's basic objection was that for all Descartes knows, some other attribute, such as extension, might be necessarily implicated in his essence together with the known attribute of thought; the only way of eliminating this possibility is to establish that one knows *all* the properties of the self. Descartes's position, however, is just that *since* he recognizes that thought is sufficient "for me to subsist with it alone", he *thereby* knows no other attribute is necessary. To claim that thought and extension are different, and that either is sufficient to determine a complete or true *thing*, is already to deny the possibility of some "hidden" necessary dependence of a thinking thing on the attribute of extension. Thus a "complete knowledge" in Descartes's originally intended sense is sufficient for the epistemological argument to go through.

We may now obtain a clearer understanding of the intended relation between the Second Meditation and the Sixth—indeed Descartes seems finally to make this relation explicit in the important passage I have quoted from the reply to Arnauld. The *cogito* reasoning and its immediate sequel are intended to establish, precisely, that "mind can be perceived clearly and distinctly, or sufficiently so for it to be considered a complete thing, without any of those forms or attributes, from which we recognize that body is a substance . . ." . I think this explains, for example, Descartes's insertion into the Second Meditation of the statement that he knows he is a true and truly existing *thing*, merely in conceiving himself as *thinking*. The role of the epistemological argument in the Sixth Meditation is merely to establish that the perception of the mind argued for in the Second Meditation (clearly and distinctly perceived as a complete thing in virtue of having the property of thought) is sufficient ground for the conclusion that the mind is *really* a distinct thing. What is primarily needed, besides the conclusions of the Second Meditation, is the validation of clear and distinct perceptions as reliable guides to reality.[4]

Discussion of the objections of Caterus and Arnauld has shown the need for some changes in the analysis of the epistemological argument offered above. I suggest, finally, the following reading:

1. If A can exist apart from B, and vice versa, A is really distinct from B, and B from A.

2. Whatever I clearly and distinctly understand can be brought about by God as I understand it.

3. If I clearly and distinctly understand the possibility that A exists apart from B, and B apart from A, then God can bring it about that A and B *do* exist in separation.

4. If God can bring it about that A and B exist in separation, then A and B can exist apart and hence, by (1) they are distinct.

5. I can clearly and distinctly understand the possibility of A and B existing apart from each other, if: there are attributes Φ and Ψ, such that I clearly and distinctly understand that Φ belongs to the nature of A, and that Ψ belongs to the nature of B, and that $\Phi \neq \Psi$, and I clearly and distinctly understand that something can be a complete thing if it has Φ even if it lacks Ψ (or has Ψ and lacks Φ).

6. Where A is myself and B is body, thought and extension satisfy the conditions on Φ and Ψ respectively.

7. Hence, I am really distinct from body and can exist without it.

How good (or bad) is the epistemological argument when interpreted in the way that (as I maintain) Descartes intended it? Well—to mention only one problem—it is at the very best no better than the distinction between clear and distinct perception and "mere" perception. And while I have made some attempt to clarify this distinction, I must admit to distrusting it very radically. (Though I do not know whether recent essentialists' appeals to intuition are on any better ground.) On the other hand, the argument seems to me stronger and much more carefully thought-out than Descartes's critics—contemporary or recent—have generally recognized. In particular, Descartes's reply to Arnauld is so direct and apposite that there can be, I think, no justification for repeating and endorsing Arnauld's objection without giving serious, systematic consideration to the reply.[5,6]

REFERENCES

[1] *Oeuvres de Descartes*, ed. by Charles Adam and Paul Tannery (AT).

[2] *Descartes: Philosophical Letters*, translated and ed. by Anthony Kenny (PL).

[3] Anthony Kenny, *Descartes* (New York: Random House, 1968).

[4] G. W. Leibniz, "Observations on the General Part of Descartes' *Principles*, in *Die Philosophischen Schriften von G. W. Leibniz*, ed. by C. I. Gerhardt (Ger).

[5] Norman Malcolm, "Descarte's Proof that His Essence is Thinking," in *Descartes: A Collection of Critical Essays*, ed. by Willis Doney (Garden City, N.Y.: Doubleday, 1967).

[6] M. D. Wilson, "Cartesian Dualism," in *Descartes: Critical and Interpretive Essays*, ed. by Michael Hooker (Baltimore: Johns Hopkins University Press, 1978) 197–211.

[7] ———, Introduction to *The Essential Descartes* (New York: New American Library, 1969).

NOTES

1. Descartes does not seem to offer justification for the transition from "I think" to "Thought belongs to my nature or essence".

2. Versions of the first objection considered here are found in [3], [4], and [5], and of the third in [3] and [5]. These objections have also been discussed by Michael Hooker in unpublished writings. The second objection is one that I have often heard in discussion, though I do not know of any source in the recent Descartes literature.

3. Although in the Sixth Meditation ([1], VII, p. 78, line 8 from bottom) he does speak of understanding himself distinctly as a "whole" without the faculties of imagination and sense.

3.5 Descartes's doctrine of the creation of the eternal truths is not brought up in this context.

4. I think these observations also help one understand Descartes's notorious tendency, in works other than the *Meditations*, to pass without visible transition from "*cogito ergo sum*" to "*sum res cogitans*".

5. Here I mean to take issue with, for example, Kenny's treatment in [3], pp. 91ff. In [7] I, too, implied it was questionable whether Descartes's reply to Arnauld is at all cogent—a suggestion that I now wish to retract.

6. I am indebted to Michael Hooker, Robert Sleigh, and James F. Ross for very valuable criticism of an earlier, longer version of this essay. I'm uncomfortably aware of not having yet been able to take account of all of their suggestions.

True and Immutable Natures

I

In the Fifth Meditation Descartes introduces the notion of "true and immutable natures." He says that these natures (or essences) are the contents of some of the "ideas" that he finds within himself; and he attempts to establish that they are quite different from any thought-contents that he might have *invented*. Initially he presents this notion as exemplified by geometrical concepts—which in turn he is trying to present as providing the fundamental principles of physical science:

> And what I here think is most worthy of consideration is that I find in me innumerable ideas of certain things which, even if perhaps they exist nowhere outside of me, nevertheless, cannot be said to be nothing; and although they are in some way thought by me at will, they are nevertheless not formed [*finguntur*] by me, but have their [own] true and immutable natures. Thus when, for example, I imagine a triangle, even if [*etiam si*] perhaps such a figure nowhere exists outside my thought, and never existed, there is really nevertheless a certain determinate nature, or essence, or form of it, immutable and eternal, which is not made [*efficta*] by me, and does not depend on my mind; as appears from the fact that various properties can be demonstrated of this triangle, as that its three angles are equal to two right angles, [or] that its largest angle is subtended by its largest side, and the like, which whether I wish or not I now recognize clearly, even if [*etiamsi*] I did not in any way think of them before, when I imagined a triangle, and hence were not made [*effictae*] by me. (AT VII, 64)

Other passages confirm that Descartes attached importance to the claim that mathematical or geometrical ideas, specifically, represent true and immutable natures.[1] But in the Fifth Meditation he quickly moves on to an exposition of a version (or perhaps one should say versions) of the Ontological Argument, in which the distinction between true and immutable natures, and merely factitious ideas, plays a major role. Much of the discussion of the notion of true and immutable natures—in Descartes, his contemporary critics, and recent philosophical interpreters—is connected with the way the notion figures in that argument, or family of arguments. In the First Replies, particularly, Descartes reinvokes and develops the distinction between true and immutable natures and factitious ideas, in attempting to fend off Caterus's objections to his purported demonstration of the existence of God in Meditation V.

A related important issue connected with the notion of true and immutable natures is that on the whole they seem to constitute for Descartes the sole content of ideas that he counts as *innate*. In the Fifth Meditation itself Descartes goes on to stress that ideas of true and immutable natures are "produced from [his] thought"; noting that a great many of them, at least, represent things that he could never have encountered in sense experience. (AT VII, 64–65) But the point is made most explicitly in the following passage from the Correspondence, which dates from the same year as the Meditations:

> By the word *Idea* I understand all that which can be in our thought, and of which I have distinguished three sorts, that is: those which are adventitious, such as the idea which one commonly has of the sun; others that are made or invented [*aliae factae vel factitiae*], in the class of which we can put that which the astronomers have of the sun by their reasoning; and the others innate, such as the idea of God, Mind, Body, Triangle, and in general all those which represent some true, eternal, and immutable essences. (To Mersenne, June 16, 1641; AT III, 383).[2]

Descartes goes on to draw out the significance of the contrast between innate and factitious ideas, by holding that it provides a grounding for a distinction between inferences from an idea that are legitimate, and those that involve a *petitio principii*. (I will return to this issue shortly.)

In a rather long-ago discussion of the notion, I argued that Descartes wholly fails to establish a clear and viable distinction between true and immutable natures and invented or factitious contents.[3] I claimed, first, that Descartes offers *different* criteria for the distinction in the Fifth Meditation, on the one hand; and in the follow-up defense in the First Replies, on the other hand. Second, I tried to show that *both* accounts are highly vulnerable to counter-examples. Much more recently, Walter Edelberg has put forward an interpretation of Descartes's position in the Fifth Meditation and the First Replies that he regards as meeting my criticisms, as well as countering some other interpreters' serious doubts about the viability of Descartes's distinction.[4] Willis Doney, in another recent paper, generally endorses Edelberg's understanding of Descartes's intentions.[5] Doney seems to follow Edelberg in holding that the distinction between true and immutable natures and factitious contents can be maintained successfully, despite certain difficulties in establishing a clear and consistent interpretation across various passages. (What he actually says is, "Though we may be inclined to agree with Wilson that Descartes' notion of a true and immutable nature is less than entirely clear and distinct, it is hard to believe that it is quite as confused as she makes out." [419])[6]

I first learned of Edelberg's paper when Doney presented his own paper at a conference in Paris in 1992. I was immediately impressed with the inherent interest of Edelberg's approach (as explained by Doney); and the plausibility of his (and following him, Doney's) reply to my line of criticism. Even now I don't want to defend my original criticisms of Descartes very far. My counter-example approach was too quick, given that there are no doubt significant philosophical concerns involved. Further, I'm now inclined to hedge somewhat my claim that there is a sharp difference between Descartes's accounts of true and immutable natures in the Fifth Meditation, and in the First Replies. Also, with the benefit of Edelberg's and Doney's papers, as well as an interesting 1980 paper by Gregory Brown,[7] and the various sources they cite, I see that my earlier remarks were lacking in scope. So, on the one hand I don't pretend fully to defend what I said before, against objections of Edelberg and Doney. But, on the other hand, I'm still dubious about the distinction Descartes tries to draw between true and immutable natures and mental constructs. Even after studying Edelberg's and Doney's papers, I tend to question whether the texts are fully coherent. And, ingenious and resourceful as Edelberg's paper is, there is a fair amount in it that I find untenable or unclear.

My purpose in this paper is to begin to reevaluate the issue, in light (mainly) of Edelberg's discussion.

I'll begin by briefly reviewing—with some side commentary—the main points of my original treatment. I'll then go on to sketch and respond to the most directly opposed portions of the analysis that Edelberg provides, with some reference to Doney's discussion. Edelberg's treatment is very detailed (even technical), very inventive, and (I find) in some ways rather hard to get a handle on. Certainly my main concern here is not to "refute" his interpretive position; but to rather to bring into question certain elements of it. I do believe he has at least established that there is room for advancing the discussion of the topic in useful ways; though I'm inclined to think that there are too many problems with his treatment for it to be accepted as a satisfactory clarification of Descartes's distinction.

II

In my earlier account I took Descartes, in the Fifth Meditation, to be holding that the distinction between true and immutable natures, and factitious ideas (or idea contents) rests on the fact that the former, but not the latter, have "unforeseen and unwilled consequences." (*Descartes*, 172) I took this view to be expressed at the end of the passage from Meditation V that I previously quoted (at note 1), where Descartes explains that the status of the triangle as a true and immutable nature,

> appears from the fact that various properties can be demonstrated of this triangle . . . , which whether I wish or not I now recognize clearly, even if [*etiamsi*] I did not in any way think of them before, when I imagined a triangle, and hence were not made [*effictae*] by me. (AT VII, 64)

Unfortunately, it now seems to me that I strengthened the plausibility of my reading by a slightly tendentious translation of *etiamsi* as "even though" (rather than "even if").[8] Another passage I cited from the Fifth Meditation—one which relates the notion of true and immutable natures to the necessity of affirming that God exists—now seems to me even less precisely supportive of the view that Descartes is making the distinction between true and immutable natures, and factitious ideas depend on the issue of "unforeseen and unwilled consequences." That passage goes as follows:

> [F]rom the fact that I cannot think of God except existing, it follows that existence is inseparable from God, and that he really exists; not that my thought brings this about, or imposes any necessity on any thing, but on the contrary because the fact itself, that is of the existence of God, necessarily determines me to this thought: for I am not free to think God without existence (that is the most perfect being without the most perfection), as I am free to imagine a horse either with or without wings. (AT VII, 67; cf. Wilson, *Descartes*, 171)

Surely there is indeed an emphasis in these passages on the notion that Descartes is *compelled* to make certain affirmations on the basis of the given contents of his ideas of true and immutable natures; and on the denial that he has any volitional control in the matter. Additionally, the first-quoted passage allows that the inferences or consequences he is faced with, in the case of true and immutable natures, *may well* include some that were unforeseen by him. But I would not, now, go so far as to hold that he is asserting in Meditation V that "unforeseenness" is a necessary feature of the situation.

(I should observe, though, that the relevance of "unforeseenness" of consequences is stressed more definitely in the continuation of the passage from the letter to Mersenne that I quoted above. Obliquely defending himself against the charge that his Ontological Argument involves a *petitio principii*, Descartes writes:

> Now if from a made idea I should conclude something that I explicitly put into it when I made it, that would manifestly be a *petitio principii*; but if I draw out from an innate idea something that was implicitly contained in it, *but that I still at first did not notice in it*, such as from the idea of triangle, that its three angles are equal to two right angles, or from the idea of God, that he exists, etc., that is so far from being a *petitio principii* that rather it is, even according to Aristotle, the most perfect mode of demonstration, for it has the true definition of the thing as a middle term. (AT III, 383; emphasis added)

In any case, I'd want today to offer a more nuanced account of the Fifth Meditation text itself. Still, I don't think that the relatively minor adjustments would in themselves invalidate the counter-example I originally proposed to the account as I first understood it. For, it seems, the counter-example is itself amenable to the adjustments that might be needed.

The counter-example I offered (discussed by both Edelberg and Doney) was the idea of Onk, defined as "the first non-terrestrial life-form to be discovered by man." I took this to be a clearly factitious idea; yet one that may well have consequences that were not at first foreseen, but on reflection are undeniable. For instance, the "maker" of the idea of Onk may only *on reflection* realize that for something to be a life-form it must have the ability to assimilate nourishment, and have reproductive potential. Therefore "Onk assimilates nourishment" and "Onk has reproductive potential" will be unforeseen necessary consequences. (Today I would say, "volition-independent consequences, which may have been unforeseen.")[9]

I then proposed that in the First Replies Descartes substitutes a quite different criterion of true and immutable natures: namely, *unanalyzability into components "by a clear and distinct mental operation."* This criterion would of course take care of Onk, as well as "winged horse" and "existent lion" (Caterus's example, in his First Objections criticism of the Fifth Meditation).[10] Unfortunately, I observed, it also seems to eliminate, say, *triangles*; since the notion of angle(s) can surely be clearly distinguished from the notion of three. But the idea of triangle is one of Descartes's paradigmatic examples of an idea whose content is a true and immutable nature.

Since the exact phrasing of the First Replies passage has turned out to be rather important, I here quote it at length, in three stages. The reply begins as follows:

> (a) We must notice that those ideas, which do not contain true and immutable natures, but only ones that are made [*fictitias*] and put together by the intellect, can by the same intellect be divided, not merely by abstraction, but by a clear and distinct operation; so that those which the intellect cannot divide in that way, without doubt were not put together by it. So, for example, when I think of a winged horse, or an actually existing lion, or a triangle inscribed in a square, I easily understand (*facile intelligo*) that I can also on the contrary think a non-winged horse, a non-existing lion, a triangle without a square, and the like, and hence that they do not have true and immutable natures [*nec proinde illa veras & immutabiles naturas habere*]. (AT VII, 117)

(This is my own translation; but I think it diverges in no significant respect from Cottingham's—on which Edelberg relies; and only in one from Doney's. Doney translates "*facile intelligo*" as "I readily conceive that," rather than as "I easily understand that," thereby suggesting a more limited epistemic commitment.)

Descartes goes on to contrast with such "made" ideas the case of a triangle or square (parenthetically remarking, in a rather tantalizing way, that he will not speak about the lion or the horse, "because their natures are not fully perspicuous to us"). For instance, he says,

> (b) even if I can understand a triangle, abstracting from the fact that its three angles are equal to two right angles, nevertheless I cannot deny that of it by a clear and distinct operation, that is correctly understanding what I say. (117–118)

Then he adds (surprisingly to some of us readers):

> (c) Besides, if I should consider a triangle inscribed in a square, not to attribute to the square what pertains only to the triangle, nor to the triangle what pertains to the square, but only to examine what arises out of the conjunction of the two, then the nature of it will be no less true and immutable than of the square or triangle alone; but indeed it can rightly be affirmed that the square is not less than double the

triangle inscribed in it, and the like, which pertain to the nature of this composite figure. (118)

I originally took the beginning of this whole passage to imply that if the content of an idea *can* be analyzed into "parts" (by a "clear and distinct" operation) the idea does *not* represent a true and immutable nature. (That is, I took the implication to be that such analyzability constitutes a sufficient as well as a necessary condition of factitiousness.) I claimed that the test failed to capture adequately a necessary condition of "true and immutable naturehood," because, for example, some of Descartes's favored examples of true and immutable natures seem to fail it. I also held that the unanalyzability test is entirely different from the criterion of unforeseen, ineluctable consequences that I took to be the focus of the Fifth Meditation account.

III

I turn now to consideration of Edelberg's paper. At its core is a two-part statement of a criterion for isolating true and immutable natures, which he believes captures the sense of both the Fifth Meditation and the First Replies passages. Before getting to that, though, I will first sketch some of Edelberg's comments specifically on the First Replies (in continuation of the end of my previous section).

Edelberg denies that in the First Replies Descartes means to hold that if the content of an idea is analyzable into parts, then we are *not* dealing with a true and immutable nature. According to Edelberg, in the First Replies passage Descartes is merely indicating that if one finds one can clearly and distinctly divide an idea (or its content) into parts, *we so far have no reason to believe that* we are dealing with a true and immutable nature.

Now, even Doney (who is basically friendly to Edelberg's case) considers this reading too weak to be textually acceptable. He advocates a slightly different version: namely, that analyzability provides *a reason* for thinking that we are *not* dealing with a true and immutable nature: but a *defeasible* reason. Thus, when we first notice that we can distinctly conceive of a triangle apart from the square in which it is inscribed, we should lean to the view that "triangle inscribed in square" does not count as a true and immutable nature. But this reasoning, in Doney's words, "is overridden when we reflect on another fact, that is, that this complex has consequences that are not attributable to one or the other of its components." (420) (More on the "overriding" consideration shortly.)

I take it that Doney is right that Edelberg's reading is implausible in the way he says; but it seems that his emendation is one that Edelberg could easily live with. Either of their readings is admittedly more charitable to Descartes than mine; and it is true (as Doney mentions) that I did not cover—nor even touch on—the fact that Descartes concludes the First Reply paragraph by saying that the triangle-inscribed-in-a-square *does* have a true and immutable essence (c).

Further, it now seems to me at least arguable that the *first* sentence of the whole passage (i.e., of (a)) does not go so far as to imply that divisibility ("analyzability," as I previously called it) supplies *a necessary and sufficient* condition of factitiousness. So all in all it perhaps is better to suppose that Descartes does not intend, at the beginning of the passage, to present unanalyzability or indivisibility as a *necessary* condition of true and immutable natures. Perhaps we can indeed accept the view that ability to "split up" the contents of an idea without violating a necessary connection simply provides a sort of *prima facie* reason to suppose that we are not dealing with a true and immutable nature.

I'd like to stress, though, that this does seem to me a reading that requires a certain interpretational "charity." I continue to feel that the *second* sentence of the first part of passage (a) strongly suggests the reading I originally proposed. Even Edelberg notes that, "taken literally", when Descartes remarks that ideas that can be split up or divided in the right way "do not have true and immutable natures" he "says more than he is entitled to." (511) Further, I don't think Edelberg really accounts for Descartes's introducing the "divisibility" issue at the beginning of the reply to Caterus's objection. Also, it's worth noting that, as far as either Edelberg's or Doney's treatment goes, it would still seem that exactly the same point about the limitations of the "divisibility" standard would apply to "triangle" itself (as well as "triangle inscribed in square") for the reason previously given. That is, triangle would not initially qualify as a true and immutable nature, on the basis of being undividable or (as Edelberg seems to prefer) "unsplitable."

We need now to see more clearly what, on Edelberg's view, does decisively establish that an idea is not "invented." (This will put into fuller context the logic of the First Replies passage as he sees it; while also covering his conception of Meditation V.)

Edelberg's criterion has two main components (the first foreshadowed in the quotation I read from Doney). Noting that in the Fifth Meditation Descartes posits a true and immutable nature (of a triangle) "on the basis of a certain entailment," Edelberg goes on to observe:

> . . . the entailments to which Descartes here draws our attention are ones from the *full set of defining characteristics* of the idea (or figure) to some property. The properties of being three-angled and being a polygon jointly entail the property of having the sum of your interior angles equal to two right angles; but being three-angled, or being a polygon, by themselves do not. This is a feature of every mathematical illustration Descartes gives of an idea having a true and immutable nature. (503; italics in text)

(In a footnote Edelberg indicates that talk of entailment between properties can be restated in terms of entailment between propositions.)

He secondly observes that "the entailments from the defining features of a triangle to the properties in question are not purely logical (nor analytic) entailments." Rather the correctness of the entailment in question "depends in a crucial way on facts about geometry." (504) Edelberg attempts to spell out the notion of "geometrical entailment" with reference to axiom systems and (alternatively) model-theoretic formulations (though he does not hold that Descartes himself would have analyzed "geometrical entailment" in one of these ways). He goes on to remark that of course Descartes intended his doctrine to apply to subject-matters besides geometry: "to theology, for instance." He writes:

> If we take his example from geometry to illustrate how the doctrine is supposed to work, then we must suppose that Descartes countenanced other varieties of entailment which he conceived by analogy with the case from geometry. In each case, we must suppose he countenanced a range of entailments that were neither logically nor analytically correct, but whose correctness depended in a crucial way on essential facts about the subject matter. (506)

Edelberg introduces the term "topical entailment" to refer to this criterion understood generally. Even in the theological area, Edelberg indicates, *we* can understand the relevant notion of entailment in terms of the availability of "a set of axioms and definitions for [the] subject matter . . ." (506–7) But, again, he doesn't suggest that Descartes would have understood it this way.[11]

I don't think I've been able to achieve a very good grasp of the notion of topical entailment, especially when extended to theological matters; and I'm not sure it really contributes much to Edelberg's account. One wonders, for example, about the supposed status or source of the putative "axioms," or "facts about the subject matter"; and what sort of cases can be ruled out. For example, with enough "axioms" about canine digestive systems, and "facts" about physiology and chemistry, it seems I should be able to find topical entailments in the concept of dog food—ones that would involve *both* components of the concept, too. But I have the feeling that this is a rather frivolous complaint. We know that Descartes was not much preoccupied with issues of formal validity; and it seems entirely credible to me that he "countenanced" a notion of necessary consequence that is not tied to logical form or "analytic" connections.[12]

It would be a *further* step to agree with Edelberg that for Descartes necessary connections relevant to the true and immutable natures issue *have* to be other than logical or analytic ones. One reason I'm somewhat inclined to resist this step is that (as Doney discusses) some important commentators locate Descartes's main "ontological" argument for the existence of God in the Fifth Meditation in an inference pattern (via the notions of God as a being with all perfections, and existence as a perfection) that appears to purport, at least, to be logically valid.[13] And, as noted, a major *part* of Descartes's motivation for expounding the initial distinction between true and immutable natures, and factitious ideas, is to lead up to a presentation of the Ontological Argument that will be immune to "existent lion"-type objections.

With regard to my "Onk" example, one of the objections expressed by Edelberg is that the cited "entailments" *may* be "analytic" rather than "topical."

He doesn't press this point however, since he thinks that clearly the counter-example is preempted by his other condition: that the entailed property not be a consequence of *just part of* the (putative) "nature." He writes:

> On the present reading, cases like Wilson's "onk" present no difficulty. . . . [I]f we can account for a topical entailment between "being an A" and "being F" by means of some topical entailment from one of the defining properties of A, to F, then we do not postulate a true and immutable nature of A. But this is just the sort of thing that happens in the onk example: being an onk entails having reproductive and metabolic capabilities only because being a life-form entails this. (510)[14]

It seems natural to ask at this point whether "being a life-form" is at any rate supposed to count as a true and immutable nature under this test. It is not clear to me why the answer should not be "yes" (setting aside the issue of "analytic" versus "topical" entailments). If so, then (to point out the obvious) either the idea of a "life-form" is innate, or the equivalence between true and immutable natures and *innate* ideas (or their contents)—on which Edelberg himself particularly insists—breaks down. I will return to this general issue shortly, by way of a seemingly different problem which Edelberg raises.

In a remark puzzlingly relegated to a footnote, he concedes that there appear to be counter-examples even to the two-phase criterion of true and immutable natures that he has propounded. For according to this criterion,

> it would follow that there is a true and immutable nature of the red triangle, since being a red triangle topically entails being a red trilateral, but neither being red nor being triangular entails this by itself. (507 n. 23)

Edelberg observes that it is "doubtful that Descartes would have wanted to postulate such a true and immutable nature." He attempts to deal with this problem in a brief but quite technical appendix to his paper; while stressing that he "obviously" doesn't mean to suggest that "Descartes had anything remotely as detailed . . . in mind."

The first point I want to make about this footnote is that it seems to put Onk—or at least something close to Onk [or the onks]—back in the picture as a potential counter-example. Let's simplify the defining characteristics of Onk, by defining "Onk-x" as (simply) "non-terrestrial life form." (As far as I can see, nothing hangs on this simplification.) Then we can surely get an "entailment" that satisfies the condition of requiring the *full* defining characteristics, not just *part* of the definition, along the line of Edelberg's "red triangle." Onk-x, it turns out, necessarily has the property of being *a non-terrestrial* (entity) with the ability to assimilate nourishment.

The second point is that, as far as my interpretive intuitions go, it is not merely doubtful that Descartes would have wanted to accept the red triangle as a true and immutable nature; but sure that he would *not* have—any more than in the case of Onk or Onk-x.[15]

But thirdly—and this may help clarify the last remark—the idea of "red triangle," from Descartes's point of view, contains a component which (as ordinarily understood) we fail to conceive *distinctly*. Basically, "red" is for Descartes a confused idea of sense. It is true that more distinct ideas of colors are available, on Cartesian principles, through physical theorizing (in terms of particles in motion). But it does not seem that even the physicist's idea of red would count as *innate* for Descartes: I presume he would construe it as factitious (like the "astronomer's idea of the sun," according to his remark to Mersenne). If one accepts an equivalence between true and immutable natures and the contents of innate ideas, as Edelberg apparently does, then "red triangle" should be excluded on that ground alone.[16] (I set aside here the anomalous line advanced in a certain well-known passage from the late and polemical "Notes against a Program," according to which all ideas—especially those of sense—are innate.[17] And not even that work, of course, suggests that ideas of sense are *distinct*.)

So, on the one hand, there are good reasons for not regarding the specific example Edelberg brings up as providing a relevant problem for his criterion, in the way that he supposes it does. On the other hand, consideration of this alleged counter-example brings into focus the point that the identification of true and immutable natures with the contents of *innate* ideas is potentially quite significant.

One observation related to this point is that it seems that the contents of innate ideas can be *simple*. If contents of such ideas are always immutable natures, then the latter need not, in any meaningful sense, *have* a "full set of defining characteristics." Consider, for example, the list in the First Meditation of things not rendered doubtful by the dreaming argument: that is, things that are "more simple and universal" than "eyes, head, hands and the like":

> Corporeal nature in general and its extension [Descartes says] seem to be of this sort; also the figure of extended things; also their quantity, or magnitude and number; also the place in which they exist, and the time through which they endure, and the like. (AT VII, 20)

Of these simple and universal things Descartes says that "it is at least necessary to admit that [they] . . . are real [*vera*]," a claim that he there implicitly distinguishes from the view that they "exist in nature." Given that they may not actually exist, the ideas of them are presumably not considered adventitious. Given that the natures in question are said to be the elements from which "all . . . images of things, whether true or false, which are in our thought are made," it does not seem that he regards them as factitious. That seems to lead, by elimination, to the conclusion that he considers them innate. Similarly, at the beginning of the Fifth Meditation, Descartes invokes truths about magnitudes, figures, situations, and motions that are "so open and consonant with my nature, that, when I first uncover them, I seem not so much to learn something new, as to recollect . . . what I already knew before." (AT VII, 63–64) Clearly, the implication is that these contents are innate.

But the letter to Mersenne I quoted earlier provides even more direct evidence for the view that immutable natures may be undefinable simples. Descartes there specifically mentions, for example, *Thought* as an immutable nature, innately present in our minds. I see no reason to believe that Descartes considered Thought to have any "defining characteristics."

On the one hand, then, it seems that innate ideas are supposed to include ideas of relatively simple natures, as well as ideas of triangles, etc.: I suggest that these "simples," too, have as their contents true and immutable natures. Thus, an account of the latter concept that appeals to "a full list of defining characteristics" (as Edelberg's does) is misleading.[18] On the other hand, it seems that "red triangle," and perhaps even "life-form" differ from the contents of ideas representing immutable natures, not only in virtue of being (presumably) factitious, but also in virtue of (as normally understood) lacking distinctness. Even if they *do* satisfy Edelberg's condition of non-analytic entailment involving all defining characteristics, they *still* are not candidates for the status of true and immutable natures.

Yet we've seen that Descartes, when challenged to explain why one can infer God's existence from the idea of God, but not the existence of a lion from the idea of an "existent lion," attempts a reply that does not directly appeal to notions of "distinctness" or "innateness."[19] Among the more interesting reasons that might explain his response is the consideration that there seem to be factitious ideas, all the components of which are innate (as the example of the "triangle inscribed in a square" from one point of view suggests). So, forgetting about lions, etc., one could form the idea of "existing *res extensa*." Thereby one seems to obtain the basis for an Ontological Argument for the existence of matter that doesn't require going outside the realm of distinctly perceived, innate, idea contents. Descartes would certainly want to reject this particular Ontological Argument, though, since he adhered to the traditional, pre-Spinozistic view that matter does not exist by virtue of its nature.

At this point I have to admit uncertainty about how the issue comes out. I do want to concede to Edelberg—everything considered—that the notion of defining properties *jointly* entailing a consequence captures some of what Descartes offers in the First Replies, in response to the "existent lion" objection. Yet for reasons Edelberg himself suggests, and I have discussed, this condition doesn't really seem to do the job required. For one thing, there are always going to be trivial ways of satisfying it (apart from complex, unCartesian technical manoeuvres). And, still worse, it lets in a whole lot of ideas that certainly, in Descartes's philosophy, would not be expected to begin to qualify as having true and immutable natures as their content.

There remains, I suggest, the possibility that Descartes's notion of a true and immutable natures *is*, after all (and pace Doney and Schmaltz), pretty much as confused as I earlier made out (even though I don't want to defend my earlier treatment in all details).

In conclusion, I want to touch on one loose end, having to do with the relation between true and immutable natures and innate ideas. As I noted in passing, Descartes remarks parenthetically to Caterus that the natures of the horse and lion are "not fully perspicuous to us." In a paper I mentioned earlier,

Gregory Brown attributes to Descartes a quite Lockean position: the view, that is, that there are or may be natural kinds essences which are not accessible to us, and certainly not innate. I can hardly believe that Descartes was seriously willing to "countenance" such "natures"; but I admit that I so far don't see how otherwise to interpret the remark in question. It does seem to me just possible that he thought that the scope of "true and immutable natures" was broader than our innate ideas; but that those not perspicuous to us counted for nothing within the realm of our thought.[20]

NOTES

1. See, especially, AT VII, 380–2 (Fifth Replies).
2. Descartes is responding to some objections forwarded to him by Mersenne from an unnamed critic, which focussed on the Cartesian concept of idea, and argued that Descartes's Ontological Argument is question-begging. (Cf. AT III, 375–7)
3. *Descartes*, London: Routledge and Keegan Paul, 1978, ch. 5.
4. "The Fifth Meditation," *Philosophical Review*, October 1990, 493–533. In addition to my own critical discussion, Edelberg cites those of Anthony Kenny (*Descartes*, New York: Random House, 1968) and Edwin Curley (*Descartes Against the Sceptics*, Cambridge: Harvard UP, 1978).
5. "On Descartes' Reply to Caterus," *American Catholic Philosophical Quarterly*, vol. 67, no. 4 (1993), 413–30.
6. Similarly, in the paper cited in the next note, Tad Schmaltz observes that he "agree[s] with Edelberg that there is more to Descartes' distinction between immutable and invented essences than his critics contend." (p. 135 n. 16) I am the only "critic" specifically mentioned there.
7. "*Vera Entia*: The Nature of Mathematical Objects in Descartes," *Journal of the History of Philosophy*, vol. 18 pp. 23–37.
Also of interest is Tad M. Schmaltz's "Platonism and Descartes' view of immutable essences," *Archiv fuer Geschichte der Philosophie*, vol. 73 (1991), 129–70. As Schmaltz mentions in a footnote, though, his concern in the paper is with the ontological status of immutable essences in Descartes (particularly in view of apparent conflict between the claims of the Fifth Meditation, and what Descartes says about universals in the *Principles of Philosophy*). That is, he is not concerned to discuss "Descartes' distinction between invented and immutable essences." (As mentioned in the previous note, he does express one relevant opinion.)
8. Possibly under some influence from the old Haldane and Ross translation (HR, vol. I, p. 180).
9. In a footnote to my discussion in *Descartes* I referred to a passage in the *Conversation with Burman*, which raises the question whether even strictly fictional entities might satisfy Descartes's criterion. Burman records raising the following objection:

But then [on your view] not even a chimera will be a fictitious entity [*ens fictum*], since I am also able to demonstrate various properties of it.

Descartes's reply is given as follows:

Everything in a chimera that can be clearly and distinctly conceived is a true entity; it is not fictious [*fictum*], since it has a true and intellectual essence, and this essence is as much from God, as much as the actual essence of other things [*quam actualis aliarum rerum*]. It is said, however, to be a fictional entity [*ens fictum*], in so far as we suppose it to exist [*cum nos illud existere supponimus*]. (AT V, 160)

Burman's objection makes clear that he understood the notion of "demonstrable consequences" to be central to Descartes's distinction. Descartes's reply doesn't directly address Burman's point. Descartes indeed seems to back off from any "consequences" criterion, to an appeal simply to distinct perception.

10. Possibly Chimera, too: see previous note.

11. Edelberg's most formal statement of "the general principle Descartes relies on in arguing for the true and immutable natures" reads as follows:

Suppose that X is a set of properties {A1, A2 . . ., AN} and that property A is defined as a thing having all the properties in X. Then there is a true and immutable nature of A iff:

(i) the properties in X jointly and topically entail some property F, but

(ii) no proper subset of X does so. (507)

12. In the last two sections of his paper (VII-VIII; pp. 518–32) Edelberg develops the "hypothesis" that Descartes thought that the *principal attribute* of a substance determines the topical entailments found in that substance (or its modes). Thus, for instance, "entailments among the modes of extended substance are determined by its principal attribute [extension]." (521) He continues:

If this is right, it raises the possibility that he held analogous views for the other two kinds of substances: finite minds and God. Entailments among the modes of the mind would be determined by the attribute of thought, entailments among the modes of God (or rather, among his various specific perfections) would be determined by the attribute of supreme perfection. (521–22)

Possibly this final phase of Edelberg's paper could provide material for further clarifying the notion of topical entailment itself; as well as meeting other concerns I express below. Edelberg himself, however, does not present his "hypothesis" as leading to any direct clarification of, or qualification upon, the explication of the notion of true and immutable natures provided in the earlier sections. Since these very dense sections certainly present interpretive difficulties of their own, I will not attempt to take account of them here, in any detailed way.

13. Doney, *op. cit.*, 425–27.

14. Edelberg substitutes 'onk' (or 'the onks') for my 'Onk', in order to "obviate problems about existence presuppositions" in my argument. (499 n. 10)

15. Doney himself, without directly commenting on Edelberg's note, offers "the idea of a purple triangle" as an example of a "constructed" idea, as opposed to one representing a true and immutable nature. (*Op. cit.*, p. 416.)

16. Edelburg constructs a principle that he takes to provide a necessary and sufficient condition for innateness (for Descartes) on the basis of his account of true and immutable natures (see note 11, above). This principle adds to the latter account a third condition, having to do with "mental compulsion":

(iii) the mind under certain conditions (when the entailment is clearly and distinctly perceived) lacks the power to deny that the A is F. (509)

In principle, the addition of (iii) allows that the set of innate ideas is smaller than the set of true and immutable natures. It is not clear to me, though, that Edelberg wants to make anything of this possibility. Near the beginning of his paper he does introduce as an assumption (merely) that "all innate ideas have true and immutable natures" (i.e., he does not suggest the converse). But a little later he writes:

> The true and immutable natures are introduced, I will be arguing, as the semantical ground of the truth of certain entailments; innate ideas are introduced as the psychological or metaphysical ground *of a corresponding set of mental compulsions* that are manifested under certain ideal conditions. (502; emphasis added)

17. AT VIIIB, pp. 357ff.

18. As mentioned above (note 16), Edelberg in the last sections of his paper ties his previous discussion of the notion of immutable natures to an hypothesis that the principal attributes of substances—Extension, Supreme Perfection, and Thought (the last for finite mental substances; the second for God)—dictate the topical entailments that obtain in the respective cases. These attributes he himself takes to define the natures or essences of the respective types of substance. (See, e.g., p. 520.) But, as far as I can see, he does not explain how these "attributes" relate to his earlier conditions for true and immutable natures.

19. The passage from the *Conversation with Burman*, cited in note 9, seems to be an exception.

20. Although this issue is not mentioned (as far as I've noticed, anyway) by Edelberg, his formal accounts of true and immutable natures, and innate ideas, would accommodate it. (See notes 11 and 16, above.)

I want to mention here that Professor Edelberg has provided, in private correspondence, detailed responses to aspects of this paper. It would have been too unwieldy, I thought, to try take these responses into account here; but I hope he may find occasion to make them public later.

The first draft of this paper was prepared for a conference in honor of Willis Doney's retirement (Dartmouth College, July 1995; organized by Robert Fogelin). Other occasions on which it was presented included a Descartes conference in Rio de Janeiro in October 1996, which resulted in its publication (in Portuguese translation by Ethel Rochas) in the Brazilian journal *Analytica* (March 1998); and colloquia at several American universities. Among many stimulating comments on all these occasions, I would particularly like to acknowledge the discussions during and after my presentation at the University of Wyoming.

Can I Be the Cause of My Idea of the World?
(Descartes on the Infinite and Indefinite)

. . . If the objective reality of any of my ideas is so much that I
am certain that it is not in me either formally or eminently, and
hence I myself cannot be the cause of this idea, it necessarily
follows, that I am not alone in the world, but some other thing,
which is the cause of this idea, also exists.

—*Meditation III, AT VII, 42; HR I, 163*

But as to the ideas of corporeal things, nothing occurs in them,
which is so great that it does not seem that it could have
originated from myself.

—*AT VII, 43, HR I, 164*

Therefore there remains only the idea of God, about which it must
be considered whether it is something that could not originate
from myself . . .

—*AT VII, 45; HR I, 165*

. . . Although a certain idea of substance is in me from the fact
that I am a substance, nevertheless there would not be on that
account an idea of infinite substance, since I am finite, unless it
originated from some substance which really is infinite.

—*AT VII, 45; HR I, 166*

It is repugnant to my conception, or, what is the same, I think it
implies a contradiction, that the world is finite or bounded . . .

—*Letter to Henry More, 15 April 1649: AT V; PL, 251*

I

In his first argument for the existence of God in Meditation III, Descartes argues that his idea of God requires a cause outside himself. As a finite substance, Descartes (considered as a mind) possesses within himself enough reality or perfection to be the cause of each of his other ideas. The implication is that all of these other ideas represent only finite substances, or their (finite) modes. "There remains only the idea of God" which, representing an infinite substance, cannot be explained by Descartes' own causal resources.

This reasoning has a strange feature, when considered in relation to other prominent Cartesian texts. In Meditation III Descartes writes as if all his ideas of the corporeal world were ideas of particular subparts of this world (like the idea of a stone). Yet many other texts reveal that *res extensa*, or the material world, is conceived of as a substance that exceeds any limits we can assign it, and may in fact be limitless. This conception is not even mentioned in the survey in Meditation III.[1] Nor are any of the nonsubstantial conceivables that Descartes also mentions elsewhere as exceeding (at least) our powers to assign limits, such as the natural number series.

It is true that Descartes—as he says in the *Principles*—reserves the term *infinite* "for God alone." The extension of the world, the divisibility of matter, the series of numbers—all apparently limitless from our point of view—are instead characterized as *indefinite*. Still, they are specifically not conceived as finite. Can *these* conceptions then be accounted for by the causal resources of a finite mind, according to Descartes' theory?

In the next sections of this paper I will try to delineate the nature and grounds of Descartes' distinction between the infinite and indefinite.[2] (Some of my remarks will particularly concern indefinite substance, or *res extensa*, but most will apply to the indefinites in general.)[3] I will show that Descartes uses two distinct considerations to ground this distinction. The first has to do with God's greater perfection: I call this the metaphysical criterion. Much more interesting and difficult is Descartes' further claim that we have different epistemological relations to God and to the indefinites. I call this the epistemological criterion. Clarification of the infinite/indefinite distinction—and particularly of problems surrounding the epistemological criterion—will then provide background for dealing with the question of how exactly conceptions of the indefinite fall within Descartes' theory about adequate causes of ideas. I will return to this question, and some of its implications, at the end of the paper.

II

The infinite/indefinite distinction, as it relates, for example, to *res extensa* and the number series, figures in most of Descartes' central works, including *The World, Discourse on the Method*, Replies to Objections, and *Principles of Phi-*

losophy, as well as the *Conversation with Burman* and a number of important letters.[4] Sometimes the distinction is associated with theologico-political or other strategic concerns in a way that has suggested doubts about its theoretical genuineness. For example, the heading of *Principles* I, 26 reads:

> [We] must not dispute about the infinite, but only regard as indefinite those things in which we perceive no limits [*in quibus nullos fines advertismus*], such as the extension of the world, the divisibility of the parts of matter, the number of stars, etc. (AT VIII-1, 14–15, HR I, 229)

Descartes' elaboration of the Principle continues the theme of "avoiding disputes":

> We will thus never tire ourselves with disputes about the infinite. For surely, since we are finite, it would be absurd for us to determine anything about it, and thus try, as it were, to limit [*finire*] and comprehend it. We will not, therefore, bother to reply to those who ask whether, if an infinite line be given, half of it is also infinite; or whether an infinite number is even or odd and so on: because it seems that no one ought to think about these things, unless they judge their mind to be infinite. We however will not indeed affirm all those things, in which we can find no limit under any consideration, to be finite, but rather we will view them as indefinite. (AT VIII-1, 14–15; HR I, 229–230)

Considerations of piety seem to be evoked at the beginning of the next Principle:

> And we shall call these things indefinite rather than infinite: first so that we may reserve the name of infinite for God alone . . . (AT VIII-1, 15; HR I, 230)

And in at least one other place—a later letter to Chanut—Descartes mentions the issue of Church censure in connection with the question of the infinity of the world. He seems to indicate that affirmation of the infinity of the world need not lead to objection, but that in any case his own position is even less problematic. Chanut had reported from Stockholm Queen Christina's concern that man's conception of his position in the world might be threatened by conceiving the world "in this vast extension" which Descartes calls indefinite (AT V, 22). Descartes does not reply directly to this interesting concern, but offers the following observation instead:

> . . . I recall that the Cardinal of Cusa and several other Doctors have supposed the world to be infinite without ever being reproved by the Church on this account; on the contrary, one is thought to honor God by having his works conceived as very great. But my opinion is less difficult to accept than theirs; because I do not say that the world is *infinite*, but only *indefinite*. (6 June 1647: AT V, 51; *PL,* 221

These passages show that Descartes saw his characterization of *res extensa* as indefinite, rather than infinite, as having strategic advantages. They may lead one to wonder whether the distinction really is introduced as a theoretically cogent one—or merely as a way of evading trouble. Several scholars have indeed suggested or assumed that the distinction, especially as it applies to *res extensa*, is in effect specious. In E. M. Curley's words: "Perhaps Descartes merely wishes to avoid offending the theologians; as he might, if he called any created thing infinite."[5] But whatever the advantages of the distinction from this point of view, Descartes also persistently represents it as conceptually grounded. It is the nature of this conceptual grounding that I now wish to examine. (I will return later to the issue of theoretical sincerity.)

III

Principles I, 27 is concerned specifically with "the difference between the indefinite and the infinite." Descartes writes:

> And we shall call these things indefinite rather than infinite: first so that we may reserve the name of infinite for God alone, because in him alone in every respect [*omni ex parte*], not only do we recognize no limits, but also we understand positively that there are none; then too, because we do not in the same way positively understand other things in any respect [*aliqua ex parte*] to lack limits, but only negatively admit that their limits, if they have them, cannot be found by us. (AT VIII-1, 15; HR I, 230)

In this passage, I suggest, we find combined two distinct reasons for denying the designation "infinite" of "these things" and calling them "indefinite" instead. First, we "positively understand" that there are no limits in God, while with respect to other things we only "negatively admit" that we cannot discover their limits if they have them. That is surely the dominant point. But there is present, too, a more muted contrast between God's unlimitedness *in all respects*, and the fact that other things, if unlimited, are unlimited *only in some respect*. In my terminology these are the "epistemological" and the "metaphysical" criteria for the infinite/indefinite distinction.[6] I will now show that Descartes sometimes uses each criterion in separation from the other, and critically discuss each in turn. I begin with the metaphysical criterion.

IV

A typical statement of the metaphysical criterion is found in a letter to Clerselier, written in 1649. Descartes explains:

> By infinite substance, I understand substance that has actually infinite and immense true and real perfections. This is not an accident superadded to the notion of substance, but the very essence of substance taken absolutely, and bounded by no defects; which defects, *ratio substantiae*, are accidents; but not infinity or infinitude. And it must be noted that I never use the word 'infinity' to signify only not having limit, which is negative and to which I have applied the word 'indefinite', but to

signify a real thing, which is incomparably greater than all those which have some limit. (23 April 1649: AT V, 355–356; *PL*, 254; italics omitted)

A passage from a letter to Henry More, written about the same time, contains a somewhat similar statement:

> I say . . . that the world is indeterminate or indefinite, because I recognize no boundaries [*terminos*] in it; but I would not dare to call it infinite, because I perceive that God is greater than the world, not *ratione extensione*, which, as I have often said, I do not understand as a property in God, but *ratione perfectionis*. (15 April 1649: AT V, 344; *PL*, 250–251)

Descartes' point in the latter passage is that God is appropriately called infinite, and the world is not, because God exceeds the world in perfection. In the Clerselier letter Descartes similarly indicates that he uses 'infinity' to signify something "incomparably greater than all those which have some limit." The point is put still more sharply in Descartes' reply to the First Objections—a reply that clearly foreshadows some of the language of *Principles* I, 26–27:

> And here indeed I distinguish between 'indefinite' and 'infinite', and only call that properly 'infinite' in which in no respect are limits found [*in quo nulla ex parte limites inveniuntur*]: in which sense only God is infinite; those things, however, in which under some respect only [*sub aliqua tantum ratione*] I do not recognize a limit, as extension of imaginary space, the multitude of numbers, the divisibility of the parts of quantity, and the like, I indeed call 'indefinite', because they do not lack limit in all respects [*quia non omni ex parte fine carent*]. (AT VII, 113; HR II, 17)

Perhaps the main difficulty raised by the metaphysical criterion is the following: how are we to conceive the relation between that which lacks limit in all respects, and that which lacks (or may lack) limit in some respect only? For example, if *res extensa* is thought without limit in some respect, should it not follow that God is thought without limit in that respect among others? From such an interpretation of the metaphysical criterion it would seem a short step to the Spinozistic conception of *res extensa* as an infinite attribute of God—a view that Descartes explicitly rejects in the letter to More just quoted.

Descartes evidently thinks this result can be avoided on the traditional grounds that extension implies divisibility, an imperfection, and hence cannot be attributed to God.[7] Spinoza rejected this argument with the claim that Cartesian extension, which does not admit of vacuums, cannot be conceived as really divisible.[8] Whether or not this objection of Spinoza's is right, there does at least seem to be something incomplete or loose in Descartes' statement of the metaphysical criterion of the infinite/indefinite distinction. Perhaps a more precise formulation could readily be constructed, but I will not attempt to do so here.

The metaphysical criterion, at any rate, suggests one possible answer to my original question about whether Descartes would think that his finite mind is sufficient to cause his conceptions of the indefinite. The indefinite, we are told, differs from the infinite in being unlimited, at most, in some respect only. But according to Meditation IV Descartes (as mind) *is* unlimited in some respect, namely with respect to his will or power of willing.[9] One might conjecture that Descartes' possession of unlimitedness in one respect would be sufficient, in his theory, to account for the possibility of his originating ideas of indefinite things, though not of infinite things (according to the metaphysical account of this distinction). This suggestion, though, seems incompatible with Descartes' few remarks on the subject, as I will try to show later.

V

In *Principles* I, 26–27 Descartes observes that we positively know that God is limitless, but lack such positive knowledge with respect to *res extensa*, the number series, and so on. He clearly holds, however, that we are in some kind of epistemological relation to these latter things, which prevents us from construing them as finite. There is in the texts some haziness about just what this epistemological relation is. Sometimes the relation is stated weakly and non-modally: we "notice no limits" in the things he calls indefinite. But more typically Descartes bases his characterization of something as indefinite (rather than finite) on conceptual considerations, which seem to yield (in his view) a conclusion about what is possible for us:

> Thus because we cannot imagine an extension so great, that we do not understand a greater to be possible, we should say that the magnitude of possible things is indefinite. And because it is not possible to divide any body into such parts, that we do not understand each of these parts still to be divisible, we will think that quantity is indefinitely divisible. And because it is not possible to conceive [*fingi*] such a number of stars, that we do not believe yet more could have been created by God, we will also suppose their number indefinite; and so of the rest. (*PP* I, 26: AT VIII-1, 114–15; HR I, 230)

Sometimes, as we will see, Descartes even endorses the apparently stronger claim that we encounter some sort of conceptual repugnancy or contradiction in attempting to suppose that *res extensa* has limits. Although these vacillations in formulation are inconvenient to the commentator, I do not think that they reflect any significant fluctuation in Descartes' conception of the status of *res extensa* as indefinite. (I will develop this point in greater detail below.)

We have seen that Descartes' metaphysical account of the infinite/indefinite distinction, subordinated to the epistemological criterion in the *Principles*, is put at the forefront in certain other passages. The epistemological criterion is sometimes mentioned alone, however, particularly in several discussions of *res extensa*. Such passages tend to suggest that *only* our lack of positive knowledge, rather than some inherent limitation of perfection in comparison with God, precludes applying the term *infinite* to matter and so forth. The letter to Chanut cited above provides one example. Having noted the theological advantage of calling the world "indefinitely great" rather than "infinite," Descartes continues:

> There is a quite notable difference [between the two]: for in order to say that a thing
> is infinite, one must have some reason which makes it known as such [*la fasse
> connoistre telle*], which one can have concerning God alone; but to say that it is
> indefinite, it's enough not to have any reason by which one could prove that it has
> limits. Thus it seems to me that one cannot prove, nor even conceive, that there are
> limits in the matter of which the world is composed. (AT V, 51–52; *PL,* 221)

Descartes goes on to explain the latter point as follows. Where there is three-
dimensional spatiality, there is, *ipso facto,* matter (according to Descartes' theory of matter). But if one tries to suppose that the world is finite, "one imagines
outside its limits some spaces which have their three dimensions"; and will
therefore themselves contain matter. Hence one cannot successfully imagine a
limit to the world. Then,

> Having therefore no reason by which to prove, and even not being able to conceive
> that the world has limits, I call it 'indefinite'. But for all that I can't deny that there
> may perhaps be some [reasons] which are known by God, although they are incom-
> prehensible to me: that is why I do not say absolutely that the world is 'infinite'.
> (AT V, 52; *PL,* 221)

A very similar line is taken by Descartes in another letter to More (5 February
1649). More had criticized Descartes' use of the term *indefinite* with respect to
res extensa on the grounds that the world is in itself either infinite or not. More
seems to be saying that introducing a term like *indefinite,* tied to our way of
conceiving the world, merely obscures the issue. He further seems not to take
seriously the idea that Descartes is genuinely motivated by views about the
inadequacy of our knowledge. Descartes replies:

> It is not indeed from affected modesty, but, on my view, necessary caution, that I
> say that some things are indefinite rather than infinite. For it is only God whom I
> positively understand to be infinite; of the rest, such as the extension of the world,
> the number of parts into which matter is divisible, and similar things, I acknowledge
> that I do not know whether they are infinite simpliciter or not; I only know that I
> recognize no limit in them, and on that account with respect to me I say they are
> indefinite.
>   And although our mind is not the measure of things or of truth, it certainly should
> be the measure of those we affirm or deny. For what is more absurd, what more
> inconsidered, than to want to render judgement of those things to which we admit
> the perception of our mind cannot attain? (AT V, 274; *PL,* 242)

Descartes goes on to make again the point that matter must not be conceived as
surrounded by empty space, since there can be no space without matter.

Principles I, 27, the letter to Chanut, and the letter to More, despite their
differences in formulation, suggest a reasonably constant perspective on the
infinite/indefinite distinction, in so far as it is to be construed epistemologically.
We do not perceive that *res extensa,* for example, is limited; we have no reason
to believe it is limited; indeed we cannot conceive it as limited (for to do so
would require an unacceptable conceptual divorce of *res extensa* from space).

Therefore, on one hand, it must not be considered finite. On the other hand, while we positively know God to be unlimited, we cannot have this positive knowledge in other cases.

To modern ears this dictum will sound particularly odd as it applies to number series and the like. In fact, some of Descartes' own remarks raise questions about the viability of the epistemological criterion: but, as it happens, these mainly concern *res extensa*. Thus, if the conceptual argument about matter and space that Descartes presents to both Chanut and More has any value in showing that we cannot conceive *res extensa* as limited, why doesn't it suffice as "reason" for affirming that *res extensa* is unlimited? Certain other passages from the More correspondence intensify the question. In the letter dated 15 April 1649, Descartes writes:

> It is repugnant to my conception to attribute any boundary [*terminus*] to the world, and I have no other measure of those things which I should affirm or deny, than my own perception. I say therefore that the world is indeterminate or indefinite, because I recognize no boundaries in it (AT V, 344; *PL*, 250–251)
>
> It is repugnant to my conception, or, what is the same, I think it implies a contradiction, that the world is finite or bounded, because I cannot not conceive space beyond whatever limits are assumed of the world; but according to me such a space is a real body. (AT V, 345; *PL*, 251)

If my conception is the only measure of my affirmation, and if it is repugnant to my conception that *res extensa* is limited, then must I not affirm that *res extensa* is unlimited?

Such statements have been taken to support the view, mentioned above, that Descartes' infinite/indefinite distinction is insincere or specious (at least as it applies to the physical world). Alexandre Koyré has held that the last quoted passages are significantly more definitive than the earlier remarks to More on the subject, and show Descartes' true view slipping out. According to Koyré they commit Descartes to the positive view that the world has no limits, since "it would be contradictory to posit them."[10]

Although Descartes' language does become somewhat more forceful in the latter statements to More, I find quite doubtful Koyré's conclusion that Descartes has made a new admission. He still speaks, as he did earlier, of "not recognizing" limits to matter, of not being able to conceive a limit to matter without space (and hence without matter) beyond it. Descartes' view all along has been, I suggest, that there is *something inconceivable to us* in the idea that the world has limits, some conceptual barrier to positing limits to matter. Yet he seems to hold that this fact does *not* commit him to the view that the world lacks limits. I don't think that the mention of "repugnancy" does more than point up a problem of intelligibility that has been there all along: the problem, namely, of reconciling the claim that the limitation of matter is *inconceivable*, with the claim that we don't know matter to be limitless. Does Descartes really think this makes sense?

Recall that Descartes told Chanut that he refrained from calling the world infinite because God might know some reasons for regarding it as having limits, even though these reasons are inaccessible to Descartes. A similar remark is cited by Burman:

> As far as we are concerned, we are never able to discover any limit in these things [extension of the world, number, etc.], and so with respect to us they are indefinite. . . . But as far as God is concerned, maybe he conceives and understands certain limits in the world, number, quantity, and understands something greater than the world, number, and so on; and so for him these things may be finite. As for us, we see that the nature of these things is beyond our powers, and since we are finite, we cannot comprehend them, and so with respect to us they are indefinite or infinite. (AT V, 167; *CB*, 33–34)[11]

Descartes' position seems to be that our conceptual experiments don't allow us *simply to affirm* that such things are limitless, because what is inconceivable to us may still be true from God's point of view.

This alleged dichotomy between what is conceivable to us, and what may be the case for God, might suggest a tie-in between Descartes' position on the indefinite and another, more famous feature of his philosophy. For Descartes of course maintains in many places—the More correspondence among them—that our conception does not impose a limitation on God's power: he can do anything that we distinctly perceive as possible, but we can't say that he cannot do what appears to us contradictory.[12] Perhaps the conceptual repugnancy in supposing that *res extensa*, for example, is limited requires interpretation in a similar context. When we consider the limitations of our minds in relation to the limitlessness of God, we see that our sense of contradictoriness may be merely a function of the former.

The doctrine of God's superiority to our conceptual "repugnancies," however, as it is normally interpreted, implies only that God could have made, say, two plus two not equal four; it does not restrain us from rationally judging now that two plus two equals four. In fact, insofar as the latter judgment rests on clear and distinct perception, it is precisely Descartes' doctrine that our knowledge of God warrants it. So it seems that Descartes' caution about affirming the infinity of the world, or numbers, or the divisibility of matter cannot rest simply on his general views about God's power over the eternal truths.

It seems, therefore, that Descartes' refusal positively to affirm that such things are unlimited can be construed as theoretically honest only if we assume the following. Descartes must believe that the "repugnancy" or other conceptual difficulty we find in supposing them to be limited is epistemologically weaker than the repugnancy or "manifest contradiction" we encounter in trying to suppose that two plus two does not equal four. The conceptual difficulty cannot, in other words, amount to *a clear and distinct perception that matter is unlimited.*"[13]

This suggestion would seem to derive emphatic support from the French version of *Principles* I, 27 (already cited in note 5, above). The relevant statement reads:

As to other things [than God] . . . , although we sometimes notice in them some properties which seem to us to have no limits, *we do not fail to know that that proceeds from the defect of our understanding, and not from their nature* (AT IX-2, 27, italics in text)

I do not think, however, that we should regard as conclusive this reference to the "defect of our understanding" in connection with the seeming apprehension of limitlessness in things other than God. First, the passage presents the familiar problem of judging whether a deviation from the original in an "authorized" translation of Descartes is due to Descartes or the translator. Second, the French version seems inherently confused, since it indicates that the considerations just quoted are needed to show that things like *res extensa* "are not . . . absolutely perfect"—yet surely Descartes does not think that unlimitedness in some property is sufficient for absolute perfection. Finally, the passage deals with the apparent limitlessness of the indefinites only in the weakest terms ("which seem to us not to have limits"): that is, the issue raised elsewhere of "repugnancy in conception" isn't addressed.

I am thus not inclined to count the French version of the *Principles* as providing decisive textual support for the suggestion that Descartes denied the status of clear and distinct perception to the conceptual repugnancy he found in the supposition that, for example, *res extensa* has limits. Nor do I find other direct support for the suggestion. So, on balance, I can only propose that this *might* be the position that Descartes is trying to convey.

The main alternative reading—that, epistemologically interpreted, Descartes' infinite/indefinite distinction is merely a pragmatic ploy—is by no means incredible. But I do want to hold that this alternative reading is not as evidently correct as its proponents tend to indicate. Descartes' statements that the limits of matter are inconceivable—or even that it implies a contradiction to suppose that matter has limits—do not *necessarily* mean to him that (he knows that) matter is limitless. For the statements *may* be dissociated in his thinking from an affirmation of clear and distinct perception. Certainly passages that have been taken specifically to imply knowledge of the limitlessness of matter (etc.) sometimes appear in close proximity to denials that we have such knowledge.

Now even the supposition that Descartes never means to hold that we have a clear and distinct perception of limitlessness in the things he calls indefinite will not solve all riddles about the epistemological criterion. There will remain the objection that it is not strictly true that this criterion grants "God alone" the title "infinite." For, as we've seen in passing, Descartes also thinks that the human will is *known* to be unlimited. Perhaps more important, there remain difficulties in grasping the grounds for a Cartesian claim that we do have positive knowledge of the unlimitedness of God, yet do not achieve clear and distinct perception of the limitlessness of (for example) matter. Descartes implies that our attempts at knowledge are thwarted in the case of the indefinites because such things *exceed our comprehension*, since we are finite. But this warrant for agnosticism is either incomplete or misleading. For Descartes holds that his idea of infinite God is clear and distinct to the highest degree.[14] In the next section I will examine this problem more closely.

VI

Descartes' use of the epistemological criterion requires that some things that we cannot conceive as limited are such that we do not positively know them to be unlimited. It further assumes that we do have positive knowledge of unlimitedness, at least in the case of God. But if, as finite beings, we are unqualified to judge that *res extensa* and so forth are unlimited, why are we not similarly disqualified from knowing such a fact about God?

Notice that the question I am raising here is not quite the same as the more familiar question of how Descartes reconciles his claim that we have a clear and distinct idea of God with his denial that we comprehend God.[15] What I am asking is rather: How is Descartes' claim that our finitude disqualifies us from asserting the limitlessness of things other than God (like the material world) to be reconciled with the claim that we have positive knowledge that God is infinite?

There are some passages in Descartes' writings that make this question seem very problematic indeed. For some of Descartes' statements seem to suggest that our epistemological relation to God and his attributes is after all closely similar to our epistemological relation to things called indefinite. In the Third Objections, for example, Hobbes observes:

> . . . to say that God is *infinite* is the same as if we say that He is among those objects the limits of which we do not conceive, (AT VII, 187; HR II, 72)

It is difficult to see how Descartes can accept such a negative characterization of our epistemological relation to God's "limitlessness," without undermining his distinction between our knowledge of God and matter in this respect. And yet his reply to Hobbes seems more to endorse than to reject the characterization:

> Who is there who does not perceive that he understands something? And hence who does not have this form or idea of understanding, which being indefinitely extended, forms the idea of the divine understanding, and so of the rest of his attributes? (AT VII, 188; HR II, 73)[16]

A remark to Regius similarly suggests that our idea of God is formed by indefinite extrapolation from the finite, while also touching on a comparison of God and quantity in this respect:

> In your first [objection] you say: from the fact that there is in us a certain wisdom, power, goodness, quantity etc., that we form the idea of an infinite or at least indefinite wisdom, power, goodness, and the other perfections which we attribute to God, as also the idea of infinite quantity; all of which I freely concede, and am fully

convinced that there is in us no idea of God except one that is formed in this manner. (24 May 1640: AT III, 64; *PL,* 73, italics omitted)

Descartes goes on to say:

But the whole point of my argument [sc. for the existence of God, Meditation III] is that I contend I cannot be of such a nature that I can by thought extend these perfections, which are minute in me to infinity, unless we have our origin in an Entity in which they are actually infinite. (Ibid.)

(Although Descartes admittedly does speak here of extending something finite *in infinitum,* it's not clear he means this in a strict sense distinct from indefinite extension.)

This is, however, by no means the only, or usual, picture that Descartes presents of our epistemological relation to God's limitlessness. Certain passages suggest that while our *idea* or *conception* of God's limitlessness is formed in the way just indicated, we still have some *additional,* positive knowledge that God is unlimited. Other texts—including, notably, Meditation III—insist straightforwardly that our idea of God is wholly prior to our ideas of finite things.

The "additional knowledge" picture is found in such passages as these:

We do not conceive, but understand the perfections and attributes of God: or, rather, that we may conceive them, we conceive them as indefinite [*concipimus illa tanquam indefinita*]. (AT V, 154; *CB,* 14–15)[17]

Besides I distinguish between *rationem formalem* of the infinite or of infinity, and the thing which is infinite; for as to infinity, even if we understand it to be something maximally positive, we do not nevertheless understand it except in some negative way, that is from the fact that we notice no limit in the thing. (First Replies: AT VII, 113; HR II, 17)

These passages indicate that the negative, or indefinite, conception is not the whole story about our knowledge of the infinite. Of course they leave unexplained how the idea derived by extrapolation from the finite happens to be transcended by positive knowledge in the *one* case of God (or, perhaps, in the *two* cases of God and the will).

Sometimes, though, Descartes straightforwardly maintains that the idea of the infinite, and hence of God, must be in me prior to the ideas of myself and other finite things. According to Meditation III:

And I should not think that I do not perceive the infinite by a true idea, but only by negation of the finite, as I perceive rest and shade by negation of motion and light; for on the contrary I manifestly understand that there is more reality in an infinite substance than in a finite one, and hence in some way the perception of the infinite is prior in me to the perception of the finite, that is that of God to that of myself. (AT VII, 45; HR I, 166. Cf. letter to Clerselier, 23 April 1649: AT V, 355–356; *PL,* 254; also Fifth Reply: AT VII, 365; HR II, 216; also letter to Hyperaspistes, August 1641: AT III, 426–427; *PL,* 114)

This passage seems to contradict the concession to Regius that we "have no idea of God except" one formed by some kind of extrapolation from the finite. An even more straightforward contradiction of the statement to Regius is found in a remark that Descartes makes to Gassendi:

> Whence can be the faculty of amplifying all created perfections, i.e. of conceiving something greater or more ample than they, except from the fact that the idea of something greater, or God is in us? (AT VIII, 365; HR II, 216)

According to this passage the idea of God must be in us prior to that power of amplifying which, in the Regius letter, is presented as the only source of the idea of God!

It does seem, in any case, that Descartes' application of his epistemological account of the infinite/indefinite distinction requires him to hold that we have knowledge of God's infinity independently of our power of amplifying (which can yield only "negative" knowledge). Further, consistently with his use of this criterion he must hold that such positive knowledge of God's infinity cannot yield positive knowledge of the limitlessness of the extension of the world, the number series, and so forth. In fact, if "God alone," or God plus the human will, are the only things admitted as "infinite" by the epistemological criterion, we can have no source of positive knowledge of infinity in any other case. But why should this be so? Is it merely a brute fact about what clear and distinct ideas we happen to possess?

Another, perhaps more satisfying explanation might be found in the suggestion that only God is *unlimited by nature*. (See AT IX-2, 37, and the end of note 5, above.) We have clear and distinct ideas both of God's essence and of, for example, the essence of matter. God's essence, but not the essence of matter, includes or entails unlimitedness. Hence a clear and distinct perception of unlimitedness is available to us in the former case. In the case of matter (and the indefinites generally) a final determination about unlimitedness is denied us by the *combined* factors that there is no essential unlimitedness, and that our limited minds cannot take in all features of the immense entity. Again, when Descartes says there is a repugnancy in conceiving *res extensa* as limited, he would not be claiming to have grasped an essential truth about it.

Of course this suggestion merely serves to draw out the story a little. It indicates that there is more to our ignorance about the ultimate limitlessness of matter than a mere contingent fact about what sort of innate ideas we happen to possess. But, it seems, the weight of "brute fact" is merely shifted to the claim that God alone possesses unlimitedness essentially. A Spinozist who claimed that it's an essential truth that the attributes (such as extension) are unlimited (and a truth that is distinctly perceived) would still find no rationally compelling response in Descartes' position.

I conclude by returning to the question with which I began: namely, would Descartes consider a finite mind sufficient to originate conceptions of the indefinites?

VII

We have seen that in the Third Meditation Descartes includes in his survey of ideas only the ideas of finite things, and the idea of God. He simply does not mention the ideas of things he calls indefinite, *res extensa* in particular. Gassendi, however, partially made the connection, in effect asking Descartes whether reasoning analogous to his causal argument for the existence of God could not be deployed to infer from certain philosophers' ideas of an infinite world, or an infinity of worlds, the claim that such a world, or worlds, exist (AT VII; 295, 299; HR II, 165, 168). Descartes says in reply that only the idea of God permits us to infer the *existence of that of which it is the idea* (AT VII, 369; HR II, 219). There is sound logic behind this answer: According to Descartes' principles, we only know of the causes of our ideas that they have at *least as much* reality as is contained in the idea. The idea of a being of infinite reality and perfection must have as its cause a being of infinite reality and perfection; but then the reality contained in any other idea, however great or small, could have this *same* being as its cause. Still, the question stands: Is the idea or conception of, for example, *res extensa*, as opposed to the ideas of particular bodies and their modes, sufficient from Descartes' point of view to prove the existence of *something* outside of, and greater than, himself? If so, contrary to the suggestion of Meditation III, the idea of God would not provide a *unique* bridge to external reality.

Two passages bearing on this question have already been quoted. Descartes told Regius that the perfections of wisdom, power, and goodness are so minute in him that he wouldn't be able to extend them to infinity "unless we have our origin in an Entity in which they are actually infinite." He adds the further comment (which I did not quote):

> . . . and neither could I conceive an indefinite quantity by inspection of a very small quantity, or finite body, unless the magnitude of the world also was or at least could be indefinite. (24 May 1640: AT III, 64; PL, 73)

This last comment, of course, would take some reconciling with the point just made that God is sufficient to cause any idea. But this much seems clear: Descartes is saying that his finite nature is not sufficient to generate (even) indefinite conceptions. We also noted that Descartes tells Gassendi that the power of amplifying created perfections requires the existence in us of the idea of something greater. Finally, consider this statement from the Second Replies:

> . . . I contend that from the fact alone that I attain in whatever way by thought or understanding any perfection which is above me, for example from the fact alone that I notice that in the course of numeration I can not arrive at the greatest of all numbers, and hence I recognize that there is something in *ratione numerandi* which exceeds my powers. I conclude necessarily, not indeed that an infinite number exists, . . . but that this power of conceiving that a greater number is thinkable than

could ever be thought by me, is received in me not from myself but from some other entity more perfect than I. (AT VII, 139; HR II, 37; cf. AT V, 157; *CB*, 18; letter to Hyperaspistes, August 1641: AT III, 427–428; *PL,* 114)

Textually speaking the answer seems clear: Descartes *does* think his power of generating conceptions of the indefinite cannot be accounted for by his own nature, but requires the existence of something outside himself. The fact that he ascribes to himself an unlimited power of willing doesn't seem to affect this judgment. Even though the number series, for instance, differs from God in not being "unlimited in all respects" (according to the metaphysical criterion), Descartes holds that his power of numbering still requires an external cause. Similarly the presumptive lack of a clear and distinct perception that the number series, for instance, is unlimited does not seem to affect the judgment that our conception of it requires an external cause. Thus Descartes seems to hold that merely negative knowledge that something is such that we cannot find its limits (if it has them) is sufficient to generate a causal argument for *some* external existent. In this respect, then, the idea of the infinite and conceptions of the indefinite—however otherwise distinguished by Descartes—have a similar significance in his thought.[18]

NOTES

1. See also *Discourse on the Method*, Part IV (AT VI, 33–33; HR I, 102–103). In the *Discourse* Descartes, noting his own imperfection as a doubter, reports raising the question where he had "teamed to think of something more perfect" than himself: ". . . and I knew evidently that this must be of such a nature that was in effect more perfect." Here, too, only the idea of God is recognized as that of something more perfect. In the next paragraph, however (which concludes with an affirmation that existence is included in God's essence), Descartes does mention "the object of the Geometers, which I conceive as a continuous body, or a space indefinitely extended in length, width and height . . ." (AT VI, 36; HR I, 103).

In the *Meditations*, Descartes speaks repeatedly of "corporeal nature in general and its extension," "that quantity which philosophers commonly call continuous," "this corporeal nature which is the object of pure mathematics," etc., but the issue of limits or indefiniteness isn't touched on (AT VII, 20, 63, 74; HR I, 146, 179,187).

Descartes seems to acknowledge that the idea of an angel involves more perfection than he possesses, and is itself dependent on the idea of God: AT VII, 41, 124, 138–139; HR I, 164; II, 26, 37.

2. Contrary to an odd comment in the *Conversation with Burman*, the distinction between infinite and indefinite was hardly "invented" by Descartes (AT V, 167; *CB*, 33). See Alexandre Koyré, *From the Closed World to the Infinite Universe* (New York: Harper, 1958), chap. 1, for discussion of a pre-Cartesian version of the distinction in Nicholas of Cusa.

3. It is sometimes said that Descartes held that the speed of light is "infinite": see, for example, Spyros Sakellariadis, "Descartes' Experimental Proof of the Infinite Velocity of Light and Huygen's Rejoinder," in *Archive for History of Exact Sciences* 26 (1982): 1–12; also Gerd Buchdahl, *Metaphysics and the Philosophy of Science* (Cambridge: MIT

Press, 1969), 99. And of course Descartes does speak of light as extending its rays "in an instant"—which might well *seem* to come to the same thing. (See for instance *La Dioptrique* I [AT VI, 84]; letter to Beeckman, 22 August 1634 [AT I, 307]). However I haven't so far found a case where Descartes actually uses the term *infinite* in connection with the propagation of light. Certainly Sakellariadis doesn't quote any. Buchdahl puts *infinite speed* in quotation marks, but without a supporting reference.

4. I cite relevant passages from most of these works below. See also AT XI, 32–33 (*Le Monde*); AT VIII-1, . . . (*PP* II, 34–35). Toward the end of Meditation III Descartes speaks of himself as "a thing incomplete and dependent on another, and a thing aspiring to greater and greater or better," and of God as having in himself "all these greater [things] not only indefinitely and potentially, but *reipsa infinite*." (Cf. AT V, 154; *CB*, 14–15.)

5. E. M. Curley, *Descartes against the Skeptics* (Cambridge: Harvard University Press, 1978), 223. Curley also mentions "paradoxes involved in the notion of infinity which might well have given Descartes a philosophical reason for avoiding use of the term outside of the theological contexts." Descartes also refers to the "paradoxes" somewhat more provocatively in an early letter to Mersenne (15 April 1630: AT I, 146–147; *PL*, 12). See also Koyré, *From the Closed World*, chap. 5; and *CB*, 101–102.

6. Cf. Jean Laporte, *Le rationalisme de Descartes* (Paris: Presses Universitaires de France, 1945), 260–261. Laporte recognizes the appearance of two foundations of the distinction in Descartes, but considers it clear that the two "come to the same": ". . . for what positive reason can one have to think that a being has no limits, except that this being possesses in itself a perfection, a superabundance, a power of existing that repels all limitation—and which only belongs to the *Ens amplissimum*?" I think there is something to what Laporte says here: as I will suggest later, the epistemological criterion ultimately seems to require some sort of metaphysical backing. But Laporte goes too far in saying the two foundations "come to the same." For one thing, his rhetorical question is far from unanswerable (see, e.g., note 9, below). For another, the two criteria have the potentiality for yielding different results (insofar as Descartes sometimes indicates that he would be entitled to call *res extensa* infinite if he could know that it really is of unlimited size). Incidentally, the letter to Clerselier that Laporte cites (p. 261, n. 2) doesn't really support his point, since it says nothing at all about "positive reason" for believing that something lacks limits.

As Roger Ariew has pointed out to me, the French translation of *Principles* I, 27 differs from the original Latin in clearly indicating that the appearance of unlimitedness, even in single properties, of things other than God "proceeds from the defect in our understanding, and not from their nature" (AT IX-2, 37). I suppose this declaration could be read as implying that *res extensa*, the number of stars, etc., are *not* unlimited in *any* respect, thereby rendering the metaphysical criterion nugatory. However, this implication would not hold if it could be true that something is unlimited even though unlimitedness doesn't follow from its nature. Certainly there are numerous passages besides the Latin version of I, 27 which seem to leave open the *possibility* that things other than God are in some respect unlimited.

7. *PP* I, 23 (AT VIII-1, 13; HR I, 228); cf. Étienne Gilson, *Index Scolastico-Cartésien* (Paris: Vrin, 1979; 2d ed.), 80, 82.

8. *E* I, xv, Scholium. Alan Donagan has argued that Spinoza's argument is question-begging. See "Spinoza and Descartes on Extension," *Midwest Studies in Philosophy* I, ed. Peter A. French et al. (Morris, MN: University of Minnesota Press, 1976), 31–33.

9. Descartes says he experiences his will or freedom of choice "as circumscribed by no limits": *sane nullis illam limitibus circumscribi experior* (AT VII, 56; HR I, 174). (Further, "it is the will alone, or freedom of choice, that I so experience in myself, that I apprehend the idea of none greater" [whereas he does have the ideas of greater powers of understanding and memory than his own]: AT VII, 57; HR I, 175.) It is principally the will by virtue of which he understands that he bears "a certain image and likeness of God" (ibid.).

Principles I, 35 goes further: "In fact the will can in a certain manner be called infinite [*Voluntas vero infinita quodammodo dici potest*]" (because we never notice anything that can be an object of any other will to which our will can't extend, too): AT VIII-1, 18; HR I, 233.

If *experior* signifies positive knowledge, something besides God evidently does satisfy the epistemological criterion of infinity.

10. Koyré, *From the Closed World*, 124. See also Cottingham's commentary, *CB*, 102. Cottingham thinks that Descartes' argument to Chanut, in particular, is intended "to demonstrate the logical impossibility of a finite universe."

11. I have omitted here a remark to the effect that we may perhaps say that the world, number, etc., are infinite, because repeated multiplication of the indefinite is the same as infinity. (For a very similar remark, see AT V, 154; *CB*, 14–15.) Cottingham interprets this talk of "multiplying the indefinite" in terms of the example of being able to conceive of space, and hence body, beyond any boundary we try to assign to the world. Therefore he takes the Burman passage, too, as acknowledging the "logical impossibility" of a bounded universe. (See note 10, above.) What Cottingham does *not* note is that in this very passage Descartes distinguishes between what we can conceive on this subject, and what may be true from God's point of view. In my opinion, Cottingham (like Koyré) is over-hasty is assuming that Descartes' thought-experiments amount for him to a clear and distinct perception of logical impossibility.

12. For discussion of this doctrine, and references, see my *Descartes* (London: Routledge & Kegan Paul, 1978), 120 ff.

13. This seems to be Laporte's conclusion, too: cf. *Le Rationalisme*, 263. (Laporte refers to a letter to More [5 February 1649] on the indefinite divisibility of matter; Descartes claims that even though he can't number the parts of matter, he can't say that God couldn't complete the division [AT V, 273–274; PL, 241–242].)

14. See, for instance, Meditation III (AT VII, 46; HR I, 166).

15. This issue is already discussed at some length in the *Objections and Replies*: cf. e.g., AT VII, 112–114; HR II, 17–18.

16. See also AT VII, 137; HR II, 36: "I grant . . . that the idea we have, e.g., of the divine understanding, does not differ from that which we have of our understanding, except only as the idea of an infinite number differs from idea of a number of the fourth or second power . . ."

17. Cf. Cottingham's commentary (*CB*, 76) and, especially Jean-Marie Beyssade, "Création des vérités éternelles et doute métaphysique," *Studia Cartesiana* 2 (1981): 86–105. Beyssade shows that Descartes normally distinguishes "conceiving" and "understanding": "*on concoit l'indefini, on entend l'infini*" (p. 91). Correspondingly, Descartes speaks of *concepts* of the indefinite, *ideas* of the infinite (although he does not always insist on this distinction: cf. AT VII, 139 11, lines 23–24; HR II, 38). We can form indefinite conceptions of certain of God's perfections (e.g., understanding) by extrapolation by the limited instances of these perfections in us. Of some other divine perfections (e.g., absolute unity) we have no representational conceptions (since we are acquainted

with no instances), but only pure ideas. See also Beyssade, "RSP ou Le Monogramme de Descartes" in his edition of *L'entretien avec Burman* (Paris: Presses Universitaires de France, 1981), 171–181.

Perhaps when Descartes told Regius that we "have no idea of God" except from amplification of the finite, he meant *conception* of God. This emendation would greatly help to reconcile the letter to Regius with this and other texts.

18. I wish to thank Desmond Clarke, Daniel Garber, Amélie Rorty and, especially, Roger Ariew for comments that have resulted in revisions of this paper. The research for this paper was supported by a grant from the American Council of Learned Societies under a program funded by the National Endowment for the Humanities.

Objects, Ideas, and "Minds": Comments on Spinoza's Theory of Mind

I

Both specialist commentators and writers of textbooks commonly take Spinoza to have staked out a position on "the mind-body problem" of modern western philosophy. There is, of course, much disagreement on how his position should be characterized. Some are willing to endorse such labels as "a sort of materialism," a "double-aspect theory," or whatever. Others deny that Spinoza's position fits neatly into any of the commonly accepted categories—though they may suggest *limited affinities* with central state materialism, the Strawsonian theory of persons, and so forth. In the recent English-language literature, at least, critics who hold different views about how the position should be described, tend remarkably to agree in regarding it as admirable.[1]

While I admire Spinoza's philosophical system very much, I do not think it includes an admirable position on "the mind-body problem." In this paper I am going to argue that what passes for an important theory of the mind-body relation in Spinoza is an obviously implausible candidate for that role when rightly interpreted. (I also hold, though I will not explicitly argue the point, that the theory is not aptly assimilated to any influential present-day positions.) My procedure will be to consider seriously the implications of an absolutely fundamental tenet of Spinoza's system: the identification of *minds* with *God's ideas of* finite things insofar as they are finite—and vice versa. I will try to show that this understanding of what a "mind" is does not yield a plausible or tenable account of the human mind in its relation to the human body, despite Spinoza's attempt to use the notion in this way. Contrary to what some commentators have said, Spinoza is unable to reconcile his theory of "minds" with any intelligible conception of mental representation, or any coherent and credible account of the scope of conscious awareness. Thus my objection will not be the familiar (and still important) one that it is difficult really to comprehend Spinoza's conception of the relation between the corresponding modes of different attributes. My contention is that *however* this relation be conceived, the theory of "minds" has unacceptable consequences when construed as the basis for a theory about human minds[2]—as Spinoza tries to construe it.

To focus attention on the significance of Spinoza's identification of minds with God's ideas, I will begin by sketching a few points of comparison and contrast between the Spinozistic position and Leibniz's theory of complete concepts. As a further preliminary, I will also point out some of the major differences between Spinoza's "minds" and Cartesian *res cogitantes*. The purpose of this section will be to clarify the nature of Spinoza's conception, and to insist (particularly) on some of its more unusual features. Subsequent sections will examine in detail some obstacles to construing Spinoza's position as a plausible response to the traditional mind-body problem.

II

In Leibniz's philosophy there are major metaphysical differences between God's ideas, and existing particulars, the ideas of which are in God. In the first place, the ideas *are* in God, whereas existing (finite) particulars are merely God's *creatures* (and not "in" him as their metaphysical subject). In the second place, there is in God the idea of every *possible* entity—and according to Leibniz the realm of possibles is much wider than the realm of actual entities. Hence some of God's ideas have corresponding objects, but others (infinitely many) do not. Third, God's ideas and particular entities belong to different ontological categories: at least some particular finite existing entities are *substances*, whereas (I take it) Leibniz did not think of God's ideas of substances—the "complete concepts"—as themselves substances.

There is, on the other hand, one important sort of intimate relation between complete concepts (on Leibniz's theory) and their existing objects (if any). The complete concept (as its designation suggests) must "in some manner comprise" everything true of its object.[3] In at least one place Leibniz relates this claim to the doctrine of God's omniscience.[4] And of course it also follows from God's omniscience that *every* existent has its complete concept in God.

In Spinoza's system God's ideas are (we may say) metaphysically closer to their objects than in Leibniz's. In the first place, the objects like the ideas are merely modes of God: they too are "in God." Second, Spinoza seems to deny that there are *more* ideas in God than there are objects to correspond to them. (Sometimes he seems to hold that the realms of the possible and the actual are coextensive.[5] At other times he affirms there are "ideas of non-existent objects," but holds that they too somehow have correspondents ["essences"] in the attributes other than thought.[6]) Further, whereas God's ideas and their objects belong to different ontological categories for Leibniz, for Spinoza both are of course included in the *same* category, as modes of God.

Spinoza's denial of metaphysical distance between God's ideas and their objects (in the first instance, modes of extension) is indeed thorough enough to yield the conclusion that they are in some sense *the same thing*. In the Scholium to the crucial proposition, *E* II, P7 ("The order and connection of ideas is the same as the order and connection of things"), he writes:

Here, before we go further, we must recall to memory what we showed above; namely, that whatever can be perceived by the infinite understanding, as constituting the essence of substance, all of that belongs to only one substance, and consequently that substance thinking and substance extended is one and the same substance, which is comprehended now under this attribute, and now under that. So also a mode of extension, and the idea of that mode is one and the same thing, but expressed in two ways [*modis*]; which indeed the Hebrews seem to have seen as if through a cloud, who assert that God, the understanding of God, and the things understood by it are one and the same. For example, a circle existing in nature, and the idea of the existing circle, which is also in God, is one and the same thing, which is explained [*explicatur*] by different attributes. . . . (Geb II, 90)

Admittedly, it is difficult really to grasp the sense of the claim that a circle existing (in God), and God's idea of it "is one and the same thing, *quae per diversa attributa explicatur.*" What is important here is that the assertion of identity between a mode of thought and its object derives from a conception about the relation of God's understanding to the world—a conception which makes this relation much closer and more intimate than in the more traditional Leibnizian system.

This lack of metaphysical space between God's ideas and their objects is, I take it, an important condition behind Spinoza's calling the former the "minds" of the latter (see the Demonstration of *E* II, P12). The two need to be in some sense *united* for this terminology to make much sense. Still, talking of God's ideas as the "minds" of their objects might in itself constitute no more than a curious terminological move. What makes it more than this is Spinoza's identification of God's idea of the human body with *the human mind* (see, e.g., *E* II, P12). This identification carries with it a commitment to the relevance of the theory of God's ideas to traditional issues and assumptions about mentality. I am going to argue that the attempted identification has thoroughly unmanageable consequences, and leads Spinoza to confusion and incoherence.

Now we must take note of an important point of similarity between Spinoza's position on God's ideas and that of Leibniz. For Spinoza, as for Leibniz, God's knowledge of particulars is infinite and unlimited. There is no particular object of which God lacks an idea (*E* II, P3), and God's idea of any particular includes knowledge of whatever happens in its object (*E* II, P9C). It follows that the human mind will contain a knowledge of *every* occurrence in the human body. It further follows that all bodies whatsoever are "minded" in just the sense that the human body is. Spinoza explicitly draws these conclusions. Thus Proposition 12 of Part II reads:

Whatever occurs [*contingit*] in the object of the idea constituting the human Mind, that must be perceived by the human Mind, or there necessarily is given an idea of the thing in the Mind: That is, if the object of the idea constituting the human Mind is a body, nothing can occur in this body, which is not perceived by the Mind (Geb II, 95).

The Scholium to the following proposition tells us that

. . . these things we have so far proved are completely common [*admodum communia sunt*], and do not pertain more to men that to other individuals, all of which, though in different degrees, are animated [*animata*]. For of anything at all, there is necessarily given in God an idea, of which God is the cause, in the same way as of the idea of the human Body; and hence, whatever we say of the idea of the human Body, that necessarily is to be said of the idea of anything at all (Geb II, 96).

(Spinoza goes on to explain that one idea is superior to another when the body that is the object of the former "contains more reality" than the body that is the object of the latter. I will return to this passage later.)

Of course these brief remarks do not pretend to exhibit fully the relations and differences between Leibnizian complete concepts and Spinoza's "minds." To do so would require consideration of such highly complex matters as the differences between the two philosophers' views about the reality of extension, the possibility of interaction between finite particulars, and the distinction between confused and adequate knowledge.[7] (Spinoza, for example, both maintains that whatever occurs in a given body is perceived by its "mind," and *denies* that God has *adequate* knowledge of a given particular insofar as He constitutes its "mind"—since adequate knowledge may require knowledge of external causes as well.) For present purposes, the main points are just the following. First, Spinoza facilitates identifying certain of God's ideas as the "minds" of their objects by not allowing the metaphysical space between those ideas and existent particulars that one finds in Leibniz's system. Second, he holds that human minds are just a sub-class of these "minds." Third, in virtue of being God's ideas, these "minds" have certain things in common with the Leibnizian complete concepts. In particular, no existent fails to "have" one, and everything that occurs in an object is comprised in or (as Spinoza rather puts it) perceived by its "mind."

We may now briefly contrast the features of Spinoza's "minds," as so far presented, with those ascribed to the human mind by Descartes. Everyone knows, of course, that on Descartes's theory the human mind is a substance (*res cogitans*), whereas Spinoza regards human minds as modes. But this is barely the beginning. Descartes's conception of mind rests squarely on the indubitable self-consciousness provided by the *cogito*. Descartes repeatedly claims to have established that "there's nothing in me, that is, in my mind, of which I'm not in some manner conscious."[8] But it can hardly be claimed that I'm conscious of all, or even of most, of what occurs in my body. And I don't think it will do to say cheerfully that, after all, Spinoza thinks of the mind's ideas in pretty much the same way as Descartes, *only he recognizes unconscious ones*. Consider the force of "everything that occurs in my body": this carries right down to changes of the relation of the simplest parts—the smallest molecules, the atoms, the electrons of each of the millions of cells. I don't think one can even make sense of the claim that I have something like Cartesian ideas of these things (without, however, being conscious of them, or explicitly conscious, or whatever).

Similarly, a Cartesian *res cogitans* entertains or has in it ideas of very many different things, existent or otherwise. These are just the things it is aware of thinking about. On the one hand, as just noted, these do not include "everything that happens in the human body." On the other hand, they do include many,

many things other than the human body. However, the idea that constitutes the human mind is, for Spinoza, just the idea of the human body; the ideas included in it are all ideas of parts, processes, or aspects of the human body. Also, a Cartesian *res cogitans* can represent its objects (the objects of its thought) accurately or otherwise. But Spinoza's "minds," being just God's conceptions of particulars, cannot be inaccurate (although they can, as already observed, by inadequate).[9]

Finally, a Cartesian *res cogitans* is an entity supposed to explain the capacity of certain other entities (live human beings) for rational behavior. If an entity does not behave rationally, that is grounds for denying it has a *res cogitans*. But Spinoza's position seems to entail that there is *no* relation between whether or not a thing behaves rationally, and its possession of a "mind." It seems to entail (even) that there is no relation between whether a thing's behavior and constitution suggests *sentience*, and whether it has a "mind." Once again, to say of something that it posseses a "mind" is just to say that the idea of it is in God.

Descartes's position on the mind-body issue is notoriously beset with difficulties. Still, the theory of *res cogitantes* does recognize and take account of certain propositions about the mental that seem either self-evidently true or fundamental to the whole concept. These include most (I do not say all) of the features just mentioned: that the mind (in a straightforward and common sense of the terms) *represents* or *has knowledge of* external bodies; that it *is ignorant of* much that happens in "its" body; that having a mind is associated with thinking and being conscious; that mentality is recognizable from behavior of a certain sort, and the absence of mentality from "behavior" of other sorts. Will not Spinoza's theory of "minds" simply *fail to be a theory of the mental* if it carries the denial of all or most of these propositions? More exactly will it not fail to make sense of the specific phenomena of human mentality by attempting to construe the human mind as just a circumscribed piece of God's omniscience?

In the next two sections I will consider two parts of a possible response to this challenge on Spinoza's behalf. In section III I consider an attempted defense of the claim that Spinoza *is* able to develop out of his theory of "minds" an account of knowledge or representation of the external world—one that captures the relatively straightforward Cartesian notion while improving on the Cartesian theory. I will try to show that the defense fails utterly as a defense, though I am not concerned to deny that it may correctly explain Spinoza's *intentions*. In section IV I consider versions of the suggestion that Spinoza does want to draw commonsensical distinctions between human minds and mere "minds"—particularly with respect to consciousness—and that his system provides him with adequate materials for doing so. I will argue in detail that his system provides him with no adequate materials for such a distinction. I believe that these arguments and their conclusions show that Spinoza's theory of "minds" provides little basis for a coherent, plausible position on the traditional, post-Cartesian mind-body problem.

III

It is a classical feature of human minds (one particularly stressed by Descartes) that they are able to represent or exhibit to themselves "external objects," whether near or remote; whether existent, possible, or altogether "unreal." The question of how minds do this has, of course, long been considered significant. And it has long been supposed that the answer—at least for many sorts of representation—will have something to do with the human brain and its causal relations to the sense organs and to objects outside the human body. But the question of how it is that representation occurs (or of what goes on in the body when it does) has traditionally been kept distinct from the question of what it is that is represent*ed*, of what is the "object" of the thought or idea. The answer to the latter question is supposed to be in some sense unproblematic, and more or less independent of theory. The object of my thought is just what I'm thinking of—and surely *I* know what *that* is. Answering the former question is generally supposed to require both theorizing and physiological investigation.

Now suppose one identifies the human mind (as Spinoza does) with an idea in God *of the human body*. Can one still make sense of the claim that the human mind represents to itself objects other than the human body? Well, given that states of the human body are causally dependent on states of external bodies, one can develop a *sort* of account of representation: the one that Spinoza in fact gives.[10] Just as states of a given body may have explanations involving external bodies, so many of the ideas that constitute the corresponding "mind" will have their explanation in other, "external," ideas. We may stipulate that such dependent ideas "represent" the objects of the external ideas.

The question I want to raise is whether "representation" will do as an account of the sort of representation classically attributed to human minds. It seems obvious to me that it will not. According to Spinoza's account, my mind "represents" *every* object or physical state that causally affects my own body. So, five minutes ago my mind was "representing" a number of air molecules, the movement of earth in space, cosmic radiation, etc. But (I would claim) none of these things were objects of my thought in the ordinary sense—even if some degree of non-conscious representation is allowed in the latter category. Further it follows straightforwardly from Spinoza's theory that *every* "*mind*" "*represents*" (if you doubt this, look again at the proof of *E* II, P16). For a "mind" "represents" something just in case its body is causally affected by that thing. And of course all finite modes are in constant causal interaction with other finite modes. It seems then that "representing" is in no way a sufficient condition of representing.

This point can be made still clearer if we look at the arguments offered as a partial defense of Spinoza in a well-known paper by Daisie Radner.[11] Radner suggests that Spinoza's theory of representation was meant to overcome certain difficulties of the Cartesian account, according to which (she says) an idea represents an object by resembling it. Among the alleged difficulties is the consideration that since thought and extension have radically different natures, it seems that modes of the two couldn't have enough in common to "resemble" each other.[12] According to Radner, this difficulty is overcome by Spinoza in the following way. The mode of extension which is the object of a given "mind," and the mode of thought which is the "mind," are "related as formal to objective reality" (I do not think she explains these familiar but obscure scholastic terms in any non-tautologous way). Then,

> The key to Spinoza's theory of the nature of representation is his distinction between the object of the idea and that which the idea represents. The term "the object of the idea" is not synonymous with the term "that which is represented by the idea," although in some cases the two terms have the same reference. The object and the thing represented stand in two different relations to the idea. The relation between the idea and its object is explicated in terms of the distinction between objective and formal reality. The relation between the idea and what it represents is explicated in terms of the resemblance of the thing represented to the object of the idea.[13]

But what, we must ask, is the relevant "relation of resemblance of the thing represented to the object of the idea"? Radner notes that for Spinoza (as for Descartes) what is present in the effect must have existed in the cause. Hence the affections of the human body which have external bodies as their causes, must "have something in common with external bodies."[14] Because they do, ideas of these affections of the human body (ideas in the human mind) may be said to represent the external bodies.

> For example, suppose I have an idea which represents the sun to me. This idea is not a mental picture of the sun. It is the objective reality of an affection of my body, an affection which is produced by the action of the sun upon the parts of my body. Since the sun is cause of this bodily affection, and since there must be something in common between cause and effect (*E* I, P3), there is something in common between the sun and my bodily affection. My idea represents the sun to me, by virtue of the fact that its object is an affection which has something in common with the sun (op. cit., 350).

This attempt to clarify Spinoza's position seems still to allow us to conclude that my mind represented object 0 just in case 0 causally interacts with my body. Further, my mind represents 0 merely "by virtue of the fact that" 0 has something in common with the effect it occasions in my body. But Spinoza's theory is then open to charges of being too vague as well as charges of being much too broad. For, obviously, *every* candidate for being a physical cause has "something in common with" every candidate for being a physical effect. Such minimal resemblance does not seem likely to provide any useful clarification of the notion of the client's *representing* the cause.

It should be stressed that the critical point I have just been developing is not the same as either of two other objections that have sometimes been urged against Spinoza (and that are discussed by Radner at the beginning of her article). Thus, some critics have objected that Spinoza uses the term 'idea' ambiguously (and equivocates on it in arguments).[15] On one of these usages 'idea' is tied (definitionally?) to the body of which the idea is the "mind"; an idea can have no other object than this body. On the other usage an idea is a representation or concept, which may be of something external. Now perhaps Spinoza *is* guilty of equivocation on 'idea of' in proofs, but that is not my point. My point is that he is unable to provide within his system a satisfactory conception of the human mind's consciously representing external bodies. This is one major respect in which the theory of "minds" (God's ideas) fails to provide an acceptable model of human mentality. Another objection, also different from mine, lies in the claim that Spinoza confuses "the process by which we come to have ideas with the relation that an idea has with its object."[16] In other words, he fails to notice that a particular brain state might be a necessary condition for our having a particular sort of thought, without the thought having the brain state as its object, in any ordinary sense of "object." In my opinion, this objection underestimates Spinoza's intelligence, and also misses the fundamental point that Spinoza's "minds" are God's ideas of particular physical modes. The problem is not that Spinoza has succumbed to such an elementary sort of "confusion." It is rather that he falsely thinks he can handle the classical (and Cartesian) concept of representation within the peculiar theocentric parameters of his own theory.

IV

I turn now to the question whether Spinoza's theory of "minds" can admit of rational distinctions between conscious and non-conscious entities, or between conscious and non-conscious states of a particular individual. But perhaps we should ask first whether he wants to make such a distinction. (Perhaps he really *intends* to hold that all things are in some degree conscious, and that the mind is in some degree conscious of all that happens in the body?) The textual evidence relating to these latter questions is not plentiful.[17] I will consider four texts that have been presented as evidence that Spinoza did recognize and make room for the ordinary distinction between conscious and non-conscious states or beings. I will argue that the first two are quite inconclusive on this point. The second two do seem to support the claim that Spinoza wanted to distinguish conscious ideas (or "minds") from non-conscious ones. Unfortunately, neither of these shows how such a distinction can intelligibly and plausibly be drawn within his system. Further the two are inconsistent with each other on the question of what is necessary for consciousness to be present. I conclude that Spinoza's system provides no plausible, clear or reasoned view on this fundamental aspect of the traditional mind-body problem.

All four of the texts I will consider have been pointed out by E. M. Curley, either in writing or in discussion. Curley deserves credit for giving careful, critical attention to the problem of consciousness in Spinoza's philosophy—even though his conclusions are, on my view, overly optimistic.

In *Spinoza's Metaphysics* Curley holds that Letter 58 (Geb IV, 266) "implies quite plainly that such things as stones do not possess consciousness."[18] This seems to me an overreading of the text. In this letter Spinoza asks his correspondent to "conceive if you please that [a] stone, while it continues in motion, thinks. . . ." Curley evidently interprets this as an intended counterfactual supposition—which is reasonable but not, I think, strictly required by the text. Curley further suggests that *E* II, P19 shows that having an idea of an affection of the body isn't sufficient for being conscious of that affection.[19] I find this suggestion even more dubious. *E* II, P19 reads: "The human Mind does not know the human Body itself, and does not know it to exist, except through ideas of affections, by which the Body is affected" (Geb II, 107). Curley takes "this as meaning that it is not simply in having an idea of an affection of the body that the mind knows the body" (Curley is taking "knows" to imply "has consciousness of").[20] I don't see this distinction in the text at all. The point Spinoza is making in this proposition is that God does not know *the human body itself* insofar as he constitutes the nature of the human mind. Thus the human mind knows the *affections* of the human body, but not the body itself. There is no implied contrast, so far as I can see, between having an idea of an affection and being conscious of that affection.

However, two propositions of the *Ethics* do contain remarks that suggest Spinoza does recognize some significant distinction between conscious and non-conscious "minds" or states of "minds." The first is *E* III, P9, the second, *E* V, P39 (or, more exactly, the Scholium to the latter). Let us examine these two passages in turn, and consider how they might underpin a distinction with respect to consciousness among and within Spinoza's "minds."

Spinoza first speaks of the mind being "conscious of itself" in *E* III, P9, which reads:

> The mind both insofar as it has clear and distinct [ideas], and insofar as it has confused ideas, endeavors to persevere in its own being for some indefinite duration, and it is conscious of this endeavor (Geb II, 147).

Spinoza first argues for the existence of this endeavor, and then for the claim that the mind is conscious of it. It is the latter proof that interest us. It goes:

> But since the Mind (by Prop. 23, Pt. 2) through the ideas of the affections of the Body necessarily is conscious of itself [*necessario sui sit conscia*], therefore the Mind is (by Prop. 7 of [Pt. III]) conscious of its endeavor (Geb II, 147).

The second proposition referred to here—7 of Part III—tells us that a thing's "endeavor" is just the actual essence of the thing itself. Spinoza seems to take this as sufficient to establish the hypothetical: If a thing is conscious of itself, it is conscious of its endeavor. And evidently *E* II, P23 is supposed to establish the antecedent with respect to the mind: i.e., to establish that the mind is conscious of itself "through the ideas of the affections of the Body." Now when we turn to *E* II, P23 itself, we find that it has to do with *ideae idearum*. It says that the mind "only knows [*cognoscit*] *itself, insofar as it* perceives the ideas of the affections of the Body." The word "conscious" doesn't appear either in the Proposition or the proof. But, reading backward from Part III, we may interpret Spinoza as implying here that the mind is conscious of itself insofar as it knows itself—and it knows itself insofar as it perceives its ideas, or forms second-order ideas of them. If we add the assumption that "consciousness" occurs only when a mind is conscious *of itself*, we get the result that having an idea of 0 is not the same as being conscious, or as being conscious of 0: one must additionally form an idea of one's idea.

Curley regards the doctrine of *ideae idearum* as providing sufficient basis for a distinction between conscious human minds, and other "minds" that are not conscious. He comments,

> We can equate having an idea of an idea with being conscious. . . . It is worth noting in this connection that, while every individual thing has a "mind" containing ideas of the affections of its body (*E* II, P135), the existence of ideas of ideas is proven only for human minds (*E* II, P20). I infer from this that, although Spinoza is willing to assert that everything is animate (in a very odd sense of the term), he is not prepared to say that anything except a human being is conscious.[21]

I believe (from his preceding discussion) that Curley also wants to hold that the doctrine of *ideae idearum* provides a basis for distinguishing between ideas in the human mind that involve consciousness, and those in the human mind that do not. I want to deny these suggestions.

It is true that *E* II, P20 is specifically "about" the human mind, in the sense of referring specifically to it. The proposition reads:

> There is given in God an idea, or knowledge [*cognitio*] of the human Mind, which follows in God in the same way, as the idea of knowledge of the human Body (Geb II, 108).

But the specificity is of doubtful significance, given that Propositions 11 through 13 of Part II also refer specifically to the human mind, yet Spinoza *tells* us (in Proposition 13) that they apply not only to men, but to all individuals whatsoever. *And examination of the proof of E II, P20 fails to reveal, I think, any basis for holding that it applies only to the human mind, and not to "minds" generally.* The proof turns on the claim that there must exist in God "an idea of all of his affections, and consequently (by Prop. 11 [of Part II]) of the human Mind." And Proposition 11 is one of those that Spinoza explicitly holds to apply generally, and not just to the human mind. I conclude that there must be in God ideas of all ideas. Hence the doctrine of *ideae idearum* cannot provide the basis for a satisfactory distinction between minds and "minds," or between conscious thought and non-conscious ideas within the human mind— *whether or not* Spinoza himself supposed that it could.[22]

If the doctrine of *ideae idearum* does not provide us with a rationale for ascribing consciousness and hence (as it were) special *mentality* to the idea of the human body, is there any other doctrine of the *Ethics* that does provide such a rationale? The one important passage we have not so far considered appears in the Scholium to *E* V, P39. There Spinoza comments:

> He who, like an infant or a child, has a body that is fit for very few things [*paucissima aptum*], and is very greatly dependent on external causes, has a mind which considered in itself is for the most part conscious of nothing of itself, of God, or of things; and on the other hand, he who has a Body fit for many things, has a Mind which considered in itself is conscious of much of itself, of God and of things.

He continues:

> In this life therefore we should try before all to change the body of infancy into another (insofar as its nature permits, and conduces to this) which is fit for many things, and which is related to a mind [*ad Mentum referatur*] which is conscious of itself, and of God, and of many things; and thus [*sic*] that all which is related to the memory itself, or imagination, is hardly of any moment in comparison to the understanding. . . . (Geb II, 305)

This passage partly recalls the Scholium to *E* II, P13 referred to earlier, where Spinoza explains that what distinguishes one "mind" from another, and in particular the human mind from inferior "minds," is that the object of the one is more excellent (or "real") than the object of the other:

> I say . . . in general that insofar as any Body is more fit than others to do or suffer many things at once; and insofar as the actions of one body depend more on itself alone, and the less that other bodies concur with it in acting, the mind of that body is more fit for distinctly understanding [*aptior est ad distincte intelligendum*] (Geb II, 97).

The latter passage tells us that Spinoza recognizes *degrees* of excellence and of distinct understanding among "minds"; the former relates this difference to a difference in degrees of "consciousness."

These passages may seem promising, in that they at least take the plausible step of relating the quality of a given "mind" to the degree of complexity of "its" body. So maybe the theory will come out right after all: aren't beings with nervous systems and sense organs more "complex" than those without them? Without attempting to address this rhetorical question, or to examine all the many puzzling features of the two passages, I will try to show briefly why they do not enable us to attribute to Spinoza a coherent and plausible position on the mind-body issue.

First, it is hard to see how the linking of consciousness with intellect or distinct ideas in these two passages can be reconciled with *E* III, P9 and its proof, which we have previously cited. In *E* III, P9 Spinoza says that the mind "necessarily is conscious of itself" through the ideas of the affections of "the Body," and specifically links this consciousness to the possession of "confused" as well as "clear and distinct" ideas. This suggests that if Spinoza does regard the human mind as distinguished from other "minds" with respect to consciousness, he has no *consistent* account of this distinction. Second, setting aside the issue of internal consistency, we must observe that Spinoza offers us no way at all of understanding why the adult body's fitness for many things should be linked to *consciousness* in the adult mind. It is not even very clear what "conscious" *means* in *E* V, P39, nor how it might relate to the phenomenon of sentience and subjectivity that seem to provide the core of the traditional mind-body problem. (What does *consciousness* have to do with the priority of understanding over memory and imagination? Do we really want to say that a child "is for the most part conscious of nothing of itself, of God, or of things"?) Finally, even if one does accept the linkage of consciousness with distinct ideas, it turns out that one *still* has not found a way of identifying a subset of God's ideas ("minds") as peculiarly *mental*. For, contrary to what *E* V, P39 may seem to suggest, Spinoza's principles in fact commit him to the view that every "mind" whatsoever possesses distinct or adequate ideas. Let us see why this is so.

Propositions 38 and 39 of Part II read as follows:

> Prop. 38—Those things which are common to all, and which are equally in the part and in the whole, can only be adequately conceived (Geb II, 118).

> Prop. 39—That which is common and proper to the human Body, and to any external bodies, by which the human Body is affected, and which is equally in any of their parts and in the whole, of this also there will be an adequate idea in the mind (*Ibid.*).

The proofs of these Propositions turn on the claim that the ideas of the affections of the human body are adequate in God insofar as he constitutes the nature of the human mind. But this claim is ultimately based on Propositions 12 and 13 of Part II, which (as we've seen) are said to apply to all modes without distinction. That is, God has adequate ideas of what is common to all insofar as he constitutes the "mind" of any mode. *All* "minds," and not just human minds, must contain adequate or clear and distinct ideas (cf. *E* II, P38 C, Geb II, 119).

This result is largely confirms by propositions 45 and 46 of Part II. P45 is explicitly universal:

> Any idea of any body or singular thing, actually existing, necessarily involves an idea of the eternal and infinite essence of God.

And so is P46:

> The knowledge [*cognitio*] of the eternal and infinite essence of God, which any idea involves, is adequate, and perfect. (127)

It is true that *E* II, P47 seems implicitly to restrict *having* adequate cognition (as opposed to "involving" it) to the human mind. The Proposition reads:

> The human mind has an adequate cognition of the eternal and infinite essence of God (Geb II, 128).

But the proof rests, again, on the doctrine of *ideae idearum*. It reads as follows (omitting some references):

> The human mind has ideas by which it perceives itself, and its body, and external bodies, as actually existing; hence (by Props. 45 and 46) it has an adequate knowledge of the eternal and infinite essence of God.

But, as we've seen above, it is an apparent logical consequence of Spinoza's system that *every* "mind" has "ideas by which it perceives itself. . . ." By this reasoning, then, every "mind" must not merely "involve knowledge of" the eternal and infinite essence of God. Rather, by Spinoza's principles, every "mind" of every body must like the human mind be said to *have* adequate, or clear and distinct, knowledge of the eternal and infinite essence of God. To tie consciousness to distinct cognition will therefore *not* restrict it to those entities normally thought of as minded. Apparently this awkward result was not intended by Spinoza; it is, however, dictated by the logic of his system.

V

My fundamental claim in this paper has been that Spinoza's system does not provide a plausible or coherent position about (real) minds and their relations to bodies. The basis of Spinoza's account of the relation of the human mind to the human body is a conception of the relation of God's ideas to their objects. This approach has features that have understandably been found attractive by many commentators—including the rejection of the two-substance human being, and avoidance of the problems of mind-body interaction. I hope to have shown, however, that the drawbacks of identifying the human mind with God's idea of the human body are too fundamental to be outweighed by the advantages. They include the consequences that the human mind has to include knowledge of everything that happens in the human body, and that all bodies turn out to have minds just as the human body does. I regard these results as implausible and even unintelligible on any understanding of "the human mind" that has anything much to do with the traditional "mind-body problem." I have further argued against other critics that Spinoza is not successful in accommodating traditional views of mental representation and of consciousness within his theory—even though there is evidence that he wished to do so. (With respect to consciousness, logical difficulties in developing a satisfactory position within the theory of "minds" may well have been compounded by vacillation on Spinoza's part about what view he *wanted* to hold.) I conclude that Spinoza's interpretation of the human mind as God's idea of the human body does not only fail to provide a satisfactory theory of the mind-body relation (who has *not* failed on this score?). It fails to address with even minimal cogency certain issues that lie at the very base of the mind-body problem as it is commonly understood—issues such as the relation between sentient experience and material existence, and the power of "the mind" to represent remote, non-existent, or impossible things.

Spinoza's attempt to integrate the "mind-body problem" inherited from Descartes into a theory of God's ideas and their objects was brilliant, elegant, creative and resourceful. It avoids the major impasses of Cartesian dualism and suggests (if somewhat obscurely) the move to a sophisticated modern theory that brooks no nonsense about the human mind as an "immaterial substance." These notable assets should not blind us to the facts that it has extremely exotic implications of its own, that it fails to capture ordinary notions of the mental, and that it suffers from internal imprecision and inconsistency. In short, it does not work at all.[23]

Notes

1. Some representative recent articles are the following: Stuart Hampshire, "A Kind of Materialism," Presidential Address in *Proceedings of the Eastern Division of the American Philosophical Association*, 1970; Wallace I. Matson, "Spinoza's Theory of Mind," and Douglas Odegard, "The Body Identical with the Human Mind: A Problem in Spinoza's Philosophy," both in Maurice Mandelbaum and Eugene Freeman, editors, *Spinoza: Essays in Interpretation* (La Salle, Illinois: Open Court, 1975); Errol E. Harris, "Body-Mind Relation in Spinoza's Philosophy," in *Spinoza's Metaphysics: Essays in Critical Appreciation*, ed. J. B. Wilbur (Assen, The Netherlands: Van Gorcum, 1976). Harris' careful essay touches on several of the problems in Spinoza's theory that I will examine below, as does Odegard's to a lesser degree. Both are, in my view, overly conciliatory to Spinoza. A non-conciliatory critic, whose detailed criticisms occasionally parallel those to be developed in this paper, is H. Barker, "Notes on the Second Part of Spinoza's *Ethics*," Parts I, II, and III, *Mind*, vol. XLVII (1938), reprinted in S. Paul Kashap, ed., *Studies in Spinoza: Critical and Interpretive Essays* (Berkeley: University of California Press, 1972). I particularly admire the spirit of the following statement of Barker's (though I don't agree with all the details of the reasoning leading up to it).

> In the opening sentence of the scholium [to E II, P13] Spinoza claims that we can now understand what is meant by the union of mind and body, and the commentators seem inclined to endorse his claim and to think that in his doctrine of body and mind he has made a great advance upon the other Cartesians. I cannot see that he deserves these praises. The statements that the mind is the idea of the body and the body is the one object of mind do not really throw any light upon the relationship— naturally, since they are not true. (Kashap, 148–149)

2. Although my way of speaking throughout the paper may suggest otherwise, I do not really mean to imply that *only* human beings are subjects of consciousness and the other mental qualities that give rise to "the mind-body problem." My assumption is rather that many, many things that have "minds" in Spinoza's system (all the tennis balls in the world, for instance) are not in any degree self-conscious, sentient, decision-makers like ourselves (though whales, for example, might be).

3. See, e.g., Ger, vol. IV, 433 (*Discourse on Metaphysics*, §viii). Leibniz explicitly construes the complete concept of an individual as allowing derivation of all past, present, and future states of that individual's world. This important feature of Leibniz's

theory, bound up with his theory of truth, provides a fundamental limitation on the comparison I am going to suggest between the complete concept theory and Spinoza's theory of God's ideas of particulars.

4. Ger II, 131; cf. *ibid.*, 49, 50.

5. See Ger II, 60, 76. The references are to *E* I, P16 and P135.

6. *E* II, P8 (Ger II, 90–91). I confess I find this Proposition one of the most baffling in the *Ethics*, especially when compared with those mentioned in note 5.

7. See also note 3, above. Leibniz himself, incidentally, explicitly criticized Spinoza's identification of minds with God's ideas. He argues, among other things, that mind is unlike an idea in being an active, changing entity (whereas an idea is unchanging and abstract). See Georges Friedmann, *Leibniz et Spinoza* (nouvelle edition) (Paris: Gallimard [Bibliotheque des Idées], 1962), 171 ff.

8. For a detailed discussion of this point, with references, see my *Descartes* (London: Routledge and Kegan Paul, 1978), Ch. IV, §2.

9. See *E* II, P32 and P33. It is notorious that Spinoza has serious difficulties in providing a coherent and consistent account of false ideas. See, e.g., Thomas Carson Mark, *Spinoza's Theory of Truth* (New York: Columbia University Press, 1972), and my review of Mark in *The Journal of Philosophy*, vol. 72, no. 1 (January, 1975), 22–25.

10. *E* II, P17 S, *E* III, P27. Dm. Radner's article discussed immediately below gives further references.

11. "Spinoza's Theory of Ideas," *The Philosophical Review*, vol. LXXX (July, 1971), 338–359.

12. *Ibid.*, 345.

13. *Ibid.*, 346.

14. *Ibid.*, 349.

15. *Ibid.*, 338–340.

16. *Ibid.*, 340.

17. Although Spinoza speaks of the mind as "perceiving" everything that happens in its body, this need not imply anything about conscious awareness. (Leibniz, of course, uses the term "perception" even for the states of those minds that wholly lack consciousness.)

18. E. M. Curley, *Spinoza's Metaphysics* (Cambridge: Harvard University Press, 1969), 126. See Wolf 295.

19. *Op. cit.*, 128.

20. *Ibid.*

21. *Ibid.*

22. Peggy Nicholson has suggested to me that Spinoza might intend the following distinction: the ideas of ideas belonging to the human mind are in God in so far as he constitutes the nature of the human mind, whereas the ideas of ideas of non-human minds are in God but not in so far as he constitutes these minds. This is a natural move to try, but I have so far been unable to find textual warrant for it.

23. I am grateful to Alan Donagan and Joel Friedman for valuable critical comments on an earlier version of this paper. The research for the essay was supported in part by a grant from the Guggenheim Foundation.

Spinoza's Causal Axiom (*Ethics* I, Axiom 4)

TREATMENTS of causality in seventeenth-century philosophy present the inter-preter with a peculiar problem. On the one hand, the notion of causality is central to the period's major positions and disputes in metaphysics and epis-temology. On the other hand, few of the most prominent figures of the period enter into detailed or precise accounts of the relation of causal dependence or causal connection. As a result, one is often left with only the most exiguous materials for dealing with some of the most important and far-reaching interpre-tive issues.

Spinoza is an interesting case in point. Most of the best-known, most charac-teristic features of his system—the conception of substance as *causa sui*, the thorough-going determinism, the distinction between *Natura naturans* and *Na-tura naturata*, the denial of mind-body interaction, the doctrine of thought-matter parallelism, the theories of perception and knowledge, the doctrine of the passions and the account of freedom—are all firmly centered on notions of causal order and dependence. Yet Spinoza says very little to elucidate directly the concept or concepts of causality he relies on.

The treatments of Spinoza's conception of causality that appear in the litera-ture—most of them quite brief—typically focus on his use of geometrical anal-ogies to indicate that causal necessity is truly ineluctable, and in some manner essential, as in the following, often-cited passage:

> . . . from God's supreme power or infinite nature . . . all [things] have necessarily
> flowed forth [*effluxisse*], or always follow with the same necessity, in the same way,
> as from eternity and to eternity it follows from the nature of a triangle that its three
> angles are equal to two right angles (*E*Ip17s).[1]

According to a number of commentators, such passages indicate that Spinoza assimilates or conflates the causal relation with the relation of logical entail-ment, or of "ground" and "consequent."[2] There are plenty of objections that might be made to this interpretive claim, beginning with the observation that its meaning isn't very clear. One thing it might mean is that Spinoza holds that the conjunction of the assertion of the cause and the denial of the effect, under some sort of canonical descriptions of each, will yield a formal contradiction. Or it might mean that, on Spinoza's view, physical things or facts somehow literally *logically entail* each other. Or perhaps some combination of these two notions is intended. Each of these readings goes well beyond anything actually present in the text, however, and all of them involve formidable conceptual difficulties.[3] In the passages quoted (and elsewhere) Spinoza himself offers no

direct clarification of the notion of essential consequence involved in the triangle analogy—or the "necessity" that it exemplifies.[4]

In the present essay I wish to widen interpretive discussion of causality in
Spinoza's system by turning from the geometrical analogies and the issues they
bring to mind to systematic consideration of an axiom that has been characterized as a "definition of cause," axiom 4, *Ethics* I,[5] which reads:

Effectus cognitio a cognitione causae dependet, & eandem involvit,

"*Cognitio*" is normally translated "knowledge." Although some have raised objections to this practice, I propose to continue it here, but with the understanding that the concept in question may be only loosely connected with the normal
connotations of "knowledge" in modern English.[6] So I translate this axiom as:

Knowledge of an effect depends on knowledge of the cause, and involves it.[7]

This axiom plays a key role in the development of a number of the central
Spinozist doctrines mentioned above, and others as well.

Axiom 4 has not been wholly neglected by Spinoza scholars. For example,
among recent and relatively recent commentators, Martial Gueroult, Louis Loeb
and Jonathan Bennett have each devoted a few pages to it; and Harold Zellner
has published a short article focusing on the axiom.[8] The variety of views and
suggestions about the axiom advanced in just these few brief treatments is
rather astonishing. Unfortunately, however, little of what has been proposed
really stands up to scrutiny when one looks closely enough at a range of actual
applications of the axiom. Although I will not attempt here to discuss in detail
all the argumentative uses of *E*Iax4 in the *Ethics*, I will discuss several important applications. These include, first, its intimate connection with the mode-
attribute relation in the early parts of the *Ethics*; second, Spinoza's exploitation
of this connection in setting up his case against Cartesian interactionism; third,
his use of the axiom at the beginning of *Ethics* II to establish the proposition
that the modes under the different attributes are "connected" in the same way;
and, finally, its role in Spinoza's remarkable and peculiar theory of perception
of external bodies.

Each of these contexts, as I will try to show, contributes elements and constraints to the interpretation of the axiom. In light of them I will argue that
various proposals found in the literature are either utterly untenable or (in some
cases) at least highly misleading. I will be particularly concerned to show that
"*cognitio*" in axiom 4 cannot be restricted to adequate knowledge, as Gueroult
insists. I shall also dispute certain other readings, connected with the sense of
"*cognitio*," proposed by Loeb and Bennett. I will try to show that—contrary to
a suggestion found in Bennett—the axiom is not a straightforward expression
of "causal rationalism," of an assimilation of the cause-effect relation to that of
logical ground and consequence. I will present a reason for rejecting Zellner's
thesis that the axiom should be read as the expression of a "transmission" view
of causality. I will argue that the axiom must be sharply distinguished from
Descartes' causal principles. (Bennett and Zellner touch on the possible relation

of these to Spinoza, though without definite commitment.) And I will question the reasoning behind Bennett's claim that Spinoza moves from a "logical" to a "psychological" interpretation of the axiom when he draws on it to establish the Thought-Extension "parallelism" thesis at *E*IIp7.

Besides addressing specific misconceptions, my discussion will provide support for the view that the significance of the particular terms of the axiom, and of the whole proposition, cannot really be understood in isolation from the actual contexts in which it plays a role and the highly original doctrines which it is used to develop. Not only "*cognitio*," but also "*causa*"—and perhaps "*dependet*" and "*involvit*" as well—take on peculiar technical significance as the axiom becomes entwined with the unfolding of Spinoza's system. Having noted the importance of contextual factors in interpreting the axiom, one is still confronted with problems of intelligibility and consistency in its various uses in the *Ethics*. I will briefly address one of these toward the end of the paper. (I will not otherwise be very much concerned here to assess the cogency of demonstrations that rely on the axiom, however.)

Before proceeding to direct consideration of Spinoza's arguments, I will sketch a little more fully some of the claims or suggestions about axiom 4 with which I will later take issue.

On first acquaintance, axiom 4 presents an appearance of paradox. For it appears incompatible with both common sense and ordinary forms of scientific inquiry. Surely we often know what's happened without at all knowing what brought it about; and it certainly seems that scientific research customarily begins with known effects and attempts to discover their initially unknown causes. Such reflections already suggest that the terms in Spinoza's axiom need to be interpreted with care, if the axiom is not to be regarded as denying the obvious. At the very least one would like to have a reading that would make it possible to understand its appeal *for Spinoza*. The range of readings that have been proposed at least partly reflects such systematic and philosophical concerns.

One reading, versions of which have been proposed by several commentators, renders the axiom virtually tautologous in Spinoza's system, by imposing an extremely restrictive reading on "*cognitio*." Probably the most uncompromising version of the restrictive approach is found in Gueroult. He writes: "l'*Axiome 4* et le parallélisme qu'il implique entre l'ordre des idées et l'ordre des causes ne sauraient valoir pour les idées inadéquates. . . . *L'Axiome 4* ne concerne . . . que les idées vraies."[9] And as he also explains, no true knowledge will be acquired as long as "all the causes are not known,"

that is as long as [*tant que*] the idea of the thing is not total or adequate, the adequate idea being that which includes in itself the integral knowledge of the causes of its object. In other words, since any singular thing is such only through the infinity of causes which it envelops, an idea which does not include this infinity in itself only knows the thing partially, mutilates it, does not conform to it, and, consequently, is false.[10]

Loeb's account of the axiom, while expressed in less peculiarly Spinozist terminology, has elements in common with Gueroult's. Loeb claims that in axiom 4 Spinoza is employing a special technical sense of "knowledge" such that one doesn't have knowledge of something *unless* one knows about its causal history.[11] (It is thus his view that axiom 4 is not intended *generally* to rule out the possibility of knowledge of an effect—say "by acquaintance"— which does not include knowledge of the cause.) He further explains that one will lack *perfect* knowledge in the sense at issue as long as one fails to know "the entire or complete causal history of the entity."[12]

It is not entirely clear whether Loeb ultimately means to hold that the "*cognitio*" of axiom 4 must be interpreted as perfect causal knowledge. It seems that this probably is what he means, though: for he goes on at once to stipulate that he will use the expression "SP-knowledge" just to mean perfect knowledge in the sense defined; and he subsequently discusses *E*Iax4 in terms of this expression. Similarly, it is not entirely clear whether Loeb's "perfect causal knowledge" is to be understood as something like Gueroult's "adequate idea." The use of the term "perfect," and Loeb's indication that this knowledge is a special sort of knowledge, do seem to suggest such a restrictive notion, however.[13]

The most decisive evidence against taking axiom 4 to concern only adequate knowledge of a thing, or knowledge of its whole causal history, is found in Spinoza's use of the axiom to develop his theory of sense in *Ethics* II. But the development of other implications of the axiom, from the very beginning of *Ethics* I, also shows the untenability of any such restrictive reading. It turns out, in fact, that *all* forms of "knowledge," *all* "ideas," are taken to satisfy the axiom.

At one point, Bennett, too, entertains the possibility that, in enunciating *E*Iax4, "Spinoza is thinking of some stratospherically high standard of cognitive perfection—some sort of utterly comprehensive knowledge—which we cannot have of a thing unless we have just as good knowledge of its cause."[14] But elsewhere Bennett provides a nice example of an extremely weak and common-sensical reading, according to which the axiom only means "that one's intellectual grasp on any item is weakened by one's ignorance of its cause."[15] This reading is, he suggests, most likely to yield a plausible axiom if understood in terms of instances like the following: "I would have a better grasp of the French Revolution if I knew more about what led up to it."[16] But this bland reading has little connection with any of the roles the axiom is given to play in the *Ethics*.[17] I will try to make this clear shortly, in connection with the contexts I consider. If I am right, then interpreting "*cognitio*" weakly in terms of an ordinary "intellectual grasp" (such as I might have of the French Revolution) is no sounder than restricting it to "adequate" or perfect causal knowledge.

Zellner avoids the problem of interpreting "*cognitio*" in the axiom by treating *E*Iax4 as essentially a metaphysical, rather than an "epistemological," principle. He construes axiom 4 as expressing a "transmission theory of causality"—as "saying that" the cause and effect "share" a property which the cause transfers to the effect.[18] Zellner defends his interpretation by complex reasoning which I won't attempt to assess in detail. It does seem though, that his reading is unsatisfactory insofar as it renders the actual phrasing of the axiom—in terms, precisely, of "*cognitio*"—so far out of accord with what he thinks it is meant to "say."[19] In any case, I think it can be shown that axiom 4 cannot be expressing a "transmission" theory, in virtue of some of the same considerations that tend to undercut Gueroult's view. (Without doubt, though, it is quickly *tied in with* some form of "causal likeness principle," the relevance of which Zellner advocates more plausibly.) Indeed, I think it can be shown that Spinoza did not hold a transmission theory of causality, in any general form, in the *Ethics*.[20]

According to another viewpoint *E*Iax4 is an expression of Spinoza's "deductive" conception of causality. Bennett appears more-or-less to exemplify this viewpoint, too. He says that *E*Iax4 must be read in a "logical" way in all its uses, except at *E*IIp7, where a "psychological" reading is required. Setting aside the issue of a "psychological" reading (which I'll return to later), one may ask what Bennett means by a "logical" reading of the axiom. He writes: "If 1a4 is read in a logical way, it says that if x causes y then there is a conceptual link between them, this being a version or a part of causal rationalism" (p. 127). "Causal rationalism," he has earlier explained, is the view that "a cause relates to its effect as a premise does to a conclusion which follows from it."[21] It is hard to guess what Bennett means by "a version or a part" of causal rationalism. Thus it is hard to know whether he means to imply that axiom 4 represents *cognitio* of an effect as requiring *cognitio* of a cause, such that the latter logically entails the former. But there is at least the suggestion of this view in his wording.

I earlier indicated reservations about the "logical entailment" interpretation of Spinoza's conception of causality. Even setting those aside, though, one may still dispute a reading of the axiom that construes it as an expression of a "deductivist" conception of the cause-effect relationship.[22] Although the axiom quickly becomes implicated in *some* assumptions about "conceptual relations" between cause and effect, these appear to go in the opposite direction than that required by "causal rationalism" as Bennett defines it. For, in some uses of the axiom, it appears that the "knowledge" of the cause is supposed to follow from "knowledge" of the effect (but, perhaps, not vice versa). Or, to express the point epistemically, knowledge of the effect is sufficient for knowledge of the cause (but not vice versa).

In the next section I will try to establish some of these points by examining Spinoza's development of the implications of his axiom in the early propositions of *Ethics* I and some of the middle propositions of *Ethics* II, with particular reference to the attribute-mode relation. Afterward I will show how this development underlies his repudiation of mind-body interaction, while also indicating the importance of sharply distinguishing axiom 4, on its Spinozist interpretation, from Cartesian causal principles. Subsequent sections will be concerned with Spinoza's unique applications of axiom 4 to support Thought-Extension parallelism, and to explain the possibility of sense perception without inter-attribute causation.

I

One thing that emerges at once, with respect to this axiom, is that Spinoza seems to take the following as equivalent formulations: "the knowledge of B depends on and involves the knowledge of A"; "the concept of B depends on and involves the concept of A"; and "B is understood through A." One can see this by considering *E*Iax5, and the way that Spinoza employs it in conjuction with *E*Iax4. Axiom 5 reads:

> Things that have nothing in common with each other, also cannot be understood by means of each other, or the concept of the one does not involve the concept of the other. [Quae nihil commune cum se invicem habent, etiam per se invicem intelligi non possunt, sive conceptus unius alterius conceptum non involvit.]

The "understanding" and "conceptual involvement" of this axiom are then merged with the "*cognitio*" of *E*Iax4 in the proof of *E*Ip3:

> If things have nothing in common between them, one of them cannot be the cause of the other.

The short proof goes:

> If they have nothing in common with each other, then (by Axiom 5) they cannot be understood through each other, and thus (by Axiom 4) one cannot be the cause of the other.

Similarly, the definition of substance as "conceived through itself" is combined with axiom 4 to yield a proof of *E*Ip6: "One substance cannot be produced by another substance." Thus, axiom 4 must be read as asserting—or at least implying—that the *concept* of an effect depends on the *concept* of a cause, and involves it.[23] (Spinoza's use of axiom 4 in *Ethics* II expands the list of substitutions for "*cognitio*" to include "*idea*" and even "*perceptio*," as further explained below.)

But does this not mean that the "knowledge" of an effect (by the implications here ascribed to axiom 4) always follows logically from that of its cause? The answer, I think, is "No." To understand this point one needs to consider the relation between the "conceptual dependence" asserted by axiom 4, and the conceptual dependence of modes on substance, which is built into the definition of modes.

A substance, by definition, is that which

> is in itself, and is conceived through itself: that is that, the concept of which does not need the concept of another thing, from which it must be formed (*E*Idef3).

A mode, however, is an affection of substance,

> or that, which is in another, through which also it is conceived (*E*Idef5).

This definition of "modes" appears quite harmonious with the Cartesian notion. As Descartes says of the distinction between modes and substances (*PP*, I, §61):

> [W]e can clearly perceive substance apart from the mode which we say differs from it, but we cannot, conversely, understand that mode without the substance. Thus figure and motion are modally distinguished from corporeal substance, which they are in [*cui insunt*]; so also affirmation or recollection [are modally distinguished] from the mind.[24]

Of course, the modes of body and of mind pertain to separate substances for Descartes, whereas Spinoza recognizes only one substance. There is, nevertheless, an analogous dualism in the order of modes for Spinoza. For modes pertain to substance just insofar as it is understood under a particular attribute, as one can see from *E*Ip25c:

> Particular things are nothing but affections of the attributes of God, or modes, which express the attributes of God in a certain and determinate way.

Or, as the point is expressed even more explicitly in *E*Ip28:

> [B]esides substance, and modes, there is nothing . . . , and modes are nothing except affections of the attributes of God.[25]

But attributes are "really distinct" from each other (*E*Ip10). And however exactly we interpret Spinoza's position on unknown attributes, Thought and Extension are, as Bennett says, the only specific ones relevant to the *Ethics*.[26]

The coherence of the Cartesian system certainly requires that the relation of causal dependence *not* be conflated with the conceptual dependence of modes on substances (or their attributes). Thus God causes motion, but motion is a mode of *res extensa*, which is entirely distinct from God. Similarly, the human mind, through the volitions which are *its* modes, causes changes in brain states, or modes of body. Spinoza, however, definitely runs together the conceptual dependence of modes on substance and the conceptual "involvement" of effect and cause.

This point can be briefly established by considering the proof of *E*Ip25: "God is the efficient cause not only of the existence of things but also of their essence." The core of the proof goes as follows:

> If you deny this, then God is not the cause of the essence of things; and so (by Axiom 4) it is possible to conceive the essence of things without God: but this (by Prop. 15) is absurd.[27]

And the relevant part of the proof of *E*Ip15 is simply:

> Modes however (by Def. 5) cannot be, nor be conceived, without substance.

This intimate connection between axiom 4 and the mode-attribute relation is further reflected in *E*IIp45. Because substance is God, and an attribute is just "what intellect perceives of substance, as constituting its essence" (*E*Idef4), Spinoza can reason as follows:

[S]ingular things (by Prop. 15 p. I) cannot be conceived without God; but because
. . . they have God for a cause, insofar as he is considered under the attribute, of
which the things themselves are modes, the ideas of them (by Axiom 4, p. I) must
necessarily involve the concept of their attribute, that is . . . the eternal and infinite
essence of God.[28]

(This passage exemplifies the point mentioned above, that in Part II *"idea"*
joins *"conceptus"* as an evidently equivalent substitute for *"cognitio"* in axiom
4; *"perceptio"* is employed in place of *"idea"* in certain contexts of *Ethics* II.)[29]
It follows, Spinoza thinks, that *"each* idea of *every* body, or singular thing,
existing in act, necessarily involves the eternal and infinite essence of God"
(*E*IIp45; emphasis added).

These passages, which stress the "involves" component of axiom 4, indicate
that the *cause* is conceptually included *in the effect.* Thus, if an "entailment"
relation figures here at all, it is an entailment of the cause by the effect—not a
"deduction" of effect from cause. Thus the axiom cannot rightly be construed
simply as an expression of "causal rationalism."

Notice too that the application of the axiom at *E*IIp45 is readily intelligible as
long as a more-or-less Cartesian understanding of the mode-attribute relation is
assumed. For on this understanding there is no longer much mystery in the
claim that we *don't* "know" *anything*—even in the sense of "know by acquaintance"—without having some knowledge of its cause. It is, after all, very easy
to see why someone who believes that all "effects" are either mental or physical
might consider it evident that all effects "depend on and involve knowledge" of
either Thought or Extension. While I may not know just what occurrence
brought about the stain on the rug—so that the specific nature of that occurrence forms no part of my conception of the stain—I wouldn't deny that in
conceiving of the stain I conceive it *as extended.* Similarly, while I might be
quite perplexed about what made my fantasies take a certain form, I have to
admit that I can't really conceive of them without conceiving of them *as
thoughts.*

We see already why axiom 4 cannot be restricted to adequate knowledge.
Admittedly, Spinoza holds that all knowledge of God's essence, through our
knowledge of particular things, is adequate. ("Those things which are common
to all, and which are equally in the part and in the whole, can only be conceived
adequately"; *E*IIp38; cf. *E*IIp47.) But the *knowledge of modes/effects* through
which we possess such adequate knowledge of substance/cause is *not* itself
adequate. It is the human mind's ideas "from which it perceives itself, . . . its
own Body, and . . . external bodies as actually existing" (*E*IIp47d) which establish (by *E*IIp38) its claim to possession of adequate knowledge of God's essence. But such ideas are not adequate in the human mind. We have, for instance, "only completely confused knowledge of our Body" (*E*IIp13s). (Later,
in discussing Spinoza's account of perception of external things, I will show
that both occurrences of *"cognitio"* in the axiom can be satisfied by inadequate
knowledge.)[30]

Of course I do not mean to deny that *"cognitio" encompasses* adequate knowledge. In *E*IIp47 Spinoza in fact goes on to link our possession of adequate knowledge of God's essence with the possibility of achieving the "third kind of knowledge," which "proceeds from an adequate idea of the formal essence of certain attributes of God to adequate knowledge of the essences of things" (*E*IIp40s2). He comments in *E*IIp47s:

> Since all things are in God, and are conceived through God, it follows that from this knowledge [*ex cognitionem hac*] we can deduce many things [*nos plurima posse deducere*], which we know adequately [*quae adaequate cognoscamus*), and thus form that third kind of knowledge, of which we spoke in Scholium 2 of Proposition 40 of this Part. . . .

But for present purposes "can" is a key word in the passage just quoted. By virtue of our adequate knowledge of God's essence, we are *able* to form the third kind of knowledge; but the use of axiom 4 to show that we have adequate knowledge of God's essence does not construe *cognitio* of the effect as itself of this kind.

Neither do I mean to deny that *E*Iax4 is in some ways connected with the view that finite modes are "deducible" from the attributes that are their "causes"—however exactly this "deducibility" relation is to be understood. That Spinoza holds such a view is evident from the passage just quoted, as well as from others concerned with *scientia intuitiva*. This view is the cognitive mirror of the claim at *E*Ip16 that all things "must follow from the necessity of the divine nature" (which is explicated through the triangle analogy at *E*Ip17s).[31] *E*Ip16 and *E*Iax4 are joined in the proof of *E*Vp22, "In God . . . there necessarily is an idea, which expresses the essence of this and that human Body under the form of eternity." (Because God is the cause of such essences, they must—by *E*Iax4—be conceived through him, "with a certain eternal necessity (by Prop. 16, p. I)"; a later proposition is then adduced to establish that the ideas of such essences "must be in God.") Rather, I have simply been trying to show that *E*Iax4 plays a broader role in the *Ethics*: that it is not restricted to contexts where the *cognitio* is assumed to be adequate, or the manner in which effect "follows from" cause is assumed to be evident.

We are now in a position to see some reasons for the untenability of some of the other readings mentioned above. Consider Zellner's suggestion that Spinoza held a "transmission" view of causality, and that axiom 4 should be read as an expression of this position. I believe that the application of the axiom I have just traced rules out this interpretation. Insofar as axiom 4 covers the relation of substance to its modes (as we have just seen that it does), it cannot be interpreted in terms of the transmission of a property from one thing to another. The model of a quantity of motion being transferred from a moving to a previously stationary billiard ball (Zellner's example)[32] simply fails to apply when the cause is God or substance—an immanent, not a transitive cause, by *E*Ip21— and the effect is an affection or expression of an attribute of God. There appears in this case to be no *transmission* at all, and certainly not a transmission of a *property* from one entity to another distinct one. In fact, the dependence of modes on attributes seems basically to consist in the fact that modes have no being apart from their respective attributes.

Finally, one may also see from this application of *E*Iax4 that the axiom need have little to do with "improving one's intellectual grasp" of a thing or event, by expanding one's knowledge of the causes in the conventional sense. Causes, in the conventional sense, do not come into the picture; and in the case of "knowing" the attribute through the mode one's intellectual grasp is in any case *always* "adequate."[33]

II

Although I deny that axiom 4 is just an expression of "causal rationalism" as defined by Bennett, I of course agree with Bennett that, in light of the propositions immediately following it, axiom 4 must be interpreted as indicating connections of some kind between the concepts of the cause and of the effect. (In my view, then, it is important to distinguish the "conceptual involvement" notion from the claim that "knowledge" of the cause logically entails "knowledge" of the effect.) This requirement of conceptual connection is the basis of Spinoza's repudiation of the Cartesian assumption of mind-body interaction, and the Cartesian view that God, an immaterial entity, is the creative cause of a substance of a different nature (the material universe). To clarify the significance of Spinoza's axiom, it is important to see its role in these anti-Cartesian arguments. I will now focus on the former of these. I particularly want to emphasize the difference between axiom 4, as Spinoza employs it, and the restrictions on causality espoused by Descartes, with which it is sometimes too uncritically compared. As mentioned above, the Cartesian must certainly repudiate Spinoza's partial conflation of the dependence of effect on cause with the relation of dependence between substance (or attributes) and modes. The Cartesian also must reject axiom 4 as Spinoza interprets it. Consideration of the relation between Descartes' causal principles and *E*Iax4 helps show that he is in a position to do so consistently.[34]

Spinoza's "refutation" of mind-body interaction begins with his definitions of "substance" and "attribute." An attribute is (just) what intellect perceives of substance, "as constituting its essence." In *E*Ip10 Spinoza makes clear that he takes the latter clause to mean that an attribute must conform to the definition of substance, in respect of being "conceived through itself" (and not through another). (Spinoza of course indicates that, unlike Descartes, he does not permit an inference from such independent conception to independent *entities*, i.e., distinctness of *substance*.) According to *E*IIp1 and *E*IIp2 thoughts (or "ideas") and bodies are just "modes expressing the nature of God in a definite and determinate way" (by *E*Ip25c).

> Therefore [in the case of thought] there belongs to God (by Def. 5, p. I) an attribute, the concept of which all singular thoughts involve, and through which they are conceived. Therefore Thought is one of the infinite attributes of God (*E*IIp1d).

Similarly, for body or extension, mutatis mutandis. But the status of Thought and Extension as attributes is then sufficient to show—by *E*Iax4—that thoughts (or ideas) and bodies, as modes of the respective attributes, never stand in causal relation to each other:

> Neither can the Body determine the Mind to think, nor can the Mind determine the Body to motion, nor to rest. nor to anything else (if such there is) (*E*IIIp2).

For it follows from the conceptual independence of the attributes that:

> [T]he modes of any attribute involve the concept of their attribute, but not of another; and so (by Axiom 4, p. I) have God for a cause, insofar only as he is considered under that attribute, of which they are modes, and not insofar as he is considered under another (*E*IIp6d; cf. *E*IIIp2d).

Q.E.D.[35]

The primary Cartesian argument for mind-body distinctness of course relies on the independent conceivability of (oneself as) a thinking thing, on the one hand, and *res extensa* on the other hand. Further, Descartes seems committed to the view that there is in some sense a conceptual connection between cause and effect: he holds that one cannot conceive a (total) cause as having less reality or perfection than is contained in the effect; or, indeed, as failing itself to contain the effect, "formally or eminently."[36] Some have held that this principle—sometimes called a "causal likeness principle"—is inconsistent with the postulation of mind-body interaction. Some have held, in fact, that Descartes himself saw an inconsistency in maintaining mind-body interaction. Bennett, while acknowledging that Descartes "freely allowed" mind-body interaction in "some of his works," claims that:

> Usually, however, Descartes was uneasy about allowing causal flow between thought and extension.[37]

Bennett goes on to relate Descartes' followers' rejection of mind-body interaction to the causal principle of *Meditations* III, interpreted as indicating that an effect cannot receive a property not possessed by the cause. (It is not entirely clear whether Bennett means to suggest that Descartes' own "uneasiness" had something to do with his causal principle.)

In fact, however, Descartes decisively rejected any claim that the postulation of mind-body interaction involves inconsistency. As he writes to Clerselier, it is a "false" supposition, "which cannot in any way be proved,"

> that if the soul and body are two substances of different nature, that prevents them from being able to act one upon the other.[38]

It is perfectly credible, moreover, that this position is compatible with Descartes' causal principle (or principles). The key points are (1) that Descartes initially states his causal restriction in terms of "reality or perfection"; and (2) that he permits "eminent" containment (of effect in cause). The "reality" aspect of the principle rules out only the causation of the more perfect by the less perfect; thus it absolutely does not rule out the causation of matter by God, or of a physical mode by a mental one. Even the requirement that the cause must "contain" the effect does not rule out cross-attribute causation per se, precisely because "eminent containment" is allowed. Admittedly, there is some problem in reconciling Descartes' restrictions with *body-mind* causation, on the assumption that mind is more perfect than body. One move by which Descartes might cover this point—and perhaps one which he does actually make—is to hold that a bodily state is never more than a partial cause of a mental state (amplified by further causes which are themselves mental).

If one takes Descartes' causal principle(s) to imply that the concept of the effect "involves" the concept of a cause with equal or greater perfection, one might conclude that, in a marginal sense, Descartes accepts a version of *E*Iax4. But he does not accept *E*Iax4 as Spinoza interprets it. As the statement to Clerselier in effect shows, Descartes sees no difficulty in the notion that conceptually distinct substances can satisfy such conceptual conditions as exist on causation: the distinctness of *res cogitans* from *res extensa* does not prevent the substances or their modes being suitably comparable in terms of degrees of reality or perfection. Unlike Spinoza, Descartes does not accept a specific identification of the conceptual restriction on causation with the conceptual involvement of attribute in mode: and there seems to be no obvious "inconsistency" in his position.

One may still ask, however, whether Spinoza's argument against interactionism from axiom 4 has intrinsic plausibility. On the one hand, the popularity over the centuries of the view that mind-body interaction is *somehow* "inconceivable" would seem to suggest that Spinoza has *some* sort of intuition on his side. On the other hand, it does not seem that the exact nature of the alleged problem has ever been made very clear; and it is certainly doubtful that Spinoza's argument does very much to clarify it. For there seems to he no great difficulty, for Cartesians or others, in rejecting *E*Iax4 on its Spinozist interpretation: as requiring that the concept of an effect "involve" the concept of a cause in a way that presupposes identity of attribute between the two.[39]

In summary, the main points I have so far made about *E*Iax4 are the following. First, Spinoza takes the mode-attribute relation to satisfy the axiom. Insofar as an attribute is considered as cause, knowledge of an effect is sufficient for knowledge of the cause (and it is not too hard to see why this should be so). Second, the knowledge of the effect involves knowledge of the cause, under the mode-attribute interpretation, even when the former is inadequate. Third, Spinoza views the "conceivability" relation between effect and cause indicated by *E*Iax4 as ruling out inter-attribute causality: for he construes it as inconsistent with the conceptual distinctness that obtains between attributes. (I have also held that the Cartesian can coherently resist the latter move, without totally denying the spirit of *E*Iax4, because his causal principle requires only a more abstract, less restrictive condition on causal conceivability.)

I turn now to Spinoza's use of axiom 4 in connection with certain positive doctrines about mode-mode causality. Of greatest interest are its roles in grounding the "parallelist" thesis developed in *Ethics* II, and in underpinning the crucial theory of external perception presented later in the same part. I will take these up in order.

III

Perhaps the most striking use of *E*Iax4 occurs in the proof of *E*IIp7, one of the foundation stones of Part II, and subsequent sections of the *Ethics*. The proposition reads:

> The order, and connection of ideas is the same, as the order, and connection of things.

The demonstration is stunningly simple:

> This is evident from Axiom 4, p. I. For the idea of whatever is caused depends on the knowledge of the cause, of which it is the effect. [Patet ex Ax. 4. p. I. Nam cujuscunque causati idea a cognitione causae, cujus est effectus, dependet.]

It is here that the transition occurs to the use of "*idea*" as a substitution for "*cognitio*." In addition, "depends" is here the operative verb, whereas the arguments previously considered (and one to be considered later) rely on "involves." What is the significance of these changes?

Bennett holds that in this application of *E*Iax4 "*idea*"/"*cognitio*" must be understood as a "mental" or "psychological" term (as opposed to the "logical" interpretation that he considers appropriate to other contexts).[40] It seems to follow that the appeal to *E*Iax4 is specious, for a *different* "axiom" must really be involved: one concerned with the relation of "mental" items, as opposed to an expression of the relation of "logical" items, or concepts. Bennett's reason for this view is that Spinoza soon begins identifying "the human mind" with "the idea of" the human body. He is able to find, however, no satisfactory account of the new "axiom."[41]

There are a number of reasons to reject Bennett's view. For one thing, Spinoza has just defined an idea as a concept: "a concept of the Mind that the Mind forms insofar as it is a thinking thing" (*E*IIdef3). Admittedly, one may object to Spinoza's combining this definition with the identification of minds *with* ideas; but the definition does rather clearly indicate that Spinoza sees no sharp break between terms that Bennett considers "logical" and those that he considers "psychological." Further, it is at best misleading to construe the term "idea" in the *Ethics* as "psychological" or "mental." Bennett seems to take for granted that the meaning of "mental" or "psychological" at least is clear: but this is something one emphatically must not take for granted in dealing with Spinoza.[42] Finally, up to *E*IIp7 Spinoza has been talking exclusively of ideas *in God*. Making sense of the claim that there actually exists an ordered series of "ideas," in one-to-one correspondence with the series of things, really depends on thinking of "ideas" in this way, as bits of God's omniscience. (At any rate, one could hardly make sense of the claim if one thought of ideas as items just of human—and perhaps other higher animal—awareness.) Thus, *E*IIp3, which provides necessary background for *E*IIp7 (though not explicitly invoked in the "demonstration"), reads:

> In God there is necessarily the idea both of his essence, and of all things that necessarily follow from his essence.[43]

I conclude that, since the need for interpretation of Spinoza's terminology in relation to ordinary usage extends to the term *"idea"* itself, and to *"mens"* as well, it is misleading to insist that *E*Iax4 takes on a new, "psychological" sense when introduced in the proof of *E*IIp7.[44] Of course this observation does not settle the question whether the axiom is susceptible of a single interpretation in all of its applications; and does not conflict with the point that *E*Iax4 turns out to have important connections with Spinoza's *theory* of "the human mind."

Whatever significance one attaches to the substitution of "idea" for "knowledge" at *E*IIp7, one should recognize that this application of the axiom also includes a different shift, which truly is important: the switch from "involves" to "depends on." Whereas "involves" connotes a relation of internal conceptual inclusion, "depends" connotes a sort of external relation between ideas or items of knowledge. This distinction between internal and external causal and cognitive relationships is in fact the basis for Spinoza's distinction between adequate and inadequate knowledge, between "God insofar as he is affected by the human Mind," and "God insofar as he is considered as affected by other ideas" (*E*IIp28d). That Spinoza is able to make such a distinction shows something important about *E*Iax4: that the "involvement" of cause in effect is somehow limited. For, if all ideas in the human mind involved the full chain of their causes without limit, then, it seems, there could only be adequate knowledge, or knowledge that contains the "premises" as well as the "conclusions" (*E*IIp28d). Spinoza in fact stresses that the human mind knows things only insofar as they relate to its body; whereas God knows things in all their relations, and specifically (by *E*IIp7 itself) knows them as effects of causes that are "prior in nature" (*E*IIp25).[45] This is the point at which the dual occurrence of *"cognitio"* in the axiom appears to create problems, though. For it appears to tie knowledge of anything, in *any* mind, to knowledge of the whole regress of causes: by the terms of the axiom, to have knowledge of anything is to have knowledge of *its* cause.

This consideration may well lie behind Gueroult's claim that the axiom concerns only adequate knowledge. (Certainly the wording of his discussion of the axiom suggests that he had its use at *E*IIp7 prominently in mind.) I have shown already that Gueroult's claim cannot be sustained, however; and I will strengthen my refutation in the next section. Thus, the problem of interpreting the axiom for inadequate knowledge must be faced. I will return to it in the next section.[46]

There is one other important point about the interpretation of *E*Iax4 that emerges from its use in the demonstration of *E*IIp7: namely, that the dependence relation between ideas is *the same as* the relation that holds between material causes and effects. This is clear from the fact that the axiom is supposed to support the *idem* of *E*IIp7: the order and connection of ideas is *the same as* the order and connection of things. Further, Spinoza actually begins speaking of the order of *ideas* as *causal* in *E*IIp9d:

> [T]he order and connection of ideas (by Prop. 7 of this part) is the same as the order and connection of causes [or things].[47] Therefore, the cause of one singular idea is another idea, *or* God, insofar as he is considered to be affected by another idea . . . and so on, to infinity.[48]

Thus it is clear that Spinoza does not distinguish (from the theocentric point of view) between the relation of necessary determination that holds among physical things and that which obtains among *cognitiones*. There may actually be less information here than appears to meet the eye, however. To tell us that the same relation holds among physical causes that holds among bits of God's omniscience does not really tell us all that much about the relation. In particular, it does not directly tell us that the relation in question should be construed as "logical entailment." For in order to tell us this, it would have to make clear—as it does not—that the envisaged relation among *ideas* is one of logical entailment.

IV

The final application of *E*Iax4 that I will consider occurs at *E*IIp16. This proposition is concerned with our knowledge of external bodies, i.e., bodies external to our own bodies. To understand the problem of external perception as it presents itself to Spinoza, it will be helpful again to consider Descartes' position briefly for purposes of contrast.

Descartes uses a causal argument to justify his belief that there are bodies, starting from the solipsistic viewpoint of the thinking self. His causal-containment principle yields, he insists, the conclusion that the cause of his sensory ideas of bodies must contain as much reality as is contained in the ideas themselves, considered as ideas *of bodies*. But to obtain conclusions that the causes of these ideas must be *physical*, Descartes introduces further premises about both his "disposition to believe" that the ideas are caused by bodies, and God's veracity. After he has obtained this general conclusion that "corporeal things exist," Descartes proceeds to conclude, more specifically, that he "has" a body and feels sensations according to its needs; and, further, that there are other bodies which exist around his body, and can do it good or harm.

Subsequently in the *Meditations*—and also in such other works as the *Dioptrics* and the *Principles*—Descartes explains the process of sense perception more concretely. Motions transmitted from bodies form impressions in the brain, there giving rise to sensory ideas in the mind, according to a "natural convention," or system of regular correlations, established by God. These ideas in turn may lead the mind to make judgments about external things. Because the ideas tend to be confused, the judgments are very likely to be mistaken unless carefully subordinated to reason.

A number of aspects of Spinoza's general position underlie the fundamental differences between his position on the perception of bodies and that of Descartes. Among them are the fact that Spinoza eschews the Cartesian solipsistic starting point, in favor of a theocentric one; that he accords little epistemological priority to the mental; and (most important in the present context) that he repudiates causal interaction between mind and body. According to Spinoza, the human body is that "existing thing" which (by *E*IIp11, citing *E*IIp7) is the "object" of the idea which "constitutes the being of the human Mind." Thus, according to *E*IIp13:

> The object of the idea constituting the human Mind is the Body, *or* a certain mode of Extension actually existing, and nothing else.

Hence it follows, Spinoza says, "that man consists of Mind and Body, and the human Body, as we sense it [*prout ipsum sentimus*] exists" (*E*IIp13c).

One thing we know about this mysterious "object of" relation is that it is non-causal: the mind's objects are *never* causes of it or of (the formal being of) its subsidiary ideas. Thus, as Spinoza says in *E*IIp5:

> [T]he ideas both of God's attributes and singular things do not admit as their efficient cause the objects [*ideata*] themselves, or the things perceived, but God himself, insofar as he is a thinking thing.

Yet *E*Iax4 does enter into Spinoza's account of sense perception in a crucial way.

Descartes, as mentioned above, uses a causal argument to establish the existence of body, reasoning in a general way from ideas of sense; he then moves specifically to claims about his own body and external bodies. Spinoza first establishes the existence of the human body as the "object," but not cause, of the human mind. But he then faces the problem of providing an account of the "perception" of *external* bodies (i.e., bodies external to the human body), given that he takes "perception" to be strictly mental, and that he denies any physical-mental causality. If the relation between sense perception and thing perceived cannot at all be explained in terms of a causal relation between the two, how are we to understand it? In addressing this problem Spinoza again enlists the aid of *E*Iax4.

Important in the analysis is *E*IIp12:

> Whatever happens in the object of the idea that constitutes the human Mind must be perceived by the human Mind, or there necessarily is given in the Mind the idea of this thing. That is, if the object of the idea constituting the human Mind is a body, nothing can happen in this body which is not perceived by the human Mind.

Thus, the idea or knowledge of any change of state in the body will occur in the mind, of which the body is the "object." But, when the change of state is the effect of an external body, then it would seem to follow directly by *E*Iax4 that knowledge of this change of state "involves" knowledge of its cause, i.e., that in virtue of having knowledge of the bodily changes, the mind also has knowledge of, or perceives, the external bodies which cause them.

This is in fact *roughly* the line that Spinoza does take, but two points of mild complication need to be noted. First, in developing his theory of sense perception, Spinoza relies on the following additional "axiom," presented as Axiom 1' in the midst of the lemmata about bodies that follow *E*IIp13:

> All the modes in which any body is affected by another body follow from the nature
> of the affected body, and at the same time from the nature of the affecting body. . . .

Such modes, in other words, have as causes both the affected and the affecting bodies. So, by *E*Iax4, the ideas of these modes will involve the knowledge or ideas of the affected, as well as the affecting bodies. This enables Spinoza to conclude that sense perception reflects the nature of our own body as well as external bodies, a view which he relates to the subjectivity of sense perception.[49]

Second, Spinoza's phrasing of the key proposition about sense perception fails to reflect the phrasing of *E*Iax4 in a puzzling way, despite the explicit citation of the axiom in its demonstration. "Knowledge of an effect . . . knowledge of the cause" is altered to "knowledge of an effect . . . *nature* of the cause." Thus, *E*IIp16—which has as its first corollary the claim that "the human Mind perceives the nature of a great many bodies together with the nature of its own body"—reads as follows:

> The idea of any mode in which the human Body is affected by external bodies must
> involve the nature of the human Body, and at the same time the nature of the
> external body.

For (according to the demonstration), the idea of such a mode will (by *E*Iax4) necessarily involve the nature of both the bodies from which (by the special lemmata axiom) the mode follows: the human body itself, and the external body.

I see no great significance in the omission of the second "*cognitio*" (or "*idea*") in *E*IIp16, and shall not comment on it further.[50] But the fact that our perceptions of the states by which we know external bodies at the same time reflect the nature of our own bodies connects with a point on which I want particularly to insist. Both the ideas of the affections of the human body and the ideas of external bodies with which *E*IIp16 is concerned manifestly include *confused or inadequate* ideas. Since the derivation of *E*IIp16 turns on *E*Iax4, then, we see again that the latter cannot be construed as restricted to adequate ideas.

Spinoza directly asserts at *E*IIp25:

> The idea of any affection of the human Body does not involve an adequate knowl-
> edge of the external body.

The proof of *E*IIp25 depends on the claim that (by *E*IIp7) God has knowledge of any external body, not merely insofar as it affects the human body, but also insofar as he has an idea of something *outside* the human body, something "prior in nature" to the external body. But *E*IIp16 is concerned only with knowledge of the external body insofar as the latter is a cause of an affection of the human body—from which point of view the knowledge must thus be inadequate. Again, Spinoza maintains at *E*IIp28:

> The ideas of the affections of the human Body, insofar as they are related only to the human Mind, are not clear and distinct, but confused.

Now, *E*IIp16 is of course not *restricted* to "ideas of the affections of the human Body, insofar as they are related only to the human Mind." But it must be taken to *encompass* ideas considered in this way: otherwise the crucial inference from *E*IIp16 to its first corollary would be incomprehensible. Hence the ideas of the affections of the human body, and the perceptions of external bodies which (by *E*Iax4) they "involve," include inadequate and confused ideas. In other words, the axiom is supposed to be satisfied under conditions where *both* occurrences of "*cognitio*" denote *inadequate* knowledge.

Axiom 1′ from the lemmata section is not formally involved in the proof of the inadequacy of the ideas which (by *E*IIp16) we have of external bodies. It is clear, though, that Spinoza does connect the claim that our ideas of external things involve the nature of our own body as well as (indeed, by *E*IIp16c2, more than) the nature of external bodies with the error of confusing our own physiological responses with actual properties of objects. For this is precisely the point of the examples he cites at *E*IIp16c2. Thus Spinoza appears to explain the "inadequacy" or "confusion" of our perception of external things through their effects on our bodies in two ways. On the one hand, he holds that adequate ideas of the things require knowledge of them through "things prior in nature" (or prior "in the order of nature"), and not merely through their effects. On the other hand, he indicates that our ideas of external bodies are thoroughly contaminated with "the nature of our own bodies," through which we perceive them.

Beside refuting the view that *E*Iax4 applies only to "*idées vraies*," its use in the proof of *E*IIp16 also tells strongly against any attempt to construe the axiom as an expression of "causal rationalism," as explained by Bennett. The notion that we know or perceive external things confusedly through their effects on our bodies is perhaps consistent with the notion that the effects are "logical consequences'" of the causes (assuming one can make any sense at all of the tatter view). But, certainly, no such deductivist view is involved in the account of knowledge that Spinoza goes on to describe as "confused" and "mutilated" (*E*IIp28d and *E*IIp29c,s).[51]

Earlier I suggested that the notion that "knowledge of an effect involves knowledge of a cause" is susceptible to an obvious and commonsensical interpretation, once one notes that attributes count as "causes" of their modes (assuming a more or less Cartesian conception of attributes). I now want to suggest that it is possible to interpret, in commonsensical terms, the "involvement" of knowledge of cause in knowledge of effect that might be at issue in

*E*IIp16—as long as one is ready to follow Spinoza in saying that the mind "knows" its body. For if one thinks of sense perception, as an "effect" of external things, it is hard to see how to avoid thinking of it as an effect that "involves the nature" of its cause or its causes. Even if one restricts oneself, as Spinoza's system requires, to intra-attribute causation, the notion of "involvement" makes obvious sense. One need only think of retinal images, let alone of the impressions of external objects lodged in the center of the brain, on standard Cartesian theory. The internal states do not merely follow on external stimuli—do not only follow *with necessity* from external stimuli: they in some sense incorporate the external entity (or so it seems).

It would be a mistake to rely too far, though, on this homely view of Spinoza's application of *E*Iax4 in developing his theory of our perception of external bodies: at best, it constitutes a sort of partial interpretation. I have already mentioned in passing Spinoza's claim that the human mind perceives *everything that happens in the human body*. What we must now acknowledge is that his use of axiom 4 in *E*IIp16 and its corollaries appears to commit him also to the view that we perceive *everything that causes any change whatsoever in our body*. Retinal images (or for that matter the cortical mappings of contemporary perceptual theory) can have no favored status as effects relevant to external perceptions, as opposed, for instance, to X-rays transmitted through one's hand, odorless and colorless gasses that have subtle metabolic effects, and so on.[52] (Such considerations are also sufficient to show what a very technical sense "*cognitio*" has taken on by the middle of *Ethics* II; we are far indeed from such routine illustrations as "improving our intellectual grasp on the French revolution by learning more about its causes.")

I return, finally, to the problem sketched toward the end of the last section: that of reconciling the cognitive regress implicit in *E*Iax4 with the claim—essential to the notion of inadequate knowledge—that we have only limited knowledge of the causal chains that impinge on our bodies. As recently noted, the proofs of *E*IIp24 and *E*IIp25 lay some emphasis on the notion that God's possession of adequate knowledge of external things consists in the fact that he knows them through his ideas of things "prior in the order of nature" to them. One might take this to mean that God, "insofar as he is affected with other ideas," has ideas of the *causes* of external things, whereas God, "insofar as he constitutes the nature of the human mind," has ideas only of their *effects*. It does not seem, however, that Spinoza can categorically deny, consistently with *E*Iax4, that *our* causal knowledge, too, in some sense extends to infinity.

Perhaps the problem of reconciling inadequate knowledge with *E*Iax4 can be more satisfactorily resolved by focusing on another theme prominent in these passages: the observation that we know things only in relation to our *own* body, whereas God knows them in *all* their relations with *all* bodies—and in the correct, "internal" order. Thus (one might propose) it does not really matter how *many* cause-ideas are somehow "involved" in the idea that constitutes the human mind; the knowledge will remain inadequate and partial as long as each of these presents its object only in its limited relation to us. (Whether this is a

160　　　　　　　　　　　• *CHAPTER 10* •

completely satisfactory solution—one consistent with other aspects of Spinoza's treatment of adequate and inadequate knowledge—I will not attempt to determine here.)[53]

CONCLUSION

I have tried to show how several attempts to explain or interpret *E*Iax4 fail to fit well with—or are actually contradicted by—some of the most important uses of the axiom in the *Ethics*. One moral I draw from all this is, of course, that there is not much point in trying either to explain or to justify the axiom in an off-the-cuff manner, without considering in detail what Spinoza does with it. This moral applies to attempts to interpret the axiom in terms of other Spinozist doctrine (such as the theory of adequate ideas); to attempts to give commonsensical readings; to efforts to relate it to previous or contemporary causal theories. It applies as well to attempts to connect the axiom with "causal rationalism" or (more specifically) the "logical entailment" view of causality supposedly expressed in *E*Ip16–17, and elsewhere in Spinoza's work. I have also argued that Bennett's claim, that the axiom has a different sense at *E*IIp7 from its other applications, fails to take adequate account of the context of that proposition, and of the oddities of Spinoza's use of "mental" terms. I have not claimed that the axiom is used in a consistent and univocal way throughout the *Ethics*, though. Indeed, the fact that the "involves" component figures essentially in certain contexts, while "depends" does the work in others, shows at least that appeal to "*E*Iax4" does not come to exactly the same thing in all cases. Further, the fact that the axiom unquestionably applies *across* the distinction between adequate and inadequate knowledge introduces additional interesting complications into the interpretive problem.[54]

NOTES

1. Sometimes Spinoza speaks in similar terms of the determination of one finite mode by another: "These [human dispositions] follow from this [human] affect as necessarily as [it follows] from the nature of a triangle that its three angles are equal to two right angles" (*E*IVp57s).

Translations throughout the paper are substantially my own. Translations of Spinoza are based on the Gebhardt edition. I have, however, consulted Shirley's and Curley's versions of most passages.

2. Henry E. Allison, *Benedict de Spinoza* (Boston: Twayne, 1975), p. 71; G.H.R. Parkinson, *Spinoza's Theory of Knowledge* (Oxford: Clarendon Press, 1954), p. 64; Jonathan Bennett, *A Study of Spinoza's Ethics* (Indianapolis: Hackett, 1984), p. 30. For a relatively detailed discussion, see E.M. Curley, *Spinoza's Metaphysics* (Cambridge, Mass.: Harvard University Press, 1969), pp. 45 ff.

3. Curley's exposition of the "logical entailment" interpretation, while not entirely clear, is the clearest I know. (For reference, see n. 2.)

4. At *E*Ip33s1 Spinoza offers an "explanation" of how "necessary" should be understood. This turns out to consist of explaining that things are "necessary" either by reason of their essence or by reason of their cause! The account he offers here of impossibility is perhaps slightly more suggestive: a thing is said to be impossible "either because its essence or definition involves a contradiction, or because no external cause is given, determined to produce such a thing." (See Curley, chap. 3, for some other passages relevant to this issue from the *Ethics* and other works.)

5. Charles Jarrett has said of the axiom in question that it "might in fact be taken as a definition of 'cause' "; "The Logical Structure of Spinoza's *Ethics*," *Synthese* 37 (1978): 29. This suggestion derives support from Spinoza's definition of "adequate cause" and "inadequate cause" at the beginning of *Ethics* III.

6. Among those who have objected to translating "*cognitio*" as "knowledge" are Jonathan Bennett (*Study*, p. 127) and Alan Donagan (in conversation). I prefer to use "knowledge" because the one likely alternative, "cognition," sounds so strained and contrived as to be distracting. The term employed in *E*Iax4 is the same used by Spinoza in *E*IIp40s2, where he expounds (what are usually known in English as) the three kinds of knowledge. Later I will emphasize that "*cognitio*" in *E*Iax4 is not restricted to adequate knowledge, i.e., to knowledge of the second or third kinds.

Spinoza, of course, also uses the term "*scientia*," which has a more restricted sense for him than "*cognitio*." Thus, in *E*IIp40s2, the third kind of knowledge is identified as "*scientia intuitiva*."

7. I see no justification for the practice followed by most English-language translators—including both Curley and Shirley—of simplifying the structure of the axiom by incorporating "*et eandem involvit*" into the first clause: "The knowledge of an effect depends on, and involves, the knowledge of its cause" (*The Collected Works of Spinoza*, ed. and transl. E.M. Curley (Princeton: Princeton University Press, 1985), vol. I, p. 410; see also Spinoza, *The Ethics and Selected Letters*, transl. Samuel Shirley, ed. Seymour Feldman (Indianapolis: Hackett, 1982), p. 32). Although this move does not change the literal sense of the axiom, it does create a slight shift of emphasis away from "*involvit*," as a distinct relation. But as I shall show, this is really the operational term in most of the important applications of the axiom, and the distinction between "*involvere*" and "*dependere*" is genuinely significant. (By contrast, Louis Loeb maintains that "*involvit*" does not figure essentially in any application, and accordingly "simplifies" axiom 4 by dropping the term; *From Descartes to Hume* [Ithaca: Cornell University Press, 1981] p. 102.) I take it that the antecedent of "*eandem*" is clear on either reading.

8. See vol. I of Gueroult's *Spinoza, Dieu* (Paris: Aubier-Montaigne, 1968), pp. 95–98; Loeb, *From Descartes to Hume*, pp. 102–103, and 167 ff.; Bennett, *Study*, p. 50 and 127 ff.; Zellner, "Spinoza's Causal Likeness Principle," *Philosophy Research Archives* 9 (March 1986): 453–462.

9. "Axiom 4. and the parallelism between the order of ideas and the order of causes that it implies, does not hold for inadequate ideas. . . . Axiom 4 concerns nothing but true ideas." Gueroult, *Spinoza*, I, pp. 96–97.

10. Ibid., p. 96. It will turn out that "including in itself the integral knowledge of the causes of its object" may not be a sufficient condition of adequate knowledge for Spinoza: confused and inadequate ideas, by virtue of *E*Iax4, contain knowledge of their causes, considered in certain relations.

11. Loeb, *Descartes to Hume*, p. 102.

12. Ibid., pp. 102–103. (Loeb cites a relevant passage on knowledge of effects from the *Treatise on the Emendation of the Intellect*.)

13. Ibid., pp. 103, 175. As indicated in note 10, above, I will suggest later that, in a sense, all ideas may have to involve infinite causal knowledge. This result derives from the double appearance of "*cognitio*" in the axiom, which of course suggests a regress: if the cause is itself an effect, then *cognitio* of it will require *cognitio* of *its* cause, and so forth. This consideration seems to underlie the longer passage quoted from Gueroult. His error, in my view, is to assume that the regressive aspect of the axiom ties it exclusively to the domain of adequate knowledge.

14. Bennett, *Study*, p. 129. Bennett notes that on such an understanding the axiom would require "an infinite mental embrace—a cognition of something, and of its cause, and of *its* cause, and so on." (At this point he is considering what he takes to be the "psychological" version of the axiom; unsurprisingly, then, he considers it less than evident that on this strong interpretation there will exist a "cognition" that satisfies it.)

15. Ibid., p. 179. Bennett is here discussing *E*IIp16, and hence assuming what he calls the "logical" understanding of *E*Iax4; see ibid., pp. 127–128, and p. 128, n. 1.)

16. Even on this understanding, Bennett doesn't seem to think the axiom is especially plausible, though it's hard to see why not.

17. Bennett does not say it does. In fact, on p. 179 he is indicating that, on its most "plausible" reading, the axiom cannot help with the problem at hand: of explaining why inadequate ideas are "mutilated." His approach throughout is to generate freely possible "meanings" of the axiom, evaluating each one in terms of (1) whether it is "plausible," and (2) whether it produces a valid argument in the context under discussion. (It appears that none of the readings of the axiom that he considers in connection with particular arguments passes both tests.) My approach here, by contrast, will be to try to get a better understanding of Spinoza's conception of the axiom by close consideration of its use.

18. "Spinoza's Causal Likeness Principle," pp. 453–456.

19. "*Cognitio*" also appears prominently in *E*Iax5, discussed below, which Zellner regards as providing a partial interpretation of axiom 4.

20. Bennett, like Zellner, interprets a remark that Spinoza makes in correspondence with Oldenburg (Letter 4) as indicating a "transfer" view of causality, which would rule out mind-body interaction. He expresses agnosticism, however, about "[w]hether this line of thought was at work in [Spinoza's] later years, encouraging his view that if one thing has nothing in common with another it cannot be its cause" (p. 50).

The gist of the comment to Oldenburg is that an effect must have something in common with its cause; otherwise "whatever the effect had, it would have from nothing" (Letter 4; Geb4/10–11; Curley transl., vol. I, p. 172). I do not think this comment actually establishes a transfer view of causality. (It is compatible as well with, for example, a "copy" view of causality.) The passage from Spinoza's exposition of Descartes' *Principles*, which Zellner also cites in this connection, seems to me even less strongly indicative of a transfer or transmission view.

21. Bennett, *Study*, pp. 29–30.

22. It of course cannot be assumed that a philosopher influenced by Descartes understands "deduction" as a formal relation.

23. This point seems to be generally accepted in the literature; cf., e.g., Jarrett, "Logical Structure . . . , p. 32; and Bennett, *Study*, p. 127.

24. AT vol. VIII-1, p. 29.

25. See also *E*IIp45d: "[Particular things] have God for their cause, insofar as he is considered under the attribute, of which the things themselves are modes."

26. Bennett, *Study*, pp. 75–79.

27. As Jarrett remarks ("Logical Structure . . . ," p. 29), the respective uses of *E*Iax4

in *E*Ip3 and *E*Ip25 show that it must be interpreted as a biconditional. In the former, Spinoza takes it that *x* causes *y* only if knowledge of *y* depends on knowledge of *x*. In the latter, the operant assumption is that knowledge of *y* depends on knowledge of *x* only if *x* causes *y*. A less charitable view is taken by Bennett (*Study*, p. 128, n. 1), who accuses Spinoza of an "illegitimate conversion" of the axiom at *E*Ip25.

28. *E*IIp45d. The omissions indicated by the ellipses are references to *E*IIp6 and *E*Idef6, respectively.

29. Given the transition from "*cogintio*" to "*conceptus*" at the beginning of *Ethics* I, the substitutability of "*idea*" appears to be licensed by the definition of that term at the beginning of *Ethics*II.

30. Because the attributes are "self-caused," the knowledge of them does not require any further knowledge under *E*Iax4; and a regress problem does not emerge at this point. The use of *E*Iax4 in connection with external perception—where both cause and effect are finite modes—does present such a problem, though. I will return to this issue in Section IV.

31. I have tried to demonstrate the integral connection between *E*Ip16 and "the third kind of knowledge" in "Infinite Understanding, *Scientia Intuitiva*, and *Ethics* I.16," *Midwest Studies in Philosophy VIII*, ed. Peter A. French et al. (Minneapolis: University of Minnesota Press, 1983), pp. 181–191 (Chapter 11 of this volume).

32. Another example that Zellner mentions is that of transfer of heat from one body to another.

33. See *E*IIp46.

34. The discussion in this section owes a considerable debt to Loeb's vigorous arguments in *Descartes to Hume*, chaps. 3 and 4.

35. The proposition Spinoza derives at *E*Ip3 with the aid of *E*Iax4—"if two things have nothing in common, one cannot be the cause of the other"—no doubt qualifies as a causal likeness principle. But this proposition is largely an idle part, and plays no role in the formal "refutation" of mind-body interaction. On this point, see Loeb's excellent discussion in *Descarte to Hume*, pp, 186–190.

36. AT, vol. VII, pp. 40–41; cf. the French version, vol. IX-1, p. 32. This principle figures both in Descartes' first argument for the existence of God and his later proof of the existence of bodies.

37. Bennett, *Study*, pp. 49–50.

38. AT, vol. IX-1, p. 213; Descartes goes on to observe (in the same sentence) that others don't hesitate to affirm that "accidents" like heat and weight can act on a body; yet, he says, there is "more of a difference" (*plus de différence*) between accidents and substance than between two substances.

On this point and related ones about Descartes' position, I largely follow Loeb's work and contributions by Robert Richardson and Eileen O'Neill. See especially Richardson, "The 'Scandal' of Cartesian Interactionism," *Mind* 91 (1982):20–37; and O'Neill, "Mind-Body Interaction and Metaphysical Consistency: A Defense of Descartes," *Journal of the History of Philosophy*, 25:2, pp. 227–245. O'Neill's interpretive position is developed more fully in *Mind and Mechanism: An Examination of Some Mind-Body Problems in Descartes' Philosophy* (unpublished Ph.D. thesis, Princeton University, 1983).

39. These points are cogently urged by Loeb, pp. 171–190.

40. Bennett, *Study*, pp. 127–131.

41. Ibid., p. 129: "I have done nothing to make 1a4 believable on a psychological reading, and that task is too much for me. It is hard even to suggest reasons for Spinoza's finding it plausible. He may have been influenced by its plausibility when read logically."

42. For a detailed defense of this claim, see my paper, "Objects, Ideas, and 'Minds': Comments on Spinoza's Theory of Mind," in *The Philosophy of Baruch Spinoza*, ed. Richard Kennington (Washington: Catholic University of America, 1980), pp. 103–120 (Chapter 9 of this volume).

43. Bennett stresses the importance of *E*IIp3 for the "parallelism" thesis. But his treatment of *E*Iax4 in connection with *E*IIp7 is rendered very confusing by his failure to consider the relevance of *E*IIp3 until after he has defended the need for a "psychological" reading for several pages, and raised objections to Spinoza's position read in this way.

44. One could even say that, in a sense, *E*IIp7 requires a *less* "psychological" reading of *E*Iax4 than the other uses considered in this paper. The uses considered previously involve "*cognitiones*" of mind and body that are (on *one* interpretation of the mode-attribute relation, anyway) directly and consciously accessible to the human mind; the one to be considered last has to do with human sense perception.

45. See also *E*IIp24.

46. It is true, of course, that the use of *E*Iax4 at *E*IIp7 has an important connection with the concept of adequate knowledge. The dependence relation among ideas with which proposition 7 is concerned is, precisely, the system of ideas *in God*; and "All ideas . . . insofar as they are related to God, are true . . . and . . . adequate" (*E*IIp36d). It does not follow, though, that truth or adequacy is presupposed as a *condition* on "*idea*"/ "*cognitio*," even in its application at *E*IIp7. For *E*IIp36d bases the claim about adequacy directly on *E*IIp7c, and the claim about truth on *E*IIp32, which is itself based on appeal to the same corollary (together with *E*Iax6, "A true idea must agree with its object"). In other words, claims about truth and adequacy are posterior to this application of the axiom.

47. See Curley's note in his translation of Spinoza's works, vol. 1, p. 453.

48. See also *E*IIp6c: "[T]he objects of ideas follow and are inferred [*consequuntur, & concluduntur*] from their attributes in the same way, and with the same necessity as we have shown ideas to follow from the attribute of Thought."

49. Indeed, according to *E*IIp16c2, our ideas of external bodies indicate the nature of our own body *more* than of external bodies. It is doubtful that Spinoza is strictly entitled to *this* conclusion by his preceding argument: see Curley's edition, vol. I, p. 463, n. 42.

50. Cf. Gueroult, *Spinoza*, vol. II, pp. 194–195, for a different view (which I think is mistaken).

51. It is perhaps worth mentioning that, inasmuch as *E*IIp16 is specifically concerned with *external* causes, its reliance on *E*Iax4 implicitly rules out an attempt to interpret the axiom strictly in terms of *constituent* causes (where "knowing the effect" would be understood as knowing the *nature* of the effect, and knowing the nature of the effect would mean knowing its molecular structure, underlying chemical processes, or other microstructural factors). I do not discuss such an interpretation in the body of the paper because it does not seem to have been advocated by publishing scholars, though I have occasionally heard it proposed in both seminars and informal discussion.

52. This consequence is indeed more fundamental to Spinoza's account of perception than the claim that the human mind perceives everything that happens in the human body. See n. 49, above.

53. At one time I believed that the axiom's assertion of "involvement" actually came into conflict with the assertion of "dependence," since ideas of affections have to *depend on* ideas of remote causes, but (given the existence of inadequate knowledge) could not generally *involve* the ideas of remote causes. The solution I now propose in effect allows

one to say that ideas of effects do, generally involve ideas of remote causes, but only in a limited or partial way, working outward from effects, rather than "concluding" to effects from causes.

54. A confused and mutilated earlier version of this paper was presented at a Philosophy Department colloquium at the University of Pittsburgh, as well as at the Jerusalem Spinoza Conference. I'm grateful to the participants on both occasions, and especially to Annette Baier, for helpful and constructive comments. Work on the paper was undertaken during a year of leave, with support, from Princeton University, for which I also wish to express my thanks.

Infinite Understanding, *Scientia Intuitiva*, and *Ethics* I.16

I

Spinoza defines 'substance' partly in terms of the way in which substance is conceived: "By substance I understand that which is in itself, and is conceived through itself: that is, that the concept of which does not need the concept of another thing, from which it must be formed" (*E* I.Def. 3).[1] But the following definition of 'attribute' suggests an even more central connection between *this* concept and that of a certain way of knowing: "By attribute I understand that which understanding perceives of substance, as constituting its essence" (*E* I.Def. 4). And the link between attributes and understanding is emphasized by Spinoza even more strongly in an early letter to de Vries (Letter IX). He writes:

> . . . [B]y substance I understand that which is in itself and is conceived through itself: that is, the concept of which does not involve another thing. I understand the same by attribute. Except that it is called attribute with respect to understanding. Attributing to substance a certain such nature.[2]

Some scholars have held that this definition of 'attribute' in terms of the perception of understanding indicates that the attributes in Spinoza's system are merely subjective or ideal.[3] Others have argued very persuasively against this reading.[4] Perceptions of understanding—and particularly understanding's ideas of the divine attributes—are held by Spinoza to be intrinsically true and adequate (II.37, 38, 41). But a true idea by definition has an agreeing ideatum. It follows that there are (formally) attributes that correspond to understanding's perceptions of attributes. And I take it further to follow that the attributes really do constitute and "express" God's essence, for otherwise they could hardly be said to "agree" with understanding's perception of them. Indeed, *Ethics* I.15, scholium, contrasts extension or quantity as conceived *abstractly* or *superficially* ("as we imagine it"), with the same conceived by understanding ("as substance"). This contrast suggests that the stress on understanding in Spinoza's account of attributes is particularly *meant* to carry the implications of truth and adequacy.

The subjective interpretation did, of course, have a reasonable motive: it was intended to resolve the problem of reconciling the unity of substance with the plurality of attributes. This remains a very difficult problem in interpreting Spinoza—one that I will not address here. Rather, I will argue that the definition of 'attribute' in terms of understanding ties in with conspicuous but initially mysterious references to understanding and "infinite understanding" in a key proposition concerning the causality of God, *Ethics* I.16. (Though conspicuous, these references to understanding have received relatively little notice in the literature on Spinoza.[5]) My approach involves the claim that *Ethics* I.16 involves the exemplification on the level of infinity of *scientia intuitiva* or the third (and highest) "kind of knowledge." It is *scientia intuitiva* that gives rise to the intellectual love of God and our highest possible peace of mind; it is also involved in the eternity of our minds. Hence, one consequence of my argument will be the demonstration of important continuity between the latter notions, which dominate the discussion of freedom and salvation in Part V, and the more broadly "metaphysical" definitions and propositions of Parts I and II. My reading also has significant implications for the interpretation of God's causality, as asserted in *Ethics* I.16.

II

Spinoza alludes to "understanding" in several of the early propositions of Part I, as well as in the definition of attribute. I want to focus though on I.16, where the expression "infinite understanding" also appears (and for the first time). The proposition reads as follows:

> From the necessity of the divine nature, infinite [things] in infinite ways (that is, all [things] which can fall under infinite understanding) must follow.

> *Ex necessitate divinae naturae, infinita infinitis modis (hoc, est, omnia, quae sub intellectum infinitum cadere possunt) sequi debent.*

The demonstration of this proposition consists of just two sentences. In the first Spinoza asserts that the proposition "ought to be evident to anyone" who only considers that:

> from the given definition of anything understanding infers (*concludit*) a number of properties, which indeed necessarily follow from it (that is, from the essence itself of the thing), and the more, the more reality that the definition of the thing expresses, that is, the more reality that the essence of the thing involves.

But, Spinoza concludes:

> Since the divine nature has absolutely infinite attributes, each of which also expresses infinite essence in its kind [all this follows from the definition Spinoza has given of God], from its necessity therefore infinite [things] in infinite ways (that is, all [things] which can fall under infinite understanding) must necessarily follow.

On initial reading, at any rate, *understanding* and *inference* certainly seem to be playing some important role in this proof. Comparing the first with the second sentence, we might even suppose that infinite understanding's inferential power plays some kind of *accessory* role in the derivation of things from the divine nature. But *this* cannot be right, for surely, on Spinoza's view, things just *do* follow with necessity from the divine nature: they do not need something different from that nature to bring them about. And Spinoza's remarks elsewhere clearly indicate that infinite understanding is *not* part of the divine nature; it is merely the *idea Dei* or an infinite mode under the attribute of thought.[6] So perhaps we should, taking heed of the parentheses, construe the references to infinite understanding in this proposition and proof as merely some sort of unimportant *obiter dictum*. But then why are the references there at all? Why would Spinoza muddle one of his key propositions with such distractions?

A more satisfying but (I am going to suggest) still inadequate explanation is the following. Spinoza clearly wishes to oppose the idea that God's creative activity involves a voluntary selection among the things existing in his understanding (as in the Leibnizian picture). He therefore mentions infinite understanding in the statement and demonstration of Proposition I.16 just to underline his view that God's understanding of things does not exceed in scope the things he actually brings into existence.

This explanation is inadequate because—I hope to show—the references to understanding in I.16 have a broader significance for the overall interpretation of the *Ethics*. They signal, namely, the involvement of this proposition, together with the definition of attribute, with *scientia intuitiva*.

In *Ethics* II.40 Scholium 2 Spinoza explains *scientia intuitiva* in the following terms: "This kind of knowing proceeds from an adequate idea of the formal essence of some attributes of God to an adequate knowledge of the essence of things."[7] I will argue that this definition fits exactly the role ascribed to infinite understanding in I.16—with several interesting implications for the interpretation of the content of the proposition.

As we noted in connection with the definition of 'attribute', understanding perceives the attributes adequately, and indeed can only perceive them adequately. Further, I think it is clear enough from what has been said that in perceiving the essence of substance, understanding perceives it "under" an attribute—or "attributes to substance a certain such nature." (See also *E* I.10S.) But the notion of inference or conclusion introduced in Proposition I.16 certainly suggests a "proceeding from . . . to."[8] So, to show that Proposition I.16 involves an exemplification, on the level of infinity, of *scientia intuitiva*, I think that we need to do only one thing. We need only show that Spinoza conceives of infinite understanding as proceeding (inferring) from its adequate ideas of the formal essences of the attributes of God *to an adequate knowledge of the essence of things*.

Now, Spinoza makes quite clear in the subsequent propositions and demonstrations that the "*infinita infinitis modis*" do at least *include* the essences of things. For example, in Proposition 25 of Part I (scholium), he observes that "God is the efficient cause not only of the existence of things but also of their essence," citing I.16. But does infinite understanding form *adequate* ideas of the essences of things that it infers from the essence of God's attributes (as the definition of *scientia intuitiva* would further require)? There are strong grounds for saying it does. According to Proposition 40 of Part II, "Those ideas are . . .

adequate which follow in the mind from ideas which are adequate in it." And in I.16 *infinita infinitis modis* are precisely said to "follow" (*sequi*) from the ideas of God's attributes in infinite understanding—which, as we have noted, must be adequate. Also, Spinoza asserts in the proof of V.17 that "all ideas, as they are related to God, are true; that is to say, are adequate." I will take this as sufficient evidence at the present stage of argument. (There are some difficulties about the point, though, which I will mention later.)

It seems then that I.16 does portray infinite understanding as proceeding from the "adequate idea . . . of some attributes of God to an adequate knowledge of the essence of things"—and hence as complying with the definition of *scientia intuitiva*. But, one might object, I.16 still does not conform exactly to the definition. For, as we have just seen, Spinoza relates this proposition to the claim that the essences *and existences* of things follow from the divine nature. But *scientia intuitiva* seems to have to do with essences in contrast to existences.

This is a reasonable objection but one that can be answered. And the answer bears in an interesting way on the interpretation of I.16 itself.

Later in the *Ethics*, when Spinoza refers back to this proposition, he at least twice indicates the sort of existence or reality that it asserts to follow from the divine nature must *not* be confused with "existence at a certain time and place." On the contrary, it has to do with a type of existence that Spinoza gives us rather clear license to construe in terms of "essence." Consider the scholium to Proposition 45 of Part II. The proposition itself reads: "Any idea of any body, or singular thing, existing in act, necessarily involves the eternal and infinite essence of God." The scholium refers us back to I.16.

> Here by existence I do not understand duration, that is, existence as it is conceived abstractly, and as a certain kind of quantity. For I speak of the very nature of existence, which is attributed to singular things, because [*propterea quod*] infinite [things] in infinite ways follow from the eternal necessity of the nature of God (see Prop. 16., p. I). I speak, I say, of the existence itself of singular things, as they are in God. For, even though any singular thing is determined by another to a certain mode of existing, nevertheless the power, by which any thing perseveres in existence, follows from the eternal necessity of the nature of God.[9]

But the power, by which a thing perseveres in existence, is characterized by Spinoza as the "actual essence" of the thing itself (*E* III.7). This characterization suggests that "the existence itself of singular things, insofar as they are in God" may be identified with the essences of things (in a certain special sense). And this is just the sort of "existence of things" that I.16 asserts to follow from the attributes of God. Hence, infinite understanding's inference even of "existences" in Proposition I.16 actually is subsumable under Spinoza's account of *scientia intuitiva*.

Ethics V provides further support for the proposed interpretation of I.16. For example, Proposition 29 of Part V reads as follows:

> Whatever the mind understands under the aspect of eternity, it does not understand
> from the fact that it conceives the present actual existence of the body, but from the
> fact that it conceives the essence of the body under the aspect of eternity.

The scholium to this proposition refers specifically to II.45, which I cited just above. The scholium reads:

> Things are conceived by us as actual in two ways, either as they exist with relation
> to a certain time and place, or as we conceive them to be contained in God, and to
> follow from the necessity of the divine nature. But those which are conceived in
> this second way as true or real, we conceive them under the aspect of eternity, and
> their ideas involve the eternal and infinite essence of God, as we showed in Proposi-
> tion 45 of Part II.[10]

Taken together these two passages—and others from Part V could be cited—seem clearly to indicate that Spinoza distinguishes two senses of 'existence' or 'being actual', only one of which relates to what infinite understanding infers according to *Ethics* I.16. The "existence" of things that infinite understanding infers from the divine attributes must be distinguished from their duration through time or at a certain place. Proposition I.16 specifies the inference of the essences of things from the essence of God: it tells us that (in the words of V.22, which also makes use of I.16) "in God there necessarily exists an idea which expresses the essence of this or that body under the aspect of eternity."

If I am right, then, Proposition I.16 has considerably broader significance and implication than is usually noticed. It does not merely tell us that all things follow "from the necessity of the divine nature" (or by necessity from the divine nature)[11] and that *everything* comprehended by infinite understanding does so "follow." It also relates this fundamental statement about the origin of beings in God to the concept of the third kind of knowledge, which is only explicitly developed later. Both Proposition I.16 and *scientia intuitiva* play important roles in Spinoza's development of his ethical and (loosely speaking) eschatological views in Part V. I hope that my interpretation, by showing the connection between this key proposition of Part I and the concept of knowledge explained in Part II, will be suggestive also as to the interpretation of Part V. More particularly, I hope it will advance efforts to interpret the *Ethics* as a truly unified work, in which metaphysical, epistemological, ethical, and eschatological themes are quite rationally and purposively intermingled.

I will not attempt here to apply my interpretation of I.16 to the detailed interpretation of the proposition of Part V. However, the proposed reading of I.16 as relating to the concept of *scientia intuitiva* does have one particular implication that seems worth pointing out. I mentioned above that the references to infinite understanding in the proposition might be construed as Spinoza's way of underscoring his opposition to the voluntarist view that God *selects* the things to be brought into existence from among the things he understands. But, at least in its Leibnizian version,[12] the voluntarist position has to do with creation in the sense of bringing into existence it a time and place. And, according to my reading of I.16, nothing about existence at a certain time or place (or about "actual" being in the corresponding sense) is supposed to be established by I.16. If this reading is correct, then, the proposition does not establish quite as complete and direct an opposition between Spinoza's metaphysics and, say, Leibniz's as might be supposed. Spinoza need not—indeed cannot—be construed as saying that everything that falls under the divine understanding exists in the sense of being instantiated at a time and place or of "having duration." Rather, he holds that everything that falls under the infinite understanding has *some sort of being* in the divine attributes (such as extension). (This result also accords well with Spinoza's statement that the "ideas of non-existent modes" have their ideata "in the attributes of God"—a claim crucial to his proof [in Propositions V.21–40] that the human mind is eternal.) Of course, even on this reading of I.16, Spinoza still differs from Leibniz in holding that all of God's ideas have *ideata* or objects that are *in some sense* actual. However, at least as far as Proposition I.16 goes, he need not be differing from Leibniz to the extent of denying that in *one* sense of 'existent' or 'actual' not everything in God's understanding is existent or actual.[13] (What is most peculiar is that Spinoza regards the notion of existence or being-actual involved in this second, commonsensically more obvious sense as an "abstraction."[14])

Now to consider some problems.

III

The reading of I.16 that I am proposing leads us into several difficulties. I believe that only one—the first to be considered—is a problem for the interpretation itself. The other difficulties I will mention seem to arise within Spinoza's system independently of the connection I am suggesting between I.16 and *scientia intuitiva*. They are relevant to my interpretation without being generated by it.

The first problem I want to consider has both a philosophical and a textual aspect. Philosophically, one may argue that my interpretation implausibly leaves the determination of existence *in the sense of duration* (or existence at a time and place) outside the scope of Spinoza's major statement on the origin of things in God. In fact, my reading of I.16 leaves the significance of I.16 rather unclear in general, for *what* is the "very nature of existence" in contrast to "existence at a time and place" or duration? Textually, the interpretation of I.16 that I am proposing runs up against the fact that some later propositions of Part I (and Part II) seem to suggest that the "causality of God" delineated in *Ethics* I.16 does after all include the determination of things' duration. In particular, in the corollary to Proposition 24 of Part I—"The essence of things produced by God does not involve existence"—Spinoza comments: ". . . [T]he essence [of things] cannot be the cause either of their existence *or of their duration*, but God only, to whose nature alone it pertains to exist" (italics added). This statement certainly suggests that Spinoza is including the duration of things in the scope of God's causality. And subsequent propositions explicitly presuppose that I.16 has established that God is the cause of all things, *both* of their essence and of their existence.

Now, I believe that the *textual* aspect of this objection to my interpretation can be met, though admittedly not in a philosophically satisfying manner. Spinoza does indicate that God is the cause of things' duration in I.24, but he does *not* there refer us back to I.16. And the subsequent passages, which do refer back to I.16, contrast existence and essence under the divine causality but make no mention of duration. It is, therefore, possible after all to tender these propositions consistent with II.45 and V.29, which I have relied on in defending the view that I.16 exclusively exemplifies the third kind of knowledge. For one can, consistent with the former texts, construe Spinoza's position in the following way: (1) Though Spinoza may assume that God is the cause of the duration of things, he does not base this claim on *Ethics* I.16. (2) When he speaks of God as cause of the essences and existence of things in the later propositions of Part I, he has in mind existence in the recherché sense he later contrasts with duration ("the very nature of existence"). Existence in this recherché sense may (according to II.45 and III.7) be identified with "the actual essence" of things.

Unfortunately, this reading does leave the reference to the causing of duration in I.24 a seemingly inexplicable loose end. But such a loose end seems unavoidable in any case, for Proposition 45 of Part II does quite explicitly imply that the divine inference of I.16 is *not* an inference to the existence of things at a certain time and place.

The second problem that needs to be considered has to do with the transition in Spinoza's system from infinite attributes to finite modes. It is a problem that is often mentioned in the literature, and it does not particularly weigh against my concept of *scientia intuitiva*.[15] But it does have a special connection with my reading.

How is it *possible* that infinite understanding should infer adequate ideas of the essences of things from adequate ideas of the formal essences of certain attributes of God? Spinoza tells us in I.21 that "all [things] that follow from the absolute nature of any attribute of God" must be infinite and eternal, i.e., the infinite modes. In the proof he comments: "Hence that which so follows from the necessity of the nature of any attribute cannot have determinate existence or duration." The language here is highly reminiscent of that of I.16. The statement, in fact, can happily be seen as confirming my claim that I.16 does not have to do with the origin of things' duration. Unfortunately, though, I.21 goes further than this, for it seems to indicate that only *infinite* and eternal modes— or ideas of such modes—could follow or be inferred from "the necessity of the divine nature."[16]

E I.21 thus presents grave difficulties for interpreting the "*sequi*" of I.16, difficulties that arise independently of my attempt to relate that proposition to the concept of *scientia intuitiva*. To express the point bluntly, Spinoza seems both to affirm and to deny that finite things "follow from" the divine nature. But we are now in a position to see some further complications of this problem. It is not *just* a problem for the reading of *E* I.16 but *also* a problem for the concept of *scientia intuitiva*—even if I am wrong in regarding the two as intimately related—for we can have *scientia intuitiva* just insofar as we *can* proceed *from* adequate knowledge of the essence of God's attributes *to* adequate knowledge of the essences of things. If this is not possible in the case of finite things, then it appears that they cannot at all legitimately be included under *scientia intuitiva* any more than under the derivation of I.16 (even if these are, contrary to my suggestion, distinct). The texts do seem to me confusing and unsettled on this point—quite a fundamental one, unfortunately, for Spinoza's "necessitarianism," his epistemology, and his theory of human happiness and salvation.

In originally relating I.16 to *scientia intuitiva* I partly relied on a proposition affirming that all ideas in God are adequate. I used this to show that infinite understanding conforms to *scientia intuitiva* in that it infers to adequate ideas of the essences of things, but I also mentioned having some reservations about the point. We have just seen that there are general difficulties in understanding the possibility of inferring, or proceeding, from the divine attributes to anything finite. It is now appropriate to note that the arguments Spinoza offers for his claim about the adequacy of God's ideas (V.17; II.36) are not very satisfactory. In these arguments Spinoza in effect holds that the *truth* of all ideas as related to God entails the *adequacy* of all ideas related to God. But God's ideas are all true just because they all have corresponding ideata. And "adequacy," as Spinoza himself defines it, seems to involve the additional condition of possessing all the *intrinsic properties* of a true idea (II. Def. 4). This awkward fallacy in Spinoza's argument may be a reflection of his deep difficulty in rationalizing the transition (in God) from infinite attribute (or its idea) to finite mode (or *its* idea).

The study of I.16 brings up another problem. This again, I think, is a difficulty that could not be avoided by any reasonable reading of I.16. As I briefly suggested in a previous remark, Spinoza clearly and firmly distinguishes the status of infinite understanding from that of the attribute of thought. He argues that infinite understanding is a *mode* of the attribute of thought. This, of course, means it is not self-caused, or "conceived through itself." Yet, by I.16 it has ideas of the attributes of God. Now, surely if it is a mode, all its ideas (including our minds) must be modes. But, famously, Spinoza holds that ideas and their ideata must be causally parallel. There seems to be an outright contradiction between the latter notion and the supposition that "other-caused" ideas take as their ideata self-caused attributes. Maybe there is an obvious answer to this dilemma, but I have not been able to see it.

Thus, my interpretation of I.16 in terms of the concept of *scientia intuitiva* by no means solves the major problems of interpretation and problems of apparent inconsistency in Spinoza's system. Indeed, it leads directly into some of them. However, I do not think it creates any *new* problems of this sort. And it does, I hope, help to illuminate the important intimacy among the metaphysical, epistemological, and ethical aspects of Spinoza's thought.

IV

In conclusion, I wish to turn to a different sort of issue. It is, I think, a common experience of students of Spinoza to feel torn between—or to alternate between—two conflicting conceptions of his philosophical stature. Some of the time, one is mainly of the opinion that his system is just too hopelessly shot through with inconsistency, fallacy, obscurity, and idiosyncrasy to *deserve* the painstaking analysis it seems to demand of the reader. At other times, one may be more impressed with the startlingly original and even powerful character of Spinoza's underlying philosophical conceptions. The treatment of creation, or the origin of dependent being, in Part I—and perhaps particularly in I.16— provides a good example of why this should be so. We have already surveyed a number of serious—indeed critical—problems with which it is bound up. On the other hand, the idea that things arise *necessarily*, as if by deductive inference, from God or nature is surely a bold and provocative one, however exactly it should be interpreted. It is a view that in some ways, at least, does provide a direct and intriguing alternative to the more traditional voluntarist conception defended (for instance) by Leibniz. Therefore, I would like finally to comment briefly on the following question: How successful is Spinoza in his attempt to establish that his form of necessitarianism is more in conformity with reason than is traditional voluntarism?[17]

The core of the voluntarist position is, I take it, the following: The world is, and is *as* it is, because God *chose* that this be so. He could have chosen differently and so things could have been different. It could even have been the case that he abstained from creating anything. Spinoza surely does make some cogent or plausible points against this view. Some are familiar, such as the argument that an all-perfect God would have no reason to decide to bring into being any thing outside himself. (This precise sort of difficulty does not arise for Spinoza, since his God does not do anything on purpose and hence *requires* no "reason for acting."[18]) Some of Spinoza's other objections to voluntarism are much more original, he argues, for instance, that, if God could have chosen differently, there must be more than one possible divine nature. Bur the ontological argument will apply to each. Therefore, there would have to be more than one God! (I. 33).[19] But one of the most interesting and fundamental points of contrast between Spinoza and his voluntarist opponents is found in their respective concepts of omnipotence. And, although Spinoza makes great fun of his opponents' views on this subject, I do not think he provides a coherent refutation.

Spinoza, as I read him, holds that God's omnipotence requires that everything in God's power actually comes into being. In other words: "G is omnipotent" entails "G brings about everything in its power to bring about." His opponents, he indicates, deny this proposition on the ridiculous grounds that, unless there are unrealized possibles in God's understanding, his power to create would have come to an end! (And, hence, I suppose, be limited.)

. . . [A]lthough they conceive God as actually understanding to the highest degree, they nevertheless do not believe he can bring it about that all [things] which he actually understands, exist; for they think they would in that way destroy God's power. They say that if he had created all [things] that are in his understanding, then he would be able to create nothing more, which they believe is inconsistent with God's omnipotence . . . (*E* I.17s).

Now, I do not know whether any of Spinoza's contemporaries actually argued like this, but certainly the voluntarist position can be stated in more plausible terms. The voluntarist may contend that omnipotence requires the power *to bring about or prevent* any possible state of affairs and therefore requires choice—the choice of which to do. In other words: "G is omnipotent" entails "it is in G's power to determine, for any possible contingent state of affairs, whether or not it obtains."[20] Presumably, Spinoza would insist that such a conception of omnipotence rests on an illegitimate anthropomorphization of God, an extrapolation from a common conception of human power to God. But he does not systematically defend or explain his own intuition. Perhaps he supposed that the demonstration of I.16 was sufficient to settle the issue in his favor. If so, I think he was wrong.[21]

NOTES

1. *E* is used as abbreviation of *Ethica*. Translations are my own. Geb. (below) refers to *Spinoza opera*, ed. C. Gebhardt.

2. Geb. IV, p. 46. (The peculiar punctuation follows Gebhardt's text.) Throughout the paper I translate '*intellectus*' as 'understanding'. In an earlier version of the paper, I frequently used 'the understanding'. At a Spinoza symposium, E. M. Curley objected to this phrasing on the grounds that it introduces a specious definiteness where (on Curley's view) Spinoza is only talking about *an* understanding or *some* understanding or other. (The Latin, of course, has no article at all.) Curley made this point in connection with more substantive criticisms. Although I was not persuaded by his other substantive criticisms, I have dropped the definite article throughout for the sake of consistency and to avoid the appearance of question-begging on the issue.

3. See especially H. A. Wolfson, *The Philosophy of Spinoza* (Cambridge, Mass.: Harvard University Press, 1934), pp. 142–57.

4. See especially Francis S. Hascrot, "Spinoza's Definition of Attribute," in S. Paul Kashup, ed., *Studies in Spinoza* (Berkeley: University of California Press, 1972, originally published 1953); Martial Gueroult, *Spinoza: Dieu (Ethique, 1)* (Paris: Aubier-Montaigne, 1968), p. 50.

5. One exception is an unpublished manuscript by Genevieve Lloyd, *The Eternity of the Mind: A Study of Spinoza's Ethics*. Lloyd's approach is in some ways congruent to mine, though there are also substantial differences between our interpretations.

6. Cf. *E* II.4; 1.34.

7. Geb. II, p. 122.

8. My linking of the third kind of knowledge with E I.16 seems to entail a different understanding of 'proceeds' in the definition of the former than that sketched by Guttorm

Fløistad, "Spinoza's Theory of Knowledge Applied to the *Ethics*," in Kashap, pp. 271–72. Fløistad, incidentally, provides a useful gloss on the term 'formal essence'.

9. Cf. *E* V.22. See also E. M. Curley, *Spinoza's Metaphysics* (Cambridge, Mass.; Harvard University Press, 1969), pp. 141–42.

10. This passage is also cited, in a similar connection, by Joel I. Friedman in "Spinoza's Denial of Free Will in Man and God," in Jon Wetlesen, ed., *Spinoza's Philosophy of Man: Papers presented at the Scandinavian Spinoza Symposium, 1977* (Oslo: 1978), pp. 51–84.

11. It is not unreasonable to wonder whether "follow *from the necessity* of the divine nature" implies "follow *with necessity from* the divine nature"; however, both the demonstration of *E* I.16 and Spinoza's subsequent use of the proposition indicate that he does intend this implication.

12. I mention Leibniz in this connection because his philosophy seems to provide in some ways an *excellent* example of the *type* of view Spinoza wants to oppose (and one with which I happen to be familiar). I do not mean to suggest that Spinoza was reacting against his successor!

13. I have learned in discussion that quite a few people want to attribute to Spinoza the view that everything in God's understanding has temporal or durational existence at some time or other. This issue seems to me an obscure one textually. There is also the problem of compossibility: Is it reasonable to hold that everything in God's understanding is compossible with everything else in the sense that, given enough time, it is possible that all these things exist? Alan Donagan attributes to Spinoza a view about incompatible essences in "Spinoza's Proof of Immortality" (*Spinoza: A Collection of Critical Essays*, Marjorie Grene, ed. [Notre Dame, Ind.: University of Notre Dame Press, 1979; originally published 1973], pp. 253–55). (Like Fløostad [see n. 8], Donagan gives some help with the concept of "formal essence," which he contrasts with "actual essence." However, Donagan does not appear to take note of the fact [argued above] that Spinoza recognizes *two* senses of 'actual'.)

14. '*Abstracte*' and '*abstractus*' are not words that Spinoza uses often. See, however, *E* I.15S (Geb. II, p. 59), and Letter XII (to L. Meyer) (Geb. IV, pp. 56–57).

15. See, for instance, Alasdair MacIntyre, "Spinoza, Benedict (Baruch)," *The Encyclopedia of Philosophy*, ed. Paul Edwards (New York: Macmillan, 1967), Vol., 7, p. 535.

16. In "The Causality of God in Spinoza's Philosophy," *Canadian Journal of Philosophy*, Vol. II, No. 2 (December 1972), A. J. Watt argues that the direct causality of God, as asserted in E I.16, should be understood as the causing of *essences*. On this point, of course, my own interpretation largely follows his. But Watt also seems to hold—what I would deny—that this construal of I.16 helps avoid problems about the emergence of the finite from the infinite.

17. Of course, if my foregoing argument is right, there is not a *complete and direct* opposition between Spinoza and traditional voluntarism, at least as far as *E* I.16 goes (since Spinoza is not there concerned with the bringing about of temporal existence). I think there is still enough opposition to consider intelligibly the issue taken up in this section.

18. However, the problem about "how" the finite modes arise from the infinite attributes in his system may perhaps be regarded as somewhat parallel.

19. I sketch a similar line of reasoning in relation to a problem of interpreting Leibniz's views about modality in "Possible Gods," *The Review of Metaphysics*, Vol. XXXII, No. 4 (June 1979), pp. 717–33 (Chapter 27 of this volume).

20. Curiously, Spinoza himself touches on this conception at the beginning of the scholium to *E* 1.17.

21. I am grateful to more people than I could reasonably name here for helpful comments on earlier versions of this paper, many of which have led to changes in argument and structure. But I must particularly thank Eyjolfur Emilsson, E. M. Curley, George L. Kline, and Joel Friedman for detailed comments and criticisms.

"For They Do Not Agree in Nature with Us": Spinoza on the Lower Animals

I

Spinoza is often praised for maintaining an anti-Cartesian conception of "the mind" which conforms, at least in some respects, to certain mainstream present-day philosophical positions. The human mind, for Spinoza, is not an absolute, simple entity radically distinct from the natural order (as Descartes held): an autonomous substance lodged within the bodily machine, and capable of inter-vening in the material world through free acts of will with causal impact on the body. On the one hand, Spinoza maintains that all physical phenomena what-soever, including (one must suppose) what we think of as "intelligent behav-ior," are susceptible of explanation within the realm of physical causes exclu-sively. Mental "determination" of anything material is, according to his system, inconceivable. (And, likewise—and perhaps less attractively from a present day perspective—he holds that material explanation of mental occurrences is ruled out.)[1] On the other hand, the mental aspect of finite things is, like the material, a "part of nature": minds themselves belong to "nature's order." Minds, like the bodies of which they are the "ideas," are compounds of sub-units; and the changes of the ideas that compose minds are subject to deterministic explana-tion in some way parallel to explanation of material change according to the laws of matter-in-motion. This notion of the mental seems to allow for a domain of psychological explanation which, while no less rigorous than the material, can proceed according to a distinct form of conceptualization—with-out implying that minds somehow function independently of their material substrata.

Spinoza himself draws from his position the conclusion that one mind is "superior" to another, just insofar as its body has certain superior capacities. In one or two passages he suggests that relatively superior minds possess a higher degree of consciousness than others. But he further seems by implication com-mitted to the modern view that even within the most superior minds, many of the components are unconscious. For he holds that the human mind includes ideas of "whatever happens in" the human body (and *surely* wouldn't hold that even the most superior human mind is *conscious* of everything that happens in its body).[2] Besides, his theory of the affects or passions is bound up with the contention that many of our attractions and aversions are dictated by past en-counters which leave their mark without our having noticed.

Apart from Spinoza's conception of the human mind specifically, his related views about the minds of non-human animals may seem to represent a major improvement over Descartes. According to Descartes's rather notorious position, humans alone operate (in part) through the activities of an immaterial, intelligent mental substance, which contains no states of which we are not "in some manner conscious."[3] Other animals are purely material, mechanical entities, lacking any form of conscious "thought."[4] But both "common sense" (from Descartes's time to our own) and Darwinian ethological theories tend to reject the notion that there is a radical ontological chasm between humans and non-human animals, inferable from their respective behaviors. Spinoza's unequivocal assertion (in *EIIIP57S*) that "brutes feel," together with *certain aspects* of his conception of the pervasiveness of mentality in nature, can well seem a useful corrective to the stringent Cartesian position.

I have small inclination to defend Descartes's claims about the strictly "mechanical" nature of beasts. But I do wish to question some prominent accounts of Spinoza's views about animals that generally seek to portray his position in a favorable light. Apologetic commentators tend to play down Spinoza's truly ruthless conception of our "rights" with regard to other animals, *in the face of* his acknowledgement that they "feel." And on this issue, the problem is not *only* his ruthlessness, but also (what seem to me) insufficiently acknowledged theoretical unclarities in his reasoning. But even before one considers the ethical issues, one needs to try to understand Spinoza's *systematic grounds* for opposing Descartes on the mental status of animals. I think that some interpreters have been too quick to interpret Spinoza as presenting a clear, coherent, and commonsensical position on the topic of animal minds in the *Ethics*.

I begin the next section (II) with an example of recent philosophical treatment of animal mentality which—while not directly concerned with Spinoza—provides a sympathetic contemporary background for evaluating his position. I go on to cite several commentators' favorable accounts of his views on the mentality of brutes. In section III I will argue that the theoretical basis for Spinoza's assertion that "brutes feel" is not as straightforward as some have supposed. And I will raise a question—relying on considerations I presented in an earlier paper—of whether Spinoza is entitled, given tenets laid down in Part II, to distinguish human from bestial nature on the basis of the possession of "reason" (as he may seem implicitly to try to do in Part IV). In the last main section (IV) I critically assess Spinoza's defense of the view that we are entitled to treat the beasts in any way convenient to us, despite the fact that they "feel."

II

In a recent book pervaded by anti-Cartesian themes (to take one prominent example), Daniel Dennett argues that much can be inferred by empirical considerations—anatomical, behavioral, and evolutionary-ecological—about the "phenomenology" of languageless animals: about what sorts of things they are conscious of, or "what it is like" to be them.[5] Dennett maintains that we can be sure that such creatures lack "many of the advanced mental activities that shape our minds"; that their minds differ greatly in "structure" from ours. "Does this mean," Dennett asks, "that languageless animals 'are not conscious at all' (as Descartes insisted)?" Dennett thinks that this question rests on an outdated assumption:

> . . . it presupposes something [he says] that we have worked hard to escape: the assumption that consciousness is a special all-or-nothing property that sunders the universe into two vastly different categories: the things that have it (the things that it is like something to be . . .) and the things that lack it. Even in our own case, we cannot draw the line separating our conscious mental states from our unconscious mental states. The theory of consciousness we have sketched allows for many variations of functional architecture, and while the presence of language marks a particularly dramatic increase in imaginative range, versatility, and self-control . . . , these powers do not have the *further* power of turning on some special inner light that would otherwise be off. (447)

Spinoza's conception of mentality, in opposition to Descartes's, seems to lend itself readily to an understanding of the "difference between men and brutes" along the lines proposed by Dennett. This suggestion receives support from accounts of his position offered by several of his most prominent interpreters. Edwin Curley, for instance, approaches Spinoza's position on the brutes by first sketching his view of the physical world as consisting of increasingly complex individuals (beginning with the simplest particles, progressing through compounds (including the human body) whose individuality depends on their maintaining a constant proportion of motion and rest, up to "the whole of nature.") Curley continues:

> One moral of this picture seems to be that man's distinctive mental capacities are a reflection of the great complexity of the body that is associated with them (*E*2P14). But the intellectual difference between man and the "lower" animals appears to be a function of the differences in the complexities of their respective bodies, not of man's possessing an immortal soul radically different from any soul "beasts" might be thought to have.[6]

Genevieve Lloyd, noting that Spinoza explicitly attributes feelings and affects to beasts, comments:

> Spinoza thinks, contrary to Descartes, that animals are sentient beings. This follows from his account of minds as ideas of bodies. Any idea of a body with a requisite degree of complexity will be for him a sentient mind. But being of a different nature from ourselves—being, that is, ideas of bodies of a different structure—their emotions are different from ours . . . .[7]

R. J. Delahunty asserts, wrongly, that Spinoza differs from Descartes in attributing "life" to beasts. (As Descartes points out to such contemporary critics as Henry More, he by no means denies that beasts are alive; rather, he understands "life" itself as a condition to be conceived in mechanistic terms.)[8] But Delahunty further observes, more nearly accurately, that Spinoza disagrees with Descartes in holding that animals "feel and sense, that they are to some degree rational or 'sagacious'":

> In many respects, their sagacity even exceeds ours (*E*III, 2S); nor can we doubt that they have sensation—even insects, birds and fish experience lust and appetite, and live contentedly, taking pleasure in their own natures (*ibid.*).[9]

Spinoza's views on the beasts, Delahunty adds,

> are in many respects an improvement over Descartes': in particular, it is encouraging to see him returning to the animals many of the features of which Descartes had stripped them. (210)

Curley, Lloyd, and Delahunty all note (with varying degrees of apparent regret) that Spinoza's conception of the "mindedness" of brutes does not lead him to the conclusion that we owe them special consideration in our treatment of them. On the contrary, Spinoza maintains that we are fully entitled to use the beasts—and indeed all non-human parts of nature—according to our pleasure and convenience. Thus, Spinoza's view of man as "part of nature," and of non-human animals as possessing various mental capacities at least analogous to those of humans, does not lead Spinoza himself to espouse an ecological ethics, a position which would (in Curley's words),

> recognize that non-human nature has either rights which must not be violated, or at least some intrinsic value, some value which does not derive merely from its being instrumental to human needs.[10]

The efforts of some writers (especially Arne Naess) to construe Spinozism as a sort of proto-ecologism collapse before Spinoza's own interpretation of the implications of his metaphysical position with regard to our dealings with non-human nature.[11] Similarly, Spinoza's relatively positive views on the mentality of beasts are detached from recent efforts to derive moral restraints on our treatment of non-human animals from claims about their mental capacities.[12]

I will return to Spinoza's position on our unrestrained "rights" with regard to the treatment of non-human animals later on. Although his conclusion is certainly unequivocal, the reasoning he offers in support of it is not very clear (or so I'll suggest). But first I want to consider more closely the status of animal minds in Spinoza's system. The main questions I'll take up in this connection are the following. First, what is the theoretical basis for Spinoza's assertion that "brutes feel"? Is Lloyd right in thinking that this claim reflects a conception of the "complexity" of brute bodies?[13] (I will suggest that her interpretation, attractive as it may seem, lacks direct textual basis, and in fact seems to be undermined by textual considerations.) Second, how, specifically, does Spinoza see the human mind as differing from that of brutes? In the possession of "reason"? *Does* the *Ethics* present a coherent position on the question whether human minds alone are "rational"? I will claim that it does not; while also arguing that

Delahunty's apparently supportive reading of Spinoza on the rationality of beasts rests on a misconstrual of the main text he cites.

III

Is it true that Spinoza stakes out a view about the "sentience" of animal minds, grounded in the "sufficient complexity" of animal bodies, of which their minds are ideas? I don't think so. Of course it *is* an important part of Spinoza's conception of the mind-body relation that one mind is superior to another mind, just insofar as its body is superior to that of the other. For, after asserting that "all [individuals] are animate, though in different degrees" (IIP13S), Spinoza adds:

> However, we also cannot deny that ideas ["minds"] differ among themselves, as the objects themselves do, and that one is more excellent than the other, and contains more reality, just as the object of one is more excellent than the object of the other and contains more reality. And so [he continues], to determine what is the difference between the human Mind and the others, and how it surpasses them, it is necessary for us . . . to know the nature of its object, i.e., of the human Body.

He goes on to indicate that a body which is more able than others to act and be acted on in many ways at once, and to act in a way more dependent on itself alone, will be a body with a superior mind.

But these observations about relative "excellence" and "reality" evidently do not amount to, nor directly entail, an assertion that "sentience" is correlative with "requisite degree of complexity" in a given "idea's" body. And, in fact, Spinoza's praised conclusion that "brutes feel" involves no mention at all of bodily "complexity." In one of his two direct statements on this subject in the *Ethics* (in connection with an observation about the "difference in nature" between the affects of humans and brutes), he merely observes, parenthetically, that "after we know the origin of Mind, we cannot in any way doubt that brutes feel (*bruta enim sentire nequaquam dubitare possumus, postquam Mentis novimus originem*)." (IIIP57S) I take this aside to refer to the general account of "mind" offered in Part II—of which the title is, "Of the Nature, and Origin, of Mind." But, according to the early Propositions of Part II (leading up to IIP13), *all* modes of extension have corresponding "minds," or "ideas," which express the nature of God, conceived under the attribute of Thought. For (by the argument of Part I, especially IP16), everything conceivable follows from God's essence; and, by IIP3, "In God there is necessarily an idea, both of his essence and of everything that necessarily follows from his essence." The specific issue of "origin of Mind" is most directly addressed in IIP5:

> The formal being of ideas recognizes God as cause only insofar as he is considered as a thinking thing . . . ; that is, ideas, both of God's attributes and of singular things recognize as their efficient cause not the objects themselves (*ideata*), nor the things perceived, . . . but God himself, in so far as he is a thinking thing.

One notion that the early reasoning of Part II certainly conflicts with is that minds have their "origins"—assuming that this term is to be understood in a causal sense—in *any* physical state or circumstance: including, obviously, the "complexity" of a body. But, as we've seen, Spinoza cites his account of the "origin" of mind, in sole support of his assertion that "brutes feel." Thus, I think that his position on the "feeling" of beasts must be construed as *independent of* his further remarks on what explains the "superiority" of one mind over another. And if Spinoza's claim that beasts are sentient is indeed grounded in his *general* account of the origin of minds, it utterly fails to distinguish beasts from presumably less "complex" entities—even rocks or tennis balls, let alone plants—with regard to the presence of "feeling." It is not, in other words, something about *beasts* that is said to show that they feel—nothing about their specific types of behavior or physiological structure. If this interpretation is right, Spinoza's position has no genuine relation to the kind of considerations that make issues of animal cognition so intriguing today. Rather, his account of "the origin of mind" seems to have the implication that *every* individual "feels"; he merely draws the conclusion specifically with regard to beasts.[14]

There is one passage in the *Ethics* that does definitely link degree of consciousness—and hence, perhaps, "feeling"—to the capacities of a mind's body occurs much later, in the Scholium to *Ethics* VP39:

> . . . he who, like an infant or child, has a Body that is capable of very few things, and very greatly dependent on external causes, has a Mind which, considered solely in itself, is conscious of almost nothing of itself, of God, or of things; and on the other hand, he who has a Body capable of very many things, has a Mind which considered solely in itself, is very much conscious of itself, of God, and of things.

In an earlier paper I observed that this tying of levels of consciousness to bodily autonomy (and, by implication, to the possession of adequate, or clear and distinct, ideas) is not easy to reconcile with Spinoza's statement, in Proposition 9 of Part III, that the mind *is conscious of* the "endeavor to persist in being" which constitutes its "nature," *both* "insofar as it has clear and distinct ideas, and insofar as it has confused ideas."[15] But even apart from that issue of textual consistency, it does *not* appear that VP39 tells us that sentience is *restricted* to ideas of bodies, or minds, possessing a "requisite degree of complexity."

It may seem comfortably commonsensical to attribute to Spinoza the view that beasts must be regarded as sentient just because they have appropriately complex bodies (whatever exactly that may be taken to mean).[16] But I see no clear basis in the *Ethics* for ascribing that position to him; and Lloyd does not offer directly supporting textual citation. And, again, the wording leading up to the claim that brutes feel seems to hark back to the account of the "origin of mind" in Part II, which is bound up with Spinoza's *general* attribution of "minds" to natural things.

Still, we *are* left with the result that "brutes feel," even if it is presented against a panpsychist background unlikely to be favored by Dennett, or other philosophers who try to take account of the recent ethological and animal be-

havioral literature, in arriving at theories about the minds of beasts.[17] The view
that beasts do feel has, unsurprisingly, been favored throughout Western history,
despite such striking exceptions as Descartes and some of his followers. A
more consistently contentious issue is whether beasts differ from humans in
lacking the faculty of "reason." This question, of course, can mean different
things to different people. Again unsurprisingly, many who are prepared to
attribute reason to beasts do not claim that there is *no difference between* brute
reason and human reason.[18] Leibniz, whose position on the subject was more
than usually precise, attributes to brutes a "shadow of reason," but not the
genuine thing. That is, he holds (especially in the *New Essays*) that brutes can
make a sort of inference on the basis of past experience of repeated sequences
of events; even humans, he thinks, rely on such purely empirical "inference"
three-quarters of the time. But, he says, brutes have no access to necessary
truths, as we humans do.[19]

As far as I can see, Spinoza presents no *explicit* position on the question of
whether "brutes reason," under any natural interpretation of it.[20] Delahunty, as I
mentioned, cites the Scholium of *Ethics* IIIP2 in support of his claim that Spinoza opposed Descartes in recognizing the "reason" of brutes. But, in fact,
Spinoza's remark about brutes in this Scholium is quite in line with Descartes's
position. The Proposition (IIIP2) itself asserts that,

> The body cannot determine the mind to think, nor can the mind determine the body
> to motion or rest, or to anything else (if there is anything else).

The issue of the "sagacity" of brutes comes up in support of *the causal efficacy
of the merely material*. Spinoza writes:

> . . . Nobody has as yet determined what the body can do; that is, nobody as yet has
> learned from experience what the body can and cannot do, without being deter-
> mined by mind, solely from the laws of its nature insofar as it is considered as
> corporeal. For nobody as yet knows the structure of the body so accurately as to
> explain all its functions, not to mention that in the animal world we find much that
> far surpasses human sagacity, and that sleepwalkers do many things in their sleep
> that they would not dare when awake;—clear evidence that the body, solely from
> the laws of its own nature, can do many things at which its mind is amazed.

The message here is, clearly, that animal "sagacity" can be explained wholly by
material principles. Descartes, quite similarly, remarks in the *Discourse* that
beasts "show more skill than we do in some of their actions." (AT VI, 58–59;
CSM I, 141) He goes on to claim that such superior skills, restricted as they are
to very limited types of behavior, show that brutes act from material "dispositions of their organs," rather than mind or intelligence. For (he says) if their
superior skills derived from mind or intelligence (*esprit*), "they would have
more intelligence than any of us and would excel us in everything." In later
writings Descartes continues to maintain that he can explain, for instance, "the
astuteness and cunning of dogs and foxes . . . as originating from the structure

of their bodily parts." (AT V, 276; CSMK III, 365) The major differences between Spinoza and Descartes on this issue have to do not with "animal sagacity," but (to a considerable degree) with issues of explanation. Spinoza, that is, differs fundamentally from Descartes in apparently holding, first, that all *human* physical behavior whatsoever is susceptible of thoroughly materialist explanation; and, second, that the issue of "mindedness" is a separate one, having to do not with the explanations of behavior considered physically, but with the status of Thought as an attribute, through which everything in nature can be conceived. (Additionally he denies "free will" to all minds without exception.)

Certain Propositions of Part IV (especially P35-P37) seem to be trying to suggest a close connection between reason and *human* nature; and since Spinoza goes on at the end of Scholium 1 to P37 (to be discussed below) to allude to differences between human nature and the nature of brutes, one might conclude that he does mean to hold that brute minds differ essentially from human minds in lacking reason. But the passages are (I think) pretty murky; and do not unequivocally support this reading. And, perhaps, Spinoza has a particular systematic reason for being vague, relating (again) to the panpsychist implications of Part II.

Above I cited Spinoza's claim that *all* "individuals" are animated, as the basis for his conclusion that "brutes feel." But Spinoza seems to be committed (in Part II) to much stronger panpsychic tenets as well. In particular, it seems that even non-human minds must, within the logic of his system, include *adequate* ideas; that is, ideas of "reason," in a special honorific sense.[21] For according to IIP45, "Every idea of any body or singular thing existing in act necessarily involves the eternal and infinite essence of God"; and according to IIP46, "The knowledge of the eternal and infinite essence of God which each idea involves is adequate and perfect." So, Spinoza's ensuing claim at IIP47, that "The human mind has adequate knowledge of the eternal and infinite essence of God," must be understood to apply to minds generally. (The Proposition underlying this phase of his argument is IIP38: "What is common to all can only adequately be conceived.")[22] Similarly, every consideration that supports the intriguing Corollary of IIP11—"The human mind is part of the infinite intellect of God"—equally supports the conclusion that *every* body has a "mind" that is "part of the infinite intellect of God," and is therefore, presumably, (in some sense) *intelligent*. (And indeed, this Corollary falls within the scope of what IIP13 *explicitly decrees* to be "completely general.")[23]

Further, Spinoza's very definition of "idea," combined with the notion that every body has its corresponding idea ("mind"), seems in another sense to commit him to acknowledging that "reason" is not restricted to humans (among finite modes).[24] For, an idea is just a "conception of Mind, which Mind forms because it is a thinking thing (*propterea quod res est cogitans*)." (IID3) And, he explains, the term "conception" is meant to connote activity: as he later maintains, ideas are not images, or "dumb pictures on a tablet," but affirmations or denials: in other words, *judgments* (IIP49S). So, it seems, animal minds (actually, minds of *all* bodies) not only "feel," in the sense of passively receiving sensations, but judge (affirm and deny).[25]

In what, then, do "man's distinctive mental capacities" consist, according to Spinoza? Well, first, the lines already quoted from VP39S show that the question, so phrased (following Curley), is somewhat misleading, in so far as it suggests that all human minds possess the *same* distinctive mental capacities, in an all-or-nothing way. Spinoza not only represents "the human mind" as *improving* from infancy to normal adulthood; he particularly stresses that it is vitally important for adult men to strive to increase their understanding of things ("under a species of eternity"), thereby continuing to increase the "perfection" or "excellence" of their minds. (In this way, and this way only, a human being can enlarge the portion of his [or her?] mind which is itself "eternal.")[26]

I mentioned earlier that Leibniz distinguishes the "shadow of reason"—an empirical association which he thinks wholly governs brutes' inferences—from the access to necessary truths that he takes to distinguish human grasp of natural processes (in about one-quarter of our thinking). In Spinoza's *Ethics* there is no sign of such a sharply conceptualized distinction between human and brute mental capacities, "reason," or "knowledge." But, still, Spinoza's implicit comparisons of minds with regard to adequacy of knowledge perhaps foreshadows Leibniz's. In the Scholium to IIP29 Spinoza writes:

> I say that . . . the Mind has, not an adequate, but only a confused [and mutilated] knowledge, of itself, of its own Body, and of external bodies, so long as it perceives things from the common order of nature, i.e., so long as it is determined externally, from fortuitous encounters with things, to regard this or that, and not so long as it is determined internally, from the fact that it regards a number of things at once, to understand their agreements, differences, and oppositions. For so often as it is disposed internally, in this or another way, then it regards things clearly and distinctly. . . .

External determination from fortuitous encounters with things seems to be something very much like the kind of "inference" based on past experience of conjunction of events which Leibniz attributes to brutes. Internal determination—based on understanding agreements, differences, and oppositions, and (I suppose) their necessary consequences—involves a grasp of necessary truths. Spinoza's system (I've suggested) implies a less sharp distinction between brute and human cognitive capacities than we find in Leibniz's late work. Still, Spinoza seems to advance a notion similar to Leibniz's, that minds differ according to how many of their "thoughts" are based on insights into necessities, as opposed to mere "confused" association. That is, even if the minds of brutes, like those of all singular things, cannot *wholly* be denied some perceptions that are "adequate," *their* conceptions are much more extensively "inadequate" or "confused" than ours.[27] (I stress, though, that this is a very speculative interpretation. I do not deny that it is very unclear exactly what Spinoza *meant* to say about the cognitive capabilities of brutes [or, for that matter, other non-human minds]; and unclear also that he had considered views on the subject, to anything like the extent that Descartes and Leibniz, among other early modern figures, did.)

My suggestion, at any rate, is that Spinoza does not draw an absolutely sharp line between humans and non-humans with regard to various attributions of cognitive capacities (even *apart from* bare "sentience"). But within the human race, and across nature, there are very great differences in the degree of adequacy of the minds' conceptions, directly related to the differences in the capability of their bodies.[28]

I now turn to my final topic: Spinoza's conclusion concerning our "rights" with regard to the brutes, in relation to their sentience, nature, and "affects."

IV

Aside from a couple of definite indications that "brutes feel," Spinoza's most direct assertions in the *Ethics* about the mentality of the beasts are focused on their "affects." In one particularly evocative passage he writes:

> . . . the affects of animals which are called irrational . . . differ from men's affects as much as their nature differs from human nature. Both horse and man are driven by a Lust to procreate, but the one is driven by an equine Lust, the other by a human Lust. So also the Lusts and Appetites of Insects, fish, and birds must vary. Therefore, though each individual lives content with its nature, which constitutes it, and rejoices in it, nevertheless that life with which each is content and that joy are nothing but the idea or soul of the individual, and so the joy of the one differs in nature from the joy of the other as much as the essence of the one differs from the essence of the other.[29]

This passage occurs in the Scholium to Proposition 57 of Part III, "Each affect of each individual differs from the affect of another as much as the essence of the one from the essence of the other." Spinoza's theory of the affects in fact ties them to the conatus, or endeavor to persist in being, that he takes to constitute the essence of any individual. Thus, strictly, the affects, such as the "joy" of *any* two individuals must "differ." No doubt Spinoza supposes it to be clear that the essences—and hence the affects—of two humans are in some significant way much more *alike* than the essence of any human and the essence of any horse. But beyond that he does write, in more realist-sounding terms, of "human nature" in contrast to the "natures" of brutes.[30] In the first Scholium to Proposition 37 or Part IV he seems to draw a severe conclusion in part from this contrast:

> . . . the law against killing brutes is based more on empty superstition and womanish compassion than sound reason. The rational principle of seeking our own advantage teaches us the necessity of joining with men, but not with brutes, or things, whose nature is different from human nature; but the same right that they have against us, we have against them. Indeed, because the right of each one is

defined by its virtue, *or* power, men have a far greater right against the brutes than they have against men. Nevertheless I do not deny that the brutes feel (*bruta sentire*); but I deny, that we are therefore not permitted to consider our own advantage, use them at our pleasure, and treat them as is most convenient for us. For they do not agree in nature with us, and their affects are different in nature from human affects (see IIIP57S).

It is rather difficult to work out what exactly the pattern of reasoning is supposed to be in this associative and allusive passage.[31] Clearly, the "principle of seeking our own advantage" plays the *dominant* role in Spinoza's drive to the conclusion that we are permitted to treat brutes as we please. But there seem to be two other notions somehow involved in the argument (if such it is), in a kind of intermediate way. First, the principle requires us to join with other men, but not with brutes. And, second (and more perplexingly, I think), the fact that their *affects* are different in nature from ours—as argued in IIIP57S—has some important bearing on the lack of moral contraint on our behavior toward them.

But how, exactly, is the "difference in nature" between men and brutes supposed to contribute to the argument that brutes fall wholly outside of the constraints of human moral consideration? And why is the difference in "affects" so important specifically? I would like to pursue these questions a bit further, beginning with the introduction of one later passage from Part IV: a passage which draws the same conclusion as the Scholium to IVP37 just quoted; but which adduces some more straightforward claims about the potential of human-animal association.

In the Appendix to Part IV, section xvi, Spinoza asserts:

Apart from men we know no singular thing in nature whose Mind we can enjoy, and which we can join to ourselves in friendship, or some kind of association. And so whatever there is in nature apart from men, the principle of seeking our own advantage does not demand that we preserve it. Instead, it teaches us to preserve or destroy it according to its use, or to adapt it to our use in any way whatever.[32]

The basic idea, I take it, is that the "principle of seeking our own advantage" "demands" that we "preserve" just those things whose minds we can enjoy, and to which we can join in friendship, or "some kind of association." Otherwise, it "demands" that we preserve or destroy any given thing according to our convenience. Now, the claim that beasts never satisfy the exempting conditions specified here is bound to be roundly disputed. (And of course there seems to be a spread of *different* conditions offered. For instance, I believe that I have surely joined myself in "some kind of association" with several beasts, though I would not strictly count any of them among my "friends"; and am unsure how to answer the question whether I enjoy their minds—though I lean to saying yes.) But, even extending a lot of charity to Spinoza on these points, one can still press on with the question: How exactly does "difference in nature" between human and brutes help to underpin the conclusion that we need observe no moral constraints on our treatment of them?

What I am getting at is this. It really does not seem surprising that an ethics grounded on the principle of seeking our own advantage would fail to yield moral constraints on the treatment of beasts, or non-human nature generally. (Perhaps it would be *unenlightened* to limit constraints on destruction or harmful treatment to *short-term* advantage, where conditions of friendship and the like do not apply. And Spinoza's statements, while of course not opposing this observation, may be considered not sufficiently to address it. Further, Spinoza does not address the issue of *sharp conflicts* among human advantages: the birdwatcher's versus the land developer's, for example. But these are separate matters.) People who think that certain kinds of behavior toward non-human animals are clearly morally unacceptable (and I am one) are entitled to consider the conclusion Spinoza draws with regard to our treatment of the brutes at least a *prima facie* reductio of his general ethical position, insofar as it is based on the principle of seeking our own advantage. (We should just not be *surprised* that it turns out to have this particular consequence.) But I am not really concerned here with ethical criticism. I am, rather, interested in the question of how far Spinoza's position on our "rights" with regard to beasts connects with what we can discern of his views about the relation of brute and human minds, *beyond* the bare appeal to "seeking our own advantage."

The Appendix passage just quoted suggests that one consideration Spinoza wants to convey is this: the difference in nature between the minds of humans and non-humans *disqualifies the former from bonds of friendship (and the like) with humans*; so the brutes fail to be exempt from human exploitation according to the principle of seeking our own advantage. (The fact that they "feel" is beside the point.) But what, exactly, do claims about "difference in nature" turn on? And how, exactly, do they help undershore, or give added depth to the conclusion that our unlimited "rights" over animals derive from the principle of seeking our own advantage?

Over the centuries, as Richard Sorabji has shown in detail, many philosophers who concede sentience to brutes still maintain that we are justified in exploiting them *ad libitum*, on the grounds that we are "rational" and they are not. (It seems that sometimes the alleged impossibility of "friendship," or the like, with a non-rational being is implicated in the argument; and sometimes not.)[33] I've suggested that Spinoza's position on "the mind" does not permit an entirely sharp line to be drawn between humans and brutes with regard to "rationality." But, on anyone's interpretation, he does emphasize that there are *at least* large differences in understanding, or possession of adequate ideas, both among humans and across species. And in fact there is considerable emphasis, in IVP37 and preceding Propositions, on common adherence to "the guidance of reason" as the grounding of positive human relationships. So it seems quite likely that in his mind *part* of the relevant "difference in nature" that deprives the brutes of any "right" to restraint on our part is connected with the deficiency (if not complete lack) of "reason" in them, because of its implications for "friendship," or other relevant "association."[34]

What seems most striking about Spinoza's position, however, is his explicit appeal, at the end of the passage from IVP37S1, to his remarkable observations in IIIP57 concerning the *affects* of brutes, together with his stress on "friendship, or other association" in the Appendix to Part IV. We are, he says in IVP37S1, entitled to use brutes at our pleasure, "*For* they do not agree in nature with us, *and their affects are different in nature from human affects*" (see IIIP57S). And in the Appendix passage he also seems to signal an inference to a moral conclusion from a claim about enjoyment of minds, and the possibility of "joining in friendship," etc: "*And so* whatever there is in nature apart from man. . . ." My question is whether these allusive references to the difference of affects, and the possibility of "friendships and other associations" between men and beasts contribute in any clear and credible way to Spinoza's position about our unlimited "rights" with regard to the treatment of non-human animals. Here is one way of explaining why I think they do not.

It seems to me entirely plausible that an "essential" difference in affects between two beings, as well as differences in "rationality," should have bearing on the question of what kind of "associations" the two can form. Thus, insofar as our unlimited "rights" with regard to non-humans depends on a supposed impossibility of "friendships," or other relevant associations, between them and us, it makes sense that any essential difference of affects should be considered relevant to the case. But in a way this concession makes it all the more mysterious why issues of "friendship" (etc.) should be regarded as so crucial, with regard to our "rights" over beasts.[35]

Why *should not* my belief (after Spinoza) that a squirrel in my yard, or an osprey over the water—or for that matter a centipede in the bathtub—experiences joy in the life that it has, inhibit my eliminating that life, even *if* I think that its joy is "different in nature" from mine, and that accordingly I cannot be "friends" with it? Why shouldn't my perception of the affection that my dog or cat has towards me rationally enlist a sense of responsibility toward the creature, even *though* I acknowledge that "its essence is different from mine," and *agree* that therefore its affection toward me is different in nature from mine toward it? (Why, that is, apart from the naked principle of seeking my own advantage, as distinct from the more abstract issue of difference in nature, and specifically of affects, across species?)

The very evocativeness of Spinoza's own account of "the affects of animals which are called irrational" seems to undercut rhetorically his dismissal of their claim to any kind of moral consideration from us. And it reinforces the sense of a peculiar *argumentative* gap in Spinoza's inference from the lack of certain kinds of "association" between man and beasts—even supposing he is right about that—to the absence of moral constraints on our treatment of them.[36]

V

To sum up, in conclusion. Among the aspects of Spinoza's view of "mind" likely to seem attractive within the context of present-day philosophy is his anti-Cartesian conception of the mentality of brutes. I have argued, however, that his explicit attribution of sentience, and affects, to brutes is grounded in his general panpsychism, rather than any particularities of their bodies and behavior. In this important respect his position can hardly be seen as an antecedent of contemporary interest in animal cognition, bound up as that interest tends to be with evolutionary, ethological, and behavioral approaches. In passing, I have tried to assess what implications Spinoza's position might have with regard to the traditionally more controversial issue of the intelligence and rationality of beasts. Despite seemingly contrary implications of IVP35–37, it appears to me that he is committed to attributing some degree of understanding and reason to "other" minds, again on grounds deriving from his general panpsychism. Spinoza, in any case, explicitly opposes the view, often advanced today, that the mental capacities of non-human animals dictate moral restraints on our treatment of them. I have tried to sort out, to a degree, the reasoning he offers on behalf of this negative claim. Largely it derives, no doubt coherently, from the "principle of seeking our own advantage," which is fundamental to his general ethical position. But it is involved, as well, with notions about the limits of human association, which can be disputed to some extent. Additionally, Spinoza seems to aim at a distinct metaphysical grounding in the "difference in nature" between humans and beasts, particularly with regard to the affects. I have suggested that this line of thinking is unclear, and probably lacking in force.[37]

NOTES

1. See, especially, *E*IIP6 and IIIP2.

2. *E*IIP12. Below I cite and discuss Spinoza's specific statements about the "superiority" of minds, and consciousness.

3. See, for instance, AT VII, 160 ("First Replies").

4. Descartes's main assertion of this position—backed up in several of his *Replies to Objections*—occurs in Part V of the *Discourse on the Method*.

5. *Consciousness Explained* (Boston: Little, Brown, 1991), ch. 14, section 2.

6. "Man and Nature in Spinoza," in *Spinoza's Philosophy of Man*, edited by Jon Wetlesen (Oslo: Universitetsforlaget, 1978), 22.

7. "Spinoza's Environmental Ethics," *Inquiry*, 23, 295. For related discussion, see her book, *Part of Nature: Self-Knowledge in Spinoza's "Ethics"* (Ithaca: Cornell University Press, 1994), 155–58.

8. This is not to deny that Spinoza's "conatus" theory provides the basis for a conception of a living being different from Descartes's. Still, Delahunty's bland repetition of More's error, persisting through his discussion of the beast-man issue, amounts to a serious flaw. (*Spinoza* [London: Routledge, 1985], ch. 6, section 6)

9. Delahunty, *Spinoza*, 208. The second internal reference should actually be to *E*IIIP57S.

10. "Man and Nature," 22–23.

11. Naess does not ignore Spinoza's comments on our rights over beasts and other non-human individuals, but he tends to play them down. Among his several papers on

the subject is "Spinoza and Attitudes towards Nature," in *Spinoza—His Thought and Work*, edited by Nathan Rotenstreich and Normal Schneider (Jerusalem: Israel Academy of Sciences and Humanities, 1983).

12. See, for instance, Tom Regan, *The Case for Animal Rights* (Berkeley: University of California Press, 1983), 243; and Richard Sorabji, *Animal Minds and Human Morals* (Ithaca: Cornell University Press, 1993), 212. Sorabji also provides detailed information about a wide range of older—especially ancient and medieval—views about the moral implications of beasts' mentality.

13. In the comments mentioned in my final note, Curley seemed to endorse this view, too.

14. Curley observes, in a footnote to IIP13S (in his translation of the *Ethics*), that Spinoza's statement that all individuals are animate, though in different degrees, is "open to very different interpretations." Many would deny that Spinoza is committed to "feeling" throughout nature. While I make no apology for my own interpretation on this point, I want to stress that the *main* question at issue in the preceding paragraph is simply how to understand Spinoza's brief remark in support of the claim that brutes feel.

15. "Objects, Ideas and 'Minds': Comments on Spinoza's Theory of Mind," *The Philosophy of Baruch Spinoza*, edited by Richard Kennington (Washington, D.C.: Catholic University of America Press, 1980) (chapter 9 of this volume).

16. Perhaps a natural interpretation is that Spinoza has in mind *brain* complexity (as Rocco Gennaro has suggested in comments on an earlier draft of my paper). Maybe so; but, again, it needs to be explained what exactly "complexity" is supposed to mean, if this suggestion is to help much in illuminating a distinction between the sentient and the non-sentient—even supposing that Spinoza *does* intend to accommodate such a distinction in the face of his panpsychism. (I touch on a related point in note 28, below.) Incidentally, one needs to be careful about reading twentieth-century notions about the "complexity" of, say, mammalian or specifically human brains into seventeenth-century work—as I believe the briefest look at Descartes's account of the human brain in the *Treatise on Man* will show.

17. Even if I am right about Spinoza's grounds for this attribution, it is still the case that Spinoza offers a *reasoned* position against Descartes, unlike a surprising number of other philosophers of the period who opposed him. (See my "Animal Ideas," *Proceedings and Addresses of the American Philosophical Association* 69, no. 2, November 1995 [Chapter 31 of this volume].)

18. See Sorabji, *op. cit.* and Wilson, "Animal Ideas."

19. Leibniz addresses the issue, for example, in the Preface to the *New Essays On Human Understanding*, and elsewhere in that work. (I provide fuller citations in "Animal Ideas.") See also Rocco Gennaro's paper in *New Essays on the Rationalists*, edited by R. Gennaro and C. Huenemann (Oxford: Oxford University Press, forthcoming), section 6.

The issue of the "rationality" of brutes has surfaced again in recent times in, especially, Donald Davidson's essay "Rational Animals" (in *Actions and Events*, edited by Ernest LePore and Brian P. McLaughlin [Oxford: Blackwell's, 1985]). Davidson, like certain ancient thinkers, as well as Descartes, maintains that the legitimate attribution of rationality to beings is tied up with the beings' possession of linguistic capabilities. Spinoza, however, does not directly relate rationality to linguistic competence.

20. In comments on an earlier version of this paper (see final note), Edwin Curley observed that "unfortunately [for my argument] Spinoza does deny that brutes possess reason." The texts he cited are from TTP (Geb. III/8; xx, 12, III/124). They concern the opinion that the end of the State is not to change men "from rational beings into beasts"

(or "automata"). The remarks relate to the role of the state in ensuring human freedom. I would hesitate to put much weight on them in interpreting the logic of the *Ethics*, with regard to the assumption of "adequate ideas" throughout nature, or more subtle questions about the cognitive capacities of brutes. (See also note 27, below.)

21. Cf. IIP40S2#3.

22. Here again (I think) I disagree with Lloyd, who seems to suppose that a mind's capacity to form the common notions of reason requires its being the idea of a body "of a sufficiently complex structure." (*Part of Nature*, 159) Compare her comment on the previous page: "Reason is an expression of human nature, and it arises from the complexity of bodily structure that distinguishes human bodies." Here, as in the case of her remarks on sentience, I think she is too free with the term "complexity," and not sufficiently precise about textual support.

23. It is, of course, possible to argue that some of the implications of the *Ethics*, particularly with regard to the issue of "panpsychism," are unintended; that they should be dismissed as mere spin-offs of an overly optimistic pretension to argumentative rigor. I concede that Spinoza in the *Ethics*, makes no specific assertions about whether beasts lack or possess "reason" or "understanding" (but see note 20 above, on the *TTP*). Still, it seems to me that on this particular issue the implication that I take his system to yield— that beasts have some degree of understanding—is neither more implausible, *prima facie*, than its denial, nor uniformly opposed by his contemporaries.

24. See, again, IIP40S2#3.

25. This conclusion can also easily be reached from Spinoza's remarks on the affects of beasts, which I discuss below.

26. It seems to be widely agreed that Spinoza is quite derogatory in what he states and implies about the mentality of non-male humans. Ruth Barcan Marcus and Anne Jaap Jacobson have both suggested to me that it is worthwhile to consider the relations between major philosophers' views about non-male humans and their views about non-human animals. I think they are probably right; but here I am only concerned with seeing what can be established about Spinoza's position on the difference between man and beast. So, for one thing, I deal more casually with certain translation issues than I would have if questions of the mental significance of gender differences had been central to my concern.

27. It would follow that a tiny, but only a tiny, portion of brutes' minds is "eternal." (As much or more as in the case of human babies? Who can tell?) I doubt that this is what Curley had in mind in remarking that, for Spinoza, humans are not distinguished from brutes by having an immortal soul; but it is not necessarily an awkward consequence for a reading to yield. The issue of the "immortality" of beasts', as opposed to human, souls was a live one in seventeenth-century philosophy. Leibniz, for instance, seems rather proud of being able to affirm—against the Cartesians—the "natural indestructibility" of the souls of brutes as well as humans (though only the latter are granted admission into the Kingdom of Grace). While Spinoza's concept of "eternity of mind" is different from the generality of seventeenth-century conceptions of immortality, I think there are enough affinities for this comment to be relevant.

28. It might be objected that Spinoza's correlation of the superiority of a mind to its body's "capacity to do and suffer many things" does not straightforwardly yield the result that even a brilliant human mind, let alone an average one, is "superior" to the minds of all beasts. Consider a paralyzed theoretical physicist, who while unable to feed or clothe himself, or walk or even speak, can still function mentally at a high level. Is it right to attribute to such a person a "body capable of very much"; a *more capable body*

than, say, that of a physically unimpaired eagle, wolf, or whale? I think that Spinoza's sympathetic commentators tend to assume that when he writes of more capable bodies, he has in mind primarily the physical substratum of theoretical understanding, as opposed to (say) ability to move the limbs. I have no real problem with this particular sympathetic reading; but there does seem to be something rather perverse about his phrasing, if that is what he intends.

29. Note the *"are called* irrational," in connection with note 20, above.

30. I set aside here the issue, touched on by Lloyd in *Part of Nature*, of how to reconcile such realist-sounding talk about "natures" with the nominalist vein in Spinoza's thought, as expressed (especially) in the first Scholium of *E*IIP40.

31. Mary Midgeley observes, after citing this passage: "Many people today would, I think, simply echo this, including all the evident confusions. What principles are involved here?" (*Beast and Man: the Roots of Human Nature* [Ithaca: Cornell University Press, 1978], 352) Midgeley goes on to suggest that Spinoza is trying to acknowledge the importance of emotions in love, despite holding that the moral restraints we owe to other humans are based on our common possession of reason. Or at least, that's how I understand her. She observes that Spinoza's ethical position has very attractive features, while deploring the results of his "egoism."

32. According to the next paragraph (xvii), "The principal advantage which we derive from things outside us—apart from the experience and knowledge we acquire from observing them and changing them from one form into another—lies in the preservation of our body."

33. As Descartes observes to More, his denial of thought to beasts is not so much cruel to them as indulgent to humans, since it absolves us from the suspicion of crime when we kill and eat them. (AT V, 278–79; CSM-K, 366)

34. Curley, Lloyd, and Delahunty all place emphasis, in connection with the issue of "association," on the fact that beasts are unable to enter *political* associations with men—which may be tied to the lack of "reason." (They also cite remarks from TTP.) I don't deny that this is a relevant aspect of the issue, but to me it seems clearly not fully to accommodate the main passages on beasts in the *Ethics*, especially the comments about "difference of affects," and "friendship."

Sorabji, incidentally, sketches a variety of historical views about the possibilities of natural association, "belonging," or community between humans and brutes. (*Animal Minds and Human Morals*, especially ch. 10)

35. See also Midgeley, *op. cit.*, 351–53.

36. In *A Study of Spinoza's Ethics* (Indianapolis: Hackett, 1984) Jonathan Bennett offers a detailed and rather scathing critique of Spinoza's effort to move from the principle of seeking one's own advantage to "conservative," "collaborative" moral principles governing *inter-human* conduct, via appeal to "likeness" among humans (section 69). In a way my discussion here is (as far as I can see) complementary to his, in that I question Spinoza's movement from non-likeness between man and beast, to a dismissal of moral constraints on human treatment of the animals.

37. Edwin Curley provided detailed comments on an earlier version of this paper—with which he indicated total disagreement—at an American Philosophical Association (Pacific Division) symposium on Spinoza and contemporary philosophy of mind, arranged and chaired by Don Garrett (1995). Although in general I have not been converted to Curley's views on Spinoza on animals, his comments have led to fairly substantial revisions in presentation; and I cordially thank him. Other improvements have been made in response to comments by Jonathan Bennett, Michael Della Rocca, Rocco

Gennaro, and Charles Huenemann, for which also I'm very grateful. I'm only too well aware of not having been able to reflect all of their perceptive criticisms and suggestions adequately in the revised version.

The paper was also presented at colloquia at Union College and Carleton College in the spring of 1997. On both occasions the discussions were imaginative and stimulating. The lack of a detailed record of them has resulted, unfortunately, in my losing track of some of the points that impressed me at the time; but I thank the contributors for reinforcing my interest in the subject, and apologize for probably neglecting changes they proved I should make.

Superadded Properties: The Limits of Mechanism in Locke

I

Locke's official, familiar position on the affections of body runs as follows. All the qualities of a body belong to one of the following classes; primary, secondary, or the "third sort" (known in the literature as tertiary). Primary qualities are all and only the essential or universal qualities of body,

> such as are utterly inseparable from the Body, in what estate soever it be; such as in all the alterations and changes it suffers, all the force can be used upon it, it constantly keeps; and such as Sense constantly finds in every particle of Matter, which has bulk enough to be perceived, and the Mind finds inseparable from every particle of Matter, though less than to make itself singly be perceived by our Senses. (*Essay* II, viii, 9, pp. 134–5)[1]

In this passage the list Locke gives of the primary qualities is: Solidity, Extension, Figure, Motion, or Rest, and Number. (Other lists in the *Essay* vary slightly from this, especially in the tendency to include Position.) Locke also identifies the primary qualities as "the real" qualities of bodies, and says that they "are always [in bodies] . . . and are sometimes perceived by us" (*Essay* II, viii, 22, p. 140). More exactly (Locke does not make this qualification explicit, but he clearly does conform to it) primary qualities are either these "universal qualities of bodies" or their determinates.

Secondary and tertiary qualities are not simply extra properties a body may have, over and above its primary qualities. Rather, they are only "powers" a body has to produce certain effects on other entities *by virtue of its primary qualities*. Thus, secondary qualities are identified with a body's powers to produce *sensible ideas in us* (other than the ideas of primary qualities). Or, as Locke says, they are

> . . . nothing in the Objects themselves, but Powers to produce various Sensations in us by their *primary Qualities*, i.e. by the Bulk, Figure, Texture, and Motion of their insensible parts, as Colours, Sounds, Tasts, *etc*. (*Essay* II, viii, 10, p. 135)

Tertiary qualities, on the other hand, are those powers that bodies have to produce changes in the primary qualities of other bodies, thereby affecting the ways the latter operate on our senses (*ibid.*).

As the passage about secondary qualities partly shows, Locke's official position is not just that a body's secondary and tertiary qualities derive from its primary qualities. Rather he holds specifically that the former qualities—and indeed all of a body's "Powers and Operations"—"flow from" the primary qualities of the body's "insensible corpuscles" or "inner constitution"—in other words, from its "real essence." Many passages show that Locke conceives the relation of real essence to derivative properties as analogous to that between the definition of a geometrical figure and the properties deducible from the definition. Because God and (probably) angels know things through the real essences, these beings do possess an a priori, deductive science of nature. Human beings, on the other hand, lack faculties to obtain knowledge of the insensible constitutions of things. Hence we can obtain knowledge of the properties co-existing in bodies only through the very limited, slow, and imperfect means of experimenting upon them.[2]

Much recent scholarship on the *Essay* has stressed Locke's indebtedness for the distinction between primary and secondary qualities (as well as the notion of inner constitution of insensible parts) to the corpuscularian science of his day—and particularly the work of Robert Boyle [1], [7], [8], [9]; see also [15], pp. 5f.; [6] p. 204; [4], pp., 102–106. A number of these critics have been concerned to set the record right, as they see it, by arguing that Locke's commitment to the distinction did not rest on the flimsy philosophical "arguments" presented in the *Essay*. (Hence Berkeley's attempts to overthrow the distinction by attacking these arguments were beside the point.) On this view Locke's real basis for his primary-secondary qualities distinction is the "modern" scientific assumption that only a few sorts of qualities figure in the correct scientific explanations of phenomena. The "support" or "basis" for the distinction may then be seen to lie primarily in the "success" of this science in providing adequate explanations of phenomena [9], p. 3; [8], pp.18–19, 23, 71.[3]

I do not in any way deny the influence of the corpuscularian theory of nature on what I have called Locke's official position. However, I want to show here that Locke's official, familiar position is in conflict with another set of views he espouses in the *Essay*, the Correspondence with Stillingfleet, and elsewhere. My primary objective is not the relatively sterile one of establishing yet another group of "inconsistencies" in Locke. My main aim is rather to indicate the extent to which Locke grasped the *limitations* of the explanatory capacities of Boylean mechanism, from both philosophical and scientific points of view. Specifically, I will argue that, his official position notwithstanding, Locke does not consistently maintain that all a body's properties stand in comprehensible or conceivable relations to its Boylean "primary qualities," or can be said to flow from them. (At the same time, in his self-assigned "underlaborer" capacity, he was not able to free himself from corpuscularian presuppositions about matter; hence the two inconsistent points of view remained side by side throughout his work.) At the minimum, Locke's claims that some presumed properties of matter *cannot be conceived* as "natural" consequences of Boylean primary qualities imply that human ignorance about bodies is not entirely a question of our lacking access to the details of any particular body's "insensible corpuscles." (Locke himself sometimes makes this point explicitly; cf. *Essay* 545.) Beyond this, however, Locke holds doctrinairely with respect to some properties—and hints with respect to others—that they *cannot be* the natural consequences of the operations of Boylean corpuscles. We must rather regard them as "super-added" or "annexed" to such operations by God.

I will begin by considering Locke's treatment of thought or mind in relation to body—a neglected subject in the literature. While it may at first appear that his views on this issue constitute only a limited and unsurprising qualification on the official position, I will go on to argue that this is not the case. Rather, Locke's views about the relation of thought and matter turn out ultimately to undercut the central claim that a body's sensible qualities flow from the primary qualities of insensible particles—and with it the notion that secondary qualities are explainable in terms of primary ones. In a subsequent section I will go on to show that Locke's sense of the intrinsic inadequacy of Boylean principles of explanation goes well beyond the problem of understanding thought and its modes.

II

It is, of course, well known that primary, secondary, and tertiary qualities of bodies are not the only properties or affections of substances that Locke recognizes. For he maintains that by reflection on "the operation of our own minds within us" we receive ideas of the various qualities and modes of thought:

> which Operations, when the Soul comes to reflect on, and consider, do furnish the Understanding with another set of *Ideas*, which could not be had from things without: and such are, *Perception, Thinking, Doubting, Believing, Reasoning, Knowing, Willing*, and all the different actings of our own Minds; which we being conscious of, and observing in our selves, do from these receive into our Understandings, as distinct *Ideas*, as we do from Bodies affecting our Senses. (*Essay* II, i, 4, p. 105)[4]

Now, Locke's recognition of mental properties and "operations," over and above the primary, secondary, and tertiary qualities of body, may not at first sight seem to conflict in any way with his official position concerning the properties of body. For it may at first appear that Locke accepts the Cartesian view that mental properties are *not* properties of body. Much of Locke's discussion of mind in the *Essay* strongly suggests a Spirit-Body dichotomy—with spirits, like bodies, being attributed an inscrutable, distinct real essence of their own (*Essay* II, xxiii, 28–30, pp. 311–13). And sometimes in the *Essay* Locke even speaks of spirits as *immaterial* substances (cf. *Essay* II, xxiii, 15, pp. 305–306). Yet when (in the *Essay* and later works) Locke considers the question directly, he always affirms it is *possible* that our thoughts do not pertain to an immaterial substance, but rather inhere in our bodies. (Cf. *Essay* IV, iii, 6, pp. 540–41 ; *CS* p. 33.) (In these contexts Locke maintains that "spirit" should really be taken to mean just "thinking thing.") It is true that Locke also holds in such passages that it is "probable" that the subject in our thoughts is immaterial (*Essay* II, xxvii, 25, p. 345; IV, iii, 6, p. 541; *CS* p. 33). But in fact he offers no good reason for even this qualified leaning toward mind-body dualism. (In fact, Locke does ascribe sensation and even "thought" to animals; yet he shows no inclination to attribute immaterial souls to *them*. It seems to follow that on Locke's principles thought not only *can* inhere in a corporeal subject but in many cases actually does.)[5] It appears that Locke would have been more warranted in maintaining unqualified agnosticism on the immaterial substance issue.

At the minimum, anyway, it is *possible* that modes of thought (including human thought) inhere in bodies.[6] Suppose then that they do. Can they be brought within the scope of the official doctrine? That is, can we say that an organism's thoughts or sensations may either count among the primary qualities of the body's insensible corpuscles? The answer to this question is straightforwardly negative. Locke certainly doesn't want to count thought and sensation among the primary and inseparable qualities of matter (cf. e.g. *Essay* IV, x, 10, p. 624). But further he insistently and repeatedly (and, of course, plausibly) denies that thought can conceivably be produced by the interactions characteristic of Boylean corpuscles:

> It is as repugnant to the *Idea* of senseless Matter, that it should *put into itself* Sence, Perception, and Knowledge, as it is repugnant to the *Idea* of a Triangle, that it should put into itself greater Angles than two right ones. (*Essay* IV, x, 5, pp. 620–21)

Moreover:

> Matter, *incogitative Matter* and Motion, whatever changes it might produce of Figure and Bulk *could never produce Thought* . . . (*Essay* IV, x, 10, p. 623)

Or as Locke also puts it, the only change of which matter is susceptible, that of change in "juxtaposition" of its parts, could never in itself account for the production of thought:

> Unthinking Particles of Matter, however put together, can have nothing thereby added to them, but a new relation of Position, which 'tis impossible should give thought and knowledge to them. (*Essay* IV, x, 16, p. 627)

Locke maintains the "repugnancy" or contradiction in the notion of incogitative matter producing thought is akin to that in the notion of matter's coming to be from nothing.[7]

Locke draws two related conclusions from these observations. First, since thought does exist in the world, yet cannot have been produced by matter, there must be an eternal cogitative being.[8] This claim provides the basis for Locke's argument for the existence of God, on which he places considerable weight in the *Essay* and elsewhere. Second, the presence of thought and sensation in creatures can only be due to acts of "superaddition" on the part of this eternal cogitative being. What we cannot know is whether he has "superadded" to our bodies just the property of thought itself, or rather an immaterial thinking substance (*Essay* IV, iii, 6, pp. 540–41). This position is reiterated in the Correspondence with Stillingfleet and elsewhere.

Now Locke's claim that thought cannot be produced by material corpuscles does lead to certain problems. It yields the somewhat anomalous result that a property as traditionally "essential" to us humans as rational thought may lack natural connection with our Lockean real essences.[9] It raises the question of what can be meant by saying a property belongs to or inheres in an object, when that property does not derive from the object's real essence.[10] Also, it seems flatly inconsistent with the interesting Lockean position (noted above in passing) that thoughts and sensations, like any other "observable" properties, must flow from some hidden inner constitution.[11] In other respects, however, the result may seem only an unremarkable adaptation of a traditional argument to the effect that matter cannot produce thought.[12] And one might simply conclude that Locke is after all a sort of doctrinaire dualist with respect to the mind-body issue—distinguishing the natural properties of matter (the traditionally, physical ones) from those properties which cannot at any rate be *natural* properties of matter: the traditionally mental ones. That the position requires an *ad hoc* modification in the familiar Lockean scheme of properties, and raises some problems of consistency and interpretation with respect to other Lockean notions may seem not especially surprising or troubling.

But Locke does not restrict his observations concerning the impossibility of a mechanical explanation or "production" of thought to the question of the possible relation of "the mind" to "the body." He also argues that mechanistic processes cannot be conceived as capable of producing certain of our sensible ideas except by divine annexation:

> 'Tis evident that the bulk, figure, and motion of several Bodies about us, produce in us several Sensations, as of Colours, Sounds, Tastes, Smells, Pleasure and Pain, *etc*. These mechanical Affections of Bodies, having no affinity at all with those *Ideas*, they produce in us, (there being no conceivable connexion between any impulse of any sort of Body, and any perception of a Colour, or Smell, which we find in our Minds) we can have no distinct knowledge of such Operations beyond our Experience; and can reason no otherwise about them, than as effects produced by the appointment of an infinitely Wise Agent, which perfectly surpass our Comprehensions. (*Essay* IV, iii, 28, pp. 558–59)

It seems to follow that the ideas in our minds may be doubly "superadded": they occur because God has (perhaps) superadded to our bodies the property of thought, and has *also* annexed to certain motions of matter the power to "produce" particular ideas in us. In the following passage Locke in fact links the two levels of superaddition:

> What certainty of Knowledge can any one have that some perceptions, such as e.g. pleasure and pain, should not be in some bodies themselves, after a certain manner modified and moved, as well as that they should be in an immaterial Substance, upon the Motion of the parts of Body: Body as far as we can conceive being able

only to strike and affect body; and Motion, according to the utmost reach of our *Ideas*, being able to produce nothing but Motion, so that when we allow it to produce pleasure or pain, or the *Idea* of a Colour, or sound, we are fain to quit our Reason, go beyond our *Ideas*, and attribute it wholly to the good Pleasure of our Maker. For since we must allow he has annexed Effects to Motion, which we can no way conceive Motion able to produce, what reason have we to conclude, that he could not order them as well to be produced in a Subject we cannot conceive capable of them, as well as in a Subject we cannot conceive the motion of Matter can in any way operate upon? (*Essay* IV, iii, 6, p. 541)

The notion that there is a merely "arbitrary" connection between motions of matter and sensations is of course familiar from Descartes.[13] (Locke is perhaps self-consciously putting an anti-Cartesian twist on the familiar Cartesian notion in the passage just quoted.) But Locke's espousal of this view has a special interest and importance. On the one hand it leads to conflict with the official view that an object's sensible qualities flow with a sort of geometrical necessity from the primary qualities of its insensible corpuscles. On the other hand, it shows rather more sensitivity to the problem of what would constitute an "explanation" of a secondary quality that is evident in the work of Boyle—or, I think, in some recent pro-Lockean commentaries.[14]

To see that this is so, we need to consider more carefully what might be meant by Locke's official doctrine that a body's secondary qualities flow from the primary qualities of its inner constitution. It is true, as we've seen, that Locke identifies secondary qualities as powers in bodies to produce ideas in us, thus distinguishing the quality in the body from the idea or sensation the quality causes us to have. And at first thought it might seem that Locke could consistently hold that a body's powers to produce ideas flow naturally from its real essence, while also maintaining that the ideas themselves are arbitrarily annexed to whatever motions of matter habitually "cause" them. But of course this is not really the case. For it follows from Locke's account that a body has its powers to produce ideas only *because of* the divine acts of annexation. Therefore, even when we keep Locke's distinction between qualities and ideas or sensations firmly in mind, we find conflict with the official position that there is in reality an a priori conceptual connection between a body's real essence and its secondary qualities.

There is one other move to consider here. One recent critic has argued that a secondary quality for Locke is just a "texture" [2]. So we might suppose that when Locke says the secondary qualities flow from the real essence like the properties of a triangle from its definition, he means that a body's surface textures derive from the primary qualities of its insensible corpuscles. On this view there is surely no conflict between the official position and the claim that the matter-sensation relation is arbitrary.

There are, however, numerous reasons for rejecting this interpretation of the claim that secondary qualities flow from primary ones. Two should suffice for present purposes. First, as the same critic acknowledges (indeed argues) what

Locke calls the names of secondary qualities—such as "colour", "gold," etc.—actually refer to the ideas of secondary qualities (sensations), not the textures that cause them.* Yet Locke cites the "particular shining yellowness" of the gold ring on his finger as an *example* of a "quality" supposed to flow from its real essence (*Essay* II, xxxi, 5, p. 379). Second, the proposed interpretation makes nonsense of the passages where Locke says "there is no discoverable connection between any *secondary Quality*, and those *primary Qualities* that it depends on," contrasting this "more incurable part of Ignorance" with our "Ignorance of the primary Qualities of the insensible Parts of Bodies." The problem Locke sees here is precisely that "our Minds [are not] able to discover any connexion between these primary qualities of Bodies, and the sensations that are produced in us by them" (*Essay* IV, iii, 12–13, p. 545). For these and other reasons I conclude that Locke's talk of secondary qualities flowing from primary ones cannot be freed from the implication that a body's sensible appearances flow from its real essence. But this implication is evidently contradicted by his claims about the arbitrary relation of sensation to the operations of matter.

It is true there is another, quite different way of trying to reconcile Locke's talk of divine annexation of sensation to matter with his official position. Thus, someone might object to my interpretation of Locke that there is no need to construe such passages with metaphysical literalness. Perhaps all Locke really means to say is that *we* are unable in any way to conceive the rational connection between primary qualities and ideas of colors, tastes, etc.—not that there is no such connection to be grasped.[15]

This suggestion raises a complex textual problem which I do not have space to deal with adequately here. But for present purposes a few observations may suffice. First, the notion that sensations really can be derived rationally from material causes (had we but faculties to perceive the connection) is at best of doubtful consistency with Locke's firm doctrine that matter cannot naturally produce thought. Second, Locke's famous passage about a man with "microscopical eyes" (*Essay* II, xxiii, 12, p. 303) seems to indicate that someone who did grasp the real essences of things would not thereby come to have a rational explanation or derivation of their sensible appearances. (Rather, the original appearances would drop out of his conception of things altogether.) Third, as we will soon see, Locke says doctrinairely of other properties—especially gravity—that they cannot naturally arise from matter (sc. as Locke and other corpuscularians conceive it). But finally, even if we grant that Locke "only" means to deny there is any conceivable (to us) connection between material cause and sensation, we are still left with some important problems for Locke's official position, and for recent interpretations (and partial defenses) of his primary and secondary quality distinction. For one thing, the reasons and motivation for holding that secondary qualities do flow from primary ones are still, at the least, brought sharply into question. For another, the notion that the primary-secondary quality distinction can be made to rest on the "explanatory success" of Boylean science obviously fares no better on the epistemological interpretation of the "annexation" and "superaddition" passages than on the metaphysical one.

The important point, at any rate, is that Locke's reflections on the fundamental incomprehensibility of the primary-secondary quality relation seem to show more philosophical originality and insight than does the official position itself.

III

I will now briefly argue that Locke's reservations about the explanatory capacities of Boylean principles are not restricted to areas implicated in the "mind-body problem," but also extend to phenomena that unequivocally fall within the range of physics. The most explicit case is that of gravity. In the *Essay* Locke remarks that impulse is the only way in which we can conceive bodies to operate. (This is good Boyleanism.) However, after studying Newton's *Principia* he became convinced of the reality of gravitational attraction. Interestingly enough, his subsequent treatment of the property of gravity closely parallels his treatment of thought.[16] Thus he writes in *Some Thoughts Concerning Education*:

> . . . it is evident, that by mere matter and motion, none of the great phaenomena of nature can be resolved: to instance but in that common one of gravity, which I think impossible to be explained by any natural operation of matter, or any other law of motion, but the positive will of a superiour Being so ordering it. (*TE*, p. 184)

Or, as he writes to Stillingfleet (*CS*, p. 463):

> You ask "how can my way of liberty agree with the idea that bodies can operate only by motion and impulse?" Answ. By the omnipotency of God, who can make all things agree, that involve not a contradiction. It is true, I say [*Essay* II, viii, 11] "that bodies operate by impulse, and nothing else." And so I thought when I writ it, and can yet conceive no other way of their operation. But I am since convinced by the judicious Mr. Newton's incomparable book, that it is too bold a presumption to limit God's power, in this point, by my narrow conceptions. The gravitation of matter towards matter, by ways inconceivable to me, is not only a demonstration that God can, if he pleases, put into bodies powers and ways of operation, above what can be derived from our idea of body, or can be explained by what we know of matter, but also an unquestionable and every where visible instance, that he has done so. (*CS*, pp. 467–68)

Since "our idea of body" is precisely what is supposed to be codified in Locke's list of primary qualities, I take this pronouncement about gravity to be an indication that the powers of a body are not fully derivable, even in principle, from the primary qualities of its insensible particles.

The first of these passages indicates that gravity is just an *illustration* of the general truth that the phenomena of nature are not in general intelligible through Boylean concepts alone. The claim is illustrated in other ways in various passages of the *Essay*. Consider for example the following:

> In some of our *Ideas* there are certain Relations, Habitudes, and Connexions, so visibly included in the Nature of the *Ideas* themselves, that we cannot conceive them separable from them, by any Power whatsoever. And in these only, we are

capable of certain and universal Knowledge. Thus the *Idea* of a right-lined Triangle necessarily carries with it an equality of its Angles to two right ones. Nor can we conceive this Relation, this connexion of these two *Ideas*, to be possibly mutable, or to depend on any arbitrary Power, which of choice made it thus, or could make it otherwise. But the coherence and continuity of the parts of Matter; the production of Sensation in us of Colours and Sounds, *etc.* by impulse and motion; nay, the original Rules and Communication of Motion being such, wherein we can discover no natural connexion with any *Ideas* we have, we cannot but ascribe them to the arbitrary Will and good Pleasure of the Wise Architect. (*Essay* IV, iii, 29, pp. 556–60; cf. II, xxiii, 28, p. 311)

"Coherence and continuity of the parts of Matter" have no more claim to being "natural" consequences of the primary qualities of matter than thought or gravity. The point is made again in those places where Locke is arguing that thought is no more opaque to our understanding than body; for example:

'tis as *easie . . . to have a clear idea how the Soul thinks, as how Body is extended.* For since Body is no farther, nor otherwise extended than by the union and cohesion of its solid parts, we shall very ill comprehend the *extension* of Body, without understanding wherein consists the union and cohesion of its parts; which seems to me as incomprehensible, as the manner of Thinking, and how it is performed. (*Essay* II, xxiii, 24, p. 309)

In such passages as these Locke again goes well beyond his customary claim that we cannot have a priori knowledge of the powers and operations of bodies because we do not have "faculties" suited to comprehending the structures of their insensible corpuscles. He is in effect indicating (though he would never put the matter in this way) that most of what goes on in the world is incomprehensible from the point of view of Boylean mechanism. From that point of view, even the "primary" qualities of body, understood in general terms, involve features as incomprehensible as thinking itself. However, it does not occur to Locke directly to challenge the Boylean concept of matter. Rather he once again has recourse to gestures in the direction of arbitrary divine acts of combination and addition.[17]

IV

Recent commentators, wanting to free Locke from a history of Berkeleyan "misunderstandings," have stressed his scientific realism and Boylean orthodoxy. I have tried in the present essay to show that Locke also had some significant insights into the limitations of Boyleanism as a philosophy and even as a science. I have argued, however, that these insights led him into inconsistency with other central doctrines of his philosophy.

It is sometimes noted that Locke, for all his incorporation of Boylean theory into his philosophy, explicitly characterized that theory as an uncertain "hypothesis." It is less frequently noted (but also true) that Locke seems to have believed it was the best theory of matter we could possibly arrive at, even though there was no way of establishing its truth (*Essay* IV, iii, 16. pp. 547–48). Now we know Locke was wrong in thinking the conceptual and empirical limitations of Boyleanism were in principle unsurmountable. It is natural to wonder what the effect on other aspects of Locke's philosophy would have been, had he in fact come to envisage a more modern, dynamic theory of nature (one that incorporated for example the concepts of attractive and repulsive forces as straightforwardly physical). Rather than speculating directly on the answer to this question, I will offer in conclusion a few reflections on why it is hard to arrive at any sense of what the answer should be.

First, Locke does not tell us why he embraces the rationalist notion of an a priori deductive science of nature to the extent that he does (namely, for "superior beings"). It may be that a relatively simplistic notion of the primary qualities of body was necessary for this notion to maintain its hold. (Although, as Locke's case proves, the *strictly* geometric Cartesian concept is not required.) Hence if Locke had given up the Boylean theory of matter, he might also have abandoned all notion of a divine deductive science of nature, even though problems of "comprehensibility" (e.g. of cohesiveness and gravity) in some ways would have become less intractable.

Second, one often has the sense in reading Locke that the talk of superaddition, annexation, and inherent incomprehensibility, while partly a reflection of the inadequacies of accepted contemporary scientific principles, also masks still deeper philosophical insights. Materialist principles far more advanced than Boyle's have not so far thrown much light on the problem of how the operations of body "produce" conscious experience—or on the problem of how to avoid the problem. And when Locke maintains that we could never thoroughly comprehend what holds the world together, he may partly have been pointing to certain philosophical problems about the nature of causal interaction that are, indeed, still with us (see, especially, *Essay* II, xxiii, 23–25, pp. 308–10).

Finally; it must be conceded that Locke sometimes simply ignored the limitations of mechanism, even with respect to so intractable a problem as the relation of thought to matter. We have noted that Locke argues insistently that thought could not arise naturally from Boylean corpuscles—and hence, it would seem to follow, from the real essences of bodies as he conceived them. Alas, there are passages too where Locke quite cheerfully treats human "Sense, voluntary Motion, and Reason" as consequences of the *same* real essence as e.g. our "peculiar Shape" (*Essay* IV, vi, 15, pp. 589–90; cf *CS*, p. 410). It is possible to take these passages as evidence that the Boylean assumptions of Locke's official position, and the difficulties they lead him into, are not even as central as I have made them here. If this is so, one might hold that the issue of the adequacy or inadequacy of any particular science is not very relevant to the correct understanding of Locke's philosophy. While I myself do not accept this result, I freely acknowledge that such passages raise questions about the order of priorities among Locke's various commitments—and in particular about the level at which his Boylean commitments operate.[18]

REFERENCES

[1] Alexander, Peter, "Boyle and Locke on Primary and Secondary Qualities," in I. C. Tipton (ed.), *Locke on Human Understanding* (reprinted from *Ratio*, Vol. 16 (1974)), pp. 51–67.

[2]——, "The Names of Secondary Qualities", *Proceedings of The Aristotelian Society*, n.s. v. 77 (1976–7), pp. 203–220.

[3] Ayers, M. R., "The Ideas of Powers and Substance in Locke's Philosophy," in Tipton (reprinted from *Philosophical Quarterly*, Vol. 25 (1975)), pp. 1–27.

[4] Bennett, Jonathan, *Locke, Berkeley, Hume: Central Themes* (Oxford, 1971).

[5] Bolton, M. B., "The Origin of Locke's Doctrine of Primary and Secondary Qualities," *Philosophical Quarterly*, Vol. 26 (1976), pp. 305–16.

[6] Buchdahl, Gerd, *Metaphysics and the Philosophy of Science* (Cambridge, Mass., 1969), Ch. IV.

[7] Curley, E. M., "Locke, Boyle, and the Distinction Between Primary and Secondary Qualities," *Philosophical Review*, vol. 81 (1976), pp. 438–64.

[8] Mackie, J. L., *Problems from Locke* (Oxford, 1976).

[9] Mandelbaum, Maurice, *Philosophy, Science and Sense Perception* (Baltimore, 1964), Ch. 1.

[10] Mattern, R. M., *Locke on the Essence and Powers of Soul*, Princeton University, June 1975 (unpublished Ph.D. dissertation).

[11] Mijuskovic, B. L., *The Achilles of Rationalist Arguments* (The Hague, 1974).

[12] Schofield, R. K, *Mechanism and Materialism: British Natural Philosophy in an Age of Reason* (Princeton, 1970).

[13] Wachsberg, M. M., "Locke on the Substance of the Mind," Princeton University, July 1977 (unpublished).

[14] Wilson, M. D., review of [15], *Synthèse*, vol. 26 (1973), pp. 172–78.

[15] Yolton, J. W., *Locke and the Compass of the Human Understanding*, (Cambridge, 1970).

[16]——, "The Science of Nature" in Yolton (ed.), *Locke: Problems and Perspectives* (Cambridge, 1969).

[17] Hall, M. B. *Robert Boyle on Natural Philosophy: An Essay with Selections from His Writings* (Bloomington: Indiana University Press, 1965).

NOTES

1. The abbreviation *Essay* is used throughout for John Locke, *An Essay Concerning Human Understanding*, edited with an Introduction, etc. by Peter H. Nidditch (Oxford, 1975). For numbered references, see above.

2. One representative passage is the following:

The whole extent of our Knowledge, or Imagination, reaches not beyond our own Ideas, limited to our ways of Perception. Though yet it be not to be doubted, that Spirits of a higher rank than those immersed in Flesh, may have as clear Ideas of

the radical Constitution of Substances, as we have of a Triangle, and so perceive
how all their Properties and Operations flow from thence: but the manner how they
come by that Knowledge, exceeds our Conceptions. (*Essay* III, xi, 23, p. 520)

See also, e.g., IV, vi, 11, p. 585; IV, iii, 25, pp. 556–7; II, xxxi, 6, p. 379. The latter
passages make explicit the view that knowledge of real essences provides a priori knowledge of derivative properties, and the identification of real essences with primary qualities of insensible corpuscles.

3. Of course Locke's twentieth-century commentators are aware that the move from
"only these properties are needed for scientific explanation" to "only these properties are
really in bodies" involves (as Mackie puts it) "a philosophical step" [8], p. 19. A number
of them seem to me rather too tolerant of this "step," but that is another matter.

4. Locke normally speaks of "powers" or "operations" or "actions" of spirits, rather
than "properties" or "qualities." While I do not regard this tacit terminological distinction
as trivial, I believe it is unimportant for my purposes here. Locke does sometimes speak
of "Qualities or Properties of Spirit"; cf. *Essay* II, xxiii, 30, p. 313.

5. The claim that Locke has no good philosophical basis for holding that it is probable
our minds are immaterial substances has been argued persuasively and in detail by Mil-
ton Wachsberg [13]. Wachsberg places stress on Locke's statements about animals, and
also shows that the notion of an immaterial substance of mind does no real work for
Locke, since he holds that the issue of immateriality is irrelevant to such concerns as
personal identity and immortality. I am grateful to Wachsberg for permitting me to cite
this so-far-unpublished work, which has influenced the present essay considerably.

6. "Possible" here may be read metaphysically as well as epistemically, since Locke
holds God can bring about anything that does not involve a repugnancy or contradiction;
see below, pp. 200–201.

7. Locke tries to maintain a distinction between (on the one hand) perceiving a repugnancy or contradiction in the idea of something (e.g. matter producing thought), and (on
the other hand) not being able to conceive how something is possible (e.g. how thought
can inhere in body). In the former case we can conclude the thing is really impossible,
but in the latter case we cannot. This distinction is, I'm afraid, both tenuous and ill-
defended; however, I cannot discuss it further here.

8. Locke does not consider the possibility that something other than matter or thought
might have originated thought.

9. There are, however, passages where Locke says just the opposite—a point I will
consider below.

10. Martha Bolton has argued that Locke adopted the doctrine of primary qualities in
the final draft of the *Essay* partly to solve the problem of what it is for various powers to
belong to the same thing ([5], p. 316). Somewhat similarly, M. R. Ayers holds it is
Locke's view that when we say a group of properties all belong to one thing what we
mean is more or less that they "are reasonably presumed due to the same underlying
structure" [3] p. 85.

11. Oddly enough, Locke's agnosticism about the substance of mind sometimes seems
to be partly based on the observation that we are ignorant of inner constitutions: cf. e.g.,
Essay IV, iii, 6, p. 543.

12. See Mijuskovic [11] for the historical antecedents of Locke's reasoning.

13. Descartes seems to treat sensible ideas of primary qualities and of secondary
qualities as alike in this respect, whereas Locke often stresses the inconceivability
of how motions produce ideas of *secondary* qualities. (But sometimes Locke too indi-

cates that there's a *general* problem about the relation of motions to ideas: see next note.).

14. In *EM* Locke explicitly concedes his inability to explain or render intelligible "how I perceive" or "how ideas are incited in me by motion." See e.g. §10, p. 217 and §16, p. 219. Sometimes, though, Locke talks about explainability of phenomena, or even of the ideas of secondary qualities, just as cheerfully as Boyle. Cf. *Essay* 286–7 (II, xxi, §73. Cp., e.g. [17], 234–5, 238–9, and [6], pp. 204–205.

*Here I misstated Peter Alexander's view. He holds that the "names of secondary qualities" in Locke refer to physical textures, not sensations. I'm grateful to George Pitcher for pointing out this error, shortly after the article appeared.

15. This is Ayers' view: cf. [3], p. 100. He presents it rather doctrinairely, without considering the possibility of arguments on the other side. I do not deny it has some textual support, even beyond the contradictions generated for Locke by the metaphysical interpretation (cf. *Essay* 388). Yolton seems to hold a similar view; unfortunately, his textual reference does not support it ([16], p. 118). Alexander gives a more "metaphysical" reading to Locke's talk of there being no conceivable connection between primary qualities and the ideas of secondary qualities ([I], p. 76). At the same time, however, Alexander provides an excellent example of what I find puzzling in most recent Locke scholars' approach to this issue. *On the one hand*, he holds that what recommends the primary-secondary quality distinction is the explanatory power of the corpuscularian hypotheses: "In terms of matter and motion, Boyle's two grand principles, we can explain the effect of bodies upon one another, and upon us to produce ideas." ([1], p. 70). *On the other hand*, he holds that the inconceivability of a mechanical explanation of sensation is "not particularly involved in the distinction between primary and secondary qualities" (p. 76). I think these two views are inconsistent. (See also [14], p. 176, for some further doubts about the uses of "explanation" in Locke scholarship.)

16. In [10] Ruth Mattern devotes a section to "The Extent of Mechanism in Locke's Early and Later Views." She argues that even before he acknowledges the non-mechanical power of gravity, Locke "does admit some cases of non-mechanical causation in bodies" (p. 86). She cites his account of the initiation of motion in animals that "follows upon sensation" (*Essay* II, ix, 11–12; [10], p. 91), and also mentions his refusal to rule out the possibility that human thought is a superadded property of body. (But she also holds that gravity is not, for Locke, an "active power" in quite the same sense as is the human power of initiating motion through acts of mind).

17. Locke was by no means alone in denying that gravity could be a "natural" property in body, or in attributing its presence to special acts of God. The view was espoused both by Newton and post-Newtonians. Cf. [12], pp. 9 ff.

18. The research for this essay was supported by a grant from the Guggenheim Foundation. A number of people have offered interesting comments on previous versions which (I regret) strict limitations of space have prevented me from discussing here. I particularly wish to thank Margaret Atherton, Martha Bolton, Norbert Hornstein, Edwin McCann, Ruth Mattern, Thomas Nagel and George Pitcher for their criticisms and suggestions.

Discussion: Superadded Properties:
A Reply to M. R. Ayers

Author's note: The following discussion piece qualifies and may help to clarify some parts of the previous paper. I have commented more directly on Ayers' views about superaddition in my review of his *Locke* (London: Routledge, 1991, 2 volumes), in *Philosophical Review* 102 (Oct. 1993), pp. 577–84. For more recent discussion of the issue of "superaddition" in Locke's philosophy see also Edwin McCann, "Locke's Philosophy of Body," in *The Cambridge Companion to Locke*, ed. Vere Chappell (Cambridge University Press, 1994); and Ayers' review of the *Cambridge Companion* in *The Locke Newsletter*, ed. Roland Hall, 1997, pp, 162–64. (As the latter citation shows, Ayers and I still differ a great deal on what the texts "require.")

IN A RECENT article M. R. Ayers has indicated that my paper, "Superadded Properties: The Limits of Mechanism in Locke," involves an erroneous interpretation of Locke.[1] It seems clear to me, however, that Ayers has seriously misconstrued the purpose and content of my paper. I acknowledge that there may be some significant differences between Ayers' and my readings of Locke's position on mechanistic explanation and superaddition. But it is hard to determine exactly what these are, given Ayers' peculiarly misleading and oblique account of my views. Most of the points he insists on I never deny; and he emphatically denies points that I do not affirm.[2]

My paper, as I quite explicitly stated, is about Locke's position on the explanatory power of the *Boylean* concept of matter, particularly in relation to the primary-secondary quality distinction. Many recent critics—whose works I cited at some length—have maintained that Locke's conception of the "explanatory success" of the Boylean science was far more important to his metaphysics than earlier writers on Locke have recognized. They feel that our understanding of the basis for his distinction between primary and secondary qualities, especially, has suffered as a consequence of this neglect of the Boylean influence. My main purpose, as I explained towards the beginning of the paper, was:

> to indicate the extent to which Locke grasped the *limitations* of the explanatory capacities of Boylean mechanism, from both philosophical and scientific points of view. Specifically I will argue that, his official (Boylean) position notwithstanding, Locke does not consistently maintain that all a body's properties stand in comprehensible or conceivable relations to its *Boylean* "primary qualities" or can be said to flow from them.[3]

I go on to note that Locke makes both the weaker claim:

(a) some presumed properties of matter *cannot be conceived* as "natural" conse-quences of *Boylean* primary qualities;

and the stronger claim:

(b) some properties *cannot be* the natural consequences of the operations of *Boylean* corpuscles.

It is properties that thus cannot be said to "flow from" the operations of *Boy-lean* corpuscles that, I suggest, Locke tends to regard as "superadded" or "an-nexed" to such operations by God. (Emphasis on 'Boylean' added here; other italics are in the original article.)

Ayers himself has relatively little to say about Locke's Boyleanism, and in fact does not relate his discussions at all directly to the primary-secondary qual-ity distinction. He does reject my characterization of Locke's Boyleanism as his "official" position: according to Ayers, Locke's "official" position is "an ag-nosticism (sc., about the nature of matter) shared with Newton and Gassendi."[4] In arguing this claim Ayers proceeds to make some of the very points that I was concerned to stress: namely, that Locke perceives that cohesion, gravity, thought, and certain other salient features of reality cannot be rendered intellig-ible in terms of Boylean primary qualities.[5] At the same time, Ayers does him-self acknowledge that Locke sometimes writes like a doctrinaire Boylean.[6] I suppose there is not much point in quibbling over which of two incompatible strains in Locke's writings in general deserves the title "official position" (though I do fail to see how my characterization could be faulted with respect to Locke's treatment of the *primary-secondary quality distinction*). In any case Ayers and I apparently agree in regarding Locke's critical perspective on Boy-leanism as more philosophically interesting than his orthodox tendencies.[7]

In his paper, Ayers seems primarily concerned to refute the supposition that Locke's theory of "superaddition" (e.g., of cohesion, or of gravity, or—in case some thinking things are material—of thought to matter) involves "an act pos-itively against the nature of matter," a "metaphysical absurdity," or the bringing about (by God) of what is "intrinsically impossible."[8] And he seems to attribute this supposition to me.[9] My claim, however, was just that Locke thought these qualities cannot "arise naturally" from Boylean primary qualities, in the sense that the former cannot be "explained" (through something like geometrical demonstration) in terms of the latter.[10] I still believe that this is true, both as an interpretation of Locke's position and in reality.

Somehow Ayers has formed the opinion that I see Locke as an occasionalist. He writes:

The question of thinking matter she [MW] connects, as Locke himself connected it, with another question, that of the unintelligibility of the processes by which ideas of secondary qualities are caused in sense perception. Both issues concern the mind-body relationship, and *she associates Locke's views on both with a tendency, which she claims to discern in what he says, to look with approval on Malebranche's Occasionalism.*[11]

I'm afraid, however, that "claims to discern" here are all on Ayers' side. I do not mention either Malebranche or occasionalism anywhere in my article.[12] I am (and was) perfectly aware that Locke rejected occasionalism. It is still true, though, that he modestly acknowledged that he could not counter Malebranche's theory with a satisfactory account of his own of the causal origin of perceptual experience.[13]

Ayers charges that my interpretation saddles Locke with two unexplained "contradictions."[14] He does not say exactly what these "contradictions" are. The first he has in mind seems to have something to do with an "ambivalent" attitude toward occasionalism.[15] But, as already noted, I never say that Locke has positive feelings toward occasionalism. (And, in any case, an "ambivalent attitude" would hardly amount to a "contradiction.") The second seems to have to do with a purported suggestion that Locke "intertwines" the view that we are ignorant of the real essence of matter or of that which thinks with "an argument assuming certain knowledge that a standing miracle would be required for materialism to be true."[16]

Now I do not in my paper invoke the concept of "miracles," standing or otherwise.[17] Even apart from this consideration I simply do not understand what Ayers means when he attributes to me this attitude toward Locke's view of "materialism." I do in my paper call attention to Locke's dictum that thought cannot *arise from* senseless matter. This is an early step in my demonstration that Locke does not consistently hold that all of a physical substance's properties are explainable in Boylean terms. (To establish the relevance of this point, I stress that Locke does allow that thought may (for all we know) *inhere in bodies*, rather than in immaterial substances.)[18] All of this seems entirely compatible with Ayers' views about Locke, so far as I understand them. So I am unable to see what unexplained contradiction Ayers thinks my reading gives rise to that his avoids.

Nevertheless, I must admit that in trying to understand Ayers' objections in relation to my paper I have come to realize that I probably do unjustifiably accuse Locke of a contradiction (not, as far as I can see, one that Ayers has in mind). Thus, I observe that Locke denies categorically (1) that thought can arise naturally from incogitative matter (in motion); yet sometimes affirms (2) that thoughts and sensations, like any other "observable" properties, must flow from some hidden inner constitution. And I allege that these two views are "flatly inconsistent."[19]

In alleging that these two positions are inconsistent I did *not* mean that Locke both affirms and denies that thought is incompatible with, or repugnant to, the essence of matter. (I never say or imply that Locke would affirm this proposition, contrary to what Ayers seems to imagine.) My idea was rather that Locke's affirmation of (2) contradicts his denial of (1), in that the "inner constitution" in question is presumably material (or anyway possibly material). I now think, though, that Locke's position is probably the following one, which is consistent in itself (though not with a thorough mechanism about real essences):

> We must distinguish what can follow from the (real) essence of matter by itself (or,
> indeed, matter plus motion) from what follows from the essences of material *sub-*
> *stances* (gold, peach trees, human beings, etc.). Thought may be supposed to follow
> from the latter, but not from the former.

As Locke says, God superadds the properties of a peach tree to matter (to
which motion has already been superadded).[20] Perhaps in so doing he *creates* a
real essence (which could not come into being through matter-in-motion by
itself). Insofar as my paper was mainly concerned to show Locke's awareness
of the explanatory limitations of Boyleanism, this resolution is quite compatible
with my main argument. For it *entails* that mechanistic principles, or primary
qualities, have limited explanatory power in Locke's considered view: the purposive action of an eternal thinking being is also required to account for phenomena.[21] (The "contradiction" in question was noted incidentally and in passing; I found it puzzling.)

In conclusion I would like to address an interesting terminological question
on which Ayers places emphasis. According to Ayers,

> In ordinary seventeenth-century usage the phrase "superadded properties" (the title
> of Wilson's article) would be a contradiction or solecism.[22]

Ayers observes that in ordinary seventeenth-century usage properties are distinguished from "accidents." Properties, unlike accidents, are attributes that flow
from the determinate "real essence" of a thing, and therefore by definition are
not superadded.[23] This point of Ayers' is, to a degree, well-taken; I did use the
term 'properties' without observing this precision. I would like to point out,
though, that the expression "superadded properties" can in fact be given a perfectly good Lockean interpretation. Consider the following passage from one of
Locke's letters to Stillingfleet (quoted by Ayers himself):

> For example, God creates an extended solid substance, without the superadding any
> thing else to it, and so we may consider it at rest: to some parts of it he superadds
> motion, but it still has the essence of matter: other parts of it he frames into plants,
> with all the excellencies of vegetation, life, and beauty, which are to be found in a
> rose or a peach tree, etc, above the essence of matter in general, but it is still but
> matter: *to other parts he adds* sense and spontaneous motion, *and those other prop-*
> *erties* that are to be found in an elephant. Hitherto it is not doubted but the power of
> God may go, and that *the properties of* a rose, a peach or an elephant, *superadded*
> *to matter*, change not the properties of matter . . .[24]

Here one may agree, in partial acknowledgment of Ayers' point, that "sense and
spontaneous motion" are considered *properties* with respect to elephants (i.e., to
follow from *their* essence), but *superadded* with respect to matter (do not follow from *its* essence, as "matter in general").[25] It still seems perfectly correct to
say that some properties of (the different sorts of) material things are superadded to that essence which they possess merely *as* material things. Similarly, I
take it, Locke would say that thought, a *property* of spirits (thinking things) is

in every case superadded to any created entity that in fact thinks, insofar as the entity is considered just as material or immaterial thing.[26] So it can indeed rightly be styled a "superadded property"—though admittedly with a more subtle and convoluted significance than I originally had in mind.

Notes

1. M. R. Ayers, "Mechanism, Superaddition, and the Proof of God's Existence in Locke's Essay," *The Philosophical Review*, 90 (1981), 210–51. For my paper see *American Philosophical Quarterly*, 16 (1979), 143–50 (Chapter 13 of this volume).

2. Ayers says that he is advancing an "alternative" to my interpretation (*op. cit.*, 220). Of course, this does not mean that every aspect of his interpretation is supposed to differ from mine. My problem has been to determine just which aspects *are* supposed so to differ.

3. Wilson, 144 (197 in this volume). My use of the term 'properties' here reflects that in the original paper, which needs some qualification; see below, p. 251.

4. Ayers, 222.

5. *Ibid*; cf. Wilson, 144–46, 148–49 (197–200, 203–04 in this volume).

6. Ayers, 248.

7. Cf. Wilson, 148 (203 in this volume), and Ayers, 248.

8. Ayers, 217, 246, 247.

9. This is admittedly an inference. Ayers clearly thinks that he is arguing against someone, and mine is the only contemporary discussion that he considers at any length. (He briefly mentions two others.) Also, he does directly imply that I think Locke's theory of "superaddition" involves the postulation of a "standing miracle" (222).

10. Cf. Wilson, 143 (196–97 in this volume).

11. Ayers, 219, emphasis added.

12. I do give one reference to Locke's critical *Examination of P. Malebranche's Opinion of seeing all Things in God*.

13. Cf. Wilson, 147, n. 14 (208 in this volume).

14. 220 ff.

15. *Ibid.*, 220.

16. *Ibid.*, 222.

17. Ayers observes that Locke understands by 'miracle' "an event contrary to the normal course of our experience" (*ibid.*, 221). If so, talk of a *standing* miracle would be at best a bit paradoxical.

18. Wilson, 145 (198 in this volume).

19. *Ibid.*, 146 (200 in this volume).

20. *Second Reply to Stillingfleet*: cf. Ayers, 238.

21. Ayers claims that the introduction of rational teleology does *not* involve the introduction of a "supermechanical" principle (246; cf. 241–42). I find this claim incomprehensible.

22. Ayers, 228.

23. *Ibid.*, 226–28.

24. See note 20 (my emphasis).

25. It would be quite a task to work out the interrelations of the property-accident distinction with Locke's distinction between real and nominal essences (of elephants, of matter, etc.). I merely note the problem here, without attempting to deal with it.

26. Cf. *Essay*, II, xxiii, 30, p. 313. Ayers stresses that thought, on Locke's view, must be "superadded" to any created substance—material or immaterial—that thinks (*op. cit.*, 247).

Did Berkeley Completely Misunderstand the Basis of the Primary-Secondary Quality Distinction in Locke?

I

According to leading seventeenth-century philosophers and scientists, our sensory "ideas" of physical objects are of two importantly different types. Certain sorts of ideas, the "ideas of primary qualities," *resemble* qualities actually existing in the object. While there are some differences about what *exactly* these comprise, size, shape, motion or rest, and number are among the accepted examples. (Locke, notoriously, includes "solidity"; he sometimes mentions position. Gravity, as we will see below, was sometimes included later.) On the other hand, the "ideas of secondary qualities" do not resemble any quality really existing in the object, although they are systematically produced by the interactions of the objects' primary qualities with percipients. Ideas or sensations of colors, odors, tastes, sounds, and temperature (hot and cold) are among the traditional "ideas of secondary qualities."[1]

Berkeley is the best known early critic of this distinction—although, as we shall see, he did have predecessors. In the early twentieth century, the distinction was vigorously attacked by Whitehead, who considered it a prominent manifestation of the "fallacy of misplaced concreteness"—which, he claimed, has "ruined" modern philosophy.[2] More recently, D. J. O'Connor, after critically expounding Locke's doctrine of qualities, dismisses it with the comment:

> Clearly all this is a great muddle. The doctrine of primary and secondary qualities is, in truth, nothing but some scientific truths dangerously elevated into a philosophical doctrine.[3]

But since O'Connor's article was published in 1964, the primary-secondary quality distinction has increasingly been treated with respect, especially by philosophers sympathetic to "scientific realism." In terms of historical criticism, this development has been accompanied by an increasingly sympathetic construal of Locke's philosophy in general, and a tendency to dismiss Berkeley as having had a very poor understanding of Locke's position. The following views, in particular, have been espoused by a number of writers. (1) Locke's distinction should be viewed as principally grounded in the explanatory success of Boylean atomism. (2) Berkeley erroneously and misleadingly construed the distinction as one supposed to rest on ordinary experience of macroscopic objects. More specifically (some have held), Berkeley misinterpreted the "arguments" of the *Essay Concerning Human Understanding*, bk. II, chap. viii, sect. 16–21—having to do with illusion and the relativity of perception—as Locke's main foundation for the distinction, and therefore falsely supposed that he could refute the distinction by showing that primary-quality perceptions are also subject to relativity considerations. But in fact the issue of perceptual relativity plays no such central role in Locke's thought. (The reasoning of *Essay*, II, viii, 16–21 should be read either as some incidental "bad arguments" for the distinction, or simply as an attempt to bring out the explanatory power of the Boylean conception of body.) (3) Berkeley is responsible, through his stress on relativity considerations, and epistemological issues generally, for a long subsequent history of misinterpreting Locke as relying on such considerations. He is correspondingly responsible for the widespread failure to recognize the truth stated above under (1). (4) When Locke's distinction is correctly reinterpreted as resting on a tacit appeal to the "explanatory success" of contemporary science, it is a much stronger position than traditionally believed. (In fact, at least one prominent philosopher has firmly endorsed Locke's position, with only minor qualifications, relating mainly to scientific progress since Locke's time.)[4]

I fully agree with the view that Locke's distinction was heavily influenced by Boylean science. However, I do not think there is strong reason to suppose that Berkeley seriously "misrepresented" or "misinterpreted" Locke in this connection, is "wholly unfair" to him, read him "carelessly," or produced arguments against Locke that are "wholly [or "simply"] beside the point," as various critics allege.[5] As Barry Stroud has recently noted, this conception of Berkeley, "like the old view of Locke, is a purely fictional chapter in the history of philosophy. . . ."[6] Stroud persuasively demonstrates this claim by a careful examination of the arguments of the *Principles* and the *Dialogues*, in relation to the primary-secondary quality distinction. Stroud stresses throughout that Berkeley is primarily concerned with what he sees as his predecessors' "faulty notion of existence"—specifically, their assumption that something unperceived and unperceiving could exist.[7] It is this assumption that Berkeley sees as their major error, rather than mistakes about the relativity of primary quality perceptions, or the epistemological appearance-reality distinction generally.

In the present essay I will defend a point of view that is similar to Stroud's, but with a somewhat different approach.[8] I will focus on the claims of three commentators—Mandelbaum, Alexander, and Mackie—who hold that Berkeley falsely believed Locke's primary-secondary quality distinction to rest on facts about ordinary perception. After quoting some passages from their writings, I will argue that there is in reality very little basis for attributing this interpretation of Locke to Berkeley. I will suggest, however, that there *is* something of a puzzle about the role of relativity arguments in the history of the primary-secondary quality distinction. (As we will see, the puzzle in question goes back beyond Berkeley; I am unable to resolve it.) I will then show that there is ample evidence that Berkeley was aware that Locke's distinction was supposed to derive major support from arguments from scientific (or corpuscularian) explanation. He in fact deals with such arguments repeatedly, searchingly, and—at least in part—astutely. I will also sketch the variety of considerations by which he tries to meet them.

It is so easy to show that Berkeley was aware of the supposed corpuscularian grounding of the distinction that what really requires explanation is the fact that he has so long been accused of missing it. In conclusion I will point out that two of the three critics indeed seem to acknowledge obliquely that Berkeley is far from simply ignoring the alleged scientific basis of Locke's distinction. But—perhaps out of sympathy for Locke's philosophy?—they do not sufficiently consider the implications of these concessions for their other charges against Berkeley.

While this is strictly an interpretive essay, I would like to mention in passing that I am in some respects quite sympathetic to Berkeley's position on the subject under discussion. That is, I share his view that the primary-secondary quality distinction is an affront to common sense, and I am not convinced that a satisfactory version of the argument from explanation has so far been brought forward to establish it.[9]

II

A key passage from Mandelbaum's influential essay on "Locke's Realism" reads as follows:

> The upshot of our argument . . . is that the basis on which Locke established his theory of the primary qualities was his atomism; it was not his aim to attempt to establish the nature of physical objects by examining the sensible ideas which we had of them. Thus instead of viewing Locke's doctrine of the primary and secondary qualities as a doctrine which rests on an analysis of differences among our ideas, his doctrine is to be understood as a theory of physical entities, and of the manner in which our ideas are caused. To this extent the Berkeleian criticism of Locke's distinction between primary and secondary qualities is wholly beside the point, for it rests on an assumption which Locke did not share—that all distinctions concerning the nature of objects must be based upon, and verified by, distinctions discernible within the immediate contents of consciousness.[10]

Mandelbaum does not explain exactly what he means by "distinctions discernible within the immediate contents of consciousness." However, in a footnote he cites *Essay*, II, viii, 21 as the only passage in Locke where it might seem that the theory of primary and secondary qualities is being supported by such a distinction. (This is the passage in which Locke observed that the corpuscularian theory of warmth in our hands as merely a motion of animal spirits enables us to understand how the same water can feel warm to one hand and cold to another, "Whereas it is impossible that the same Water, if those *Ideas* were really in it, should at the same time be both Hot and Cold."[11] He goes on to indicate that "figure" does not present the same problem, "that never producing the *Idea* of a square by one Hand which has produced the Idea of a Globe by another.") Mandelbaum remarks that the passage is primarily concerned with the causal story of the origin of ideas of secondary qualities, and he suggests that "the contention that we are not deceived by tactile impressions of shape plays no significant part in the discussion."[12]

Rather similarly, Peter Alexander writes in the introduction to "Boyle and Locke on Primary and Secondary Qualities":

> Locke has been seriously misrepresented in various respects ever since Berkeley set critics off on the wrong foot. I wish to discuss just one central view the misunderstanding of which has been particularly gross, namely, the distinction between primary and secondary qualities and, especially, the alleged arguments for this distinction in *Essay* II, viii, 16–21. Robert Boyle is often mentioned in connection with Locke but the extent and importance of his influence on Locke has seldom been realized. [Alexander here cites Mandelbaum as one of two "honourable exceptions."] If the arguments of II, viii were intended, following Berkeley, to *establish* the distinction between primary and secondary qualities then Locke was both foolish and incompetent; a study of Boyle can help us to see that he was neither of these things by making it clear what he was driving at.[13]

And, finally, some excerpts from Chap. 1 of John Mackie's book, *Problems from Locke*:

> But Locke [after well arguing that the corpuscularian science can explain the "illusion" of lukewarm water feeling cold to one hand and hot to the other] throws in, for contrast, the remark that 'figure'—that is, shape—'never produce[s] the idea of a square by one hand [and] of a globe by another.' Though literally correct, this is unfortunate because it has led careless readers from Berkeley onwards to think that Locke is founding the primary/secondary distinction on the claim that secondary qualities are subject to sensory illusion while primary qualities are not. It is then easy for Berkeley to reply that illusions also occur with respect to primary qualities like shape, size, and motion, and hence that there can be no distinction between the two groups of qualities. . . . But of course Locke's argument does not rest on any such claim . . . ; it is rather that the corpuscular theory is confirmed as a scientific hypothesis by its success in explaining various illusions in detail.[14]

The textual support offered for these negative characterizations of Berkeley's understanding of Locke is surely, by anyone's standards, singularly meager. Neither Mandelbaum nor Alexander cites any texts at all, while Mackie refers us (in the paragraph after the one partially quoted) to "especially . . . the First Dialogue." What, then, do they have in mind? Following up Mackie's clue, let us turn first to that Dialogue. One feature of Berkeley's strategy there does afford at least *prima facie* support for the charge against him.

In the first part of the Dialogue, Philonous has argued in a variety of ways (*not* just through notions of relativity or illusion) that sensible colors, sounds, heat and cold, tastes and odors exist "only in the mind." Hylas, reluctantly persuaded of this conclusion, suddenly bethinks himself of the distinction between primary and secondary qualities. "Philosophers," he points out, assert that all of the properties so far covered in the Dialogue "are only so many sensations of ideas existing nowhere but in the mind." The primary qualities however—"Extension, Figure, Solidity, Gravity,[15] Motion, and Rest"—"they hold exist really in bodies." Hylas concludes his speech as follows: "For my part, I have been a long time sensible there was such an opinion current among philosophers, but was never thoroughly convinced of its truth until now."[16] Philonous then introduces the next phrase of the argument for immaterialism in the following terms: "But what if the same arguments which are brought against Secondary Qualities will hold good against [extensions and figures] also?"[17] He then proceeds to argue that perceptions of extension are relative to the condition and situation of the percipient. This discussion includes a passage that does indeed recall the argument of *Essay*, II, viii, 21:

> *Phil.* Was it not admitted as a good argument [cited in our previous discussion] that neither heat nor cold was in the water, because it seemed warm to one hand and cold to the other?
>
> *Hyl.* It was.
>
> *Phil.* Is it not the very same reasoning to conclude, there is no extension or figure in an object, because to one eye it shall seem little, smooth and round, when at the same time it appears to the other great, uneven, and angular?[18]

In response to Hylas' expression of skepticism as to whether this ever happens, Philonous goes on to cite the instance of the microscope.

Now, does this passage, together with Philonous' subsequent development of relativity arguments for motion and solidity, show that Berkeley seriously over-estimated the importance of relativity considerations for Locke? This seems to me a rather extravagant supposition, for several reasons. First (and least important), surely there really is a suggestion in *Essay*, II, viii, 21 that relativity considerations show that hot and cold as we perceive them are not really in the water; and *some* contrast is suggested in this respect between hot-and-cold and figure. Second, as Michael Ayers has pointed out, the fact that there is an "association" of Philonous' reasoning with Locke's brief remarks about relativity scarcely shows that Berkeley *sees Locke* as resting the distinction between subjective ideas and real qualities on considerations of relativity or the possibility of illusion.[19] And, finally, the argument of the First Dialogue is clearly not presented in the form of *ad hominem* reasoning at all. That is, the overt strategy is not simply to take a premiss from the opposition—that relativity considerations establish the subjectivity of the "secondary qualities"—and show that anyone who holds *that* can logically be forced into immaterialism. Rather, Berkeley first had Philonous systematically *persuade* Hylas (through relativity and other considerations) that colors, odors, etc., are mere ideas in the mind. Following Ayers, then, I would deny that Berkeley's treatment of relativity arguments in the First Dialogue tends to convict him of a misunderstanding or "careless reading" of Locke.[20]

It might be suggested, however, that the *Principles* actually provide more direct proof than do the *Dialogues* that Berkeley saw Locke and his followers as resting the primary-secondary quality distinction on considerations of perceptual relativity. For we do find in *Principles*, I, sect. 14 the following statement:

> I shall farther add, that, after the same manner as modern philosophers prove certain
> sensible qualities to have not existence in Matter, or without the mind, the same
> things may be likewise proved of all other sensible qualities whatsoever. Thus, for
> instance, it is said that heat and cold are affections only of the mind, and not at all
> patterns of real beings, existing in the corporeal substances which excite them; for
> that the same body which appears cold to one hand seems warm to another.[21]

He goes on to claim that the same relativity considerations hold in the cases of extension and motion. It is true, as Ayers points out, that Berkeley immediately goes on (in sect. 15) to observe that this reasoning does not establish the mind-dependence of *either* class of qualities:

> Though it must be confessed this method of arguing does not so much prove that
> there is no extension or colour in an outward object, as that we do not know by
> sense which is the true extension or colour of the object.[22]

The passage does, however, provide direct evidence that Berkeley thought that "modern philosophers" drew on relativity arguments to establish the subjectivity of secondary qualities. It appears to imply that he thought they had not noticed that perception of primary qualities, too, could be affected by the position or condition of the percipient. What does this tell us about his reading of Locke?

The first point to observe is that the idea that relativity considerations extend to primary as well as secondary qualities did not originate with Berkeley—nor did the use of this point as a criticism of the view that perceptions of primary qualities possess superior objectivity. The passage quoted above from Berkeley's *Principles* has an extremely close parallel in section G of the article "Zeno of Elea" in Bayle's *Dictionary*, published years before.[23] The likelihood that Berkeley adopted this part of his reasoning from Bayle was apparently first demonstrated by Richard Popkin in 1951, and has frequently been noted in subsequent writings by Popkin and others.[24] Bayle is criticizing "the 'new' philosophers." The following passage is representative:

> . . . all the means of suspending judgment that overthrow the reality of corporeal
> qualities also overthrow the reality of extension. Since the same bodies are sweet to
> some men and bitter to others, one is right in inferring that they are neither sweet
> nor bitter in themselves and absolutely speaking. The "new" philosophers, although
> they are not skeptics, have so well understood the bases of suspension of judgment
> with regard to sounds, smells, heat, cold, hardness, softness, heaviness and light-
> ness, tastes, colors, and the like, that they teach that all these qualities are percep-
> tions of our soul and that they do not exist at all in the objects of our senses. Why
> should we not say the same thing about extension? . . . [N]otice carefully that the
> same body appears to us to be small or large, according to the place from which it is
> viewed; and let us have no doubts that a body that seems very small to us appears
> very large to a fly.[25]

Now, against whom, exactly, does Bayle suppose that such reasoning is effective? In another article Bayle credits Simon Foucher with influencing his views on the indefensibility of the primary-secondary quality distinction.[26] He specifically cites Foucher's *Critique de la Recherche de la Verité*, an attack on Malebranche published in 1675.[27] This would take the criticism of the primary-secondary quality distinction back to fifteen years *before* the publication of Locke's *Essay*. While Foucher does argue that the primary-secondary distinction is indefensible, however, he does not, as far as I can find, focus on the issue of the comparable relativity and variability of primary qualities.[28] It is perhaps logical that he should not, since Malebranche himself makes much of the relativity of perceptions of extension in the *Recherche*![29] Bayle himself notes that such arguments are found in Malebranche and the *Port Royal Logic*, among other sources.[30] It is therefore presently unclear to me just whom Bayle thought he was refuting in the passage quoted, and just what he thought their error was. (Not noticing that perceptions of primary qualities are variable? Not drawing the right conclusion from the observation?)—There certainly seems to be no good reason to suppose he had in mind specifically *Essay*, II, viii, 16–21. The same difficulties then come up at one remove about Berkeley's closely comparable reasoning (and even wording) in *Principles*, sects. 14–15. That is, there may have been "modern" or "new" philosophers who fit the role that Bayle and Berkeley cast them in more closely than Locke—and Bayle and Berkeley may have had them in mind. Or there may not have been, in which case Berkeley will have taken over from Bayle a piece of reasoning without a proper target. In contrast to this rather murky situation, however, it is possible to show clearly that Berkeley (if not Bayle) fully appreciated the importance of the alleged success of corpuscularian explanations as a basis for the primary-secondary quality distinction. Let us now turn to this task.

III

It is an interesting fact that Mandelbaum, Alexander, and Mackie in arguing that the explanatory success of corpuscularianism is the main basis for Locke's distinction, particularly cite the ability of this science to explain the production of ideas in us, including the ideas of secondary qualities. But this is, as it happens, a topic with which Berkeley deals repeatedly and emphatically. For instance, at the very beginning of the Second Dialogue, Hylas first admits that he can see no false steps in the reasonings of the previous day. But, he says,

> when these are out of my thoughts, there seems, on the other hand, something so satisfactory, so natural and intelligible, in the modern way of explaining things that, I profess, I know not how to reject it.[31]

The conversation proceeds as follows:

> *Phil.* I know not what you mean.
> *Hyl.* I mean the way of accounting for our sensations or ideas.

Phil. How is that?

Hyl. It is supposed the soul makes her residence in some part of the brain, from which the nerves take their rise, and are thence extended to all parts of the body; and that outward objects, by the different impressions they make on the organs of sense, communicate certain vibrative motions to the nerves; and these being filled with spirits propagate them to the brain or seat of the soul, which according to the various impressions or traces thereby made in the brain is variously affected with ideas.

Phil. And call you this an explication of the manner whereby we are affected with ideas?[32]

In objecting to this reasoning, Philonous first points out that by the previous day's reasoning the brain is just one sensible object among others, and hence itself exists "only in the mind." How could one idea or sensible thing reasonably be supposed to cause all the others? But, he continues, Hylas' position is intrinsically inacceptable, even apart from conclusions previously arrived at.

Phil. . . . for after all, this way of explaining things, as you called it, could never have satisfied any reasonable man. What connexion is there between a motion in the nerves, and the sensations of sound or colour in the mind? Or how is it possible these should be the effect of that?[33]

As this passage shows conclusively, Berkeley was perfectly aware that the primary-secondary quality distinction was supposed to derive support from the alleged ability of contemporary science to explain perception in terms of materialist mechanism—and hence of primary qualities. His response is straightforward: the purported "explanation" is a sham. In presenting this response he invokes the notion that the production of ideas by states of matter is not "possible." Such an a priori stricture on causal relations would be considered untenable by many philosophers today. It was, however, accepted by Locke, who argued at length that states of matter cannot "naturally" produce "Sence, Perceptions, and Knowledge."[34] Far from missing Locke's point, Berkeley has come down on a crucial weakness—and problem of consistency—in the Lockean system.[35]

Berkeley raises this issue repeatedly.[36] However, he also deals in other ways with the notion that the contemporary concept of external matter characterized (just) by primary qualities is justified by its "explanatory success." Some of his arguments draw on problematic—even idiosyncratic—views about causal relations. For present purposes there is no need to analyze the relevant passages in detail. I will merely summarize the main considerations he advances.

(1) From the contention that only spirits are active, Berkeley argues that extension, motion, etc.—or unthinking matter characterized by these qualities—cannot be causes of anything. Hence they cannot "explain" the production of any effect.[37]

(2) Even apart from the impossibility of understanding how a motion of matter could produce an idea, or how an "inert" entity could be a cause, con-

temporary materialism is far from explanatorily adequate. Have the materialists, Berkeley demands,

> by all their strained thoughts and extravagant suppositions . . . been able to reach the mechanical production of any one animal or vegetable body? . . . Have they accounted, by physical principles, for the aptitude and contrivance, even of the most inconsiderable parts of the universe?[38]

(3) The explanatory successes that the new science has had can readily be accommodated within the immaterialist philosophy. They have to do mainly with uncovering regularities and "analogies" in nature. Nothing but confusion results when it is thought that these regularities are leading to the discovery of productive material causes (e.g., "gravitational attraction"). Rather they should be conceived as part of an increasingly comprehensive theory of ideal "signs" to significata. The underlying ground of *this* relation is the causality of the infinite spirit, orderly producer of these ideas or sensible objects that constitute nature.[39]

These contentions range, clearly, from prodigious metaphysics to simple common sense. Taken together, however, they hardly indicate unawareness of the explanatory claims of contemporary mechanism—or of the philosophical significance attributed to these claims.

Two final points should be added, in concluding this discussion of Berkeley. First, the specific considerations against arguments from "explanatory success" for the Boylean concept of matter are offered despite the fact that Berkeley (in the *Principles*, anyway) believes that he can demonstrate the *unintelligibility* of the notion before the issue of its "explanatory power"—which surely is in some sense posterior—is even raised. Second, it would be wrong to suppose (as Mandelbaum sometimes seems to)[40] that Berkeley neglects the prevailing view that qualities of material bodies are supposed to derive from their inner real essences or constitutive corpuscles. He clearly states and disputes this Lockean conception in more than one passage.[41]

IV

In conclusion, I want to acknowledge that both Mandelbaum and Alexander show some recognition that Berkeley's attack on Locke was not wholly a matter of misinterpretation. In the case of Mandelbaum, the recognition is extremely oblique and in several ways puzzling. Mandelbaum points out that Berkeley did not merely overlook the fact that Locke's philosophy was founded on scientific considerations; rather he consciously "sought to free philosophic questions from any direct dependence upon science."[42] From this observation Mandelbaum somehow moves to the conclusion that it is *accordingly* "misleading" to interpret Locke in the light of Berkeley's criticisms. He also seems to think that Berkeley's efforts "to free philosophic questions from any direct dependence upon science" entail his reading the *Essay* "as an epistemological treatise devoid of a scientific substructure."[43] But none of this really follows, unless it be supposed that Berkeley's attempt to free philosophy from dependence on science was somehow a mere blind turning away from the earlier "tradition" without any direct confrontation with its assumptions. Perhaps this inference is tied in with Mandelbaum's undefended claim that Berkeley simply assumes that all distinctions among ideas must be drawn within the contents of ordinary experience of macroscopic objects. In any case, I hope to have shown that Berkeley did understand these "scientific" aspects of Locke's position that Mandelbaum is concerned to stress—and still had reason to regard the position as incoherent.

At the end of his article, Alexander does allow that "perhaps the most difficult objection for Locke to meet," with respect to the primary-secondary quality distinction, "is an argument about causality put by Berkeley. . . ."[44] It appears at first that Alexander means (surprisingly) Berkeley's argument that everything except spirit is "inert" and hence causally inefficacious. But the whole passage gives the impression that "the most difficult objection" that Alexander has in mind is really Berkeley's observation, expounded at some length above, "that no philosopher even pretends to explain 'how matter should operate on a spirit'."

In my opinion, this has to be a crucial point of contention between Berkeley and Locke's present-day apologists, with respect to the primary-secondary quality distinction.[45] Berkeley, I have argued, *rejected* the argument from the explanatory success of mechanistic physics; he did not merely ignore it. And I have also claimed that, insofar as Berkeley was pointing out an inconsistency in the philosophy he opposed, his position is solidly grounded. It is apparently open to the contemporary philosopher, concerned with philosophical truth as well as Locke exegesis, to deny that there is, after all, any special problem about causal relations between the mental and the physical, and hence about "explaining" perceptions in physical terms. (In this, I stress again, he would have to disagree with *both* Berkeley and Locke.) Mandelbaum and Mackie do not address this point; they do not seem to see it.[46] Alexander does at least partly see it. But rather than reject the eighteenth-century assumption that there is some special problem about mind-body interaction, he attempts to help Locke out of the difficulty by invoking an unexplained distinction between scientific and philosophical issues:

> Locke believes, as does Boyle, that the facts of experience force dualism upon us; the consequent problem is not scientific but philosophical and is therefore not particularly involved in the distinction between primary and secondary qualities.[47]

But surely the whole drift of Berkeley's attack on Locke's distinction is that the "facts of experience" do *not* force dualism upon us—so the philosophical inconsistency that Locke falls into can be avoided. Berkeley thinks that his immaterialism lets us accommodate the facts of experience without *having* a problem—whether "philosophical" or "scientific"—about how matter could possible produce ideas in the mind. Alexander has not only conceded to Berkeley a relevant, if not powerful, objection to Locke's system.[48] He has unintentionally pointed to one of the strongest positive features of Berkeley's anti-Lockean metaphysics.

NOTES

1. See John Locke, *Essay Concerning Human Understanding*, bk. II, chap. viii. Descartes, Galileo, and Boyle are among the other prominent exponents of the distinction.

2. A. N. Whitehead, *Science and the Modern World* (1925; repr. New York: The Free Press, 1967), chap. 3.

3. "Locke," in D. J. O'Connor, ed., *A Critical History of Western Philosophy* (New York: The Free Press, 1964), p. 211.

4. J. L. Mackie, *Problems From Locke* (Oxford: Clarendon Press, 1976), chap. 2. Other sources for the views cited (with less explicit philosophical endorsement of Locke's distinction) are found in the works of Mandelbaum and Alexander, cited below. At the beginning of the paper cited in n. 6, Barry Stroud gives many references to works advancing the "old" interpretation of Locke.

5. All of these comments are from Mackie, Alexander, and Mandelbaum. Some of them occur in the passages I cite from their works at the beginning of pt. II.

6. "Berkeley v. Locke on Primary Qualities," *Philosophy* 55 (April 1980): 150. See also Daniel Garber, "Locke, Berkeley, and Corpuscular Scepticism," in Colin M. Turbayne, ed., *Berkeley: Critical and Interpretive Essays* (Minneapolis: University of Minnesota Press, 1982), pp. 174–94.

7. Stroud, "Berkeley v. Locke," pp. 150–51 and passim.

8. To the best of my knowledge, my views about the interpretation of Berkeley developed in complete independence from Stroud's. I did not become aware of the similarities between our ideas on this matter until I came across the published version of his paper, after an earlier version of the present article had been submitted for publication. I must acknowledge, however, that I had in my possession all the while a manuscript version of his essay, which constituted part of a much longer paper on Locke and Berkeley, and had indeed misremembered the paper as being wholly on Locke. (My oversight came to light as a result of recent correspondence with Stroud.)

I have extensively revised pt. I of the present essay to take account of Stroud's prior work. For reasons of structure and exposition, it has proved impractical to remove all overlap from later sections, however. In particular, my treatment of Berkeley on relativity arguments is in several respects close to Stroud's. Stroud also touches briefly on Bayle's precedence to Berkeley, which I discuss in more detail, and on the issue of materialist explanation.

9. I critically discuss Mackie's exposition of the argument in "The Primary-Secondary Quality Distinction: Against Two Recent Defenses," 1979, unpublished.

10. Maurice Mandelbaum, "Locke's Realism," in *Philosophy, Science, and Sense Perception* (Baltimore: Johns Hopkins Press, 1974), pp. 27–28; see also p. 20.

11. John Locke, *Essay*, p. 139.

12. Mandelbaum, "Locke's Realism," p. 28, n. 52.

13. In I. C. Tipton, ed., *Locke on Human Understanding* (Oxford: Oxford University Press, 1977), p. 62; see also p. 73. (Originally published in *Ratio* 16 [1974].)

14. *Problems From Locke*, pp. 22–23; cf. p. 24.

15. The inclusion of gravity constitutes an important departure from Locke: cf. Margaret D. Wilson, "Superadded Properties: The Limits of Mechanism in Locke," *Ameri-*

can Philosophical Quarterly 14 (April 1979): 148–49 (Chapter 13 of this volume). On the other hand, Berkeley does not always include gravity in the list of primary qualities: cf. *PHK*, I, sect. 9. (In *Works*, vol. II, p. 44).

16. *Works*, II, pp. 187–88.

17. Ibid., p. 188.

18. Ibid., p. 189.

19. "Substance, Reality, and the Great Dead Philosophers," *American Philosophical Quarterly* 7 (January 1970): 43. Ayers is disputing a rather different allegation of Berkeleyan misunderstanding—that of Jonathan Bennett—but some of his remarks are relevant to the present context as well.

20. Ayers points out that Berkeley's deployment of relativity arguments in the First Dialogue can well be read as the outcome of "his own quasi-sceptical reflections on the fact that the state, position, etc. of the perceiver help to determine how *any* aspect of the world is perceived." However, as I explain below, there is considerable reason to believe that the "quasi-sceptical reflections" in question were strongly influenced by Bayle.

21. *Works*, II, pp. 46–47. In *PHK*, sect. 14–15, Berkeley specifically mentions relativity considerations as applying to color and taste, as well as hot and cold, among the secondary qualities, and extension, figure, and motion among the primary qualities.

22. Ibid., p. 47. A similar point is made by Bayle in the section of "Zeno" cited in the next note.

23. Pierre Bayle, *Dictionnaire historique et critique*, nov. éd., tome XV (Paris: Desoer, 1820), pp. 44–45; *Historical and Critical Dictionary*, ed. Richard H. Popkin (Indianapolis: Bobbs-Merrill, 1965), pp. 364–66. Subsequent references are to Popkin's edition. The *Dictionary* was originally published in 1697.

24. Richard H. Popkin, "Berkeley and Pyrrhonism," *Review of Metaphysics* 5 (1951–52): 223–46. See also his notes to his edition of Bayle's *Dictionary*, s.v. "Pyrrho" and "Zeno of Elea." See also Richard A. Watson, *The Downfall of Cartesianism, 1673–1712* (The Hague: Martinus Nijhoff, 1966), p. 3: and his *Introduction* to Simon Foucher, *Critique de la Recherche de la Verité* (New York and London: Johnson Reprint Corporation, 1969), p. xxix. I am grateful to Phillip Cummins for calling my attention to Bayle's (and Foucher's) relevance to the present inquiry.

25. *Dictionary*, pp. 364–65.

26. S.v. "Pyrrho," ibid., p. 197.

27. Reprinted 1969: see n. 24. See esp. pp. 76–80 of this work. Foucher's influence on Bayle has been noted by Popkin and Watson in the works cited above. Watson's *Downfall of Cartesianism* contains an especially detailed discussion of Foucher and his relationship to Malebranche, Bayle, Berkeley, and others. See also Phillip Cummins, "Perceptual Relativity and Ideas in the Mind," *Philosophy and Phenomenological Research* 24 (December 1963): 202–14. Cummins notes Bayle's seemingly erroneous emphasis on the issue of perceptual relativity and provides an interesting analysis of his (and of Foucher's) conception of the issue.

28. Popkin indicates that he does: cf. Popkin, "Skepticism," in Paul Edwards, ed., *The Encyclopedia of Philosophy*, vol. 7 (New York: Macmillan and The Free Press, 1967), p. 454. He does not give an exact reference, however. Watson, in his detailed discussion of Foucher's anti-Malebranche works, does not seem to point to the presence of an "equal variability" argument in Foucher. (I have personally had access to only the first of Foucher's critical works.)

29. *Recherche de la verité*, bk. I, chap. vi, sect. 1, in Nicholas Malebranche, *Oeuvres*

complètes, ed. A. Robinet, vol. I (Paris: J. Vrin, 1958), pp. 79ff. However, Malebranche does claim that judgments about bodies' primary qualities involve truths about proportions and relations, while judgments about secondary qualities are more wholly erroneous: cf. Watson, *Downfall*, p. 44.

30. Bayle, *Dictionary*, s.v. "Zeno," nn. 66 and 67, pp. 365–66.

31. *Works*, II, p. 208.

32. Ibid., pp. 208–09.

33. Ibid., p. 210.

34. Cf. Wilson, "Superadded Properties," pp. 144–48 (Chapter 13 of this volume, pp. 198–203); and Stroud, "Berkeley v. Locke," p. 158.

35. Foucher had already observed this inconsistency—and some related ones—in the dualist, realist philosophies of his day, and had dwelt on it emphatically and at length. As noted above, however, his targets were post-Cartesian continental philosophers, especially Malebranche. Foucher's critical arguments and their influence on Berkeley and others have been meticulously detailed by Watson in *Downfall*.

In "Berkeley on the Limits of Mechanistic Explanation" in *Berkeley: Critical and Interpretive Essays*, ed. by C. Turbayne (Minneapolis: University of Minnesota Press, 1982), pp. 95–107, Nancy L. Maull also stresses Berkeley's use of this line of argument, and mentions its *ad hominem* relevance. Unfortunately, I did not learn of Maull's essay until the present paper had been submitted for publication. While there are a number of points of contact between our approaches, I disagree strongly with Maull's conclusion that we can now see that Berkeley's criticism of contemporary materialist philosophy was "ultimately ineffectual and irrelevant." That is, I do not believe that Berkeley's criticism has been shown to reflect a merely dogmatic distinction between the mental and the physical (as she seems to imply), or that is has been discredited by the subsequent development of psychophysiology.

36. See *PHK*, I, sect. 50 (*Works*, II, p. 62):

> . . . you will say there have been a great many things explained by matter and motion: take away these, and you destroy the whole corpuscular philosophy, and undermine those mechanical principles which have been applied with so much success to account for the phenomena. . . . To this I answer, that there is not any one phenomenon explained on that supposition, which may not as well be explained without it. . . . To explain the phenomena, is all one as to shew, why upon such and such occasions we are affected with such and such ideas. But how matter should operate on a spirit, or produce any idea in it, is what no philosopher will pretend to explain.

See also *PC*, sect. 476, ed. A. A. Luce (London: Thomas Nelson and Sons, 1944), p. 161.

37. Cf. *PHK*, I, sect. 25, and I, sect. 102, *Works*, II, pp. 51–52, 85.

38. Third Dialogue, ibid., p. 257.

39. *PHK*, I, sects. 58ff. and 103, ibid., pp. 65ff., 86. Compare *PC*, sect. 71 and 403, in Luce, ed., pp. 19 and 131. (See also Stroud, "Berkeley v. Locke," pp. 158–59.) As the first of the two passages from the *Commentaries* suggests, Berkeley felt that the mechanists were faced with certain problems in merely understanding *physical* causality, problems that his system avoided. Probably he had in mind, for instance, some of Locke's statements about the incomprehensibility of cohesion on materialist principles: cf. Wilson, "Superadded Properties," p. 149 (Chapter 13 in this volume).

40. Cf. Mandelbaum, "Locke's Realism," p. 3.

41. *PHK*, I, sect. 65 and 103, *Works*, II, pp. 69, 85; *PC*, sect. 533, in Luce, ed., p. 185. See also Garber's detailed discussion in *Berkeley*, ed. by Turbayne.

42. "Locke's Realism," p. 3.

43. Ibid.

44. Alexander, "Boyle and Locke," in Tipton, ed., p. 75.

45. At least those discussed in this paper. Jonathan Bennett's defense of the distinction does not focus on the issue of explanatory adequacy, and to this extent avoids completely any problem about body-mind causation: cf. his *Locke, Berkeley, Hume: Central Themes* (Oxford: Oxford University Press, 1971).

46. As becomes clear in a later chapter, Mackie does see a problem about "reducing" phenomenal properties or sensations to states of matter: see *Problems From Locke*, pp. 167ff.

47. "Locke and Boyle," p. 76.

48. Alexander also concedes at the end of his article that he has not "dealt adequately with Berkeley's conclusion from his various arguments that the idea of matter is unintelligible." It seems, then, that Alexander concedes in conclusion that there is *a good deal* that is relevant, if not powerful, in Berkeley's attack on Locke's distinction, and the "idea of matter" that is tied to it.

Berkeley on the Mind-Dependence of Colors

BERKELEY developed his theory that physical objects are just congeries of sensory "ideas" in deliberate opposition to the materialist scientific realism of his seventeenth century predecessors. An important component of his position is the claim that physical things are as they are perceived: that the senses do not systematically mislead us about the physical world. In maintaining this view Berkeley self-consciously sides with "common sense" against the prevailing philosophical assumption that mechanistic corpuscularian science provides a conception of physical reality superior to the vulgar. Thus he defends the status of perceived (or phenomenal) colors, tastes, warmth and cold, and so on as real, irreducible qualities of objects, against the scientific realist contention that these putative qualities are mere subjective manifestations or effects of corpuscular structures. A well-known speech by Philonous in the Third Dialogue highlights this aspect of Berkeley's position, which I will call phenomenal (or sensory) realism:

> I am of a vulgar cast, simple enough to believe my senses, and leave things as I find them. To be plain, it is my opinion that the real things are those very things I see, and feel, and perceive by my senses. These I know; and, finding they answer all the necessities and purposes of life, have no reason to be solicitous about any other unknown beings. . . . It is likewise my opinion that colours and other sensible qualities are on the objects. I cannot for my life help thinking that snow is white, and fire hot. You indeed, who by *snow* and *fire* mean certain external, unperceived, unperceiving substances, are in the right to deny whiteness or heat to be affections inherent in *them*. But I, who understand by those words the things I see and feel, am obliged to think like other folks. (*Works*, II, 229–30)[1]

Berkeley's position, however, also includes the claim that physical things are nothing but sensory appearances in the mind, or sets of sense experiences; and in maintaining *this* view he clearly does *not* think like other folks. This idealist conception of physical reality as mind-dependent brings Berkeley directly into conflict with common sense.[2]

Berkeley's phenomenal realism certainly appears to be logically distinct from his idealism. To hold that things are, by and large, just as we sensibly perceive them, does not seem to imply that they are only ideas in the mind, or that their existence consists in being perceived. This observation suggests that the two tenets need to be separately assessed with respect to their motivation and grounds. Further, the fact that Berkeley's phenomenal realism and his idealism so clearly weigh on opposite sides of the "common sense" issue makes one wonder to what extent their respective bases in Berkeley's thought can even be mutually compatible.

Berkeley's defense of phenomenal realism consists largely in showing that the materialist challenge to this position has not been coherently formulated. I have dwelt on this aspect of his philosophy—which I regard as basically correct—in other work; I will not be further concerned with it here.[3] Berkeley's grounds for maintaining idealism are more elusive, however. Indeed, passages from both the *Principles* and the *Dialogues* may suggest strongly that this fateful philosophical thesis rests on nothing more forceful than an uncritical acceptance of the Cartesian and Lockean identification of immediate objects of perception with ideas. For instance, the passage quoted above (on the side of common sense) from the Third Dialogue continues:

> Wood, stone, fire, water, flesh, iron, and the like things, which I name and discourse of, are things that I know. And I should not have known them but that I perceived them by my senses; and things perceived by the senses are immediately perceived; and things immediately perceived are ideas; and ideas cannot exist without the mind; their existence therefore consists in being perceived. . . . (230)

Here the mind-dependence thesis seems to rest on a bald identification of "things immediately perceived" with ideas. In the *Principles* the claim that what we perceive are just our own sensations similarly figures as a premiss in Berkeley's argument that the notion of unperceived existence of sensible things is self-contradictory:

> It is indeed an opinion strangely prevailing amongst men, that houses, mountains, rivers, and in a word all sensible objects have an existence natural or real, distinct from their being perceived by the understanding. But with how great an assurance and acquiescence soever this principle may be entertained in the world; yet whoever shall find in his heart to call it in question, may, if I mistake not, perceive it to involve a manifest contradiction. For what are the forementioned objects but the things we perceive by sense, and what do we perceive besides our own ideas or sensations; and is it not plainly repugnant that any one of these or any combination of them should exist unperceived? (I.4; 42)

Other commentators, such as Ian Tipton and George Pitcher, have pointed out that "what we immediately perceive is always an idea" is a central claim for Berkeley, and further that it is a claim that he seems uncritically to accept from his opponents.[4] Tipton has also shown that many of the arguments that Berkeley offers in defense of idealism are vitiated by his failure to consider the option that what is immediately perceived is a mind-independent physical thing. This position, Tipton stresses, constitutes an alternative to both Lockean-type theories that distinguish ideas from objects, and Berkeley's own identification of objects with mind-dependent ideas. Insofar as Berkeley neglects it, his attempted refutations of the Lockean position, even if successful, fail to establish his own.[5]

It's important to notice, too, that insofar as Berkeley's mind-dependence thesis rests on a claim adopted from his opponents, it rests on considerations that Berkeley cannot even accept. In the work of the scientific realist theorists the claim that the immediate objects of perception are mind-dependent entities derives its primary support from the very assumptions that Berkeley is most dedicated to opposing. For seventeenth century theorists of perception the immediate objects of sense must be mind-dependent entities because they—or large classes of them, anyway—have no place in the materialist scientific account of physical reality.

As is generally acknowledged, however, Berkeley does offer some arguments of his own for the claim that the immediate objects of perception are mind-dependent entities. These arguments, which he deploys in the First Dialogue, center on two basic types of consideration. First, Berkeley tries to establish that certain sense presentations, such as great heat and sweet tastes, are indistinguishable from sensations acknowledged to be mind-dependent, namely pain and pleasure. The second, more complex line of reasoning focuses on considerations of perceptual variability. Both Tipton and Pitcher point to these arguments as the primary support that Berkeley offers for the claim that sensible objects are mind-dependent.[6] They do not regard the arguments as successful, however. In fact I think it would be fair to say that neither regards the arguments as worth very much at all. If they are right, it would seem to follow that the most characteristic and notorious feature of Berkeley's philosophy—the idealism—really lacks any serious foundation. His arguments against materialist scientific realism, according to this line of thought, may provide a respectable defense of *phenomenal* (or *sensory*) *realism*, but this, as I've been indicating, isn't the same as defending idealism.

I would personally prefer it to turn out that idealism with respect to sensible qualities is false. Nevertheless, I think that Berkeley's arguments in the First Dialogue are better arguments (some of them anyway) than Tipton or Pitcher recognizes.[7] Here I will not try to dispute the prevailing negative assessment of the pleasure-pain argument, but I do wish to reexamine the questions of whether and how the facts about perceptual variability that Berkeley cites lend support to his thesis that sensible qualities are mind-dependent. I will focus on Berkeley's treatment of color. I am going to hold that Berkeley's arguments— although certainly not demonstrative and in several other ways defective—do provide serious considerations on behalf of the claim that the colors we normally attribute to physical things are mind-dependent. (Throughout this discussion I will treat "mind-dependent," "perceiver-dependent," and "ideal" as roughly equivalent terms, and will ignore all questions about their relations to metaphysical spiritualism.)

I will finally have to concede, however, that Berkeley's defense of the mind-dependence of colors (among other sensible qualities) is itself inconsistent with his phenomenal realism (though not, of course, for the same reason that the *scientific realist* argument for the mind-dependence of colors is incompatible with phenomenal realism). Thus, even if I succeed to some degree in showing that his arguments from perceptual relativity provide some reason to regard sensible qualities are perceiver-dependent, I will not have done much to vindicate the tenability of his whole position.

I

Arguments from perceptual variability of the sort I have in mind begin with assertions that the sensible appearances of things alter according to the condition or circumstances of the perceiver. From such premisses they proceed to the conclusion that in sense experience (or certain important classes of sense experiences) we are not presented with qualities that exist in things independently of our own acts of perception. The premisses of such an argument may be more or less specific. I am going to claim that Berkeley uses at least three versions of variability argument with respect to color: the first two involve premisses having to do with specific types of perceptual variability, while the third proceeds from more general considerations. Before turning to the arguments, though, I want to set forth certain assumptions that will govern my discussion, and specify certain limitations of its scope.

1. I will assume that to see a color is normally to see something as colored; I won't try to defend this assumption, however; and I won't otherwise be concerned with the relation between "perceiving a color" and "perceiving a thing."

2. I will assume that the issues in question are not bound up with problems of hyperbolic doubt or Cartesian certainty. (I believe that this assumption is consonant with Berkeley's procedure.)

3. I will assume that the following statement is intelligible and acceptable: If an object, or part of an object, appears one determinate color at one time to one observer, and another, contrasting, color at another time and/or to another observer, then either the object has changed or at least one of the color-appearances is perceiver-dependent ("in the eye of the beholder").

4. I will not claim that Berkeley's arguments help in any way to establish that there *is no such thing as* a perceiver-independent color. I believe that the arguments don't have to establish such a strong conclusion in order to be important, and I do not think that Berkeley even intends them to establish the non-existence claim. (On this point I disagree with a central point in Pitcher's critique of the First Dialogue.)

5. I assume that questions about an object's "true color" are almost always resolvable in ordinary life by recourse to reasonably unproblematic "standard conditions" of visual observation. For instance, a flower that looks red in daylight to a normally sighted human, and gray at twilight, is correctly said to be red, not gray. (This fact has some bearing on how arguments from perceptual variability should be developed; however, it does not settle the question whether or not colors are perceiver-dependent.)

6. I assume that the fact that a certain perceptual vantage point is required to perceive a particular quality or circumstance does not in itself show that the quality or circumstance is mind-dependent. For example, the fact that one had to be stand-

ing on the third base line to see whether a particular drive was fair or foul would not show that the fairness-or-foulness of that drive was mind-dependent.

7. Further, the fact that a certain quality or circumstance can be perceived only by someone possessing certain kinds of sense organs, functioning in some "normal" way, does not suffice to show that that quality or circumstance is mind-dependent. (A very loose analogy may serve to illustrate this point: the fact that a certain kind of radiation could be detected only with a properly functioning Geiger counter doesn't necessarily establish that that kind of radiation is Geiger-counter dependent.)

8. Finally, I assume that some perceptual phenomena—things we may say we "see"—really are most plausibly regarded as perceiver-dependent. Examples include "Mach bands,"[8] the "convergence" of railway tracks as they recede from our viewpoint, the "straightness" of the Parthenon columns, stroboscopic motion, the reddish cast a gray square will take on if surrounded by bright green. I will refer to such phenomena as perceptual projections. In a way, we could say that the central issue between Berkeley and his opponents comes down to the question whether the whole physical world is perceptual projection, whether perceptual projection is all there is, besides perceiving minds. At present, however, I am concerned only with a small and qualified piece of this question: namely, whether it is reasonable to regard the colors we normally attribute to objects around us as perceptual projections. More specifically, I am concerned with whether Berkeley's arguments from perceptual variability tend to show that colors should be regarded in this way.

II

As already mentioned, Berkeley's attempt to establish the mind-dependence of color by reasoning from perceptual variability or relativity in fact comprehends at least three distinguishable arguments or argument stages. (Tipton and Pitcher don't clearly demarcate these stages, although Tipton more or less touches on all three of them.) The first I will call the Argument from Close Examination; the second, the Argument from Species Relativity; the third is a generalized form of the Argument from Perceptual Variability. None of these arguments is presented in a fully persuasive form by Berkeley, and the third is surely the worst presented of the three.

In the earlier part of the First Dialogue Philonous has persuaded Hylas that warm and cold, tastes, smells, and sounds "have no being without the mind." Hylas, however, tried to dig in his heels when the discussion turns to colors.

Phil. And I hope you will make no difficulty to acknowledge the same of colours.

Hyl. Pardon me: the case of colours is very different. Can anything be plainer, than that we see them on the objects?

Phil. The objects you speak of are, I suppose, corporeal substances existing without the mind.

Hyl. They are.

Phil. And have true and real colours inhering in them?
Hyl. Each visible object hath that colour which we see in it. (183).

This last naively unqualified assertion is of a type frequently put forward by Hylas in the First Dialogue, making some of Philonous' "refutations" rather too easy. The reader may quickly conclude that Berkeley's arguments would have no force against an intelligent opponent—one who does not, in Tipton's words, "accept some grossly implausible principle such as that which Hylas accepts."[9] Some later phases of Berkeley's discussion of color are in fact vulnerable to objection for this reason, as I'll explain later. The first argument for the mind-dependence of colors, however, does not rely on Hylas' commitment to the presence in objects of the colors we see in them, without qualification. It rather turns, precisely, on a qualification that is quickly introduced.

i. The Argument from Close Examination. "Only be pleased to let me know," Philonous challenges, "whether the same colours which we see, exist in external bodies, or some other." "The very same," Hylas ingenuously replies. "What!" Philonous responds, "are then the beautiful red and purple we see on yonder clouds really in them? Or do you imagine they have in themselves any other form, than that of a dark mist of vapour?" (184) At this point Hylas adjusts his position by introducing a distinction between real and apparent color:

> *Hyl.* I must own, Philonous, those colours are not really in the clouds as they seem to be at this distance. They are only apparent colours.
> *Phil.* *Apparent* call you them? how shall we distinguish these apparent colours from real?
> *Hyl.* Very easily. Those are to be thought apparent, which appearing only at a distance, vanish upon a nearer approach.

Philonous now leads Hylas on to concede that "the nearest and exactest survey" of an object is that made by a microscope, rather than by the naked eye.

> But (Philonous continues) a microscope often discovers colours in an object different from those perceived by the unassisted sight. And in case we had microscopes magnifying to any assigned degree; it is certain, that no object whatsoever viewed through them, would appear in the same colour which it exhibits to the naked eye. (1984)

Philonous now draws from Hylas' "own concessions" the conclusion that:

> all the colours we see with our naked eyes, are only apparent as those on the clouds, since they vanish upon a more close and accurate inspection, which is afforded us by a microscope. (184)

The presentation of this argument winds up with a defense of the claim that microscopes, rather than altering colors through "artificial management," in fact provide a more accurate view of an object, by making our sight more sharp and penetrating. (Microscopes, Philonous says, "represent objects as they would appear to the eye, in case it were naturally endowed with a most exquisite sharpness." They thus can better discover than the naked eye "the real and natural state of an object"; colors that are "more genuine and real.")[10]

This argument is a refutation of the claim that "the same colours which we see exist in external bodies," proceeding from the assumption that the "real" colors are those revealed by the most near and exact survey. The colours which we (normally) see are not, on this assumption, the "real" ones, and must be reconstrued as "apparent" or (ultimately) mind-dependent. (Because the argument depends on this *specific* assumption, it is not *simply* an argument "from perceptual relativity.")

At first sight it may seem that it is easy to dispose of this argument simply by pointing out the untenability of its key assumption. Tipton, for example, rejects this assumption on the ground that standard conditions for determining an object's "real color" do not include microscopic examination. (A shopper may take a piece of cloth into daylight to ascertain its color, but is not likely to subject it to microscopic inspection.)[11] Speaking more generally, it is easy to resist the "slippery slope" reasoning on which this argument depends. Someone who dismisses as "merely apparent" colors seen at a great distance (when different colors are expected on nearer approach), is not thereby committed to dismissing as "merely apparent" colors seen with the naked eye (because different colors are expected upon microscopic examination). There might perfectly well be an ideal point of observation for seeing the real colors—one that is neither too far *nor too near*.

If Berkeley's argument is not conclusive, however, neither is Tipton's response. The columns of the Parthenon are constructed to look straight from the perspective of the usual viewer—not to someone suspended within a few feet of the architrave. Yet we would normally accept the claim of the latter viewer that the columns aren't, after all, straight. The shopper for fabric, like the designers of the Parthenon, is mainly concerned with how the object in question will look from the normal distances of daily human life. That he is satisfied with the "redness" of a cloth that looks red when held at arm's length does not tell us whether or not the redness is, like the straightness of the columns when viewed from the ground, "merely apparent," or whether it is perceiver-dependent.

Further, there is something more that can be said on Berkeley's behalf. Imagine you are standing on a terrace, a few yards from a pink wall. At least, the wall *looks* pink from this fairly normal wall-viewing distance. Suppose, however, that you approach the wall, till it is only a few inches from your nose. From this vantage point you see that the surface of the wall is composed entirely of small bits of red tile and small bits of white tile mixed together. Would not this second observation at least somewhat incline you to say that the pinkness you previously perceived was an appearance arising from your perspective (as well as from certain facts about the wall surface—which do not include any part of it actually being pink)?[12] For myself, I do find that any initial belief in a mind-independent pinkness "in the wall" would be subverted in the circumstances described. Certainly I would not be even slightly inclined to say that the wall has, perceiver-independently, the quality of pinkness, though it can be made to *look* red and white if approached too close.

Thus I agree with Berkeley's basic line of thought on this issue, rather than Tipton's. Close inspection can alter one's original impressions about the color of things, even if the things in question aren't standardly viewed up close. And when such alteration occurs, one may well come to regard the colors originally "seen" as perceiver-dependent appearances, or perceptual projections. Now if we agree with Philonous' claims that, with respect to color, microscopes merely provide a "more close and accurate inspection," *and* that under powerful enough microscopes no object would look the same color as to the naked eye, then I think the reasoning sketched provides at least a good prima facie case for the claim that all the colors we *ordinarily ascribe* to objects are perceiver-dependent appearance, rather than qualities "really inherent" in external things, independent of perception. (Of course this argument cannot support the general conclusion that *all* colors are mind-dependent.)

For now I will leave evaluation of the argument from close examination in this rather inconclusive stage—claiming only to have shown that Tipton's effort to refute it is not successful, and that the position sketched by Philonous has a reasonable intuitive basis.

ii. The Argument from Species Relativity. The previous argument depended on the assumption that the colors perceived by a more "close and accurate" inspection are the more "real," "genuine," or "natural." As Berkeley moves to his next argument, he at first seems to be only developing the earlier line of thought, by substituting the eyes of tiny animals for microscopes:

> Besides, (Philonous continues) it is not only possible but manifest, that there actually are animals, whose eyes are by Nature framed to perceive those things, which by reason of their minuteness escape our sight. . . . Must we suppose they are all stark blind? Or, in case they can see, can it be imagined their sight hath not the same use in preserving their bodies from injuries, which appears in that of all other animals? And if it hath, is it not evident, they must see particles less than their own bodies, which will present them with a far different view in each object, from that which strikes our senses? (185)

The last sentence signals, however, that the terms of argument have changed in an important way. Philonous is now taking as a premiss not the claim that animals able to see tiny particles have a *better* view of the colors of objects, but only that they have a *different* view. Thus, the passage continues:

> Even our own eyes do not always represent objects to us after the same manner. In the *jaundice*, everyone knows that all things seem yellow. Is it not therefore highly probable, those animals in whose eyes we discern a very different texture from that of ours, and whose bodies abound with different humours, do not see the same colours in every object that we do? (185)

From the proposition that animals with different types of eyes from ours and different bodily chemistry see different colors in every object than we do, Berkeley has Philonous draw the desired conclusion without further ado:

> From all which, should it not seem to follow, that all colours are equally apparent, and that none of those which we perceive are really inherent in an outward object? (185)

It's interesting to notice that Berkeley has adduced two types of scientific consideration in sketching this argument. First, there is what we would today identify as the evolutionary consideration: animals' perceptual systems are tailored to their survival needs; and their characteristic visual images of the world may be expected to vary accordingly. Second, we can observe many different visual structures ("textures") across different species, together with other biochemical differences ("humours") which we take to be more or less relevant to perception. Today, for instance, the variation across species of types and groupings of retinal cells provides evidence of differing visual capabilities, which of course link up with the species' characteristic modes of hunting and self-protection.

Particularly vivid, up-to-date illustrations of Berkeley's points in this passage are provided by the fascinating "Nature" film, *Through Animal Eyes*.[13] By combining advanced knowledge of physiology and ethology with advanced computer and photographic techniques, this film seeks to give us some idea of how cheetahs, hawks, owls, and even rattlesnakes see their prey; how motion may be perceived by creatures with compound eyes; and the like. Of most direct relevance to the present discussion are the film's dramatic illustrations of how the colors of familiar flowers and foliage may be transformed if "seen through the eyes" of bees or other insects visually sensitive to ultraviolet radiation. According to the film, certain flowers that humans see as an undistinguished pale mauve may be brilliant yellow to a bee, while our standard white and yellow blossoms from the bee's point of view are fiery, psychodelic red-blue. Further, where we see a homogeneously colored petal surface, the bee may see a range of shades intensifying towards the center—the business end of a flower for a bee. Fascinating as these considerations are, however, Berkeley is surely overoptimistic in taking them straightforwardly to establish that all colors are merely apparent, and none which we perceive are really inherent in outer objects. In fact, his statement of the argument from species relativity exhibits a singularly conspicuous logical gap between the more or less scientific premises and this "philosophical" conclusion. Tipton finds in this passage the point (which he credits to some extent) that our standards of "normal" color vision are incurably anthropocentric: a flower that looks yellow to a normal-sighted human may look greige to a normal Martian, or ultra-violet to a normal bee. He seems to think it relevant to reply that "we have every reason" for taking normal human sight as our standard: in other words (I take it) for accepting the judgment that the flower is yellow.[14]

Berkeley, however, is not really concerned with the point that Tipton addresses: the question, that is, of whether we are justified in asserting that certain flowers are such and such colors. (Even the materialist, after all, is entitled to assert *in a certain sense* that roses are red and violets are blue.) The question Berkeley is trying to settle is whether the colors that we see are mind-independent qualities inhering in external things, or merely perceptual projections. Now why, exactly, are considerations about the variation of color perceptions across different species supposed to resolve this question in favor of the latter alternative?

Perhaps Berkeley does imagine that no one can consistently hold that colors are mind-independent qualities, while admitting that animals of different species may perceive the same things differently with respect to color. He may think, that is, that such differences in the perception of colors would *show* that colors are perceptual projections. This position would not be correct, however, as is clear from the following consideration. It is always *possible* to interpret observations about the species relativity of color perceptions in light of analogies with preferred perceptual vantage points, or non-distorting instruments. Just as you may need to be at a particular position on the ball field to see whether a drive is fair or foul, so (one may propose) you need a *certain type* of eye—say diurnal, non-color-blind mammalian—to see the *real* colors of flowers.

Nevertheless I think the hypothesis that different species see different colors "in things" than we do does help somewhat to establish the plausibility of the mind-dependence thesis (though certainly not to demonstrate its truth). First, although the hypothesis is not logically inconsistent with the view that the colors humans see are real qualities in things, it does manage to make this position look rather ill-founded. In this respect it needs to be contrasted with the variability of color perception associated with, say, color-blindness. If I contend that the red and green I see in the tulip are real, inherent qualities of the tulip, independent of my perception, then I must say that my colorblind friend's perception of the tulip as uniform brown is a *mis*perception. But since color blindness is naturally considered a perceptual defect, this characterization of my friend's conflicting color perception is itself quite natural. Similarly, it seems, if I say that the yellow I see in the buttercup is a real, inherent, mind-independent quality of the buttercup, I must hold that the bee's putative vision of the buttercup as ultraviolet is a misperception. In this case the move seems less natural, however, since it is much less natural to hold that the bee's vision is abnormal or defective relative to my own.

Second, the species relativity hypothesis provides at least prima facie reason to question the apparent *grounds* for our normal *assumption* of the mind-independent status of colors. That things' colors have an outthereness, a constancy, a predictability, a fixedness, an intersubjective verifiability—all features we associate with independence of ourselves—*seems* to be what convinces us that colors are qualities picked up by our perceptual systems, rather than projections of them. The hypothesis of species relativity, however, suggests strongly the idea that the colors of the world could have all these "objective" features, and yet be to a perceiver systematically different, without any changes in the colored things.

Of course we do not really know that flowers "look ultraviolet" to bees—or indeed that they look any way at all to them—and it would be even rasher to say that, for bees, buttercups are fixedly, constantly, predictably ultraviolet.[15] This important consideration places another limitation on the power of the argument from species relativity. Again, my claim is not that the argument can establish idealism with respect to colors, but only that it is relevant to this enterprise, and of some value in making Berkeley's position seem reasonable.

iii. The Argument from Perceptual Relativity. Finally, Berkeley has Philonous state the Argument from Perceptual Relativity in its more famous general form. The argument, as Berkeley presents it, has two phases. First, Philonous appeals to all the changes "the colors of an object" can undergo without a change "in the object," concluding that colors are therefore not themselves in the object. If this phase of the argument is isolated from the second, it appears entirely futile. I will quote enough of the passage to give the idea, omitting, however, several of Berkeley's examples.

> The point will be past all doubt, if you consider, that in case colours were real properties or affections inherent in external bodies, they could admit of no alteration, without some change wrought in the very bodies themselves: but is it not evident . . . that upon the use of microscopes, upon a change happening in the humours of the eyes, or a variation of distance, without any manner of real alteration in the thing itself, the colors of any object are either changed, or totally disappear? (185–86)

After running through the rest of his illustrations Philonous concludes:

> . . . now tell me, whether you are still of opinion, that every body hath its true real colour inhering in it. . . . (186)

As Pitcher and Tipton point out in different ways, Berkeley's argument seems incompetent, insofar as he neglects to consider any possible distinction between the *real* and the *apparent* colors of things.[16] (In fact, a premiss of the reasoning appears to be Hylas' initial, naively unqualified assertion that every object has that color we perceive in it.) Surely, what is "evident" is just that an object may appear different colors under different circumstances without undergoing any intrinsic change (in any ordinary sense). From this it perhaps follows that objects do not always have "the colors we perceive in them," independently of our perceptions. It certainly does not follow either that they never do, or that we cannot know when we are perceiving the real, mind-independent color.

The second phase of this last argument does, however, address this crucial point—though admittedly in a rather offhand way:

> . . . now tell me, whether you are still of opinion that every body hath its true real colour inhering in it; and if you think it hath, I would fain know farther from you, what certain distance and position of the object, what peculiar texture and formation

of the eye, what degree or kind of light is necessary for ascertaining that true colour, and distinguishing it from apparent ones. (186)

Since Berkeley does reintroduce the putative distinction between real and apparent colors in a relevant way at the end of the passage, it is perhaps unfair to insist that his whole deployment of the relativity argument rests on a shallow blunder. A more charitable interpretation would go as follows:

> If you hold without qualification that colors we perceive in objects are really in them, your position reduces to absurdity (for then the qualities of an object could change without the object changing). Thus you need to distinguish real from apparent colors. But to establish this distinction you will need to specify the precise conditions under which the true colors emerge, and this is impossible to do.

Pitcher argues that even if Berkeley is right on this last point, his argument at most establishes the epistemological claim that we can never know what the true color of something is; it cannot establish that colors are not inherent in outer objects, that they are mind-dependent.[17] It seems to me, however, that if Berkeley is able to establish that the distinction between real and apparent colors is without basis, he will have made some progress towards defending idealism. For he will have put his opponent, who wishes to uphold the claim that the colors we perceive in things are independent of our minds, in a rather awkward position. ("Some of the colors we perceive in things are, or may be mind-independent qualities, but we can never know which ones, if any, fit this description": this would surely be a bizarre position for an anti-Berkeleyan to undertake to defend.)

The really fundamental failure of Berkeley's concluding argument for the mind-dependence of colors lies in the fact that the rhetorical question in which it culminates isn't enough to establish Berkeley's point. Leaving aside strange and special considerations such as those adduced in the Arguments from Close Examination and Species Relativity, there seems to be no great difficulty about specifying standard conditions for determining "real colors": we do it all the time.[18] If general considerations about perceptual variability are going to yield any significant support for the mind-dependence thesis, they will have to be supported by conscientious consideration of normal ways of determining standard conditions, rather than by mere tacit dismissal of the latter. The earlier arguments do raise specific problems about the usual concept of standard conditions, which (I have suggested) are not without effect. Lacking further consideration of this issue, the last phases of Berkeley's defense of the view that colors are mind-dependent make no further useful contribution, even if some objections against them can be met.

I mentioned at the beginning that Berkeley is of course not entitled to scientific realist arguments for the mind-dependence of colors. It should now be clear that the arguments he offers in the First Dialogue for the mind-dependence of colors are themselves incompatible with the simple common sense ascriptions of colors to things ("the wall is white") that he elsewhere identifies as his own position. Most directly incompatible with common sense color ascriptions are the premises of the Argument from Close Examination: that the true colors of things are only revealed by microscopic examination, and are always different from those that appear to the naked eye (even under favorable conditions). In addition, however, Berkeley's last two arguments in this section of the *Dialogues* attempt to establish that colors are mind-dependent by undermining the conception of things as having *one* true color. Of course the idealist conclusion of these arguments ("colors are mind-dependent") conflicts with common sense in one way (insofar as we do normally take colors to "inhere" in mind-independent things). But, even more important for the coherence of Berkeley's philosophy, the assumptions of the arguments conflict with that part of common sense notions about colors that Berkeley explicitly tries to embrace: the view that things really do, literally, have colors—the very colors we commonly ascribe to them. I conclude that Berkeley cannot maintain both his own perceptual variability arguments for idealism, and his claim to side with common sense on the presence of colors in things.[19]

NOTES

1. *Works*, vol. II, p. 229. All passages from Berkeley cited in this paper are from this volume. Henceforth I give the page references only.

2. Nicholas Sturgeon has observed (in comments on a version of this paper presented at a Cornell University Philosophy Department colloquium) that it is unclear what "mind-dependent" is supposed to mean. This is a question which clearly requires a far deeper and more detailed response—both historical and critical—than I am able to offer here. For present purposes I can only indicate that what I mean by the term in this paper is something like this: to say that a thing or quality is "mind-dependent" is to say that *it is just* an appearance to a perceiving subject (or subjects). (The statement of identity is not intended ultimately to rule out the possibility that mind-dependent entities are "well-founded," in some quasi-Leibnizian sense, in non-appearances—though this is of course not an issue with respect to Berkeley's own views.)

In the same comments Sturgeon also suggests that the version of phenomenal realism that Berkeley tends to endorse is not the "moderate," commonsensical view I ascribe to him—that things are by and large as we perceive them—but rather an "extreme" phenomenal realism, according to which things are *exactly* as we perceive them. On this interpretation Berkeley's claims to be an ally of common sense are unsustainable even considered just in relation to the phenomenal realist dimension of his position. There is much to be said for this interpretive position. I regret that time constraints have prevented me from taking it into account more fully in the text of the paper.

3. "Did Berkeley Completely Misunderstand the Basis of the Primary-Secondary Quality Distinction in Locke?" in Colin Turbayne, editor, *Berkeley: Critical and Interpretive Essays*, Minneapolis: University of Minnesota Press, 1982, pp. 108–23 (Chapter 15 of this volume). See also, "Berkeley and the Essences of the Corpuscularians," in John Foster and Howard Robinson, editors, *Essays on Berkeley*, Oxford: Clarendon Press, 1985, pp. 131–47 (Chapter 17 of this volume).

4. I.C. Tipton, *Berkeley: The Philosophy of Immaterialism*, London: Methuen, 1974, 63ff. and *passim*; George Pitcher, *Berkeley*, London: Routledge and Kegan Paul, 1977, 94ff.

5. *Berkeley*, 65–71; 179–81.

6. See Tipton, *Berkeley*, 227ff; Pitcher, *Berkeley*, 100–106.

7. D.M. Armstrong offers a more favorable assessment of Berkeley's perceptual variability arguments than either Pitcher or Tipton: see "Colour Realism and the Argument from Microscopes" in *The Nature of Mind and Other Essays*, Ithaca: Cornell University Press, 1981 (ch. 7). My own treatment, in fact, has a number of points in common with Armstrong's, although when I first developed it I did not know about his paper. Armstrong's position is criticized by David R. Hilbert in *Color and Color Perception*, Stanford: CSLI Lecture Notes, Number 9, 1987, ch. 2. Although I am not persuaded by his counterarguments, I will not attempt to reply to them in the present context.

8. Mach bands are bright and dark "stripes" that appear on a figure shading from light to black, where there are no corresponding changes in physical luminance: see, e.g., Lloyd Kaufman, *Perception: The World Transformed*, New York: Oxford University Press, 1979, 304–305. One could also instance the bright "triangles," "spots," and "streets" that appear in the patterns discussed in "The Amateur Scientist" section of *The Scientific American*, January, 1988, pp. 96–99.

9. *Berkeley*, 241.

10. In the Third Dialogue Berkeley has Philonous present the quite different view that the same object is *not* perceived by the microscope, "which was by the naked eye" (245). On the conflict between the statements about microscopes in the First and Third Dialogues see Bruce Silver, "The Conflicting Microscopic Worlds of Berkeley's *Three Dialogues*," *Journal of the History of Ideas*, vol. 37 (1976), 343–49.

11. Tipton, *Berkeley*, 244–45.

12. A similar example is discussed by Armstrong in "Colour Realism."

13. This film was shown in the "Nature" series on Public Television in (I believe) the spring of 1985.

14. *Berkeley*, 251.

15. The film, it should be stressed, does not pretend to have established otherwise.

16. Tipton, *Berkeley*, 253–55; Pitcher, *Berkeley*, 104–106.

17. *Berkeley*, 106.

18. I do not in the least mean to suggest that the notion of "standard conditions" for determining things' colors is wholly free of difficulty, considered from a sophisticated philosophical or scientific perspective. (On this issue see Clyde L. Hardin, "Colors, Normal Observers, and Standard Conditions," *The Journal of Philosophy*, vol. lxxx (1983), 806–13.) My point is only that the type of argument Berkeley is deploying cannot succeed by simply ignoring (or implicitly denying) the fact that we do commonly distinguish with confidence a thing's "real" color from the colors it merely "looks" under special circumstances.

19. A number of people have made significant criticisms and suggestions concerning my arguments in this paper, some of which have influenced the present form of the work, others of which I hope to take more adequately into account in subsequent presentations. I would particularly like to thank Nicholas Sturgeon and Edward Wilson Averill for detailed comments. I would also like to thank Emmett Wilson, Jr. for invaluable last-minute technical and editorial assistance in preparing the manuscript.

Berkeley and the Essences of the Corpuscularians

I

In the *Principles and the Dialogues* Berkeley repeatedly connects his defence of the unproblematic reality of things as we sensibly experience them with the denial that we are ignorant of 'the internal constitution, the true and real nature' of physical objects. The issue is raised insistently in the *Third Dialogue*, particularly towards the beginning. Hylas keeps asserting that the restriction of our knowledge to the sensible appearances of things means that it is not possible for us ever to know the real nature of any thing in the universe, 'what it is in itself' (*Dialogues*, 227). As he further explains to Philonous:

> You may indeed know that fire appears hot, and water fluid: but this is no more than knowing what sensations are produced in your own mind, upon the application of fire and water to your organs of sense. Their internal constitution, their true and real nature, you are utterly in the dark as to *that*.

Philonous, in return, stigmatizes these pessimistic views as 'wild and extravagant' contending that Hylas is led into them by the belief in material substance:

> This makes you dream of those unknown natures in every thing. It is this occasions your distinguishing between the reality and sensible appearances of things. It is to this you are indebted for being ignorant of what every body else knows perfectly well. (*Dialogues*, 229.)

The same point is expressed more colourfully in a later exchange;

> *Hylas.* . . . you may pretend what you please; but it is certain, you leave us nothing but the empty forms of things, the outside only which strikes the senses.
> *Philonous.* What you call the empty forms and outside of things, seems to me the very things themselves. Nor are they empty or incomplete otherwise, than upon your supposition, that matter is an essential part of all corporeal things. (*Dialogues*, 244.)

In the *Principles* Berkeley explicitly describes the doctrine of hidden inner natures as a primary source of scepticism, and maintains that his philosophy removes this ground for challenging the adequacy of human knowledge. He goes so far as to indicate that his position allows us to claim 'perfect comprehension' of physical things.

> . . . all that stock of arguments [the sceptics] produce to depreciate our faculties, and make mankind appear ignorant and low, are drawn principally from his head, to wit, that we are under an invincible blindness as to the *true* and *real* nature of

things. . . . We are miserably bantered, say they, by our senses, and amused only
with the outside and shew of things. The real essence, the internal qualities, and
constitution of every the meanest object, is hid from our view; something there is in
every drop of water, every grain of sand, which it is beyond the power of human
understanding to fathom or comprehend. But it is evident from what has been
shewn, that all this complaint is groundless, and that we are influenced by false
principles to that degree as to mistrust our senses, and think we know nothing of
those things which we perfectly comprehend. (*PHK*, 101.)

These passages appear to develop a theme already sounded in the *Philosophical
Commentaries*: 'My Doctrine affects the Essences of the Corpuscularians'.[1]

Daniel Garber has recently focused on Berkeley's remark about hidden natures in an original and interesting paper, 'Locke, Berkeley and Corpuscular
Skepticism'.[2] Garber plausibly relates Berkeley's statements to Locke's contention that the real essences of things are unknowable to us because of the limitations of our faculties.[3] As Garber notes, Locke connects his conception of inaccessible real essences with the corpuscularian theory of matter: our inability to
know real essences is linked by Locke to the view that we are unable to perceive the inner corpuscular structure of things, because of the grossness of our
senses.[4] (Locke acknowledges that corpuscularianism may not provide the ultimate truth about the nature of physical things; however, he evidently thinks it
is the best theory we will ever have. And if real essences are not, in fact,
corpuscular structures, they consist in something 'still more remote from our
comprehension'.[5]) Garber stresses that this 'corpuscular skepticism' 'infects'
Locke's *Essay*. He observes that it is an issue of more persistent and systematic
interest to Locke than the 'veil of perception skepticism' engendered by the
view that we do not immediately perceive material things, but only the 'ideas'
they supposedly cause in us. Part of the purpose of Garber's paper is to insist
on the distinction between corpuscular and veil-of-perception scepticism, and to
call attention to the fact that commentators have tended to ignore Berkeley's
repudiation of the former, while dwelling on his concern with subverting the
latter.[6]

Garber's discussion indicates, however, that Berkeley's position on corpuscular scepticism is considerably more complex than his position on absolutely
existing matter. Berkeley, we know, is able to reject this 'matter' as a useless
hypothesis: not only is it unperceivable (as the wholly 'external' cause of our
perceptions); it also lacks any prospect of explanatory value, since the materialists themselves admit that they are unable to explain how it is *possible* or
conceivable that matter should produce ideas of sense. (See, for instance, *PHK*
50.) But, Garber holds, Berkeley does not categorically take such a position
with respect to the corpuscular theory of inner structures. In *Principles* 60–6, in
particular, Berkeley seems to assume the existence of inner mechanisms, and to
ascribe genuine explanatory power to this conception. Garber goes on to argue
that (1) Berkeley accepted the reality of corpuscles insensible to us; (2) Berkeley had at hand the theoretical resources for satisfactorily reconciling this position with his idealistic immaterialism (though he did not explicitly utilize them

in this connection); and (3) Berkeley's explicit rejection of scepticism relating to our ignorance of inner natures is also reconcilable with his manner of embracing corpuscularianism.

I wish to dispute—with varying degrees of opposition—Garber's conclusions on each of these points. First, I will try to show that Garber overreads *Principles* 60–6 in taking these sections to imply endorsement of an 'immaterialist corpuscularianism'. (He says that these sections provide 'the most convincing evidence' (in the early works) that Berkeley accepted a form of corpuscularianism.[7]) Second, I will challenge his claim that Berkeley could successfully reconcile immaterialist corpuscularianism with the fundamental principles of his philosophy in the way that Garber proposes, while also exploring some further complexities in the problem of insensible entities. Third, I will examine Garber's reasons for holding that Berkeley's reconception of the doctrine of inner structures enables him to retain such a doctrine while avoiding the 'corpuscular scepticism' of his opponents. Although I think that part of what Garber says in support of this view is interestingly correct, I will suggest that his conclusion is still overly optismistic. I will also try to show that the interest of this latter issue does not wholly depend upon whether Garber is warranted in ascribing 'immaterialist corpuscularianism' to Berkeley. For it is at least clear that Berkeley accepts in some form the view that microscopic science is capable of vastly extending our comprehension of nature, presumably in an open-ended, non-terminating way. And it is at least prima facie doubtful whether the acceptance of such a view can be reconciled with his rejection of inner qualities and constitutions, or his affirmations that we 'perfectly comprehend' physical things.

II

In *Principles* 60–6 Berkeley is attempting to answer a quite specific objection to his position. On Berkeley's view ideas are 'inert' or causally inefficacious, and physical things are only ideas of sense or collection of such ideas. All causal efficacy with respect to the production of ideas of sense is ascribed to God, who causes these ideas in our minds directly, or without material intermediary. According to the objection that Berkeley wants to meet, his theory about God's direct causation of ideas renders *unaccountable* 'that curious organization of plants, and the admirable mechanism in the parts of animals'—or for that matter the relevance of inner springs and wheels to the observed movement of the hands of a watch.

> . . . might not vegetables grow, and shoot forth leaves and blossoms, and animals perform all their motions, as well without as with all that variety of internal parts so elegantly contrived and put together, which being ideas have nothing powerful or operative in them, nor have any necessary connexion with the effects ascribed to them? If it be a spirit that immediately produces every effect by a *fiat*, or act of his will, we must think all that is fine and artificial in the works, whether of man or Nature, to be made in vain. (*PHK*, 60)

If it is 'an intelligence' that directs the hand of a watch, why may he not do it without the artisan going to the trouble to construct the inner movements; 'Why does not an empty case serve as well as another?' Berkeley concludes the objection:

> The like may be said of all the clockwork of Nature, great part whereof is so wonderfully fine and subtle, as scarce to be discerned by the best microscope. In short, it will be asked, how upon our principles any tolerable account can be given, or any final cause assigned of an innumerable multitude of bodies and machines framed with the most exquisite art, which in the common philosophy have very apposite uses assigned them, and serve to explain abundance of phenomena. (60.)

In 64 the objection is restated this way:

> . . . ideas are not any how and at random produced, there being a certain order and connexion between them, like that of cause and effect: there are also several combinations of them, made in a very regular and artificial manner, which seem like so many instruments in the hand of Nature, that being hid as it were behind the scenes, have a secret operation in producing those appearances which are seen on the theatre of the world, being themselves discernible only to the curious eye of the philosopher. But since one idea cannot be the cause of another, to what purpose is that connexion? And since those instruments, being barely *inefficacious perceptions* in the mind [according to Berkeley's philosophy], are not subservient to the production of natural effects; it is demanded why they are made, or, in other words, what reason can be assigned why God should make us, upon a close inspection into his works, behold so great variety of ideas, so artfully laid together, and so much according to rule . . . ?

Berkeley's response to this objection includes two basic claims. First, the 'ideas' we observe on 'close inspection' of God's works are indeed no more causally efficacious than any other ideas, but are rather to be understood as *signs*. Secondly, the fact that there are such ideas, beheld on close inspection, is necessary for *regularity* in nature; it accounts for our ability to systematize and make more predictable, 'what we are to expect from such and such actions, and what methods are proper to be taken for the exciting such and such ideas' (*PHK*, 65).

Garber acknowledges that 'Berkeley does not explicitly use the *word* "corpuscle" in these passages'.[8] Nevertheless, he interprets *Principles* 60–6 as supporting the attribution to Berkeley of an 'immaterialist corpuscularianism'. In defending this reading Garber first notes, correctly, that 'never once in the course of his lengthy response does [Berkeley] suggest that the objects in question do not really have internal parts'.[9] Secondly, in portraying 'mechanisms' as necessary to the order and regularity of natural phenomena, 'Berkeley does not say that God set things up in such a way that we can always *actually discover* the mechanism behind the manifest properties of things'.[10] Further, Berkeley does not in any way imply an *instrumentalist* conception of the inner constituents of things (as he does, for example, in the case of gravitational attraction).

But even if all this is granted, why should we suppose that Berkeley 'meant to include the hidden corpuscular substructure of things'[11] when he argues, in these passages, that his conception of the causation of phenomena does not actually render explanatorily nugatory the inner mechanisms of organic bodies or human machines? Garber offers the following reasons for supposing that Berkeley had 'insensible corpuscles' in mind.[12] First, corpuscles are after all needed to explain magnetic and chemical and physical phenomena just as wheels and springs are needed to explain the movement of a watch hand. Second, although Berkeley doesn't mention corpuscles by name, 'his language is virtually identical with the language that Locke uses when talking about corpuscles'. For example, like Locke, Berkeley speaks of the 'size, figure, motion, and disposition of *parts*'.[13] (Garber also cites other examples.) Finally, 'Berkeley makes use of the most characteristic metaphor of the corpuscularians when he compares the mechanisms of nature to the workings of a clock'.[14]

I do not find these arguments convincing. In these sections Berkeley is confronting an opponent who simply argues that on his principles the organization of nature as we know it makes no sense. Berkeley contends that this organization does have a point, though not a causal role. It is true that the passage shows that Berkeley shares an important component of the corpuscularians' conception of nature: the notion of natural mechanisms. This is no evidence, however, that he shared the specifically corpuscularian component: the notion of *imperceptible* mechanisms. The fact that the language Berkeley uses in this passage (or puts into the mouth of his objector) resembles Locke's language when he talks about corpuscles need reflect no more than the fact that Locke, like other corpuscularians, models corpuscularian theory on observable mechanistic structures (like clockworks). It need not be taken to imply that Berkeley himself accepts this extension.

Of course the discussion in this passage may legitimately raise the question *whether* Berkeley has in mind 'imperceptible' as well as observable mechanisms. But in considering this question I think one must note that throughout these sections Berkeley persistently phrases both objection and response in terms of mechanisms that are at least minimally perceivable by us: that are, in fact among our 'ideas'.

> The like may be said of all the clockwork of Nature, great part whereof is so wonderfully fine and subtle, as scarce to be discerned by the best microscope. . . . (*PHK* 60) . . . *ideas* are not any how and at random produced, there being a certain order and connexion *between them* . . . there are also several combinations *of them* . . . which *seem* like so many instruments in the hand of Nature, . . . *being themselves discernible only to the curious eye of the philosopher.* (*PHK*, 64; emphasis added.)

Berkeley's account of the order of nature in terms of the relationship, among ideas, of sign to thing signified seems especially to imply that he is conceiving the problem in terms of observables.

> . . . the reason why ideas are formed into machines, that is, artificial and regular combinations, is the same with that for combining letters into words. That a few

original ideas may be made to signify a great number of effects and actions, it is necessary they be variously combined together: and to the end their use be permanent and universal, these combinations must be made by *rule*, and with *wise contrivance*. By this means abundance of information is conveyed unto us, concerning what we are to expect from such and such actions, and what methods are proper to be taken, for the exciting such and such ideas: which in effect is all that I conceive to be distinctly meant, when it is said that *by discerning* the figure, texture, and mechanism of the inward parts of bodies, whether natural or artificial, we may attain to know the several uses and properties depending thereon, or the nature of the thing. (*PHK*, 65; last emphasis added.)

According to this picture mechanisms are conceived in terms of 'original ideas' that function as signs *to us*. Similarly, Berkeley does not merely fail to mention imperceptible corpuscles: he couches his whole account in terms of figures, textures, and mechanisms that we discern.[15]

I would claim, then, that nothing in these sections strongly indicates that Berkeley is trying to establish the consistency of his principles with any doctrine of imperceptible corpuscles—materialist or 'immaterialist'—and a good deal indicates that he is not. Still, the first point raised by Garber remains significant: aren't insensible entities *needed* for a comprehensive predictive science of nature? Indeed, this is a crucial reason for concern about Berkeley's position on insensible corpuscles: it certainly seems that a science recognizing only correlations on the level of sensible appearances must be explanatorily deficient in comparison to one that admits 'theoretical entities'. Despite the importance of the question, however, it seems to me wishful to think that Berkeley implicitly addresses it in *Principles* 60–6.[16]

Further, there is an additional important point that must be kept in mind. To the extent that Berkeley's opponent is conceived as a Lockean 'corpuscular skeptic', he is not being conceived as someone in a position to claim much explanatory superiority over Berkeley in this area. Such a sceptic (as personified by Hylas) holds that we are altogether ignorant of the specific natures of things (not just that our knowledge of them is imperfect or partly conjectural). We are not likely to find *this* figure opposing Berkeley by arguing that a realism about insensible entities is needed to provide ontological grounding for elegant explanations of why gold is fusible and wood not!

III

After ascribing a version of corpuscularian doctrine to Berkeley, Garber goes on to raise the question how Berkeley can 'recognize the existence of insensible corpuscles if external objects are to be clusters of *ideas*'.[17] He notes that Berkeley doesn't address this question directly, but he believes that a satisfactory answer can be proposed on Berkeley's behalf. In effect, Berkeley's appeal to ideas in God's mind to provide for the existence of ordinary sensible objects, when they are not being perceived by finite minds, may be extended to 'insensible corpuscles' as well.

This proposal, while resourceful, runs into several weighty problems. I will first summarize the details of Garber's explanation, then sketch some objections to his strategy.

Garber expresses Berkeley's position concerning 'the real existence of external objects when no one is sensing them' in the following terms: 'sensible things, when not being perceived by finite minds, exist as ideas in God's mind, ideas that He would produce in us if we were in appropriate circumstances'.[18] Garber argues that Locke did not regard corpuscles as *in principle* unobservable: that is, we *would* be able to observe them if we had more acute senses or more powerful instruments. But Berkeley too refers to microscopes, and the possibility of more acute sense organs than we in fact have. So he too may be supposed to distinguish between things that are in fact observable, and things only observable in principle. Thus,

> Given that it is not in principle impossible to observe the corpuscles, one can give an account of their real existence that is exactly parallel to Berkeley's account of the real existence of the hidden wheels of the watch. The insensible corpuscles may be said to exist as ideas in God's mind, which we would have if we were in appropriate circumstances. Of course, the specification of appropriate circumstances involves more than just opening the watch case; it involves positing appropriately strong microscopes or appropriately penetrating sense organs. But this makes no difference with regard to the question of their real existence.[19]

It is true that in the *Dialogues* Berkeley holds that sensible things 'depend not on my thought, and have an existence distinct from being perceived by me . . .' (*Dialogues*, 212). He regards this claim, together with the fundamental doctrine that sensible things cannot exist otherwise than in a mind or spirit, as showing that there must be some other mind in which they exist: 'As sure therefore as the sensible world really exists, so sure is there an infinite omnipresent spirit who contains and supports it'. (*Dialogues*, 212.) Unfortunately, this and other related passages invite many questions about just what conception of existence in God's mind Berkeley means to advance, and how it relates to other tenets of his philosophy.

Aspects of these questions have been explored by other writers.[20] Here I need only indicate a few central points. First, although Berkeley does sometimes talk of God's 'perceiving' things, he cannot really mean that God has sensuous awareness like ours. For he definitely tells us that God, a wholly active being, 'perceives nothing by sense as we do', 'can suffer nothing, nor be affected with any painful sensation, or indeed any sensations at all'. God, he says, 'knows or hath ideas; but His ideas are not convey'd to Him by sense, as ours are' (*Dialogues*, 241). The divine ideas, it later emerges, may be considered 'archetypes' to which our various ideas of sense are referred' (*Dialogues*, 248; cf. 254).

These moves, if taken seriously, render it very unclear what, after all, the existence of sensible objects consists in for Berkeley (not entirely, it would seem, in being *perceived*); or indeed what they *are* (not, it would seem, just congeries of sensations). Certainly, the remarks render very problematic Garber's claim that 'insensible corpuscles may be said to exist as ideas in God's mind, which we would have if we were in appropriate circumstances'.[21] Assuming it is of the nature of an idea of sense to be 'conveyed by sense' the infinite all-active spirit can hardly be said straightforwardly to *'have' such ideas*— though I suppose he might be ascribed some intellectual comprehension of *what it is to have* such ideas. Further, Berkeley's statements leave unilluminated the question of what existence in God's mind might consist in, if not in 'being perceived'. In being understood? But then, it seems either Berkeley must subscribe to the unpopular Spinozistic view that everything in God's understanding is actual,[22] or he must provide some way of conceptualizing the distinction between *mere* existence in God's understanding, and the way that *actual* things exist in God's understanding.[23]

I conclude, therefore, that the allusions to existence in God do not provide us with a way of establishing that Berkeley can coherently maintain the existence of insensible corpuscles. For the statements about existence in God are themselves both exceedingly unclear, and very hard to reconcile with other fundamental Berkeleian doctrines.

Of course not all attempts to explain 'unsensed existence' in Berkeleian terms rely directly on appeal to existence in God's mind. But is there any other way than the one chosen by Garber that will help reconcile the postulation of insensible corpuscles with the basic tenets of Berkeley's position?[24] Consideration of this issue will at least serve to show the need for greater precision in the statement of the problem.

Consider first George Pitcher's explication, within Berkeleian constraints, of the notion that ordinary sensible objects continue to exist when no one is in fact perceiving them. Sensible objects are, for Berkeley, collections of ideas of sense. But, Pitcher asserts, the ideas belonging to the 'collection' that is the physical object are by no means all actual ideas.

> . . . for Berkeley, what we ordinarily call a (single) physical object—e.g., a fig tree—is actually a huge metaphysically grounded family of ideas of sense. Some of these are actual ideas of sense, but most of them are non-actual, possible ideas of sense. The series of *actual* ideas of sense that belong to the family that constitutes any given object is almost certain not to be temporally dense—that is, there will be moments at which none of them occurs. These are the moments when the object is unobserved. But Berkeley's system by no means entails that the object lapses into non-existence at such moments.[25]

(Pitcher explains 'possible sense ideas' in terms of God's intentions or dispositions; see note 24 above.) A key statement in this passage is the remark, 'some of these are actual ideas of sense'. As Pitcher elsewhere expresses the point, possible ideas of sense 'give an *extra degree* of reality to any object'.[26] The explicit wording of this analysis restricts its relevance to objects that are in fact, actually, sometimes perceived, or in other words can be considered as families of the ideas that include some actual ones. It may be extended to 'insensible corpuscles' just in case such entities are only, so to speak, temporarily or partially unsensed—just in case, that is, they are actually sensed at some (future) time by us.[27]

A good deal depends, therefore, on exactly how we understand Garber's phrase 'sensible in principle', as it allegedly applies to corpuscles. If we take it to imply that corpuscles, while insensible in respect of not being among our present objects of observation, will come to be sensed, then the case of corpuscles does collapse to that of Pitcher's fig tree.[28] Suppose, on the contrary (as Garber seems to suppose)[29] that Berkeley regarded corpuscles as 'sensible in principle' in some sense that does not assume that they will ever be sensed by us. Then there are two options to consider. The phrase could mean only that corpuscle-perceptions are a logical possibility: that their imperceptibility to us has to do with the system of regularities that God has ordained in our world—in simple terms, with the laws of physics and physiology. Various complications would then ensue. For example, we could not simply say 'God stands ready to cause sensible ideas of corpuscles—to make them [the ideas] actual—in case any finite mind should be in a position to perceive them'.[30] We should have further to tie the possible perception of corpuscles to God's willingness to suspend the laws of regular association that he has ordained. The notion of 'being in a position to perceive them' would be tied to the possibility of a miracle. We might even wonder whether, on this understanding, the 'perceivability in principle' of corpuscles is sufficient to ground their actuality, or *only* their possibility. (In some possible world, different from the actual one, human beings perceive corpuscles, which therefore exist in that world.)

Perhaps on these assumptions the case of corpuscles would be similar to that of *other* kinds of entities that we want to postulate even though it is, or *seems*, physically impossible that human beings should ever perceive them, such as extremely distant stars, or the primal soup. It is at least worth considering, though, whether the case with respect to corpuscles would not be even worse. For one thing, at least many of the physical things that we want to say exist though we will never be able to perceive them, are of the same sort as things that we do perceive, for example, stars. They have, so to speak, a generic perceivability. We may therefore say, 'Stars exist, though some are too far away to be perceivable', anchoring this generic actuality statement in actual star perceptions. No similar claim can be made about corpuscles, on the present assumptions.[31]

Suppose, finally, that when we say that corpuscles are perceivable in principle we mean not that they *are* perceived (at some future time, though not yet), nor, on the other hand, that they are merely possible perceptions in the sense that there exist in God's mind possible worlds, with different 'laws' than ours, in which corpuscles are perceived. Suppose we mean that there is no 'physical impossibility' in perceiving corpuscles, but that corpuscle perceptions are absent from our world because (say) no one gets around to constructing a powerful enough microscope. (Whether we could be entitled to claim that corpuscles are forever unperceived *only* for such reasons is of course a separate problem.) In this case corpuscles would be more problematic, in Berkeley's system, than the unobserved fig tree in the quad, but arguably they would be very near in status to the tree that grows and perishes in an unexplored forest. (Though here again the issue of generic perception might need to be considered.)

I do not claim, then, to have shown that the hypothesis of insensible corpuscles, on every natural understanding of that hypothesis, raises problems within Berkeley's system different from every problem that may be raised about ordinary physical things. I only claim that the hypothesis raises considerably more difficulties than Garber recognizes. These have to do mainly with the general significance of 'existence in God', but partly also with special problems that arose with respect to 'insensible' entities. The problems are not avoided by claiming that corpuscles are 'perceptible in principle'; and weaker interpretations of the latter phrase—such as Garber seems to intend—make them more difficult than the stronger ones I have also sketched.

It might seem in any case, that the supposition that corpuscular structures exist as mysterious archetypes in God's mind—*at least* presently inaccessible to us because of the grossness of our faculties—runs Berkeley dangerously near to the assumption of unknowable inner natures that he was so bent on denying. Garber evidently believes, however, that Berkeley can accept immaterialist corpuscles, while avoiding corpuscular scepticism. In the last section I will evaluate this claim.

IV

Garber assumes that Berkeley will grant that the corpuscular substructure of things is 'unknown and for all practical purposes unknowable'.[32] He believes, however, that this position does not entail corpuscular scepticism, because it does not entail ignorance of real natures. Corpuscular substructures are only collections of ideas, albeit ideas that we can or will never have. As such they are causally inefficacious: in particular, they do not satisfy the Lockean conception of a real nature as the productive source of the appearances a thing presents to us. Garber observes:

> . . . this removes the principal motivation for considering the corpuscular substructure to constitute the real nature of body. Since the corpuscular substructure is not the productive cause of the manifest properties of bodies, it has no claim to represent the real nature of bodies.[33]

In a sense Berkeley's philosophy does not reduce the scope of our ignorance, in comparison to Locke's, but it does transform that ignorance 'from a matter of great importance' to 'ignorance of a much more benign sort'.[34] We need no longer think of ourselves as ignorant of the '*true* and *real* nature of things', but only of 'empirical facts about the interconnection of ideas'—an inevitable and non-demeaning consequence of the fact that our minds are finite.[35]

At first sight this victory over 'corpuscular skepticism' may well seem far too cheap. It does not seem clear why the denial of genuine causal efficacy in nature should be in itself sufficient to resolve the problem of unknown 'real natures'.[36] After all, even if corpuscular ideas do not strictly cause anything, they must evidently be ascribed the same systematizing and predictive—even 'explanatory'—role as what we ordinarily *treat* as causes (when we say, for example, that the watch hand's movement is caused by inner wheels and springs). Why shouldn't 'corpuscular substructures' still be regarded as inner natures of things, when they are reinterpreted as fundamental 'original' elements of the divine system of ideas?

There is, however, another consideration that lends support to Garber's distinction between 'ignorance of corpuscular structures' and 'corpuscular skepticism' of the non-benign sort. Locke's real essences, it seems, do not merely stand in the relation of efficacious cause to sensible properties; they also stand in the relation of transcendental reality (what a thing 'is in itself', as Berkeley puts it) to *mere* subjective ideas in our minds. The immaterialist corpuscularianism that Garber ascribes to Berkeley would enable him to retain corpuscular theory, while denying both that corpuscular structures stand as unknown causes to the effects we observe, and that they stand as transcendental realities in contrast to the mere sensible appearances with which we are amused. Although Garber emphasizes the first point, the second may actually be more persuasive.

The second point is persuasive, that is, *provided* that the status of corpuscles as divine archetypes, different from our ideas of sense and (perhaps) wholly inaccessible to us, does not itself generate a reality-appearance distinction closely analogous to the materialists'. This concern is very similar to one expressed by Samuel Johnson, to which Berkeley disappointingly failed to reply. As Johnson implies, the more archetypes are divorced from our ideas of sense, the more they threaten to play the role of matter all too well.[37] From this point of view, too, reliance on existence in God's mind seems a problematic and potentially self-destructive device within Berkeley's empiricist system.

Finally, I would like to mention two problems connected with this discussion that arise whether or not one follows Garber in ascribing immaterialist corpuscularianism to Berkeley. The first is rather obvious. It seems that Berkeley's acknowledgement, in *Principles* 60–6, of the scientific extension of our knowledge of nature, cuts directly against his ebullient claim that we 'perfectly comprehend' physical things, his dismissal of the view that there is something that exceeds our comprehension in every drop of water or grain of sand. Of course these claims fare even worse if one agrees with Garber that Berkeley means to affirm the reality of corpuscular substructures that are 'unknown and for all practical purposes unknowable'.[38] But they remain quite baffling even if one merely assumes that the divine language of nature, however accessible to us, is also inexhaustible.[39]

Another problem is this. Part of what Berkeley means when he says that we perfectly comprehend sensible objects is, presumably, that things should not be supposed to be systematically *different* in reality from how they appear to the senses. For instance, they do not in reality lack the colours that we perceive 'in' them. A theory of 'inner structures', whether sensible or insensible, may not at first seem to cause any trouble for *his* position. Just as a thing can look different from the front and the back, so it can look different (to us, or so to speak, to God) from the outside and the inside. Different aspects or ideas may to this extent non-competitively constitute a thing. Berkeley attempts to extend this analysis to the distinction between the ordinary appearance of something and the way it appears under a microscope. Thus, Hylas introduces the example of the microscope to challenge Philonous' defence of the common-sense image of reality:

> *Hylas.* You say you believe your senses; and seem to applaud your self that in this you agree with the vulgar. According to you therefore, the true nature of a thing is discovered by the senses. If so . . . why should we use a microscope, the better to discover the true nature of a body, if it were discoverable to the naked eye? (*Dialogues*, 245.)

Philonous replies that microscopes just give us new ideas to add to our collections of appearances of things. They do not get us any closer to 'the nature of the thing'. Hylas' assumption that there is an 'inconsistency' among our ideas of sense—with those derived from microscopic examination to be regarded as the more accurate—is just one more noxious outcome of his 'preconceived notion of (I know not what) one single, unchanged, unperceivable, real nature' (*Dialogues*, 245). But in fact the example Hylas has adduced raises a problem that is not at all closely tied to either 'corpuscular' or 'veil of perception' scepticism. One may reject nearly every aspect of the doctrine of unperceivable real natures, and remain convinced that the ordinary sensory experience of things is not to be 'trusted'. Berkeley's position that microscopic examination merely adds to our ordinary sensible ideas of things, without correcting them, may well be a consistent one; the problem is just that it is so very hard to believe. Similarly, it is equally hard to believe that things are *on the surface* just as we ordinarily experience them—smooth, homogeneous, etc. In other words, the issue whether ordinary sense experience is challenged or corrected by microscopic examination is not at all the same as the question whether things have 'true natures'—imperceptible, transcendentally real, causally potent material essences—that are inaccessible to us. From this perspective the problem for Berkeley's vindication of the reality of ordinary sensible appearances lies less in the fact that we are ignorant of some inaccessible inner natures, than in the fact that we know too much.

NOTES

1. *PC*, 234.
2. *Berkeley: Critical and Interpretive Essays*, ed. Colin Turbayne (Minneapolis, 1982), pp. 174–93

3. It would be incorrect, however, to suppose that Berkeley had Locke in mind exclusively. Cf. *Dialogues*, 214, where he ascribes the doctrine of unknown real natures to Malebranche.

4. Garber, pp. 174ff.

5. *Essay*, IV iii, 11, p. 544.

6. As Garber recognizes, the distinction between corpuscular and veil-of-perception scepticism is by no means sharp in the texts. At the beginning of the *Third Dialogue*, for example, the scepticism about the existence of physical things that arises from materialist principles is presented as a sort of intensification of the problem about knowing natures: 'we are not only ignorant of the true and real nature of things, but even of their existence'. (*Dialogues*, 228.)

7. Garber, p. 182. Like Garber (see his note 8, p. 193) I will ignore here the complex question of Berkeley's attitude toward corpuscularianism in works later than the *Dialogues*. For an interesting discussion of aspects of this question, see I. C. Tipton, 'The "Philosopher by Fire" in Berkeley's Alciphron', in Turbayne, pp. 159–73, especially section III. Tipton also touches on the issue of corpuscles in the early works.

8. Garber, p. 184.

9. Ibid., p. 182.

10. Ibid., p. 183.

11. Ibid., p. 184.

12. Ibid.

13. Ibid., Garber's emphasis.

14. Ibid.

15. Cf. R. J. Brook, *Berkeley's Philosophy of Science* (The Hague, 1973), pp. 100–1.

16. Tipton also indicates that *PHK* 60–1 are concerned just with sensible mechanisms: op. cit. note 7 above, p. 168.

17. Garber, p. 185.

18. Ibid.

19. Ibid. Both Garber and Tipton point out that if Berkeley is to conceive corpuscles as perceivable in principle, they must be ascribed more than just primary qualities. Cf. Garber, p. 193, n. 17, and Tipton, 173, n. 33.

20. See, for instance, R. A. Lascola, 'Ideas and Archetypes: Appearance and Reality in Berkeley's Philosophy', *Personalist* 54 (1973), pp. 42–59; George Thomas, 'Berkeley's God Does Not Perceive', *Journal of the History of Philosophy* 14 (1976), pp. 163–8, and, especially, George Pitcher, *Berkeley* (London, 1977), Ch. X.

21. Garber, p. 185.

22. In fact, this is an oversimplification even with respect to Spinoza. See M. D. Wilson, 'Infinite Understanding, *Scientia Intuitiva*, and *Ethics* I, 16', in *Midwest Studies in Philosophy* VIII, ed. P. A. French, T. E. Uehling, Jr., and H. K. Wettstein (Minneapolis, 1983), pp. 184–5 (Chapter 11 of this volume).

23. See Pitcher, pp. 171–2. Pitcher holds that Berkeley *should* have given an account of unperceived existence in terms of God's will or intentions (sc. to cause appropriate ideas, belonging to a given object, in us in appropriate circumstances). Pitcher's account is well-motivated (by glaring defects in the likely alternatives), but it is not very precisely formulated. For instance, sometimes Pitcher phrases his analysis in terms of 'a dispositional state of God's will' (p. 179): but *can* an all-active being have 'dispositions'? Sometimes he formulates it in terms of intentions, leading to grammatical incoherence: 'there is a readiness, indeed a positive intention, on God's part, to create whatever members of the family would have been required if various circum-

stances had existed'. (p. 165.) Despite these flaws, his treatment of the problems is very illuminating.

24. A nice text that seems to count for Garber's view that Berkeley in some sense countenances corpuscles is the following statement in *Dialogues* 213: 'Let any one of these abettors of impiety but look into his own thoughts, and then try if he can conceive how so much as a rock, a desert, a chaos, or *confused jumble of atoms*; how anything at all, either sensible or imaginable, can exist independent of a mind . . .' (emphasis added). But of course this doesn't tell us that Berkeley thinks corpuscles are *real*.

25. Pitcher, p. 166.

26. Ibid., p. 164; emphasis added.

27. Garber seems to hint that corpuscles could be counted among the unperceived *properties* of objects, some ideas of which are actual (p. 182, middle). I cannot make good sense of this passage; perhaps I have misunderstood it completely.

28. It is another question whether Berkeley could be *justified in claiming* that they exist.

29. Garber, p. 190 (quoted below).

30. Cf. Pitcher, p. 165.

31. I mention this notion simply because it seems somewhat intuitive. I do not know whether it is consistent with Berkeley's nominalism.

Tipton suggests that, 'for Berkeley in *Siris*, there is nothing corporeal that is "insensible," except in the sense that, because it is "inconceivably small" (sect. 261), it lies, and may always lie, beyond the range of our most powerful microscopes'. (p. 168.) This suggestion is indeterminate between the second and third of the interpretations of 'sensible in principle' that I sketch—or perhaps among all three. Tipton adds parenthetically, 'One would expect Berkeley to hold that if no human will ever perceive the aether [postulated in *Siris*], other spirits can or could'. The significance of the disjunction of modalities at the end of this sentence is not clear; it seems simply to leave us with a regress of the problem of interpreting 'sensible in principle'. Berkeley is not above invoking 'other created intelligences' (besides men) to help adjust his doctrine to ordinary conceptions of what exists (or did exist). Cf. *Dialogues*, 252. It is not clear in Berkeley's own text whether he is invoking them as a possibility or an actuality—or, for that matter, whether he is invoking them as *perceivers*, or quasi-divine understanders.

32. Garber, p. 190.

33. Ibid.

34. Ibid.

35. Ibid.

36. Garber himself observes that 'Berkeley's answer to the corpuscular skeptic, as I have interpreted it, may look like a mere linguistic move'. He goes on to claim that 'this is not entirely fair to Berkeley', because Berkeley, in denying that ignorance of corpuscular substructures is ignorance of real natures, renders the ignorance relatively innocuous. Garber, however, does not consider the line of reply to this claim that I sketch in the text.

37. See his letters in Berkeley's *Works*, ii. 274–6; 285–6. Berkeley did not reply to most of Johnson's other objections.

38. Garber cites these remarks at an earlier phase of his discussion (p. 179), but does not return to them.

39. See Tipton, p. 173, n. 29, for a relevant quotation from *Siris*.

The Issue of "Common Sensibles" in Berkeley's *New Theory of Vision*

CLAIMS about similarity or likeness on the one hand, and heterogeneity or difference on the other hand, figure prominently in many of the most characteristic arguments of Berkeley's philosophy. For instance, Berkeley relies on a "resemblance" notion of representation in denying that we have ideas of spirits;[1] in maintaining that our own spiritual selves provide knowledge of other finite spirits and even of God;[2] and in holding that ideas of imagination represent actual ideas of sense by virtue of being copies or resemblances of them. Further, "likeness and conformity among phenomena" are the basis of our ability to formulate laws of nature. (*PHK* I.104) But perhaps his most interesting and provocative application of the similarity/heterogeneity distinction is the claim, central to the *New Theory of Vision*, that objects (or ideas) of sight and touch are wholly "heterogeneous" from each other.[3]

The importance of this claim for Berkeley goes far beyond its role in the relatively technical *New Theory of Vision*. It constitutes an attack on the traditional notion of "common sensibles," often linked with mind-independent material reality, and the primary/secondary quality distinction.[4] And it underpins Berkeley's own central metaphysical concept of a physical object as just a congeries of sense-based ideas. The main concern of this paper will be to examine and evaluate his explanation and defense of this position—the "heterogeneity thesis."

It will be somewhat important for my discussion that in the *New Theory of Vision* Berkeley alternates the 'similarity'/'heterogeneity' terminology with assertions about two sets of ideas being of different "species" or "sorts." One needs to ask whether he is able to explain what is required for ideas to count as "similar"; what is required for them to be "of the same sort"; and whether one of these notions is more fundamental than the other to his thinking on this issue.

In the first section, as background to my discussion of the *New Theory*, I will examine some aspects of Berkeley's use of the notion of "sorts" in his attempt to provide an account of "how ideas become general" that will avoid the incoherence he finds in Locke's theory of abstract general ideas (*PHK* Intro.).[5] I will point out that he here uses the notion of "sorts" as an unexplained primitive—despite the fact that Locke himself regards the problem of explaining sorts as a central task of his abstract ideas theory. A main aim of this section is to establish the extent to which Berkeley could simply take for granted the notion of "same sort of idea," which proves to be strongly implicated in his defense of the heterogeneity thesis in the *New Theory*. At the same time, however, I want to set the stage for a more positive point in Section II: namely, that in the *New Theory*, unlike the *Principles* Introduction, Berkeley at least makes a gesture at explaining "being of the same sort": it seems to emerge that "similarity" is the more fundamental notion. In the *New Theory* Berkeley offers explicit arguments that ideas of sight and touch are not of the same sort, proceeding from the claim that they are not similar or resembling.

Despite finding a small advantage of explicitness in the *New Theory* position, I will try to show that the heterogeneity thesis is not well defended there. (Hence Berkeley's attack on the common sensibles doctrine is not effective.)[6] Apart from weaknesses in the direct arguments for the conclusion that ideas of sight and touch are of different sorts, problems are presented by Berkeley's own concession that certain ideas of sight are more "fit" than others to "signify" certain ideas of touch.

In the final section I will turn to another important point at which the concept of similarity is prominent in Berkeley's system: his familiar claim that an idea cannot be "like" a non-idea. This claim of course plays an important role in his attack on "unperceived matter," and on the primary/secondary quality distinction. I will suggest that his position on the heterogeneity of ideas of sight and touch can help illuminate this dictum. But, again, his concession about the relative "fitness" of certain ideas of sight to signify certain ideas of touch will be found to present a difficulty.

I

Berkeley's direct arguments against abstract ideas, so thoroughly examined by other commentators, need not be considered here. All I am interested in for present purposes is his own alternative account, in the Introduction to *Principles of Human Knowledge*, of how ideas become general. Still, a few words about the background of this account are needed.

Berkeley notes that part of the underlying motivation for the abstract ideas doctrine is to help explain the meaning of general terms, such as 'man' or 'dog' or 'triangle.' According to the abstract ideas theorist—Locke in particular—such terms become general by coming to stand for an abstract idea of *man* or *dog* or *triangle*, an idea which encompasses "all and none" of the determinations which distinguish particular individuals of the kind in question. In the published version of the Introduction, though, Berkeley entirely fails to mention an important feature of Locke's position. Locke claims explicitly that abstract ideas, functioning as nominal essences, *determine which* individuals fall under a given term by (conventionally) setting the boundaries of kinds, species, or sorts:

> . . . it being evident, that Things are ranked under Names into sorts or *Species*, only as they agree to certain abstract *Ideas*, to which we have annexed those Names, the *Essence* of each *Genus*, or Sort, comes to be nothing but that abstract *Idea*, which the General, or *Sortal* . . . Name stands for. (*Essay* III.iii.15 [Nidditch, 417])

George Pitcher has criticized Berkeley for failing to provide any account of the "word-world link" for general terms; or any analysis of "the relation that binds a general term to just the particulars it denotes."[7] This criticism is nearly correct, but it needs to be clarified a bit. Berkeley does, in a sense, have an account of what "binds" general terms to particulars. He explains that the relation of particulars to general terms can be understood by considering "how ideas become general," that is to say in the following way:

> . . . an idea, which considered in itself is particular, becomes general, by being made to represent or stand for all other particular ideas of the same sort. (*PHK* Intro., #12)

A word, too, we must infer, becomes general by being made to stand for other ideas (things) of the same sort.[8]

"Sorts," then, are the key to the (general) word-world link in Berkeley. But on the fundamental point Pitcher's criticism is quite correct: Berkeley provides in this context no analysis whatsoever of the relation "same sort as." Whereas Locke tries to *explain* this relation in terms of conformity to an abstract general idea, Berkeley uncritically *assumes* it in his account of generality. (Despite Berkeley's reputation as a nominalist, his uncritical reliance on sorts to explain the generality of ideas or terms leads one to wonder whether some simplistic realist conception of sortals lurks behind the passage just quoted.)

Did Berkeley simply fail to see that "sorts" in themselves present a philosophical problem?[9] Given the amount of space and ingenuity Locke, whom Berkeley is directly criticizing, devotes to this issue, it would seem, *prima facie*, all but incredible that the problem could have escaped Berkeley. So one naturally turns to the *Philosophical Commentaries* and the so-called "Draft Introduction"—an early version of the published Introduction to the *Principles*—for indications of Berkeley's awareness of this aspect of Locke's position. And in both works one finds Berkeley duly noting Locke's conception of abstract ideas as determining sorts—and himself endorsing this view.[10] For some reason, then, he simply chose to suppress all reference to this role of Lockean abstract ideas in the published version of the Introduction.

The tactical reason for this change can only be conjectured, but it seems to me most probably to lie in two considerations. First, Berkeley had originally supposed that the mind-dependence of sorts would aid his cause of establishing the mind-dependence of physical things; he subsequently recognized that this line of reasoning was not effective.[11]

Second, Berkeley came to realize that the issue of whether general terms designate real or conceptual entities was merely a distraction from his own principal objectives in attacking the abstract ideas doctrine. It is an opinion strangely prevailing among Berkeley scholars that the "meaning of general terms" is the central issue behind the abstract ideas debate. As already indicated, there is *some* textual evidence even from the published Introduction that Berkeley was concerned with this semantic issue. The problem is that this reading, as its proponents recognize, makes it impossible to understand why Berkeley presented his attack on the notion of abstract ideas as fundamental to his broad philosophical objectives. In response to this problem, certain recent writers have emphasized the metaphysical and epistemological objectives of Berkeley's position on abstraction; and I think they are on the right track.[12] Berkeley wants to deny that we can separate mentally the existence of physical objects from their being perceived; that we can mentally contemplate visible extension abstracted from color or texture, or tactual extension abstracted from hardness or softness; that we can legitimately postulate an actual substance abstracted from any sensory modality. The basis we may have for classifying particular entities as dogs, humans, triangles, or other "kinds," and the semantic grounding for such general terms, are incidental issues relative to these concerns. (Though Berkeley does, of course, want to avoid postulating any *inaccessible* "real essence" behind the data of sense.)

For present purposes, in any case, the main point is simply that Berkeley leaves the notion of "same sort as" wholly unexplained in the Introduction—even while relying on it to provide an alternative to what is, in part, a theory of sorting. In the *New Theory*, by contrast, he at least makes *some* effort to elucidate the concept.

II

Traditionally a "common sensible" is a quality perceived by more than one sense, notably sight and touch. This formulation can be accommodated within the "ideas" terminology in the Cartesian tradition, since Descartes himself distinguishes two senses of 'idea': idea as state of the perceiver, and idea as object or content of perception (or partial content).[13] For Descartes the question of whether there are common sensibles comes to the question of whether two types of ideas-as-perceptions have in common some particular idea-as-content (or partial content). Berkeley, however, does not normally observe a distinction between idea as perception and idea as object or content. In his philosophy, therefore, the issue of whether there are common sensibles must be understood simply as a question whether (certain) ideas of sight and touch have something in common. At the beginning of the *NTV* the issue is presented as a question whether "there is any idea common to both senses":

> My design is to shew the manner wherein we perceive by sight the distance, magnitude, and situation of objects. Also to consider the difference there is betwixt the ideas of sight and touch, and whether there be any idea common to both senses. (#1)

In the absence of a perception-content distinction, however, it may seem that this question may be answered trivially—too trivially—in the negative, simply on the grounds that ideas as perceptions are individuated (in part) by their respective sensory modalities: a visual perception *is not* (identical with) a tactual one. Berkeley himself eventually relaxes the formulation in terms of *iden-*

tity of ideas into a formulation in terms of identity of ideas *or of sorts or species* of ideas: can ideas of sight and touch be of the same sort? Of course this reformulation would not represent much progress, if the *sort* an idea belongs to is strictly tied to its modality. Toward the end of the *New Theory*, in addressing the sortal issue, Berkeley offers *arguments* against the claim that ideas of sight and touch are sometimes specifically the same. These arguments indicate that he is trying to avoid trivializing the sortal question. Their thrust is to establish that the fact that both visual and tactual ideas are said to be, for example, "of triangles" does not establish that visual and tactual ideas are of the same kind, because the "triangularity" presented in visual and tactual ideas is not of the same species. I will try to show, however, that these arguments fail to make a case for the specific distinction of visual and tactual figure, or other visual and tactual ideas. But before considering these arguments, I need to sketch certain aspects of Berkeley's reasoning in earlier portions of the *New Theory of Vision*.

These earlier portions are largely concerned with showing the difference between ideas of sight and touch with respect to certain specific perceptual qualities: distance, magnitude (with a word about figure as well), and position or situation. With respect to distance perception, Berkeley's main conclusions are as follows. First, we do not immediately perceive distance by sight (for this would require perceiving "a line directed end-wise to the eye") (#2); second, we do not visually perceive distance by means of something necessarily connected to it, i.e., by geometrical constructs (for it would be "incomprehensible" that I make judgements on this basis without being conscious of doing so (#19)); third, "perceiving distance by sight" is simply a matter of learning to associate certain features of visual ideas, such as "faintness," with a likely sequence of tactual (and kinesthetic) ideas. (#45) Thus, "a man born blind, being made to see, would, at first, have no idea of distance by sight," for

> The objects intromitted by sight would seem to him (as in truth they are) no other than a new set of thoughts or sensations. . . . (#41)

Berkeley's refusal to distinguish ideas-as-perceptions (thoughts) from ideas-as-objects is particularly evident in this passage. In a similar vein he goes on to assert emphatically that ideas of sight and touch are "widely different and distinct"—as indeed "the ideas intromitted by each sense" are from each other. (#46) Although it may be more difficult to "discern the difference there is betwixt the ideas of sight and touch" than between, say, those of hearing and touch, it nevertheless is certain that "a man no more sees and feels the same thing than he hears and feels the same thing." The "objects of sight and touch are two distinct things"; "we never see and feel one and the same object." (#49)

Two important features of Berkeley's treatment of distance perception, carried over to his discussions of magnitude and situation and to the general heterogeneity arguments, are the claims that (a) (what we call) visual perceptions "of distance" are only *contingently* connected with their tactual counterparts; and (b) we may denominate ideas thus contingently connected by the same term, when their connection is sufficiently reliable to allow us to infer the one from the other. (Thus, what we call visual ideas of distance are simply ideas with those features that enable us to anticipate relevant differences of tactual (and kinesthetic) experience.)

Berkeley's commentators often follow him in emphasizing the point about contingency—perhaps because his position on this point is plausible and imaginatively argued. I believe, though, that the "contingency" arguments actually offer more confusion than illumination, with regard to the defensibility of the heterogeneity claim. The main point I want to make is the following: while it may be plausible to hold that ideas of sight might ("conceivably") have been associated with ideas of touch in a way that varies from the associations that prevail "in our world," it simply does not follow that in our world ideas ideas of sight and touch "have nothing in common." I will try to clarify this observation with reference to Berkeley's discussion of the perception of magnitude.

In discussing magnitude Berkeley particularly emphasizes that the connection between features of visible ideas and features of tangible ideas is wholly contingent: "Nor will it be found that great or small visible magnitude hath any necessary relation to great or small tangible magnitude. . . ." (*NTV* #59) Although magnitude or extension of the visible object tends to be correlated with tangible magnitude or extension ("big look" goes with "big touch"), this presumption can be overridden if the visual idea is confused or faint. (#56) Further, the connection could well have been even weaker than it is, if our eyes had been framed differently than they are.[14] From which considerations, he concludes,

> it is manifest that as we do not perceive the [tangible[15]] magnitudes of objects immediately by sight, so neither do we perceive them by the mediation of anything which has a necessary connexion with them. Those ideas that now suggest unto us the various magnitudes of external objects before we touch them, *might possibly have suggested no such thing*: or they might have signified them in a direct contrary manner: so that the very same ideas, on the perception whereof we judge an object to be small, might as well have served to make us conclude it great. Those ideas being in their own nature equally fitted to bring into our minds the idea of small or great, or no size at all of outward [i.e., tangible] objects; just as the words of any language are in their own nature indifferent to signify this or that thing or nothing at all. (#64; emphasis added)

The man born blind and made to see

> would not consider the ideas of sight with reference to, or as having any connexion with, the ideas of touch. . . . (#79)

In these passages Berkeley moves from the claim that visual and tactual ideas of magnitude might not have been correlated as they are, to the claims that our actual visual ideas of magnitude have no "fitness" to suggest the tactual ideas they do suggest, and no "connexion" with them. The implicit premiss, I take it, is that "suggestion" is the only relevant relation, and that this depends only on contingent association between (types of) ideas.

Now some aspects of what Berkeley is saying here seem quite plausible. In particular, it does seem in some sense *conceivable* that the sequences of visual and tactual "ideas" characteristic of our experience might not have obtained: if you like, that the relations are contingent. What is not clear is why this concession should be taken to imply that ideas of sight and touch are, categorically, "widely different and distinct" in a sense relevant to the common sensibles issue; or that we never, in fact, see and touch the same thing. Similarly, it might be the case that certain de facto, contingent relations among, say, our visual and tactual perceptions of magnitude—of the type Berkeley himself mentions—are important to our *belief* that we do (often) see and touch the same thing; but how does this tend to show that the belief is untrue, *given* these correlations?

Perhaps the point I am getting at can be made clearer with an example. Suppose a world in which, literally, all that is "seen" are flashes of color (though shapes and sizes are still "felt"). We might further suppose, if we like, that the color spectrum as we know it correlates with, say, increasing size as indicated by tactual perceptions. Thus, a violet flash comes to signify the immediate availability of a tactual impression of something tiny; green something of medium size, and so on. It *might* be the case that in this world we *would* say that magnitudes are visually signified, rather than "seen." (And one can go on to imagine "inverted spectrum" worlds; worlds lacking consistent correlations, and so on.) My claim is that this supposition, which underlines the supposed contingency of the connection between visual and tactual ideas, tells us *nothing* about the common sensibles issue as it arises within our world. (It *might* have been that all our visual triangle-perceptions were green, and all our green perceptions were triangular; this scarcely throws light on the question whether our actual green [visual] triangle perceptions have something in common with our red triangle perceptions.) In other words, the question whether our visual and tactual ideas *in fact* have "anything in common" is quite distinct from the question whether it is conceivable that our visual and tactual ideas *might have had* nothing in common (yet might still have given rise to mental association, by virtue of repeated correlation).[16]

It is important to note that Berkeley himself gives grounds for insisting that the spectral flashes situation is relevantly different from our own, with regard to visual ideas. For he assumes throughout most of the *New Theory* that we do have *immediate* visual perception of magnitude and figure: that is (in his terms), there is, *apart from* association with tangible ideas, such a thing as *visual* magnitude, and *visual* figure, capable of being assessed as "large" or "small."[17] In fact, this assumption appears clearly in his reasoning, quoted above, from the *contingency* of association between the visual and the tactual. (In view of some quotations to be considered shortly, I want particularly to stress that Berkeley does repeatedly and explicitly indicate that sight presents us *immediately* with visual magnitude or extension: besides *NTV* #59, already quoted, see especially ## 54 and 130.)[18]

From magnitude we proceed (briefly) to situation and figure. I have indicated in passing that Berkeley adduces the case of the "man born blind, and made to see" in connection with his discussion of the perception of both distance and magnitude. This same figure (hereafter "the Molyneux Man") again appears in his subsequent discussion of the perception of situation. The man born blind, and made to see, Berkeley holds, would not be able to apply terms such as 'higher' and 'lower' on the basis of his new visual ideas alone, for

> The objects to which he had hitherto been used to apply the terms *up* and *down*, *high* and *low*, were such only as affected or were some way perceived by his touch: but the proper objects of vision make a new set of ideas, perfectly distinct and different from the former, and which can in no sort make themselves perceived by touch. (#95)[19]

To reinforce this point he offers a "particular comparison" between the ideas of sight and touch:

> That which I see is only variety of light and colours. That which I feel is hard or soft, hot or cold, rough or smooth. What similitude, what connexion have those ideas with these? Or how is it possible that anyone should see reason to give one and the same name to combinations of ideas so very different before he had experienced their coexistence? (#103)

Finally, the previously established distinction between visible and tangible magnitude yields the conclusion that visible and tangible *figure* are distinct,

> For figure is the termination of magnitude; whence it follows that no visible magnitude having in its own nature an aptness to suggest any one particular tangible magnitude, so neither can any visible figure be inseparably connected with its corresponding tangible figure: so as of itself and in a way prior to experience, it might suggest it to the understanding. (#105)[20]

In the latter of these two argumentative passages Berkeley (again) runs together denial of "necessary connection" between visual and tactual ideas with denials of relations of "fitness" (here, "aptness") of one to suggest the other. The prior passage stresses the denial of "similitude," implying, oddly, that visual and tactual ideas have no similitude on the grounds that the two senses are restricted to their respective traditional "special" sensibles. (This point will come up again.) The objects of sight and touch make, in short, "two sets of ideas which are widely different from each other." (#111) "[T]here is no resemblance between the ideas of sight and things tangible." (#117)

We come now to Berkeley's more general and systematic discussion of the issue whether sight and touch have "ideas" in common. It is necessary, he says, "to inquire more particularly concerning the difference between the ideas of sight and touch, which are called by the same names, and see whether there be any idea common to both senses." (#121) This is not an inquiry about numerical difference: Berkeley maintains that he has already shown that figure and extension perceived by sight are numerically different from tangible figure and extension. Further, Berkeley does not stick to the original formulation in terms, exclusively, of whether there is "any idea" common to both senses. The question, he says,

> is not now concerning the same numerical ideas, but whether or not there be any one and the same sort or species of ideas equally perceivable to both senses; or, in other words, whether extension, figure, and motion perceived by sight are not specifically distinct from extension, figure, and motion perceived by touch. (#121)

This statement is a little confusing, since, as we have seen, Berkeley has not in fact restricted himself in his argument so far to the issue of "numerical distinctness": he has made claims, as well, about the lack of "similitude" and "fitness" between ideas of sight and touch.[21] He has not, however, posed the question of their relation in terms of "sorts" or "species" (except at the very beginning of the treatise).

His first move, in responding to this question, is to deny the existence of an abstract idea of extension, singled out from all other tangible and visible qualities. He claims in general that a line or surface cannot be conceived *in separation from* qualities of the particular senses (color, roughness, etc.); and more specifically that *determination of magnitude depends on* variation in such qualities. (121–24)[22]

Berkeley then moves on to "the question now remaining," namely,

> whether the particular extensions, figures, and motions perceived by sight be of the same kind with the particular extensions, figures, and motions perceived by touch? (#127)

The proposition that he "ventures to lay down" in answer to this question is italicized:

> *The extension, figures, and motions perceived by sight are specifically distinct from the ideas of touch called by the same names, nor is there any such thing as one idea or kind of idea common to both senses.* (#127)

The issue of whether there are common sensibles of sight and touch is thus finally understood as the question whether there is any "idea *or kind of idea* common to both senses." The proposition that there are no such ideas or kinds of ideas can be collected, Berkeley notes, from what he's already said. But because it is so much at variance with received notions, he undertakes to demonstrate it with direct arguments.[23]

Berkeley's stress on sorts here gives rise to hopes that he will say something illuminating about this notion, later used so casually and problematically in the *Principles* Introduction. And in fact he seems to try to. For he proceeds to offer an explicit account of 'same sort as'—or, more exactly, of 'ranging' things under the same sort:

When upon perception of an idea I range it under this or that sort, it is because it is perceived after the same manner, or because it has a likeness or conformity with, or affects me in the same manner as, the ideas of the sort I rank it under. In short, it must not be entirely new, but have something in it old and already perceived by me. It must, I say, have so much at least in common with the ideas I have before known and named as to make me give it the same name with them. (#128)[24]

In this statement Berkeley assumes that there are ideas already classified into sorts: the question is simply whether a new idea does or does not belong to an existing classification. Thus the original basis of classifying ideas into sorts is not examined. Further, the basis for classifying new ideas into an existing sort is surely not explained with any precision. That a new idea "is perceived after the same manner as" ideas of an existing sort is, in particular, a criterion likely to seem question-begging in the context in question (if, as seems natural, "after the same manner as" implies "within the same sensory modality"—or, what comes to the same thing, "conjoined with the same traditional special sensibles"). But we may conclude that Berkeley must not intend this trivializing interpretation—otherwise his discussion would be much shorter than it is.

It seems appropriate, then, to focus on the "likeness or conformity" criterion. And this formulation does allow at least some sense of progress in understanding Berkeley's position on sorts: for it suggests that the notion of *resemblance among ideas* is the main issue, and is more fundamental than the notion of "same sort as."

What establishes, then, whether two ideas are "like" in the relevant way? The comment at the end of the quotation suggests that our being prepared to give them the same name is some kind of criterion. But of course we *do* give the same names to certain tactual and visual ideas (as Berkeley himself has recently observed): 'circular' or 'squarish,' for example. Berkeley, however, holds that *this* form of common naming rests purely on contingent association, not on the true likeness that underlies sorting. To see whether the likeness relevant to sorting actually obtains between visual and tactual ideas we must, Berkeley says, consider the case of the man born blind and then made to see, whose naming practices won't have been influenced by contingent associations. And, he says, it has been "clearly made out" that such a man would not recognize visual and tactual ideas as sharing a common nature, and so would not call them by the same name. (#128)[25] This is his first "argument" for the position that visual and tactual ideas are specifically different.

I do not believe that this "argument" is at all effective. For one thing, Berkeley's earlier statements about the Molyneux Man generally *assume* the difference or non-resemblance as well as the numerical distinctness of ideas of sight and touch. (Cf. ##79; 94–95.) According to these statements, it is *because* visual and tactual ideas are not similar that (Berkeley claims) we can be confident that the Molyneux Man would not recognize the visual sphere as a result of his experiences with tangible spheres. In fact (given that we are relying only on a priori considerations) it's hard to see how the case of the Molyneux Man could provide the slightest *independent* grounds for claims about the heterogeneity of visual and tactual ideas. For another thing, someone's inability to *recognize* resemblance without experience—even if this were established empirically—need not at all prove the absence of resemblance. (I may need to *learn* to see photographs as resembling their subjects.)[26]

Berkeley's second argument (#1290) turns on the claim (already recently foreshadowed) that light and colors are the only immediate objects of sight; but everyone allows that light and colors constitute a species different from the ideas of touch. (#129) Now, how are we to reconcile this argument with his talk throughout the *Essay* of visible figure, extension, etc.—explicitly claimed to be immediately perceived? One possibility is that he is trying to get across the idea that we cannot see figure or extension (or anything else) independently of color and light—or perhaps that we see figure and extension by virtue of seeing color and light.[27] But this consideration in itself is not sufficient to show that what we see by color and light is not of the same kind as what we feel in conjunction with other qualities (hardness, roughness, etc.): namely, for instance, a triangle. If the visual ideas of a red triangle and of a green triangle can be of the same sort, then why not the visual idea of a red triangle and the tactual idea of a warm triangle? (And if not even diverse *visual* ideas of triangles can be of the same sort, then Berkeley's account—so much emphasized in the *Principles* Introduction—of how ideas and terms become general is defeated. By the same token, this criticism of Berkeley's second argument does not seem to depend on the possibility of "separating" triangularity, say, from all other sensible determinations; and hence does not depend on opposing his denial of abstract ideas in the *New Theory*.) Once again, the alleged argument for the heterogeneity of sight and touch appears question-begging.[28]

Berkeley's third heterogeneity argument (#131) goes as follows: any two magnitudes of the same kind can be added together; visual and tactual magnitudes can't be added together; therefore they aren't of the same kind.[29] Berkeley leaves it to each of us individually to determine whether the adding of visual and tactual magnitudes is conceivable. For myself, I find no problem in this; and I think in fact that Berkeley's own (later) account of physical objects as congeries of sensations in a certain way requires the "addability" of the visual and tangible. Suppose I have a visual idea of a "length of pipe" that terminates in a dark hole in the basement wall (apprehended visually, of course). Where I see the hole I (visually) place my hand, and lo and behold I tactually experience "a length of pipe" ("beyond" the scope of vision). Surely these respective visual and tactual ideas belong to the "congeries" which (on developed Berkeleyan theory) *is* the pipe; and equally surely they must relate to each other differently than the visual and tactual ideas "of" *the portion of pipe in the lighted part of the basement*. In the former case, but not the latter, the relation has to be additive; one has to consider oneself to be dealing with "one continued sum or whole." Thus, I think, Berkeley's third argument fails on intuitive grounds, and is also one that seems to conflict with an important feature of his metaphysics.[30]

For his fourth argument (#132) Berkeley returns to the Molyneux Man. He notes that Locke and Molyneux both hold that the man would not be able to recognize previously touched objects from his new visual ideas. Thus either ideas of sight and touch are of different kinds, "or else . . . the solution of this problem given by those two thoughtful and ingenious men is wrong." (#133) This bald appeal to authority is, I think, the only novelty presented in this phase of his reasoning.[31]

Berkeley goes on to consider some objections to his position. To the question of how it can be that visible and tactual ideas are called by the same name, if they are not of the same kind, he predictably responds that their universal association with each other is sufficient to account for this fact. (It would seem to follow that his own attempt to tie "same sort of" with "called by the same name as" is sheerly nugatory.) The next objection, and Berkeley's reply, are much more interesting, however.

> But, say you, surely a tangible square is liker to a visible square than to a visible circle: it has four angles and as many sides: so also has the visible square: but the visible circle has no such thing, being bounded by one uniform curve without right lines or angles, which makes it unfit to represent the tangible square but very fit to represent the tangible circle. Whence it clearly follows that visible figures are patterns of, or of the same species with, the respective tangible figures represented by them: that they are like unto them, and of their own nature fitted to represent them. . . . (#141)

Berkeley, as we've seen, has previously denied that any particular visual *magnitude* is fitter than another to suggest (or represent) a given tactual magnitude. It is significant, and perhaps surprising, then, that he does *not* take this hard course with respect to figure. Rather, he replies that a visible square is indeed "fitter" than a visible circle to represent a tangible square; but he insists it is not on that account more like, or "more of a species with it." The visible square, like the tangible square, has four distinct parts (sides): that is the reason for its "fitness" to signify the tangible square. But, Berkeley continues, for the two to be like or of the same species, they must have not only the same number of parts, but the same *kind* of parts as well. The case is the same, he indicates, with spoken and written speech.

> It is indeed arbitrary that, in general, letters of any language represent sounds at all: but when that is once agreed, it is not arbitrary what combination of letters shall represent this or that particular sound. (#143)

A simple sound, like *a*, should have a simple visual designation; and a spoken word of several parts, like 'adultery,' should be represented by a written word of several parts.

While Berkeley's point is reasonably clear, his distinction between homogeneity and fitness is shaky. It certainly does not appear to be a general truth that two things must have the same kind of parts to be "like"—or even to be of the same sort. (An oil portrait on canvas can be *very* like a photograph on paper, or a papier-mâché sculpture like a hologram. Two machines can both be lawn mowers even though one has a gasoline motor and the other doesn't.) Further, it seems unlikely that "number of parts" is really at the heart of the "fitness" issue. For instance, in considering the fitness of visual equilateral triangles, as opposed to visual right triangles, to suggest tactual equilateral triangles, symmetry considerations would seem more salient. And, in any case, how can Berkeley establish that the *parts* of a visual square are not "of the same kind as" the *parts* of a tactual square? We may allow, as he claims, that the respective parts are bound up with different kinds of special sensibles: greenness and warmness, for instance. But the very question at issue is whether this consideration is sufficient to establish a *thorough* heterogeneity of ideas: whether visual and tactual ideas are indeed of different species (where this question is not *trivially* to be answered in the negative simply on the grounds that they belong to different sensory modalities).

The crux of the matter is this: if Berkeley is prepared to allow differences of "fitness" even for a subset of visual-tactual correlations, he needs to do much better than he does in explaining both his understanding of "fitness" and the relevant criterion of "resemblance" that "fitness" fails to satisfy. Until this better explanation is provided, the notion of "same sort as," insofar as it is predicated on resemblance, itself remains in conceptual limbo, together with the claim that ideas of sight and touch are invariably heterogeneous. And, in the context of Berkeley's philosophy, the important denial of common sensibles stands or falls with the defense of the heterogeneity claim.

III

In conclusion, I will try to connect my discussion of Berkeley's position on the heterogeneity of visual and tactual ideas with his firm assertion that "an idea can be like nothing but an idea." (*PHK* I.8) This claim is an important feature of his attack on the views of his scientific realist predecessors. It is a response to a somewhat characteristic tenet of their position as expressed, for example, in the following passage from Locke's *Essay*:

> . . . the *Ideas of primary Qualities* of Bodies, *are Resemblances* of them, and their Patterns do really exist in the Bodies themselves; but the *Ideas, produced* in us *by* these *Secondary Qualities, have no resemblance* of them at all. (II.viii.15)

The notion of "resemblance" is left largely unanalyzed by Locke and others of similar persuasion. It constitutes a vulnerable aspect of their position which Berkeley *could* have exploited simply by arguing that they fail to give clear sense to this notion. (Obviously, *one* salient account of what it is for x to resemble y—that x *appears similar to y*—is not available to an ideas theorist of scientific realist persuasion in this context.)[32] In fact, however, Berkeley does not choose to question the scientific realist's notion of "resemblance" *per se*; rather he takes the more dogmatic course of denying that ideas can resemble non-ideas. He thus shifts to himself the burden of explaining why this is so.

Unfortunately he does not actually discharge this burden by explaining *why* he is right, and the scientific realist wrong, with respect to the resemblance issue.[33] Perhaps, however, his case can be strengthened—or at least clarified— by connecting his claim that an idea cannot resemble what is not an idea with his *NTV* position on the heterogeneity of ideas of sight and touch.

Suppose that Berkeley has successfully made his case that visual and tactual ideas never do resemble each other. Then, first, he is in a position to make a strong further point against the position expressed by Locke. For if visual and tactual "ideas of shape" do not resemble *each other*, then it is going to be hard to explain how *both* resemble the same extra-mental quality—at least if "simplicity" of ideas and quality is assumed. (Are we supposed to think that our visual ideas of roundness resemble *one aspect* of "real" roundness, and our tactual ideas another?) But Locke categorically asserts that "ideas of primary qualities"—not just, say, *tactual* ideas—resemble qualities in extra-mental objects.

Suppose, though, that the scientific realist restricts himself to claiming that, say, *tactual* ideas of shape resemble qualities really existing in extra-mental matter. Then Berkeley's *NTV* argument can still be adapted as an objection to the scientific realist's position. What I have in mind can most easily be explained with reference to Pitcher's objection to Berkeley's repudiation of Locke. Pitcher writes:

> Berkeley is surely right that a color, as such, or a shape, as such, can exactly resemble only a color or a shape . . . But—and this is the really important question here—how does that speak against the Lockean hypothesis? It speaks against it if, and only if Lockean material objects do not have colors, and do not have shapes. Locke himself concedes that his material objects do not have colors, but he insists that they do have shapes—and it is only with respect to shape and the other so-called primary qualities that he claims a resemblance between characteristics of our ideas of sense, on the one hand, and characteristics of material objects, on the other. But then Berkeley's dictum, [that an idea can be like nothing but an idea] . . . has no force whatever against the Lockean hypothesis: Locke could simply agree with it—e.g. could agree that a figure can be like nothing but another figure—and then add: But of course Lockean material objects do have figures . . . , and so, as I have always maintained, our ideas of sense do resemble material objects with respect to figure and the other primary qualities. (116–17)

In a later phase of his discussion Pitcher suggests that the requirements of scientific explanation give us "good reason for thinking that unobservable material objects resemble our ideas of sense in certain respects . . . ." (119)

We might expect Berkeley to reply that Pitcher's objection assumes the availability of an abstract idea of shape, existing in separation from ideas of the special sensibles. But (he thinks) he has defeated this assumption, in both the *New Theory* and the *Principles*. This move is not sufficient to vindicate Berkeley, however, if (as I've suggested in passing) one can talk of resemblance in a respect without supposing that the "respect" *exists separately from* all special determinations. (I have already pointed out that Berkeley's account of general ideas in the *Principles* Introduction requires that we be able to talk of resemblance between ideas involving different determinate special sensibles at least within a modality.)

But, secondly, the arguments discussed at the end of the last section seem to show that Berkeley thought he could establish the heterogeneity of visual and tactual ideas without placing emphasis on his own understanding of what "abstraction" would consist in. I have suggested that Berkeley's case for heterogeneity seems to come down to the view that tactual and visual shapes cannot resemble each other because they are respectively bound up with different special sensibles. This point can be adapted to the present context in an obvious way. If, for instance, a "shape" experienced through one type of special sensible—say a warm triangle—can never be homogeneous with, or "resemble," a "shape" experienced through another type of special sensible (say a green triangle) then (one may reason) a "shape" experienced through any type of special sensible (as all "shapes" must be experienced) can never resemble a posited "shape" *not experienced through a special sensible at all* (as Pitcher's defense would seem to require).

Once again it comes down to the question whether Berkeley is able to establish that "warm triangle ideas" and "green triangle ideas" are not univocally ideas of *triangles*—are not, in respect of being triangle ideas, similar to each other, or of the same sort. I have claimed that his defense of the position in the *New Theory* is not very successful. Even if it *were* successful, though, the scientific realist might *still* have at least a partial *ad hominem* riposte.

Suppose Berkeley were able to make out a distinction between (a) the claim that visual triangle ideas "resemble" tactual triangle ideas, and (b) the claim that the former are "more fit" to suggest (or represent) the latter than are visual square ideas. (Suppose, that is, that my earlier objections to his position on this subject are answered.) And suppose we agree that visual triangles do not resemble tactual triangles, but are merely "fit" to suggest them. Then, I think, the scientific realist might argue as follows.

> Never mind the claim about "resemblance." Consider only the issue of "fitness." Just as (on your own testimony) visual triangles are "fit" to represent or suggest tactual triangles whereas visual squares are not, so (I claim) tactual triangles "fit" material triangles and fail to "fit" material squares. In the case of secondary quality ideas, however, there are no fitness relations whatsoever between them and specific qualities of matter. Thus an essential part of my position is preserved: some significant informational relation obtains beween at least certain *favored* ideas of primary qualities and qualities as they exist in matter which simply does not obtain in the case of secondary quality ideas.

I do not mean to claim that the materialist has the last word in this debate with Berkeley—only that he has, so to speak, the *next* word. Nor did I mean to imply earlier that Berkeley is *wrong* to deny common sensibles. My view is that he has raised some interesting issues, but handled them inconclusively. Among the most critical problems for his position are its apparent internal inconsistencies and incompleteness.[34]

NOTES

1. Berkeley denies that (active) minds or spirits can resemble "inert" ideas: mind is "more distant and heterogeneous from [ideas/bodies] than light is from darkness." (*PHK* I.27; cf. 137–38; 141)

2. . . . [A]s we conceive the ideas that are in the minds of other spirits by means of our own, which we suppose to be resemblances of them: so we know other spirits by means of our own soul, which in that sense is the image or idea of them, it having a like respect to other spirits, that blueness or heat by me perceived hath to those ideas perceived by another." (*PHK* 140)

This statement invites certain questions which I won't further consider here. How, for instance, do we *know* that our spiritual selves are "similar to" other selves? And what is the exact content of this claim? Again, do *notions* "represent" spirits, granted that ideas do not? If so, is the representation in *this* case grounded on resemblance? (Berkeley says he has, "though not an inactive idea, yet in myself some sort of active thinking image of the Deity." (*Dialogues* 232) This curious phrasing suggests that Berkeley may in fact be trying to insinuate a resemblance between the representing notion and the active thinking being represented.)

3. Although I will not be primarily concerned with Berkeley's conception of representation, in relation to the *New Theory*, it is worth noting that in that work Berkeley does not adhere to the "resemblance" conception that figures so prominently in the *Principles*. For ideas of sight are definitely said to "signify," and according to certain passages even "represent," the heterogeneous ideas of touch (*NTV* ##142–44); although according to other passages they do *not* "copy or represent" them (#117).

4. In *Theory of Vision Vindicated*, Berkeley himself draws the connection between the primary/secondary quality distinction and the assumption of common sensibles: *TVV* 15; cf. Margaret Atherton, *Berkeley's Revolution in Vision* (Ithaca: Cornell University Press, 1990), p. 174.

5. He also employs the notion of "same sort as" in explaining how it can be correct, even on the assumptions of his philosophy, to say that different people perceive the same thing: "Words are of arbitrary imposition; and since men are used to apply the word *same* where no distinction or variety is perceived, and I do not pretend to alter their perceptions, it follows, that as men have said before, *several saw the same thing*, so they may upon like occasions continue to use the same phrase. . . . Let us suppose several men together, all endued with the same faculties, and consequently *affected in like sort by their senses*, and who had yet never known the use of language; they would without question agree in their perceptions. Though perhaps, when they came to the use of speech, some regarding the uniformness of what was perceived might call it the *same* thing: others especially regarding the diversity of persons who perceived, might choose the denomination of different things." (*Dialogues*, 247–48; ll. 7–8, emphasis added)

Berkeley's account of the way ideas are united under one name, so as to constitute one thing, probably also rests on implicit postulation of *sorts* of ideas, although Berkeley doesn't employ either the 'similarity' or the 'sortal' terminology in this context. (". . . [I]deas are united into one thing (or have one name given them) by the mind; because they are observed to attend each other." (3D, 249) But presumably it is the same *sort* of ideas which attend each other, not numerically the same ideas.)

6. I will not try to defend the stronger thesis that there *are* common sensibles.

7. Pitcher, *Berkeley* (London: Routledge and Kegan Paul, 1977), pp. 89–90.

8. It seems to me that Pitcher is entirely correct in holding that Berkeley's account of how ideas become general relates to the issue of how a term acquires a general reference only by analogy. That is, Berkeley is *not* proposing that words become general by virtue of standing for ideas which have become general. I think Pitcher is also right in suggesting that Berkeley backed off the Draft Introduction position that *only* words (not ideas) are general simply because he decided to advocate relying on naked ideas, to avoid verbal confusions. Unfortunately the move to general ideas, as Berkeley phrases it, seems totally inadequate to resolve the problem to which it's presumably addressed. Suppose I try to think a proposition of the form, "Remus is a handsome dog," while focusing on the naked ideas (no confusing *words* allowed). My idea of Remus has to be some kind of image of Remus; but my idea of *dog* may also be, on Berkeley's account, an image of Remus, which is taken to stand for other particulars of the same sort. How exactly do I avoid the inference that what I'm really thinking is that Remus is a handsome Remus? (Or, supposing my dog-idea is an image of a different dog, say Norman, that I'm entertaining nonsense to the effect that Remus is a handsome Norman?)

9. Pitcher believes that Berkeley "sees no need for anything, idea or non-idea, to serve as a connecting link between general terms and their referents [i.e., the particulars they 'denote']." My view is that Berkeley helps himself to "sorts" as the connecting link; but then one can ask, again, whether he "sees no need" for an account of sorts.

10. *PC* 836; 288, 289; in *Philosophical Commentaries by George Berkeley*, edited by George H. Thomas (New York and London: Garland, 1989 [reprint of c. 1976 edition], pp. 34, 109). *George Berkeley's Manuscript Introduction*, edited by Bertil Belfrage (Oxford: Doxa, 1987), pp. 67–69.

11. See Luce's comments on *PC* 271 and 287–90, Thomas edition, pp. 197 and 200.

12. See, especially, Margaret Atherton, "Berkeley's Anti-Abstractionism," and Martha Brandt Bolton, "Berkeley's Objection to Abstract Ideas," both in *Essays on George Berkeley*, edited by Ernest Sosa (Dordrecht: D. Reidel, 1987).

13. Preface to the Meditations, AT VII, 8; see Vere Chappell, "The Theory of Ideas," in A. O. Rorty, ed., *Essays on Descartes' Meditations* (Berkeley and Los Angeles: University of California Press, 1986), pp. 177ff.

14. He also argues that indefinitely many visual ideas of *varying* magnitude are correlated with the same tangible magnitude. This point is emphasized by Atherton in *BRV*.

15. Berkeley uses 'magnitude' in the specific sense of 'tangible magnitude' throughout this passage. This usage is not typical of *NTV*, however. See, for instance, #54: ". . . there are two sorts of objects apprehended by sight; each whereof hath its distinct magnitude, or extension. The one, properly tangible, *i.e.* to be perceived and measured by touch, and not immediately falling under the sense of seeing: the other, properly and immediately visible, by mediation of which the former is brought in view."

16. For an interesting discussion of various conceivability issues, with particular reference to Thomas Reid's criticisms of Berkeley (as well as more recent writings) see David H. Sanford, "The Perception of Shape," in *Knowledge and Mind: Philosophical Essays*, edited by Carl Ginet and Sydney Shoemaker (New York: Oxford University Press, 1983).

17. He is at pains to deny that the same holds true of distance, but the reasons for this interesting discrepancy need not detain us here.

On the point that Berkeley does assume that there is such a thing as visible extension, figure, etc., see Pitcher, *Berkeley*, pp. 51, 53–54. On the "immediate" visual perception of magnitude see *NTV* #59.

18. Further, as we shall see, Berkeley himself later concedes that—at least in certain

cases—particular types of visual ideas do have an intrinsic "fitness" to represent particular types of tactual ideas.

19. There is some suggestion here of a semantic argument, to the effect that words such as 'up' and 'down' would have their meanings supplied (for the Molyneux Man) only by tangible ideas. This is not really a distinct argument, though. If the meanings are supplied by ideas, then if the ideas of sight and touch have something in common, the meanings of 'up' and 'down' (etc.) will not be strictly equivocal across modalities.

20. This argument seems to neglect the fact that there may be triangles of different sizes (whether visual or tactual).

21. Atherton makes this point (see *BRV*, p. 173).

22. He also offers an anticipation of his *Principles* attack on Locke's account of the abstract idea of a triangle. (#125)

23. As Atherton points out, Berkeley is not only reinforcing his previous results here, but also generalizing them (*BRV*, pp. 173–74). That is, he has previously focused on distance, magnitude, and position (with brief mentions of figure); now he is concerned with ideas of sight and touch unrestrictedly. One may also note that he now will give special attention to the idea of figure.

24. Pitcher notes that "[i]n this passage of atypical wooliness, Berkeley hardly says anything more helpful than that he classifies a new thing under such and such an old heading because he feels right about doing so!" (*Berkeley*, p. 51). He goes on to say, though, that Berkeley's understanding of 'of the same kind' may be gathered from his defense of the claim that ideas of sight and touch are heterogeneous.

25. In the first edition of *NTV* Berkeley had added that ". . . the judgment of such an unprejudiced person is more to be relied on in this case, than the sentiments of the generality of men: who in this, as in almost everything else, suffer themselves to be guided by custom, and the erroneous suggestions of prejudice, rather than reason and sedate reflection." This passage was later deleted.

26. See Pitcher, *Berkeley*, p. 56. Further, it would seem that the ability of the Molyneux Man to "recognize" a sphere or a cube visually need not imply a resemblance between the visual and tactual ideas: God, for instance, could have arranged for the necessary (brute) association relations to be innately wired in.

Some parts of Berkeley's earlier discussion suggest that even *visual* ideas of (as we would say) the same object—say the moon seen from Earth and the moon seen up close—lack resemblance to each other. (#44) Are these then supposed to be of different "sorts"? How much, and what kind, of resemblance is required for ideas to count as of the same sort?

27. Pitcher takes him to be holding that visible extension and figure are *identical* with color and light (*Berkeley*, p. 54). I agree with Atherton's rejection of this reading (*BRV*, 188).

28. As Berkeley notes a little later (#136) something might, in theory, affect the sight and touch in different manners, yet it still be the case that besides the new manner of affection, there is something, "the angle or figure, which is old and known," and which the newly sighted person could recognize in the new sensation.

29. Note, again, that this argument supposes "visual magnitudes."

30. Atherton criticizes a somewhat similar rebuttal by David Armstrong, on the grounds that Armstrong's counter-example disregards Berkeley's position on distance perception. (*BRV*, p. 190) Mine avoids any direct dependence on distance perception. It does of course still implicitly adduce some sort of (rough and intuitive) common metric between vision and touch. In fact I think that it tends to show that there *is* some such

common metric: this is, after all, the basic issue at stake in the argument. Atherton (in comments on an earlier formulation of my example) maintained (plausibly) that Berkeley would hold that we don't actually add the visual and tactual ideas, but rather the directly experienced tactual idea, and the potential tactual idea of which the visual idea serves as "sign." It seems to me, though, that this position relies on Berkeley's heterogeneity claim, rather than providing independent support for it.

Bernard Williams has suggested (in discussion) that Berkeley would do better to argue that visual and tactual ideas *can't be compared with respect to size*. (But in fact, as we've seen, he in a way holds that we can!)

31. Atherton takes Berkeley to be indicating that Locke's position is internally inconsistent: if, as Locke says in his treatment of simple ideas, the same idea (e.g. of shape) can enter through sight or touch, then he should allow that the Molyneux Man can recognize by vision shapes previously perceived only by touch. If so, Berkeley is making a good point: Locke's position *is* internally inconsistent. This does not settle, of course, which part of it is wrong.

32. Berkeley touches indirectly on this point in *PC*: "A man cannot compare 2 things together without perceiving them each, ergo he cannot say any thing which is not an idea is like or unlike an idea." (*PC* 51, Thomas ed., p. 6.) It isn't really clear, though, whether the point he means to express is semantic or merely epistemological.

33. The closest he comes to offering an argument for the claim that an idea cannot resemble mind-independent matter is a passage in *PHK*:

How . . . is it possible, that things perpetually fleeting and variable as our ideas, should be copies or images of anything fixed and constant [as material things are supposed to be]? Or, in other words, since all sensible qualities, as size, figure, colour, &c. that is, our ideas are continually changing upon every alteration in the distance, medium, or instruments, of sensation; how can any determinate material objects be properly represented or painted forth by several distinct things, each of which is so different from and unlike the rest? (II.205–6)

The first part of this passage seems to be saying that ideas are too radically different in temporal quality (fleetingness) to be said to resemble supposed external reality (allegedly fixed). Despite the suggestion of equivalence ("in other words") the second part seems to make the quite different point that the variability in all our "perceptions of" any supposed perception-independent quality makes it hard to maintain that any particular perception resembles that supposed quality.

Even this latter argument is reminiscent of a phase of his defense of the dissimilarity of visual and tactual ideas in *NTV*: in discussing the perception of magnitude he notes that one fixed tactual magnitude is correlated with a wide range of visual magnitudes (and so cannot be claimed to "resemble" visual ideas). But the very fixedness of tactual magnitude invoked in the NTV argument creates a problem for the strategy as applied in the more general context of the *PHK*: our ideas of sight may be fleeting and various, but what we think of as tactual experiences of the same object are not really "so different and unlike" each other.

34. My approach to the topic of heterogeneity has been influenced by discussions in my Berkeley seminar in the spring of 1989, and by the written work of the participants. I am also grateful to Kenneth Winkler and Margaret Atherton for detailed comments on earlier versions of the paper (on separate occasions).

Kant and "The *Dogmatic* Idealism of Berkeley"

I

In the "Critique of Pure Reason" Kant maintains that space and time are (merely) *a priori* conditions of our perceptual experience—mere "forms" under which our sensible objects must appear. Thus space and time have no claim to reality independent of us, of our experience: they are "transcendentally ideal." Similarly, the objects we perceive *in* space and time are also said to be transcendentally ideal: since their character is determined by the spatial and temporal conditions of our experience, they have an intrinsic dependence on *us*. Kant contrasts these mind-dependent or conditional perceptual objects ("appearance") with the realm of the unconditioned, transcendentally real "thing in itself." Our knowledge is limited to sensible objects, to appearance.[1]

One of Kant's most insistent claims is that his "transcendental" idealism differs radically from all previous idealisms, and indeed vindicates "empirical realism" against them. Whereas earlier idealisms deny or call into question the reality of the physical world, Kant contends that transcendental idealism provides a uniquely secure basis for the claim that we do have knowledge of real things in space. He holds that knowledge of spatial reality is possible if and only if space is regarded as a condition of our perception, and things in space are distinguished from things in themselves.

Specifically, Kant represents himself as a defender of realism against *two* idealist positions. One is "problematic idealism"—defined as the doctrine that we can have no *immediate knowledge* of objects in space; that such objects can at best be inferred as *causes* of the immediately perceived ideas in our own mind. Kant claims that such inference can never lead to certainty; hence on this view the existence of outer objects would always remain problematic or doubtful. Not too surprisingly, Kant associates problematic idealism with Descartes and his followers.[2] He discusses this position in the first edition of the *Critique* ("Paralogisms" section),[3] in the *Prolegomena*,[4] and in a new section inserted in the second edition of the *Critique*, titled "Refutation of Idealism."[5] (As we shall have occasion to note below, there is a clear change in Kant's manner of replying to problematic idealism in the course of these three works.)

The other idealist position to which Kant explicitly contrasts his own is called "dogmatic idealism." The dogmatic idealist is said to hold that there *can be* no real things in space, that space (and everything in it) is "false and impossible," or that spatial appearances are mere "illusion." Dogmatic idealism is mentioned only briefly in the first edition (in the course of the reply to Descartes);[6] it is not attributed to any particular philosopher. In the *Prolegomena* and second edition, however, Kant repeatedly associates this doctrine with the name of Berkeley.[7] And he seeks to emphasize the merits of his own position, and especially his conception of space, as an answer to the "dogmatic idealist." As Kant openly indicates, the new polemical interest in Berkeley resulted from the critical reception of the first edition: more than one reader, to Kant's displeasure, thought there were significant affinities between transcendental idealism and Berkeley's philosophy.[8]

Kant's conception of problematic idealism is quite perspicuous. Further, while there are points of obscurity in all of Kant's anti-Cartesian passages the general line of attack is sufficiently clear in each case. His treatment of dogmatic or "Berkeleyan" idealism, on the other hand, is full of difficulties. The aim of this paper is to present and deal with some of the most serious of these difficulties. (The replies to Descartes will be considered just in so far as they are bound up with questions about Kant's relation to Berkeley.)

There is, first, an obvious historical problem connected with Kant's remarks about dogmatic idealism. For Kant's allegation that "Berkeley degraded bodies to mere illusion"[9] appears to be altogether without foundation in Berkeley's actual position; it is certainly in contradiction to Berkeley's own understanding of his position. Another thesis that Kant attributes to Berkeley is, if anything, even more incongruous: in the *Prolegomena* Kant cites Berkeley as a latter-day Eleatic who believed that "only in the ideas of the pure understanding and of reason is there truth."[10] Such characterizations make it very doubtful whether Kant's repudiations of dogmatic idealism can have any significant relevance to the position of the historical Berkeley.

Apart from the issue of historical relevance, moreover, one is forced to question whether Kant had *any* plausible conception of what he was attacking and repudiating under the rubric "dogmatic idealism." The difficulty here is that Kant's different remarks on dogmatic idealism in general, and Berkeley in particular, do not seem to add up to any coherent position. Thus, in the *Prolegomena* Kant first groups Berkeley with the Eleatic rationalists, placing in contrast his own position that knowledge depends on sensory experience.[11] Immediately afterwards he comments approvingly that Berkeley, like Kant himself, treated space as mere appearance:

> Space and time, together with all that they contain, are not things in themselves or their qualities, but belong merely to the appearances of the things in themselves. Up to this point I am one in confession with the above idealists [i.e. "all genuine idealists, from the Eleatic school to Bishop Berkeley," who hold that "only in the ideas of . . . reason is there truth"].[12]

However, Kant goes on to say that Berkeley was unable to avoid illusionism because he regarded space as merely empirical:

> But these [idealists], and among them more particularly Berkeley, regarded space as a mere empirical representation that, like the appearances it contains, is, together with its determinations, known to us only by means of experience or percep-

tion. . . . It follows from this that, as truth rests on universal and necessary laws as its criteria, experience, according to Berkeley, can have no criteria of truth because its phenomena (according to him) have nothing *a priori* at their foundation, whence it follows that experience is nothing but sheer illusion. . . .[13]

In this passage Kant claims that the way to avoid Berkeley's "illusionist" conclusions is by accepting the Critical conception of space as an *a priori* form of sensibility.

In the second edition of the *Critique*, on the other hand, Kant twice seems to allege that Berkeley drew illusionist conclusions because he could not free himself from the *transcendental realist* conception of space.[14] That is, he concluded that a real world in space was impossible on the grounds that the very notion of space leads to absurdities, conceiving space as an independently existing entity, or as a property of things in themselves. Here Kant indicates that the remedy to Berkeleyan illusionism or dogmatic idealism lies in the view that space is ideal. The following passage is representative:

[Berkeley, as dogmatic idealist] maintains that space, with all the things of which it is the inseparable condition, is something which is in itself impossible; and he therefore regards the things in space as merely imaginary entities. Dogmatic idealism is unavoidable, if space be interpreted as a property that must belong to things in themselves. For in that case space, and everything to which it serves as condition, is a non-entity.[15]

It seems, then, that taking together the *Prolegomena* and the second edition of the *Critique* Kant attributes to Berkeley (1) mainstream rationalism; (2) some form of empiricism; (3) the view that space is a property of appearances only (or ideal); and (4) the view that space is a property of things in themselves (or transcendentally real). Kant's claims that his own system provides a bulwark *against* dogmatic idealism reflect these varying (and apparently inconsistent) characterizations.

In this paper I will try to show that Kant's various characterizations of Berkeley's "dogmatic idealism" can, despite appearances, be reconciled with each other in a rather interesting way. I will also suggest some ways in which Kant's replies to "dogmatic idealism" do happen to reflect significant differences between his conception of the problem of external reality and that of Berkeley— even though Berkeley's position is hardly what Kant represents it to be.

It is not strictly essential to this part of my thesis that Kant *genuinely believed* Berkeley to have held the views attributed to him in the *Prolegomena* and the *Critique*. Nevertheless, the supposition is both significant and convenient for my purposes, and I will begin my discussion by defending it.

It may at first seem unlikely that this supposition needs much defense. For the assumption that Kant's misrepresentations of Berkeley as an illusionist result from ignorance is surely a natural one, and has been made almost automatically by many commentators.[16] However, certain features of Kant's successive treatments of *Cartesian* idealism do seem to suggest a different view of Kant's relation to Berkeley. Thus, the first edition reply to Descartes ("Fourth Paralogism," A 366 ff.) turns on the reduction of objects in space to representations or ideas. It does have, therefore, a distinctly Berkeleyan character. In this passage Kant accepts the Cartesian premiss that we have immediate knowledge only of our own ideas (representations), but argues that this premiss does *not* lead to the conclusion that we have at best inferential knowledge of objects in space. If space is transcendentally ideal, then spatial objects are *nothing but* a "species of representations."[17] Hence the transcendental idealist ". . . may admit the existence of matter without going outside his mere self-consciousness, or assuming anything more than the certainty of his representations, that is, the *cogito ergo sum*."[18] This explicitly reductionist line of reply is not relied on in the *Prolegomena*, however, and in the second edition of the *Critique* the passage in which it had originally occurred is suppressed. (Kant therefore seems to move away from his argument just at the time he becomes interested in repudiating charges of Berkeleyanism.) The new Refutation in the second edition is an argument for the seemingly opposite conclusion that "I have immediate consciousness of a permanent (substance) in space *distinct from* my representations."[19] *This* argument can easily be construed as unBerkeleyan or even as anti-Berkeleyan.

Such considerations have led commentators to some of the following conclusions: (a) Kant did not reply to Berkeley in the first edition because he could not do so without refuting himself; (b) Kant, in developing his first refutation of Descartes, was directly influenced by Berkeley's rejection of causal realism; (c) Kant abandoned the first edition argument for immediate knowledge of material things *because* he recognized the difficulty of distinguishing his original reply from Berkeley's position; (d) the second edition argument, which concludes that I have immediate knowledge of a real thing in space distinct from my ideas, is Kant's actual answer to Berkeley.[20]

Each of these propositions carries the implication that Kant was not as ignorant of Berkeley as his remarks on that philosopher suggest. At least three of them imply that Kant could not seriously have regarded his doctrine of space as itself the basis for an adequate answer to Berkeley.

In the next sections I will briefly consider the views of two scholars, Norman Kemp Smith and Colin Turbayne, who accept some of the four propositions listed above. I will try to show that neither offers compelling reasons to believe that Kant was aware of the "realist" intentions of Berkeley's empiricism. Once this point has been made clear, we can go on to consider what Kant may really have had in mind in his various remarks about Berkeley.

II

In his *Commentary* Kemp Smith concludes from Kant's misrepresentations of Berkeley's philosophy that Kant was essentially ignorant of his predecessor's position.[21] (He suggests that Kant must have relied on inadequate secondary sources, such as Beattie and Hume.) However, Kant's successive arguments against *Cartesian* idealism do lead Kemp Smith to accept (a), (c), and (d) of the above propositions. His account of *these* arguments therefore involves a much more positive view of Kant's understanding of Berkeleyan doctrine. (Kemp Smith himself seems unaware of this apparent inconsistency in his interpretation.) With respect to the first edition reply to Descartes, Kemp Smith writes:

> Kant refutes the problematic idealism of Descartes by means of the more subjective idealism of Berkeley. The "dogmatic" idealism of Berkeley in the form in which Kant here defines it, namely, is consisting in the assertion that the notion of an independent spatial object involves inherent contradiction, is part of his own position. For this reason he was bound to fail . . . to refute such dogmatic idealism. Fortunately he never even tries to do so.[22]

According to Kemp Smith, the conclusion of the second edition Refutation is "the direct opposite of what is asserted in the first edition." "This difference," he continues,

> is paralleled by the nature of the idealismus to which the two proofs are opposed and which they profess to refute. The argument of the *Paralogisms* of the first edition is itself Berkeleyan, and refutes only the problematic idealism of Descartes. The argument of the second edition, though formally directed only against Descartes, constitutes a no less complete refutation of the position of Berkeley.[23]

In these passages Kant is represented as attributing to Berkeley the denial of bodies in space *conceived as distinct from perceptions*, rather than the denial of physical reality or matter *simpliciter* (illusionism). On this view, the doctrine Kant attributes to the "dogmatic idealist" is very close to, though not quite the same as his own position in the first edition Paralogisms, and also very close to a central tenet of the historical Berkeley. In the second edition, we are to believe, Kant finds it necessary to "refute Berkeley" by arguing that there is *immediate knowledge* of a distinct spatial entity—thereby negating his own earlier position.

Inspection of Kant's text, however, reveals little or no real basis for such an interpretation. In the first place (and most importantly) Kant does *not* in fact define dogmatic idealism as the doctrine that "the notion of an independent spatial object involves inherent contradiction." If this *were* Kant's definition his own position would indeed satisfy it. But what Kant actually says in the first edition Paralogisms is that the dogmatic idealist regards *matter* as a notion involving contradiction.[24] It is precisely Kant's point in this passage that one can deny the possibility of "independent spatial objects," in the transcendental realist sense, while affirming the existence of matter—*provided* Kant's transcendental idealism is accepted. In other words, Kant is insisting that a distinction must be recognized between independent or non-representational existence, and external (spatial) reality. Without such a distinction, discovery of contradiction in spatial existence as conceived by the transcendental realist might well seem to entail the general denial of physical reality. (As I shall try to make clear below, this is exactly what Kant regards as the dogmatic idealist's error.)

Contrary to Kemp Smith, then, Kant's denial of *independent spatial objects* in the first edition Paralogisms by no means commits him to "dogmatic idealism" (or the outright denial of "matter"). Nor does Kant's first edition definition of dogmatic idealism bring it closer to the position of the historical Berkeley than his characterizations in the later works.

It may further be noted against Kemp Smith's view, that the *second* edition Refutation in no way "professes" to refute any position except Descartes'. (Berkeley, Kant claims, has already been answered in the Transcendental Aesthetic.)[25] Indeed, this Refutation has an *intrinsic* feature that marks it as a specifically anti-Cartesian argument. Having remarked in this passage that Berkeley regards space "with all the things of which it is the inseparable condition" as "impossible," Kant continues:

> Problematic idealism, which makes no such assertion, but merely pleads incapacity to prove through immediate experience, any existence save our own, is, in so far as it allows of no decisive judgment until sufficient proof has been found, reasonable. . . . The required proof must, therefore show that we have experience, and not merely imagination of outer things; and this, it would seem, cannot be achieved save by proof that even our inner experience, which for Descartes is indubitable, is possible only on the assumption of outer experience.[26]

Kant then proceeds to the proof itself, which begins with the premiss, "I am conscious of my own existence as determined in time." He thus rests proof on a premiss which (he stresses) Descartes himself would accept. At no point, however, does he attempt to establish a connection between this premiss (or any other part of the argument) and Berkeleyan doctrine.

In general, Cartesian idealism is viewed by Kant as a doctrine which uses the indubitability of inner experience (self-consciousness *in time*) as a basis for calling into question the real existence of outer things. Dogmatic idealism, on the other hand, is said to deny the reality of outer things on the basis of certain intrinsic difficulties in the concept of space and the nature of outer appearances. Kant says of Berkeley that he "did not consider" time.[27] The two positions, as Kant conceives them, have quite different starting points, and therefore require different answers.[28] In his discussion, Kemp Smith has not sufficiently observed these important distinctions. Contrary to what he implies, there is no obvious reason to doubt that what Kant intended as his real answer to dogmatic idealism is identical with his apparent answer, and has to do with his doctrine of space.[29]

The main strength of Kemp Smith's account is that it does provide an explanation of the change in Kant's treatment of Cartesian skepticism. Yet it is perfectly reasonable to suppose that the early charges of idealism or Berkeleyanism[30] affected Kant's later discussion of Descartes, without concluding that Kant himself would have viewed his earlier argument as a form of dogmatic idealism. Kant may have come to realize that his original reductionist argument did suggest—contrary to his intentions—the reduction of all reality to the flux of inner sense. (This would help account for the emphasis placed on the concept of *permanence* in the second edition.) The dogmatic idealist, however, is said to argue that space and matter in space are impossible or illusory.

III

Colin Turbayne is even more impressed than Kemp Smith with the "Berkeleyan" character of the first edition reply to Descartes. In his paper, "Kant's Refutation of Dogmatic Idealism,"[31] Turbayne traces the "systematic similarity" between Kant's position and the "main argument of Berkeley's *Principles* [*of Human Knowledge*] and [*Three*] *Dialogues* [*Between Hylas and Philonous*]"[32] Kant's vindication of the reality of bodies in space, he maintains, parallels in its essential steps Berkeley's refutation of both causal realism and the skepticism or illusionism which this doctrine dialectically engenders. According to Turbayne, both Kant and Berkeley find the answer to skepticism in the repudiation of independent existence (existence outside the mind) for physical objects, and the affirmation of the reality of sensible appearances. Turbayne recognizes that in itself the similarity can support only the thesis that Berkeley anticipated Kant. He would like to claim, however, that the resemblance is a result of direct influence: that "Kant was thoroughly familiar with Berkeley's doctrine and learned from it."[33] He acknowledges that this supposition is in apparent conflict with Kant's various misrepresentations of Berkeley. However, he thinks he can show that, despite appearances, the textual evidence actually favors the view that Kant had a "sure comprehension" of Berkeley's philosophy. The misrepresentations must therefore be construed as "deliberate . . . perversions."[34]

Turbayne's case for this rather startling thesis rests partly on the observation (developed at some length) that Kant's remarks about Berkeley are not *wholly* inaccurate or hostile. While I think Turbayne somewhat overstates Kant's acknowledgement of affinity with Berkeley,[35] it does not seem necessary to deal with this part of his argument in detail. Even if every textual point in this part of Turbayne's paper were accepted, it would follow only that Kant's view of Berkeley is not unrelieved fantasy. It would not follow that Kant had sound first hand knowledge of Berkeley's writings, or that he secretly knew of Berkeley's own claims to empirical realism.

The key point in Turbayne's case however is his contention that Kant's attribution of illusionism to Berkeley can be seen on close inspection to reflect knowledge rather than ignorance. This paradoxical claim is supported ingeniously (but I think ultimately unconvincingly). First Turbayne points out that Kant customarily ascribes to other philosophers doctrines which *he* regards as logical consequences of their positions, rather than what he knows to be their real views.[36] Secondly, he alleges that close reading of Kant's main anti-Berkeley passage in the *Prolegomena* shows that this is exactly what is behind the ascription of illusionism. In this passage (which I have quoted in part above) Kant claims that Berkeley's "illusionism" derives from his purely empirical understanding of spatial concepts. After distinguishing his own a priorism from Berkeley's empiricism, Kant produces the following sentence:

> It follows from this that, as truth rests on universal and necessary laws as its criteria, experience, according to Berkeley, can have no criteria of truth because its phenomena (according to him) have nothing *a priori* at their foundation, whence it follows that experience is nothing but sheer illusion; whereas with us, space and time (in conjunction with the pure concept of the understanding) prescribe their law to all possible experience *a priori* and, at the same time, afford the certain criterion for distinguishing truth from illusion therein.[37]

In his interpretation Turbayne focuses on the clause, "whence it follows that experience is nothing but sheer illusion." He comments (without argument):

> Kant thus holds that illusion is a necessary consequence of Berkeley's view, not that it is Berkeley's view. This highly significant admission makes it more than likely that Kant's repeated assertions elsewhere to the effect that Berkeley actually believes in dogmatic idealism are instances of Kant's habit of ascribing to other philosophers what are, in fact, consequences drawn by Kant himself.[38]

Now the proposition that Kant did not think Berkeley was a deliberate illusionist is doubtless consistent with the rather erratic syntax of the *Prolegomena* sentence in question. It is certainly not accurate to say that Kant "admits" the point, however. To hold that illusionism is a necessary consequence of Berkeley's view (as Kant clearly does) of course does not *preclude* also believing that Berkeley drew that consequence himself. The passage is merely compatible with Turbayne's thesis; it surely does not provide the direct confirmation he requires.

Therefore, Turbayne's arguments that Kant deliberately and almost systematically misrepresented Berkeley's position seem to me quite tenuous. Turbayne somewhat mitigates the obstacles to assuming that Kant had a close familiarity with Berkeley's writings; but he is far from establishing that this assumption provides the "only adequate explanation"[39] of the facts pertaining to Kant's treatment of Berkeley. On the contrary, as I shall show in the next section of this paper, there is an alternative way of interpreting all the passages we have referred to, on the assumption that Kant did think of Berkeley as an avowed illusionist.

But what of the alleged similarities between Kant's reductionist argument and Berkeley's position? As I will explain below, I think Turbayne also overstates this aspect of his case.[40] On the other hand, there are without question some striking parallels. These could be wholly coincidental. Yet it should be observed that one does not have to choose between denying *any* influence and accepting a position as strong as Turbayne's (that Kant had detailed first hand knowledge of Berkeley's philosophy). Information need not be "direct" or fully accurate in order to be influential.

Recognition of a distinction between the historical Berkeley and Kant's Berkeley is helpful in several ways. First, it promotes a more accurate reading of Kant's statements about other idealisms. (This should be evident from our discussion of Kemp Smith.) Secondly, it completely eliminates a question which should have been troubling to both Kemp Smith and Turbayne (neither mentions it). Namely, assuming Kant does need an argument like the second edition refutation in order to answer Berkeley, why should he so austerely refrain from openly using this argument against Berkeley? Thirdly, this distinction prescribes a specific approach to a question that does trouble Turbayne: what can Kant have been thinking of in urging his doctrine of space against Berkeley?[41] (One must first form a picture of "Kant's Berkeley.") Finally, the distinction shows that evaluation of Kant's *philosophical* relation to the *actual* Berkeley may require a broader perspective than the explicitly anti-idealist passages provide. For these are apt to bear only obliquely on the arguments of the *Dialogues* and *Principles*.

I will now try to explain in more detail Kant's conception of "the *dogmatic* idealism of Berkeley."[42]

IV

As a result of some interesting recent scholarship, it is now known that Berkeley was repeatedly characterized both as an illusionist and as a rationalist in the pre-Kantian literature of the eighteenth century.[43] Let us assume that Kant uncritically accepted these contemporary misrepresentations. We will then require two additional assumptions, neither of which seems especially bold: first, that Kant knew that Berkeley was one of the most outspoken critics of the Newtonian conception of space;[44] and second, that he had learned in some perhaps indirect manner that Berkeley reduced space and spatial appearances to "mere empirical representations." Let us also bear in mind that vindication of knowledge of the natural world was inseparably connected in Kant's thought with the possibility of knowing synthetic truths *a priori*. The possibility of establishing that there are necessary truths valid of outer experience was in turn regarded by Kant as dependent upon the doctrine that space is *a priori* and transcendentally ideal.

Now from these observations and assumptions we can develop a quite cohesive account of Kant's conception of "Berkeleyan" or dogmatic idealism. Kant credits Berkeley with the following views:

1. A real thing in space (or "matter") is properly conceived as an entity existing "outside the mind" in an independently and necessarily existing absolute space such as that conceived by Newton.

2. But there are contradictions and anomalies in the notion of such an entity.

3. Hence there are no real things in space.

4. There are of course representations or ideas of "outer things." (These constitute the data of the senses.)

5. As "mere empirical representations" with nothing *a priori* or rational or necessary at their foundation they must be classed as illusion.

On this interpretation it finally becomes clear how Kant could attribute all empiricist view of space to Berkeley, while at the same time characterizing him as a rationalist. If Berkeley was a rationalist, and if he held there was no rational basis for spatial representations (but merely a sensationalistic one), he would *naturally* hold that spatial appearances are mere illusion. Of course all this seems preposterous in relation to Berkeley's actual views,[45] but (as we have just noted) it is not out of conformity with his eighteenth century reputation, nor with Kant's own anti-empiricist patterns of thought.

We can also now see how Kant could consistently have believed both that Berkeley regarded space as "mere appearance" and that Berkeley suffered from transcendental realist preconceptions. What Berkeley, on Kant's view, failed to grasp is that a "real thing in space" could at the same time be "mere appearance"; that to affirm space and bodies cannot exist independently of the knowing subject is *not* equivalent to affirming that there is no such thing as spatial *reality*.

Kant's position, as he was himself at pains to point out, turns on the possibility of distinguishing "transcendental externality" (existence unconditioned by the knowing subject) from empirical externality or existence in space.[46] He seems to assume that Berkeley, together with Descartes and other transcendental realists, failed to grasp the cogency of such a distinction. As a result they failed to appreciate that denial of the possibility of subjectively unconditioned objects in space was not equivalent to denying the possibility of "real things in space."[47]

It remains true, even on this interpretation, that Kant gives slightly different versions of the logical basis of Berkeley's "illusionism" in the *Prolegomena* and in the second edition of the *Critique*. To hold that spatial appearances are illusory because there can be no transcendent causes in space outside the mind is not quite the same as to conclude spatial appearances are illusory because they have nothing *a priori* "at their foundation." These two positions do not seem to conflict with each other, however. For instance, Berkeley could be thought of as assuming that the existence of real things in space requires that *one* of the following propositions be true: either "spatial appearances have some basis in reason, some grounding in necessary truths," or "spatial appearances have cognitively unconditioned causes in space outside the mind." Other possibilities could be suggested. But there is really no need to speculate further on this question, nor need we assume that an intricately developed conception of the logic of "dogmatic idealism" dictated the details of Kant's treatments in the two works. I have been interested only in showing that the major apparent conflicts within and between these treatments can be resolved.

V

Now I would like to make two suggestions concerning the historical relevance of Kant's remarks about Berkeley. We have noted that Kant may have been influenced by contemporary misrepresentations of Berkeley as an illusionist and a rationalist to assume that Berkeley shared some of Kant's own antipathies to radical empiricism. To this extent his "replies" do not have the *ad hominem* effect that Kant presumably intended, for it is not true that Berkeley linked radical empiricism with illusionism. However, a first hand acquaintance with Berkeley's works would probably not have dissuaded Kant from holding that Berkeley's attempt at vindicating empirical realism is unworkable. For since *Kant does* hold the view that "truth requires something *a priori* at its foundation," an empiricist analysis of the external world—no matter how realist in intent—must be for him ultimately a philosophy of illusion. Hence, even if Kant had had a sound knowledge of Berkeley's intentions, his reply might not have been altogether different. The doctrine of the *a priori* status of space is not merely (as Turbayne says) a "legitimate difference" between Kant's philosophy and Berkeley's; it is from Kant's point of view a doctrine of absolutely fundamental importance for the vindication of external reality.[48] Whether Kant's position on this matter is justifiable to any degree is of course another, very complicated question—one that I shall not attempt to deal with in this context.

There is, however, a rather curious respect in which Kant's remarks about Berkeley's view of space do have significant *ad hominem* relevance. For there is one respect in which it is not entirely far-fetched to claim that Berkeley *was* an illusionist with respect to space. Consider the following well-known passage from the *Principles of Human Knowledge*:

> . . . That we should in truth see external space, and bodies actually existing in it, some nearer, others farther off, seems to carry with it some opposition to what has been said of their existing nowhere without the mind. The consideration of this difficulty it was that gave birth to my *Essay Towards a New Theory of Vision*, which was published not long since, wherein it is shown that distance, or outness is neither immediately perceived by sight, nor yet apprehended or judged of by lines and angles, or anything that has a necessary connection with it; but that it is only suggested to our thoughts by certain visible ideas and sensations attending vision, which in their own nature have no manner of similitude or relation either with distance or things placed distance. . . .[49]

Berkeley goes on to remark that the "ideas of sight and touch" are two distinct species, and that in his *Theory of Vision* the argument had been directed only to the former:

> That the proper objects of sight neither exist without mind, nor are the images of external things, was shown even in that treatise.[50]

He acknowledges that the contrary was there supposed to hold of tangible objects, but indicates that this "vulgar error" was not disputed only because the point was irrelevant in a treatise on vision. He continues:

> So that in strict truth the ideas of sight, *when we apprehended by them distance and things placed at a distance, do not suggest or mark out to us things actually existing*

at a distance, but only admonish us what ideas of touch will be imprinted in our minds at such and such distances of time, in consequence of such and such actions.[51]

This passage, together with its correlate in the *Three Dialogues*,[52] suggests not only that we merely seem to perceive things "existing at a distance," but also that if the contrary were allowed, it might count against the doctrine that nothing exists outside the mind. And it is a notably accurate characterization of such a position to say that "space [or spatial distance] must be a property of things in themselves." That is, Berkeley's problem arises (at least partly) from what Kant would regard as a failure clearly to distinguish empirical or spatial externality from "transcendental externality," or existence altogether "outside the mind." Kant's reply would then be that his doctrine of space as an *a priori* form of intuition allows for the avoidance of transcendental realism (things exist "nowhere outside the mind"), without requiring an empiricist reduction of space to a purely temporal order among empirical representations.[53] (The transcendental ideality of space, Kant insists, does not entail that "bodies merely seem to exist outside me.")[54]

In recent decades Berkeley's commentators have tended to dismiss as a strange aberration his notion that irreducible perceptions of spatial distance would somehow conflict with his "idealism" or immaterialism. To this extent they have evidently endorsed a central tenet of Kant's transcendental idealism: that existence "actually at a distance" is not incompatible with existence "in the mind" or "in us."[55] Certainly Berkeley's discussion of the issue reveals considerable confusion, and doubtless on more than one level. This need not mean, however, that his worry is completely without basis. It is not easy to deny *all* connection between spatial existence and what Kant would call transcendental externality—as philosophers other than Berkeley have sometimes observed. H. W. B. Joseph suggests that perception of space-relations is in some sense a sufficient condition for belief in a "real world outside the mind":

> The relation of what we feel or hear to the feeling or hearing of it is not the same with that of what we see or touch to the seeing or touching it. Where the apprehension of figure and space-relation enters, there enters the thought of a difference between what is, and how it appears to us, which is immediate; this . . . is what presupposes the existence of 'things outside me'.
>
> And there one is tempted to leave the matter, and say that these things are real and independent of mind, and that we come alone and get to know them.[56]

More recently, P. F. Strawson has contended that distance or some close analogue of distance is at least a necessary condition for our possessing the concept of independently existing objects.[57]

Perhaps, then, there is need for more thorough discussion of the problem (with careful separation of logical and strictly genetic questions), before we conclude that Berkeley's intuitions are wholly spurious. It is possible that the notions of spatial externality and independent existence cannot be so sharply separated as Kant assumes. Such considerations could weigh against the cogency of grounding an empirical realism in a "transcendental idealism." On this point Kant's advantage over the historical Berkeley may not be as secure as it seems.

<h2 style="text-align:center">CONCLUSION</h2>

I have argued that Kant conceived of Berkeley as an illusionist, who denied the reality of bodies in space because he had discovered absurdities in the current (Newtonian) conception of space. Kant must have wrongly assumed that Berkeley's critique of Newton formed the basis for his metaphysical conclusions—which in the eighteenth century were widely reputed to be of an illusionist nature. Kant could thus represent his own doctrine of space, which he thought avoided the difficulties in the Newtonian view, as an answer to Berkeley. (I have tried to show that the "Berkeleyan" strategy Kant uses against Descartes in the first edition Paralogisms need not be taken to indicate a more accurate knowledge of his predecessor than is consistent with these errors.) I have also pointed out that there actually is an important difference between Kant and Berkeley with respect to the status of space. While Berkeley's philosophy may have been, in intent, as "realist" as Kant's, it must be acknowledged that Berkeley found it desirable to deny the reality of spatial distance in order to meet a possible objection to his metaphysical position. The thesis that Kant imagined to be the polemical essence of Berkeley's philosophy, derived from the critique of Newton, in fact emerges as a sort of defensive footnote unconnected with any claims about "absurdities" in the concept of space.

<h2 style="text-align:center">NOTES</h2>

1. Kant characterizes his position as "transcendental idealism" at A 369 ff. Cf. A 28 = B 44; A 36 = B 52. The quotations in this paper are from Norman Kemp Smith's translation (London: Macmillan, 1958).

2. The attribution of problematic idealism to Descartes does involve some license, of course, since Descartes himself concluded that the transcendental causal inference can be guaranteed. But Kant, like many post-Cartesian philosophers, evidently felt that the most significant of Descartes' arguments were those developed in the first two Meditations.

3. A 366 ff.

4. *Prolegomena to Any Future Metaphysics*, §49. The *Prolegomena* (1783) was published between the first (1781) and second (1787) editions of the *Critique*.

5. B 274 ff. Cf. Kant's note on this passage in the Preface to the second edition, B xxxix ff. In this note Kant seems to use the expression "psychological idealism" as an alternative to "problematic idealism."

6. A 377. Kant here says that the dogmatic idealist will be answered in the next section after the "Paralogisms—i.e., the "Antinomies." He does not mention dogmatic idealism in the latter section.

7. *Prolegomena*, Appendix; *Critique*, B 274; cf. B 69 ff. In Remark III at the end of

§ 13 of the *Prolegomena* Kant speaks of the "mystical and visionary" idealism of Berkeley.

8. Cf. *Prolegomena*, Appendix. As this passage shows, the prime offender was the (now infamous) Garve-Feder review published in the *Göttinger gelehrten Anzeigen* of January 19, 1782) (Zugabe, Stück III). The passage in this review which contains the comparison with Berkeley reads as follows:

> Auf disen Begriffen, von den Empfindungen als bloßen Modificationen unserer selbst (worauf auch Berkeley seinen Idealismus hauptsächlich baut) vom Raum und von der Zeit berüht der eine Grundpfeiler des Kantschen Systems.

B. Erdmann has written in detail about the impact of this review on Kant, in the introduction to his edition of the *Prolegomena* (Leipzig: Voss, 1878). (But see introduction to Karl Vorländer's edition [Hamburg: F. Meiner, 1957] for evaluation of Erdmann's results.)

It is perhaps worth stressing that this is the *sole* mention of Berkeley in the entire (nine page) review, since one often encounters exaggerations in the Kant literature. A. C. Ewing, for instance, can only have this review in mind when he writes: "Kant was considerably offended by a review of the first edition which accused him of being an idealist and of out-Berkeleying Berkeley. . . ." (*A Short Commentary on Kant's Critique of Pure Reason* [London: Methuen 1961; first ed. 1938], p. 182.)

9. *Critique*, B 71.

10. *Loc. cit.*

11. *Ibid.*

12. *Ibid.* Quotations from the *Prolegomena* follow the L. W. Peck translation (Indianapolis: Bobbs-Merrill, 1950 [Library of Liberal Arts]).

13. *Ibid.*

14. B 69 ff. and B 274.

15. B 274. The statement relating to Berkeley at B 69 is very similar:

> It would be my own fault, if out of that which I ought to reckon as appearance, I made mere illusion. That does not follow as a consequence of our principle of the ideality of all our sensible intuitions—quite the contrary. It is only if we ascribe *objective reality* to these forms of representation [i.e. space and time], that it becomes impossible for us to prevent everything being thereby transformed into mere *illusion*. For if we regard space and time as properties which, if they are to be possible at all, must be found in things in themselves, and if we reflect on the absurdities in which we are then involved [Kant here itemizes absurdities], . . .— we cannot blame the good Berkeley for degrading bodies to mere illusion.

16. See, for instance, Ewing, *loc. cit.*; H. J. Paton, *Kant's Metaphysics of Experience* (London: George Allen and Unwin, 1936), Vol. II, p. 376; T. D. Weldon, *Kant's Critique of Pure Reason*, second ed. (Oxford: Clarendon Press, 1958), pp. 9 f.

17. A 370.

18. *Ibid.*

19. Cf. B 274 ff. This is a paraphrase of Kant's conclusion, not an exact quotation.

20. See sections II and III, below, for some references; cf. Robert Paul Wolff, *Kant's Theory of Mental Activity* (Cambridge: Harvard University Press. 1963), pp. 200, 300; also Ewing, *loc. cit.*

21. *A Commentary to Kant's* Critique of Pure Reason (New York: Humanities Press, 1962; reprint of second ed. [1923]), pp. 156–157.

22. *Ibid.*, p. 305; cf. p. 157, where Kemp Smith observes that Kant does not keep his

promise to answer Berkeley's idealism in the "Antinomies," "doubtless for the reason" that his own teaching "frequently coincides with that of Berkeley."

23. *Ibid.*, p. 313.

24. A 377.

25. B 274 f.

26. B 274–275.

27. *Prolegomena loc. cit.* This remark might suggest an acquaintance with Berkeley's *De Motu*, where discussion is concentrated on the concept of absolute *space*. See n. 34.

28. Because of this distinction, I believe commentators have erred in regarding Kant's reply to an idealist argument in A 36 = B 53 ff. as directed against Berkeley and/or dogmatic idealism. (Cf. Kemp Smith, *op. cit.*, p. 157, and Arnulf Zweig's introduction to *Kant: Philosophical Correspondence, 1759–1799* [Chicago: University of Chicago Press], pp. 10–11, n. 11.) It is rather the distinct, "Cartesian" line of thought that Kant here has in mind.

29. It might be objected that regardless of Kant's intentions he *in fact* needs the second edition argument to distinguish his position from (the historical) Berkeley's, so Kemp Smith is right on the one point of real philosophical significance. To this there are two replies: (1) *Apart from* this argument Kant would have reasons to hold that his position provides a stronger defense of the reality of spatial appearances than Berkeley's (see sec. V, below); (2) The historical Berkeley does not deny that the natural world is lasting or enduring. Of course it might be possible to define *some* philosophical position that would be contradicted by the second edition refutation, but not by Kant's doctrine of space.

30. The doctrine of the first analogy is linked with the enterprise of avoiding Berkeleyan implications in a letter written to Kant by his disciple J. S. Beck:

> [A man] becomes aware [of the proceedings of the understanding in accordance with the categories] when I ask him to suspend all the objects in space and, after the passing of 50 years, set up a world again. He will assert that both worlds go together and that no empty time has passed, that is, that he can only conceive of time in connection with something persisting. Attention must be paid to this, in order to lay the ghost of Berkeleian idealism. (Zweig, *op. cit.*, p. 228)

In an earlier letter Beck writes, à propos of the issue of "Berkeleyanism":

> Appearances are the objects of intuition, and they are what everybody means when he speaks of objects that surround us. But it is the reality of just these objects that Berkeley denies and that the *Critique*, on the other hand, defends. (*Ibid.*, p. 195)

James Beattie, with whose work Kant was familiar in translation, remarks that Berkeley's doctrine includes the position that things cease to exist as soon as they ceased to be perceived. (And Beattie makes no mention of the role of God in Berkeley's philosophy.) Cf. *Essay on the Nature and Immutability of Truth*, revised ed., *Essays*, vol. I, p. 49.

31. *Philosophical Quarterly*, vol. 5 (1955), pp. 225–244.

32. *Ibid.*, p. 229. Turbayne thinks this position is reflected in all Kant's anti-idealist passages except the second edition Refutation. However, throughout his paper he relies very heavily for citations on the first edition "Paralogisms," and eventually he admits that Kant is closer to Berkeley in this passage than anywhere else (p. 243).

33. *Ibid.* Turbayne also contends that Kant does not attempt to refute Berkeley in the first edition because of the close similarity between their views (p. 243). Thus he accepts both (a) and (b) of the propositions listed on p. 263, above. Of the second edition argu-

ment Turbayne says only that Kant here utilizes "a method of proof of the external world" different from that of the other anti-idealist passages (p. 229).

34. *Ibid.*, pp. 242–243. Turbayne maintains in particular that Kant had read the *Three Dialogues* and *De Motu*. He stresses that a German translation of the former work was available prior to the publication of the first edition of the *Critique*, contrary to a claim made by Kemp Smith. (The *Principles* would not have been accessible in German. It is generally believed that Kant did not read English.) Turbayne's observation that Kant could well have read *De Motu* is important; I have no quarrel with this suggestion (see sec. IV, below). My contention is only that Turbayne fails in his attempt to show that Kant manifests an accurate knowledge of Berkeley's general philosophical position, as elaborated in the *Dialogues* (but not, of course in *De Motu*).

35. Turbayne claims that the two statements about Berkeley in the second edition of the *Critique* correctly ascribe Berkeley Kant's "own denial of transcendental realism" and "his own insight into the relation of transcendental realism and illusionism" (p. 241). But what Kant seems actually to ascribe to Berkeley in these passages (which have been quoted above) is a denial of the reality of space *based on a failure to comprehend the possibility of an alternative to transcendental realism*. Kant there seems unquestionably to view Berkeley as accepting the transcendental realist *conception* of space, but as denying that there *can exist* anything satisfying that conception.

36. *Ibid.*, pp. 240 f. He supports this claim with a citation from Kemp Smith's *Commentary*, and some reference to Kant's treatment of Leibniz.

37. *Op. cit.*, pp. 242 f. Turbayne seems to follow the Beck translation in his citations from the *Prolegomena*.

38. *Ibid.*, p. 243. The sentence reads in German:

Hieraus folgt: daß, da Wahrheit auf allgemeinen und notwendigen Gesetzen als ihren Kriterien beruht, die Erfahrung bei Berkeley keine Kriterien der Wahrheit haben könne, weil den Erscheinungen derselben (von ihm) nichts *a priori* zum Grunde gelegt ward; woraus denn folgte, daß sie nichts als lauter Schein sei, dagegen bei uns Raum and Zeit (in Verbindung mit den reinen Verstandesbegriffen) *a priori* aller möglichen Erfahrung ihr Gesetz vorschreiben, welches zugleich das sichere Kriterium abgibt, in ihr Wahrheit von Schein zu unterscheiden. (Vorlander ed., p. 145)

39. *Op. cit.*, p. 240.

40. *Ibid.*, pp. 238, 243.

41. See p. 22, and n. 48.

42. *Critique*, B 274.

43. See Harry M. Bracken, *The Early Reception of Berkeley's Immaterialism: 1710–1733* (The Hague: Martinus Nijhoff, 1959), *passim*. Bracken traces the development of Berkeley's eighteenth century reputation as an idealist and a skeptic, as one who rejects the evidence of the senses and reduces bodies to "phantoms." He also notes that Jesuit writers of the period characterized Berkeley as a "Malbranchiste de bonne foi," who went beyond his master by actually denying the existence of matter. A sentence quoted by Bracken from one of their reviews reads in part: "Mr. Berkley (sic) continues to sustain obstinately *that there are no bodies and that the material world is only an intelligible world . . .*" (p. 17). Bracken himself tentatively suggests a link between Kant and Berkeley's early critics (see esp. pp. 87–88).

44. As noted above, it seems possible that Kant was familiar with *De Motu*.

45. The late work *Siris*, however, has sometimes been interpreted as Platonist. It cer-

tainly does exhibit a more "mystical and visionary" pattern of thought than Berkeley's early (and now better-known) books.

46. *Critique*, A 370 (for instance).

47. Or, in Descartes' case, that denial of immediate knowledge of such unconditioned objects is not equivalent to denial of immediate knowledge of real things in space.

48. Turbayne regards the doctrine of space as an *a priori* form of sensibility as essentially irrelevant to the defense of empirical realism. Hence, while this doctrine constitutes a genuine difference between Kant's position and Berkeley's, "Kant's appeal to it . . . as a guard against illusion, which Berkeley lacked . . . creates difficulties" (p. 243). The antidote to the illusionism generated by transcendental realist assumptions "is not the *a priori* nature of space, but its ideality or subjectivity" (*ibid.*).

Turbayne, however, points out himself that Kant (like Berkeley) appeals to the criterion of lawfulness or coherence to distinguish reality from illusion within experience. He seems further to acknowledge that on Kant's view the availability of such a criterion presupposes validity of synthetic *a priori* judgements (*op. cit.*, pp. 237–238). But he regards this aspect of Kant's position as incidental to the "central argument" against skepticism or idealism allegedly shared with Berkeley (*ibid.*).

I find it difficult to determine precisely what Turbayne is claiming here. Surely the grounds for distinguishing reality from illusion cannot be incidental to a defense of empirical realism. On Kant's view the distinction depends on knowledge of universal laws; and this in turn presupposes synthetic *a priori* knowledge of objects of experience—which ultimately depends on the *a priori* character of space. It is highly dubious, then, that Kant shares Berkeley's "central argument" to the extent of endorsing a vindication of empirical realism that could function completely independently of the "a priorist" Critical framework. If this is Turbayne's position, I think it requires modification.

49. § 43.

50. § 44.

51. *Ibid.* My emphasis.

52. *Works*, vol. II, p. 202 (First dialogue).

53. Max Jammer has also seen in Berkeley's conception of space an "extreme subjective idealism . . . the final conclusion of an empiricistic approach," to which Kant's position provides a significant alternative. Cf. *Concepts of Space* (New York: Harper, 1960 [Harper Torchbook]), pp. 133–134. J. L. Borges is another who ascribes appropriate significance to Berkeley's reductionism with respect to space:

> Hume noted for all time that Berkeley's arguments did not admit the slightest refutation nor did they cause the slightest conviction. This dictum is entirely correct in its application to the earth, but entirely false in Tlön. The nations of this planet are congenitally idealist. . . . The world for them is not a concourse of objects in space; it is a heterogeneous series of independent acts. It is successive and temporal, not spatial. ("Tlön, Uqbar, Orbis Tertius," trans. by J. E. Irby.)

54. *Critique*, B 69.

55. Cf. Luce, *Berkeley's Immaterialism*, pp. 8, 119–120; D. M. Armstrong, *Berkeley's Theory of Vision* (Melbourne University Press, 1960), pp. 26 ff. Armstrong writes (p. 31):

> Suppose we accept immaterialism. How must we modify the New Theory of Vision? It is clear that we must now deny that tangible objects exist independently of

their being perceived, but we do not have to deny that these objects are at a distance from our bodies and set in circumambient space.

56. "A Comparison of Kant's Idealism with That of Berkeley," *Proceedings of the British Academy*, vol. XV (1929, Henriette Hertz Trust Lecture), p. 22.
57. See esp. *Individuals* (London: Methuen, 1959), p. 75.

The "Phenomenalisms" of Berkeley and Kant

BERKELEY AND KANT

Of all the major modern philosophical systems the views of George Berkeley have probably met with the most resistance, ridicule, and distortion. Among Berkeley's many detractors and distorters was Kant, who represented Berkeley as a "dogmatic idealist" who "degraded bodies to mere illusions." (*B*71)[1] As has frequently been pointed out, however, Kant's few direct remarks about Berkeley are not unrelievedly negative. In the *Prolegomena* particularly, Kant acknowledges a limited affinity with Berkeley, pointing out that they agree in treating space as idea;.[2] Kant goes on to indicate that he differs from Berkeley in regarding space as a priori rather than merely empirical, and for this reason is able to avoid Berkeley's illusionism. In the second edition of the *Critique of Pure Reason* Kant also points to his doctrine of space as the answer to dogmatic idealism—though the logic of his claim there is at least superficially quite different from that in the *Prolegomena* (*B*274; cf. *B*69).[3]

The historical and philosophical relations between Kant and Berkeley are topics of long debate among Kant scholars. It is generally acknowledged—at least by twentieth century critics—that Berkeley was far from considering himself an "illusionist." According to one strong tradition Kant's own position is in important respects quite close to Berkeley's *real* position.[4] Within this tradition one finds disagreement over whether Kant was simply ignorant of this fact, as a result of lacking firsthand knowledge of most of Berkeley's writings, or whether he deliberately misrepresented Berkeley's position to conceal an intellectual debt.[5] According to another viewpoint, more recently developed, Kant's empirical realism/transcendental idealism is in fact significantly different from Berkeley's position—and in approximately the ways Kant indicates that it is different.[6] Some commentators in arguing this viewpoint have presented rebuttals to their predecessors' claims that Berkeley's works would in general have been inaccessible to Kant, because he did not know English. (In fact, various works were available in Latin, French, and even German during Kant's lifetime.) Some recent writers further hold that Kant's system is philosophically superior to Berkeley's in at least some of the ways Kant took it to be.[7]

The earlier *and* the more recent critics have tended to portray Kant and Berkeley as united by a common concern: that of vindicating the certainty of our knowledge of bodies in the wake of Cartesian doubt. Both philosophers, it is held, sought to achieve this result by denying the Cartesian (and Lockean) interpretation of physical objects as the mind-independent causes of our subjective perceptions. Berkeley responded with the theory that bodies *just are* sets of subjective sense-perceptions, which are presented in orderly fashion to human minds according to the well-disposed will of God. Therefore, our certain knowledge of our own subjective states in itself guarantees the certain knowledge of bodies: there is no need for a tenuous, extraexperiential causal inference that must inevitably succumb to skeptical challenge. Against the view that Kant's idealist solution to skepticism is essentially similar to Berkeley's, recent critics have held that Kant secures unproblematic knowledge of bodies while avoiding Berkeley's sensationalistic reductionism. Kant's position, in other words, allows him to enjoy the sweets of phenomenalism without the bitters of subjectivism.[8] Kant's theory of space and time as a priori forms of intuition, together with the transcedental deduction of the categories (and the ensuing elaboration of the "principles" of causality and substance), allow him to hold that objects are as immediately known as the series of inner experiences. At the same time they allegedly allow him to preserve such essential features of objectivity as permanence, publicity, and the distinction between truth and illusion— results not achieved by Berkeley's cruder theory. It sometimes is also stressed that Kant's and Berekely's idealisms have quite different implications for the interpretation of Newtonian science, and that the two philosophers do not take the same view of the primary–secondary quality distinction.[9]

In my opinion the earlier tradition that assimilated Berkeleyan and Kantian phenomenalism is clearly erroneous. Further, I grant that Kant's own view of his relation to Berkeley may be accurately captured by some of the recent commentators. Nevertheless, the full difference between Kant's and Berkeley's position has still not been correctly expressed. For both Kant and his recent commentators (including myself) have tended to overlook a radical difference in the philosophical motivations of the two systems. It seems to me that this difference of concern would give Berkeley good reason to regard Kant's position as alien to, rather than an improvement of, his own in a quite fundamental respect. It is therefore quite wrong to represent Berkeley as getting about halfway to a result that Kant finally achieved. Development of this idea leads me to touch on some features of Kant's theory of 'appearances' that I find rather strange. Without attempting to assess further the recent claims about Kant's philosophical superiority to Berkeley, I suggest that clarification of the differences between the two philosophers' goals is a necessary step towards such assessment.

BERKELEY ON THE REALITY OF SENSIBLE QUALITIES

The principle claim I want to defend is that Berkeley understood the challenge posed by Descartes's (and Locke's) transcendental realism very differently than did Kant. Berkeley's mission, at least in the great early works, was to vindicate the reality of the objects of ordinary sense experience, *as sensed*. The *primary* foe in this connection is not the historically somewhat fictitious position of "Cartesian skepticism." It is rather the historically quite real and (in modernized form) still current position of Cartesian scientific realism.[10] But Kant's empirical realism *is* a form of scientific realism. It is *not* a vindication of ordinary sense experience (or "common sense") as Berkeley conceived it. In other words, whatever Kant may have achieved in demonstrating the claims to reality of appearances as he understood them, he has not demonstrated (or tried to demonstrate) the reality of phenomena as Berkeley understood them. For Kant, what is empirically real is primarily the material world of the science of his time—a world that does not possess colors, tastes, and the like in any literal, irreducible sense.[11]

Berkeley, on the contrary, takes as empirically real the objects of ordinary sense experience, literally and richly endowed with colors, tastes, and the other 'secondary qualities'—and perhaps with aesthetic, religious, and emotive 'qualities,' too. This position of course leaves Berkeley with problems about how to accommodate the more esoteric concepts of contemporary mechanism, and the explanatory successes achieved through these concepts. Berkeley did make earnest efforts to confront these problems—at times taking refuge in instrumentalist accounts. I certainly do not claim that he was fully successful in these efforts. But the goal itself of vindicating the reality of the sensible world as concretely sensed and experienced, as against the "abstractions" of the scientists, is in my view a far from frivolous one. After citing some passages that show Berkeley doing just that, I shall consider a variety of passages from Kant's first *Critique* which seem to indicate the great difference between Berkeley's and Kant's position concerning the relations among real appearances, sensations, and the entities of science.

Consider the opening of Berkeley's first *Dialogue*. Berkeley's spokesman Philonous is in a garden, where he encounters his prospective antagonist, Hylas. Hylas has endured a night of intellectual unrest; as a result he has risen early. In what superficially appears to be mere indulgence in scene setting, Philonous is made to respond with the following effusion:

> It happened well, to let you see what innocent and agreeable pleasures you lose every morning. Can there be a pleasanter time of the day, or a more delightful season of the year? That purple sky, those wild but sweet notes of birds, the fragrant bloom upon the trees and flowers, the gentle influence of the rising sun, these and a thousand nameless beauties of nature inspire the soul with secret transports.[12]

But the passage is far from being as intellectually innocuous as the casual reader may suppose. Berkeley's citation of the beauties of nature (those, presumably, that are not "nameless") systematically touches on each of the commonly mentioned traditional 'secondary qualities,' omitting only taste. Thus we encounter in the garden color ("that purple sky"), sound ("those wild but sweet notes"), odor ("fragrant bloom"), and warmth ("gentle influence") of the rising sun. The emotive or affective aspects of the sensuously experienced natural scene are also lightly stressed.

Later, when the antagonist Hylas has been driven to concede that sensible objects have no reality "without the mind," and has thence concluded that there is no certain reality in nature, Philonous counters: "Look! are not the fields covered with a delightful verdure? Is there not something in the woods and groves, in the rivers and clear springs, that soothes, that delights, that transports the soul?"[13] And so on, at length. The speech concludes: "What treatment, then, do those philosophers deserve, who would deprive these noble and delightful scenes of all *reality*? How should those Principles be entertained that lead us to think all the visible beauty of the creation a false imaginary glare"?[14]

Elsewhere, in somewhat similar circumstances, Philonous emphasizes that the reality of the full range of the sensed qualities of a cherry is all that matters to us:

> *Hyl.* . . . But, after all, Philonous, when I consider the substance of what you advance against *Scepticism*, it amounts to no more than this:—We are sure that we really see, hear, feel; in a word, that we are affected with sensible impressions.
>
> *Phil.* And how are we concerned any farther? I see this cherry, I feel it, I taste it: and I am sure *nothing* cannot be seen, or felt, or tasted: it is therefore *real. Take away the sensations of softness, moisture, redness, tartness, and you take away the cherry, since it is not a being distinct from sensations.* A cherry, I say, is nothing but a congeries of sensible impressions, or ideas perceived by various senses: which ideas are united into one thing (or have one name given them) by the mind, because they are observed to attend each other. Thus, when the palate is affected with such a particular taste, the sight is affected with a red colour, the touch with roundness, softness. [etc.]. Hence, when I see, and feel, and taste, in sundry certain manners, I am sure the cherry exists, or is real; its reality being in my opinion nothing abstracted from those sensations. But if by the word *cherry* you mean an unknown nature, distinct from *all those sensible qualities*, and by its *existence* something distinct from its being perceived; then, indeed, I own, neither you nor I, nor any one else, can be sure it exists.[15]

According to the common interpretation I have sketched, Berkeley is driven into empiricistic reductionism, and hence (unfortunately) into subjectivism, just because he supposes this is the only way to avoid the external world skepticism that is virtually built into Cartesian or Lockean scientific realism. I agree that there is clear evidence of this concern—for example at the end of the passage just quoted. Yet the several passages quoted indicate that Berkeley was not merely interested in affirming the reality of sensible appearances or qualities as a *means* to making a case for the reality of body in some form or other. It was precisely the reality of the world of experience, as experienced, that he was concerned to establish. Even if the Cartesian inference to *res extensa*, or the Lockean inference to (epistemologically indeterminate) real essences of physical substances were certain above all skeptical challenge, too much of reality as we conceive and experience it in ordinary life would have to be construed as "false imaginary glare." This at least is the reading I propose.

One further issue about Berkely's conception of the reality of the world as we experience it is worth mentioning. Frequently in the *Dialogues* Hylas attempts the move of distinguishing the "real" sound or color or other quality (as the scientist understands it) from the mere sensation, with the aim of maintaining that the former at least is not simply "in the mind." Philonous in turn makes fun of the idea that real colors are unseen, real sounds unheard, and so forth. The following passage is representative.

> *Hyl.* I own myself entirely satisfied, that [colors] are all equally apparent, and that there is no such thing as colour really inhering in external bodies, but that it is altogether in the light. And what confirms me in this opinion is, in proportion to the light colours are still more or less vivid; and if there be no light, then are no colours perceived. . . . It is immediately some contiguous substance, which, operating on the eye, occasions a perception of colours: and such is light.
>
> *Phil.* How! Is light then a substance?
>
> *Hyl.* I tell you, Philonous, external light is nothing but a thin fluid substance, whose minute particles being agitated with a brisk motion, and in various manners reflected from the different surfaces of outward objects to the eyes, communicate different motions to the optic nerves; which, being propagated to the brain, cause therein various impressions; and these are attended with the sensations of red, blue, yellow, [etc.].
>
> *Phil.* It seems then the light doth no more than shake the optic nerves.
>
> *Hyl.* Nothing Else.
>
> *Phil.* And consequent to each particular motion of the nerves, the mind is affected with a sensation, which is some particular colour.
>
> *Hyl.* Right.
>
> *Phil.* And these sensations have no existence without the mind.
>
> *Hyl.* They have not.
>
> *Phil.* How then do you affirm that colours are in the light: since by *light* you understand a corporeal substance external to the mind?
>
> *Hyl.* Light and colours, as immediately perceived by us, I grant cannot exist without the mind. But in themselves they are only the motions and configurations of certain insensible particles of matter.
>
> *Phil.* Colours, then, in the vulgar sense, or taken for the immediate objects of sight, cannot agree to any but a perceiving substance.

Having received Hylas's acquiescence in this restatement, Philonous concludes:

> *Phil.* Well then, since you give up the point as to those sensible qualities which are alone thought colours by all mankind beside, you may hold what you please with regard to those invisible ones of the philosohers. It is not my business to dispute about *them*; only I would advise you to bethink yourself, whether, considering the inquiry we are upon, it be prudent for you to affirm—*the red and blue which we see are not real colours, but certain unknown motions and figures which no man ever did or can see are truly so.* Are not these shocking notions, and are not they subject to as many ridiculous inferences, as those you were obliged to renounce before in the case of sounds?[16]

Viewed in one way, this passage of course shows Berkeley making a case for his general position that sensible objects have no existence without the mind.

Roughly stated, a *sensible* color is a color as consciously experienced—not a stream of minute particles of which no one is directly aware in ordinary seeing. And Hylas admits that the *former* exists only in the mind. But at the same time, I suggest, the passage shows Berkeley insisting on the point that a *real color* is a color as consciously experienced—and that colors as consciously experienced are real colors, colors of things. Kant's position about perceptual reality is quite different, as we shall see.

KANT'S POSITION CONCERNING SENSIBLE QUALITIES

Throughout the first *Critique* Kant consistently seems to distinguish objects of experience or appearances (*Erscheinungen*) from sensations (*Empfindungen*). Sensations are the mere subjective results of the effects of "the real in appearances" on our peculiar organs of sense. The secondary qualities are assimilated by Kant to sensations. According to this complicated theory, then, bodies in space are transcendentally ideal because space is only the form of our sensibility, but their primary qualities are empirically real. Their perceived colors, odors, tastes, and so forth are not even *empirically* real.

Other commentators have pointed to this feature of Kant's position as an important difference between his idealism and Berkeley's.[17] I believe, however, that its profound significance for the difference in motivation and concern between the two philosophers has not yet been sufficiently appreciated.[18] Further, the attempt to affirm the primary-secondary quality distinction within an idealist or phenomenalist philosophy of body raises a perplexing issue about Kant's concept of appearance—an issue that surely deserves more consideration than it has received. Before articulating the problem I have in mind, I shall cite some relevant passages from three different parts of the *Critique of Pure Reason*: the Aesthetic, the Anticipations of Perception, and the Fourth Paralogism in the first edition (which has often been construed as an *especially* Berkeleyan passage.)

In *B44*–45 of the Transcendental Aesthetic Kant writes:

> With the sole exception of space there is no subjective representation, referring to something *outer*, which could be entitled objective *a priori*. For there is no other subjective representation from which we can derive *a priori* synthetic propositons, as we can from intuition in space. . . . Strictly speaking, therefore, these other representations have no ideality, although they agree with the representation of space in this respect, that they belong merely to the subjective constitution of our manner of sensibility, for instance, of sight, hearing, touch, as in the case of sensations of colors, sounds, and heat, which, since they are mere sensations and not intuitions, do not of themselves yield knowledge of any object, least of all any *a priori* knowledge.
>
> The above remark is intended only to guard anyone from supposing that the ideality of space as here asserted can be illustrated by examples so altogether insufficient as colors, taste, etc. For these cannot rightly be regarded as properties of

things, but only as changes in the subject, changes which may, indeed, be different for different men.[19]

Part of the passage just quoted (toward the beginning) replaced a perhaps even more committed statement in the *A* edition, which includes the following sentences:

> The taste of a wine does not belong to the objective determinations of the wine, not even if by the wine as an object we mean the wine as appearance, but to the special constitution of sense in the subject that tastes it. Colors are not properties of the bodies to the intuition of which they are attached, but only modifications of the sense of sight, which is affected in a certain manner by light. [*A*28–29]

It may be noted that in this last passage Kant seems to agree with Berkeley that colors *are* sensations—not properties of light or nonsensational surfaces. But Kant is clearly distinguishing, in a most un-Berkeley-like way, between mere subjective effects of bodies, and objective properties of the bodies, considered as appearances.

In the Anticipations of Perception Kant's theory of perception comes through even more clearly. He reiterates the view that "sensation is not in itself an objective representation." (*A*166/*B*208). Appearances, however, besides intuition contain "the real of sensation as merely subjective representation, which gives us only the consciousness that the subject is affected, and which we relate to an object in general" (*A*166/*B*207–208). All sensation possesses intensity or degree, however, and this may be in turn taken to correspond to the "degree of influence on the sense." As Kant also says, "what corresponds in empirical intuition to sensation is reality [*realitas phaenomenon*]" (*A*168/*B*209). He continues:

> If this reality is viewed as cause, either of sensation or of some other reality in the appearance, such as change, the degree of the reality as cause is then entitled a moment, e.g., the moment of gravity. . . .
>
> Every sensation, therefore, and likewise every reality in the appearances, however small it may be, has a degree, that is, an intensive magnitude which can always be diminished. [*A*168–69/*B*210–11]

According to Kant's theory, then, physical causes (as understood by the scientist, such as gravity) affect our senses, giving rise to sensations which, while not resembling properties of the object, nevertheless bear some correspondence to the latter, owing to the proportionality of cause and effect.

The Fourth Paralogism of the first edition is a passage that has been cited by commentators as showing Kant at his most Berkleyan. Some have been held that Kant abandoned the argument of this passage in the second edition *because it was too Berkeleyan*.[20] There are in fact a few phrases in the passage that seem a bit discordant with Kant's distinction elsewhere between sensation on the one hand, and the real in space that gives rise to sensation on the other hand. We find, for example, the following statement. "All outer perception thus directly proves something real in space, *or is rather the real itself* . . ." (*A*375, italics added). But this very sentence continues: ".... and in this way is empirical realism thus beyond doubt, i.e. *there corresponds to* our outer intuitions something real in space" (*A*373, italics added).[21] And other statements in the Paralogism in *A* seem completely consonant with the account of perception we have noted in the Aesthetic and the Anticipations of Perception. For instance, Kant writes:

> Space and time are indeed *a priori* representations, which dwell in us as forms of our sensible intuition, before a real object has determined our sense through sensation, so as to represent the object under those sensible relations. Only this material or real, this something that is to be intuited in space, necessarily presupposes perception, and can not independently of it, which indicates (*anzeigt*) the reality of something in space, be composed and produced by any power of imagination. .... It is unquestionably certain that whether one takes the sensations of pleasure and pain, or even the outer ones, such as colors, heat, etc., perception is that through which the stuff to think objects of sensible intuition must first be given. This perception thus represents . . . something real in space. [*A*373–74]

Here again the theory Kant is propounding appears to be a causal one, for all the "noninferential" or "direct" knowledge perception is said to afford us of "something real in space." Perception and sensation have a necessary dependence on such reality, which is not itself reducible to the mere *forms* of sensible intuition. The ideality of the forms assures that 'the real in space' will itself count as mind dependent, however. Kant seems to suppose that this fact is sufficient to counter the challenge of problematic idealism.

I will not attempt to assess here how strong a response to "external world skepticism" this theory really is. (Kant himself, as noted, did not stick by it.) What I do want to stress is that it is not a Berkeleyan response. The "something real in space" *etwas Wirkliches im Raume* is not in the least the same thing as, for instance, Philonous's cherry, *comprised of* the sensations of softness, moisture, redness, tartness. It is rather merely the *cause* of such sensations, shaking the optic and the other sensory nerves.

It follows, I think, that Kant's theory of the relation of perceptual experience and reality is much closer to Descartes's than it is to Berkeley's. Unlike Descartes, Kant thought that space had to be construed as ideal or mind-dependent, if we are to evade the skeptic's challenge concerning the reality of 'outer objects.'[22] And unlike Descartes *and* Berkeley, Kant seems completely untroubled by the discrepancy between the subjective world of 'sensation' (colors, tastes, warmth, and so on) and the world of bare matter (or forces) portrayed by scientific theory.[23] But like Descartes, and unlike Berkeley, Kant construes the world of science, and not the world of sensation, as empirically real. Like Descartes, and unlike Berkeley, Kant holds that our experiences of colors, tastes, and so on are mere "subjective sensations" that do nothing to "determine an object."[24]

If my remarks on Kant's theory of perception are correct, Kant is a very peculiar sort of 'phenomenalist' indeed. He cannot think that things just are the way they appear in ordinary sense experience, for the secondary qualities with which they appear to be endowed are only subjective sensations, sensations caused by the objects. The "something real in space" must, it seems, retain its mystery until its true nature is revealed by sophisticated scientific-philosophical inquiry. The reality of this sensorily remote, mysterious 'matter' is, of course, just what Berkeley would want to deny. Granted, for Kant the fundamental concepts of scientific understanding of this matter are also implicit in the ordinary experiential ordering of the world. This concession does not affect the fact that Kant—like Descartes and Locke before him and numerous "scientific realists" after him, and very *un*like Berkeley—is a *critic* of what might be called the naive empiricist world view. Kant can be styled a phenomenalist not because he accords 'reality' to the ordinary 'image,' but only because the scientist's sophisticated reductive explanation of that image is, on Kant's view, elaborated within the framework of merely ideal 'forms of intuition.'

Thus, it may be that from one point of view Kant offers us the sweets of idealism without the bitters of subjectivism. From another point of view, I suggest, Kantianism yields the bitters of idealism, without the sweets of Berkeley's commonsense empiricism. In the Critical philosophy, as in the more naive materialism that Berkeley was attacking, a significant portion of our ordinary sense-world is rendered, in Berkeley's poignant expression, a false imaginary glare.

A corollary of this reading of Kant is that his conception of what constitutes 'experience' has to be, at best, somewhat recondite. The most interesting recent English-language commentaries—the works of P.F. Strawson and Jonathan Bennett—seem to me to go wrong in completely overlooking this important complexity.[25] Defense of this point would require, however, a far more detailed discussion than is appropriate here.

CONCLUSION

If my interpretation is right, Berkeley and Kant are very far apart in their views about physical reality, in relation to sense experience and science. I would like to point out, though, one widely overlooked point of apparent communality between the two 'phenomenalists'; namely, their respective concepts of a *non-human* apprehension. Both Berkeley and Kant stress the passivity of human sense experience, and contrast this way of experiencing objects with the wholly active, "archetypal" intelligence that can be attributed to God.[26] Of course both philosophers introduce the latter notion in a quite sketchy way, and there is much room for uncertainty about the exact nature of their views and speculation about disanalogies between them. For example, it will immediately be noted that Berkeley is dogmatically assertive where Kant is critically circumspect in observations about the relation between God's mind and its 'objects'. Further, Berkeley succumbs to the temptation to appeal to archetypal intelligence as a basis for resolving objectivity problems that arise within his phenomenalist account of things: the problem of their continuous existence in particular. (Things are always in God's mind, even though human perceptions are intermittent.)[27]

Kant, on the contrary, evidently construes the resolution of such problems as an essential and integral requirement of the phenomenalist enterprise itself. All the same, Kant notoriously does hint that the appearances which for us constitute "empirical reality" are in some sense grounded in the things in themselves—where the latter may be at least speculatively identified with the objects of (God's) nonsensible intuition (See *B*xxvi–vii). On the other hand, Berkeley's casual attempt to *integrate* the flow of human sense perceptions with the divine archetypal apprehension is surely undercut by his acknowledgment of the radical discrepancy, between the two modes of apprehension.[28] To this extent, it seems, Berkeley as well as Kant must be attributed a qualified empiricism: a position that ultimately acknowledges that ordinary human sense perception is not the very last authority on the truth about things. And both philosophers, by introducing at least the possibility of a strictly active apprehension, leave room for the relative "mereness" of appearances to us.[29]

NOTES

1. I use Kemp Smith's translation of the *Critique* but with some modifications.

2. See the Appendix of the *Prolegomena*.

3. I compare the *Critique* passages with the *Prolegomena* statement in my "Kant and 'the *Dogmatic* Idealism of Berkeley'," cited in note 4.

4. See Norman Kemp Smith's *A Commentary to Kant's Critique of Pure Reason* (London: Macmillan, 1923), pp. 156–57; Colin M. Turbayne, "Kant's Refutation of Dogmatic Idealism," *Philosophical Quarterly* 5 (1955), 225–44. I critically discuss Kemp Smith's and Turbayne's views in "Kant and 'the *Dogmatic* Idealism of Berkeley'," *Journal of the History of Philosophy* 9 (1971), 464–70 (Chapter 19 of this volume).

5. Kemp Smith maintains the former view, Turbayne the latter.

6. See George Miller, "Kant and Berkeley: The Alternative Theories," *Kant-Studien* 64 (1973), 315–35; Henry E. Allison, "Kant's Critique of Berkeley," *Journal of the History of Philosophy* 11 (1973), 43–63; Richard E. Aquila, "Kant's Phenomenalism," *Idealistic Studies* 5 (1975), 108–26; G. D. Justin, "On Kant's Analysis of Berkeley," *Kant-Studien* 65 (1974), 20–32; and Wilson, "Kant and 'the *Dogmatic* Idealism of Berkeley'." In "Berkeley's Immaterialism and Kant's Transcendental Idealism," M. R. Ayers defends and extends Allison's position in *Idealism—Past and Present*, ed. Godfrey Vesey (Cambridge, England: Cambridge University Press, 1982), pp. 51–69. I have also seen unpublished work by William Harper on a similar theme.

7. Aquila, "Kant's Phenomenalism," 125–26; Allison, "Kant's Critique of Berkeley", pp. 52 and 56; Miller, "Kant and Berkeley", 321–23; 334–35.

8. I use the term 'idealism' more or less alternatively to 'phenomenalism' to characterize Berkeley's system as well as Kant's. For expository purposes it is convenient to follow the practice of Kant and several of his commentators in this respect. I am aware that some Berkeley scholars vehemently oppose the characterization of his position as 'idealist', but I do not really accept their strictures, and in any case the issue is not crucial to the points I want to make.

9. Allison, in particular, provides a perceptive discussion of these issues ("Kant's Critique of Berkeley").

10. I defend this perspective on Cartesianism in my book, *Descartes* (London: Routledge, 1978).

11. This use of the term 'literal' is borrowed from John Mackie, *Problems from Locke* (Oxford: Clarendon Press, 1976), pp. 14–15.

12. *Works*, vol. 2, p. 171.

13. *Works*, vol. 2, p. 210.

14. *Wroks*, vol. 2, p. 211.

15. *Works*, vol. 2, p. 249. Italics added.

16. *Works*, vol. 2, pp. 186–87.

17. Cf. Allison, *"Kant's Critique of Berkeley,"* pp. 52ff.

18. I am aware of one important exception. In his Ph.D. thesis, "The Idealism of Kant and Berkeley" (University of Pittsburgh, 1979), George John Mattey stresses that Kant and Berkeley held quite different views on the primary-secondary quality distinction, and emphasizes the significance of this difference in comparing their idealisms.

19. Allison also cites and discusses this passage and its predecessor in *A* ("Kant's Critique of Berkeley," pp. 56ff.).

20. Kemp Smith, for instance. See my discussion in "Kant and 'the *Dogmatic* Idealism of Berkeley'," pp. 463ff. (Chapter 19 of this volume, pp. 278 ff.) On the alleged "Berkeleyanism" of the Fourth Paralogism, see Allison, "Kant's Critique of Berkeley," pp. 45ff.

21. Kemp Smith introduces a sentence break that is not in the German.

22. Cf. A27–28. Amazingly, some commentators seem to take the view that Descartes's conception of material substance as mind-independent *logically bars* him from holding that we can have knowledge of matter: see, in this connection, Allison, "Kant's Critique of Berkeley," p. 47. As far as I can tell, this interpretation completely overlooks the theory of innate ideas and the "divine guarantee."

23. In *Descartes* I argue that this discrepancy was a serious concern of Descartes's, relating closely to him preoccupations with the problem of God's veracity, and the respects in which the senses can be said to "deceive."

24. Cf. Descartes's discussion in *Principles of Philosophy*, part 2, 3–4; part 4, 197–99, in *AT*, vol. 8–1, pp. 41–42; 320–23.

Here I assume the point of view argued earlier: that Berkeley was not merely concerned to refute the transcendental reality of matter, and correlatively to answer "Cartesian skepticism," but also to reinstate the reality of the sensible world as we experience it in ordinary life.

25. See Jonathan Bennett, *Kant's Analytic* (Cambridge, England: Cambridge University Press, 1966), pp. 22; and P. F. Strawson, *The Bounds of Sense* (London: Methuen, 1966), p. 32. In the latter passage I take Strawson to be interpreting Kantian phenomena in terms of "ordinary reports" and "ordinary descriptions" of "what we see, feel, hear." On pp. 40–41 of *The Bounds of Sense* Strawson rather startlingly *contrasts* Kant with "the scientifically-minded philosopher"!

26. Berkeley discusses the archetypal-sensible distinction in *Works*, vol. 2, pp. 241, 254, and in his 1729–1730 correspondence with Samuel Johnson (*Works*, vol. 2, pp. 271–94). See also Russell A. Lascola, "Ideas and Archetypes: Appearances and Reality in Berkeley's Philosophy," *The Personalist*, 54 (1973), 42–59 (especially pp. 52ff) and George H. Thomas, "Berkeley's God Does Not Perceive," *Journal of the History of Philosophy* 14 (1976), 163–68. At *B*72 Kant contrasts our sensible intuition, to which

objects have to be *given*, with "original" intuition, "which so far as we can judge, can belong only to the primordial being." Elsewhere, notably in Phenomena and Noumena, Kant does claim that we cannot even comprehend the possibility of an original intuition. (If Thomas's thesis as stated in his title is correct, then Berkeley's "to be is to be perceived (or to perceive)" thesis seems to require fundamental rephrasing. For it is surely Berkeley's view that both God and the archetypes in his mind have being.)

27. Berkeley, in his youthful works, tried to use God's archetypes to ground the permanence and perhaps the "publicity" of the objects of outer sense: see *Works*, vol. 2, pp. 212; 230–31. Perhaps he later gave up on this idea. He makes hardly any reply to Samuel Johnson's queries about archetypes—especially in relation to the issue of permanence—even though Johnson expresses his questions clearly and rather persistently (*Works*, vol. 2, pp. 274–6; 285–6). (Berkeley does reply appositely to most of Johnson's other inquiries.) Allison, "Kant's Critique of Berkeley," p. 61, quotes a striking, often overlooked passage in Kant's *Gesammelte Schriften* in which Kant comments on Berkeley's recourse to "the mystical [intuition] of God's ideas." Although the passage is obscure, I take Kant to be saying that he, unlike Berkeley, does not need to call on the divine understanding to provide for the connection of appearances. The passage is also cited by Graham Bird in a different connection in *Kant's Theory of Knowledge* (New York: Humanities Press, 1962), p. 37.

28. According to Berkeley, "God perceives nothing by sense as we do" (*Works*, vol. 2, p. 241, and Thomas, "Berkeley's God Does Not Perceive," p. 166). Of course, the assimilation of Berkeleyan archetypes to nonsensible *intuitions* (in the Kantian sense) will not hold fully if the former are understood platonically, as universal forms—as Johnson *may* be understanding them in section 1 of his second letter (Berkeley's *Works*, vol. 2, pp. 285–86). I conjecture God's archetypes must be particulars for Berkeley's purposes in the early works—from which it would follow that their relation to our ideas is not one of form to instances.

29. This paper was completed under a grant from the American Council of Learned Societies, through a program funded by the National Endowment for the Humanities.

The Phenomenalisms of Leibniz and Berkeley

THE TWO great German philosophers of the early modern era, Leibniz and Kant, overlapped Berkeley's life at opposite ends. Each was aware of Berkeley, and had at least some knowledge of his early philosophy. (Berkeley's *Principles of Human Knowledge* was published in 1710, when Berkeley was about twenty-five, and Leibniz was in his sixties. When Berkeley died in 1753, Kant was about thirty years old.) Kant's philosophy–which he himself called "transcendental idealism"—has been linked to Berkeley's idealism or phenomenalism through a long tradition, going back to the contemporary Garve-Feder review of the first *Critique*. Numerous works in English have contributed to this tradition, including several papers of the past decade or so. Commentators have often viewed Berkeley and Kant as united in a common concern with answering Cartesian skepticism, and as generating their respective phenomenalisms or idealisms at least partly in response to this concern. Some have, in effect accepted Kant's own assessment that Berkeley embraced an extreme reductionistic subjectivism only because he failed to grasp the possibility of an a priori grounding of empirical knowledge in "forms of intuition" and the categories. (Berkeley, in other words, failed to appreciate that one could mount an idealist response to external world skepticism without giving up "objectivity.")

Efforts to connect Berkeley's position to that of Leibniz have been fewer, more limited, and (as far as I can determine) mostly pretty recent.[1] Possibly Leibniz's notable *lack* of preoccupation with external world skepticism, accompanied by his uninhibited espousal of a rationalistic metaphysics, has made the comparison of his philosophy with Berkeley's seem a less natural and inviting enterprise. Nevertheless, there are now at least the beginnings of a tradition linking their respective "phenomenalisms." Montgomery Furth, in an article published in 1967, proposed that Leibniz should be interpreted as a phenomenalist, and discussed some of the relations between Leibniz's position and Berkeley's. Just as critics commenting on the relation between Kant's phenomenalism and Berkeley's have held that Kant does fuller justice to our objectivity concepts than Berkeley, so Furth holds that Leibniz's special form of phenomenalism "helps to dispel the feeling, voiced about phenomenalistic theories from Berkeley's day down to our own, that . . . we have been swindled out of the real world of corporeal substances . . ."[2] Furth further states that Leibniz

> . . . perceived the essential problem set by Descartes—namely that of explicating the notion of a *matter of objective fact* within terms of objects of possible experience, much as that problem was later perceived by Berkeley, by Kant, and for that matter by C. I. Lewis.[3]

A recently published study by Robert Adams continues the discussion of Leibniz's phenomenalism with some reference to Furth's paper. Adams gives more detailed consideration to the relation between Leibniz and Berkeley, stressing different issues. While Adams perceptively expounds some major differences between Leibniz's phenomenalism and Berkeley's position, he notes that Leibniz "did not fail to see that he and Berkeley were fundamentally on the same side."[4] J. J. MacIntosh in a 1971 paper has maintained that "Berkeley and Leibniz . . . held strikingly similar philosophical views," and implies that English-speaking chauvinism accounts for the fact that this point hasn't been more widely recognized.[5]

I believe that attempts to assimilate Berkeley's phenomenalism either to Kant's position or to Leibniz's give insufficient weight to certain fundamental and unique features of Berkeley's philosophical doctrines and objectives—features which in fact place him in opposition to both Leibniz and Kant. Of course, I do not deny that these three philosophers share *some* common views and objectives. Certainly, each was concerned to counter the apparently anti-religious implications of materialist philosophies by endorsing, or leaving room for, the primacy of "spirit." Each may be said to hold in some sense that the physical world is "mind-dependent." Also, each was, in his own way, a critic of Newton's "transcendental realist" theory of space. And antiskeptical concerns do figure prominently in Berkeley's philosophical writings as well as in Kant's. But Berkeley, for all the oddities of his sensationalistic reductionism, was a "commonsense" philosopher in a way that Leibniz and Kant never were. Berkeley was a phenomenalist in the straightforward sense that he construed the appearances of ordinary sense experience—the purple skies, "wild but sweet notes of the birds," fragrant blooms, and warm sunshine—as *the real world*.[6] He was deeply concerned to *deny*—in the early works, at any rate—that either science or metaphysics reveals truths about reality which provide a corrective to ordinary sense experience. As Philonous remarks in the Third Dialogue:

> I am a vulgar cast, simple enough to believe my senses, and leave things as I find them. To be plain, it is my opinion, that the real things are those very things I see and feel, and perceive by my sense . . . It is likewise my opinion, that colours and other sensible qualities are on the objects. I cannot for my life help thinking that snow is white, and fire hot.[7]

Neither Leibniz nor Kant accepts this position of deliberately naive empiricism. In this important respect they follow closely in the tradition to which Berkeley most resolutely opposed himself. Both hold that materialistic science provides a *relatively* objective and true account of nature, which to some degree contrasts with that of ordinary experience. Of course, they are not strictly scientific realists, since they both hold that the scientific account of things is not a true account of things as they are in themselves, of the ultimate reality. This ultimate reality they take to lie beyond the reach of materialistic science as well as beyond the immediate data of sense. (Leibniz differs from Kant, of course, in regarding it as the appropriate subject of human metaphysics.) Still, they do both accept the view that our ordinary sensory experiences of colors and tastes are *merely* subjective; that the materialistic scientific account is *relatively* objective and real. In my opinion, this aspect of both of their positions is sufficient to place them directly at odds with Berkeley. It is true that Berkeley attributes the philosophers' distinction between the reality and the sensible appearances of things to the belief in mind-independent, material substance.[8] It does not follow, however, that he would have no objective to the distinction if it were detached from this belief (as it is, in different ways, by Leibniz and Kant). Similarly, while there are legitimate senses of "phenomenalism" (or "idealism") in which Leibniz and Kant are both phenomenalists (or idealists), it simply does not follow that their views and concerns are fundamentally similar to Berkeley's. Failure adequately to recognize this point is partly the result of insufficient attention to variations of meaning, across different contexts, of the term "phenomenalism" itself and terms commonly used in the definition or characterization of "phenomenalism"—like "perception" and "experience".

In an earlier paper I have argued this case in detail with respect to the relations between Berkeley and Kant.[9] Here I would like to develop a similar case against attempts to assimilate the "phenomenalisms" of Berkeley and Leibniz.

                                              I

Berkeley, I have said, denies any distinction between the appearances or phenomena or ordinary, direct sense experience and the real physical world. *His* "phenomenalism" consists basically in the view that the sensory phenomena *are the real things*. (Because he identifies the objects of sense experience as "ideas," Berkeley's position may also be called an idealism.) What reasons are we given for construing Leibniz as a phenomenalist? Furth writes:

> Thus [Leibniz's] theory is a phenomenalism, for it offers a reductive explication of statements about material things as translations or abbreviations of statements about perceptions . . .[10]

MacIntosh examines "the extent to which Leibniz moved towards phenomenalism," or to "full-blown phenomenalism";[11] he seems to take this as much the same thing as an examination of the extent to which Leibniz moved towards Berkeley's metaphysical position. Nowhere in his paper does MacIntosh offer an explicit account of the meaning of "phenomenalism." He does say, though:

> One version of phenomenalism may be plucked from the *Monadology* (1714): Monads are windowless (7) and are subject to change (10) resulting from an internal principle (11) which acts by bringing about perceptions (15). In short what is, is internal, and what is internal is what is perceived.[12]

In light of this comment I take it that MacIntosh's underlying conception of "phenomenalism" is much the same as Furth's: there is no material reality that is not in some sense reducible to "perceptions." Adams, while stressing that bodies are the *objective content* of perceptions for Leibniz, comments: "In calling [bodies] phenomena Leibniz means that they have their being in the awareness that perceivers have of [the] story [told or approximated by perception, commonsense, and science]."[13]

Of course, Leibniz, or any of his commentators, is entitled to his own interpretation of the terms "phenomena" and "phenomenalism." Yet we should be wary of attempts to assimilate Leibniz's position to Berkeley's, on the grounds that they both think that reality may be fully explicated in terms of perceivers, their wills or appetites, and their perceptions or perceptual contents. What if the concepts of "perceivers" and "perceptions" differ drastically between the two philosophers? And what if there are corresponding radical differences in their conceptions of "phenomena"? This issue arises, for example, when Adams writes:

> Part of Leibniz's point in saying that extended things as such are phenomena is to claim that they have their existence only in substances that perceive them, *and in this he agrees with Berkeley.* (emphasis added)[14]

Certainly there is *nominal* agreement between Leibniz on Berkeley on this point (ignoring the question whether the archtypes of bodies in God's mind really count as "perceptions" for Berkeley). But there is, one may point out, *nominal* agreement between Berkeley and Descartes that physical things really exist, and are different in nature from minds. Nominal agreement may conceal radical philosophical differences. This is the case, I want to hold, with respect to Berkeley's and Leibniz's positions on the "phenomenal" status of bodies. What Leibniz means by "perception" is *utterly* different from what Berkeley means by "perception," and their understandings of the relations between physical reality and sensations are also sharply in conflict. I believe the difference is so significant that it is incorrect to say they "agree."

Before arguing this point I want to acknowledge that Adams, at least, is quite aware of the sorts of differences between Leibniz's and Berkeley's views that I am about to discuss. They are among those that he expounds in some detail. Similarly, Furth has to be aware of certain important differences: for they are to some extent preconditions of the philosophical advantage he claims that Leibniz's phenomenalism holds over Berkeley's. MacIntosh also comments on differences between the two philosophers, though not, in my opinion, as precisely as Adams. My argument here, in any case, will not hinge very much on dispute about textual details. Rather I hope that by highlighting the contrasts between more or less familiar aspects of Berkeley's and Leibniz's positions I can make clear that they are fundamentally at odds with each other with respect to both motivation and doctrine.

Let us consider first the suggestion that Leibniz and Berkeley are basically in agreement about the nature of bodies in so far as they both reduce physical things to perceptions. To evaluate this claim we surely need to ask what they respectively understand by "perceptions." To take the easier case first, it seems both evident and uncontroversial that when Berkeley speaks of perceptions he means conscious awareness. The most explicit statement of this point that I know of occurs in the early *Philosophical Commentaries*, where Berkeley notes:

Consciousness, perception, existence of Ideas seem to be all one.[15]

Consciousness is not, as far as I can find, explicitly discussed in the *Principles* or the *Dialogues*; but I also find in those works no indication that Berkeley entertained even the possibility of unconscious mental states. In *The New Theory of Vision* Berkeley seems to reject as "incomprehensible" the postulation of unconscious mental processes.[16]

In general when Berkeley speaks of perception he means, more specifically, conscious awareness *of ideas of sense*. This is, indeed, invariably the case when he is talking about our perception of physical objects—except in the special context of "indirect perception," or association from present ideas of sense to other imagined or anticipated sensory ideas. Thus, when Berkeley says that for a physical thing to be is to be perceived, he means that a physical thing exists just in case it (or one of the sensible qualities that constitute it) is (a) the object of a conscious sensory experience for humans; and/or (b) exists in God's mind, though not as an object of sense. *Occasionally*, Berkeley will use the terms "perceive" and "perception"—even in connection with physical objects—when he does not have sense perception in mind: for instance, although he is clear that God "perceives nothing by sense as we do," this does not *always* prevent him from saying that things are "perceived by God."[17] And of course he does hold that we know by reflection, or have notions of, ourselves as spiritual substances, and our inner operations, such as willing:

. . . I have a notion of spirit, though I have not, strictly speaking, an idea of it. I do not perceive it as an idea or by means of an idea, but know it by reflexion.

. . . I know or am conscious of my own being; and that I myself am not my ideas, but somewhat else, a thinking active principle that perceives, knows, wills, and operates about ideas.[18]

But, in any case, knowledge of spirits is always sharply contrasted by Berkeley with knowledge of physical things; and when he speaks of spirits he has in mind nothing very unusual—just you, me, other humans, God, and perhaps animals and angels.[19]

Before turning to Leibniz I would like to mention one further point about Berkeley's treatment of perception. While he does sometimes say that ideas may be more or less "clear" or "distinct," this terminology is generally used in his system to mark the commonsense difference between genuine sense experiences and mere imaginings or dreams:

the ideas formed by the imagination are faint and indistinct; they have besides an entire dependence on the will. But the ideas perceived by sense, that is, real things, are more vivid and clear, and being imprinted on the mind by a spirit distinct from us, have not a like dependence on our will.[20]

I will return to this point later, in comparing Berkeley's position with that of Leibniz.

II

I now turn with a trepidation that everyone familiar with it will appreciate to the topic of Leibniz's understanding of the term "perception." Fortunately, present purposes do not require a deep and searching analysis of the difficulties surrounding this issue—although the *seriousness* of the difficulties is indeed germane to my purpose.

Leibniz, as is well known, restricts the term "perception" neither to conscious experience nor to sense perception. He defines the term, rather mysteriously, as "the expression of many things in one."[21] "Expression" implies a "constant and regulated relation between what can be said of the one and of the other."[22] The "one" in which perception occurs is invariably a simple substance, or monad. Also, although not all cases of expression are perceptions, I take it that all cases of expression *in monads* are perceptions.[23] The perceptual states of monads include intellection in rational beings or spirits, sensations in spirits and animals, and states which are neither intellection nor sensations. Only the latter sort of "perceptions" occur in the bare monads, which "are wholly destitute of sensation and knowledge."[24] Further, the perceptual states of spirits and animal minds must also include subsensational perceptions, as well as sensation and (in the case of spirits) thought. For every monad "expresses the whole world from its own point of view," but Leibniz does not suppose that a human or animal mind has knowledge or sensation of everything in its world.

It should already be clear that a Leibnizian "reductive explication of statements about material things as translations or abbreviations of statements about perceptions," need be nothing *at all* like a Berkeleian one. The question indeed is whether such a purported "reductive explication," in so far as it involves appeal to "perceptions" which are neither intellectual nor sensory—and may even be states or entities that *have* neither intellect nor sense—offers us anything intelligible. I can only say that I myself can make little serious sense of this broad Leibnizian concept of "perception," and that I note that other commentators—Adams, for instance—also acknowledge its extreme obscurity.[25] One point I would particularly like to stress in this connection is that it seems very dubious practice to refer to subsensational perceptions as "awarenesses," "experiences," or even "mental events," as Furth and other commentators comfortably do.[26] It may be all right to say, "I must have experienced the closeness of the room from the moment I entered, though I didn't really become aware of it till now." But in this sort of example we are talking about a perception that has a role in a readily identified mental life, and that in fact is continuous with related conscious experiences. I do not think that the intelligibility of this sort of context shows we can talk meaningfully of the "awarenesses" or "experiences" of "mind-like substances with neither understanding nor sensation."

The point is relevant to Furth's conception of the advantage of Leibniz's phenomenalism over Berkeley's. Furth holds that Leibniz is able to satisfy a "no-residue" condition on phenomenalistic translations that Berkeley either cannot meet, or can handle only through such objectionable strategies as appeal to subjunctive conditionals or to an all-perceiving God. Leibniz, that is, "can deliver the full content of the ostensible material-thing statements in their pre-systematic form."[27] His advantage here lies in the fact that he doesn't stop short at any "paltry population" of observers; "every conceivable point of view in the universe is already enlisted among the monads . . ."[28] For Leibniz there is no problem of "gaps" in the population's actual experience, or "unrepresented viewpoints and interrupted conscious histories," such as a phenomenalist of Berkeleian stripe, who admits minds only where we normally *think* there are minds, must hopelessly confront.[29]

I suggest that Leibniz obtains this "advantage" at the very high cost of leaving it quite unclear exactly what it is that bodies are being reduced to, in so far as they are reduced to "perceptions" in his system. To the extent that Leibniz's reduction relies on the doctrine of pre-established harmony among *all* "perceivers"—the view stressed by Furth—it simply lets go of the more familiar conceptions of perceptions, appearances, and experience that have been the mainstay of the more familiar forms of phenomenalism, such as Berkeley's. (For this reason I would reject Furth's claim that Leibniz saw the problem of explicating the notion of a matter of objective fact within "terms of objects of possible experience" in much the same way as Berkeley—or for that matter C. I. Lewis.)

Other radical differences between Berkeley's and Leibniz's positions relate in various ways to the one I have just been considering. For one thing, Leibniz, as is well known, denies that we can have demonstrative knowledge of the existence of bodies.[30] This is really a remarkable concession for a phenomenalist to make. I take it to derive precisely from Leibniz's conception of the reality of bodies as grounded in the harmonized perceptions of infinitely many "perceivers"; whereas, as individual minds, each of us is directly aware only of (some of) our own perceptions. (The more one thinks of Berkeley as focusing on the refutation of external world skepticism, the more deeply divided will he appear to be from Leibniz on this point.) But Leibniz's "phenomenalism" is not only compatible with the denial of certainty concerning the existence of bodies. It is in fact tightly bound up with a double-layered critique of the ordinary sense-conception of bodies that Berkeley seeks to defend. The key points are, first, that Leibniz denies all of what he counts as "perception" is on an epistemologically equal footing; and second, that he denies that even our best perceptual representations of bodies accurately present to us what really is. Elaboration of these points will help clarify further the opposition between Leibniz's view of "phenomena" and Berkeley's.

III

Berkeley's defense of the unproblematic reality of the objects of ordinary sense experience includes, as an essential feature, rejection of the primary-secondary quality distinction. He holds that all the standard types of sensible qualities are equally objective and real, just as they are perceived or experienced by us. Some have imagined that the reason for this aspect of his position is that he overlooked the original scientific realist reasons for the distinction (in Descartes, Locke, and numerous other predecessors), and thus thought it sufficient to point out that primary quality perceptions are no less perceiver-relative than secondary quality perceptions. Elsewhere I have tried to show that this notion of Berkeley's historical ignorance and philosophical naivete is completely unfounded.[31] He was in fact a well informed and intelligent—I would say deep—critic of the scientific realist conception of the relation of bodies to our experience. His rejection of the primary-secondary quality distinction is the cornerstone of this critique. I will approach the comparison of his position on this issue with Leibniz's by considering MacIntosh's attempt to establish close similarity between them.

According to MacIntosh, Leibniz's position resembles Berkeley's since Leibniz, too, "runs together" the primary and secondary qualities.[32] MacIntosh bases his conclusion on passages like the following from Leibniz's writings:

> . . . the whole nature of body does not consist solely in extension, that is to say in size, figure and motion, . . . there must necessarily be recognized in it something which is related to souls and which is commonly called substantial form, though it brings about no changes in phenomena . . . It can even be demonstrated that the notion of size, figure and motion is not so distinct as is imagined, and that it includes something imaginary and relative to our perceptions, as are also (although much more so) colour, heat and other similar qualities, of which it can be doubted whether they are truly present in the nature of things outside us.[33]
>
> Concerning bodies I can demonstrate that not merely light, heat, colour and similar qualities are apparent but also motion, figure, and extension. And that, if anything is real, it is solely the force of acting and suffering, and hence that the substance of a body consists in this (as if in matter and form). Those bodies, however, which have no substantial form, are merely phenomena or at least only aggregates of the true unities.[34]

I think, however, that these passages bring out the *contrasts* between Leibniz's and Berkeley's views of qualities much more than any similarities. Indeed, the type of "phenomenalism" that Leibniz subscribes to in such passages is almost the opposite of Berkeley's position.

Berkeley thinks that perceptions of secondary and of primary qualities equally and adequately present to us the real qualities of bodies (bodies themselves being only congeries of sensations). A cherry is literally red, soft, tart-tasting, *and round*.[35] Or, as Berkeley expresses the point in the *Principles*:

. . . whoever shall reflect, and take care to understand what he says, will, if I mistake not, acknowledge that all sensible qualities are alike *sensations*, and alike *real*;
and that where the extension is, there is the colour too, to wit, in his mind . . . and
that the objects of sense are nothing but those sensations combined, blended, or (if
one may so speak) concreted together.[36]

The first point to be noted about Leibniz's position in this connection is that
he does, in his own way, recognize and accept the traditional distinction between mere sensations in us, and their physical causes. The latter he characterizes in terms of extension, figure, and motion. Sensations like color and taste he
characterizes as "phantoms," saying that they strictly merit this name, rather
than that "of qualities, or even of ideas."[37] Behind this terminological precision
is Leibniz's view that sensations are indecipherably blurred appearances of the
figures and motions that give rise to them.[38]

Leibniz further holds, however, that *even* the primary quality perceptions
have to be contrasted with the reality of things, although they are in some way
less subjective than the secondary quality perceptions. As sensations like color
and taste are blurred appearances of the figures and motions that cause them, so
figure and extension are only ways in which infinite aggregates of unextended
substances appear to our limited minds.[39] Thus size, figure, and motion are also
"relative to our perception," although color, heat, and other similar qualities are
"much more so."

The very fundamental opposition between Berkeley and Leibniz on the primary-secondary quality issue may now be stated succinctly. The aim of Berkeley's "phenomenalism" is to reclaim as equally "real" qualities that had come to
be classified as non-objective, as *mere* subjective appearances. Berkeley, in
other words, was centrally concerned to vindicate the reality of the world as
presented in ordinary sense experience, against the abstractions of the philosophers and scientists of his time. Leibniz, on the contrary, agreed to the superior
reality or objectivity of the physicist's conception of the world. As Adams says:
"for Leibniz the universe of corporeal phenomena is primarily the object not of
sense but of science."[40] But Leibniz further holds that qualities construed by
physics as "real" are themselves *mere* phenomena, relative to their monadic
"foundations." For him the term "phenomenon" thus carries the pejorative connotation of being in some degree subjective, unreal, or "imaginary." To quote
Adams once more: " 'Phenomenon' [in Leibniz's discussions] contrasts not only
as intramental with 'extramental'; it also contrasts as apparent with 'real.' "[41]
Thus, while both Berkeley and Leibniz construed the physicists' theory of reality as an "abstraction," they developed this notion in completely opposite directions. Berkeley construed it as an abstraction in relation to the concrete reality
presented in ordinary sense experience. Leibniz thought that ordinary sense
experience was still less reflective of reality, more "relative to our perception,"
than physical theory, but considered the latter as unreal or abstract in relation to
some still more remote and basic concrete metaphysical truth.

I mentioned earlier that when Berkeley, in the *Principles* and *Dialogues*, distinguishes among perceptions in terms of clarity or distinctness he is trying to characterize in phenomenological terms the difference between normal sense perceptions on the one hand, and dreams, hallucinations, and imaginations on the other hand. Leibniz, too, sometimes draws a similar distinction in terms of "vividness."[42] Leibniz uses the characterizations of clarity and distinctness, however, in distinguishing among normal waking perceptions and states of knowledge. While his usage of these terms involves subtle and difficult issues, we may at least note here that when Leibniz speaks of a perception as relatively distinct, he is, in part, marking its relative informativeness with respect to the world of substances outside the individual perceiver, and also its relatively intellectual status.[43] His distinction among normal waking perceptions in terms of clarity and distinctness is particularly reflected in his remarks about primary and secondary qualities. On the one hand he will say, echoing Descartes: "we perceive nothing distinctly in matter save magnitude, figure, and extension."[44] On the other hand, as we've seen, he will also insist that "the notion of size, figure and motion is not so distinct as is imagined." Berkeley, however, denies that there is any world of substances external to our perceptions for our ideas to be informative about, and denies any intellectual knowledge of body superior to the sensible. Accordingly, he lacks a use for the Cartesian epistemological concept of distinctness, and for the whole rationalist framework within which Leibniz's doctrine of "perception" unfolds.

IV

In summary, we have now noted several fundamental points of divergence between Berkeley's conception of the perception-dependence, and hence the "phenomenality," of bodies and Leibniz's. First, Berkeley reduces bodies to conscious sense perceptions; but Leibniz uses the term "perception" in a far wider, and far less easily grasped way. Second, Leibniz does not interpret his position concerning our perceptions of bodies as providing a conclusive basis for the repudiation of skepticism concerning the existence of bodies—in whatever sense bodies may be said to exist. Third, Berkeley's phenomenalism is explicitly directed at denying any superiority to the "scientific," as opposed to the ordinary sensible, conception of bodies. Leibniz maintains the traditional scientific realist stance concerning the relative superiority, with respect to reality, of the scientific story (as Adams calls it). Finally, when Leibniz says that even extension and figure are phenomenal, involve "something relative to our perceptions," he is saying that even these qualities are *merely* apparent—that they are to be contrasted with the true reality of things, understood as aggregations of monads. Berkeley, on the other hand, deliberately identifies the (sensorily) perceived with the real.

Some further specific differences between their positions—touched on by Adams and MacIntosh—are closely connected with the latter two of these three fundamental ones. Thus, Berkeley's contention that nothing smaller than a minimum sensibilium is physically real, and his related rejection of "infinitesimals," are not—contrary to what MacIntosh suggests—reflections of a lack of sophistication in mathematics.[45] They are consequences of his new principle that (for a physical thing) to be is to be perceived by sense. (Of course Berkeley also had other reasons for regarding the contemporary notion of infintesimals as incoherent.)[46] Leibniz's insistence on the infinite divisibility of matter correspondingly reflects his lack of empiricist or sensationalist commitments as much as his mathematical genius. Similarly, Berkeley's espousal of an instrumental interpretation of certain scientific conceptions, notably the conception of force, is closely connected with his sensationalistic criterion of physical reality. For Leibniz, who wholly lacks such motivation, physical force is at least as well founded a phenomenon as are extension and shape.

On another matter of considerable importance to Berkeley his general systematic commitments also lead him in quite an opposite direction from the one that Leibniz takes. Berkeley's opposition to skepticism, and his accompanying determination to establish that ordinary sense knowledge is perfectly in order just as it is, leads him resolutely to reject the Lockean corpuscularian notion of unknown inner constitutions.[47] The materialists, he implies, lead us into unnecessary and extravagant skepticism and doubt of our faculties by holding that:

> The Real essence, the internal qualities, and the constitution of even the meanest object is hid from our view; something there is in every drop of water, every grain of sand, which is beyond the power of human understanding to fathom or comprehend.[48]

According to Berkeley the doctrine of hidden inner natures is entirely bound up with the chimerical notion of material substance, and must happily vanish along with it. Leibniz, despite his opposition to purely material substances, has no qualms at all about hidden natures or real essences, construed as entities within the realm of *phenomena bene fundata*. It is true that he does not follow Locke in treating these constitutions as intrinsically unknowable; but he does certainly allow that they are to a large degree unknown, stressing the highly provisional and speculative status of current thought about them.[49]

V

In the paper I have often cited, Robert Adams takes up the interesting issue of Leibniz's own assessment of his relation to Berkeley. As he notes, Leibniz's best known statement about Berkeley suggests that Leibniz was under the common misapprehension that Berkeley's attack on the reality of matter was intended as, or amounted to, an attack on the reality of bodies or the objects of perception. Leibniz comments to des Bosses:

> The Irishman who attacks the reality of bodies seems neither to offer suitable reasons nor to explain his position sufficiently. I suspect that he belongs to the class of men who want to be known for their paradoxes . . .[50]

But Adams also quotes a less well known annotation to Leibniz's copy of Berkeley's *Principles*, in which Leibniz gives Berkeley a bit more credit: "Much here that's right and in agreement with my opinion (*ad sensum meum*)."[51] It is this notation that leads Adams to remark that Leibniz saw that he and Berkeley were fundamentally on the same side. Leibniz does not verbally repeat the error he makes in the des Bosses correspondence, of saying that Berkeley attacked the reality of bodies. He does, however, go on again to accuse Berkeley of being paradoxical. And, much more to the point, he adds an explanation of the ways that Berkeley's philosophy needs to be corrected by the principles of Monadology that I think Berkeley would have found hair-raising. Here is the complete notation:

> Much here that's right and agrees with my views. But too paradoxically expressed. For we have no need to say that matter is nothing, but it suffices to say that it is a phenomenon like the rainbow; and that it is not a substance, but a result of substances; and that space is no more real than time, i.e. that it is nothing but an order of coexistences as time is an order of subexistences. The true substances are Monads, or Perceivers. But the author ought to have gone on further, namely to infinite Monads, constituting all things, and to their preestablished harmony. He wrongly or at least pointlessly rejects abstract ideas, restricts ideas to imaginations, despises the subtleties of arithmetic and geometry. He most wrongly rejects the infinite division of the extended; even if he is right to reject infinitesimal quantities.[52]

These comments certainly indicate that Leibniz *thought* that he and Berkeley were on the same side—to the extent of advising that what Berkeley "needs to say" is just what Leibniz does say.[53] But Berkeley is perhaps entitled to his own opinion of his goals. In the *Third Dialogue* he lists "the novelties, . . . the strange notions which shock the genuine uncorrupted judgment of all mankind; and being once admitted, embarrass the mind with endless doubts and difficulties."[54] "It is against these and the like innovations," he continues, "I endeavor to vindicate common sense." The list indeed includes two or three points which Leibniz would join with Berkeley in rejecting, e.g., "that there are in bodies absolute extensions, without any particular magnitude or figure," and, more importantly, the postulation of inactive matter operating on spirit. But consider some of the other views that Berkeley lists as his primary targets:

> That the qualities we perceive, are not on the objects; that we must not believe our senses; that we know nothing of the real nature of things, and can never be assured even of their existence; that real colours and sounds are nothing but certain unknown figures and motions; . . . that the least particle of a body contains innumerable extended parts.[55]

To a very large degree these views which Berkeley has dedicated himself to overthrowing are views that Leibniz embraces. Who are we, and who is Leibniz, to say that Berkeley has "no need" to reject him?

Because of the novelty of the idealist positions developed in the late seventeenth and the eighteenth centuries, it is quite easy to see the philosophers classifiable as idealists as constituting a united front against their materialist and dualist predecessors. It is easy to forget that Berkeley saw himself not merely as the enemy of stupid matter, but also as the staunch proponent of common sense, and of the unproblematic reality of the immediate objects of sense. With respect to the latter aspects of his position, Berkeley was deeply opposed to Leibniz, even if Leibniz may himself have overlooked or downplayed the opposition in the spirit of idealist ecumenicism.[56]

Notes

1. For an astute brief comparison from a work much earlier than those discussed below, see Eugen Stäbler's Inaugural Dissertation, *George Berkeley's Auffassung und Wirkung in der Deutschen Philosophie bis Hegel* (Zeulenroda: Bernhard Sporn, 1935), pp. 8–10. Herbert Wildon Carr comments even more briefly on the relationship between Berkeley and Leibniz in *Leibniz* (Boston: Little, Brown, 1929), pp. 191–92. Both Stäbler and Carr mention Leibniz's conception of bodies as *phenomena bene fundata* as a major point of difference with Berkeley. (I am indebted to Douglas Jesseph for these references, and for other valuable assistance in the preparation of this paper.)

See also Willy Kabitz, 'Leibniz and Berkeley,' *Sitzungsberichte der Preussische Akademie der Wissenschaften*, Philosophisch-Historische Klasse, 24 (1932), pp. 623–36. In this article, which is also cited by Adams in the paper discussed below, Kabitz comments on Leibniz's reading of Berkeley, with particular reference to his marginal comments in his copy of *The Principles of Human Knowledge*.

2. Montgomery Furth, 'Monadology,' *Philosophical Review* (1967), pp. 169–200; reprinted in *Leibniz: A Collection of Critical Essays*, ed. Harry G. Frankfurt (Garden City, NY: Doubleday [Anchor Books], 1972). The passage quoted is on p. 117 of the Frankfurt edition; subsequent references are also to this edition.

3. *Ibid.*, p. 123.

4. Robert Merrihew Adams, 'Phenomenalism and Corporeal Substance in Leibniz,' in *Midwest Studies in Philosophy VIII*, ed. Peter A. French, *et al.* (Minneapolis: University of Minnesota Press, 1983), p. 222.

5. J. J. MacIntosh, 'Leibniz and Berkeley,' *Proceedings of the Aristotelian Society* (1970–71), pp. 147–63: p. 147

6. Cf. the opening *mise en scene* of *Dialogues*, 171.

7. *Dialogues*, 229–30.

8. *Dialogues*, 229.

9. Margaret D. Wilson, 'The "Phenomenalisms" of Berkeley and Kant,' in *Self and Nature in Kant's Philosophy*, ed. Allen W. Wood (Ithaca: Cornell University Press, 1984), pp. 157–73 (chapter 20 of this volume).

10. 'Monadology', p. 116.

11. 'Leibniz and Berkeley,' pp. 151–52.

12. *Ibid.*, p. 151.

13. 'Phenomenalism . . . in Leibniz,' p. 218.

14. *Ibid.*, pp. 223–24.

15. *PC*, 578; in George H. Thomas' edition (Mount Union College, 1976), p. 76. Cf. *PC*, 24 (Thomas, p. 3): "Nothing properly but persons . . . i.e. conscious things do exist . . ."

16. See especially *NTV*, 19.

17. See *Dialogues*, 241 and 235, respectively.

18. *Dialogues*, 233; cf. 231–32.

19. Berkeley, unlike Leibniz, has very little to say about the status of animals as perceivers (or non-perceivers). In *NTV*, 80 and Appendix, and again in *Dialogues*, 188–90, the perceptions of minute animals (like mites) are invoked to make different points. In his letter to Berkeley dated 5 February 1730, Samuel Johnson raises a difficulty connected with the supposed status of animals as perceivers (in Berkeley's system), but Berkeley fails to reply. (*Works*, ii. 289) (I must again acknowledge Douglas Jesseph's assistance, in connection with this issue.)

20. *Dialogues*, 235; cf. *PHK*, 30–33.

21. See, e.g., Ger, vol. II, pp. 121, 311, etc.

22. *Ibid.*, p. 112.

23. Adams suggests, however, that not all of a monad's expressions of a given thing count as perceptions *of that thing*: 'Phenomenalism . . . in Leibniz,' p. 221.

24. 'Discourse on Metaphysics,' 35, in Ger, vol. IV, p. 460–61.

25. See 'Phenomenalism . . . in Leibniz,' p. 223. For a recent discussion of issues relating to consciousness in Leibniz's monadology, see Robert B. Brandom, 'Leibniz and Degrees of Perception,' *Journal of the History of Philosophy*, XIX (October 1981), pp. 447–79. Difficulties in understanding Leibniz's general conceptions of perception and expression are explored in the following two papers by Mark Kulstad: 'Some Difficulties in Leibniz's Definition of Perception,' in Michael Hooker, ed., *Leibniz: Critical and Interpretive Essays* (Minneapolis: University of Minnesota Press, 1982), pp. 65–78; and 'Leibniz's Conception of Expression,' *Studia Leibnitiana*, IX (1977), pp. 55–76.

26. Cf. Furth, 'Monadology,' p. 115; Brandom, 'Leibniz and Degrees of Perception,' p. 462.

27. 'Monadology,' p. 117.

28. *Ibid.*, p. 118.

29. *Ibid.*

30. See especially 'On the Method of Distinguishing Real from Imaginary Phenomena,' Ger, vol. VII, 320–21; trans. and ed. by Leroy E. Loemker, *Leibniz: Philosophical Papers and Letters* (Dordrecht-Holland: Reidel, 1969 (2nd edition), p. 364. See also the letter to Foucher, Ger, vol. 1, 372f.; 'Discourse on Metaphysics,' 32, in Ger, vol. IV, pp. 457–58; Loemker, p. 324; *NE* IV, ii, 14, in DA, Series 6, Vol. 6, pp. 373–75. Adams provides a detailed discussion of this issue in section 4 of 'Phenomenalism . . . in Leibniz.'

31. 'Did Berkeley Completely Misunderstand the Basis of the Primary-Secondary Quality Distinction in Locke,' in *Berkeley: Critical and Interpretive Essays*, ed. Colin M. Turbayne (Minneapolis: University of Minnesota Press, 1982), pp. 108–123 (chapter 15 of this volume).

32. 'Leibniz and Berkeley,' p. 157; cf. pp. 152f.

33. Leibniz, 'Discourse on Metaphysics,' 12; MacIntosh, pp. 152–53.

34. Leibniz, 'On the Method of Distinguishing Real from Imaginary Phenomena,' Ger, vol. VII, p. 322; Leomker, p. 365; MacIntosh, p. 153. (MacIntosh's reference is erroneous.)

35. Cf. *Dialogues*, 249.

36. *PHK*, 99.

37. *NE*, IV, vi, 7; DA, p. 404.

38. Cf. 'Discourse on Metaphysics,' 33, in Ger, vol. IV, pp. 458–59; also *NE*, II, viii,

13–15; DA pp. 131–33. For discussion and further references see Margaret D. Wilson, 'Confused Ideas,' *Rice University Studies*, 63 (Fall 1977), pp. 127ff. (chapter 22 of this volume); and Adams, 'Phenomenalism . . . in Leibniz,' p. 225. In *Philosophical Commentaries* Berkeley too entertains the supposition that ideas of colors contain "component ideas" that "we cannot easily distinguish & separate" (153; Thomas ed., p. 16). Berkeley particularly connects this point, as Leibniz did, with the fact that green is "compounded" out of blue and yellow. See, e.g., *PC*, 502–4; Thomas ed. p. 65.

39. Leibniz connects the "mere phenomenality" of a standard primary quality such as shape to the fact that it involves an abstraction or simplification of the infinite divisibility and complexity of nature. (Cf. Adams, 'Phenomenalism . . . in Leibniz,' pp. 225–26.)

40. 'Phenomenalism . . . in Leibniz,' p. 223. See also p. 224.

41. *Ibid.*, p. 224. In his later discussion Adams particularly stresses Leibniz's view that bodies can have only "phenomenal" status because they lack "true unity"—are mere aggregates which own their unity to the perceiving mind. (See pp. 241ff.) Berkeley regards the mind as responsible for unifying distinct ideas of sense—those that go constantly together—into single things; but he does not seem to see even this form of "mind dependence" as having negative implications for the reality of bodies. See, e.g., *Dialogues*, 246.

42. Cf. 'Method for Distinguishing Real from Imaginary Phenomena,' Ger, vol. VII, pp. 319f.; Loemker, p. 363. Of course, both Berkeley and Leibniz also mention other marks besides vividness for distinguishing "real" from imaginary phenomena—e.g., coherence.

43. Robert Brandom, in the paper cited in note 25 discusses Leibniz's conception of distinctness in considerable detail with particular emphasis on the issue of information content. Leibniz frequently links "distinctness" with the "intellectual" as opposed to the sensible; cf., e.g., 'On the Elements of Natural Science,' Loemker, p. 277. See also Wilson, 'Confused Ideas,' and Adams, 'Phenomenalism . . . in Leibniz,' pp. 223, 225.

44. 'On the Elements of Natural Science,' Loemker, p. 288. (It should be noted that this is a relatively early work, believed to have been written before the 'Discourse on Metaphysics.')

45. Cf. 'Leibniz and Berkeley,' pp. 156; "One difference [between Leibniz and Berkeley] . . . concerns infinity and infinite divisibility. It is a difference which seems to reflect the fact that Leibniz was a mathematician of genius while Berkeley was not . . ." Adams, however, points out that their difference on this issue directly reflects Berkeley's insistance that everything real is perceivable by sense, on the one hand, and Leibniz's rejection of sensationalism on the other hand. ('Phenomenalism,' pp. 222–23.)

46. See G. A. Johnston, *The Development of Berkeley's Philosophy* (London: MacMillan, 1923), chapter V.

47. For detailed discussion of Berkeley's position see Daniel Garber, 'Locke, Berkeley, and Corpuscular Scepticism,' in Turbayne, pp. 174–93, and Margaret D. Wilson, 'Berkeley and the Essences of the Corpuscularians,' in J. Foster and H. Robinson, eds., *Essays on Berkeley* (Oxford: Clarendon Press, 1985), pp. 131–47 (chapter 17 of this volume).

48. *PHK*, 101; *Dialogues*, 85.

49. *NE*, III, vi, 38, DA, p. 325; IV, vi, 4–8, DA, pp. 401–5.

50. The statement is found in Leibniz's letter of 15 March, 1715, in Ger, vol. II, p. 492; Loemker, p. 609.

51. Adams, 'Phenomenalism . . . in Leibniz,' p. 222: This notation was originally published by Kabitz, in the article cited in note 1, above. Kabitz also describes Leibniz's

other marks on the copy of Berkeley, including underlining. He concludes that Leibniz gave most attention to specific passages that fit best with his own interests, and probably had not read the whole book through carefully (see p. 627).

52. Kabitz, p. 636; Adams, p. 222 (I use Adams' translation).

53. Kant sometimes takes a similarly patronizing approach in his comments on Berkeley: see *The Critique of Pure Reason*, B 71.

54. *Dialogues*, p. 244.

55. *Ibid.*

56. Cf. Stäbler's comment at the end of the passage cited in note 1: "Leibniz in seinem Streben nach Harmonie und in seiner Flucht vor Einseitigkeiten konnte an dem extrem gehaltenen System seines englishen [*sic*] Zeitgenossen nur das anerkennen, was sich als Baustein in sein universales Gedankengebäude hätte einfügen können."

Confused Ideas

INTRODUCTION

It is widely known that Leibniz was severely critical of Descartes's use of the notions of clear and distinct (versus obscure and confused) ideas. Commentators frequently cite with approval Leibniz's various statements that a "criterion" or "mark" of clarity and distinctness is required, if the notions are to have any epistemological value. Leibniz's own, very pervasive, use of the notions of distinctness and confusion in ideas is less frequently examined. With the exception of some excellent, but largely expository work by Robert McRae, this aspect of Leibniz's philosophy does not seem to have received much systematic consideration in the English language literature.[1] I believe that this relative neglect is unwarranted. One purpose of the present paper is to argue that Leibniz's treatment of confused and distinct cognitions involves a very fundamental advance over Descartes's, although the feature in question is not one that Leibniz himself stressed. Unlike Descartes, Leibniz fairly consistently observes a distinction between *concepts* on the one hand, and *particular presentings* on the other hand.[2] (His position can therefore be construed as an important and perhaps influential antecedent to Kant's celebrated distinction between intuitions and concepts.) That is, Leibniz defines 'confused' and 'distinct' in one way to distinguish different levels of conceptual ability, and in another way to distinguish (alleged) features of perceptions. (There is also a third sense of 'confused' in Leibniz's writings that may apply to both categories of cognition.[3]) It is particularly interesting to compare Leibniz's treatment of sensory ideas with Descartes's. Leibniz, like Descartes, regards sense *perceptions* as necessarily and ineluctably confused; and he also uses sensory *concepts* as paradigms of the sort of confusion that may be ascribed to one's conceptual repertoire. Recognition of the fact that he does not regard the two as "confused" in the same sense of the term is important both in interpreting some puzzling Leibnizian passages, and in understanding his relation to Descartes. After developing these points in more detail, I will go on to discuss critically Leibniz's notion of confused *concepts*, and his use of sensory paradigms in this connection. I will not, however, attempt to evaluate in any detail his theory of confused *perception*; nor will I consider here his most central and original use of the notion of confusedness: his doctrine that every substance "expresses in a confused way" all of its past and future states, and everything that happens in its world. The latter notions certainly merit critical examination, and they are closely interrelated with the points I do discuss. They are so complex and difficult, however, that they seem to demand separate and systematic treatment.

I will begin with a brief review of relevant features of Descartes's position.

I

Descartes speaks variously of clear and distinct (or obscure and confused) knowledge, comprehension, ideas, perceptions, conception, notions, and so forth. In the *Principles* a "clear perception" is defined as one "that is present and open to an attending mind: just as we say that that is clearly seen by us, which, being present to the viewing eye, affects it sufficiently strongly and openly" (I, xlv: AT VIII–1, 21–22). A "distinct perception" is one which is not only clear, but also "so separate (*sejuncta*) from all others and (so) precise, that it contains in itself nothing else at all, except what is clear" (ibid., 22). A perception that is not clear and distinct is obscure and confused. The terms of these definitions suggest that what is at issue is the way in which particular entities are presented to the mind—as of course does the word 'perception' itself. And, in fact, in the next Principle Descartes proceeds to apply his distinction to the "perception of a pain." Two points need to be noted, however. First, Descartes thinks we clearly and distinctly perceive things (e.g., the nature of a body) "by the understanding," and he implies (for instance in the "wax passage" towards the end of Meditation II) that achieving clarity and distinctness in one's cognition is at least partly a matter of getting straight about what is contained in one's basic concepts. Second, while Descartes invariably characterizes sense perceptions—or at least those not "exhibiting" extension, figure, or motion—as confused, it is not at all evident how his definition of the "distinct" fails to apply to them. In what way do *they* "contain in themselves" what is not clear?[4] In fact, what he usually seems to mean in calling sensations "confused" is that they have very limited cognitive content (if any): they do not "exhibit to us" "real" properties in any intelligible way. (Similarly, Descartes's original sensible notion of the wax was amiss, not because there were undistinguished elements *of the sense experience(s)*, but because the true (intelligible) notion of wax was not yet before his mind's eye.)[5] What Descartes should probably say is that our "perception" (understanding) of the nature of body, and of physical properties, is confused insofar as we rely on sense perceptions. Only internal reflection and analysis enable us to grasp accurately "what is contained in" the idea of body, and distinguishes body "from all else." Sense perceptions, or sensations, can themselves be called "confused," within Cartesian parameters, only by a sort of conflation. They *fail to help us toward* the distinct and conceptually perfect understanding of the nature of things that our innate ideas can ultimately yield, once the discerning "attention of the mind" is directed toward them. This observation is very important to understanding the major differences between Descartes's position and that of Leibniz.

II

Leibniz too uses 'clear,' 'distinct,' 'confused,' and 'obscure' to qualify a wide range of terms: 'idea,' 'expression,' 'representation,' 'notion,' 'cognition,' 'perception,' 'thought,' even 'attribute,' to mention some of the most important examples. But whereas Descartes seems to move from talk of clear and distinct *x*'s to talk of clear and distinct *y*'s without observing any definite and significant distinctions, this is not at all the case with Leibniz. Although certain qualifications will have to be spelled out later, it is generally the case that when Leibniz talks of distinct or confused *notions* or *ideas*, he has in mind questions about conceptual abilities. When he speaks of distinct or confused *perceptions*, on the other hand, he is concerned with features of particular-presentings. Confusion in our *ideas* is to a considerable extent correctable; but the sort of confusion found in perceptions is largely ineluctable, unremovable: indeed, it belongs to the nature of the perceptions themselves. I will now consider these two types of "confusion" in turn—with brief mention of a third sense of 'confusion' that may apply more broadly than the other two.

According to the *Meditations on Knowledge, Truth, and Ideas*, we have a clear but confused notion or idea of things of a certain sort (say ϕ's), if we can recognize them when we encounter them, but cannot explain what distinguishes them from other entities (see Ger IV, 422). Our notion is distinct as well as clear if we can state a "mark" of ϕ-ness—in other words give an account of our ability to pick out ϕ's. This essay dates from 1684. In a much later work, the *New Essays*, Leibniz makes the same point, saying that we have a distinct idea when we can give "the definition or the reciprocal marks" (II, xxxi, §§1, 2: DA ed., p. 266).[6] The one exception to this rule is constituted by genuinely "primitive" notions; as Leibniz writes:

> There is, however, also a distinct cognition of an indefinable notion, when it is *primitive* or known by itself, that is, when it is irresolvable and only understood through itself. (Ger IV, 423)

Leibniz identifies the primitives with "the absolute Attributes of God" (ibid., 425).

It seems evident that these distinctions between clear and obscure, and distinct and confused ideas are distinctions of conceptual abilities. I can be said to "have" the concept of a Darwin tulip, for example, if I can pick out, identify, Darwin tulips reliably. I have the concept in a fuller sense if I can perform the further feat of providing explicit identifying marks of this type of tulip. It is also possible to ascribe to someone a sort of marginal possession of a concept, when he can make some accurate marginal use of a term: this would correspond to having an obscure idea, as opposed to having no idea at all. Thus I may have an obscure idea of a Darwin tulip if I know, at least, that it is not the same thing as a Parrot tulip, that it is much larger than a Botanical, and so forth. Lacking *all* these abilities I can hardly be said to possess the concept of a Darwin tulip at all—even though I may feel some faint cognitive stirrings of recollection when I hear the term used.

According to Leibniz, "ideas of one sense," like red, sour, or warm, must be denied the status of primitives. (It would certainly be hard to see how they could be counted among "the absolute Attributes of God.") But the same distinctions apply. Therefore our ideas of these qualities must count as confused insofar as we are unable to articulate distinguishing marks. Thus, I have a clear but confused idea of red if I can identify or pick out red things, but cannot state a mark of redness (see, e.g., Ger IV, 422).

This way of looking at the confused-distinct distinctions has no strict parallels in Descartes's writings. As observed above, Descartes does relate the notion of "distinctness" to that of *distinguishing*: a distinct idea enables us to distinguish its "object" from all else. But Descartes is surely not concerned like Leibniz with the problem of recognizing presented particulars—with concept "application" or use of "kind terms" in the usual sense. Rather, he is concerned with establishing on an *a priori* level the difference between (say) the natures of mind and of matter, between mere sensation and real qualities of bodies. Whether or not we conclude that Leibniz succeeded in making the notion of a distinct idea more *philosophically valuable* than Descartes, he should no doubt be given credit[7] for recognizing the significance of the issue of conceptual competence in relation to (actually or possibly) presented entities.

Before turning to the Leibnizian notion of "confusion" that applies specifically to perceptions, I would like to mention a third sense of the term that Leibniz *may* take to apply to both ideas and perceptions. The state of a mind (or mind-like substance) is called "confused" by Leibniz when it is *wholly unconscious*. Even monads naturally incapable of consciousness have "confused perceptions" in this sense. Thus, bare monads are said to express or perceive confusedly everything that happens in their world—and also completely to lack consciousness and sensation.[8] It is, of course, unproblematic that 'confused perception' and 'confused expression' are used by Leibniz in this sense. But Leibniz also speaks of unconscious *ideas* (a concept, he says in one place, is a conscious idea).[9] And he sometimes identifies ideas as "expressions."[10] It is possible, therefore, that he might be prepared to speak of "confused ideas," in the sense of implicit or unrecognized conceptual abilities. I am, however, unable to cite direct textual support for this suggestion.

But 'confused' also carries another sense in Leibniz's writings. While this sense is related to the one just considered, it definitely applies specifically to perceptions, as opposed to conceptual abilities. In *this* important sense, a perception is confused when the person perceiving *is* conscious of *it*, but is not conscious of "all that is in it," of the elements that "compose" it. Leibniz holds that all sense perceptions are confused in this sense; that is, all are composed of "elements" that we do not—and in fact cannot—distinguish or discern.[11] The "simplicity" or homogeneity of such perceptions is therefore only *apparent*.

I pointed out above that Descartes, while treating sense perceptions as "confused," provides no way of understanding how they fail to satisfy his definition of a distinct idea, as "containing nothing at all within it except what is clear." Notice now that on Leibniz's account sense perceptions do satisfy the original Cartesian conception of confusion. It is not the case that "all that is in them" is clear to the perceiving mind.

Leibniz offers several different reasons for this rather extraordinary doctrine.

One type of reason has to do with his conception of the cause-effect relation. According to Leibniz the "effect corresponds to the cause"—i.e., *everything* present in the cause must have some corresponding element in the effect.[12] But the "motions" that cause sense-perceptions—considered either in the object or in the body—are indefinitely, indeed infinitely, complex.[13] Hence corresponding complexity *must* be present in the sensation that results from these motions, even if we are not aware of it and cannot become aware of it.

Other lines of reasoning to the same conclusion[14] derive directly from the Principle of Sufficient Reason and the Principle of Continuity, respectively. Descartes had held the position that there was only an arbitrary connection between experienced sensations on the one hand, and the events in the brain that give rise to them on the other hand. Leibniz rejects this view as contrary to the rational order of things. It is, he says, "not the custom of God to act with so little order and reason."[15] If all sensations were really simple, Leibniz seems to believe, the notion of an arbitrary relation would be unavoidable. If we suppose an implicit complexity in sensation, however, we may then further suppose that there is some rational or intelligible relation between, say, the complex physical "cause" of the sensation of yellow and that sensation itself—a relation that does not obtain between that cause and some *other* sensation (say the sensation of blue).[16]

Leibniz argues also from the Principle of Continuity that every perception of which we are aware must be composed of parts of which we are not aware. For instance he comments in the *New Essays*: "that which is noticeable must be composed of parts which are not, (since) nothing can arise suddenly, thought no more than movement" (II, i, §18: D.A. ed., p. 117; cf. II, ix, §4: p. 134). He wants to claim, then, that we cannot go "*tout d'un coup*" from a state of zero perception to a state of perceiving consciously; such abrupt transitions are not permitted by the Principle of Continuity. The suggested alternative seems to be that a conscious perception emerges from a sort of temporal summation of "*petites perceptions*" which belong to and contribute to the whole although they are not separately discerned—either in it, or as its conditions.

Additional considerations Leibniz adduces on behalf of his theory of sensation include the claim that *we know* that green is a composite of blue and yellow, yet green appears no less "simple" than the other two colors. (Thus apparent simplicity does not *entail* actual simplicity.)[17] Also, Leibniz mentions the example of a spinning cog wheel: as the wheel moves faster we are increasingly unable to discriminate the individual cogs, and eventually we "perceive" only a homogeneous blur.[18] His suggestion, I take it, is that there is no good reason to deny that the individual cogs contribute any less to our perception when they are moving fast than when they are moving slowly.[19] We should conclude rather that they contribute to and are implicit in our "blur" perception, even though not individually discerned. Sensory perceptions, such as color, odor, sound, etc., should be understood analogously.

Leibniz states very explicitly—especially in the *New Essays*—that the confusedness of sense perceptions is essential to them:

[Colors, tastes, etc.] merit [the] name of phantoms, rather than that of *qualities*, or even of *ideas*. . . . To wish that these confused phantoms remain, and that nevertheless one distinguishes (*demêle*) their ingredients by the phantasy itself, is to contradict oneself; it is to want to have the pleasure of being deceived by an agreeable perspective, and to wish that at the same time the eye see the deception, which would be to spoil it. (Ibid., pp. 403–404)

What this passage does *not* tell us is whether it is *possible* to "distinguish the ingredients" of sense perceptions by the "phantasy," supposing one is willing to give up the initial experience of the "phantom." In one place Leibniz suggests that we fail to perceive *petites perceptions* only because we are distracted by their multitude, or because they are effaced or obscured by greater perceptions.[20] This way of talking seems to leave open the possibility that by a special effort of mind we *could* become aware of the elements of which our perceptions of blue (for example) are composed. But Leibniz does not actually say this, and the view seems extremely implausible. Perhaps he means to hold that *if* we could, *per impossibile*, reduce our experience at a given time to a handful of *petites perceptions*, there would be nothing to rule out our becoming aware of them. But in fact there will always be an overwhelming multitude in any sense perception, and the mind in this situation is helpless to distinguish them.[21]

My argument so far has proceeded as if the distinction between confused ideas and confused perceptions were (at least textually) perfectly sharp and unproblematic. Now it is necessary to take account of some of the qualifications I mentioned at the outset. First, it must be conceded that throughout the *New Essays* Leibniz speaks of "ideas of sense" being confused in the sense of being constituted out of *petites perceptions*, of which we are unaware. (Note the use of the term 'idea' in the passage quoted in the previous paragraph.) I do not think this fact in itself is of any great significance. Locke, of course, speaks of "ideas of sense," meaning sensory *experiences*; Leibniz simply falls into his antagonist's terminology.[22] But there is another problem of greater importance. Even in the *Meditations on Knowledge, Truth and Ideas*, with Locke nowhere in view, Leibniz seems to run together his thesis that sensory perceptions are confused (implicitly complex) with the claim that we cannot provide a "distinguishing mark" for picking out their qualities. He writes:

Cognition [*cognitio*] is . . . *clear* when it gives me the ability to recognize the thing represented, and clear [cognition] in turn is either confused or distinct. It is *confused* when I cannot separately enumerate marks sufficient to discriminate the thing from others, even though the thing really has such marks and requisites, into which its notion can be resolved: thus colors, odors, tastes, and other particular objects of the senses we indeed recognize sufficiently clearly and discriminate from each other, but by the simple testimony of the senses, and not by statable marks; hence we cannot explain to a blind man what red is, nor can we explain such things to others, except by bringing them into the presence of the thing, and causing them to see, smell or taste it. . . . even though it is certain that the notions of these qualities are composite and can be resolved, since they surely have their causes. (Ger IV, 422–423; emphasis in text)

In this passage, and others like it, Leibniz runs together the two main senses of 'confused' that I have distinguished, to obtain the thesis that we have only "confused ideas" of "the objects of the senses." Thus, as the last few lines of the quotation reveal, the implicit compositeness of sensory experiences is taken to rule out the view that sensory ideas or notions are primitive.[23] The necessary confusedness of our perceptions of colors, odors, etc., is then taken to show that we only (*can* only?) have confused ideas of these qualities. For the confusion of these sensory experiences is such that we are unable to "notice in them" any mark that would enable us to *say* how red, for instance, is distinguished from green. Because our experience of these qualities can never be freed of "confusion," we cannot convert our conceptual power of mere *recognition* to that capacity for articulate explication signaled by the ascription of a distinct idea. Thus we cannot "explain to a blind man what red is."

I believe that Leibniz gets involved in a confusion in this and similar passages. To see that this is so, consider first the question where the physical theory of sensible qualities could fit into Leibniz's account. On the one hand, the view that sense experiences are "confused" (implicitly complex) is based to a considerable extent on the view that these experiences stand in some unique relation (causal or expressive) to the indefinitely complex motions in bodies postulated by theoretical physics. Yet on the other hand, the running together of the claim that our sense experiences are confused, with the claim that our concepts of sensory qualities are confused, seems to negate the possibility of a physical-theoretical account of sensible qualities. For if we are allowed to suppose that a *red* object, for example, is just one that reflects light waves of such and such frequency in such and such circumstances, there is no obvious reason why we could not ascribe to ourselves a distinct *notion* of red, even on the supposition that our (sense) *perceptions* are all confused. We would be able to say, for instance, that red objects differ from all others in that *they* reflect wavelengths in range l_x–l_y. Further, on this physical or scientific understanding of 'red' there is no barrier at all to explaining to a blind man "what red is"—since, presumably, he can understand physical optics as well as the next person. (*His* ideas, too, could come to be distinct.) In other words, the doctrine that our sense experiences of colors, odors, etc., are all confused will lead to the conclusion that our concepts of these qualities are all confused, only if the qualities are somehow identified with the experiences (or if we lack cognitive resources other than direct sensing).

Leibniz himself does, in a number of places, formulate theoretical identifications of sensory qualities with (potentially) describable states of physical objects. Thus he suggests that red may be the "revolving of certain small globules," and heat may be "the expansion of air."[24] With respect to colors, he specifically indicates that distinct ideas may be derived from optics, and that there is no barrier to instructing the blind in this science.[25] These statements might lead one to suppose that his linking of confused perceptions with confused ideas (in the *Meditations* and elsewhere) is meant to be contingent upon a low level of scientific understanding. That is, he *could* be saying in such passages that sense experiences *alone* will not provide distinct concepts of sensory qualities; that someone *ignorant of optics* cannot "explain to a blind man what red is," even though such a person can easily recognize red things. In my view, this is what he *should* be saying, in order to maintain a coherent position. There is evidence, however, that Leibniz did not have one consistent way of thinking about sensory qualities, and hence that such a rationalization of the *Meditations* passage is misleading. For even in passages where Leibniz seems to endorse the possibility of physical-theoretical accounts of sensible qualities, he *still* denies that one can know what red or heat is unless one has the appropriate sensations. (In these passages he tends to alternate between saying that the physical state *is* red or heat, and saying that the physical state *causes* red or heat.) For example, in *On the Elements of Natural Science* (1682–1684) he first proposes that heat must ultimately be understood in terms of physical theory:

> Simple attributes . . . are simple by their own nature and for intellectual reasons, or they are simple with respect to our senses. As an example of an attribute simple in nature can be offered 'to be itself' or 'to endure.' An attribute simple with respect to the senses, on the other hand, would be heat, for the senses do not show us by what mechanism the state of a body is produced which brings about the sensation of warmth in us, yet the mind properly perceives that warmth is not something absolute which is understood in itself but that it will only then be adequately understood when we explain of what it consists or distinctly describe its proximate cause—perhaps the expansion of air, or rather some particular motion of a fluid which is thinner than air. (Loemker, p. 285).[26]

Yet in the next breath Leibniz is telling us that we know what heat or light is, only if we actually have the sensation of heat or of light:

> Confused attributes are those which are indeed composite in themselves or by intellectual principles but are simple to the senses and whose definition therefore cannot be explained. These attributes can be imported not by description but only by pointing them out to the senses. (Ibid.)

He goes on to indicate that cold-blooded people in a sunless land could not "be made to understand what heat is merely by describing it"; to "learn what heat is" they would have to *experience* it—for instance by having a fire kindled near them. "Similarly," Leibniz concludes, "a man born blind could learn the whole optics yet not acquire any idea of light" (ibid.).

Leibniz tends to alternate, then, between saying that we can, through physics, develop distinct, verbally communicable ideas of sensible qualities, and indicating that we can acquire the ideas of these qualities only through "confused" sensory experiences (whence it follows that the ideas themselves are confused or uncommunicable). Similarly, he vacillates between saying that physics tells us what sensible qualities are or consist in, and saying that physics tells us the causes of sensible qualities. Insofar as he inclines to the former view, he thinks of sensible qualities as properties in physical objects that happen to be discriminable by the senses. Insofar as he inclines to the latter view, he thinks of the nature of a sensible quality as completely bound up with the nature of sensory experience (cf. the talk of "confused attributes" in the passage just quoted).[27]

This ambivalence about sensory qualities seems to be an unrationalized, pervasive feature of Leibniz's thinking. It tends to muddle his discussions of confused ideas, by conflating the confusedness proper to concepts (on Leibniz's own account) with that proper to perceptions. It is perhaps worth remarking, however, that the ambivalence in question is hardly trivial or idiosyncratic. It reflects, to borrow some phrases, the superposition of the manifest image on the scientific image, the naive on the causal viewpoint. Thus, we do not naturally think of "perceived red" as just a sensation like pain. For we perceive it *in* the objects of the manifest image. From this point of view it is natural to think of it as a quality in its own right, that happens to be completely bound up with perceptual experience. From this point of view, to "know what red is" *does* require seeing red. The peculiar thing about Leibniz is that he can move so flexibly between the manifest and scientific images—even within a paragraph or two—in considering the issue of "what red is." It is amazing that he was able to overlook such a conspicuous appearance of inconsistency. (Descartes's contempt for the manifest image was deeper and more consistent: for Descartes, perceived red is a "confused" sensation and nothing else.)

There is also, I think, another way of understanding Leibniz's ambivalent treatment of sensory qualities. This is found in his way of categorizing conceptual abilities as confused or distinct. Following Cartesian dogma, Leibniz seems to assume automatically that one's "idea" cannot be distinct without being clear, though it can be clear without being distinct. Given Leibniz's definitions, this hierarchical ordering would have the consequence that while one can be able to recognize without being able to state a mark, one cannot state a mark unless one is able to recognize. Now the blind person in the normal course of things does *not* have the ability to pick out or recognize red objects in his environment. It follows, on the stated assumptions, that he does not have a *clear* idea of red. *Ergo* (on this line of reasoning) he *must* lack a distinct one: there *has* to be a sense in which he does not "know what red is."

I do not mean to claim, of course, that Leibniz's treatment of knowledge of sensory qualities is consistently dominated by such a hierarchical assumption about the classification of ideas. As we have seen, he does sometimes say in so many words that a blind man can have a distinct conception of colors. The point, again, is just that his ambivalence can be understood in light of certain conflicting assumptions or perspectives, which may to some extent alternate in his thought.

To sum up the main points of my interpretation: Leibniz, in treating the issue of clarity and distinctness, recognizes clearly if implicitly a distinction between conceptual abilities and features of particular presentings or perceptions. In the case of the latter, Leibniz's theory of sense perception enables us to see why the term "confused" is supposed to be generally applicable—whereas Descartes's fails to do so. However, Leibniz's distinction between confused concepts and confused perceptions is blurred in those passages where he uses cognition of qualities proper to one sense as paradigms of "both" types of confusion. What is important to recognize, however, is that insofar as sensory qualities are identified through the concepts of physics (as Leibniz frequently does identify them) the (alleged) ineluctable confusion in our sense-perception of them does not at all entail that our ideas or notions of them must be confused. To lose sight of this fact (as Leibniz himself sometimes does) is to lose sight of one of the more satisfactory and historically significant features of Leibniz's epistemology: the distinction between the categories of conceptual abilities and perceptions.

III

I turn now to some questions of evaluation. As I indicated at the outset, I will not undertake here any systematic evaluation of the complicated theory that sense perceptions are "confused"—though I will conclude with a few peripheral remarks concerning it. I believe, however, that some fairly conclusive observations can be made concerning Leibniz's manner of defining the distinction between confused and distinct notions, and will take up that issue first.

It seems evident that *any* serious account of concept-possession must accord some fundamental place to a person's ability to *recognize* presented particulars as ϕ's or ψ's. Leibniz's focus on this level of ability makes good sense. Further, it seems unproblematic that there is a way of "knowing what ϕ's are" that goes beyond merely being able to recognize ϕ's. One of Leibniz's favorite examples is convincing: an assayer has a much better knowledge *of what gold is* than I do, even though I *can* generally *recognize gold objects* when I encounter them. While there seems to be no good philosophical reason for retaining the Cartesian terminology, we can hardly deny Leibniz the right to stipulate that mere recognitional ability counts as a "confused idea," while something more, such as the assayer's knowledge of gold, is required for one's idea to count as distinct.[28]

The problem lies in trying to lay down conditions on the "something more" in a way that seems really to support an epistemically significant distinction. There are, after all, very few sorts of cases where recognitional ability is *wholly* divorced from the ability to state *some* salient features of the sort of thing one can recognize. And I do not think it is clear that such minimal articulateness with respect to ϕ's should be one of the two or three major criteria of whether and to what degree one "knows what ϕ's are." Do we want to say, on the other hand, that a person has a distinct idea of ϕ's just in case he can state a necessary and sufficient condition of ϕ-ness—a "reciprocal mark," as Leibniz suggests in one place? This proposal seems both too weak and too strong. Too weak, because such knowledge could in many cases be relatively trivial. Thus, I might know that a certain species of mammal (of which I happen to have heard the name) is the only one in existence with greenish toenails—and know absolutely nothing else about these mammals. It would be ridiculous to compare my knowledge of this species with the assayer's knowledge of gold. The proposal seems too strong, on the other hand, because one can know so very much about different types of entities, without being able to produce with any great confidence a list of properties that members of each type have in common, and share (as a set) with no other entities. It seems that Leibniz's conception of a *distinct* idea or notion is not sufficiently developed to bear very heavy epistemological weight.

Leibniz's way of distinguishing confused and distinct ideas is also objectionable precisely because of its implication that our ideas of sense (of the manifest image) are on exactly the same regrettable epistemological footing as our most minimal abilities to recognize animals and flowers. Even if one should grant Leibniz his claim that sensory perceptions are "confused" in the relevant sense (i.e., implicitly complex), it still does not seem true that our inability to state a mark of (manifest) redness is the same sort of problem as a given person's inability to state a mark by which to recognize a particular type of bird or tree. In the latter case, but not the former, there exists the real possibility of converting one's idea from "confused" to "distinct" by reflection on, and generalization from, one's direct experiences (sensory presentings) of the entities in question. In the former case, as we have seen, the story is far more complicated. Leibniz's position on the nature and knowledge of sensory qualities involves a lot of philosophy, a lot of (not always consistent) theoretical commitments. His effort to assimilate this issue to the distinction between recognitional and articulate knowledge of "what ϕ's are" is both oversimplifying and highly misleading.

Leibniz's distinction between confused and distinct perceptions is much harder to evaluate than the distinction between confused and distinct notions, partly because it is more obscure and difficult and partly because it is much more fundamental to Leibniz's system. In the present context I will make just a few observations. First, we should resist the temptation to reject out of hand the claim that sense perceptions are "confused" (on the grounds that the notion of a perception or perception-part of which we can never become aware is inconsistent). Leibniz's *petites perceptions*, like the Kantian manifold which they prefigure,[29] are postulated because of the dictates of a fairly deeply thought-out theory. To know what to think about them we must try to understand the theory first. Second, one could agree that the arguments Leibniz presents, in the *New Essays* and elsewhere, for the implicit complexity of all sense perceptions, involve unacceptable or dubious *general* principles, without necessarily dismissing his theory. The central issue that must be addressed is the following: are there any grounds at all for inferring from complexity in the object, cause, or conditions of an experience on the one hand, to complexity in the experience itself on the other hand? Rationalist principles about the cause-effect relation, or about God's "custom," provide a handy basis for a positive answer. The question retains some interest, however, even if one rejects these principles as a basis for argument. Sometimes Leibniz himself seems to present it as simply a fact about *perception* that we could not perceive the result of the co-action of minute motions if we did not perceive the minute motions themselves.[30] This is a view that might be analyzed and evaluated independently of general dogma about the correspondence of effect to cause.

Finally, we should notice that Leibniz's theory of the implicit complexity of sense experiences follows directly from his account of representation or expression, together with the view that perception is a form of representation or expression.[31] That is, the theory of confused perceptions can be directly derived from this aspect of Leibniz's position without benefit of any rationalist premisses about the cause-effect relation in general,[32] or God's rational ordering of things. In other words, to reject the view of sense perception as intrinsically confused, one must either reject Leibniz's theory of representation or expression, or deny that sense perception is a form of representation or expression. According to Leibniz, one thing expresses another if there is a "constant and regulated" or "exact and natural" relation between what we can say of the two things, or of the relations of their elements.[33] Some of Leibniz's examples suggest that there must indeed be a one-to-one correspondence between the elements of the expressing entity and the elements of the expressed. (This is suggested, for example, by his description of a geometrical projection expressing the figure projected: "each point of the one corresponding, following a certain relation, to each point on the other" [*N.E.* II, viii, §13: D.A. ed., p. 131].) If such a condition is intended, then (it seems), a perception can express a colored object only if there is an element in the perception corresponding to every feature of the colored object (e.g., each feature of its surface that gives rise to its reflective properties). And by this reasoning we would arrive again at the full-blooded Leibnizian view that every sense perception is implicitly as complex as its infinitely complex cause. However, some of Leibniz's own examples of expression—models and maps[34]—indicate that he probably does not intend this improbably strong position when he defines 'expression.' The important point is that even if *exact* or one-to-one correspondence is not required, the theory of expression will still require *some* "regulated" relation between the features of the perception and features of the perceived. And this, I presume, would require *some* sort of internal complexity in the perceptions themselves. But suppose Locke and Leibniz are right in saying that the perception of a splotch of red or blue of a single shade is (at least) *apparently* homogeneous. It will follow immediately that there is an *implicit* or unrecognized internal complexity in such perceptions—and hence that they are, on Leibniz's definitions, confused.

I do not, of course, present these observations as any sort of defense of Leibniz's conception of sense perceptions as intrinsically "confused." What I have tried to suggest is that the theory should not be rejected either as transparently false, or as entirely dependent on transparently outdated premisses.

NOTES

For abbreviations see the list at the beginning of this volume. All translations into English are mine unless otherwise noted.

1. See R. McRae, *Leibniz: Perception, Apperception and Thought* (Toronto: University of Toronto Press, 1976). See especially pp. 36ff. and 72ff. In addition, Hidé Ishiguro provides an interesting discussion of Leibniz's use of the confused-distinct distinction in connection with the "ideas of sensible qualities": see her book, *Leibniz's Philosophy of Logic and Language* (Ithaca, N.Y.: Cornell University Press, 1972), chapter IV.

2. That Leibniz observes such a distinction is already brought out by McRae, in the sections cited above. In other respects, however, our approaches are quite different.

3. Like Descartes, Leibniz sometimes also speaks of the "criteria of clearness and distinctness" in relation to *judgments*. These contexts seem to involve yet a different issue from the three Leibnizian notions of "confusion" that I discuss in the paper: namely, the issue of (experiential or formal) *proof*. See especially Ger IV, 425–426.

4. In his discussion of pain in Principle xlvi Descartes explains that the perception itself may be clear (not distinct); however, the treatment of "material falsity" in the Third Meditation suggests that most sense perceptions should be regarded as obscure. It should be noted that Descartes does not very consistently observe the clear-distinct and obscure-confused distinctions.

5. While I will not take the space to defend this point here, I have argued it in more detail in my book *Descartes* (London: Routledge & Kegan Paul, 1978).

6. In some places in the *New Essays*, though, Leibniz suggests a much stronger criterion of "distinct ideas" than the one he usually espouses. For example, in II, xxiii, §§4–5 (p. 227 in D.A. ed.) he says "the true mark of a clear and distinct idea of an object is the means we have of knowing therein many truths by *a priori* proofs. . . ." He goes on to claim to have shown this "in a discourse on truth and ideas"—evidently a reference to the "Meditations." This is a puzzling statement. Possibly Leibniz is confusing his treatment of distinct ideas in the "Meditations" with that of "real definition"? (Cf. Ger IV, 424–425)

7. Within the context of post-Cartesian philosophy.

8. This use of 'confusion,' too, is different from any Cartesian usage, since Descartes would not have dissociated perception from consciousness to this degree.

9. *Discourse on Metaphysics*, xxvii, Ger IV, 452–453.

10. Ibid.; also in "What is an Idea?," Ger VII, 263–264.

11. *Discourse*, xxxiii, Ger IV, 458–459.

12. Cf. *N.E.* II, viii, §15: D.A. ed., p. 131. I believe Leibniz regards this principle as itself somehow a consequence of the Principle of Sufficient Reason. In fact the "different reasons" I distinguish in this and the following paragraphs are not sharply distinguished by Leibniz, as the passage just cited shows.

13. See, e.g., *N.E.* II, i, §17: D.A. ed., p. 117. Here Leibniz is invoking the doctrine that the soul expresses everything in the body, rather than any explicitly causal formulation. On Leibniz's own principles, the notion of expression is indeed more fundamental than that of causality strictly speaking, the body does *not* cause sensations in the mind. See also *Discourse on Metaphysics*, xxxiii.

14. See note 1, above.

15. *N.E.* II, viii, §13: D.A. ed., p. 131.

16. I have gone over some of this same ground in "Leibniz and Materialism," *Cana-*

dian Journal of Philosophy 3 (June, 1974): 495–513 (chapter 26 of this volume). My reason for repeating myself is that I failed to get some of the points right in the previous discussion—notably the distinction between confused ideas or notions and confused perceptions.

17. *N.E.* IV, vi, §7: D.A. ed., p. 403.

18. Ibid.

19. What Leibniz actually says is that "we don't need to suppose that God by His good pleasure gives us this phantom and that it is independent of the teeth of the wheel and their intervals . . . on the contrary we conceive that it is only a confused expression of what occurs in the movement. . . ."

20. *N.E.* II, ix, §1: D.A. ed., p. 134.

21. Sometimes Leibniz says explicitly that it will never be in our power to recognize the *petites perceptions* through sense experience. See, for instance, *N.E.* IV, vi, §7: D.A. ed., p. 403.

22. Compare McRae, *Leibniz*, p. 37, no. 15, and p. 72.

23. It is not clear whether "their causes" is meant to refer to the causes of the notions or the causes of the qualities. What he *should* mean, in my view, is that the *perceptions* have causes; which is to say that the *qualities* are complex, analyzable entities; hence our *notions* are confused until we achieve some kind of analysis.

24. Ger VI, p. 492 and Loemker, p. 285 (and cf. note 26, below).

25. *N.E.* II, ix, §8: D.A. ed., p. 137; cf. *N.E.* III, ii, §3: D.A. ed., p. 287.

26. This work is not published in Ger.

27. Ishiguro indicates (*Leibniz's Philosophy of Logic and Language*, p. 54–56) that for Leibniz the *same* quality can be represented confusedly by a sense-derived idea, or distinctly represented by the physicist. However, I think she overlooks the Leibnizian ambivalence I am concerned to call to attention.

28. Forgetting, for now, the theory of primitive ideas.

29. I owe this observation to discussion with Leon Barnhart. The "theoretical entity" conception is loosely derived from Wilfrid Sellars.

30. See for instance Ger II, 113 (letter to Arnauld).

31. Cf. Ger II, 112.

32. I am assuming that one can detach Leibniz's account of what expression is, from his view that "causation" in general is to be analyzed in terms of it.

33. Ger II, 112; *N.E.* II, viii, §13: D.A. ed., p. 131.

34. Ger VII, 263–264.

Confused vs. Distinct Perception in Leibniz:
Consciousness, Representation, and God's Mind

THE NOTION of *perception* plays a fundamental and mysterious role in the philosophical systems of both Spinoza and Leibniz. Both philosophers depart from the relatively commonplace Cartesian notion of perception as a conscious state of a rational mind (human or higher) that "exhibits" or represents to that mind some entity which may (or may not) exist outside the mind. Spinoza holds that *every* body in nature is the "object" of a "mind" that perceives it, and indeed perceives "everything that happens" in it. (*E*IIp12)[1] The mind and its proper object (its body) are in some sense one and the same thing (*E*IIp7s); and the mind in effect immediately perceives *only* what happens in its body. (A mind, however, perceives external bodies indirectly, through their effects on its own body. (*E*IIp16)) Leibniz holds that the world is constituted of infinitely many monads, each of which perceives all that happens in all the others, though only some are conscious or sentient, and fewer still are rational. (Like Spinoza, Leibniz holds that minds—and mind-like substances—perceive their own bodies immediately, and external things mediately, through their effects on the monads' bodies.)[2]

These doctrines about perception are very difficult to understand. In particular, they seem to be in conflict with ordinary connotations of the term 'perception', which fit much more naturally with the Cartesian usage. Recently commentators have tended to hold or imply, however, that their seemingly paradoxical quality can be greatly mitigated by attending to the distinction between *distinct* and *confused* perception, which is salient in both philosophers (though Spinoza tends to prefer the terms 'adequate' and 'inadequate').[3] The general tendency is to suggest that for m to perceive x *confusedly* (or inadequately) is *not* for m to be *consciously* (*explicitly*) *aware* of x (whatever else it might be). Thus, the doctrines in question do not imply that *conscious (explicit) awareness* is present throughout nature; that our minds are *consciously (explicitly) aware* of each and every event that occurs in our bodies; that awareness of external things presupposes *more direct and explicit awareness of the states of our own bodies*; and so on.[4]

I certainly agree that both Spinoza and Leibniz radically divorce the notion of perception from that of conscious, explicit awareness. I do not think, though, that this observation helps much to reduce the mystery of their views about perception; rather, it encapsulates a major part of the problem. (What, for instance, is meant by calling a state a *perception*, when it is not conscious or accessible to consciousness?)[5] Moreover, emphasis on the distinction between

distinct and confused perception is not apt to give much help with the difficulties, for this distinction is itself poorly understood in the case of both philosophers. It does not, in particular, provide a path to reconciling the two philosophers' dicta about the ubiquity of perception with ordinary assumptions about
explicit conscious awareness. For the relation between the distinct/confused distinction, and the conscious/non-conscious distinction is far from straightforward
in either Spinoza or Leibniz. Further, in the case of Spinoza, at least, the dis-
tinct-confused contrast involves claims about the relation between God's understanding and the "perceptions" of creatures that are very far indeed from common sense.

In this paper I will focus on the problem of interpreting the distinction between confused and distinct perception in Leibniz's philosophy.[6] I will certainly
not attempt to cover all aspects of this complex problem, but will limit myself
to the following steps of argument. In the first section I will assess claims that
the distinction between distinct and confused perception in Leibniz is close to,
if not identical with, the distinction between perception of which we (or other
souls) are conscious (or notice, or apperceive) and perception of which we are
not conscious. Although there is some textual basis for this suggestion, it can
readily be shown that Leibniz requires a way of ranking perceptions by degree
of distinctness that is independent of the issue of consciousness. On the latter
point I follow an interesting essay by Robert Brandom, which has not yet received its due in the literature.[7]

In section two I evaluate Brandom's alternative proposal for making sense of
the notion of degrees of distinctness in Leibniz. I argue that Brandom's proposal is unsuccessful for two reasons: first, the quasi-Leibnizian concepts he
enlists are inadequately explained and lack textual justification; and second, he
fails in his purpose of accommodating the alleged intensional features of Leibniz's notion of perception generally.

In section three I suggest that it is, in fact, a mistake to pursue an account of
the distinct/confused perception distinction in Leibniz that will preserve anything like an ordinary notion of intrinsic intensionality (i.e., representationality
accessible to the perceiver itself). I propose settling instead for a notion of
external inferability in interpreting the inter-perception of monads. (This is also
a feature of Brandom's account, although it is there in tension with the requirement of intrinsic intensionality). In explaining the distinction between distinct
and confused perception, however, we need to reinforce the notion of external
inferability with some notion of the order of reasons in God's mind. This proposal seems to accord with Leibniz's intentions, though he does not very clearly
indicate just how it is supposed to work.

In the fourth and final section I briefly relate these conclusions about Leibniz
to certain aspects of Spinoza's account of the distinction between distinct and
confused perception, particularly in relation to the order of God's ideas. On my
reading of the two philosophers their notions of distinct and confused perceptions have even more in common than is usually recognized.

I cannot claim that my efforts here will significantly reduce the mystery of the later rationalist philosophers' notions of perception. In fact, the most useful result may well be to suggest how misleading it is even to *try* to bring these philosophical theories into alignment with common sense assumptions about mind and nature.

I. DISTINCT PERCEPTION AND CONSCIOUSNESS IN LEIBNIZ

Leibniz holds, explicitly and emphatically, that the notion of perception is not tied to that of consciousness, contrary to Cartesian assumptions:

> The passing state [of any simple substance] which enfolds and represents a multitude in the unity or in the simple substance is merely what is called *perception*, which must be clearly distinguished from apperception or from consciousness. . . . It is in this that the Cartesians were very mistaken, for they disregarded perceptions which are not apperceived. It is this, too, which led them to believe that only spirits are Monads and that there are no souls in beasts or other entelechies. . . . ("Monadology," § 14; *Ger.* II, pp. 608–609)

In many passages Leibniz insists that the postulation of unconscious, or at least subliminal, perception is required to explain various phenomena of conscious experience. For instance, our conscious perception of the ocean's roar must, he supposes, be a sort of summation of perceptions of the various waves, of which we are not explicitly aware. His commitment to divorcing perception from consciousness obviously is not wholly tied to such reasoning, however. For he goes far beyond assuming that there are unconscious perceptions bound up, in the same subject, with those that are conscious. There are, he maintains, infinitely many wholly unconscious perceivers, or bare monads ("other entelechies").

Robert McRae has held that Leibniz's distinction between perceptions of which we are conscious and those of which we are not exactly matches his distinction between distinct and confused perceptions:

> The difference between distinct and confused perceptions corresponds exactly to that between perceptions of which we are conscious or which we apperceive and those of which we are not conscious or which are not apperceptible. It corresponds to that between sensible perceptions and insensible perceptions.[8]

Proceeding along somewhat the same path, G.H.R. Parkinson observes that while a (human) soul is supposed to perceive the whole universe, it does not *notice* everything that occurs in the universe. He continues:

> Leibniz puts this by saying that although the human soul perceives the whole universe, the perceptions that it (and indeed every created substance) has are 'confused.' . . . [T]o call perceptions 'confused' is to say that, because of their infinity, they cannot be distinguished by the percipient.[9]

Parkinson goes on to indicate that there are several ways in which one might try to explain the connection between distinct perception and noticing. He adds that while "[i]t cannot be said that Leibniz makes very clear just what he has in mind . . . , it is most important to try to see what he means," because "only those substances that have distinct perceptions have sensations. More than this: having distinct perceptions is not just a necessary condition of having sensations, but is both necessary and sufficient."[10] Now Leibniz very often does write as if distinct perceptions are just those that are consciously "noticed" and "distinguished", while confused perceptions are not noticed and distinguished: this much seems to me indisputable. Among the many relevant passages are several statements from the beginning of the "Monadology", including the following:

> . . . [I]f in our perceptions there were nothing distinct nor anything, so to speak, in relief and of a more marked taste (*d'un plus haut goût*), we would always be in a swoon. And that is the state of the mere bare Monads (*des Monades toutes nues*).[11]

Other passages, however, suggest that consciousness is correlated not with distinctness *per se*, but with an especially high *degree* of distinctness.

> If we wish to call Soul anything which has *perceptions* and *appetites* in the general sense which I have just explained, all created simple substances or Monads could be called Souls; but, since sensation is something more than a simple perception, I agree that the general names 'Monads' and 'Entelechies' suffice for simple substances, which have only the latter, and that we should call Souls only those which have *perception that is more distinct*, and is accompanied by memory.[12]

A moment's reflection, in any case, should be enough to establish that relative distinctness of perception cannot simply parallel the degree of conscious awareness in monads, despite the suggestions of McRae, Parkinson, and other Leibniz scholars.[13] For, as Robert Brandom has emphasized, Leibniz holds that monads *in general* differ from each other not in *what* they perceive—each perceives the whole universe—but in the degree of distinctness of their various perceptions.[14] Thus even bare monads will each have a unique mix of (relatively) confused and distinct perceptions of the world. Further, Leibniz supposes that physical relations like nearness are grounded at the metaphysical level in the relative distinctness of monads' perceptions of each other. Thus two wholly unconscious monads that are "next to" each other must perceive each other relatively distinctly. Also, "minds" are said to perceive "their own" bodies more distinctly than external bodies: but the objects of *conscious* perception, where such does exist, are often (in fact generally) external bodies.[15] What is needed, then, is an account of degrees of distinctness in perceptions which does not turn on degree of consciousness.

It is quite important, in approaching this problem, to avoid conflating Leibniz's view of *perceptions* as ranging from "confused" to "distinct", with his categorization of *concepts* as "obscure or clear", and "confused or distinct". The categorization of concepts pertains primarily to conscious, rational beings, and has to do with our ability to recognize instances of a given concept, and to explain the applicability of the concept to that instance.[16] Leibniz discusses the categorization of concepts frequently and at length. Although his accounts are not totally unproblematic or consistent, the difficulties are relatively manage-able and well-understood, compared to those presented by his distinct/confused distinction with respect to *perception*, particularly as it relates to the bare monads.

I turn now to Brandom's proposed solution to the latter interpretive problem.

II. CRITIQUE OF BRANDOM'S PROPOSAL

Turning away from the issue of consciousness, Brandom proposes the notion of "expressive range" of individual perceptions, as the basis for providing a more comprehensive account of Leibniz's distinction between distinct and confused perceptions.[17] Brandom develops his account by means of the following as-sumptions and stipulations. Every monad at any given time will express the whole universe through its total perceptual state. This is to say that by the "laws" of the world all the states of all the substances will be "deducible" or "inferable" from the perceptual state of any one of them. The perceptual state, however, comprises various individual perceptions, each of which will express a greater or lesser set of accidents of (its own or other) monads. (Brandom defines an 'accident' as a "non-maximal" property of a monad, or one that does not "contain" everything in the monad's complete concept.)[18] The number of accidents "enfolded" in *each perception* determines that perception's "expres-sive range". A perception is relatively distinct, in comparison with another, when the "expressive range" of the first properly includes the expressive range of the second.[19] A monad is more perfect, or perceives its world more distinctly, insofar as more about its world can be deduced from fewer of its perceptions (i.e. insofar as its perceptions have relatively great expressive ranges).

Brandom ingeniously expounds several advantages of this proposal which I will not attempt to cover here. I will rather pursue the more ungrateful course of sketching some problems that the proposal appears to present, which are not addressed by Brandom.

Brandom's proposal depends crucially on the possibility of distinguishing co-occurrent perceptions of a single monad. Thus, where **r** and **s** denote different accidents, it must make sense to distinguish the perceptual state of monad **M**, which includes a single perception "of" **r and s**, from the perceptual state of monad **N**, which includes a perception "of" **r**, and a *different* perception "of" **s**. Brandom deals with this issue of the individuation of perceptions only to the extent of postulating that individual perceptions, like perceiving substances, in-volve the expression of many things *in one*.[20] Now Leibniz tells us that we are familiar with the possibility of expressing many things in one, because "our soul provides us with an example."[21] If this remark is interpreted as an allusion to the unity of consciousness, it notably fails to provide for the expression of many things in several *individual* perceptions in the same substance at the same time. Leibniz does say:

> We ourselves experience a multitude in a simple substance when we find that *the slightest thought which we apperceive* enfolds a variety in the object.[22]

But does he think that we "apperceive" different such thoughts at the same time? If so, how is the *distinctness* of co-occurrent thoughts, *each* expressing a multiplicity, reconcilable with the absolute *unity* of self to which Leibniz appeals in explaining the notion of a monad? Neither Leibniz nor Brandom throws light on these questions. And even if they could be favorably resolved, we would probably not have gotten very far towards rendering intelligible the notion of various distinguishable simultaneous perceptions in an *unconscious* monad. In any case, Brandom's proposal appears to be very much a "reconstruction": an attempt to make out what Leibniz *could say* about distinct perception that bears only the most tenuous connection to what he actually does say.

The other major problem with Brandom's interpretation has to do with intensionality, or the supposed "representational" nature of all perceptions. Brandom asserts that his "deducibility" conception "allow[s] an intensional reading of expression."[23] His idea is that principles based on the harmony preestablished among the monads, by making possible inference from one monad's perception to the accidents of the others, provide content *internally accessible* to any given monad. He writes:

> A perception provides its monad with information about the rest of the world only insofar as the preestablished harmony provides principles (laws of Nature) which permit inferences from the occurrence of this particular perception, rather than any other possible one, to conclusions about facts outside that monad. We are assured of the existence of such principles only by metaphysical reasoning. The form in which that harmony manifests itself in the experience of particular monads is the physical or phenomenal world. It is accordingly facts couched in the phenomenal terms of *this* world that are the informational contents of perceptions as experienced by the monads those perceptions modify.[24]

In this passage Brandom speaks of monads as having experiences, and being provided with information, without explaining how such characterizations are appropriate for wholly unconscious substances.[25] Even if we assume that the laws of nature are somehow included in every monad, we cannot, I think, suppose that a non-conscious—indeed a non-rational—being makes "deductions."[26]

Brandom attempts to combine in his interpretation the notions of *external deducibility* and *internally accessible content or representationality*.[27] This effort is understandable, in view of the fact that the states under discussion are called 'perceptions', and that Leibniz regularly characterizes them as 'representations' (and substances in general as "representative" entities).[28] It may be, though, that part of Brandom's account can be salvaged just in case we jettison the requirement that the notions of distinct and confused perception in Leibniz be strictly tied up with that of internally accessible content. I will try to show in the next section that there is reasonable textual warrant for this move. But first I would like to digress briefly to indicate how the external-inference understanding of Leibnizian perception emerges in another passage of ingenious recent commentary: Benson Mates's attempt to refute the objection that there's something "paradoxical" in Leibniz's claim that the states of monads are just perceptions or mirrorings of the states of all the other monads.[29]

Mates cites several versions of this objection. The general drift is that the inter-perceiving substances that Leibniz posits can have no "content" for their perceptions: each perceives only the others perceiving itself perceiving the others. . . . Some have held that there is a "logical" or "quasi-logical" problem or inconsistency in the Leibnizian picture.

Mates responds by constructing a mathematical model which preserves many of the features of the monadology without a trace of paradox. I won't go into all the details here. The basic ideas can be indicated briefly, however. First, each monad in a given world (and also each world) is assigned a unique number according to the natural number series. The successive states of the monad are then represented by an ascending segment of the real number series that is systematically determined by the number of the monad. Any given real number is then cashed into a complete designation of simple properties or their complements which characterize the monad at a given time, by a correlation device involving the binary expansion of the reciprocal of the real number. Finally, monad 1 of the actual world becomes a "clock" for the world, by having its states correlated with amount of time elapsed since the Creation. In this model, as Mates notes, "Given the state of any actual monad at any time a sufficiently discerning mind will easily deduce the state of any other monad at that time."[30] The "sufficiently discerning mind" may be, presumably, a mind external to the monads in question. (And what mind, in general, would be sufficiently discerning except God's?) Mates's model, in other words, interprets "mirroring"—the mutual expression or representation of monads—wholly in terms of external inference, rather than intrinsically accessible intensionality. This feature is preserved in his (admittedly inadequate) attempt to provide for the distinction between confused and distinct perception in terms of his model.[31] He offers a "partial representation of this" in terms of the absolute values of the differences between different monadical numerical states. (Lower values will match with more distinct perception.) Mates is dissatisfied with his proposal because its results do not fit well with Leibniz's use of the distinction: for instance, it has the result that a monad will perceive its own past and future states more distinctly than those of any other monad at any time. What is of interest here, however, is just that Mates does not even consider a requirement that monadic inter-perception, and the distinct/confused distinction, be interpreted in terms of intrinsically accessible intensionality. His model is cast entirely in terms of relations between monads accessible to an *external* inferring mind.[32]

III. Mirroring without Internal Intensionality: Distinct "Perceptions" as God's Reasons

Pursuing the lines of thought of Brandom and Mates—but rejecting Brandom's spurious attempt to accommodate internal intensionality—one may propose that 'perception' in general for Leibniz connotes only external deducibility, not internally accessible intensionality or representation. One may propose, that is, that when Leibniz writes of bare monads perceiving each other, he means no more than that a suitably informed mind can make correct inferences from the state of either to that of the other. The following text seems encouraging in this regard:

> [T]he difference between intelligent substances and those which are not is as great as that between the mirror and him who sees.[33]

Mirrors, after all, do not utilize information, or represent *to themselves* external reality. Rather, they *alter in response to changes in external reality,* in a regular manner intelligible to a rational mind acquainted (explicitly or habitually) with the laws of reflection. (*I* "read off" from the mirror that the cat has just jumped onto the bed; the *mirror* knows nothing of this.) It might be objected that the reading I'm proposing collapses *perception* into *expression*—or "constant and rule-governed relation"—between the states of one thing and those of another, whereas Leibniz clearly understands perception as a special species of expression.[34] What is said to differentiate perception from expression in general, though, is just that in perception many things are expressed *in a unity* (i.e. in a substance or monad).[35] This stipulation does not by any means establish that perception requires internally accessible intensionality. And, it seems to me, Leibniz is quite willing to identify the representational feature of monadic perception in general simply with expression (in a simple substance).[36]

I have explained above (following Brandom) that Leibniz's distinction between *distinct* and *confused* perception cannot just be read as a distinction between *conscious* and *unconscious* perceptions, since it has to be applicable *within* the realm of wholly unconscious monads. For similar reasons, it cannot be identified with a distinction between perceptions that do possess internal intensionality, and those which merely "express the many in the one" in a way that allows external inference from the "perceiver" to the "perceived". For (I am supposing) bare monads do not *experience* representationally any more than they experience consciously. The question, then, is whether anything can be made of the distinction between distinct and confused perceptions that does not trade on either internal intensionality or the distinction between conscious and unconscious perceptions.[37]

Brandom's proposal, suitably purged of references to bare monads making "deductions" from "information" available to them, would be the right *type* of candidate. I have objected, however, that his proposal (in terms of "expressive ranges" of individual perceptions) requires a way of distinguishing co-occurrent perceptions independent of their respective objects, which is not supplied by either Brandom or Leibniz, and which also lacks textual basis: in fact, it sits uneasily with Leibniz's claim that a substance always has several perceptions, each of which "enfolds an infinity."

An alternative proposal, which clearly does have textual basis, goes as follows: a perceptual state **p** of monad **M** is *more distinct than* perceptual state **q** of monad **N**, insofar as **M's being p** *provides God's reason* for creating **N with q**, rather than the other way around.

Textual basis for this suggestion is found, for instance, in "Monadology" §§ 49–56. Leibniz explains that a monad is *active* in so far as it his *distinct* perceptions, *passive* in so far as its perceptions arc *confused*. One creature is said to be more *perfect* than another in so far as "there is found in the former a reason to account a priori for what is happening in the other"; and this is for the former to act on the latter. But since no created monad literally acts on another,

> [I]n the simple substances this influence of one monad upon another is but *ideal*, which can have its effect only through the intervention of God; in as much as in the Ideas of God a Monad reasonably requires that God in regulating the others from the beginning of things, have regard to it. For since one created Monad cannot have a physical influence on the interior of another, it is only in this way that one can have dependence on the other. (§.51; *Ger*, VI, p. 615)

Leibniz continues,

> And this is why actions and passions are mutual among creatures. For God, comparing two simple substances, finds in each reasons which oblige him to accommodate the other to it, and consequently what is active in certain respects, is passive according to another point of consideration . . . (§ 52)

Similarly Leibniz in the *Theodicy* links distinct perceptions with perfection and confused perceptions with imperfection, employing these concepts in an account of the mutual "dependence" of body and mind. He adds that the "actions" of simple substances upon each other should be understood along the same lines:

> That is, each is considered to act on the other according to the degree of its perfection, although this is only ideally and in the reasons for things, in that God has first regulated one substance on another, according to the perfection or imperfection that there is in each: although action and passion are always mutual in creatures, because one part of the reasons which serve to explain distinctly what happens, and which have served to cause it to exist (*a le faire exister*) is in one of the substances, and another part of these reasons is in the other, perfections and imperfections being always mixed and shared. (§ 66; *Ger* VI, 139)

This account, of course, remains on the most schematic level. It does not help us understand what the states of unconscious monads are *like*, or just how the state of one serves to explain, or give reason for, God's decision or regulation with respect to the others. And the account may present more formal problems as well. (Will it be possible to identify relative distinctness as superiority in the order of reasons in God's mind, while preserving the claim that monads "nearer to" each other perceive *each other* more distinctly than either perceives, or is perceived by, "more distant" monads?)

It is difficult, further, to see how coherently to combine this account with those passages that seem to indicate a strong association (at least) between "distinctness" of perceptions and consciousness. Apparently, conscious perceptions cannot simply be those which invariably have a rational priority in God's mind over those that are unconscious. True, Leibniz indicates that God has special care for spirits, and gives them the largest share of perfections that the universal harmony permits.[38] Still, Leibniz's way of accounting for the appearances of mind-body interaction (where there is no actual interaction between created beings) seems to require supposing that sensations (involuntary but consciously apprehended states, such as the pain of a pinprick) are harmonized with bodily occurrences, rather than the other way around.[39]

I will not attempt to deal further with these problems here. My claims with respect to the views expressed in the quoted passages are, for now, only the following. They—and not just the passages linking distinctness and consciousness—have to figure in any reasonable account of Leibniz's position on the confused/distinct distinction. Second, they allow us to suppose that the "perceptual" states of simple substances in general need not be attributed *internal* intensionality; rather, whatever they are, their relative distinctness may be understood in terms of their place in the order of reasons in *God's* mind. Third, they present us with an intriguing point of connection between Leibniz's notion of the confused/distinct distinction, and Spinoza's. In the next and final section I will briefly develop this last point.

IV. DISTINCT PERCEPTION AND GOD'S MIND: THE SPINOZA CONNECTION

Spinoza speaks of "consciousness" much less frequently than does Leibniz; his few remarks are fragmentary and unsystematic.[40] Keeping these points in mind, one may note that (first) in Spinoza, too, perception in general is conceptually separated from conscious experience; and (second) Spinoza also gives signs of postulating a link of some kind between consciousness and *distinct* perception. He holds, on the one hand, that not all appetites of a body reach consciousness—though surely, as "something that happens in the body," they must be "perceived". (*E*IIIp9s) And he asserts that even the less highly developed of *human* bodies—those less fit to do and suffer many things—have minds which are "for the most part unconscious . . ." (*E*Vp39s) On the other hand, minds, as just indicated, are to a greater degree conscious insofar as they belong to bodies fit for many things: these are the minds which are more fit for distinctly understanding.[41] At the same time, however, there is reason to resist linking distinct understanding very tightly with consciousness in Spinoza, too. For one thing, Spinoza also links consciousness to the endeavor to persist in being (which is indifferent to the distinction between distinct and confused ideas);[42] and to the existence in God of ideas (not only of bodies, but) of those ideas—distinct *and* confused—which constitute the "minds" of bodies.[43]

I would like to suggest another point of comparison between Spinoza and Leibniz before getting to what is, for present purposes, the main issue. I have claimed that it is wrong to suppose that, for Leibniz, 'perception' connotes, at least, internally accessible intensionality or representationality (even if it doesn't connote consciousness). I am inclined to think that this point holds for Spinoza, as well. To say that a mind perceives its body is not to say that it is consciously aware of its body; and it is certainly not to say that the mind holds within itself, "representatively", an entity which may or may not happen to exist on its own.[44] For these reasons, efforts to interpret "perception" in the *Ethics* as representational in the Cartesian sense seem misguided.[45]

In any case, Spinoza's understanding of the distinction between distinct (or adequate) and confused (or inadequate) perception, like Leibniz's, falls well outside the Cartesian framework. The knowledge of a body is adequate, according to Spinoza, just in case that knowledge is comprehended in the right way within the system of ideas expressing the true causal order. With respect to particular finite things human ideas derived from ordinary experience are always inadequate, because the human mind is limited to perceiving its own body, and external things through their effects on that body only.[46] The point is best expressed in the Proofs of *Ethics* IIp24 and p25. First, with respect to the mind's ideas of its own body:

> . . . [T]he idea or knowledge of any component part [of the human body] will be in God (*E*II.9) . . . in so far as he is considered as affected by another idea of a particular thing, a particular thing which is prior in Nature's order to the part itself (*E*II.7) . . . [A]nd so, of any component part of the human body there is knowledge in God in so far as he is affected by very many ideas of things, and not in so far as he has the idea only of the human body . . . So (*E*II.11c) the human mind does not involve adequate knowledge of the component parts of the human body.

Then, with respect to the (finite) mind's knowledge of external bodies:

> We have shown that the idea of an affection of the human body involves the nature of an external body in so far as the external body determines the human body in some definite way (*E*II.16). But in so far as the external body is an individual thing that is not related to the human body, the idea of knowledge of it is in God (*E*II.9) in so far as God is considered as affected by the idea of another thing which is (*E*II.7) prior in nature to the said external body. Therefore an adequate knowledge of the external body is not in God in so far as he has the idea of an affection of the human body; i.e. the idea of an affection of the human body does not involve an adequate knowledge of an external body.

The contrast between inadequate and adequate knowledge of a given bodily state, then, is presented as a contrast between ideas that God has just in so far as he constitutes the mind of that body, or of the body whose state is (partially) caused by that body; and the ideas God has in so far as his intellect is infinite. The ideas that God has insofar as he is infinite contain ideas of bodies "prior in nature"—i.e. in the causal chain—to the body whose affection is immediately in question. Perhaps, then, the distinction between confused and adequate ideas consists in a distinction between ideas considered as isolated from causes (or from causes of causes), and those which contain or include the whole infinite series of causes that determines any bodily affection. (After all, Spinoza does characterize inadequate sensory knowledge as fragmented or "mutilated," or as "conclusions without premises".)

This explanation cannot be quite right, however, for the following reason.[47] Axiom 4 of Part I, on which Spinoza's explanation of external perception explicitly turns, is regressive in structure: it stipulates that the cause of any effect is known in knowing the effect. It follows, apparently, that to know an effect is to know its cause, *and* the cause of its cause, and so on, *ad infinitum* (assuming, as Spinoza does, that the chain of (finite) causes is infinite). And from *this* it seems to follow that God in so far *merely* as he constitutes the mind of a given body will in some sense have the idea of all the causes of the affections of that body, and of *their* causes, etc. Why then would this knowledge not itself count as adequate?

To this question I propose the following answer. The distinction between adequate and inadequate knowledge consists not in a difference of the *infinite extent* of the causal chains "involved" in the two cases, but rather in the complexity and ordering of the infinite causal knowledge respectively required. Thus, God in so far as he constitutes a finite mind knows physical affections *only* in their relation to the body that is that mind's object. But God qua infinite intellect knows physical affections in *all* their relations with *all* bodies, and in the correct, "internal" order of priority.

On this account Spinoza can make good on the distinction between confused and adequate knowledge *without* supposing that the former is "fragmented" in the specific sense of not involving an infinite regress of causes. *Any* perception or "knowledge" of a (determinate) bodily affection involves an infinitely iterated series of perceptions or knowledge of bodily causes. Thus, on my reading, Spinoza like Leibniz holds that perception in general expresses the infinite.[48]

What I want particularly to stress here, however, is that Spinoza's position connects in an interesting way with Leibniz's account of the distinct/confused distinction as I have explained it above. For Leibniz the perception of one monad is distinct relative to another if the former *provides the reason for the existence or occurrence of the latter*, as mediated by God's understanding. For Spinoza, a perception is distinct in so far as it is suitably grasped in relation to other ideas prior to it in the order of nature, or (in other words) in the total causal system of ideas in God's understanding. In both cases, then distinctness is explained in relation to the causal order as understood by God.[49]

There are also important differences, of course. For Spinoza causality obtains directly among finite entities, whereas for Leibniz, causality between monads is purely "ideal". For Leibniz the perception *in a monad* is distinct in so far as *it is* a reason; whereas for Spinoza a perception is distinct *in God* in so far as it is comprehended in the right way *within the system* of reasons or causes. In each case, however, the distinction between distinct and confused perception is closely bound up with the tenets of a rationalist, theocentric, metaphysical system.[50]

NOTES

1. Translations are my own from the Gebhardt edition, vol. 2.

2. See, for instance, Leibniz's running discussion of this issue with an incredulous Arnauld, in Leibniz: Ger, vol. 2, pp. 74–75, 90–91, 112–113. (Translations are my own.)

3. Spinoza formally distinguishes 'perception' (as connoting mental passivity) and 'conception' (as connoting activity) (*Ethics* IIdf3, Explication), but does not rigorously observe the distinction in practice. He freely interchanges both terms with 'idea' and 'knowledge' (*cognitio*). (For more detailed discussion of this point see my paper, "Spinoza's Causal Axiom (*Ethics* I, axiom 4)," in *God and Nature: Spinoza's Metaphysics* (Leyden: Brill, 1991) (chapter 10 of this volume). Leibniz, unlike Spinoza (and Descartes), quite carefully distinguishes ideas (or concepts) from perceptions, using 'confused' and 'distinct' to mark differences within both categories of 'mental' states. Here I am concerned with the distinct/confused *perception* distinction in Leibniz. (I touch on this point again briefly below.)

4. Edwin Curley, Henry E. Allison, and Alan Donagan all stress, in recent works, that Spinoza does not really mean to hold such "absurd" or "wildly implausible" or "paradoxical" opinions as that all things are conscious, or that the human mind is explicitly conscious of all that happens in its body; and they tie this point in with the distinction between distinct and confused perception. See Curley, *Behind the Geometrical Method* (Princeton: Princeton University Press, 1988) pp. 70ff.; Allison, *Benedict de Spinoza: An Introduction*, revised edition (New Haven: Yale University Press, 1987) pp. 94ff. (despite the publication dates Allison's position was influenced by Curley's); Alan Donagan, *Spinoza* (Chicago: University of Chicago Press, 1988) pp. 125ff. (For a contrary view, see T.L.S. Sprigge, *Theories of Existence* (New York: Pelican, 1984).) Curley and Allison go so far as to propose that when Spinoza says that everything is animated, in virtue of there being in God an idea of every body, he means only that everything is "alive"—and *this* only in the rather idiosyncratic sense that to everything belongs a force whereby the thing perseveres in its being. This cannot be correct, however: for the endeavor itself pertains to God's modes generally (*E*IIIp6), whereas "idea" is specifically mental. The commentaries on Leibniz I particularly have in mind here are those of McRae, Parkinson, and Furth, cited below.

5. I discuss this point at somewhat greater length in "The Phenomenalisms of Leibniz and Berkeley," in Ernest Sosa, editor, *Essays on the Philosophy of George Berkeley* (Dordrecht: Reidel, 1987) pp. 8–10 (chapter 21 of this volume).

6. Although I will briefly return to Spinoza at the end of the paper, I will not be able to substantiate in detail my suggestion that recent attempts to rescue Spinoza's statements about perception from undue "paradox", by emphasis on the distinct/confused distinction, are insufficiently well worked out. The main ground of my concern (apart from the one explained in note 4) is that the attempts do not seem adequately to reflect the actual language of *E*IIp12 and its proof; namely, that the *idea, perception, knowledge* of whatever happens in the human body is necessarily in the human mind (since knowledge of that thing is in God, in so far as he constitutes that mind). This would seem, at best, a strange way of putting the point that when I step on a tack I feel pain (to follow Curley's example)—especially in view of the fact that many forms of damage (or benefit) to the body do not seem to reach consciousness *at all*. Donagan, in *Spinoza*, makes a sustained effort to deal with this problem. But it seems to me his case holds only if one allows a slide from the claim that the mind does not have *adequate* cognition of its body,

the affections of its body, etc., to the claim that the mind *doesn't cognize* the parts or affections of its body, etc. (lacking as it does a God's eye grasp of their causes, and their relations to other things). (See *Spinoza*, p. 129.) He seems to need the second, stronger assertion, but he doesn't show how to derive it, and he doesn't explain just how it relates to the proposition immediately under discussion: that the mind does perceive, or know, everything that happens in its body. (Thus I am not persuaded that he in fact answers, as he purports to, problems about Spinoza's position as I posed them in an earlier paper. Incidentally, the objection he attributes to me on p. 127 about the subject of ideas in Spinoza, and which he understandably dismisses, is not one I have ever advanced.)

7. R. Brandom, "Leibniz on Degrees of Perception," *Journal of the History of Philosophy*, 19 (1981) pp. 447–479.

8. R. McRae, *Leibniz: Perception, Apperception, and Thought* (Toronto: University of Toronto Press, 1976) p. 36.

9. G.H.R. Parkinson, "The 'Intellectualization of Appearances'", in M. Hooker, editor, *Leibniz: Critical and Interpretive Essays* (Minneapolis: Minnesota University Press, 1982) p. 6.

10. Parkinson, pp. 7–8.

11. "Monadology," §24; *Ger.* VI, p. 611; see also *Ger.* VII, p. 317, quoted by Parkinson: "If the perception is more distinct, it makes a sensation."

12. "Monadology" § 19, *Ger.* VI, p. 610; emphasis added. As Parkinson stresses, Leibniz also calls sensations "confused", even though we are conscious of the sensation, because we are not conscious of the infinitely many perceptions that constitute the sensation. See, e.g., *Ger.* IV, p. 459, and Parkinson, p. 7. (Parkinson, however, seems to alternate between treating 'confusion' as strictly a property of mixed perceptions (sensations) and treating it as a property that can apply to their elements as well.)

13. See also Montgomery Furth, "Monadology" in Harry G. Frankfurt, ed., *Leibniz: A Collection of Critical Essays* (Garden City, New York: Doubleday-Anchor Books, 1972). The essay is reprinted from the *Philosophical Review*, 1967.

14. See, for instance, *Ger.* II, p. 90 (from the Arnauld correspondence): "Monadology" § 60, *Ger.* VI, p. 617.

15. See "Monadology," §§ 60, 62; also Brandom, "Leibniz on Degrees of Perception," pp. 451–53.

16. This point is discussed in detail in the works by McRae and Parkinson already cited, as well as by Brandom. See also my paper, "Confused Ideas," *Rice University Studies in Philosophy* (1977), pp. 123–137 (chapter 22 of this volume). Conscious sensation is typically linked with confused *ideas* in Leibniz: we identify, for instance, red things by the sensory experience we have of them, but cannot articulate a "mark" or criterion of redness (i.e. we have a clear but confused idea of the quality). In so far as Leibniz *does* link consciousness with distinctness of *perception*, we would here have a case of a distinct perception joined to a confused idea. (There are, however, further subtleties with respect to this issue, having to do, especially with the fact that Leibniz tends to characterize (consciously apprehended) sensations as clear but confused. For discussion of this point see Parkinson's essay.)

17. The core of Brandom's account is presented on pp. 460–464 of "Leibniz on Degrees of Perception." He, too, notes that Leibniz links "distinctness" or "heightenedness" of perception with conscious awareness or knowledge in numerous passages. (p. 451) He concludes that distinctness is (only) a *necessary* condition for conscious *perception* in Leibniz's theory. (The idea/perception distinction, discussed above, must be kept in mind here.) This is one (partial) solution to relating the passages in which distinctness is linked

to consciousness to those concerning perceptions in bare monads. And I agree that some of Leibniz's statements can be read in this way. It seems to me, however, that Leibniz rather too often implies that consciousness *just goes with* distinct perception for this proposal to be altogether satisfactory. Below I'll make some further remarks on this problem; but I do not yet see a really good solution.

18. Brandom, "Leibniz on Degrees of Perception," p. 460. Brandom relates this understanding of 'accident' to one of Leibniz' own definitions.

19. Brandom, "Leibniz on Degrees of Perception," p. 463.

20. Brandom, "Leibniz on Degrees of Perception," p. 461.

21. Leibniz to Arnauld, *Ger.* II, p. 112.

22. "Monadology," § 16, *Ger.* VI, p. 609. Emphasis added.

23. Brandom, "Leibniz on Degrees of Perception, p. 460.

24. Brandom, "Leibniz on Degrees of Perception, p. 462.

25. Brandom himself points out the logical pitfalls in moving from conscious to unconscious "perceptions" on p. 459 of "Leibniz on Degrees of Perception."

26. This point, too, is stressed by Brandom elsewhere in his paper.

27. The distinction in question is not a very subtle one and probably requires no elaboration. Here, however, is a simple illustration of what I have in mind. Suppose a flower-lover has a "law" about the disposition of plants in her house, such that (a) there is always one plant per room; (b) the plants are changed simultaneously at the beginning of every month; (c) the same type of plant is never placed in the same room twice in a year; and (d) there is a fixed specification of what type of plant goes in each room each month. Thus in December there is a fir tree in the living room, a poinsettia in the dining room, an amaryllis in the kitchen . . . ; in April, azalea in the living room, tulips in dining room, hydrangea in the kitchen. Then any one who knows the "law" can deduce the types of plants in other rooms from what appears in any one room. But this is not to say that the plants have intensional states, nor even that the poinsettia represents the amaryllis in the kitchen . . . Of course the analogy is loose: most importantly, no simple substances appear in it. But whether "simplicity" or metaphysical unity should be taken to bring with it intensionality or internally accessible representation is, precisely, one of the points that will be at issue.

28. See e.g. "Monadology," § 60, *Ger.* VI, pp. 616–617.

29. Benson Mates, *The Philosophy of Leibniz* (Oxford: Clarendon Press, 1986) pp. 78–83.

30. Mates, *The Philosophy of Leibniz*, p. 82.

31. Mates recognizes, obliquely, that the individuation of monads depends on this distinction. I say obliquely, because Mates poses the problem in terms "of the different 'degrees of clarity' with which the various monads of the actual world are said to perceive one another." (*The Philosophy of Leibniz*, p. 83) As Brandom stresses, however, the term 'distinctness'—not 'clarity'—should be used in this context.

32. In an earlier version of this paper, presented at the Iowa Ideas Conference and also at an MIT philosophy colloquium, I asserted quite definitely that the line of objection to which Mates is replying assumes an *intensional* interpretation of mirroring—and that therefore Mate's model is beside the point. I now want to retract this claim. I still think, however, that Mates's argument needs supplementation to avoid the appearance of *ignoratio elenchi* (but for a different reason). It still seems to me that the original objections turn on a point not addressed directly by Mates: that monads' states are *nothing* but reflections of each other. This point, I think, is at least partly independent of the issue about internal intensionality. To avoid the appearance of *ignoratio elenchi*, then, Mates

needs to add to his model an explicit rejection of the view that monads' states are *nothing but* reflections of the states of other monads. I'm inclined to think that he is textually entitled to do this; but I will not carry this issue further here.

33. "Discourse on Metaphysics," § 35, *Ger.* II, p. 460.

34. See, for instance, *Ger.* II, p. 112.

35. See e.g. *Ger.* II, pp. 121, 311. Sometimes, as we've seen, infinitely many "sentiments" are said to be unified in a perception which itself is unified with others *in a simple substance*.

36. See Leibniz's remarks to Arnauld on the subject of perception in non-conscious substances, *Ger.* II, pp. 112–113. He writes, for instance, "our soul . . . will have some thought of all the motions in the universe, and I hold that every other soul or substance will have some perception or expression of them." Of course intensionality does come into perception or representation in the conscious range. In one of the passages associating consciousness with distinctness Leibniz writes: "A soul can read in itself only what is distinctly represented in it . . . " ("Monadology," § 61, *Ger.* p. 617) (This is another passage that literally fits Brandom's "necessary condition" reading of the distinctness/consciousness relationship.)

37. Ideally, of course, an account of the distinction would *both* provide an explanation of how it applies within the realm of bare monads, *and* make sense of the passages which appear to tie distinct perception to consciousness. As indicated above, however, I won't provide such a comprehensive account here (though I conclude the present section with a further note on the problem).

38. See *Ger.* IV, p. 461.

39. See, for instance, *Ger.* II, p. 114. Here, as always when discussing the mind-body relation, Leibniz is particularly concerned to inculcate the view that the soul's states arise from its own internal laws, and do not come about as the result of actual physical causality. But the account of the experience of a pinprick seems to me to accord a certain *priority* to the physical state in the order of reasons which would fit well with the account of (relatively) distinct perception I have discussed in this section. The connection, however, is admittedly not made explicitly.

40. I discuss this point in detail in "Objects, Ideas, and 'Minds'," in R. Kennington, editor, *The Philosophy of Baruch Spinoza*, Catholic University of America Press, 1980 (chapter 9 of this volume).

41. *Ethics* IIp13s, V.39. The explicit reference to consciousness occurs in the latter passage, in connection with the *body's* "fitness for many things"; but the latter phrase is linked with the mind's fitness for distinctly understanding in *E*II.13s. It should be noted that since distinct understanding is, arguably, present throughout nature according to Spinoza's system, even a tight connection between distinct understanding and consciousness would not yield a result desired for Spinoza by common sense commentators: that consciousness is not supposed to be ubiquitous throughout nature, even though perception is. See *Ethics* IIp38–p39, and my discussion of these passages in "Objects, Ideas, and 'Minds'".

42. *Ethics*, IIIp9.

43. The proof of *E*IIIp9, just cited, relies on *E*IIp23, which holds that the mind "knows itself, insofar as it perceived the ideas of the affections of the Body."

44. If the mind, which perceives the body, or has it for its object, exists, so must the body. (*Ethics*, IIp11)

45. Here again I have reservations about the discussions by Curley and Donagan cited earlier.

46. Spinoza does, however, accord to humans some capacity for achieving "knowledge of the third kind", which proceeds "from an adequate idea of the formal essence of certain attributes of God to adequate knowledge of the essence of things." (*Ethics*, IIp40s2; cf. Vp25–p29)

47. What follows is an abbreviated version of an argument from my paper, "Spinoza's Causal Axiom." It should be noted that Amy Robinson discussed the infinite regress problem still earlier, in a draft of her dissertation on Spinoza's theory of perceptions, "The Problems in Spinoza's Theory of Sense Perception" (Princeton University, 1991).

48. There are of course differences: Leibniz holds that any monad, at any time, expresses the whole world, past, present, and future. There is no suggestion in Spinoza's position that the idea of a physical state or occurrence expresses its future effects as well as its causes. (This point was made by Edwin Curley in commenting on an earlier version of my paper.)

49. Of course other interesting points of comparison exist as well. For instance, both Spinoza and Leibniz utilize the distinction between distinct and confused perception to provide for the distinction between mental activity and passivity while denying mind-body interaction. (In Spinoza this distinction paves the way for the highly intellectualistic account of virtue and human salvation that dominates the final Parts of the *Ethics*; Leibniz does not provide such a developed account of these issues.) Many specific Spinozistic turns of phrase pop up—coincidentally or otherwise—in Leibnizian texts, for example:

> God produces different substances according to the different views that he has of the universe. . . . God turning, so to speak, on all sides and in all ways the general system of phenomena which he finds it good to produce to manifest his glory, and regarding all the faces of the world in all possible manners, since there is no aspect (*rapport*) which escapes his omniscience; the result of each view of the universe, as regarded from a certain place, is substance which expresses the universe conformably with this view, if God finds it good to render his thought efficacious and to produce this substance. And since God's view is always true, our perceptions are as well, it is our judgements that are of ourselves and that deceive us.

> [God] sees the universe not only as [individuals] see it, but also quite differently than they do.

> (God of course perceives only distinctly; created substances are differentiated from divinity as well as from each other by confused perceptions.)

The quotations are from "Discourse on Metaphysics," § 14: *Ger*. IV, pp. 439–40; and (for the first) Leibniz, *Discourse on Metaphysics*, translated and edited by Peter G. Lucas and Leslie Grint (Manchester: Manchester University Press, 1953) pp. 22–3. (Lucas and Grint include the caption from the diplomatic edition which is not in Gerhardt.)

50. I wish to thank faculty and students of the MIT philosophy department for extensive discussions of an earlier version of this paper, which had the invaluable effect of making me aware of how much further work was required. I regret that time limitations have prevented me from making even further use of points raised by the discussions. I also am grateful to Edwin Curley for his comments at the conference on "Ideas: Sensory Experience, Thought, Knowledge, and Their Objects," held at the University of Iowa, April, 1989. They have had limited direct effect on the present version only because it largely omits the original portions on which his comments focussed.

Leibniz and Locke on "First Truths"

IN THE XVIIth century the venerable Aristotelian-Scholastic doctrine that the principle of non-contradiction is the first truth of knowledge became a focus of philosophical controversy. Quietly rejected by Descartes, the doctrine was finally made the object of an all-out attack by Locke.[1] The impatience of these "moderns" with the Scholastic position is understandable. If the principle was intelligibly to be regarded as the foundation of certain knowledge, it must be shown how other certain or necessary truths could be reduced to or derived from it, and this the Scholastics had not effectively done. Moreover, both Descartes and Locke were convinced that quite a large number of other truths (Locke says "almost infinitely" many) are also "self-evident": that is, can immediately be perceived to be true merely by considering the ideas involved.[2] These, they hold, constitute a large class of primary truths to which no other proposition, including the principle of non-contradiction, may intelligibly be regarded as prior. However, this modern denial of the Scholastic doctrine had its own opponents. In particular Leibniz, who was dismayed by the subjectivist tendencies which he discerned in the Cartesian intuitivist approach to knowledge, strongly defended the absolute priority (and exclusive self-evidence) of the principle of non-contradiction within the domain of necessary truth. (The principle of non-contradiction includes in Leibniz's formulation, the principles of identity and excluded middle. How many sorts of propositions he believed to fall within "the domain of necessary truth" is a difficult and obscure question,[3] but this class included for him *at least* all of logic and mathematics—disciplines from which Descartes and Locke took many of their examples of "self-evident truths.")

Leibniz's defense of the importance of the principle of non-contradiction is prosecuted with particular vigor in the *Nouveaux essais sur l'entendement humain*, in which he offers point by point replies to Locke's attack in the *Essay*.

Behind this defense lies Leibniz's view that all of arithmetic, geometry, and logic can in fact be reduced to identities by formal "geometrical" demonstration: i.e., by the substitution of definientia for definienda.[4] Since this view is now discredited, and since the exclusive primacy of the principle of non-contradiction is no longer a major philosophical question, it might be supposed that the conflict between Leibniz and Locke on this matter can safely be consigned to the realm of dead issues. However, a close comparison of Locke's attack upon, and Leibniz's defense of, the doctrine of the primacy of the principle of non-contradiction (identity), reveals some fundamental conceptual differences of more general interest and significance. Locke and Leibniz are found to be divided not only on the question whether the principle of non-contradiction (identity) *is* the "first truth of knowledge," but, more basically, on the question of what it is for a proposition to *be* a "first truth of knowledge." The depth of their opposition on this issue is, however, partly concealed by the fact that both indicate that a proposition's being non-derivative or primary is equivalent to its being "self-evident."

In this paper I shall examine the conflicting views of Locke and Leibniz concerning the dependence of one proposition upon another within the domain of necessary truth, assuming this to include at least arithmetic, geometry, and logic. I shall first show that their different conceptions of what it is for one truth to be dependent upon, or posterior to another, are bound up with quite different conceptions of the nature of a principle or "maxim." To establish this point it will be necessary to consider their respective conceptions of the relation between a maxim and its instances. Secondly, I shall argue that their apparently contradictory positions on the question whether non-identical necessary truths can be self-evident are actually predicated on different understandings of "self-evidence." Leibniz, as I shall point out, has two different ways of arguing for the exclusive self-evidence of the principle of non-contradiction: one of these approaches is incoherent; the other does not constitute a direct reply to Locke since it clearly assumes the *Leibnizian* conception of what constitutes a "first truth of knowledge."

In conclusion, I shall consider briefly Locke's well-known contention (in the chapter, "Of Trifling Propositions") that the principles of identity and non-contradiction and their instances[5] (together with definitional truths) are actually the *least* important of all certain truths—and in a class by themselves—because they alone "convey no real knowledge." Leibniz's handling of this dismissal of identities as "merely trifling" seems to me interesting, and more justifiable than has sometimes been supposed. (An incidental outcome of the discussion will be the suggestion that this phase of Locke's attack on the "magnified maxims" is inconsistent with some of his earlier arguments.)

I. THE RELATION OF MAXIMS TO THEIR INSTANCES

As one aspect of his general attack on "magnified maxims," Locke argues at some length that a particular truth is in no sense less "evident" than the general maxim of which it is an instance. "Equals taken from equals the remainder will be equal" has no "clearer self-evidence" than the following particular instance of it: "If you take from the five fingers of the one hand two, and from the five fingers of the other hand two, the remaining numbers will be equal."[6] Similarly, he claims that both the general maxim "whatsoever is, is"—Locke's usual formulation of the principle of identity—and such instances of it as "a man is a man," are perfectly and equally self-evident. But on this particular point Leibniz has no quarrel with Locke whatsoever: he merely points out the superior usefulness, in science, of the most general formulation.

It is true, and I have already remarked that it is as evident to say ecthetically in particular A is A, as to say in general, something is that which it is.[7] . . . As to the axiom of Euclid, applied to the fingers of the hand, I am ready to agree that it is as easy to conceive what you say in respect to the fingers, as to see it in respect to A and B, but in order not to do the same thing often, we mark it generally and after that it is enough to make subsumptions [il suffit de faire des subsomtions]. Otherwise it would be as if a calculus of particular numbers were preferred to universal rules, which would be to obtain less than one can.[8]

In fact, in the *Nouveaux essais* and in other writings, Leibniz sometimes remarks that the number of primitives will be "infinite" since it will include not only the general formulation of the principle of non-contradiction (identity) but also all particular immediate instances of it, such as "A rectangle is a rectangle," etc.[9]

A conflict arises between Locke and Leibniz not on the question of the "evidence" of instances, but on the question of their relation to the maxims of which they are instances. For Locke denies that what he himself calls the particular "instances" of maxims have any intrinsic relationship to the maxims of which they are instances, and this conclusion Leibniz cannot accept.

On Locke's view maxims and instances are separate and independent truths, connected only extrinsically, in as much as the mind exercises the same sort of perception in apprehending the truth of both. His formulation of this position is, in part, as follows:

Whenever the mind with attention considers any proposition, so as to perceive the two ideas signified by the terms, and affirmed or denied one of the other to be the same or different; it is presently and infallibly certain of the truth of such a proposition; and this equally whether these propositions be in terms standing for more general ideas, or such as are less so: e.g. whether the general idea of Being be affirmed of itself, as in this proposition, "whatsoever is, is"; or a more particular idea be affirmed of itself, as "a man is a man"; or "whatsoever is white is white". . .[10]

Implicit in this passage is Locke's general conception of knowledge as involving essentially *a comparison of the ideas* signified respectively by the subject and predicate terms of a proposition:

A man is said to know any proposition, which having been once laid before his thoughts, he evidently perceives the agreement or disagreement of the ideas whereof it consists. . . .[11]

To know that "a man is a man" is a true proposition is a matter, then, of perceiving the "agreement" of the idea of man (subject) with the idea of man (predicate); in precisely the same way, to know that "whatsoever is, is" is a matter of perceiving the agreement of the idea of "being" (subject) with the idea of "being" (predicate). To this extent, the "general axiom" and the "particular instance" are epistemologically on a level. Locke thus seems to hold that a separate intuition of the "sameness" of the ideas that constitute for him the meaning of the terms of a proposition is necessary to establish the truth of each of the indefinitely large number of identicals.[12]

This position may be supposed to represent the extreme of antiformalism. For it involves the implication that a principle is something generated by the comparison of ideas and dependent for its character on the character of the "ideas" compared. We recognize the truth of an identity not by recognizing a valid formal schema, but by intuiting a relationship between the subject and predicate "ideas." These ideas must therefore be determinate and fully understood: in the most general statement of the principle of identity the terms must be thought of as signifying the determinate idea of "being," and not as variables.[13] (As I shall point out below, Locke himself appears to move to a different, more "formalistic" view in a later part of the *Essay*.) This position has, therefore, the curious result that if particular identicals are to be regarded as "instances" of the principle of identity at all, it can only be in the sense that "cerulean is cerulean" is an "instance" of "blue is blue": i.e., the relation of instance to maxim is at best reduced to a matter of the extension of a more particular *term* being comprehended in that of a more general term.

It should also be noticed that while there is nothing odd about Locke's conception of which truths *are* "instances of the principle of identity" ("white is white," etc.), his comparison theory of knowledge leads him to an unusual understanding of what constitutes an "instance" of the principle of non-contradiction. Just as we apprehend the truth of the principle of identity by perceiving the agreement or sameness of the subject and predicate ideas, so, he maintains, we apprehend the truth of the principle of non-contradiction ("it is impossible for the same thing to be and not to be") by perceiving the *disagreement* or *difference* between the idea of being and the idea of not-being. Accordingly, Locke treats all statements of the disagreement or difference of particular ideas as bearing the same relation to the principle of non-contradiction as "white is white" bears to the principle of identity.[14] And of course the former category, while presumably including such uncontroversial "non-contradictories" as "red is not-red" ("red" and "not-red" signifying *different* ideas), also includes such favorite examples of Locke's as "a man is not a horse"; "red is not blue"— truths the denials of which are, as we should say, not formally self-contradictory.

Leibniz replies to this phase of Locke's argument against the primacy of "maxims" by maintaining that in an important sense maxims and their instances should not be regarded as separate truths:[15]

> To say that the body is larger than the trunk, does not differ from the axiom of Euclid [that a whole is greater than its part], except in that his axiom is limited to what is essential [se borne à ce qu'il faut précisément]: but in instantiating it and giving it body, one makes the intelligible sensible, because to say that a certain whole is larger than a certain one of its parts is in effect the proposition that a whole is larger than its parts, but with the features charged with a certain coloring or addition, as when one says AB, he says A. Thus one must not oppose the axiom and

the instance as different truths in this respect, but consider the axiom as incorporated in the instance and rendering the instance true.

It is evident from this passage that Leibniz is advancing a radically different conception of the nature of a principle from that assumed by Locke. As we have seen, Locke would regard the suggestion that "a man is a man" *incorporates* the principle of identity as nonsensical on the grounds that since the two propositions involve different ideas they are necessarily different and independent: on Locke's view no sense at all could be given to the statement that two propositions involving different ideas are "true by the same principle." A maxim or principle is, according to Locke, merely an assertion of an intuitable relation between relatively "general" ideas. For Leibniz, on the other hand, a principle may be given independently of any specific ideas, as the expression of a valid formal schema. Thus it exists, as it were, "above the level" of ideas,[16] so that it is perfectly intelligible to speak of "substituting different ideas in the same principle," and hence to speak of two different statements being true by the same principle. A principle is a matter of the "configuration" of ideas and not of their character:

> Whoever knows that ten is more than nine, that the body is larger than the finger, and that a house is too large to escape out the door, knows each of these particular propositions by the same general reason, which is, as it were, incorporated and colored in the particular [par une même, raison générale qui y est comme incorporée et enluminée], just as you see features charged with colors, where the proportion and configuration are properly constituted of the features, whatever the color may be [consiste proprement dans les traits, quelle que soit la couleur].[17]

Similarly, Leibniz had stated in a much earlier writing: "It is certain that identical propositions are necessary without any understanding or resolution of the terms, for I know that A is A, regardless of what is understood by A."[18]

In accordance with this understanding of the relation between principle and instance, Leibniz is able consistently to treat as immediate instances of the principle of non-contradiction only those truths which retain the form, A is not not-A, substituting the same term for both A's. This is, indeed, his normal procedure.[19] It is clear, however, from several passages in the *Nouveaux essais*, that he was not at all sure how to handle Locke's favorite examples of "instances" of this principle, which Leibniz characterizes as "disparates." An examination of this problem would take us too far from the present subject: it may be noted, however, that while Leibniz appears to incline at one point to the (implausible) view that such propositions as "yellowness is not sweetness" must be reducible to express instances of the principle of non-contradiction,[20] he elsewhere characterizes them as a separate class of primitive truths, which are *not* true by the principle of non-contradiction.[21]

We may now turn to Locke's and Leibniz's respective views of what it is for one truth to depend on, or be derived from, or be grounded in another. Locke, while denying there is any intrinsic relationship between a maxim and its "instances," maintains that a relation of priority may be established by considering which truth—axiom or instance—is first apprehended by the individual. And from this point of view it is clear to Locke that the "instances" must be regarded as prior to the "maxims," since particular ideas are (he claims) apprehended by the individual earlier than general ideas, with the result that a person is aware that a man is a man, for instance, well before he is ready to bear witness to the fact that everything is identical with itself:

> Cannot a country wench know that, having received a shilling from one that owes her three, and a shilling also from another that owes her three, the remaining debts in each of their hands are equal? Cannot she know this, I say, unless she fetch the certainty of it from this maxim, that *if you take equals from equals the remainder will be equals*, a maxim which possibly she never heard or thought of? I desire any one to consider, from what has been elsewhere said, which is known first and clearest by most people, the particular instance or the general rule, and which it is that gives life and birth to the other.[22]

Leibniz, in reply, seems to suggest that Locke has simply misconceived or misunderstood what is really at issue:

> It is not a question here of the history of our discoveries, which is different for different men, but of the connection and natural order of truths [de la liaison et de l'ordre naturel des veritez], which is always the same.[23]

The fact that a person may be aware of the truth that "a man is a man" before he has ever thought or heard of the principle of identity is completely irrelevant, according to Leibniz, to the question whether the one *proposition* should be regarded as prior to the other. The latter question must be understood as having to do with the relation of *logical* (or as Leibniz rather puts it, *natural*) priority.

What Leibniz fails to observe is that there is simply no room in Locke's philosophy for the notion of a logical or "natural" order of truths as Leibniz understands it. It is not the case that Locke merely overlooks the fact that a formal relation among propositions is what is in question. Rather, Locke has resolutely turned his back on the whole notion of a formal order. There is no aspect of a proposition which is in any way independent of the character of the ideas involved: i.e., there is no isolable formal aspect which it is the purpose of a general axiom to express. But this means that Leibniz's notion of a logically derivative truth is in general excluded by Locke's "comparison" theory of knowledge and the resulting conception of a principle, since, like the notion of an instance, it assumes the intelligibility of *substituting* different terms in the same principle, or of instantiating variables.

This is not to say that "derivation" of one truth from another can have no sense for Locke, but that it can have no sense wholly independent of "the history of our discoveries." Thus, Locke also speaks of a "clear and fit order" among truths, in which they should be laid out "to make their connexion and force be plainly and easily perceived"; and of "the dependence of the conclusion on all the parts." But the "order of truths" is, for Locke, dependent on the "natural order of ideas"—an expression which he uses much more frequently. And the "natural order of ideas" is nothing other than that order which allows the mind to pass from one idea to the next by a series of intuitions of agreement or disagreement. For instance, Locke points out, we are able to achieve certainty of many geometrical truths, only by first perceiving "the immediate agreement of the intervening ideas, whereby the agreement or disagreement of the two ideas under examination (whereof the one is always the first, and the other the last in the account) is found."[24] Thus, in order to apprehend the truth of "the square of the hypotenuse of a right triangle is equal to the sum of the squares of the two sides," we must discover whether the subject idea (denoted by "the square . . . triangle") is the same as the predicate idea (denoted by "the sum . . . sides"), and to make this discovery we may have to employ further propositions asserting the agreement of "intervening ideas." The conclusion may be regarded as deriving from assertions of agreement between intervening ideas, just in so far as a man's perception of the truth of the conclusion depends upon his perception of the truth of intervening statements: i.e., strictly in so far as his certain knowledge of the one derives from his certain knowledge of the others. Thus there is no room in Locke's philosophy for a distinction between order of discovering or becoming certain of a truth, and order of truths.

II. NECESSARY TRUTHS WHICH ARE NOT EXPRESSLY IDENTICAL: SELF-EVIDENT OR DERIVATIVE?

We have noted that Leibniz agrees with Locke's contention that "instances" are not less evident than the maxims of which they are instances. An important difference of opinion, however, arises with respect to propositions which while necessary (according to both of them) are not express identities (immediate "instances" of the principle of identity). For it appears that Leibniz wishes to hold that all necessary truths which are not express identities are less evident and certain than express identities. He writes, for instance, that identities and the principle of non-contradiction are the only non-contingent truths that one cannot "revoquer en doute";[25] or that cannot be proved by something "more certain";[26] they alone are "incontestable."[27] Locke, in opposition, vigorously maintains that we are as certain of the truth of, e.g., such elementary arithmetical propositions as "two and two are four, three times two are six," as we are of *any* proposition:

> Many a one knows that one and two are equal to three, without having heard or thought on . . . any . . . axiom by which it might be proved; and knows it as certainly as any other man knows, that "the whole is equal to all its parts," or any other maxim; and all from the same reason of self-evidence: the equality of those ideas being as visible and certain to him without that or any other axiom as with it. . . .

What principle is requisite to prove that one and one are two, that two and two are four, that three times two are six? . . . To which, if we add all the self-evident propositions which may be made about all our distinct ideas, principles will be almost infinite. . . .[28]

Hence, Locke says, the notion that such a proposition as "two and two are four" needs proof "takes away the foundation of all knowledge and certainty," since if one part of self-evident knowledge needs proof, so will every other.[29]

One may well wonder how such a dispute is to be decided. Are express identities the only self-evident non-contingent truths?[30] Leibniz offers in justification of his position only such dogmatic assertions as: "It is absolutely impossible that there be truths of reason [non-contingent truths] as evident as the identicals or immediates." But in what sense is it "absolutely impossible"? What justification can there be for regarding "identical" and "immediate" as equivalent, beyond the *preconception* that all and only express identities are self-evident? But if we turn to Locke we find merely the equally dogmatic assertion that elementary arithmetical truths *are* as evident as identities (or the injunction to consult our natural light and *see* if they are not as evident). Must we regard this as simply an ultimate incompatibility of intuitions—Locke's natural light yielding one result and Leibniz's another?

It might well be maintained that Locke is standing on firm ground in denying the exclusive primacy of the principle of non-contradiction, if the question of its primacy—or its status as the ground or foundation of other truths—is to be decided on grounds of self-evidence, and if a proposition is "self-evident" when we may attain perfect and unconditional personal certainty of its truth without experiment or argument from other truths. Can it really be denied that we are as certain that two and two are four as we are that two is equal to two? Can it really be maintained that a theoretical proof such as the one Leibniz offers in the *Nouveaux essais* of "2 + 2 = 4" can make us *more certain* of the truth of this proposition?

It must be acknowledged that there are times when Leibniz seems implicitly to concede this point himself. In reply to Jean Bernouilli (who had inquired whether he wished to call into question the axiom "the whole is larger than the part") Leibniz argues for a distinction between requesting a demonstration of an axiom and feeling doubt about its truth.[31] Similarly, when Philalethes in the *Nouveaux essais* demands to know what principle is needed "to prove that two and two are four," claiming, after Locke, that the truth of such propositions is known "without the aid of any proof," Leibniz does not dispute the contention that "2 + 2 = 4" is perfectly well-known to be true without proof. Instead, he replies by denying that it is an *immediate* truth—and not on the grounds that it "requires" proof in some psychological sense, but on the grounds that it is susceptible of reduction:

I am well prepared for that question. That two and two are four is not a completely immediate truth [une vérité tout à fait immédiate]. Suppose that four signifies three and one. It can then be demonstrated; and I shall show you how. . . .[32]

Having completed the proof, he puts into Philalethes' mouth the following words:

> This demonstration, *as little necessary as it may be with respect to its well-known conclusion* [quelque peu nécessaire qu'elle soit par rapport à sa conclusion trop connuë], serves to show how truths depend on definitions and Axioms [ont de la dépendance des définitions et des Axiomes].[33]

In such passages as this we again find evidence of Leibniz's preoccupation with the logical or "natural" order which he believed to obtain among propositions themselves, as opposed to the chronological order in which a given individual happens to apprehend the propositions as true. Reduction to identity is, he claims, a worthwhile undertaking regardless of whether the proposition to be reduced "needs proof" in the ordinary sense, since it is only through reduction that this formal or natural order can be brought to light. By the same token, it is intrinsically worthwhile to make clear the grounds of the necessity of a proposition whether its truth is really in question or not. Thus Leibniz writes that, aside from the question of whether or not we may be confident of the truth of an undemonstrated geometrical axiom, if we should forego reduction,

> We would be deprived of what I most esteem in geometry, with respect to contemplation [par rapport à la contemplation], which is the disclosure of the real source of eternal truths and of the way of enabling us to understand their necessity [du moyen de nous en faire comprendre la nécessité]. . . .[34]

In spite of his insistence on the distinction between the logical order of truths and the chronological order in which they are apprehended by individuals, however, Leibniz is not in the last analysis prepared to concede that a man may achieve perfect certainty of a necessary truth without any reference to its logical grounds in identity. He has two quite different ways of supporting this position against Locke's contention that many arithmetical and geometrical truths are evident to us prior to any consideration or employment of "maxims." The one I will consider first involves a revision of the ordinary conception of "perceiving the logical grounds" of a truth; the second centers on the notion of a proposition's being "perfectly certain."

The first defense of the view that our certain apprehension of truths of reason always involves the principle of identity turns on the conception of unconscious or "implicit" employment of a maxim. Thus, in several passages of the *Nouveaux essais* Leibniz concedes that an individual may acknowledge or maintain an elementary truth of arithmetic (for example) before he has ever heard of the principle of identity; but insists that this does not establish that the former truth is known independently of the principle. In the case of necessary truths, certainty always derives from perception of the fact that the proposition in question is what Leibniz calls an implicit identity—although this perception need not be "express" or conscious:

> If the truths are quite simple and evident, and quite close to identities and definitions, one hardly needs to employ the Maxims expressly in order to draw these

truths from them, since the mind employs them implicitly [virtuellement] and draws
its conclusions at a stroke without an intermediate stop [fait sa conclusion tout d'un
coup sans entrepos].[35]

In the same vein, he elsewhere likens the implicit employment of maxims in
reasoning to the omission of a premise in enthymematic reasoning:

> We ground our thinking on these general maxims [on se fond sur ces maximes
> générales], just as we do on the major premises which we suppress when reasoning
> by enthymemes; for although we often do not pay distinct attention to what we do
> in reasoning, any more than to what we do in walking and jumping, it is still true
> that the force of the conclusion consists partly in what is suppressed [consiste en
> partie dans ce qu'on supprime] and could not come from anywhere else, as will be
> found when we wish to justify it.[36]

Leibniz appears to be arguing in both these passages that if the principle of
identity is the logical ground of other necessary truths, our certainty of these
truths *must* be in some sense derivative from a knowledge of the principle.
Since, as he admits, we do not generally employ it consciously, we *must* be
employing it "implicitly" or "virtually." In order to do this we must in a sense
"know" (have in mind) the principle of identity prior to knowing the truths that
depend on it.[37] Leibniz, that is, argues from the fact that the principle of identity
is the logical ground of all necessary truths to the contention that it must be in
some sense the psychological ground of a person's certainty of all these truths
("l'esprit les employe virtuellement").

However, one does not have to accept Locke's repudiation of the conception
of a formal order to find fault with this reasoning. It seems no less paradoxical
to suppose that we *unconsciously* carry out the sort of theoretical deduction that
Leibniz offers before we are certain that two and two are four, than to suppose
that we do so consciously. The enthymeme analogy, at any rate, is of little help.
A person reasoning in enthymemes is conscious that he is drawing a conclusion, and makes some of his premises explicit; whereas whether we apprehend
"2 + 2 = 4" as a conclusion from another truth is precisely what is in question. Moreover, the criterion of a person's having a suppressed premiss "implicitly in mind" appears to be that he is able to produce this premiss when challenged. We are *not* ready to say, every time someone leaves out a step in
reasoning, that his mind has supplied the premiss "implicitly." The supposed
fact that "2 + 2 = 4" may be shown to follow logically from the principle of
identity would seem no more to establish that everyone who is certain of this
truth has (consciously or unconsciously) derived it from identity by the manipu-
lation of definitions, than the fact that "this man is rational" follows from "all
men are rational" establishes that I have arrived at certainty of the former proposition by at least "implicitly" carrying out the instantiation.[38] Leibniz seems to
argue that if a proposition is logically "justifiable," the mind which is certain of
the truth of this proposition must be in some sense in possession of the logical
justification; but why should we accept this assumption?

It seems unfortunate that Leibniz, instead of resorting to the practically un-verifiable notion of unconscious employment of maxims, does not rest his case for the value of reduction on his own enlightened and potentially fruitful dis-tinction between psychological and logical order.[39] To discover the "logical ground" of mathematical truths by deriving them from a general logical princi-ple need not increase our certainty of these truths in order to be interesting and scientifically valuable. But further, if the suggestion that we might possibly feel absolutely certain of a truth without having in any sense "perceived its logical grounds" is thought inevitably to lead to a loss of scientific objectivity by ad-mitting subjective certainty as a standard of truth, the issue has simply been misconceived. For a distinction may be recognized between scientific standards and subjective fact.[40] Leibniz himself, indeed, seems to recognize this distinc-tion in at least one place, where he allows that "imagination derived from sense experience" will not permit us to represent to ourselves more than one meeting of two straight lines. He then continues:

> But it is not this on which science should be founded [ce n'est pas sur quoi la science doit être fondée]. And if someone thinks that this act of imagination [cette imagination] gives the connection of distinct ideas, he is not sufficiently instructed in the source of truths, and many propositions that are demonstrable by other prior ones will pass with him for immediate.[41]

We may base our conviction of a truth on "imagination": *mais ce n'est pas sur quoi la science doit être fondée.* Surely it is sufficient for Leibniz's purpose in repudiating the Cartesian methodology to draw this line between the subjective and the scientifically admissible or interesting, and to place "intuitions" in the former category, admitting only reasonings set forth with the greatest possible exactitude in the latter. The attempt to establish that subjective processes funda-mentally conform to our standards of objectivity is, it would seem, as unnecess-ary as it is implausible.

Leibniz does have a second way of arguing for the view that the principle of identity must be regarded as prior to all other noncontingent truths not only in respect of logical order, but also in respect of our certainty. This second ap-proach is already suggested in the passage just quoted. It makes no essential use of the notion of the unconscious employment of maxims, but rather turns on a distinction between a "distinct" and a "confused" perception of the connection between ideas:

> To doubt seriously is to doubt with respect to practice. And certainty may be taken to be a knowledge of the sort of truth one cannot doubt with respect to practice without folly. . . . But Evidence is a luminous certainty [une certitude lumineuse], that is, a case where one does not doubt because of the connection that one sees among ideas [à cause de la liaison qu'on voit entre les idées].[42]

Clarity and evidence should therefore be regarded as "une espèce de la certi-tude." "Evidence" is absent as long as the true connection between the "ideas" of a proposition is not clearly and precisely apprehended: it will therefore be absent, in the case of a necessary truth, as long as the reducibility of the proposition to identity is not apprehended. *For as long as one has not seen that the proposition is reducible to identity one has not seen the real ("natural") grounds of the connection of the "ideas."* Thus, one may be very certain indeed of the truth of such a proposition prior to demonstration, but one's certainty will not at this point be "luminous": one's perception of the truth will be in some sense confused, as long as the identity of the ideas has not actually been exhibited by reduction to the first principle:

> What you have said [Monsieur] . . . concerning the connection of ideas as the real source of truths requires explication. If you wish to be satisfied with seeing this connection in a confused way, you will weaken the exactitude of demonstrations. . . . But if you wish this connection of ideas to be seen and expressed distinctly, you will be obliged to have recourse to Definitions and identical Axioms.[43]

It should be quite obvious to us—although it apparently was not to Leibniz—that Locke could never accept this understanding of "self-evidence," since he allows no room for the notion of logical foundation on which it depends. For this reason Locke could not and would not admit that we arrive at a more distinct or "luminous" apprehension of the connection between ideas when we have carried out a formal reduction to identity. For Locke, the true connection between ideas is exactly what we apprehend it to be by our intuition, and not something that is formally expressible. Whereas formal demonstration is regarded by Leibniz as producing a more "luminous" certainty of truths which we may have felt quite certain of prior to demonstration, it would be regarded by Locke as introducing confusion and complexity into what is already perfectly clear and simple.

But what must be observed is that, in the light in which it is now set, the issue between Locke and Leibniz can no longer be thought of as one that might or that must be decidable by simple introspection. Leibniz does not seem to be saying that we must be *aware* that our conception of the truth of "$2 + 2 = 4$" is confused before we have seen it demonstrated: we do not need to *feel* confused or doubtful about the truth of the proposition. By the same token, once the matter has been put on this ground, the fact that "$2 + 2 = 4$" does not seem to need proof, or even to be rendered more certain by proof, no longer provides the basis for an objection to Leibniz's position concerning the epistemological primacy of the principle of identity. For "luminous certainty" has come (virtually by definition) to signify *the state of mind in which the logical grounds of an arithmetical or other necessary truth are apprehended*. The criterion by which one identifies "evidence" or "luminous certainty" is the possession or perception of the "logical grounds" of a necessary truth (which is also the ground of its necessity). Leibniz is saying that this state of mind is the one which, as scientists, we should try to arrive at. Which is no more than to say that as scientists we should strive to carry out the reduction of all axioms to identity.

It should now be clear that the exclusive "self-evidence" of the principle of non-contradiction (identity) is more a *consequence* of Leibniz's views concerning epistemological priority, than a starting-point from which he argues to the need to demonstrate other (necessary) truths. It is because Leibniz believes that all necessary truths have their logical foundation in the principle of identity, and that "nothing should be admitted without proof," that he refuses to admit as thoroughly "luminous" any apprehension of these truths which does not see through them to this principle. This is virtually the opposite approach to the Cartesian-Lockean one of consulting our "natural light" to see which truths may be accepted as certain without proof, and seeking demonstrations of the rest. The possession of a proof is the criterion of luminous certainty, according to Leibniz. Whether or not we are (by subjective determination) perfectly certain is the criterion by which to decide whether or not we need a proof, according to Locke (and also Descartes). The scientific method is expounded with reference to "self-evidence" by the Cartesians; "self-evidence" is interpreted in terms of his ideal of objective science by Leibniz.

Leibniz bases his claim for the primacy of the principle of non-contradiction largely on the belief that it is possible logically to derive all other necessary truths from it. Locke argues against its primacy largely on the grounds that no reduction to the "magnified maxim" could ever make such a truth as "2 + 2 = 4" more certain. Moreover Locke implicitly denies the conception of a logical or formal order on which Leibniz's defense of the primacy of this principle depends, while Leibniz denies (somewhat unsteadily) the possibility of an order of obviousness or certainty distinct from his "natural" or logical order of truths. Now there is nothing particularly compelling about either of the latter two denials. But if these are set aside, Locke and Leibniz may well seem to be arguing, for the most part, very much at cross-purposes—the former heatedly denying one sort of priority to the principle of non-contradiction, the latter heatedly maintaining that it possesses a different sort of priority.

This conclusion will lend support to what I take to be a rather widespread conviction among readers of the *Nouveaux essais* that Leibniz's arguments and objections fail to meet Locke's position directly. On the other hand, I hope to have shown (a) that this failure of direct confrontation is traceable to interesting divergences in fundamental conceptions and assumptions; and (b) that there is something to be gained in understanding the nature, strength, and limitations of each philosopher's position by considering the two together.

III. THE ALLEGED TRIVIALITY OF IDENTITIES

Let us now take note of one final point of Locke's: his contention that all identical and all definitional truths, "though they be certainly true, yet they add no light to our understanding, bring no increase to our knowledge," and must hence be regarded as "trifling."[44] In evident inconsistency with his position, as

stated above, that knowledge of identical truths involves direct perception of
the agreement or sameness of the ideas involved in each case, Locke here
implies that knowledge of the truth of identities amounts to no more or less
than knowledge of the *general* truth that a *word* may always be affirmed of
itself (and *that* a word may always be affirmed of itself is the whole content and
significance of the principle of identity):

> Neither that received maxim ["whatsoever is, is"], nor any other identical proposi-
> tion, teaches us anything; and though in such kind of propositions this great and
> magnified maxim, boasted to be the foundation of demonstration, may be and often
> is made use of to confirm them, yet all it proves amounts to no more than this, That
> the same word may with great certainty be affirmed of itself, without any doubt of
> the truth of any such proposition; and let me add also without any real knowl-
> edge. . . . At this rate, any very ignorant person . . . may make a million of proposi-
> tions of whose truth he may be infallibly certain, and yet not know one thing in the
> world thereby. . . .[45]

Definitional truths, too, such as "every man is an animal," "a palfrey is an
ambling horse," teach us nothing but "the signification of words." Locke concludes that there are two sorts of propositions the truth of which we can know
"with perfect certainty":

> The one is, of those trifling propositions which have a certainty in them, but it is
> only a verbal certainty, but not instructive. And secondly, we can know the truth,
> and so may be certain in propositions, which affirm something of another, which is
> a necessary consequence of its precise complex idea, but not contained in it. . . .[46]

As an example of the non-trifling classes of certain or necessary truths, Locke
offers the geometrical proposition, "the external angle of all triangles is bigger
than either of the opposite internal angles":

> which relation of the outward angle to either of the opposite internal angles, making
> no part of the complex idea signified by the name triangle, this is a real truth, and
> conveys with it instructive real knowledge.[47]

One may assume, I believe, that Locke would be prepared to class geometrical
and arithmetical truths in general as non-trifling—even those elementary ones
which he regards as self-evident (since these do not, on his view, fall into either
the category of identities or of definitional truths).[48] He would want to say, I
take it, that "2 + 2 = 4" is self-evident and non-trifling ("instructive"), while
"2 is 2" is self-evident but trifling. But he would certainly find it difficult to
make this distinction on the basis of his original conception of how we apprehend identities. If it is really necessary for someone to compare the idea of 2
with the idea of 2 to know that 2 is 2, it is difficult to discern how the latter
proposition may be called more trivial than "2 + 2 = 4," which is apprehended—as Locke originally indicated—in precisely the same manner (by
comparing subject and predicate ideas). Thus, to make his point about triviality,

Locke is forced covertly to introduce the notion of a formally valid principle or schema. Locke now seems to be conceding Leibniz's point that in knowing that 2 is 2, and that "whatever is, is," we do not know two completely separate truths.

Setting aside the question of definition, which we cannot deal with here, we may consider the bearing of the view that identities are trifling on Leibniz's doctrine of the priority of the principle of non-contradiction. Although the point is not quite explicit in the *Essay*, it seems fairly evident from the passage quoted first that Locke's *aim* in emphasizing the "uninstructive" character of identities is to discredit the view that they may reasonably be regarded as the "foundation of demonstration" of all necessary and certain knowledge. The observation that identities are "merely trifling" propositions might be supposed to create a strong presumption against the reasonableness of regarding them as the first principles of all demonstration, and in particular against the view that they are the grounds of serious or "instructive" truths of arithmetic and geometry. Other thinkers, at any rate, have accepted as fact the Lockean distinction between trivial and instructive truths, and have taken it to be grounds for dismissing Leibniz's reductionistic position. Russell, for instance, in his *Critical Exposition of the Philosophy of Leibniz* (1900), having observed that for Leibniz all necessary truths are "analytic," comments that the instances which Leibniz gives of "analytic" judgments are either not truly analytic,

> or they are tautologous, and so not properly propositions at all. Thus Leibniz says, on one occasion . . . that primitive truths of reason are identical, because they appear only to repeat the same thing, without giving any information. One wonders, in this case, of what use they can be and the wonder is only increased by the instances which he proceeds to give. Among these are "A is A," "I shall be what I shall be," "The equilateral rectangle is a rectangle." . . . Most of these instances assert nothing; the remainder can hardly be considered the foundations of any important truth.[49]

Russell concludes (though not, it is true, on the strength of this argument alone) that the doctrine of the "analyticity" of all necessary truths (and, in particular, of the truths of mathematics) is false, if not actually absurd. Similarly, James Gibson observes that Leibniz "entirely failed to grasp . . . the significance of Locke's exposure of the futility" of the effort to reduce necessary truths to identities.[50]

It is in fact true that on one level Leibniz's reply seems to miss the point of Locke's remarks on the triviality of the principle of identity. Taking up Locke's statement that the assertion of identical truths is "but like a monkey shifting his oyster from one hand to the other: and had he but words, might no doubt have said, 'Oyster in right hand is subject, and oyster in left hand is predicate'. . .," he replies:

> I find that this author as full of wit as endowed with judgment has every reason in the world to speak against those who use [identities] thus. But now you see how one

should employ identities to render them useful, i.e., in showing by force of consequences and definitions that other truths which one wishes to establish reduce to
them.[51]

If Locke is taken to be arguing, in the chapter, "Of Trifling Propositions," that
identities cannot be the basis of other truths precisely because they are "trifling," Leibniz does in a sense seem to miss Locke's point when he returns that
identities are not trifling because they are the basis of other truths. However,
two things must be borne in mind. In the first place, Leibniz believes that he
has already *shown*, with his earlier proof of "two and two are four," that what
Locke regards as non-trifling necessary truths *can in fact* be derived from identities; therefore, it is not surprising that he should be unimpressed with general,
"a priori" arguments to the effect that express identities cannot conceivably be
the basis of demonstration of other truths.[52] Secondly, Leibniz's suggestion in
this reply that the "triviality" or non-triviality of a truth is a function of how the
truth is used, while perhaps indicative of a superficial reading of Locke, is by
no means wholly irrelevant. For it amounts to a disclaimer of Locke's assumption that certain truths have an intrinsic triviality which disqualifies them for
serious use.[53] The fact that certain truths are "uninstructive" in Locke's sense,
does not entail—Leibniz might wish to argue—that they cannot be put to instructive uses; nor, indeed, that they cannot be the logical basis of truths that we
find instructive. Further, if pressed on this point, Leibniz might well point out
once more that he is primarily concerned with the logical relations among
truths, not with questions of psychology; and that whether or not a given truth
is "instructive" is a question of the latter sort. Therefore, he might conclude, the
fact that proposition *p* is "instructive" and proposition *q* is not, should not
create any kind of prejudice about what sort of *logical* relations they may bear
to each other. For decisions concerning the logical grounds of various classes of
propositions we should turn from intuitivist preconceptions to serious consideration of the procedure of formal reduction.

Leibniz has, in fact, been partially vindicated, in respect of his position on
this point, by subsequent developments in logic and the philosophy of mathematics. Thus Russell by 1919 is maintaining (on the basis of the achievements
in *Principia Mathematica*) that "what can be known, in mathematics and by
mathematical methods, is what can be deduced from pure logic";[54] and he remarks that the characteristic (which he calls "tautology") that sets off logical
truths is "the one which was felt, and intended to be defined, by those who said
that it consisted in deducibility from the law of contradiction,"[55] although
Russell denies that the principle of non-contradiction has any "special pre-emi-
nence" among logical truths. Indeed, the present exalted status which Leibniz
enjoys as the "founder of mathematical logic"[56] is in part a consequence of his
refusal to admit on intuitive Lockean grounds an unbridgeable gap between
serious mathematical propositions and the "trivial" logical maxims.

NOTES

1. See Descartes' letter to Clerselier, June or July 1646, in Vol. VII of his *Correspondance*, ed. C. Adam and G. Milhaud (Paris, 1960), 84–5. Cf. *Recherche de la vérité* [Amsterdam, 1701] in AT, X, 522. Locke's arguments are cited below.

2. On Descartes, see esp. *Principia Philosophiae* [Amsterdam, 1644], ii (AT, VIII, 23–4), and *Regulae ad directionem ingenii* [ca. 1628, first published Amsterdam, 1701], iii (AT, X, 368). On Locke, see below.

3. In an early letter Leibniz indicates that a "large number" of the propositions of metaphysics, physics, and ethics are derivable from the principle of non-contradiction, as well as arithmetic and geometry. (Letter to Simon Foucher, 1675, vol. 1 of DA, 245–6.) It is apparent, however, that by the end of his life he had come to regard all physical laws as contingent (cf. L. Loemker, "Leibniz's Judgments of Fact," *J.H.I.*, VII [1946], esp. 402–409), and I find some uncertainty in his later writings concerning the status of metaphysics and morality. I have briefly discussed this problem in my Ph.D. dissertation, "Leibniz's Doctrine of Necessary Truth" (Dept. of Philosophy, Harvard University, 1965; New York and London: Garland [Harvard Dissertations in Philosophy], 1990), p. 54, n. 4; however, it would unnecessarily complicate the present essay to delve into these issues here.

4. See e.g. *Monadologie* (in letter to Prince Eugene of Savoy, 1714), §§ 33–35; Leibniz's second paper in the Leibniz-Clark correspondence (1715–16), § 1; *Nouveaux essais* (1703–1705; first published posthumously, ed. R. Raspe, Amsterdam-Leipzig, 1765), IV, ii, §§ 9–12. (Citations from *NE* follow the DA edition).

5. A slight awkwardness is created for exposition by the fact that Locke normally treats the principles of non-contradiction and identity as *two* principles, while Leibniz treats them as one. This difference is not very material, however, especially since Locke generally discusses the two together.

6. *Essay Concerning Human Understanding* (first ed. London, 1690), IV, vii, 6. All quotations in this paper are from the Dover printing (New York, 1959) of the A. C. Fraser edition (Oxford, 1894).

7. N.E., IV, vii, 2–4. Translations of Leibniz in this paper are my own. In quoting from the French, I have not altered the orthographic heterogeneity except for accents.

8. *Ibid.*, 6.

9. See e.g. *Opuscules et fragments inédits de Leibniz*, ed. Louis Couturat (Paris: Presses Universitaires de France, 1901), 186.

10. *Essay* (F), IV, vii, Cf. *Ibid.*, i, 4.

11. *Ibid.*, 8. Cf. IV, iii, 2, and IV, vii, 2, where Locke speaks of the mind's "comparing" two ideas to arrive at that immediate perception of their agreement or disagreement which is "intuitive" knowledge. Besides intuitive knowledge, he recognizes "demonstrative" knowledge (involving a *series* of intuitions), and perception of the existence of particular things by sensation. The latter Locke sometimes (e.g. IV, iii, 2) treats as falling under the general rubric of comparison of ideas; elsewhere (IV, xvii, 2), and more plausibly, as *not* involving comparison of ideas.

12. Cf. *Essay* (F), IV, i, 4; also IV, vii, 10, where Locke remarks that all self-evident propositions are "wholly independent."

13. Cf. *ibid.*, vii, 4: "the immediate perception of the agreement or disagreement of *identity* being founded in the mind's having distinct ideas, this affords us as many self-evident propositions as we have distinct ideas. . . . So that all such affirmations and

negations . . . must necessarily be assented to as soon as understood; that is, as soon as we have in our minds determined ideas, which the terms in the proposition stand for."

14. See, e.g. *Essay* (F), IV, vii, 4.

15. N.E., IV, vii, 10.

16. This characterization is borrowed from Yvon Belaval, *Leibniz critique de Descartes* (Paris: Gallimard, 1960), 71. Belaval's detailed comparison of Leibnizian "formalism" with Cartesian "intuitionism" is an invaluable aid to understanding the respective methodological aims and assumptions of the two philosophers.

17. N.E., IV, xii, 1–2.

18. Letter to Hermann Conring, Mar. 19, 1678, in DA, vol. I of series II, 398.

19. An important qualification must be noted. Propositions of the form "AB is not-A," in which the predicate is the negation of *part* of the subject, while sometimes distinguished by Leibniz from truths in which the predicate is the negation of the whole subject, are also counted by him as formal self-contradictions. Cf. e.g. *NE*, IV, ii, 1.

20. *NE*, I, i, 18.

21. *NE*, IV, ii, 1.

22. *Essay* (F), IV, xii, 3.

23. *NE*, IV, vii, 8–9.

24. *Essay* (F), IV, ii, 7.

25. *NE*, I, ii, 13.

26. *NE*, IV, ii, 1.

27. *NE*, I, ii, 13.

28. *Essay* (F), IV, vii, 10. It should be noted that *some* of the arithmetical truths which Locke claims to be "self-evident" are treated by Leibniz not as derivative truths but as definitions ("one and one" is the *definition* of "two"; "two and one" is the *definition* of "three," etc.).

29. *Ibid.*, 19.

30. In accordance with his distinction between necessary and contingent truths (truths of reason and truths of fact), Leibniz frequently speaks of a primitive truth (or truths) of fact. He is not, however, apparently consistent or uniform in his pronouncements on this sort of primitive truth. At times he characterizes one or both of the following as the first truth(s) of fact: "I exist," "I perceive different things" (*varia a me percipiantur*). (Cf. e.g. *Opuscules et fragments inédits*, 86–7, 183; N.E., IV, ix, 3–4 and IV, vii, 7.) On the other hand, in many well-known passages Leibniz indicates that, as truths of reason depend on the Principle of Identity, truths of fact depend upon the Principle of Sufficient Reason (e.g. *Monadologie*, §§ 31–6, *Discours de métaphysique* [1685–6; first published Hanover, 1846], xiii). In one place he says there are two ways of knowing contingent truths: by experience, proceeding from the distinct perception of things; and by reason, proceeding from the Principle of Sufficient Reason (cf. *De libertate* in *Nouvelles lettres et opuscules inédits de Leibniz*, ed. Foucher de Careil [Paris: Auguste Durand, 1857], 182).

31. GM, vol. III, 316. The date of the letter is Aug. 23, 1696.

32. *NE*, IV, vii, 10.

33. *Ibid.* (my italics).

34. *Ibid.*, xii, 4–6. Cf. G. Frege, *The Foundations of Arithmetic*, trans. J. L. Austin from the German, *Die Grundlagen der Arithmetik* (Breslau, 1884); 2d rev. ed. (New York: Harper and Brothers, 1960), p. 2: "The aim of proof is . . . not merely to place the truth of a proposition beyond all doubt, but also to afford us insight into the dependence of truths upon one another. . . . The further we pursue these enquiries [into the founda-

tions of mathematics], the fewer become the primitive truths to which we reduce everything; and this simplification is in itself a goal worth pursuing."

35. *NE*, IV, vii, 19.

36. *Ibid.*, I, i, 19.

37. Leibniz, of course, believes that the principle of identity is innate: the passage just cited is in fact presented as a counter to one of Locke's arguments against innate ideas.

38. Somewhat similar criticisms of Leibniz's enthymeme analogy are to be found in Keith S. Donnellan's unpublished Ph.D. dissertation, "C. I. Lewis and the Foundations of Necessary Truth" (Dept. of Philosophy, Cornell University, 1961), 68ff. This dissertation includes an interesting critique of efforts of Leibniz and more recent philosophers to base "justification" of necessary or analytic truths on formal reduction to primitives.

39. Cf. Bertrand Russell, *Introduction to Mathematical Philosophy* (London: George Allen and Unwin, 1919), 2: "The most obvious and easy things in mathematics are not those that come logically at the beginning; they are things that, from the point of view of logical deduction, come somewhere in the middle."

40. Cf. Frege, *op. cit.*, 3: "In general . . . the question of how we arrive at the content of a judgment should be kept distinct from the other question, Whence do we derive the justification for its assertion?"

41. *NE*, IV, xii, 4–6.

42. *Ibid.*, xi, 1–10.

43. *Ibid.*, xii, 4–6.

44. *Essay* (F), IV, viii, 1.

45. *Ibid.*, 2–3.

46. *Ibid.*, 8.

47. *Ibid.*

48. On the other hand, Locke would evidently treat some common non-identical maxims as trifling on the ground that they should properly be regarded as definitional: cf. *Ibid.*, vii, 11.

49. 2d ed. (London: George Allen and Unwin, 1937), 16–17. Russell seems to be implying in this passage either that "analytic proposition" is a nonsensical expression or that there are nontautologous analytic truths.

50. *Locke's Theory of Knowledge and its Historical Relations* (Cambridge: Cambridge University Press, 1917), 295. Cf. Frege's comment on the Leibnizian view that all the laws of number are analytic, *op. cit.*, 22: "But this view, too, has its difficulties. Can the great tree of the science of number as we know it, towering, spreading, and still continually growing, have its roots in bare identities? And how do the empty forms of logic come to disgorge so rich a content?"

51. *NE*, IV, viii, 3.

52. At *NE*, IV, ii, 1, Leibniz remarks that someone listening to his talk concerning the status of the principle of non-contradiction might "finally lose patience and say that we are amusing ourselves with frivolous statements, and that all identical truths are useless [ne servent de rien]. But he would make this judgment because of not having reflected sufficiently on these matters." He then remarks on the use of the principle in demonstrating logical and geometrical truths, and offers a sample "demonstration."

53. Cf. Ger, VII, 300 (ca. 1679): "Identities also have their use, and no truth, however unimportant it may seem, is entirely sterile. . . ."

54. *Introduction to Mathematical Philosophy*, 145.

55. *Ibid.*, 203–204. Cf. P. P. Wiener, "On Method in Russell's Work on Leibniz," in

The Philosophy of Bertrand Russell, ed. P. S. Schilpp (Evanston: Northwestern University Press, 1944), esp. 273–4.

56. I. M. Bochenski, *A History of Formal Logic*, trans. [from the German, *Formale Logik* (Freiburg, 1956)] and ed. Iva Thomas (Notre Dame: University of Notre Dame Press, 1961), 258. Further discussion of Leibniz's importance in the history of formal logic may be found in L. Couturat, *La logique de Leibniz* (Paris: F. Alcan, 1901); C. I. Lewis, *A Survey of Symbolic Logic* (Berkeley: University of California Press, 1921), ch. 1; and William and Martha Kneale, *The Development of Logic* (Oxford: Clarendon Press, 1962), 320–45.

Leibniz: Self-Consciousness and Immortality in the Paris Notes and After

Author's note: As indicated at the beginning, this essay developed from a paper presented at a conference focused on Leibniz's early "Paris years." The division of emphasis within the paper between Leibniz's "Paris Notes" and his mature philosophical writings may, I hope, be more understandable if the original occasion of the work is kept in mind.

I

Descartes held that the immortality of the mind followed from the indestructibility of substance[1]. According to Spinoza the mind is a mode rather than a substance; he nevertheless also believed that some form of immortality is not only true but demonstrable. Thus, according to *Ethics* V, xxiii, when the human body perishes not all of the mind is destroyed with it, but "something remains that is eternal". The Cartesian and Spinozistic approaches to the proof of immortality, different as they are, both omit to connect the doctrine of immortality with any conception of phenomenological self-consciousness, or sense of self-identity, let alone commonsensical notions of what is involved in saying a particular person continues to exist. Spinoza, indeed, expressly denies that the "something that remains" will have a memory of what is past[2]. In the case of Descartes, on the other hand, the omission seems to be tied in with the general absence in his philosophy of any systematic consideration of the problem of personal identity.

With these views may be contrasted those of Locke. In his well-known treatment of personal identity Locke stresses the fundamental importance of ordinary criteria of self-consciousness and memory, which he regards as separate in principle from the issue of identity of substance[3]. Locke further believes that we can't know for certain that "what thinks in us" is an immaterial substance—although he does incline to the Cartesian view that it is[4]. He believes this ignorance is compatible with "all the great ends of morality and religion" being "well enough secured"[5]. In particular, it should not undermine our hope of personal immortality—an article of faith, not of reason, for Locke. Locke's distinction between identity of person and identity of substance makes this position seem all the more reasonable.

Leibniz's mature position on these issues, appearing in works from the comparatively early *Discourse on Metaphysics* to the later *New Essays* and "Monadology", includes important Cartesian elements, and also anticipates Locke in fundamental respects. Like Descartes, Leibniz believes we can know that *we are* immaterial substances⁶, and also that substances cannot be destroyed by natural means. (This is, presumably, a *logical* 'cannot': there is a contradiction involved in saying a substance is destroyed in any other way than Divine anihilation⁷.) I take this to mean that we can know that 'I' denotes a monad, and that what 'I' thus denotes is indestructible by natural means. In the later writings, the monad's indestructibility is said to follow from its simplicity⁸. On the other hand, Leibniz believes that this conception of the indestructibility of "my" substance is insufficient basis for meaningful immortality. Meaningful immortality requires not only continuation of substance (indeed not *even* continuation of substance)⁹. It requires, fundamentally, memory and "consciousness of what we are and have been"¹⁰. Leibniz thinks it would be incompatible with "the order of things" for God to remove this consciousness from a particular continuing substance—in Leibnizian terms, to dissociate "moral identity" from real or "physical" identity¹¹. However, this continuing consciousness of personal identity is, Leibniz implies, logically distinct from continuation of substance. It is at most morally impossible, and not absolutely or logically impossible, that moral identity cease, without violating the principle of the natural indestructibility of substance.

Some of Leibniz's Paris writings show him already deeply concerned with the issue of personal immortality and the relation of the concept of immortality to the consciousness of self. He expressly repudiates the Spinozistic treatment of immortality, maintaining against Spinoza that "the individual mind is [not] extinguished with the body, for mind somehow remembers what has preceded, and this is over and above what is merely eternal in mind—the idea of body, or its essence"¹². He further notes that "without memory nothing that happens in death pertains to us"¹³. The Paris Notes therefore anticipate Leibniz's later doctrine that immortality involves memory and consciousness of oneself as a continuing being. Passages in these notes suggest, however, that at the time of writing them Leibniz believed it was possible to *demonstrate* personal immortality from *facts about* self-consciousness. Further, the facts in question are not the same as the consciousness of self as a "true unity" to which Leibniz appeals in later writings in developing his doctrine of naturally indestructible simple substances. There is then, an important difference between the Paris Notes and Leibniz's mature writings. In presenting his mature philosophical system Leibniz finds it necessary and appropriate to appeal to God's goodness, or "the order of things", to establish continuing moral identity, or true personal immortality. In the Paris notes, on the other hand, he seems to think that personal immortality can be argued for rigorously, without appeal to the overall architectonic of "order".

One of the primary purposes of the present essay is to provide a fuller account of the differences between Leibniz's early and his mature position, and to suggest some possible explanations for the changes. I will also argue, however, that Leibniz's mature position involves him in some difficulties and even inconsistencies that are not evident in the earlier one.

The rest of this essay is divided into four sections. In the next one I expound somewhat more fully the difficulties with a Cartesian account of immortality, that presents the immortality of "our minds" as derivable from the indestructibility of substance. It is important to have a clear view of the limitations of this account in order to grasp the motivation for Leibniz's moves away from it, in both his earlier and later writings. In the third section of the paper I will sketch in some more details of Leibniz's treatment of self-consciousness and immortality in his mature works. I will try to show that the development of his thought on these subjects leads him into very significant problems about self-consciousness. In the fourth section, I will turn to two passages in the Paris Notes that consider self-consciousness in relation to the issue of immortality. Since the arguments of these passages are presented in an allusive and disconnected way, part of the task is to try to understand what exactly Leibniz may have had in mind. I will argue that the Paris Notes, whatever their limitations, are free of the conflicts I find in the mature position. I will consider some possible explanation for Leibniz's abandonment of his earlier position in favor of the later one.

II

What constitutes, or is necessary and sufficient for, the continued existence of a person—say myself? According to Cartesian principles, *I am* just a particular *res cogitans*[14]; hence it is necessary and sufficient for my continued existence that a particular *res cogitans* continue to exist. Now apparently identity conditions on substances (*rēs*) permit the complete and total alteration of the accidents of substance[15]. Further, all my thoughts, beliefs, desires, and my specific mental capacities (excluding the general "faculty of understanding" and probably also the faculty of willing) are accidents[16]. Among these, of course, are my memories, both "corporeal" and "intellectual"[17]. It seems to follow, then, that I could continue to exist without any constancy whatever in the content of my consciousness. (If in a twinkling all my memories, desires, aspirations, attitudes, beliefs, and even specific mental capacities and incapacities, were replaced by yours, I would not lose my identity, but simply acquire new memories, desires, beliefs, etc.) Descartes indeed seems explicitly to embrace this conclusion, perhaps without really considering its implications. In the Synopsis to the *Meditations* he implies that the immortality of our minds can be demonstrated from the fact (established in the *Meditations*) that they are substances, and substances cannot perish, except by Divine anihilation. He comments:

> . . . the premises, from which the immortality of [the human] mind can be concluded, depend on the explication of the whole of Physics; first in order to know that all substances whatsoever, or things which need to be created by God in order to exist, are incorruptible by their nature, and cannot ever cease to be, unless they are reduced to nothing by the same God, denying them his concurrence . . .

Physics will show that body in general is a substance and cannot perish, but that the human body, on the other hand, considered as distinct from other bodies, is only made up of a configuration of members and other similar accidents. But

> . . . the human mind is not thus constituted [*constare*] out of any accidents, but is a pure substance: for even if all of its accidents changed, so that it understood other things, wanted others, felt others, and so forth, the same mind would not on that account become another [*non idcirco ipsa mens alia euadit*] . . .[19]

The Cartesian account thus seems to entail the possibility of identity of self through total psychological discontinuity. And, with memories surely among the *cogitationes* that have the status of accidents, it follows that one could be a continuing identical self, without the slightest awareness that this is so.

Now someone might want to suggest that the continued existence of a Cartesian *res cogitans* would not, after all, be quite as vacuous as this from the point of view of phenomenology or consciousness. We have recognized above that a Cartesian *res cogitans* must at least understand, and understanding requires *self-consciousness*[20]. But if a continuing substance S continues to be self-conscious, is it not clear that S's mental history will have at least the continuity involved in repeated awareness of the same specific individual substance? That is, even if S "forgets" the history of thought that S in fact has, an omnipotent all-knowing being could "match" different stretches of S's mental history, by noticing that all of them contain the awareness of S.

From the perspective of historical Cartesianism there is an answer to this suggestion that is both obvious and (I think) conclusive. For Descartes holds that we are not aware of substances directly, but infer their presence from observation of their attributes[21]. It appears, then, that he cannot identify the self-consciousness that accompanies understanding as awareness of a specific substantival particular. Descartes is wide-open to the Lockean objection that self-consciousness (and hence self-identity) cannot be the same thing as consciousness of a substantial self. For we are, typically, self-conscious, at least in the sense that we seem to know that it is the same I who did this, that, etc. But we are not supposed to be conscious of that substance—"whatever it may be"—which is the subject of our attribute of thought. Given all this, the Cartesian must ultimately face the question, in what way can it after all be true that I am essentially "only a thinking thing"[22]. Even if we charitably assume that Descartes means something like "one thinking thing in particular"[23], he does not seem to have allowed himself any way of relating the identity of that thinking thing to any psychological or phenomenological manifestation[24].

There is of course nothing very novel in this criticism of Descartes. I have only elaborated a little on the familiar arguments of Locke and of Kant[25]. I want now to consider Leibniz's later and earlier treatments of self-consciousness and continuing existence of the self in the light of these very fundamental problems within the Cartesian perspective. It is clear enough that Leibniz's developing position on personal identity and immortality was in part generated by appreciation of the difficulties. I claim, however, that Leibniz did not really succeed in avoiding or resolving the Cartesian difficulties; considering his position as a whole one finds that he has, instead, made the problem more conspicuous and complicated.

III

There is plenty of evidence in Leibniz's mature writings that he *both* identified the denotation of 'I' with a particular substance, and also held that consciousness of this I (self-consciousness) is what provides our original and true understanding of the nature of substance in general (as a "true unity", comprising a multiplicity within itself). It seems to follow that (for any I) self-consciousness must be consciousness of a particular simple substance (the one that is me), and further that it must involve consciousness *of* the identity, simplicity and substantiality of this entity. The following passages are representative.

These souls [rational souls or spirits] are capable of performing reflexive acts, and of considering what is called 'I' [*Moy*], 'substance', 'soul', 'mind'—in a word, things and truths which are immaterial[26].

We experience ourselves a multitude in the simple substance, when we find that the least thought which we perceive envelops a variety in its object. Hence everyone who recognizes that the soul is a simple substance should recognize this multitude in the monad. . . .[27]

Expression is common to all forms and is a genus of which natural perception, animal feeling, and intellectual knowledge are species. In natural perception and feeling it suffices that what is divisible and material, and is dispersed among several beings, should be expressed or represented in a single indivisible being, or in a substance which is endowed with a true unity. The possibility of such a representation of several things in one cannot be doubted, since our soul provides us with an example of it[28].

. . . [B]y means of the soul or form there is a true unity which corresponds to what is called 'I' in us; which could not occur in artificial machines, nor in the simple mass of matter, however organized it may be; which can only be regarded as like an army or herd. . . . If there were no true *substantial unities*, however, there would be nothing substantial or real in the collection[29].

It is very true that our perceptions or ideas come either from the exterior senses, or from the internal sense, which can be called reflection: but this reflection is not limited to just the operations of the mind, as is said [by Locke] . . . it goes as far as the mind itself, and it is in perceiving [the mind] that we perceive substance[30].

It is also clear that Leibniz did not regard the "unceasing" existence of the substance to which 'I' refers or "corresponds" as sufficient for personal immortality[31]. Thus, the title of § 34 of the *Discourse on Metaphysics* reads: "On the difference between minds and other substances, souls, or substantial forms. And that the immortality which is required includes memory." And the text of this section reads in part:

> [Animals or sub-rational souls] pass through nearly a thousand transformations like that which we see when a caterpiller changes into a butterfly, [and] it is the same for morality or practice as if one should say they had perished. . . . But the intelligent soul, knowing what it is, and being able to say this 'I' [*MOY*] which says much, not merely remains and subsists metaphysically . . . but it also remains the same morally and constitutes the same person [*fait le même personnage*]. For it is memory, or the knowledge of this 'I', which makes it capable of punishment and reward. Also, the immortality which is required in morality and religion does not consist merely in this perpetual subsistence which is common to all substances, for without memory of what one has been, there would be nothing desirable about it[32].

Similarly he tells Arnauld,

> . . . [M]inds must keep their personality [*leur personnage*] and moral qualities, so that the city of God will lose no person [*aucune personnel*], they must particularly preserve some kind of reminiscence of consciousness, or the power to know what they are, on which depends all their morality, sufferings, and punishments, and consequently they must be exempt from those revolutions of the universe which would make them completely unrecognizable to themselves, and make them morally speaking another person[33].

Implicit in these passages is the Leibnizian doctrine mentioned above, that considerations of "order" ensure that God will not allow it to be the case that minds lose their consciousness of what they have been, their personal memory. As he puts it in § 36 of the *Discourse*:

> It must not be doubted . . . that God has ordered everything in such a way that minds not only can live forever, which is inescapable, but also that they always conserve their moral status [*leur qualité morale*], in order that the city [of God] lose no person, as the world loses no substance. As a result they will always know what they are, otherwise they would not be susceptible of reward or punishment . . .[34]

Similar views are expressed at some length in the later work, the *New Essays*.

Now I do not want to claim that Leibniz's doctrine *as I've so far described it* involves apparent inconsistency. A position such as the following would seem to fit the cited texts reasonably well, and it seems consistent:

> Knowledge of ourselves (self-consciousness) requires awareness of the indivisible substances which we in fact are. However, meaningful immortality also requires consciousness of continuing personal identity. And this requires awareness of having been conscious in the past of the same substance that we are now conscious of when we reflect on ourselves. But while the very nature of substance requires that it be (naturally) indestructible, it does not logically require that a given substance be aware of having been conscious of itself in the past. God's goodness is

thus necessary to guarantee memory, and hence we must appeal to it for our doctrine of immortality.

There are indeed passages where Leibniz seems to be saying precisely this[35]. Further, we have not so far found him endorsing any principles that would preclude our apprehending ourselves as specific individual substances.

However, both the Arnauld correspondence and the *New Essays* contain important passages that do, I believe, involve Leibniz in confusion—even inconsistency—on the issue of self-consciousness. First, the complete concept theory, as Leibniz expounds it to Arnauld, seems to imply—almost as sharply as Descartes's principles—that we can have no definitive consciousness of ourselves as continuing specific substances. He writes:

> I remain in agreement that to judge of the notion of an individual substance, it is good to consult that which I have of myself, as it is necessary to consult the specific notion of the sphere to judge of its properties. Although there is a great difference. For the concept of myself in particular and of every other individual substance is infinitely more extended and more difficult to understand than a specific concept like that of the sphere, which is only incomplete . . . It is not enough in order to understand what this I is, that I feel myself [to be] a substance that thinks, it would be necessary to conceive distinctly that which distinguishes me from all the other possible minds; but I have only a confused experience of this[36].

It seems, then, that the most I can be aware of through self-consciousness is myself as *a* substance which thinks, *not* as some specific substance in distinction from others. It is true that Leibniz also writes, in another draft to Arnauld, that "my inner experience convinces me *a posteriori* of this identity"[37], i. e. of my self-identity over time, and here it is identity of substance that Leibniz seems to have in mind. However, the point Leibniz is making when he says this is, precisely, that such consciousness is *not* sufficient to establish identity of substance. "*A priori* reasons" are required, and these involve an appeal to the complete concept theory.

> There must . . . be some reason *a priori* independent of my experience that makes it the case that one says truly that it was I who was at Paris and that it is still I and not another who am now in Germany and consequently it must be that the concept of myself [*la notion de moi*] connects or comprehends different conditions. Otherwise it could be said that it is not the same individual although it appears to be the same[38].

What Leibniz seems to be concerned about in these passages is not the continuity of his memory, but the inadequacy of mere "*a posteriori*" self-consciousness *for apprehending what it is that makes it true that* the same 'I' has continued from an earlier time in Paris to a later time in Germany. Apart from grasping our own complete concepts, we are unable to apprehend our substantial selves as individuals, or the true identity of these individuals over time. But self-consciousness does *not* afford a grasp of our own complete concepts.

There are, then, conflicting tendencies in the treatment of self-consciousness in Leibniz's mature writings. On the one hand, he seems to want to hold that we are conscious of *ourselves as* unique substances that continue through time— indeed that we derive the ideas of substance, identity, and duration from reflection on ourselves. On the other hand, the account of individuation in terms of complete concepts implies that self-consciousness cannot yield knowledge of ourselves as individual substances, since it cannot provide anything like adequate apprehension of what really individuates us. We are individual, enduring substances because we have a complete concept which individuates us, which makes us complete beings and distinguishes each of us from every other. But this crucial fact about our own substantiality is, as Leibniz tells Arnauld, precisely what self-consciousness does not yield. The question then is in what sense it *does* yield awareness of substance, identity, and duration at all. This is a fundamental unclarity which, so far as I know, Leibniz never directly confronts.

A still more critical problem for Leibniz's position on self-consciousness arises from certain moves he makes explicitly in the *New Essays*, in trying to combine Cartesian and Lockean ideas. Here he continues to maintain that it would be inconsistent with "the order of things" for God to allow a particular self-consciousness-cum-memory (Lockean person) to be dissociated from the substance in which it originally inhered (the Cartesian self). However, he repeatedly suggests that this development would not be logically impossible. And he concludes that in the event it should happen, personal identity in the moral sense (the sense relevant to immortality) would remain with the identical consciousness, rather than the original substance.

> It seems that you hold, Sir, that this apparent identity [«*la consciosité ou le sentiment du moi*»] could be conserved when there is no real identity. I believe that that would be possible perhaps by the absolute power of God, but according to the order of things, the identity apparent to the person himself, who feels himself the same, supposes real identity . . .[39]

> . . . [B]ut if God should change extraordinarily the real identity, the personal [identity] would remain, provided that the man conserved the appearances of identity . . .[40]

> I confess that if God brought it about that the consciosities were transfered to other souls, it would be necessary to treat them according to moral notions as if they were the same, but this would be to trouble the order of things pointlessly [*sans sujet*] and to make a divorce between the apperceptible, and the truth which is conserved by the insensible perceptions[41].

The difficulty arises from trying to conjoin the following propositions, as this chapter of the *New Essays* seems to require:

1. I *am* a particular immaterial substance;
2. It is metaphysically possible that I continue as an identical self-consciousness and identical self, independently of this particular substance.

The first proposition implies (I have suggested above) that 'I' denotes a particular individual substance. But if this is so, I do not see how the conjunction of (1) and (2) can be regarded as a coherent position. At the minimum, we need some suggested way of dealing with the question: *How can it be*, from a logical or metaphysical point of view, that I cease to be the substance I am now identical with, and yet continue to exist? As far as I know, Leibniz provides no such suggestion; he seems not to have noticed the problem.

Once again, the *underlying* difficulty may be that Leibniz is unclear about the sense in which I am *conscious of* the particular simple substance that he wishes to identify with me. As we've seen, certain aspects of his position seem to require that this individual substance is what I am conscious of in being conscious of myself. Yet the Arnauld correspondence gives reason to believe that I can't be conscious of "my" substance as a particular individual. Now, only so far as *this* is true does it make *any* sense to say I might retain consciousness of self-identity while losing identity of substance. (It seems I wouldn't "know the difference".) But even so it does not make *enough* sense to suppose such a divorce between self-consciousness and consciousness of substance. For if I *am* just a particular substance, my self-consciousness must be consciousness of this substance. It certainly cannot be consciousness of another substance—one that is not myself!

IV

Leibniz was concerned with the problem of immortality from the very beginning of his career. Notes on ways to demonstrate the immortality of the soul are found in some of his earliest papers[42]. The Paris Notes, as I read them, show Leibniz already trying to improve on the Cartesian as well as the Spinozistic position[43], by finding a way to demonstrate the immortality of the soul, conceived as an entity that not only necessarily continues or "remains", but *is conscious of its own continuing identity*. One cryptic passage begins by commenting on the experience of becoming aware of oneself thinking, and then of this awareness itself:

> It seems that when I think of myself thinking and already know, between the thoughts themselves, what I think of my thoughts, and a little later marvel at this triplication of reflection, then I turn upon myself wondering and do not know how to admire this admiration. . . . It sometimes happens that I cannot forget something, but involuntarily think of the same thing for almost an hour, and then think of this difficulty in thinking and stupefy myself into reflections through perpetual reflections, so that I almost begin to doubt that I shall ever think of anything else and begin to fear that this direction of mind has harmed me[44].

Leibniz goes on to try to derive from this experience some conclusion about the necessity of the mind's "continuation":

I do not yet adequately experience how these different acts of the mind take place
in this continually reciprocating reflection, as it were, in the intervals between these
acts. . . . But if you observe well, this act will merely make you remember that you
already had this in mind a little previously, that is, this reflection of reflection, and
so you observe it and designate it by a distinct image accompanying it. Therefore it
already was in your mind earlier, and so perception of perception goes on perpetually in the mind to infinity. In it consists the existence of the mind *per se* and the
necessity of its continuation[45].

Here Leibniz's somewhat euphoric reasoning seems to be that since our
thoughts are attended by the consciousness that we have thought, which consciousness in turn has a slightly later reflection in consciousness, the mind
cannot fail to continue. For if it did, thought would *not* have an infinite reflective sequence. This seems to me a painfully weak argument, although it does
have historical interest as a development of the Cartesian doctrine that we cannot think without being aware of our thought, and Descartes's account of reflective cognition[46]. For example, the argument gives us no real reason to reject the
alternative story that our thought has continuing echoes *just as long as* the mind
continues to exist. Leibniz does better, and anticipates his mature doctrines
more fully, in another note:

In our mind there is perception or a sense of itself as of a certain specific thing;
this is always in us, because, as often as we use the name, we at once recognize it.
As often as we will, we recognize that we perceive our thoughts, that is, that we
have thought a little earlier. Therefore intellectual memory consists not in what we
sense but in that we sense—that we are those who sense. This is what we commonly call identity. This facility in us is independent of externals. I do not see how
a man or a mind can die or be extinguished while these reflections last. Something
remains in modifications, not as extension in itself remains in space, but as a certain
particular thing endowed with definite modifications, since, namely, it perceives one
thing or another[47].

This passage does not suggest any strict separability (in the logical or metaphysical sense) of moral and metaphysical identity[48]. Leibniz seems to be saying something like the following.

1. Personal immortality presupposes the continuing identity of "the thing that
thinks".
2. It further requires some memory that one has thought, some knowledge of the,
continuation of the thing that thinks.
3. These conditions, if satisfied, are also sufficient for immortality ("I do not see
how a man or a mind can die while these reflections last.")

Leibniz seems to regard these considerations as enough to establish personal
immortality. For he continues,

If this is the nature of the mind, and it consists in the perception of itself. I do not
see how it can ever be impeded or destroyed, as I have said earlier, because the

identity of the mind is not destroyed by any modifications and therefore is not destroyed by anything—as can easily be shown[49].

Leibniz's point seems to be that just as changes in modifications do not bring about destruction of substantival identity so they cannot bring about destruction of the continuing substance's consciousness of itself as thinking and having thought. This would suggest that without going very far beyond the Cartesian framework, one can strengthen the Cartesian conception of immortality by establishing identity of consciousness *together with* identity of substance. And whatever objections one may want to raise to this position and this argument, it does seem to avoid the difficulties I have claimed exist in the mature system. For nothing in this argument allows the separation of self-awareness from awareness of substance; in fact, the argument assumes that these are the same. Leibniz's early view that immortality is logically demonstrable seems bound up with the assumption that self-awareness is awareness of a substance capable of indefinite modifications. Awareness of oneself (this substance) as having been the subject of previous thoughts is supposed to provide a sufficient strengthening of the Cartesian and Spinozistic conceptions of immortality.

V

After the Paris period, as we've seen, Leibniz came to believe that appeal to the goodness of God—God's consideration of "the order of things"—was necessary to assure immortality. Now it is certainly possible that he abandoned the reasoning of the Paris Notes on the basis of some essentially local dissatisfactions with the particular proof or proofs. For example, the passage to which I've given most attention can be faulted on the grounds that it assumes, rather than shows, that what thinks in us can't fail to have available the possibility of moment-to-moment self-consciousness. It is still possible, however, that the change in Leibniz's approach to personal immortality may be tied in with other significant developments in his thought. For example, it is possible that his conception of the conditions of meaningful immortality were strengthened to the extent that the sort of continuing self-consciousness ostensibly guaranteed by the Paris Notes wouldn't be sufficient anyway. After considering this possibility briefly, I will go on to mention a second one, having to do with Leibniz's mature views about the epistemology of self-consciousness.

The consciousness of continuing existence that Leibniz espouses in the Paris Notes appears to be very much a matter of moment-to-moment consciousness of continuation, rather than any overarching conception of one's own long-term existence and career[50]. It may be that Leibniz decided later that this was not enough for the "moral identity" that ethical and religious considerations required. Although in the middle and late writings Leibniz does not say very much about the sort of memory he conceives as requisite for human immortality, such expressions as "memory of what one has been"[51] suggest rather more extensive remembrance than the Paris Notes' awareness "that we have thought a little earlier". Thus, he may have decided that the sort of consciousness of continuity that is "proved" in the Paris Notes even if it really *must* be available to any enduring mind—is not the sort of immortality which is "required" from the moral point of view. And the continuation of longer-term memory appears so contingent that it is hard to see how it could be argued for from logical and "metaphysical" considerations alone. Although I am not sure all the texts fully accord with this supposition, it seems for the most part plausible and warranted[52].

But the changes, documented above, in Leibniz's views about self-consciousness could also explain his reliance on considerations of "order" in his later treatments of immortality. The Paris Notes take for granted that consciousness of continuing self-identity and awareness of a continuing distinct substance are one and the same thing. But the mature Leibniz, separating "*a posteriori* conviction" of identity from "*a priori* reasons", concluded that this didn't *have* to be the case. Consciousness could not after all guarantee that one was *really* the same, in the sense of being the same substance. In the *New Essays*, Leibniz connects this point explicitly with the experience of moment-to-moment continuation of the self. With the passages we have considered from the early Paris Notes should be compared the following, written toward the end of Leibniz's career:

> I believe that [separation of moral and real identity] is perhaps possible through the absolute power of God, *but following the order of things*, the identity apparent to the person himself, who feels himself the same, supposes real identity, at each contiguous passage [*passage prochain*] accompanied by reflexion or by the feeling of the self [*le sentiment du moi*]: an intimate and immediate perception which *cannot deceive naturally* . . . [53] [emphasis added]

Leibniz is here contrasting moment-to-moment self-consciousness with long-term memory: the latter can "deceive naturally", the former cannot. However, considerations of "order" must still be brought in to guarantee that such "unnatural" deception does not occur. Thus, if the "right" kind of immortality involves consciousness of continuation together with *real continuity*, its occurrence also depends on considerations of order—even if long-term memory is *not* required.

I have already claimed that the position Leibniz holds in the mature writings, concerning the logical possibility of a dissociation between "my" original substance, and "my" continuing consciousness, is incoherent. We should now note that the distinction between long-term memory and moment-to-moment self-consciousness is basically irrelevant to this issue. Leibniz's position commits him to the following proposition:

> It is possible that it seems to me that I am the substance that I was previously; whereas in fact God has played a trick: I am now identical with substance X and was previously identical with substance Y (Y ≠ X).

But, whether 'previously' in the above proposition be read "an instant ago" or "a year ago" this proposition leads to seemingly insuperable difficulties for

Leibniz. Give the identification of selves with particular substances, and self-consciousness with consciousness of the substance that one is, it simply makes no sense to suppose that I continue to exist and be conscious of myself independently of real or substantival identity. Or at least Leibniz's position raises the question of how this *could* make sense—and provides no satisfactory answer.

Leibniz's mature position, as we have seen, relies on God's goodness and on considerations of order for the guarantee of personal immortality. This move seems acceptable, to the extent that it may be dictated by the consideration that a given self-conscious substance could after all *lose* its memory—long-term or short-term—"of having thought". On the other hand, to the extent that it is dictated by the idea that a given substance and "its" self-consciousness could go their separate ways, the move seems confused and ill-conceived. In this respect at least the Paris Notes were on the right track—so long as a substantival theory of the self be assumed.

NOTES

Some portions of this essay were originally presented at a conference, "Leibniz in Paris", in Chantilly, France, November, 1976. Sponsors of the conference include the Gottfried-Wilhelm-Leibniz-Gesellschaft, the Centre nationale de la Recherche scientifique, and a number of other organizations.

1. See Synopsis of the *Meditations*, AT Vol. VII (1973), pp. 13–14.
2. *Ethics* V, xxi.
3. *Essay Concerning Human Understanding*, II, xxvii, §§ 8ff.
4. *Ibid.*, IV, iii, § 6; cf. *Essay* (F) Vol. II, pp. 194–195.
5. *Ibid.*, p. 195.
6. See the passages cited below, notes 23–26.
7. Cf. "Monadology" (1714) § 4: "there is no conceivable manner in which a simple substance can perish naturally"; Ger Vol. vi, p. 607; Loemker, No 67, p. 643.

Emilienne Naert makes the interesting point that Leibniz regards it as contrary to *reason* that God would exercise his power of destroying substance, whereas Descartes regards this as a matter of faith. See her *Memoire et conscience de soi selon Leibniz* (Paris: J. Vrin, 1961), pp. 129–131. (Hereafter abbreviated: Naert.)

8. "Monadology", *loc. cit.* In the *Discourse on Metaphysics* (1686) Leibniz implies that natural indestructibility and indivisibility follow *separately* from his complete concept theory of substance. Cf. *Discourse* § 9, Ger II, 433–434; Loemker, No 35, p. 308. However, the position found more commonly in his writings—especially the later ones—is that the natural indestructibility of substances follows from the fact that they are simple or indivisible or "without parts". For this point I'm indebted to an unpublished paper by Eileen O'Neill, "The Incessance and Indestructibility of Individual Substances [in Leibniz's Philosophy]", Princeton University, 1976.

9. See *NE* II, xxvii, § 9; DA, Sechste Reihe, Sechster Bd., p. 237.
10. This is a composite derived from texts cited below.
11. DA: *NE* p. 237.
12. Loemker, 162. I have had to rely on Loemker's translations of the Paris Notes. I have so far been unable to gain access to the original Latin versions, as published by

I. Jagodinsky in Leibniz, *Elementa Philosophiae Arcanal de Summa Rerum* (Kazan, 1913).

13. *Ibid.*, 161.

14. AT VII, p. 78.

15. *Ibid.*, p. 14.

16. *Ibid.* and AT VII, 78–79. In the latter passages Descartes specifically excludes imagination and sensation from his essence, but not volition.

17. For this distinction see letter to Mersenne April 1, 1640 (AT III, 45) and letter to Hyperaspistes, August, 1641 (AT III, 422); *PL*, pp. 72, 112. Naert discusses this Cartesian distinction with reference to immortality (Naert, p. 136–136, n. 64). She is concerned with the question whether intellectual memory would involve memory of one's personal past. I consider more important the fact that Descartes cannot hold intellectual memory to be *necessary* for substantial endurance or the immortality based on it.

18. AT VII, 13–14.

19. *Ibid.*, p. 14.

20. For Descartes, consciousness of self is implicit in the act of thinking. Cf. e.g. Robert McRae, "Innate Ideas", in *Cartesian Studies*, ed. R. J. Butler (New York: Barnes & Noble, 1972), esp. p. 41.

21. *PP* I, lii; AT, VIII, 25. Nevertheless, Descartes *also* holds that I am conscious of myself *as* a substance or self-subsistent being: cf. McRae, *op. cit.*, p. 34. There is, then, a difficulty in Descartes' treatment of self-consciousness similar to a difficulty I discuss below in relation to Leibniz.

22. AT VII, 78.

23. Rather than holding "it is essential to me to be identical at any time with some thinking thing or other".

24. Nor, notoriously, of "individuating" the thinking thing which is himself different from other thinking things.

25. Locke, *Essay*, II, xxvii; Kant, *Critique of Pure Reason*, the "Paralogisms of Pure Reason" A 348ff.; B 406ff.

26. "Principles of Nature and of Grace" (1714) § 5, Ger VI, 601; Loemker No 66, p. 638. Cf. "Monadology" § 30, Ger VI, 612; Loemker No 67, p. 646.

27. "Monadology" § 16, Ger VI, 609; Loemker, 644.

28. Letter to Arnauld, October 9, 1687; Ger II, 112; Loemker No 36. II, p. 339.

29. "New System of the Nature and Communication of Substances" (1695) § 11, Ger IV, 482; Loemker, No 47, p. 456.

30. From Leibniz's "*échantillon*" of reflections on the Second Book of Locke's Essay, DA: *NE*, 14. This passage is cited, in the course of a useful discussion of Leibniz's treatment of self-consciousness, by Robert McRae in *Leibniz: Perception, Apperception, and Thought* (Toronto: University of Toronto Press, 1976), p. 96. Unfortunately, McRae relies upon A. G. Langley's translation which here as elsewhere is crucially inexact.

31. The point is developed at length in Naert's valuable exposition, cited above and also, from a more critical point of view, in a paper by Samuel Scheffler, "Leibniz on Personal Identity and Moral Personality" (*Studia Leibnitiana*, 8 [1976]). Scheffler's essay, though concerned with different points of criticism has influenced the present study very strongly. See also Nicholas Rescher, *The Philosophy of Leibniz* (Englewood Cliffs, N.J.: Prentice-Hall, 1967), p. 136.

32. Discourse, § 34, Ger IV, 459–460 ("titles" Ger II, 14); Loemker No 35, 325.

33. Ger II, 125; Loemker No 36, II, 347.

34. Ger IV, 452; Loemker, No 35, 327.

35. E.g. Ger IV, 527: «Car toutes les ames conservent leur substance, mais les seuls esprits conservent encore leur personalité, c'est à dire la conoissance de ce *moy*, par laquelle je me connais le même personne, ce qui me rend susceptible de recompense ou de châtiment.» This passage is cited (with an erroneous reference) by Naert, *op. cit.*, p. 134. On the same page Naert cites a Latin passage in which Leibniz more explicitly identifies continuing self-consciousness with consciousness of a continuing substance. It is perhaps significant, though, that the latter passage dates from a relatively early stage of Leibniz's career (1679). I suggest below that the serious difficultues in his position only develop (or emerge) later.

36. Ger II, 53; Loemker, No 36, I, 334.

37. Ger II, 43.

38. Ger II, 53; Loemker, No 36, I, 334.

39. DA: *NE*, 236.

40. *NE*, 237. At this point in the argument Leibniz is distinguishing "internal" appearances of continuing personal identity (self-consciousness and memory) from "external" ones (manifestations of personal identity as observable to others).

41. DA: *NE*, 242. The issue is complicated by a fundamental Leibnizian doctrine I do not discuss in the text: the claim that every substance at any time includes "traces" of all its past and future states—traces which may or may not be accessible to consciousness. It would require another paper to begin to unravel the inter-connections between this doctrine and Leibniz's distinction between moral and substantival identity. The two most interesting relevant texts I have come across are the following: Ger II, 57; Loemker, No 36, I, 337 (from the Arnauld correspondence) and DA: *NE*, 239.

42. See Naert, 123 ff. and DA VI, I, 494f.

43. As indicated above, Leibniz in the Paris notes specifically defines his position in opposition to Spinoza's. Later texts show Leibniz self-consciously opposing Descartes on the issue of immortality: cf. Naert 119 and 134.

44. Loemker, No 12, II, 161.

45. *Ibid.*

46. For a good discussion and numerous texts see Robert McRae, "Descartes' Definition of Thought", also in *Cartesian Studies*, pp. 55–70.

47. Loemker, *loc. cit.*, 161–162.

48. Cf. Naert, 132.

49. Loemker, *loc. cit.*, 162.

50. In addition to passages already cited, the following tends to confirm this suggestion: "So there will be some memory after death, such as there is in falling asleep" (Loemker, *loc. cit.*, 161).

51. *Discourse* § 34, Ger IV, 460; Loemker, No 35, 325.

52. In at least one place in the *New Essays* there is a clear suggestion that all that is required for personal identity through a series of time-intervals is that there be *intermediate* linkages of consciousness: cf. DA: NE, 236. The passage in question is the continuation of the one next cited in the text.

53. DA: *NE*, 236.

Leibniz and Materialism

SEVENTEENTH-CENTURY discussions of materialism, whether favorable or hostile towards the position, are generally conducted on a level of much less precision and sophistication than recent work on the problem of the mind-body relation. Nevertheless, the earlier discussions can still be interesting to philosophers, as the plethora of references to Cartesian arguments in the recent literature makes clear. Certainly the early development of materialist patterns of thought, and efforts on both the materialist and immaterialist side to establish fundamental points in the philosophical analysis of mind, have considerable historical interest at the present time. This paper attempts to clarify the significance of some of Leibniz's views in connection with the materialist thesis. I do not have in mind his rather notorious parallelism, though some of the points made below bear indirectly on the character of this position (or perhaps on the question whether he held it consistently). Instead, I will examine his approach to arguments against materialism.

In the first section I consider his response to some of the arguments for an immaterialist conception of the mind or self that were developed by his immediate predecessors, Descartes and Malebranche. I hope to show that his objections to these arguments consistently exhibit a particular epistemological and methodological perspective. I hope it will also be evident that the counterarguments he presents foreshadow in broader strokes strategies painstakingly developed by materialists in more recent debate (although I will not attempt to provide assiduous documentation an this point). Finally, I will argue that he does not succeed in making a clear case for the *prima facie* defensibility of materialism, although he certainly attempts to do so.

Leibniz's own acceptance of immaterialism often seems to rest on nothing more original than simple piety together with the conviction that all serious objections to the inter-actionist form of dualism were avoided by his principle of pre-established harmony.[1] However, at least a gesture toward a new argument against materialism is found in the "Monadology," in a well-known but obscure and little-discussed passage. This is considered in section two. I suggest that the phrasing of the passage explicitly indicates an effort on Leibniz's part to meet the type of objection he himself brings against his predecessors' arguments. At the same time, it is very difficult to see exactly what his argument *is* given the very fragmentary statement that Leibniz provides. I propose that Leibniz's argument can plausibly be assimilated to a much more fully stated argument criticized by Kant in the "Paralogisms" section of the *Critique of Pure Reason* (and quite *im*plausibly associated in the Kant literature with the name of Descartes). The argument as stated by Kant is still quite obscure. After clarifying it somewhat, I take up the question whether this argument against materialism really avoids the sort of difficulty that Leibniz finds in the work of his mentalist predecessors.

I: LEIBNIZ AS CRITIC OF MENTALISM

Leibniz's counters to the anti-materialist arguments of others generally reflect the following views or assumptions: (1) if a materialist 'account' or explanation of thought is possible, materialism is true; (2) efforts to establish a distinction between mind and matter which do not directly confront the question of explain*ability* are unable to distinguish mere *ignorance* of the nature of the self from knowledge that the self is not material. As we will see, Leibniz's adherence to these views depends in turn on his broad rejection of Cartesian positions on questions in epistemology and the philosophy of mind.

I will consider three arguments for immaterialism that Leibniz rejects: (1) the Cartesian claim that freedom of will is self-evident; (2) a version of the Cartesian epistemological argument for mind-body dualism; (3) an argument that can be construed as a version of the argument from Leibniz's law. The first of these will be considered only briefly, since it is not a direct argument for immaterial substance, although (on the modern determinist conception of matter) it is of course the basis for an indirect one.

The introspectionist argument for freedom of the will—Descartes defended his free will doctrine by maintaining that it is "self-evident," "evident to the light of nature," and a matter of "universal experience" that the will is free.[2] (Rather unfortunately, the example he is particularly concerned with is our freedom to "give or withhold assent" in the case of any proposition not clearly and distinctly perceived). In the *Theodicy* Leibniz replies to this position in the following terms:

> . . . [T]he reason that Descartes alleged to prove the independence of our free actions by a pretended vivid internal feeling has no force. We cannot strictly feel our independence, and we are not always aware of the causes, often imperceptible, on which our resolution depends. It is as if the magnetic needle found pleasure in turning towards the north; for it would believe it turned independently of any other cause, not being aware of the insensible movements of magnetic matter.[3]

Leibniz claims, then, that Descartes' position depends on the implicit assumption that if we are not *aware* of external causes impelling us to act we can conclude there are no such causes.[4] But this assumption is unfounded: we can easily conceive of an entity which, being unaware of the causes that in fact determine its movements (or "resolutions"), erroneously believes that the movements (or "resolutions") are purely spontaneous, or governed only by its own conscious desires and purposes.

In this instance the objection that the opponent is arguing "from ignorance" seems both straight-forward and readily intelligible. Leibniz's claim is that internal "experience of" causelessness is as consonant with mere ignorance of (the actual) causes as with the actual absence of causes. To put the matter differently, an experience or feeling of causelessness cannot be sharply distinguished from a belief that there are (were) no causes; so the former cannot provide "evidence" for the latter belief, let alone certify it conclusively. (It is unlikely Descartes would want to claim that "the will is free" is self-evident in the way that "$2 + 3 = 5$" is self-evident, so that all reference to "experience" is out of place. Certainly Leibniz does not interpret him in that way.) The objection in this case is backed up by an example that helps tie down the claim that ignorance can be confused with knowledge in this area. The point is not only that people might be in the position of the (rather fortunately disposed) hypothetical magnetic needle,[5] without knowing the difference. For, the second sentence of the quotation suggests, we do know in general what it is like to imagine that an event has no physical explanation merely because the actual cause is unnoticed or not understood; and we know in particular what it is like to come to believe that our own past behavior was determined by factors of which we were not at the time aware.

Even this passage, however, contains echoes of Leibniz's particular epistemological views—views which figure more crucially in other passages on materialism that will be cited below. For example, an essential feature of Cartesian epistemology is that with careful mental discipline one can by reflection assuredly distinguish ideas which are clear and distinct (and hence veridical) from those which are not.[6] In accepting freedom of the will as "self-evident" Descartes is, perhaps, implicitly relying on this doctrine. Leibniz, however, rejects it, as we will see below.

The Cartesian epistemological argument for mental substance—Leibniz attacks the central Cartesian argument for the independence of mind from body in his "Observations on the General Part of Descartes *Principles*."[7] He writes:

> It does not follow: I can assume or imagine that no bodies exist; but I cannot imagine that I do not exist, or that I do not think; therefore I am not a body, nor is thought an attribute of body. And I am astonished that such a distinguished man could have given so much credit to such a trivial sophism. . . .

According to Leibniz, anyone who held that the soul was a body would not allow the supposition that no bodies exist;

> but he will concede only this much: you can doubt (as long as you are ignorant of the nature of the soul), whether bodies exist or do not exist; and since you nevertheless see clearly that your soul exists, he will allow only one thing to follow from this, you can thus far doubt whether the soul is corporeal; and no torture will wrench anything more from this argument. . . .

Leibniz here rather parodistically represents Descartes as reasoning: "I know that I exist as a thinking thing; I do not know (i.e. can doubt) that matter exists; therefore the self that I know to exist is not material." He observes that all that really follows from the premises is that I do not know (can doubt) that the soul is material. But of course, the proposition that I don't know that *p* is compatible with *p* as well as with not-*p*. Thus the materialist will claim that since "the soul is a body," I can both know that I exist and doubt that matter exists, only in so far as I *remain ignorant* of the nature of the soul.

In truth, even in the *Principles* Descartes phrases his argument somewhat more subtly than this treatment would suggest. Having established in Principles i–vii that the existence of a physical world is doubtful, while the fact that he exists as a thinking thing is beyond doubt, Descartes continues the argument in Principle viii as follows:

> And this is the best way to understand the nature of the mind, and the distinction between it and the body. For *examining what we are* who suppose everything which is different from us to be false, *we clearly see* that no extension, nor figure, nor local motion, nor anything similar that is attributed to body, belongs to our nature, but only thought, which therefore we know prior to and more certainly than any corporeal thing; for this we already perceive, but so far we doubt the others.[10]

It is understandable that Leibniz should have interpreted the passage as he did. If weight is given to the italicized phrases, however, a different line of thought seems to emerge—one more consonant with Descartes' way of expressing and defending his position in the *Mediations* and the Replies to Objections.[11] According to this line of thought, certainty of one's own existence, conjoined with doubt about the existence of a physical world, may be viewed as merely a *step on the way to the realization* that one can conceive one's mind independently of any exclusively physical attribute. The weight of the argument is then borne by the latter proposition; the preceding claims about doubt and certainty may be said to prepare the way for it, but are not represented as actually entailing it. On this interpretation, Descartes' argument really turns, not on ordinary notions of knowing and doubting, but rather on his quasi-technical notion of clear and distinct conception. In order to establish the distinction between mind and body it is sufficient to have a clear (and distinct) conception of the soul or mind as existing, that is independent of any reference to matter. (In the *Mediations* he inserts a reference to God's omnipotence into the argument, with the claim that whenever he "can clearly and distinctly conceive one thing without another," he may be assured that "the one is distinct or different from another, for they can be separately set forth (*posées*), at least by the omnipotence of God.")[12]

It is not likely, however, that acknowledgment of these refinements would have changed Leibniz's response to the argument very much. Leibniz is highly critical of "clear and distinct conception" as a criterion of knowledge, regarding it as intrinsically subjective and unreliable.[13] He would probably maintain that if a state of clear and distinct perception is to be regarded as purely psychological ("feeling certain"), the possibility of error cannot be ruled out. If, on the other hand, it is a condition of being in a state of clear and distinct perception that the proposition believed be true, there is no way of arguing non-circularly from such a state to truth. And he would not be prepared to admit any third possibility. So even in the face of a more careful interpretation of Descartes' argument, Leibniz would hold that the original objection stands: you can't derive knowledge from ignorance. From 'I can clearly and distinctly conceive mind as distinct from matter' one can deduce only 'it seems to me mind is not identical with matter'; a more than purely epistemic conclusion is permitted only if non-identity is already *assumed* in the description of my state as one of clear and distinct perception. But then the description itself is problematic.

Leibniz maintains, then, that knowledge of the nature of the self as thinking being cannot be obtained by Cartesian reasoning. Such reasoning can only show what is "possible" within the limits of an individual's present knowledge. It cannot show what is actual, or what would appear possible if his knowledge were extended. The completeness or adequacy of a concept such as Descartes' 'idea' of the self cannot be expected to appear on its face, contrary to what Descartes himself assumes.

A recent writer has claimed that "[W]hat must be shown, to defeat the Cartesian argument, is that when we try to conceive of our minds without bodies, . . . we do not succeed in doing that, but instead do something else, which we mistake for it."[14] From Leibniz's point of view this statement, although on the right track, is too strong. Leibniz thinks it is enough to point out that *for all Descartes shows* his ability to "conceive the mind as distinct from the body" *could be* a function of ignorance of the (material) nature of mind. Now one might well reply that in fact this is *not* enough. The acceptability of Leibniz's objection to the free-will claim, one might argue, depends on our being able easily to understand what it would be like to decide that one's "feelings" of indeterminacy were illusory. But is it conceivable in the same way that an extension of our knowledge would result in our no longer thinking that our minds are distinctly conceivable in separation from matter? The difficulty of grasping what such an extension would be like is, surely, the strength of the Cartesian argument; it is what makes the charge that the Cartesian conceivability criterion may be satisfied as a result of mere *ignorance* less compelling in this particular case than it might otherwise seem.

Modern materialists have relied on theoretical equivalences ("water is nothing but H_2O"; "lightning is just discharge of electricity") as providing models for the identification of mind-states such as sensations with states of the body. Some philosophers have argued further that these identities must be construed as non-contingent. Thus it is not *really* conceivable that water is not H_2O—although there may be a legitimate epistemic sense in which one can assert, "Water might not be H_2O."[15] There is reason to think that this line of thought would be congenial to Leibniz, and that he would see no *prima facie* difficulty in applying it directly to the mind-body question—in the materialist's favor. In his reply to another immaterialist argument (the last we will consider before his own) he indicates that the relevant extension of our knowledge of mind would be a sort of "explanation." Further, he tries to clarify the point by giving an example by analogy—an example which at first does not seem too far removed from those cited above. I will argue that the example is quite inconclusive. It does, however, point the way to further clarification of Leibniz's critical strategy by bringing to mind relevant features of his anti-Cartesian theory of "ideas."

A "Leibniz's Law"-type argument—In a brilliant and intriguing short work called "Conversation Between Philarète and Ariste," Leibniz considers a proof, derived from Malebranche,[16] that "the modifications of the soul are not at all modifications of matter and that as a result the soul is immaterial."[17] The argument, as first expressed by Malebranche's disciple in the dialogue, is as follows:

> . . . [M]y pleasure, my desire, and all my thoughts are not at all relations of distance, and one cannot measure them by feet or by inches, like space or that which fills it.[18]

As restated by Leibniz's mouthpiece, the argument is that "thoughts are not relations of distance, because we cannot measure thoughts." The argument, in other words, appears to be that thoughts cannot be states of matter because certain things true of states of matter—that they are measurable and stand in relations of distance—are not true of thought. It therefore bears some resemblance to more recent objections to the mind-body identity thesis based on the principle known as "Leibniz's Law."[19] It is of some historical interest, then, that Leibniz explicitly rejects the argument as inconclusive. "A follower of Epicurus," he says

> Would say that [the fact we cannot measure thoughts] is due to our faulty knowledge of them and that, if we knew the corpuscles which form thoughts and their movements that are necessary for that, we would see that thoughts are measurable, and are the workings of certain subtle machines.[20]

Color, too, he continues, does not seem to consist essentially of anything measurable, yet "the reason for such qualities in objects" may be "found in certain configurations and movements." When this happens in the case of color (or if it should happen in the case of thought),

> then these qualities may at last be reducible to something measurable, material, and mechanical.[21]

It is clear from this passage, first, that Leibniz himself did not regard the applicability of "physical" predicates to mental states as straight-forwardly decidable on the basis of ordinary language or experience; and second, that he was ready to accept the view that an "explanation" of thought in materialist terms would be sufficient to establish a "reduction" of states of mind to states of matter. To this extent the issue of the reducibility of mental states to brain states seems to be presented as an open question, one requiring an empirical resolution. If the "reasons for" thought *can* be found in mechanistic principles, then materialism will "turn out" to be true. The Malebranchist cannot establish knowledge of the immateriality of thought by arguing that predicates of distance, etc., do not apply to it; rather, we cannot know for certain what predicates do or do not apply to conscious states until we know that we know what these states are states of.[22]

However, the passage suffers from a serious difficulty that arises in connection with the example. Leibniz does not make clear what he means by the color "qualities" which surprisingly turn out to have mechanistic explanations; as a result the example does not really provide illumination by analogy. If he means perceptual appearances of color (colors *as* perceptual appearances), then a mechanistic explanation of a color would already be, in some sense, a mechanistic explanation of a perception and hence (on Leibniz's terms) of a thought. (It would not of course follow automatically that *all* thoughts have mechanistic explanations.) But if he does *not* mean this, it is not immediately obvious what the *explicandum* could be, that at the outset does not seem to consist in anything measurable. One might argue that since Leibniz speaks of colors as qualities *in objects* he must be supposing that one set of *objective* qualities (the colors) are explained by another set (configuration and movements). But then, it would seem, the explanation would not establish an identification.

In fact, Leibniz normally speaks of color perceptions as "confused representations" of what is represented distinctly in physical analysis.[23] Accordingly, the premiss in the above passage might perhaps be construed as follows: In ordinary life we are not aware that the qualities we *refer to* as "red," "green," etc. *are really* particular classes of configurations and movements. He would then be arguing that we might equally discover that the occurrences we refer to as "pain," "perception of red," "fear," etc. are really particular physical occurrences, expressible in terms of figure and movement. On the basis of this analogy, though, he would presumably have to say that just as color perceptions are confused representations of the qualities in bodies, so our pain perceptions, etc. are merely confused representations of the states of our own bodies. But the analogy then does seem inadequate to support the reply to Malebranche. For what we set out to "reduce" to figure and motion was just the perception or representation itself. But what we have concluded is that our ordinary experience of pain, for instance, is just a *confused representation* of a bodily state; the notion of representation or perception is still present and unreduced.

From another point of view, however, Leibniz's example does help to clarify certain aspects of his reasoning concerning the immaterialist arguments we have considered. When Leibniz says that, e.g., our ordinary color perceptions are "confused" he does not mean merely what he sometimes says he means: that we cannot verbally *state a mark* by virtue of what we recognize something as, say, green.[24] He *also* means that perceptions of the actual complex material states of green things are somehow implicit in each perception of green, although we could never "distinguish" them individually in it.[25] (In the same way, he thinks, the perception of the ocean includes "in a confused way" a perception of each individual wave.[26]) As Leibniz sometimes puts it, "the cause corresponds to the effect,"[27] so that one can reason from the nature of the one to the "real" (if not directly evident) nature of the other. With respect to the Cartesian and Malebranchian arguments this view seems to affect Leibniz's responses in at least the following ways.

First, it helps sustain the point that the *distinctness* of our ideas is not an intrinsically *evident* property: our concepts and experiences might yield a very inadequate conception of their "objects," including our "selves," without our realizing that this is so. (If having distinct knowledge were merely a matter of being able to "state an identifying mark" it is much less obvious that we could be ignorant, in an interesting way, that our idea of something was not distinct.)[28] At the same time, distinctness or confusedness *is* an intrinsic and non-relative feature of our ideas. Thus, a conception of the self or subject of thought as immaterial is confused if the self is in fact material; but introspection cannot settle the issue.

Secondly, the views about confused perceptions lead Leibniz to take seriously the question whether a more "distinct" understanding of consciousness might not be achieved through physical investigations just as a more distinct understanding of color difference in objects has been achieved in this way. If so, we will be *clarifying our idea* of our self or consciousness, and not merely establishing external "causes" of consciousness. Establishing the causes of *x* cannot, within Leibniz's system, be sharply distinguished from clarifying the concept of *x*, given the principle of "correspondence" between causes and effects.[29]

In summary, Leibniz flirts with the materialist "identity thesis" in criticizing some of his predecessors' arguments. He takes the view that a mechanistic "explanation" of mental states would serve to establish the materialist's position. He maintains that Cartesian and Malebranchian arguments fail to show the impossibility of such explanations, and are therefore open to the objection that they proceed merely from ignorance of the nature of the soul or self. He does not, however, discuss the hypothetical "explanations" in any but the most general terms. The analogy of color does not go very far towards illuminating the possibility of establishing material "reasons' for thought, nor the bearing of such a possibility on our conception of ourselves. The example does, however, help to remind us of some relevant peculiarities of Leibniz's views about the relation of perception to object and of effect to cause.

II: Leibniz's Rejection of Materialism

As we have seen, Leibniz contends that his predecessors fail to refute materialism in so far as they fail to rule out the possibility of a materialistic explanation of thought. In the "Monadology" he appears to be reaching for a sounder foundation of immaterialism; for in that work he claims that the possibility of such an explanation can, after all, be ruled out *a priori*. He writes:

> One is besides obliged to admit that *Perception* and what depends on it is *inexplicable by mechanical reasons*, that is by figures and motions.[30]

The "reasons for" thought, unlike the "reasons for" phenomena of color, cannot be found in the operations of matter. Leibniz supports this claim with a famous but little-discussed illustration, which is evidently meant as an argument.

And imagining (*feignant*) that there were a Machine, the structure of which brought about thinking [*fasse penser*], feeling, having perception, you can conceive it enlarged while preserving the same proportions, so that you could enter it as you go into a mill. Supposing that you do, you will find in visiting the inside only parts that push each other, and never anything to explain a perception. Thus perception must be sought in the simple substance and not in the composite, or in the machine.[31]

This key statement is evidently incomplete in at least two crucial respects. In the first place, there is no justification provided for the assumption that if an explanation of perception in terms of some kind of a 'machine' is inconceivable, then the only alternative is explanation in terms of a "simple substance." In the second place there is no explication of why, or in what sense, "parts that push each other" *cannot* "explain perception."

On the first point, we may provisionally note that Leibniz did take it for granted that all (non-miraculous) physical or material phenomena were susceptible of "mechanistic" explanation.[32] This need not imply, however, that the *mill* analogy should be construed very strictly. Although it would be odd to speak of entering, say, a chemical process "as you go into a mill," a mechanistic conception of chemistry (or physiochemistry) would allow Leibniz's point to go through. (One might speak of observing a chemical change on a proposed chemical theory of mind as if it were a billiard game.) We will briefly return to this problem below after proposing a fuller statement of the argument.

On the second point, it may well seem that one is simply left to *guess* what Leibniz was getting at according to one's own prejudices about the stronger points of mentalism. Is he, for instance, suggesting that perceptions, being private to the perceiver, are necessarily omitted from any account produced by an outside observer who enters the allegedly perception-producing "machine?" I am not at all sure this suggestion can be ruled out, but evidence from both the "Monadology" context and Leibniz's other writings suggests that what he regards as not susceptible of mechanistic explanation is, more immediately, the "unity" of perceptual consciousness, or what he calls the "true unity" designated by "I."

Consider, for example, the following passage from another work:

> . . . By means of the soul or form, there is a true unity which corresponds to what is called *I* in us; which could not occur either in artificial machines, nor in the simple mass of matter, however organized it might be; which can only be regarded as an army or flock, or as a pond full of fish, or as a watch composed of springs and wheels. However if there were no true *substantial unities*, there would be nothing substantial nor real in the collection.[33]

The last sentence alludes to Leibniz's doctrine, expressed throughout his writings, that all *substances* must be indivisible, the paradoxes of division (Zeno's paradoxes), he thinks, show that extension is purely phenomenal.[34] The importance of this doctrine for Leibniz's philosophical system should certainly not be overlooked in the present context. If there must be "something real" underlying physical phenomena, and if this something real must be unextended, then (assuming the traditional mind-matter dichotomy) it may well seem to follow on this basis alone that there are mental substances—or at least "mind-like" substances.[35] However, Leibniz seems also to want to claim that we can somehow know from direct experience of ourselves and our perceptions that *we are* indivisible and hence immaterial substances. This experience provides us with a way of understanding the proposition that reality consists of "substantial unities." As he writes to Arnauld:

> A thing expresses another (in my terminology) when there is a constant and rule-governed relation between what can be said of the one and of the other. It is in this way that a projection in perspective expresses its geometrical figure. Expression is common to all the forms, and is a genus of which natural perception, animal feeling, and intellectual knowledge are the species. In natural perception and in feeling it is sufficient that what is divisible, material and dispersed among several entities, be expressed or represented in a single indivisible entity, or in substance which is endowed with a true unity. *One cannot doubt the possibility of such a representation of several things in just one, for our soul provides us with an example.* But this representation is accompanied by consciousness in the reasonable soul, and it is then that one calls it thought.[36]

Conversely, he remarks that

> We ourselves experience a multitude in the simple substance, when we find that the least thought which we apperceive includes a variety in the object.[37]

Leibniz seems to hold, then, that in analyzing conscious perception we must take account of both the "true unity" of the perceiving "I" and a manifoldness or variety in object or content. To return to the passage quoted from the "Monadology," his point seems to be (very roughly) that a materialist explanation of perception is impossible because perception does essentially involve the "true unity" of the perceiving self, while material mechanisms are always divisible into parts. What will be missing in the observer's description of any hypothetically perception-producing machine is just the essential "unity" of consciousness, or anything from which an understanding of that unity could be derived.[38]

Leibniz is, however, extremely inexplicit about the relation between our apprehension (presumably immediate) of the "true unity" of our conscious perception, and the conclusion that we are immaterial substances. It is not even clear that he consistently regards the connection as inferential: the last quoted passages almost suggest that we can self-evidently experience ourselves as simple or immaterial entities. However, Leibniz's reply to Malebranche, together with the "Monadology" statement, seem incompatible with the notion that one can counter materialist claims in such a simple-minded manner. How, then, are we supposed to understand the alleged incompatibility between the "unity of consciousness" and materialist doctrine?

Illumination of Leibniz's position can, I think, be obtained if we consider the fate of the doctrine of simple substances in the work of his successor Kant. In his pre-Critical period Kant became seriously concerned with the problem of how we can have knowledge of simple substances, and with the significance of this problem for Leibnizian rationalist metaphysics. He at first tried to resolve the problem by relying on a quasi-Leibnizian distinction between sensible appearances and things in themselves. Unextended simple substances cannot be given to sensible intuition under the conditions of space and time; nevertheless they are represented by purely intellectual concepts; they are in fact "demanded" by the intellect. This is the doctrine of the "Inaugural Dissertation."[39] In the *Critique of Pure Reason*, however, Kant abandons the view that we can have knowledge of particulars not presented to sense, and with it the view that we can know that there are absolutely simple, immaterial substances. He retains the Leibnizian characterization of perceptual consciousness as a "necessary unity." However, he now interprets this doctrine as meaning only that the distinguishable elements in the content of a perception must exist in the appropriate sort of *conceptual connection* with other elements. He denies that any metaphysical inference can be made from this "condition of thought" to the nature of what thinks or the real subject in which thought "inheres."

What is important in the present context is that Kant does not rest his repudiation of the Leibnizian metaphysics of simple substances merely on the claim that we cannot have knowledge of non-sensible entities. Rather, in the "Paralogisms of Pure Reason" he states and criticizes an argument that attempts to prove from the nature of thought or perception that the thinking self is an absolutely simple and hence immaterial entity. Commentators have shown an unaccountable tendency simply to assume the "rational psychology" under attack in the "Paralogisms" can be identified with the doctrines of Descartes. But the passage in the Sixth Meditation to which one is sometimes referred in connection with this argument hardly resembles the proposed reasoning except in its conclusion.[40] It is much more illuminating, I think, to view the argument as a more complete statement of the reasoning on which Leibniz (at least partly) based his rejection of materialism.

Kant introduces the argument as "no mere sophistical play, contrived by a dogmatist in order to impart to his assertions a superficial plausibility, but an inference which appears to withstand even the keenest scrutiny and the most scrupulously exact investigation."[41] (This build-up need not necessarily be taken too seriously; Kant could also wax effusive about the merits of the Argument from Design.) He then states the argument as follows.

Every *composite* substance is an aggregate of several substances, and the action of a composite, or whatever inheres in it as the composite, is an aggregate of several actions or accidents. Now an effect which arises from the concurrence of many acting substances is indeed possible, namely, when this effect is external only (as, for instance, the motion of a body is the combined motion of all its parts). But with thoughts, as internal accidents belonging to a thinking being, it is different. For suppose it be the composite that thinks: then every part of it would be a part of the thought, and only all of them taken together would contain the whole thought. But this cannot consistently be maintained. For representations (for instance, the single words of a verse), distributed among different beings, never make up a whole thought (a verse), and it is therefore impossible that a thought should inhere in what is essentially composite. It is therefore possible only in a *single* substance, which not being an aggregate of many, is absolutely simple.[42]

The contrast drawn in this passage between the "aggregate" and the simple seems to fit in well with the line of thought partially sketched in the "Monadology"; so, indeed, does the manner in which the challenge to materialism is expressed: the unity of consciousness cannot be understood as the "effect" of the action of an aggregate.

An immediate difficulty for interpreting the argument as Kant expresses it arises from the apparent speciousness of the example on which it relies (different words of a verse distributed among different beings). Even for *mechanical* unity it is not sufficient that certain motions or bits of matter *exist*: They also must exist in contiguity, or at least in some kind of dynamical relation. The fact that words in *different* brains don't form "one thought" hardly seems to show, even on a *prima facie* basis, that, say, different parts of one mechanical brain cannot. However, the point of the illustration can perhaps be clarified if we restate the argument as follows:

Let us suppose that the subject of thought is complex and divisible. Then each part of the complex thought will inhere in a different part of the subject. ("For suppose it be the composite that thinks: then every part of it would be a part of the thought . . .") But then the *part* of the subject in which a given part of the thought inheres may be taken as the subject of that (part of the) thought. But then the original thought must be regarded as divided among a plurality of subjects, and the consideration raised by the illustration will apply.

In other words, the supposition that the subject of thought is material (i.e. that thoughts are states of matter) leads to the absurd and contradictory consequence that every *single* thought is constituted of thoughts belonging to a *plurality* of consciousnesses. This seems also to be Kant's understanding of the argument, as expressed in the following interpretive passage:

. . . [W]e demand the absolute unity of the subject of a thought only because otherwise we could not say, 'I think' (the manifold in one representation). For although the whole of the thought could be divided and distributed among many subjects, the subjective 'I' can never thus be divided and distributed, and it is this 'I' that we presuppose in all thinking.[43]

Another difficulty is presented, however, by the seeming arbitrariness, not to say incoherence, of the consequence, "Suppose it is the composite that thinks; then each part is a part of the thought." This seems strictly parallel to the false, if not incoherent consequence: "Suppose it is the adding machine that adds; then each part of it is part of the addition." This difficulty may be somewhat mitigated, though, by the following considerations.

First, the point of the argument is to show that thoughts cannot be identical with states of matter. (To this extent the term "effect" may be misleading.) Second, the premiss in question should not be read as claiming that *every* part of any material unit (say the brain) which may be singled out as the "subject" of thought must be involved in every thought. The reasoning behind the consequence is, then, that if a thought were identical with a state of a composite *qua* composite, elements of the thought would be identical with states of elements of the composite. The next step is the conclusion that in that case different parts of the thought would be distributed among different subjects contrary to the original supposition (we are talking about the thought of *one* 'I'). Hence the 'I' cannot be identified with a composite, such as the brain.

Without denying that every step of the argument, as thus interpreted, is subject to criticism, I hope these remarks help to elucidate its nature. The following example may make the interpretation still clearer.

Suppose I am seeing something green while experiencing an odor like the smell of cabbage cooking. Now we know that stimulation of different parts of the brain are correlated with experiences of the different sensory modalities. Therefore one might expect the materialist to hold that the sensation of green is a state of my visual cortex, and the olfactory sensation a state of my olfactory cortex. Now we have located (roughly) different experiences in different parts of the brain. But we have not explicated the fact that seeing-green-and-smelling-cabbage is *one* experience (with distinguishable components), or in other words, that the sensations belong to one consciousness. According to the argument (as interpreted above) the observation that the experiences occur in a single brain not only fails to remove the difficulty, but actually leads one to conclude that it cannot be met at all within a materialist framework. For if the experiences are states of one brain, they are equally supposed to be states of different brain parts (a brain being merely the aggregate of its parts). But there is *no* sense (in the example under consideration) in which they may be said to belong to different consciousnesses.

This argument may seem to depend on, and be vitiated by, the simplistic conception of materialist "explanation" that we touched on in connection with the "Monadology" illustration. If so, it might be classed as an "argument from ignorance" insofar as it assumes that the possibilities of materialist explanation are exhausted by the forms recognized in the 18th century. There is, however, a philosophically more interesting way in which the argument fails to avoid the kind of objection that Leibniz urges against other immaterialist reasonings.

Suppose, as Leibniz does, that one has a distinct understanding of something only to the extent that he understands the causes, or can produce a correct analysis of the concept, if any is possible. Suppose further, as Leibniz seems to, that to understand the causes of thought is to know the metaphysical nature of the self—i.e. whether or not materialism is true. It follows that one cannot reason to the falsity of materialism in the way that Leibniz attempts to reason. For until one knows whether or not materialism is true, one lacks a distinct knowledge of the nature of the self or the referent of 'I'. But if one lacks a distinct knowledge of the self, one cannot confidently reason from propositions about the self to the falsity of materialism.

In other words, Leibniz's rejection of the Cartesian Theory of evidence or distinctness seems to leave him no epistemological ground for inferring from the "data" to the "causes" of perception. There is no evident reason to grant special epistemological status to the "idea" of the unity of consciousness, while rejecting arguments derived from Descartes and Malebranche on the grounds that our idea of thought or the self might be as "confused" as the ordinary idea of green.

(Kant, I think, is getting at something like this when he goes on to claim (in rejecting the argument) that 'I' is an "entirely empty expression."[44] We are, he says, ignorant of its referent precisely in so far as we are ignorant of the true causal account or "ground" of thought (which is to say totally).[45] Kant suggests that the Leibnizian (or more exactly the "rational psychologist") somehow confuses the lack of any determinate content with the *datum* of a simple entity or something that can only be explained by reference to a simple substance.)

It is perhaps worth noting, however, that there are at least two ways of understanding this objection in connection with Leibniz's system. A critic could acknowledge that there indisputably is such a thing as the "true unity of consciousness," which a materialist account of thought will at some point have to reckon with. Someone who takes this view would presumably hold that "advances in neurophysiology" (perhaps in combination with advances in philosophical analysis) can be expected to resolve the problem. On the other hand, one could maintain that the "datum" itself is suspect until the theoretical analyses (and related experimental results) are in. (Kant takes the latter course to what must be an extreme conclusion when he claims—in a perhaps excessively celebrated footnote—that (1) for all 'I' know, over time 'my' consciousness is being passed along a series of material substances; and (2) if this is so the sense of personal identity is illusory.)[46]

It has sometimes been remarked that recent materialists do not really pave the way for a thoroughly materialist ontology since they do not provide for a materialist analysis of the notion of the subject-of-experiences or person or self—but only of particular "mental states" of the person.[47] Accordingly one might want to claim that Leibniz's argument, by focusing on the problem of subjective unity, points towards a real limitation in the development of materialist theory up to this time. Obviously, the present paper makes no good case for any such claim. What I do hope to have established is that (a) Leibniz's treatment of anti-materialist arguments is closely connected with his broader epistemological commitments; (b) that his own way of arguing for an immaterialist conception of the self may have grown out of his views about the weaknesses of earlier arguments; (c) that his views about philosophical argument concerning the mind-body relation show considerable sophistication and have some contemporary interest; (d) that despite all this there is reason to doubt that his anti-materialist position could avoid his own objections. I hope also to have provided (if only rather incidentally) some reason for questioning recent assumptions about interpretation of the "Paralogisms," and, more generally, the nature and history of the philosophical endeavor that Kant calls "rational psychology."[48]

NOTES

1. "[My] system has besides this advantage, to conserve in all its rigor and generality this great principle of physics, that a body never undergoes a change in its motion, except by another moving body that pushes it. . . . This Law has been violated up to this time by all those who have admitted Souls or immaterial principles, including even all the Cartesians, The Democriteans, Hobbes and some other pure materialists, who have rejected all immaterial substance, having alone conserved this law up till now, believed they had found in this a ground for insulting other philosophers, as if they were maintaining in this respect an extremely unreasonable opinion. But the ground of their triumph was only apparent and *ad hominem*: and far from being able to aid them, it serves to bring them down. And now that their illusion has been discovered, and their advantage turned against them, it seems one can say that this is the first time that the best philosophy is shown to be also the most agreeable with reason in everything, nothing being left with which to oppose it."

Considerations on the Principles of Life, and on Plastic Natures . . . , Ger, vol. 6, p. 541; cf. Loemker No. 61. (Translations in this paper are my own unless otherwise indicated; however, the translations of Leibniz have often been influenced by Loemker's versions. In most cases I give references both to an original language edition and to a convenient translation of the work. In citing Loemker's translations I usually use selection numbers rather than page numbers, which are different in the first and second editions.) In the same paper Leibniz suggests that Descartes himself would have embraced parallelism, had he recognized that motion is conserved as a vector, and not as a scalar quantity.

2. *PP*, I, 39, 41 (HR, vol. 1, 234–35); Reply to (the twelfth part of) Objections III, *ibid.*, vol. II, 75.

3. *Theodicy*, "Essay on the Goodness of God," Part I, § 50 (Ger, vol. VI, 130; ed. Diogenes Allen, Bobbs-Merrill, 1966, p. 51).

4. One point Leibniz is making in this context is that there is no "liberty of indifference"—i.e. no *strictly* arbitrary act. But the possibility of sub-conscious causes also is relevant to cases where one believes, for example, that the whole explanation of one's having done A is to be found in one's conscious desire for X.

5. It isn't clear whether the example is supposed to suggest that desires might *just happen* to coincide with bodily movements, or rather that they might be effects rather than causes of conditions sufficient for the movement "desired." In fact Leibniz's own official view is somewhat closer to the first position: there is *no* causal connection between mental and physical states, but God sees to it that there is an appropriate "harmony" between the two series. Incidentally, Leibniz's mention of a "vivid internal feeling" seems to go beyond Descartes' relatively bland characterizations of the apprehension of freedom.

6. See, e.g. the "fourthly" clause of the Replies to Objections II, especially HR II, 42.

7. Leibniz remarks that what Descartes "adds" to the argument in the Meditations (presumably this would include the reference to God—see below) will be examined "in its proper place." As far as I know he does not carry out this promise.

8. On Article 8 of Part I, Ger IV, 359; cf. Loemker No. 42.

9. *Ibid.*

10. AT, VIII Part I, 7.

11. See, besides Meditations ii and vi, his reply to the first part of Objections II, HR II, 30ff.

12. AT, IX, 000; HR I, 190. For a later and more developed discussion of Descartes' "epistemiological argument" (in the *Meditations*) see Chapter 6, above.

13. See, for example, "Observations on . . . Descartes *Principles*," ad. Art. 43, 45, 46 (Loemker, No. 42); L. Courturat, *La logique de Leibniz*, Paris: Alcan, 1901, pp. 100 n. 2 and 203 n. 2. I have discussed some related aspects of the contrast between Leibnizian and Cartesian epistemologies in "Leibniz and Locke on 'First Truths'," *Journal of the History of Ideas*, vol, XXVIII (1967), 347–66 (Chapter 24 of this volume).

14. Thomas Nagel, "Armstrong on the Mind," *Philosophical Review*, LXXIX, July, 1970, 402. Nagel comes closer to the Leibnizian viewpoint in his previous sentence, which reads: "The real issue is whether one can know that one has conceived such a thing [as mental states existing apart from body]. . . ." From this sentence to the next Nagel seems to move without comment from "Can we know we have conceived such a thing?" to "Can we know we cannot conceive such a thing?" For Leibniz a negative answer to the *first* question is sufficient to "defeat the Cartesian argument." See also Leibniz's letter to Malebranche, June 22/July 2, 1679, (Ger I, 332; Loemker No. 22, ii):

> The distinction of the soul and the body is not yet completely proved. For since you admit that we do not conceive the nature of thought [*ce que c'est la pensée*] distinctly, it is not sufficient that we doubt the existence of extension (that is, of that which we conceive distinctly) without being able to doubt thought; that, I say, is not sufficient to draw a conclusion about how far the distinction goes between what is extended and what thinks, for one may say that it is perhaps our ignorance that distinguishes them, and that thought includes extension in a way that is unknown to us.

15. See Saul Kripke, "Naming and Necessity," in *Semantics of Natural Languages*, ed. D. Davidson and G. Harman (Dordrecht-Holland: Reidel, 1972), 253–355.

16. P. Malebranche, *Entretiens sur la metaphysique et sur la religion*, I, i. (I am grateful to Willis Doney for providing this reference.) Although there can be little question that this is the passage Leibniz draws on, his statement of the argument has a rather different character than Malebranche's own. Malebranche in effect argues that it is *just evident* that thoughts and mental states generally are one thing, and that attributes of matter something else.

17. Ger, VI, 587; Loemker, No. 64.

18. Ger, VI, 586.

19. In recent controversy a point that has particularly been discussed is whether thoughts can be said to have spatial location (and if not, what the consequences of this would be for the materialist thesis). See for instance Jerome Schaffer's well-known paper "Could Mental Events be Brain Processes?," *Journal of Philosophy* 58 (1961), 813–22. However, the argument that Leibniz here repudiates could be interpreted differently, as depending on the principle of non-contradiction rather than Leibniz's Law, viz.: "if anything is a brain state it is immeasurable; if anything is a thought it is not measurable; if

anything is a brain-state and a thought it is measurable and not measurable; hence no thought is a brain state." Whatever the importance of this distinction of logic, it does not appear that there is any need for a distinction with respect to the reply or counter-argument—especially since the one Leibniz offers here is in fact used (with some refinements) by Smart and other materialists in reply to Leibniz's Law arguments.

Note, incidentally, that Leibniz's treatment of the Cartesian epistemological argument (discussed above) suggests that he wasn't prepared even to *entertain* the idea that "Leibniz's Law" could yield the non-identity of mind and body *via* discrepancies in their (respective) "intensional" predicates.

20. Ger, *loc. cit.*

21. *Ibid.*

22. In this passage (and elsewhere, for that matter) Leibniz does not enter into subleties about the relation of language to theory.

23. See, for example, "Meditations on Knowledge, Truth, and Ideas," Ger IV, 422–26; Loemker, No. 33. That this is the correct interpretation of Leibniz's point seems strongly confirmed by the following passage, from a letter to Queen Sophie Charlotte (Weiner, 355):

> We use the external senses as . . . a blind man does a stick, and they make us know their particular objects, which are colors, sounds, odors, flavors, and the qualities of touch. But they do not make us know what these sensible qualities are or in what they consist. For example, whether red is the revolving of certain small globules which it is claimed cause light: whether heat is the whirling of a very fine dust; whether sound is made in the air as circles in the water when a stone is thrown into it, as certain philosophers claim; this is what we do not see. And we could not even understand how this revolving, these whirlings and these circles, it they should be real, should cause exactly these perceptions which we have of red, of heat, of noise.

This letter is cited by Hidé Ishiguro in "Leibniz and the Ideas of Sensible Qualities" (in *Reason and Reality*, Royal Institute of Philosophy Lectures, vol. V, 1970–71, ed. G. Vesey [London: Macmillan, 1972], pp. 49–63). Ishiguro's entire discussion bears directly on the points I discuss in the next few pages; I regret that I did not know of her interesting essay earlier. It would appear from this and other passages quoted by Ishiguro that there is an unresolved ambivalence in Leibniz's views on the reference of such terms as "heat" and "red," which may help explain the difficulties in his reply to Malebranche. In brief, he seems unable to decide whether heat, for example, should be identified with the cause of a particular sort of experience or with the experience itself.

24. See, e.g. "Meditations on Knowledge, Truth, and Ideas," *loc. cit.* Cf. *NE* III, iv, §§ 4, 5, 7 (Langley, 319; DA, 296).

25. *NE* II, ii, § 1 (Langley, 120–21; DA 120); cf. § 4. In *New Essays*, II, xxxix, §§ 9, 10, Leibniz characterizes "confusion" as "the lack (*defaut*) of the analysis of the notion that one has" (Langley, 270; DA 258). Leibniz's discussion of § 13 suggests that an idea is distinct only if it enables one to discover the nature and properties of its object.

26. Cf. *NE* Preface (Langley, 48; DA 54; also Loemker, 2nd ed., p. 339.)

27. *NE* II, viii, § 15 (Langley, 133; DA 131). Leibniz likes to claim that, applied to perception, this principle (with its implication of the internal complexity of a sensation) yields the conclusion that the correlation of a *particular* mind-state with a *particular* state of matter is not arbitrary or inexplicable, as Descartes thought. (See, e.g., *NE* Preface [Langley, 50; DA 56]). There may be reason to question the consistency of this talk of perceptions in terms of external causes with Leibniz's parallelist claim that mental

states have only mental causes. In fact, Leibniz sometimes distinguishes the causality of sensation (which is said to "be regulated on the body," and to "express the laws of motion according to the order of efficient causes") from that of the higher mental states (said to be caused by the will). See esp. Ger IV, 591.

28. Actually the matter is more complicated than this. Since Leibniz rejects conventionalism, he holds that we might assume that a definition or mark is distinct in the sense of uniquely individuating a given species when it is not. In fact, three or four separate questions are run together rather confusingly in Leibniz's various pronouncements on what it is to have a distinct idea of X:

1. Can we state a *mark* of X's, as opposed to just "knowing them when we see them"?

2. Can we give a characterization of X's which (in reality) uniquely picks out X's?

3. Do we thoroughly understand the "nature or causes" of X-ness?

4. Is our explicit knowledge of the properties of X's sufficient to allow (potentially) a full deduction of their properties, *qua* X's?

29. Ishiguro (*op. cit.*) presents a number of details relating to this point. However, at least part of the reason for the lack of a sharp distinction in Leibniz's philosophy between causally explaining, and analyzing a concept must be found in his uncertainty about whether e.g. heat is to be identified with a physical state or with the perception caused by the state (see n. 23 above). If one vaguely assumes that it is both at once, then a physical theory of heat may seem to be both an analysis of the nature of heat, and a causal account of heat.

30. *Monadology* § 17 (Ger VI, 609; Loemker No. 67).

31. *Ibid.* Cf. *Essays*, Preface (Langley, 61–2; DA 66–7).

32. Louis E. Loeb has shown, in an interesting unpublished paper ("Leibniz's Conception of Miracles," 1972) that Leibniz's criterion for determining whether a phenomenon is natural (as opposed to miraculous) is whether or not it is explainable mechanistically.

33. "A New System of the Nature and Communication of Substances," paragraph 11 (Ger VI, 482; Loemker No. 47, pt. I).

34. *Ibid.*, paragraph 3; cf. Bertrand Russell, *A Critical Expositon of the Philosophy of Leibniz* (London, G. Allen & Unwin, 1937 [2nd ed.]), ch. 8; also Ger IV, 559–60 (Loemker, 2nd ed., 577–8):

But besides the principles which establish Monads, of which composites are only the results, internal experience refutes the Epicurean doctrine: the consciousness that is in us of this *me* which apperceives the things that happen in the body; and the act that perception cannot be explained by figures and motions establishes the other half of my hypothesis, and makes us recognize in ourselves an indivisible substance, that must itself be the source of its phenomena, so that, following this second half of my hypothesis, everything takes place in the soul as if there were no body, just as according to the first half, everything occurs in the body as if there were no soul.

35. But in the Conversation of Philarète and Ariste, cited above, Leibniz himself suggests that one should not accept as axiomatic the exhaustiveness of the mind-matter dichotomy.

36. Ger II, 112; Loemker, No. 36, pt. II—2nd ed., p. 339.

37. *Monadology*, § 16.

38. Sometimes, however, Leibniz identifies our inner experience of "activity" as the key to our knowledge of ourselves as immaterial substances. See for instance Loemker, No. 2, n. 17; No. 64. As he himself seems to point out in the latter work ("Philarète and Ariste"), however, this identification appears to go through only on the Cartesian conception of matter as essentially inert—a conception that Leibniz rejects.

39. Cf. I. Kant, *Selected Pre-Critical Writings*, ed. G. B. Kerferd and D. E. Walford (Manchester: Manchester University Press, 1968), III.

40. *E.g.*, Jonathan Bennett, "The Simplicity of the Soul," in *The First Critique*, ed. T. Penelhum and J. J. McIntosh (Belmont, Calif.: Wadsworth, 1969), pp. 109–122, reprinted from *The Journal of Philosophy* (1967), pp. 648–660. (But Professor Bennett has indicated in correspondence that he too now regards the argument as more Leibnizian than Cartesian.)

41. *Critique of Pure Reason*, trans. Norman Kemp Smith (London: Macmillan, 19), A 351 (Second Paralogism: of Simplicity).

42. A351–52. In citing Kant I follow the Kemp Smith translation because it is generally reliable and widely used. The translation of this passage does contain one error affecting the sense: "that a thought should inhere in what is essentially composite" (next-to-last sentence) should read, "that a thought should inhere in the composite as composite" (the locution is the same as in the first sentence).

43. A 354.

44. A 355.

45. Kant, however, holds that the self is not presentable to sense and hence unknowable to us. So his rejection of the Leibnizian argument is not conceived as opening the way for a naturalistic account of thought or subjectivity.

46. A 363–64. But perhaps Kant offers this fable only as a *reductio* of (what he takes to be) the rational psychologist's definition of 'identical person'.

47. Roderick Chisholm, *Theory of Knowledge* (Englewood Cliffs, N.J.: Prentice-Hall, 1966), p. 102. Compare Thomas Nagel, "Physicalism," *Philosophical Review* 74 (1965), pp. 353ff (a suggestive discussion of a closely related point).

48. I wish to thank Fabrizio Mondadori and Stephen Barker for helpful comments.

Possible Gods

I

. . . The nature of an individual substance or of a complete being
is to have a concept so complete that it is sufficient to comprise
and allow the deduction from it of all the predicates of the subject
to which this concept is attributed.[1]

Certain recent commentators have convincingly argued that this famous definition from Leibniz's *Discourse on Metaphysics* is tied in with a characteristic
and unique Leibnizian position on the dependence of an individual's identity on
his properties. The latter position has been appropriately dubbed (by Fabrizio
Mondadori) "super-essentialism."[2] Super-essentialism is the view that all of a
given individual's properties are essential to him; to suppose a change of properties is tantamount to introducing a different individual. Leibniz allows that for
any individual (say Adam or Sextus) who inhabits the actual world, there will
be other possible (but non-actual) beings who share some of his more salient
properties (such as being the first man), and hence "resemble" him.[3] However,
these "other possible Adams and Sextuses" will differ from our Adam and our
Sextus with respect to certain other properties. Leibniz's super-essentialism will
thus require us to deny that they *are just* our Adam and our Sextus in other
possible worlds: rather they are different, although resembling, individuals. Following some well-known work of David Lewis on the semantics of quantified
modal logic, these commentators have recommended regarding the other possible Adams and Sextuses (or their concepts) as "counter-parts" of our Adam and
our Sextus (or their concepts).[4]

At least some of these commentators have then, rather naturally, taken a step
which it will be the business of this essay to criticize. They have suggested that
Leibniz's "counter-part theory" can be understood as providing an interpretation
of counter-factuals and certain forms of modal discourse within *his* system. For
example, Mondadori writes:

Where . . . the relevant counterfactual is—

(1) If Sextus had not raped Lucretia, he would have led a happy life, we are not
allowed [in light of Leibniz's super-essentialism] to take it to mean that Sextus has
the counter-factual property expressed by the following formula:

(2) If *x* had not raped Lucretia, *x* would have led a happy life. For to say that
Sextus has the property in question, or that he satisfies (2), is to say . . . that it is

possible that Sextus should not have raped Lucretia (and hence that it is possible that Sextus should have had a different history than the history he in fact had). A better interpretation of (1), and one which has the advantage of being compatible with Leibniz's "super-essentialism," is that (1) attributes to Sextus (not the property expressed by (2) above but) the property of having a complete concept one of whose counter-parts is such that (a) it does not entail the property of *raping Lucretia*, and (b) as a consequence of this, the property of leading a happy life follows from it.[5]

This passage shows that Mondadori interprets super-essentialism as entailing the denial of "it is possible that a given individual should act otherwise than he does." He goes on to propose that seeming direct attributions to an individual of properties like "possibly having ϕ'd" should also be interpreted in terms of other (resembling) possible individuals. This is, he says, to offer "an interpretation of *de re* modal predications which is consistent with Leibniz's super-essentialism."

> Thus, for example, when we say that Sextus (is such that he) might have ϕ'd, although we seem to be attributing to him the modal property of *possibly having ϕ'd, really* we should be understood to be attributing to him the property of having a complete concept one of whose counterparts entails the property of ϕing. We should be understood to be speaking, in particular, *via Sextus himself*, of the concept which is the counter-part in some world w_i of the concept exemplified by "our" Sextus in the actual world, and which is such that, had w_i been actualized in place of our world, it would have been exemplified by an individual one of whose properties would have been precisely that of ϕing.[6]

It is perhaps not quite clear whether or not Mondadori wants to hold there is *no* Leibnizian sense of "possible" in which one could say literally of an individual, "it's possible that he should have ϕ'd" (when in fact he didn't). I will suggest later that there is one consistent with the super-essentialism. For now we need only note what Mondadori does clearly hold: that Leibniz was a super-essentialist, and that his conception of possible worlds and possible individuals provides the basis for the interpretation of counter-factuals and *de re* modal discourse consistent with this position.

Now Mondadori does not expressly attribute these interpretations to Leibniz himself, and does not directly raise the question of whether he could have held them, consistently with other major aspects of his system, apart from the super-essentialism. However, at the end of his article he does claim to have shown that "it is possible to provide a unified treatment of the topics of reference, essentialism, and modality in Leibniz's metaphysics which centers around the notion of a complete concept."[7] And somewhat similar views have been expressly attributed to Leibniz by Hidé Ishiguro. She writes, for instance, that

> *What Leibniz meant* by saying that the opposite of "Caesar crossed the Rubicon" is possible, is that there could have been—in a different world—a person like Caesar in all respects except that of crossing the Rubicon, with its attendant consequences.[8]

She goes on to stress that the possible individual in question could not be Caesar himself. Similarly, with respect to counter-factuals:

> . . . *he* (Leibniz) *thought that* when we make such counter-factual claims as "Had Caesar not crossed the Rubicon, then . . ." we are not thinking about the historical Caesar himself, even though we do use the proper name 'Caesar'. We use 'Caesar' here to express an individual concept in which we then go on to make certain alterations by eliminating a predicate and replacing it by its contradictory. Thus although we *are* . . . thinking of a possible world, described in terms of a counter-factual in which reference is made to an individual in *this* world, the possible world so described does not contain Julius Caesar himself.[9] (Initial emphasis added, here and above.)

The first of these passages, to be sure, suggests an apparent discrepancy between Ishiguro's and Mondadori's approaches. She gives an instance of "*de dicto*" modality, while he is only concerned to interpret *de re* predication. However, I don't really think her example signals fundamental divergence in their concerns. For Ishiguro also says in the same place that the other possible worlds "show what is contingently true of the real Sextus" by exhibiting worlds in which many of Sextus's properties are exemplified by individuals who fail to do what he does. Both commentators are suggesting that ascriptions of possibility of the form "S might have ϕ'd" should be interpreted in terms of other individuals similar to S in other possible worlds.[10]

I agree, by and large, with their ascription of super-essentialism to Leibniz. That is, I agree with them[11] that for Leibniz no possible individual with properties different from those Caesar (for example) has in this world could *be* Caesar. I further agree that, for Leibniz, any two "possible Caesars" in different possible worlds must have different properties (since each individual is supposed to "mirror" all the properties of his possible world).[12] However, I want to argue that the theories of counter-factuals and *de re* modality that they sketch are *ruled out* for Leibniz, once their implications are considered more fully. More exactly, Leibniz cannot consistently subscribe to these views as general accounts of counter-factuals and *de re* modalities. While he might consistently have subscribed to them for one sort of context (the cases of Adam, Sextus, Caesar, and other created beings), to do so would have required that he make seemingly arbitrary and ad hoc distinctions. As neither Mondadori nor Ishiguro provides much evidence that Leibniz did accept these interpretations of his complete concept theory with respect to counterfactuals and *de re* modal discourse, even for the contexts they discuss, I think it better to refrain from ascribing them to him (subject, of course, to more textual evidence being produced).[13] In fact, I think my argument provides some independent support for an important, contrary conclusion developed by Robert M. Adams: that Leibniz's conception of possible individuals and possible worlds does not and cannot provide the basis for interpreting modal discourse within his system.[14] If the modal and counter-factual discourse that Leibniz accepted as metaphysically and logically correct is supposed to find its interpretation in talk of *possibilia* (or their concepts), contradictions, among other disasters, can be seen to ensue. Therefore Leibniz's notion of *possibilia* should not be ascribed this role. He is, then, a much less direct ancestor of contemporary "possible worlds semantics," than the Mondadori-Ishiguro analysis seems to suggest.[15]

The main argument I want to present will (as already noted) take us outside the Leibnizian contexts considered by Mondadori and Ishiguro themselves. Before turning to it, though, I will conclude this section by briefly pointing out some difficulties in what they say *for their contexts*. My aim is to make the rejection of their interpretations more palatable, by showing that they are subject to (so to speak) internal difficulties in any case. I will take their accounts separately, since differences of detail are relevant here.

Ishiguro's account suffers from what seems to me a serious textual error. She has Leibniz holding that, if 'xϕ is contingent, there must be in another possible world an individual "like x in all respects" up to the time xϕ's. (Subsequent divergence of properties will depend just on the difference the one (actual) individual having ϕ'd and the other (possible) individual not having ϕ'd.)[16] However, she offers no good evidence that Leibniz ever held this, and one long passage she cites implies the exact opposite: that any two possible individuals will have different properties *from the beginning*.[17]

This problem figures also in her representation of Leibniz's theory of counter-factuals. On her view, when we make a counter-factual claim like "Had Caesar not crossed the Rubicon, then . . . ," we are (according to Leibniz) thinking of one complete concept (Caesar's), which we then change by "eliminating a predicate and replacing it by its contradictory."[18] This suggests there would be no inconsistency between "not crossing the Rubicon" and the antecedent properties of our Caesar—a view which Leibniz seems explicitly to repudiate.[19] Moreover, Ishiguro does not justify her ascription to Leibniz of the view that human beings may achieve such familiarity with complete concepts (God's ideas) as to be able to manipulate them in this way.

Mondadori's account avoids these difficulties, but I think it has some problems of its own. We have seen that on his proposed (for Leibniz) interpretation of "if Sextus had not raped Lucretia, he would have led a happy life," the statement "attributes to Sextus the property of having a complete concept one of whose counter-parts is such that (a) it does not entail the property of *raping Lucretia*, and (b) as a consequence of this, the property of leading a happy life follows from it." But remember that Leibniz presents us with *many* "possible Sextuses." There seems no reason at all to believe that all those that satisfy (a) will also satisfy (b). That is, there will be possible Sextuses who don't rape Lucretia (or rather any Lucretia counter-part), yet still lead wretched lives (and others, no doubt, whose beatific happiness is altogether independent of their conduct toward women). Why should we bother to single out just one of these by uttering our counter-factual (when we could just as well have singled out another by uttering its negation)? Of course sophisticated possible worlds semanticists have ways of dealing with such questions. But Leibniz didn't, as far as I know. And this points up (I want to claim) just how far his conception of *possibilia* is from providing adequate grounds for an interpretation of counter-factual conditionals.

II

I now want to argue directly against the view that Leibniz *could* have accepted, as a general position, the sort of analyses of modal discourse and counter-factuals sketched for him by Mondadori and Ishiguro. The core of my argument is very simple—indeed elementary—although certain steps require some textual precision. Note first that Leibniz usually holds—indeed stresses—that some facts about God are contingent: it is possible that God should have done otherwise.[20] He might have prevented sin, or lacked knowledge He in fact has; He could have created a different world.[21] Further, certain counter-factuals with 'God' serving as the subject of the antecedent and/or consequent are true: e.g., "If God had created some other world, there would have been more evil than there is"; "If God had created some other world, he would have had a reason for doing so."[22] Now either these statements about God will fall within the scope of the Mondadori-Ishiguro proposal or they will not. If they do not, then it certainly does not seem warranted to claim that the account provides a "unified treatment of reference, essentialism, and modality in Leibniz's metaphysics." (And modal statements about God are hardly *incidental* features of Leibniz's metaphysics.) So let us explore the possibility that statements about God do fall within the scope of the theory.

At first the prospects may look promising. Leibniz does present his complete concept theory as an account of the nature of an individual substance as such, and without qualification: "It is the nature of an individual substance, or of a complete being. . . ." (That the complete concept theory must apply to all substances without exception is further indicated by the fact that Leibniz derives this account of substance from his "*praedicatuin inest subjecto*" theory of truth—which he explicitly tells us holds without exception for all true singular propositions.)[23] And of course Leibniz holds that God is an individual substance: He is, for instance, the "primitive simple substance" that "contain(s) in itself eminently the perfections contained in the derivative substances which are its effects."[24] Therefore we must suppose that God has a concept so complete that all his properties can be derived from it. So perhaps we should simply postulate other possible Gods (or God-concepts), the counter-parts of our God (or of His concept) and the Mondadori-Ishiguro analysis can go through. For example, the first of the statements mentioned above might be analyzed as follows: "There is for our God's concept a counter-part concept, which includes the property of choosing a different world, of which a consequence is the existence of more evil (sc. than there is in our world)."[25]

Unfortunately, this suggestion leads to contradiction and absurdity, when certain other fundamental Leibnizian views are taken into account. In various places Leibniz endorses versions of both the ontological and the modal arguments for God's existence. In the case of the ontological argument, he holds that existence does indeed follow from the notion of an all-perfect being (God), and that this fact is sufficient to establish God's existence, providing only that the notion of an all-perfect being can be shown to be free of contradiction.[26] But Leibniz holds that it follows from the definition of a perfection (as a positive quality capable of being possessed to the highest degree) that there can be no contradiction in the notion of an all-perfect being.[27] With respect to the modal argument, Leibniz argues that God can be defined as the Necessary Being, or the being that needs only be possible in order to be actual.[28] He then argues that the Necessary Being is possible, on the grounds that if He were not, no existence would be possible—which is false.[29] Now we must consider how the introduction of counter-part Gods (or God-concepts) would relate to these views. There would be no problem, of course, if we could assume that no counter-part God-concept can be supposed to include all perfections, or be the concept of "Necessary Being." But I do not see how this restriction can logically be maintained. For to say that God could have created another world, and yet that He necessarily exists, is just to say that it is (in some sense) compatible or consistent with God's having the properties from which His existence follows, that some other world be chosen. On the Mondadori-Ishiguro line of analysis, then, there must be counter-part God-concepts which do include our God's infinite perfection, or status as the Necessary Being, yet include also the choice of some other world than ours. For example, if I made the statement (true on Leibniz's view) that "God could have created some other world without ceasing to be all-perfect,"[30] I would have to mean (on their analyses) something like the following: "(Our) God has a complete concept one of whose counter-parts entails the property of creating a different world, without lacking any of the perfections included in our God's concept." But by the previous reasoning this counterpart concept must be instantiated *as well as* our God's concept, since existence follows from our God's infinite perfections. This is bad enough, but we must face the following consequence, too. The counter-part God and our God make (we are supposing) different world-decisions: that is, they choose to create different possible worlds.[31] Now among their perfections is omnipotence: thus *both* choices must be supposed efficacious. Given that both Gods exist, both world decisions are also actual. But different possible worlds are supposed to be incompossible.[32] We have reached the result, then, that incompatible worlds (i.e., worlds that cannot, logically, coexist) coexist.

Now the following reply might be made here. It might be argued that the problem we have generated exists in Leibniz's system in any case, and is not merely the product of the Mondadori-Ishiguro proposals. (Hence the problem does not constitute an objection to their proposals.) For, given that Leibniz does maintain there is no impossibility in God's having chosen some other world,[33] how *can* we rule out the reality (in whatever sense possibles are real) of a possible God who does make this alternative choice? But then, since there's nothing to rule out this other possible God's being attributed infinite perfections, He too will necessarily exist in actuality. In other words, we get our contradictions in any case.

My answer to this reasoning is that there are at least two ways of saving Leibniz's position from seeming to entail a plurality of possible Gods. Neither, however, is compatible with the Mondadori-Ishiguro proposals, construed as general interpretations of counter-factuals and *de re* modalities in Leibniz's system. In the following section I examine these two solutions. The first involves rejecting super-essentialism in the sole case of God (while still assuming a qualified version of the complete concept theory applies to Him). The second solution, derived from Robert Adams, allows us to retain super-essentialism even for God (and hence requires no special adjustment of the complete concept theory in His case either). The latter solution indeed allows a uniform account of *de re* modal predications for God and creatures. At the same time it requires us to dissociate Leibniz's conception of *possibilia* from modal attributions within his system. Following Adams, I believe this dissociation is warranted.

III

For reasons given above, I take it as unproblematic that Leibniz's statements about substances *unequivocally entail* the extension of the complete concept theory to God. Nevertheless, we could suppose that the theory holds for God in a *special sense*, compatible with *denying* super-essentialism in the sole case of God. This would allow us to say, then, that God differs from created substances in precisely the following respect: it is correct to say that He could have made a different decision, hence had a property different from those He does have, and yet still be the very same individual He is. In other words, in the place of a plurality of possible-God-concepts, each individuating a *different* possible God, we would suppose *one* complete God-concept, comprehending modal and counter-factual properties.

This suggestion is derived from an argument offered by Benson Mates, in criticism of the view that super-essentialism directly falls out of the complete concept theory.[34] For as the latter theory is normally formulated (both by Leibniz and by his commentators[35]) it says only that an individual substance must have a concept complete enough to permit the deduction of "all its (or his) properties." But this formulation by itself doesn't entail any result about whether the same individual can or cannot be present (with different properties) in different possible worlds. For example, one *could* hold, with respect to Caesar, that (a) he does exist in different possible worlds; and (b) that God has a complete concept *of him* that comprehends (under a system of "world-indexing") his properties in *all* of the worlds in which he, Caesar, exists.[36] We know that Leibniz (with whatever justification) did not accept this picture with respect to finite substances. But perhaps he *would* wish to hold it with respect to God?

Perhaps he would wish to hold there is only one *complete* God-concept, encompassing many world decisions *He* could have made, as well as the ones He does make?

In evaluating this suggestion we need to consider two different issues. One is whether Leibniz might have nonarbitrary, logical justification for rejecting super-essentialism in the case of God, in the form in which he accepts it for creatures. The other question is whether there is textual justification for supposing he did intend to make this exception.

The first question is difficult to answer for the reason that Leibniz does not provide a clear logical basis for his super-essentialism with respect to *creatures*. Indeed, his explanations of this position are exceedingly vague and unilluminating.[37] For example, he says of Adam:

> . . . The nature of an individual should be complete and determined . . . one must
> not, therefore, conceive of a vague Adam or of a person to whom certain attributes
> of Adam appertain when it is a question of determining whether all human events
> follow from his presupposition, but one must attribute to him a concept so complete
> that all which can be attributed to him may be derived from it. . . . It follows, also,
> that this would not have been our Adam but another, if he had had other events,
> because nothing prevents us from saying that this would be another. It is, therefore,
> another.[38]

Now we know what *use* Leibniz wants to make of his super-essentialism. He wants to use it as a basis for denying that God is responsible for a created individual's misfortunes or bad choices, since *that individual* couldn't have existed unless he made those choices and experienced whatever he in fact experiences.[39] But the passage just quoted seems to be as close as Leibniz ever comes to offering a *reason* for the position. And the reason is just that "nothing would prevent us from saying it is another" person if his circumstances or choices are supposed to differ in some respect from the actual world. Would something, then, "prevent us from saying" that a different world-choice would imply a different God?

Well, perhaps the fact that *not* making an exception for God leads to contradiction and absurdity would by itself constitute a "preventing" reason in His case. And there is nothing in the passage just quoted to *rule out* our making an exception to the usual form of super-essentialism in the case of God. On the other hand, once such an exception is admitted, Leibniz's position with respect to *creatures* may begin to seem even more tenuous and ill-grounded than it did to start with. The question presents itself insistently: what prevents us from *denying* it would be a different Adam if circumstances had been different (given that we *are* prepared to deny this in the case of God)? And of course, to admit that a God who "has other events" than our God would not thereby "be another," is to abandon the idea of a unified treatment of modal predication in Leibniz's system.

The textual evidence is similarly undecisive. Leibniz does speak frequently in the Arnauld correspondence of "possible decrees of God."[40] This at first seems to lend support to the notion that a God who had decreed otherwise, might still be the very individual our God is. But in fact such locutions prove very little. In the first place, Leibniz does not say that *God's* concept includes alternative possible decrees. (Possible decrees are included in the concept of possible *worlds*.) And further, Leibniz also says of *himself*, "I would be able not to take this journey" (that he in fact takes).[41] The notion of a possible alternative set of divine decrees—like any other ascription of possibility in Leibniz—requires interpretation. There must of course be a sense in which God could have chosen otherwise—but then there must be a sense in which Adam (for example) could have, too.

There is, in fact, a way of interpreting these predications uniformly in Leibniz's system, that does not require us to postulate concepts of possible Gods who act otherwise than our God. This interpretation has been developed in recent work by Robert M. Adams.[42] Adams focusses on the passages where Leibniz describes *a contingent truth* as one that cannot be proved in a finite number of steps—or, in other words, a true proposition the denial of which cannot be reduced to contradiction in a finite number of steps. According to Adams, this account of contingency "seemed to satisfy (Leibniz) pretty well"; this is what Leibniz came to mean in saying the denial of a contingent truth is possible.[43] To adapt this interpretation of contingency to the contexts that concern us, we may read "x might have ϕ'd" as: "the supposition that x ϕ'd cannot be shown inconsistent with x's concept in a finite number of steps." (This analysis will hold both for God and for creatures.) From this notion of provable inconsistency, Adams distinguishes that of a concept's involving (demonstrably or otherwise) a contradiction or conceptual falsehood. A *possible world* for Leibniz is one that is conceptually consistent in this latter sense.[44]

This distinction between provable contradictoriness and conceptual inconsistency provides, I suggest, the key to attributing contingency to God's decisions, while denying a plurality of complete God-concepts (possible Gods). Adams himself applies the notion of conceptual consistency to God: it is conceptually inconsistent (though not demonstrably contradictory) that God should do anything other than what He actually does.[45] We need add only one embellishment to Adams's account to meet the requirements of our argument here. We need to attribute to Leibniz the view that it is conceptually inconsistent (though not demonstrably contradictory) for God *qua Being of unlimited perfection* or *qua Necessary Being* to create some world other than this one. This move also allows us to maintain superessentialism with respect to God: that He creates this world follows from His concept, is a condition of this being the very individual He is. But, again, the decision cannot be derived in a finite number of steps: *this* is the sense in which "it is possible that" God should do otherwise than He in fact does.

Precisely the same analysis will apply to the cases of Adam and Sextus— leaving their "counter-parts" out of the picture altogether. To say that Sextus might not have raped Lucretia will be to say that raping Lucretia does not follow from his concept in a finite number of steps. But why, then, is it legitimate to talk of other possible Sextuses, when it is not legitimate (I am suggesting) to talk of other possible Gods? A plausible answer is the following: there is no conceptual inconsistency between certain salient features of our Sextus—say the outward circumstances of his birth—and a variety of different futures. There are then many different complete concepts that may be identified as concepts of "possible Sextuses." On the other hand, the salient features of our God—notably His perfections—are not ultimately consistent (allowing infinite analysis) with a variety of different "futures": e.g., world decisions.

This interpretation denies the direct relevance of Leibnizian *possibilia* to the analysis of Leibnizian modal discourse. (We may even say, following Adams, that Leibniz uses 'possible' *equivocally* between "possible worlds" and "possible individuals" contexts on the one hand, and "it is possible that" contexts on the other hand.[46]) The interpretation assumes that the role *possibilia* play in Leibniz's metaphysics is largely theodicidic, not logical. In a sense, this conclusion is disappointing. (We would like to be able to think of Leibniz as a *nearer* ancestor of contemporary "possible worlds semantics.") I hope, however, to have provided an additional reason—beyond the detailed textual argumentation developed by Adams—for accepting the disappointment as unavoidable.

In conclusion, I should perhaps make clear that I have no intention of endorsing Leibniz's distinction between demonstrability and "infinite analysis" as the basis for a distinction between necessary and contingent truths. (His appeal to infinite analysis in this context indeed rests only on an obscure and undeveloped mathematical analogy.) I am not even concerned to endorse Adams's view that Leibniz was "pretty well satisfied" with the "infinite analysis" account of contingent truth in his later years. (Although I'm inclined to think that dissatisfaction with the view as an interpretation of Leibniz has tended to stem from dissatisfaction with the view itself: certainly this has been true in my own case.) My claims have been only the following. First, if we try to ascribe to Leibniz a unified interpretation of counter-factuals and *de re* modal discourse in terms of *possibilia*, we can generate absurdities from his modal discourse about God. These can be avoided by restricting Leibniz's super-essentialism to the realm of creatures. But this restriction will still not allow us to claim a unified account of counter-factuals and *de re* modal discourse—and it seems an awkward and ad hoc one in any case. If we follow Adams's line of interpretation, on the other hand, we are able, without generating contradictions, to interpret modal discourse uniformly for God and for creatures. (I do not claim we can derive an account of counter-factuals—but then I have argued above that there are serious difficulties in the Mondadori-Ishiguro approach anyway, even apart from its unsuitability to counter-factual statements about God.) Adams's account also seems to have a far more solid and extensive textual grounding. I believe these considerations, taken together, provide good reason for rejecting the attribution to Leibniz of a counter-part interpretation of counter-factuals and *de re* modalities.[47]

Notes

1. *Discourse on Metaphysics*, see. 13, in Ger 4: 433. Hereafter the *Discourse* will be abbreviated *DM*.

2. See especially Mondadori, "Reference, Essentialism, and Modality in Leibniz's Metaphysics," *Studia Leibnitiana* 5 (1973): 74–101, and "Leibniz and the Doctrine of Inter-World Identity," *Studia Leibnitiana* 7 (1975): 21–75, and Benson Mates, "Individuals and Modality in the Philosophy of Leibniz," *Studia Leibnitiana* 4 (1972): 81–118. Some version of this view is also implicit in Hidé Ishiguro's *Leibniz's Philosophy of Logic and Language* (Ithaca, New York: Cornell University Press, 1972) (see pp. 119–25). Indeed I had assumed her view was *the same* as Mondadori's until she made clear in correspondence that she wishes to reject some of the consequences that Mondadori accepts. (On this distinction, see n. 10, below.)

3. This view is discussed at some length in the correspondence with Arnauld (see, e.g., Ger 2: 42–54) and in a famous passage at the end of the *Theodicy* (secs. 414–16, Ger 6: 362–64). Mondadori and Mates give many additional references in their articles cited above.

4. See Mates, pp. 110 ff.; Mondadori, "Reference, Essentialism, and Modality," pp. 94 ff. and "Doctrine of Inter-World Identity," pp. 54 ff. Both Mates and Mondadori refer to Lewis's article, "Counter-part Theory and Quantified Modal Logic," *Journal of Philosophy* 65 (March 1968): 113–26. Ishiguro also cites this article as having a Leibnizian reference (p. 11), though she makes no specific mention of the notion of counter-parts.

5. Mondadori, "Reference, Essentialism, and Modality," pp. 97–98. To simplify the form of the quotation, I have ignored Mondadori's paragraphing here.

6. Ibid, p. 99.

7. Ibid, p. 101.

8. Ishiguro, p. 123. Once again, though, it should be noted that Ishiguro doesn't apply the term "counter-part" to Leibniz's theory.

9. Ibid., p. 124.

10. Ishiguro has informed me in correspondence that she does *not* mean to deny we can say literally of a given individual that he might have had a property he in fact lacks. (It follows that her view of the matter differs somewhat from Mondadori's.) I am not yet entirely clear how she wishes to reconcile this position with the indications in her book (cited above) that individuals like our Caesar in other possible worlds, but with some different properties, are *not Caesar*. The resolution of this issue would not, in any case, affect my subsequent argument materially.

11. (And with Mates.)

12. Robert Grimm has maintained a contrary position in "Individual Concepts and Contingent Truths," *Studia Leibnitiana* 2 (1970): 200–22—but without, I think, giving due weight to the passages cited by Mates, Mondadori, and Ishiguro.

13. A shred of evidence is perhaps provided by a passage quoted (in a different connection) by Mates, p. 105, n. 69. However this passage seems to me to be more concerned with "knowing what would happen if" certain counter-factual states had been realized, than with analyzing counter-factuals per se.

14. "Leibniz's Theories of Contingency," in *Essays on the Philosophy of Leibniz*, ed. Mark Kulstad, *Rice University Studies* 63 (Fall 1977): 1–41, esp. sec. 3.

15. Ibid., p. 64.

16. Ishiguro, pp. 124–25.

17. Ibid., see also my review of her book, *Archiv für Geschichte der Philosophie* 57 (1975): 86.

18. Ishiguro, p. 124.

19. Not merely in the passage about Sextus that she cites (erroneously, in my view) but also throughout the correspondence with Arnauld.

20. It is, I think, fairly uncontroversial that Leibniz did hold this, and that (at least in his later writings) he did not normally think of the "contingency" of God's choices as reducing to the claim that more than one world is possible *in itself*, or self-consistent (where God's choosing the world He does might still be necessary). Adams's study constitutes the most comprehensive and textually conscientious treatment of this issue that I know of in English.

21. Cf. Ger 2: 44; 6: 38; 6: 362 (= *Theodicy*, sec. 414).

22. " . . . Since physical evil and moral evil are found in this perfect work (i.e., the created world), we must judge of it *without that a still greater evil would have been inevitable*. This great(er) evil would be that *God would have chosen badly if he had chosen otherwise than he did*" (*Theodicy*, sec. 130, Ger 6: 183). (The first set of italics is Leibniz's; the second mine.) "If, for example, God had ordained that bodies should move on a circular line, he would have needed perpetual miracles, or the ministry of Angels, to execute this order . . ." (*Theodicy*, sec. 355, Ger 6: 326). I owe these two references to Peggy Nicholson. See also *Theodicy*, sec. 416, Ger 6: 364: "Si Jupiter avait pris ici un Sextus heureux à Corinthe, ou roi en Thrace, ce ne serait plus ce monde." On the notion that God would have had other reasons if he'd created another world see, e.g., Ger 2: 51.

23. Cf. e.g., Ger 2: 56.

24. *Principles of Nature and of Grace* 9, Ger 6: 602; cf. *DM* 35, Ger 4: 460.

25. In "Leibniz on Necessary and Contingent Truth" (unpublished) John Earman has called attention to the fact that the interpretation of contingent truth in Leibniz through counter-part theory would require the introduction of "Counterpart Deit(ies)." (As far as I know, he was the first to point out this implication.) In his brief discussion Earman indicates that this fact leads to problems for the interpretation—although he does not consider the difficulties I'm concerned to develop here.

26. See for instance Ger 4: 358–59.

27. Ger 7: 261–62. This is an early note. During most of his later career Leibniz seems to have lost interest in proving that the concept of an all-perfect being contains no contradiction, perhaps for the reason that he came to believe that the modal argument (mentioned below in the text) was simpler and more elegant. But the issue is revived in the *Monadology*: See n. 29, below.

28. Ger 4: 358–59; 6: 614.

29. See Ger 4: 406. Nicholas Rescher calls attention to Leibniz's stress on the modal argument, calling it "the characteristically Leibnizian proof of the existence of God": *Philosophy of Leibniz* (Englewood Cliffs, N.J.: Prentice-Hall, 1967), p. 66. On this and the following pages Rescher analyzes the argument in some detail, and provides several references beyond those already cited here. However, I follow David Blumenfeld, as against Rescher, in supposing that Leibniz intended the argument to rely on the premise "It is possible something exists": rather than "something exists": see his "Leibniz's Modal Proof of the Possibility of God," *Studia Leibnitiana* 4 (1972): 132–40.

In the "Monadology," however, Leibniz argues that the Necessary Being is possible on grounds reminiscent of his earlier defense of the ontological argument: "Thus God alone (or the Necessary Being) has this privilege, that he must exist (*il faut qu'il existe*), if he is possible. And since nothing can prevent the possibility of that which includes no limits (*ce qui n'enferme aucunes bornes*), no negation, and by consequence no contradiction, that alone suffices to know the Existence of God a priori" (sec. 45, Ger 6: 614).

The notion that God is *unique* seems to be somehow implicated in Leibniz's argument here (cf. sec. 40, p. 613). But, whatever one may make of this implication, I don't think it will show us how to avoid the problems I find, with respect to God, in the "counterpart" analysis of Leibnizian modalities.

Leibniz did, incidentally, regard the uniqueness of God as demonstrable—although it's far from evident what exactly he has in mind. See David Blumenfeld, "Leibniz's Proof of the Uniqueness of God," *Studia Leibnitiana* 6 (1974): 262–71.

30. The relation between God's choice of this world and his perfection is admittedly a complicated subject. Rescher argues that one must distinguish, within Leibniz's system, between God's *metaphysical* perfection and His *moral* perfection. Metaphysical perfection is quantity of essence: "God, who exists necessarily as we have seen, *is in this sense* wholly and necessarily perfect" (p. 44; emphasis in text). Moral perfection, on the other hand, is "more akin to goodness"; God exhibits his moral perfection in the creation of the best world. According to Rescher the choice of the best world—and God's *moral* perfection in general—is contingent, not necessary, and depends on God's free will (ibid., p. 45; cf. p. 28). Adams, on the other hand, has argued (with much textual support) that Leibniz generally did not regard it as a contingent truth that God chooses the best; His choice of this world is still supposed to be contingent on the grounds that it is a contingent truth that this is the best world (see. 2.1). For the purposes of my argument it does not seem to matter which of these interpretations is correct.

31. This approach may require that there be one (or more) counter-part God-concept that includes the decision to create nothing. If this means "decides there is to be nothing," this (or these) counterpart(s) will be as troublesome as those considered in the text.

32. There can be no question that Leibniz did hold this, though I agree with an observation made by Mondadori (in conversation) that the logical foundation of the position is unclear.

33. See n. 19, above.

34. Mates, p. 106.

35. See, e.g., the initial quotation of this paper and Mondadori, "Doctrine of Inter-World Identity," p. 55.

36. See Mates.

37. A similar view is expressed by Mates, p. 105.

38. Ger 2: 42. In this and other passages from Leibniz's letters to Arnauld he attempts to dispel the latter's distress at the notion that God's mere decision to create Adam forever determined all subsequent events.

39. Cf. *Theodicy*. sec. 416, Ger 6: 364, where Athena draws the moral of possible worlds for Theodorus: "You see that my father did not make Sextus wicked; he was so from all eternity, he was always so freely: (my father) did nothing but grant him existence, which his (Jupiter's) wisdom could not refuse to the world in which he (Sextus) is included. . . ." See also Mates, pp. 104–105, for other relevant references.

40. Ger 2: 50–51.

41. Ger 2: 46.

42. See n. 13 above.

43. Adams, p. 12. Adams has argued in sec. 1 that in the earlier part of his career Leibniz depended just on the notion that more than one world is *internally consistent*, for his claims about contingency. The infinite analysis theory therefore constitutes "Leibniz's second main solution" to the problem of contingency.

44. More exactly, Adams holds that Leibniz's principal conception of a possible world is "that of a world whose *basic* concept does not involve (demonstrably or otherwise) a contradiction or conceptual falsehood, a world whose *basic* concept is conceptually consistent" (p. 35; emphasis on "basic" added here, but used by Adams on p. 32; these references are to sec. 3 of his paper). The basic concept of a possible world will include everything that happens in that world, but not everything that is true about its relation to God's will (e.g., whether he chooses to create it) (ibid. and sec. 1.2). Adams contrasts basic with *complete* concepts (the latter includes *everything* true of a world). He believes that there is a way in which the complete concepts of non-actual possible worlds do, for Leibniz, "involve, indemonstrably, conceptual falsehoods." (The latter quotation is from a letter.) I gather Adams introduces the distinction between basic and complete world-concepts *because* he believes a world-concept would involve a conceptual inconsistency by virtue of including entailing evidence that that world is not actual. I hesitate to accept this view without more explicit argument. Accepting it would not, however, fundamentally affect the argument of the present paper.

45. Adams himself applies his analysis to God's decisions: pp. 35–36.

46. Ibid., p. 36: "Thus Leibniz's main conception of possible worlds does not provide a possible worlds semantics for his main conception of possibility.

47. Spinoza pointed out a problem similar to the one I've been concerned to document here. Thus he argues as follows in the proof of *Ethics* 1.32 ("Things could not have been produced by God in any other way or in any other order than they have been produced"):

All things necessarily follow from the given nature of God (Prop. 16), and by the necessity of the nature of God are determined to exist and act in a certain way. . . . If things, therefore, could have been of a different nature, or have been determined to act in a different way, the order of nature would have been different; therefore God's nature also could have been different from what it now is; and hence (by Prop. 11 [God necessarily exists, since existence follows from His essence, etc.]) that (different nature) also would have to exist, and consequently there could be given two or more Gods. This (by Prop. 14, Coroll. 1) is absurd. (Geb 2: 73.)

It is true there are some un-Leibnizian assumptions at the beginning of this passage. But if the argument of this paper is correct, Leibniz too would have to accept the consequence that a different creation of "things" would entail a difference in God's nature.

I am very grateful to Fabrizio Mondadori for detailed criticism of a previous draft. He made me realize that the issues discussed here are considerably more complicated than I had originally thought, and his comments resulted in extensive revisions of the paper. I have not, however, tried to take account of all his suggestions and replies (which I hope he may present himself in some future work). I am also indebted to Robert M. Adams and James F. Ross for helpful comments, and to Hidé Ishiguro for the informative correspondence cited above.

Another essay criticizing the Mondadori-Mates treatment of the problem of contingency in Leibniz appeared while the final version of my paper was being typed: Dennis Fried's "Necessity and Contingency in Leibniz," *Philosophical Review* 87 (October 1978): 575–84. Fried, however, approaches the issues from a totally different point of view; as far as I can see his arguments neither overlap nor conflict with mine. I have also seen unpublished work by David Blumenfeld on some related issues.

The research for this paper was supported by a grant from the Guggenheim Foundation.

Leibniz's Dynamics and Contingency in Nature

I

In 1699 Leibniz wrote to a correspondent:

> My Dynamics requires a work to itself . . . you are right in judging that it is to a great extent the foundation of my system; for it is there that we learn the difference between truths whose necessity is brute and geometrical, and truths which have their source in fitness and final causes.[1]

And about a decade later he remarks in the *Theodicy*:

> This great example of the laws of motion shows us in the clearest possible way how much difference there is among these three cases, first, *an absolute necessity*, metaphysical or geometric, which can be called *blind* and which depends only on efficient causes; in the second place, *a moral necessity*, which comes from the free choice of wisdom with respect to final causes; and finally in the third place, *something absolutely arbitrary*, depending on an indifference of equilibrium which is imagined, but which cannot exist, where there is no sufficient reason either in the efficient or in the final cause.[2]

The claims made in these passages for the philosophical importance of Dynamics are strong and in a sense unequivocal. Yet they are also rather mysterious. Leibniz of course wants to hold that the laws of nature *are* contingent—not true in all possible worlds; this in fact is a point he often makes side by side with the claim that the existence of any individual substance is contigent, and depends on the free choice of God to create the most perfect of the possible worlds. But in these passages Leibniz seems to say more than this. He says we *learn* from Dynamics the difference between necessary and contingent truths, that the laws of motion show "in the clearest possible way how much difference there is" between the blind or brute necessity of mathematics and contingent or "morally necessary" truths that depend on the choice of perfect reason. What is more, he speaks in the first passage specifically of "my" Dynamics, while the second passage follows a long criticism of Cartesian physics and a statement of some of Leibniz's own physical principles. The suggestion, then, is that the specific principles that Leibniz believed he had established, in opposition to the Cartesians, help make evident the difference between necessary and contingent truths.

To a twentieth-century philosopher, this notion is apt to seem very odd. The question whether the laws of nature are necessary or contingent—assuming this is a reasonable question at all—does not seem in any way dependent on what laws are found to be the true ones. (Similarly, one would have difficulty making sense of the suggestion that the question whether individual existence is necessary or contingent must be answered with reference to what individuals actually exist.) And in fact, the contingency of laws as well as the contingency of particular existents seems often to be presented by Leibniz himself as a tenet of his system resting on purely philosophical intuitions. Nevertheless (as it will be the purpose of this paper to show), Leibniz's remarks in the passages quoted do reflect an important and persistent aspect of his thought. Further, his claims for the philosophical significance of his Dynamics, though largely anachronistic today, are tied up with some issues of considerable interest from the point of view of the history of ideas.

Leibniz's doctrine of contingency has, of course, been the subject of much controversy in the critical literature of the past seventy years. However, this controversy has tended to focus on the status of propositions about particular individuals—e.g., "Adam ate the apple"—and largely to neglect any problems about contingency that might be specifically related to his views about the laws of nature. Most attention has been devoted to determining how, if at all, Leibniz's claims that propositions about particular existents are contingent, and true only because God freely selected the *best* possible world for creation, can be reconciled with his further doctrine that in *every* true proposition the concept of the predicate is "in some manner" included in the concept of the subject. For the latter claim seems to imply that *all* propositions are implicit identities. But Leibniz's standard definition of a necessary truth is a proposition the negation of which implies a contradiction—in other words, an explicit or implicit identity. Thus the theory of truth suggests that even existential propositions may ultimately have to be construed as necessary, and brings in question the sense in which alternative worlds may rightly be characterized as "possible." (That another world is in itself consistently conceivable need not imply that it might have existed.) Of course, the theory of truth presents difficulties for any claim of contingency in Leibniz's system—not just for propositions about individuals. But some of the most interesting aspects of this particular problem are tied up with the treatment of individual substances.[3]

Naturally, it has not gone unnoticed that Leibniz regarded the laws of nature as contingent. However, their status tends to be touched on only incidentally in the literature, in connection with proposed solutions to problems deriving from the theory of truth. Thus, Louis Couturat cited the contingency of laws in Leibniz's system as evidence against the proposal that Leibniz regarded only existential judgments as contingent—and meant to *exempt* such judgments from the "analytic" theory of truth.[4] And as part of his effort to reestablish a version of the latter interpretation, E. M. Curley has replied that "according to Leibniz, the laws of nature are also existential propositions, so that they do not form a distinct class of contingent truths."[5] Curley quotes a passage in which Leibniz does represent the view that the laws of nature are contingent as resting on the premise that the existence of the "series of things" depends on God's choice:

[We said] these laws are not necessary and essential but contingent and existential. . . . For since it is contingent and depends on the free decrees of God that this particular series of things exists, its laws will be themselves indeed absolutely contingent, although hypothetically necessary and as it were essential once the series is given.[6]

Curley further clarifies his point by indicating that the laws of nature are "existential" in that they rule out certain possible states of affairs from the realm of actuality:

. . . "All circles are plane figures," which is given [by Leibniz] as an example of an essential proposition, says that a circle which is not a plane figure is not a possible thing. But a law of nature, such as "unsupported bodies fall to earth," says only that an unsupported body which does not fall to earth is not an actual thing, i.e., does not exist.[7]

Now one may feel some hesitation about this interpretation. In particular, it seems to deny Leibniz any distinction among universal laws, local law-like generalizations, "accidental" generalizations, and hypotheticals true by virtue of the falsity of the antecedent. (The example Curley uses is, clearly, far from being universally true—and has the special disadvantage, in this context, of *mentioning* a particular existent.) Further, it seems that a philosopher could hold that more than one "series of existents" is possible, without holding that more than one set of basic laws is possible.[8] (I will suggest below that such a view can be found in the writings of Descartes.) On the other hand, Curley is clearly right in pointing out that since Leibniz *does* believe the laws of nature are contingent, and since statements of laws of nature do have negative existential import, their truth, for Leibniz, cannot be altogether independent of God's choices of particular existents. What we need now, however, is some account of why the laws of nature should sometimes be ascribed *special importance* in illuminating the distinction between necessary and contingent truth.

In what follows I shall try to provide such an account, by placing Leibniz's interpretation of his dynamical conclusions within its historical context. Fundamentally, Leibniz was concerned to oppose—for religious reasons especially—the "geometrical" conception of natural science exemplified (in different degrees) by his predecessors Descartes and Spinoza. That is to say, he was concerned to oppose the assimilation of physics to geometry, and of physical necessity to geometrical necessity. Leibniz shared with most of his contemporaries the view that the axioms of Euclidean geometry are among the eternal truths: within Leibniz's system this view appears as the doctrine that the axioms of geometry are true of all possible (i.e., consistently conceivable) worlds for reasons connected with the concept of space.[9] He believed he could establish that this status is *not* shared by the laws of mechanics. Leibniz believed his Dynamics yielded this conclusion in virtue of showing (1) that matter cannot be adequately conceived in purely geometrical terms—that "the essence of matter does not consist in extension alone"; and (2) that physical laws manifest features of "fitness and proportion," which not only are inconsistent with the geometrical view, but which further can only be explained with reference to the purposes of a "wise author" of nature. (He thus claims to have discovered the basis for a new, updated version of the Argument from Design.) That his reasoning on these issues is logically impeccable can hardly he maintained; on the other hand, the reasoning has, for the most part, a definite *ad hominem* cogency against the assumptions of his opponents.

But Leibniz's rejection of the doctrine of blind or brute geometrical necessity, on the basis of his conclusions in dynamics, has a murkier aspect as well. For he also takes his Dynamics to reveal that the underlying causes of natural phenomena must be found in immaterial or soul-like entities that are governed by final causes and may be identified with Aristotelian forms or entelechies. Such immanent purposiveness he also takes to be incompatible with the concept of determination by "geometrical necessity" (although, amazingly, he never makes clear that this is an entirely different point from those mentioned above). This view appears to reflect a good deal of wishful thinking about the possibility of partially defending the older philosophy of nature against the atheistical and "materialistic" implications of the modern view—and, one may be tempted to think, not much else. I will suggest, however, that even this conclusion, obscure as it may be from a strictly philosophical point of view, can be partially explicated in terms of the transition away from the early geometrical conception of physics. In this case a particular sort of conceptual difficulty implicit in the transition appears partially to account for Leibniz's otherwise bewildering move.

Finally, I shall point out some ways in which attention to these aspects of Leibniz's position can contribute to a balanced and historically accurate interpretation of his views on contingency. In particular I shall try to make clear that Leibniz *is* in one important sense entitled to present his system as an alternative to "brute geometrical necessitarianism"—*even if* he does not ultimately succeed in maintaining a coherent distinction between moral necessity and absolute necessity, or necessity in virtue of the principle of non-contradiction.

II

All things, I repeat, are in God, and all things which come to pass, come to pass solely through the laws of the infinite nature of God, and follow (as I will shortly show) from the necessity of his essence.[10]

Nothing in the universe is contingent, but all things are conditioned to exist and operate in a particular manner by the necessity of the divine nature.[11]

Things could not have been brought into being by God in any manner or in any order different from that which has in fact obtained.[12]

These quotations from Part I of Spinoza's *Ethics* represent the strongest form of the geometricism that Leibniz wished to oppose through his Dynamics. Spinoza's extreme position can be expressed in the claim that whatever is (in the timeless sense of "is") cannot not be, and whatever is not, cannot be. Individual existents (modes), their relations to each other, laws of nature, the two accessible attributes of thought and extension, and the world as a whole are alike in this respect. Only God is self-caused, or has an essence that includes existence; however, the causal necessity by which modes come into existence is itself in no sense weaker than the necessity of a logical deduction from necessary premises:

> From God's supreme power, or infinite nature, an infinite number of things—that is, all things have necessarily flowed forth in an infinite number of ways, or always follow with the same necessity; in the same way as from the nature of a triangle it follows from eternity and for eternity, that its three interior angles are equal to two right angles.[13]

This passage and the whole deductive format of the *Ethics* epitomize the influence of the geometrical model on scientific thought of the seventeenth century.

The geometric model was of course also a primary influence on the thinking of Spinoza's predecessor Descartes, although in some respects Descartes did not take things quite so far. Descartes does not deny that other worlds are possible; on the other hand, there is evidence that he did regard the basic laws of nature as necessary—as holding in any worlds God "could have created." The laws of nature, like the axioms of the geometers, are, he claimed, innate in our minds, so that "after having reflected sufficiently upon the matter, we cannot doubt their being accurately observed in all that exists or is done in the world."[14] Further, he remarks that in his Physics he had

> pointed out what [are] the laws of Nature, and without resting my reasons on any other principle than on the infinite perfections of God, I tried to demonstrate all those of which one could have any doubt, and to show that they are such that even if God had created several worlds, there could be none in which these laws failed to be observed.[15]

As this passage may suggest, Descartes in fact "deduces" his laws of motion, such as the principle that the same "quantity of motion" (mv) is always conserved, by appeal to the "immutability of God"—an appeal which may have echoes in Spinoza. (Notoriously, though, Descartes elsewhere espouses the views that the "eternal truths" or standards of logical and mathematical possibility themselves depend on God's will and that God enjoys a complete "liberty of indifference" in determining what they should be. Thus he is a source both of necessitarian thought and of the seemingly opposite tendency (also opposed by Leibniz) that views the circumstances of nature and even ordinary mathematics as "arbitrary.")

Descartes' conception of the laws of nature as *a priori* and necessary (like the axioms of geometry) is accompanied by a strictly geometrical conception of matter. This conception is advanced on purely intuitive grounds in his philosophical writings. The doctrine that what is "clearly and distinctily perceived is true" yields, in the *Meditations*, the claim that the real or objective properties of body (as distinct from mere sensory appearances) are just those properties that it possesses as "the object of pure mathematics."[16] By "pure mathematics" Descartes means, especially, geometry;[17] extension, figure, and motion or movability are apprehended by the intellect as "all that remains" when we consider a body as it is in itself, stripped of "external forms."[18] In the *Principles of Philosophy* Descartes further argues that extension is the one property of bodies that is presupposed by all the other physical properties, without itself presupposing them. On this basis he holds that extension is *the* defining or essential attribute of body.[19] These purely conceptual arguments ostensibly (at least) appeal only to ordinary intuitions, rather than sophisticated scientific understanding. This concept of body or matter is assumed by Descartes in deriving his laws of motion *a priori*. (The motion in the world, on the other hand, is not represented as itself part of the nature of body, but as a quantity imposed "externally," as it were, by the prime mover.)

Extrapolating a bit from Descartes' own statements, we might suggest the following argument as an exemplar of the moderate geometricism that views the laws of nature (if not individual existents) as obtaining in any world God could have made.

1. It is a necessary truth (true in all possible worlds) that the essence of matter consists in extension alone.

2. No world could exist that is not made by God.

3. Immutability is an essential properly of God, i.e., "God is immutable" is a necessary truth.

4. The basic laws of motion, m_I–m_n, can be derived with geometrical (i.e., logical) necessity from the assumptions that the essence of matter is just extension and that any material world is created by an immutable Being. (I take it one need not suppose the existence of motion to be a necessary truth, in order to hold that the laws of motion are true in all possible worlds.)

This series of claims is, of course, based primarily on the passage quoted above from the "Discourse." (Fortunately, we need not be concerned here with the plausibility of these propositions, and particularly of the fourth.) It yields the conclusion:

5. The basic laws of motion are necessary (are "observed," as Descartes puts it) in any world God could make.

Now someone concerned to dispute the conception of physical law implicit in this line of thought might very well wish to concentrate attention on the "laws" its propounder claims to have derived in this *a priori* manner. He might, for instance, try to show that some "laws of nature" presented as necessary either do not follow from these assumptions, or are false of the actual world (and *a fortiori* not true of all worlds that could exist). He might argue that *correct* reasoning from the geometricist's premises yields false results. None of these approaches, to be sure, would suffice to show that the laws of nature are *not* necessary. However, a sort of minimal argument against that conclusion would consist in that some particular set of laws (say that espoused by the geometricist) is both possible and false (not "observed" by nature).

In other words, one good way to refute the geometricist's conception of physics is to refute the geometricist's physics (without claiming that his principles are *necessarily* false). If such an enterprise sounds somewhat farfetched today, this is, I think, largely because the geometricist's conception of physics sounds farfetched. But the quotations from Descartes and from Spinoza may perhaps serve to remind us of the grip of the geometrical model in the early seventeenth century.

Some further points about the Cartesian outlook should be mentioned before we consider Leibniz's reaction to it. First, in the minds of seventeenth-century Cartesian philosophers there seems to have been a close connection between the idea that the essence of matter consists in (the geometrical property of) extension, and the idea that the laws of nature share the *necessity* of geometrical axioms. In fact, there does *not* seem to be any direct logical route between these notions: even if we suppose that Euclidean geometry is necessarily true of the world, the doctrine that the laws of nature are necessary seems neither to entail, nor to be entailed by, the proposition that only geometrical concepts are required for the statement of them.[20] But it is understandable that these ideas should be assumed to stand or fall together as twin aspects of the notion that physics (as Descartes remarked to Mersenne) "is nothing but geometry."[21]

In the same way both necessitarianism and the Cartesian theory of matter are tied up with the exclusion of final causes from the physical world—a position shared by Descartes and Spinoza. On the one hand, it is difficult to conceive how a bare bit of extension could be endowed with a purpose or goal. On the other hand, because of the close linkage of the concept of *purpose* with that of *choice*, it might well seem natural to suppose that only efficient causality can consort with the strict necessity supposedly characteristic of geometrical axioms.[22] Thus both the necessitarianism of the geometrical conception of physics, and the attendant conception of matter, may be viewed as having *some important connection* with the denial of immanent teleology. It is understandable, therefore, that someone interested in reinstating immanent final causes should find it *necessary* to oppose the other aspects of the geometricists' view. Leibniz, as we shall see, sometimes seems to think that rejection of geometricism in physics is *sufficient* to establish that there are purposive entities throughout nature.

Finally, however, we must concede that Descartes' use of the rather inscrutable notion of *God's immutability* makes it difficult to measure with complete assurance the distance between his and Leibniz's conception of the relation between physical and mathematical truth. Thus Descartes seems to hold that the laws of nature are true in any world God could have made—on the hypothesis that God is immutable. If this hypothesis is required only for the derivation of physical laws, and not as an underpinning for geometry proper, and if, further, it is taken to introduce some reference to volition and purpose (God's immutable will), then Descartes' actual position might turn out to be much closer to Leibniz's than at first seems to be the case. It would still remain true, however, that Leibniz differs fundamentally from Descartes in his concern to emphasize rather than minimize the distinction between physical and mathematical truth.

III

In his early years Leibniz himself accepted the geometricist conception of physics. He even attempted to derive "abstract principles of motion" by reasoning *a priori* from the conception of matter as mere extension.[23] One of the propositions he "proved" in this way provides the springboard for his later attacks on the doctrine of brute geometrical necessity in nature. Briefly, Leibniz had reasoned that mere extension must be "indifferent" to both motion and rest. By this he seems to have meant that there was nothing in the purely geometrical conception of matter to provide for a force of resistance, or reaction to every action. He then proceeded to the startling conclusion that when a body in motion, however small, collides with a body at rest, however large, both bodies will then move in the direction of the original motion, and at the original speed! According to his later accounts, he was even at the time distressed by this bizarre result, and supposed that the "wise Author of nature" would not permit such a disproportion between cause and effect. Subsequently he affirms (with a rather puzzling air of informativeness) that indeed such phenomena do not occur.[24] He affirms in these later works a principle of equality of reaction, which he derives from (or perhaps equates with) the principle that there is an equality between causes and effects. This principle he seems to regard as foreign to Descartes' "geometrical" reasoning. (Elsewhere he stresses that Descartes' disregard of the architectonic or non-geometrical principle of continuity—according to which all change is gradual—also explains fundamental errors in his physical principles.)[25]

Leibniz concludes that the Cartesian conception of matter is inadequate to account for the actual phenomena of nature, so a different conception must be substituted:

> If the essence of body consisted in extension, this essence alone should suffice to explain [*rendre raison de*] all the affections of body. But that is not the case. We observe in matter a quality which some have called *natural inertia* [read "resistance" or "reaction"], through which body resists motion in some manner. . . .[26]

> In order to prove *that the nature of body does not consist in extension*, I have made use of an argument . . . of which the basis is that *the natural inertia of bodies* could not be explained by extension alone. . . .[27]

Now we may note in passing that this argument does not depend exclusively on dynamical notions. For instance, it seems to presuppose a rather uncartesian conception of the function of an essence: Descartes does not think that even the fundamental property of motion *follows from* the essence of matter alone. On the other hand, Descartes does assume a certain conception of body in his deductions of the basic laws. And Leibniz does not make clear exactly what he means by an "account" of the properties of bodies. Therefore it is not easy to pinpoint the extent of their difference on this question; fortunately it does not seem very important that we do so.[28]

In at least one later writing, however, Leibniz seems to concede that this reasoning is perhaps not sufficient to clinch the case against Cartesianism. For his conclusion about impact might be staved off if only one assumed—as Descartes had assumed—that God conserves the same quantity of motion.[29] At this point, therefore, Leibniz brings to bear another argument. This argument, based openly on the research of Galileo, purports to prove that the true conservation principle in physics is not the conservation of motion (mv), as Descartes held, but the conservation of quantity mv^2, which Leibniz identifies as *vis viva*, active force. From this fact, too, Leibniz claims, it can be seen that there is more in nature than quantity of motion, and more to matter than is dreamed of in Descartes' Geometry.[30]

(The consideration that is supposed to prove this point is, briefly, as follows. A body of 4 pounds falling freely from a height of 1 foot will rise again to a height of 1 foot (assuming elastic rebound). A body of 1 pound falling from a height of 4 feet will rise again to a height of 4 feet. This shows, Leibniz says, that the "forces" operating in the two cases are equal (as the Cartesians would have agreed). However, Galileo had shown empirically that velocity in free fall from a state of rest is proportional not to the distance of fall but to the square root of the distance. Thus if force were measured in the Cartesian manner (mv), the "forces" of the two bodies on impact would be not equal but in a proportion of 2:1; i.e., the 1-pound body would rise to 2 feet, not 4 feet. So to get the correct results, we must introduce the quantity mv^2 as the measure of force. This argument, too, is held to manifest the principle of equality of cause and effect.)

Although Leibniz does use other dynamical arguments against the Cartesians, these two seem to have been his favorites. Sometimes, as I have indicated, he uses them in tandem; more often he presents them independently of each other. There are, to be sure, puzzling features in both arguments, from the point of view merely of the physical interpretation. In particular, it is difficult to understand in what way the second argument may be said to establish the *conservation* of *vis viva*.[31] What we are concerned with here, however, is Leibniz's *philosophical* interpretation of the arguments, his claim that they show the falsity of the doctrine of brute geometrical necessity in nature.

It is worth noting, first, that Leibniz's conclusions would provide the materials for a simple-minded but plausible repudiation of necessitarian claims along lines touched on above. The collision argument pretends to derive from Cartesian assumptions, "laws" that are in fact false of the world. The free-fall argument shows (according to Leibniz) that a principle Descartes himself derived is incompatible with the true "conservation" principle. Further, Leibniz in one place seems to go out of his way to indicate that Cartesian assumptions (as he interprets them), though false, are not impossible. He writes to the Cartesian de Volder:

> And doubtless such a world could be imagined as possible, in which matter at rest yielded to the mover without any resistance; but this world would really be pure chaos.[32]

(It might be objected that Leibniz could here be saying not that a Cartesian world *is* possible but only that we could (wrongly) suppose it to be possible. One might be particularly tempted to make this objection in view of the fact that "pure chaos" seems incompatible with the Principle of Sufficient Reason, which Leibniz does regard as a necessary truth.[33] However, it appears from the context that Leibniz does *not* think such a world would violate the Principle of Sufficient Reason, though it *would* violate another, contingent principle, to the effect that the better we understand things, the more they satisfy our intellect. I admit the passage is pretty peculiar.)

If the Cartesian laws are false but not *necessarily* false, it follows of course that the basic laws of nature cannot be attributed the necessity of geometrical axioms. And, given the influence of the geometric model on seventeenth-century conceptions of physical science, this way of arguing against necessitarian conceptions might well have more effect than appeals to alleged direct intuitions of alternative possibilities. However, it does not seem that Leibniz's own reasoning ever follows quite this route.

Clearly, Leibniz thinks the need to introduce the concept of reaction, and of mv^2 as a measure of force, to describe physical phenomena shows the inadequacy of the Cartesian conception of matter, and *thereby* demonstrates the inadequacy of the conception of physics as a science of brute geometrical necessity. His reasoning here appears to be, in a way, specious, since, as we have noted, there seems to be no direct logical route between the concept of matter as mere extension and the necessitarian position concerning the laws of nature. From a historical point of view, however, Leibniz's reasoning is understandable. The Cartesian characterization of physics as nothing but geometry suggests such a close association between a necessitarian conception of the laws of nature and the conception of matter as extension, that it might well be natural to view them as standing or falling together.

Up to this point the issue of teleology has not at all entered into our discussion of Leibniz's philosophical interpretation of his results in physics. We have merely considered two ways of construing the denial of necessitarianism—one manifestly present in the Leibnizian texts, and one somewhat artificially constructed out of elements provided by the texts. This negative aspect of Leibniz's position accords well enough with the conception of the status of physical laws prevalent in contemporary philosophy—so well, in fact, that some effort of historical imagination is required to understand the prominence he accords to the contention. However, as our initial quotations clearly show, Leibniz's interest in refuting the doctrine of "brute geometrical necessity" lay not in the bare demonstration of *non*-necessity but rather in showing that nature manifests "fitness and final causes." Two points seem to be involved in this claim. First, Leibniz believes his physics provides a basis for restating and vindicating the traditional Argument from Design against the view that nature is governed not by design but by geometry. Second, he believes that his concept of force requires us to assume that underlying the phenomena of physics are purposive, mind-like metaphysical entities that somehow provide a "foundation" for the phenomena.

IV

Many passages concerning the rejection of Cartesian physics reflect Leibniz's preoccupation with vindication of the concept of design in nature against the geometricist's view. The following are representative:

> *If mechanical rules depended on Geometry alone without metaphysics, phenomena would be quite different.* . . . One notices the counsels of [the divine] wisdom in the laws of motion in general. For if there were nothing in bodies but extended mass, and if there were nothing in motion but change of place, and if everything had to be and could be deduced from these definitions alone by a geometric necessity, it would follow, as I have shown elsewhere, that the smaller body would give to the greater which was at rest and which it met, the same speed that it had, without losing anything of its own speed. . . . But the decrees of divine wisdom to conserve always the same force and the same direction in sum has provided for this.[34]

> I have already asserted several times that the origin of mechanism itself does not spring from a material principle alone and mathematical reasons but from a certain higher and so to speak Metaphysical source.
>   . . . One remarkable proof of this, among others, is that the *foundations of the laws of nature* must be sought not in this, that the same quantity of motion is conserved, as was commonly believed, but rather in this, that it is necessary that the same *quantity of active power* be conserved. . . .[35]

> Perhaps someone will . . . believe that a completely geometric demonstration can be given of [the laws of motion], but in another discourse I will show that the contrary is the case, and demonstrate that they cannot be derived from their source without assuming architectonic reasons.[36]

(Again, "architectonic reasons" means such principles as the equality of cause and effect (or of action and reaction), the principle of continuity, and certain other principles such as the law of least action, that Leibniz regards as comparable in showing the governance of a wise Author of nature.)

Leibniz himself stresses that his discernment of intelligence and a sense of perfection behind the principles that his dynamics establish (in contrast to the "chaotic" implications of Cartesian mechanics) is closely related to the traditional Argument from Design. He believes that he has advanced beyond the traditional form of the argument by showing that the general laws of nature, as well as its particular phenomena, manifest the workmanship of a beneficent intelligence. In the "Discourse on Metaphysics," for example, he first endorses the traditional form of the argument (with special reference to animals in general and eyes in particular), and makes fun of its opponents. He continues:

> Thus, since the wisdom of God has always been recognized in the detail of mechanical structure of some particular bodies, it ought also to show itself in the general economy of the world and in the constitution of the laws of nature. And this is so true that one notices the counsels of this wisdom in the laws of motion in general.[37]

In the conclusion of the passage, which has already been quoted, Leibniz cites his argument against Cartesian principles that is derived from the problem of collision. In another work he claims that the dependence of the laws of his true dynamics on the principle of fitness provides "one of the most effective and obvious proofs of the existence of God."[38]

Without wishing to endorse any version of the Argument from Design, I would like to suggest that this is a quite understandable and rather interesting move for a determinedly pious person to make in the historical situation in which Leibniz found himself. The Cartesians rejected final causes and the Argument from Design on the grounds that events in nature were determined according to a "blind" deductive system of necessary "geometrical" laws. Leibniz does not deny the lawfulness of nature, and he does not deny that physics is a deductive system. However, he holds that final causes, or considerations of fitness and proportion, may be said to enter into the system on the top level, once one recognizes that the Cartesian physics is false.

This move that Leibniz makes in defense of the Argument from Design (against, we may suppose, such ferocious critics as Spinoza)[39] has some affinity with a move later made in its defense in the face of the theory of natural selection. In the words of F. R. Tennant,

> The sting of Darwinism . . . lay in the suggestion that proximate and "mechanical" causes were sufficient to produce the adaptations from which the teleology of the eighteenth century had argued to God. Assignable proximate causes, whether mechanical or not, are sufficient to dispose of the particular kind of teleological proof supplied by Paley. But the fact of organic evolution, even when the maximum of instrumentality is accredited to what is figuratively called natural selection, is not incompatible with teleology on a grander scale . . .[40]

> . . . The discovery of organic evolution has caused the teleologist to shift his ground from special design in the products to directivity in the process, and plan in the primary collocations.[41]

Although Leibniz seems to present his reasoning as supplementing, rather than replacing, the traditional argument from the evidence of "special design in the products," he too makes use of the discovery of mechanical principles—principles at first sight inimical to teleological conceptions of nature—to argue for "teleology on a grander scale." Whereas the later teleologist finds progress and hence purpose in the process of evolution broadly considered, Leibniz insists on the evidence of wisdom in the order and proportion that are maintained throughout nature as a result of the *sort* of mechanical laws that obtain. His claim against the geometricists is that, first, these laws are *not* those of "brute geometrical necessity," and second, that they can *only* be viewed as manifesting the values and aesthetic sense of a wise Creator.[42]

Leibniz's theological interpretation of the laws or principles of his Dynamics is more asserted than argued; it could hardly be expected to carry conviction to anyone not highly sympathetic to the aims of the Argument from Design. One might, obviously, accept his negative claim—that not all fundamental principles of physics are "geometrical"—while withholding credence entirely from the teleological interpretation. For there is no need to accept as exhaustive the division of geometrical necessity on the one hand and purposiveness on the other. Leibniz's point of view is, nevertheless, readily intelligible against its historical background. Indeed, it has not been altogether absent from the science and philosophy of our century.

V

As I have indicated, however, this attempted vindication of the intrinsically teleological character of the basic principles of physics is tied up in Leibniz's own thinking with a stranger and more elusive notion. Consider the following passages, from different parts of his writings.

First, from the "Discourse on Metaphysics" (1686) following a statement of the argument for the conservation of mv^2:

> And it becomes more and more apparent, although all particular phenomena of nature can be explained mathematically or mechanically by those who understand them, that nevertheless the general principles of corporeal nature and of mechanics itself are rather metaphysical than geometrical and belong rather to some indivisible forms or natures as causes of appearances than to corporeal or extended mass.[43]

From "Critical Thoughts on the General Part of Descartes' *Principles*" (1692):

> For besides extension and its variations, there is in matter a force or power of action by which the transition is made from Metaphysics to nature, from material to immaterial things. This force has its own Laws, which are deduced from the principles, not merely of absolute, and so to speak brute necessity, but of perfect reason.[44]

And from "On the Elements of Natural Science" (ca. 1682–84):

> Certain things take place in a body which cannot be explained by the necessity of matter alone. Such are the laws of motion which depend on the metaphysical principle of the equality of cause and effect. Therefore we must deal here with the soul, and show that all things are animated.[45]

Many other similar passages could be cited from Leibniz's work. But these three should suffice to make clear that the denial of brute necessity in nature is intimately associated in his thought with the postulation of immaterial forms, entelechies, or souls as the real metaphysical basis of phenomena. Of course, Leibniz had other reasons for maintaining that extension is purely phenomenal, and that real substances are indivisible and mind-like.[46] But he seems to regard the non-geometrical nature of his "laws of force" as providing independent reason for this view.

Bertrand Russell has with justice harshly criticized this aspect of Leibniz's position.[47] As far as I know, Leibniz never fills in any of the steps that might take one from "forces" in physics to "souls" in metaphysics. He does not indicate what it might mean to say that the latter provide a "general explanation" of the former. And he does not provide elucidation of the relation between the two claims made about the "general principles of corporeal nature"; i.e., that they are "rather metaphysical than geometrical," and that they "belong . . . to some indivisible forms or natures as causes of appearances"—he merely treats the claims as if they were obviously equivalent.

I have suggested above that there would be some natural affinities for a seventeenth-century thinker among the denial that the laws of nature have the status of geometrical axioms, the rejection of the Cartesian conception of matter, and the reaffirmation of the traditional "forms" or immanent purposiveness in the (non-human) world. It is also quite clear and beyond question that Leibniz took an almost obsessive pride in the notion that his system offered a "synthesis" of traditional metaphysics and modern physics, retaining the best of both views and in particular avoiding the anti-spiritualist implications of the latter. But there is a more specific and perhaps more interesting explanation, or partial explanation, of this obscurity in his system.

Despite Leibniz's opposition to the Cartesian theory, one finds in his writings a certain tendency to assimilate the concept of the material to that of the geometrical, in just the Cartesian manner:

If nature were brute, so to speak, that is purely material or Geometric. . . .[48]

Certain things take place in body that cannot be explained by the necessity of matter alone.[49]

Of course, Leibniz uses the term "matter" in different ways in different contexts; it would be quite wrong to attribute to him without qualification the assumption that "the non-material" can be equated with "the non-geometrical." But we may still suppose that his transition from forces in physics to "immaterial things" reflects some implicit assumption that any entity in nature not fully describable through the concepts of geometry, and particularly anything suggesting changes not reducible to relative change of place, is by definition excluded from the realm of the material. Similarly, where the concept of efficient cause has been associated with that of geometric determination, the reintroduction of forms, entelechies, or final causes might well seem warranted or inevitable, once the geometric picture is abandoned.[50] In such ways we can make out a path from "mechanical" dynamics to soul-like purposive entities as underlying "causes."

Here someone might object that since Leibniz postulates force as part of the "essence of body" or even of the "essence of matter," he can hardly be said to conflate the non-geometrical with the non-material. And further support could be adduced for this objection: for example, Leibniz in one place explicitly characterizes the failure to provide a ground for the laws of force as an insufficiency in the "common notion of matter":

> . . . It is not possible to deduce all truths about corporeal things from logical and geometrical axioms alone, those of great and small, whole and part, figure and situation, but others of cause and effect, action and passion must be added, by which the reasons of the order of things may be preserved. Whether we call this principle Form or entelechy or Force is not important, so long as we bear in mind that it can only be intelligibly explained through the notion of force.
>
> But I cannot agree with the view of certain prominent men today, who perceiving that the common notion of matter does not suffice. . . .[51]

What this really shows, however, is only that Leibniz's conception of matter was ambiguous. Thus, the very next paragraph after the passage quoted begins:

> Although I admit an active principle throughout bodies which is superior to material notions and so to speak vital. . . .

Similarly, while the first quotation may suggest for a minute that Leibniz's transition from "forces" to "entelechies" or "souls" is after all a merely terminological issue, the second reminds us of the edifying talk of "higher" sources and spiritual cures for those "mired in materialist notions" that characterizes nearly all his presentations of his conclusions in physics. "Entelechy" and "soul" invariably connote for Leibniz the unequivocally mental qualities of sense and appetition.[52] The obscure inference to these from the concepts of Dynamics is an internally important aspect of his thinking; unfortunately it is also, as Russell remarks, "one of the weakest points in his system."

VI

This concludes my explication of Leibniz's claim that his Dynamics teaches us "the difference" between necessary and contingent truths, and helps to overthrow the doctrine of brute necessity in nature. I wish, finally, to make two further observations concerning the significance of this explication.

First—to take up a very specific point—my account throws new light on a question discussed at some length in an interesting article by Leonard J. Russell: namely, how much "community of structure" is held to exist (in Leibniz's system) between our world and other possible worlds.[53] In the midst of some insightful and plausible analysis, Russell writes:

. . . While the laws of physical motion may in some respects differ from those in the actual world, the fundamental principle laid down by Leibniz for the actual world, viz., the equality of cause and effect, has some claim to apply to all worlds. In Ger III 45–46, and in Ger II, 62, he describes this equality as a "metaphysical" law, and this would make it apply universally. Again he tells de Volder that if matter had no inertia the world would be a chaos (Ger II, 170)—in which case it would not be a possible world—while to Remond (11 Feb. 1715, Ger III, 636) he says that if there is inertia then cause equals effect. It is true that this law is here described as a rule of *covenance* (in which case it is not metaphysical), but it is clear that if the effect were less than the cause in accordance with a constant law, motion would in the end cease, and God would have to intervene from time to time to set things moving again—and Leibniz was never happy about a system which would involve God in a permanent need for miraculous action . . . I conclude then that the equality of cause and effect is likely to be maintained in all worlds.[54]

Russell has been misled, I think, by the fact that Leibniz frequently uses the expression "metaphysical necessity" as equivalent to "absolute" or "geometrical" or "brute" necessity—which he *contrasts* with moral necessity, or the necessity by which "perfect reason" chooses the best among all possibilities.[55] My exposition has shown that in calling the principle of the equality of cause and effect "metaphysical" Leibniz actually means the very opposite of what Russell interprets him as saying. In the relevant Leibnizian contexts, to say a law is metaphysical is to say that it is *not* geometrically necessary; that it depends on immaterial rather than material principles, that it has to do with form, entelechy, and purpose rather than brute necessity. Certainly this dual usage of "metaphysical" is confusing; but only until its existence has been pointed out.

Russell's mistake has further led him to take for granted a seemingly erroneous interpretation of the remark to de Volder.[56] Perhaps it has also led him to the mistaken view that Leibniz's "unhappiness" about a principle such as God's frequent miraculous intervention is the same as a tendency to believe that such a principle is false in all possible worlds. (A world that involved God's constant intervention would presumably be, to Leibniz's way of thinking, radically imperfect and therefore non-actual—but not in the least impossible.)

The role of the law of equality of cause and effect in Leibniz's philosophy certainly poses some interesting and difficult problems for interpreters. To deal with these problems effectively and accurately, however, one must take into consideration the prominent, if peculiar, line of thought I have examined here.

Finally, a more general consideration. There has been much controversy over whether Leibniz was (a) sincere and (b) justified in presenting his system as an alternative of Spinozistic necessitarianism. As we have noted above, his theory of truth seems to have the implication that all truths are such that their denial implies contradiction. Thus it is not in the last analysis clear that more than one world is *really* possible on Leibnizian principles. Further, even apart from the theory of truth, it is not ultimately clear in what sense it would have been possible that God create some world other than the maximally perfect one of those that he could conceive without contradiction.[57] These are, indeed, crucial problems, and problems that provide an interesting challenge to Leibniz's more analytically inclined interpreters. However, I think that in a certain sense they have been somewhat overstressed. Even if one should conclude that the denial of a truth of fact *must* lead to contradiction on Leibniz's premises, there remain vast differences between his system and the necessitarianism of Spinoza. The main point can be expressed very simply: Leibniz's philosophy requires that the explanation of any existential proposition involve reference to value, purpose, perfection. As we have seen, this idea is particularly prominent in his presentation of his conclusions in Dynamics. No one could, I think, deny that in this respect Leibniz's position is indeed antithetical to Spinoza's.[58] And the antithesis is hardly trivial.[59] Granted, if Leibniz's general theory of contingency ultimately breaks down as has been claimed, he has not succeeded in providing a coherent opposition to necessitarianism *simpliciter*. Further, on one understanding of "brute geometrical necessity"—according to which a proposition is geometrically necessary if it could not, in the last analysis, have been false—difficulties for the general theory are indeed difficulties even for Leibniz's claim to have rejected the doctrine of "brute geometrical necessity" in nature. But what *can* still be said (in the face of such difficulties) is that within *Leibniz's* system—unlike the system of (at least) Spinoza—the laws of nature do have a specifically different status from that of the axioms of geometry. The latter, but not the former, are true of all worlds conceivable by God as candidates for existence. And the laws of nature that obtain in the actual world *are* the actual laws of nature *just because* a world in which they hold is the *best* of all possible (i.e., internally possible) worlds. In other words, they reflect and even (according to Leibniz) demonstrate the valuation on the part of the creator of "fitness and proportion"—however necessary *this valuation* may itself turn out to be on Leibniz's own premises. The same claim *cannot* be made for the geometry of the world—in Leibniz's system or in Spinoza's. Thus, there is a clear if limited sense in which Leibniz's attack on the Spinozistic doctrine of brute geometrical necessity in nature may be said to survive even the most serious objections to his general theory of contingency.

Notes

Members of the philosophy faculties of Ohio State and Rutgers universities, and several other individuals, have greatly influenced the present form of this work through their comments on earlier versions. I am particularly indebted to Robert Turnbull, Wallace Anderson, and Norman Kretzmann for specific comments and suggestions, and to Fabrizio Mondadori and James F. Ross for discussion of some of the problems dealt with in the paper. I learned of some of the articles cited from a bibliography prepared by E. M. Curley.

1. Ger, 3:645.

2. Ger, 6:321. In general, translations throughout the paper are my own unless otherwise indicated. However, I quote directly from the Elwes translation of Spinoza's *Ethics*

(which is accurate for the passages cited), and from the admirable Lucas and Grint translation of Leibniz' "Discourse of Metaphysics." My versions of other passages have sometimes been influenced by the published translations cited in the notes.

3. For example, its connection with the claim that every substance has a "complete concept" from which all its properties—past, present, and future—are somehow derivable.

4. "Sur la métaphysique de Leibniz," *Revue de métaphysique et de morale* 10 (1902): 12.

5. "The Root of Contingency," in H. Frankfurt, ed., *Leibniz: A Collection of Critical Essays* (Garden City, N.Y.: Doubleday, 1972), p. 91.

6. Ibid. The original source for this quotation is L. Couturat's edition of *Opuscules et fragments inédits de Leibniz* (Paris: Alcan, 1903), pp. 19–20. I have altered Curley's wording slightly.

7. Ibid., p. 92.

8. It might be questioned whether this idea would be congenial to Leibniz. A statement in one of his letters to Arnauld could be read as suggesting that he thought no two possible worlds have a law in common: "For as there is an infinity of possible worlds, there is also an infinity of laws, some proper to one, others to another [*les unes propres à l'un, les autres à l'autre*], and each possible individual of any world includes in his notion the laws of his world" (Ger, 2:40; this passage was brought to my attention by James Alt). However, I doubt that Leibniz really means to imply that every law is peculiar to some particular possible world. Earlier in the paragraph, for instance, he indicates that the decree to create a particular substance (Adam) was distinct from the "few free primary decrees capable of being called laws of the universe."

9. Cf. J. Moreau, "*L'Espace et les verités éternelles chez Leibniz*," *Archives de Philosophie* 29 (1966): 483ff.

10. Spinoza, *Ethics*, Part I, Proposition 15, Note, translated by R. H. M. Elwes (New York: Dover Publications, 1951), 2:59.

11. Ibid., Proposition 29. p. 68.

12. Ibid., Proposition 33, p. 70.

13. Ibid., Proposition 17, Note, p. 61.

14. "Discourse on the Method of Rightly Conducting One's Reason and Seeking Truth in the Sciences," part 5, AT 6:41. Cf. HR, 1:106. There is a non-trivial error in the HR translation, however.

15. AT, 6:43; HR, 1:108.

16. Meditation VI; AT, 7:80; HR, 1:191.

17. Descartes's seventeenth-century French translator renders "*in purae Mathesos objecto*" as "dans l'object de la géométrie speculative." Cf. AT, 9:63.

18. Meditation II; AT, 7:30–31; HR, 1:154–55.

19. *Principles of Philosophy* 1:53 (AT, 8:Pt. 1, 25; HR, 1:240).

20. See A. Quinton, "Matter and Space," *Mind* 73 (1964): 347–49, for an elaboration of this point. Quinton, surprisingly, seems to go along with the view that geometry *does* provide a body of necessary truths about "spatial qualities in the external world." But perhaps I have misunderstood him.

21. To Mersenne, 1639 (AT, 2:268).

22. Spinoza, in fact, makes clear in the Appendix to Part I of the *Ethics* that he regards the claim that "everything in nature proceeds with a sort of necessity" as incompatible with the supposition of final causes (Dover ed., 2:77).

23. Ger, 4:228–32. This paper of 1671 is translated in Loemker, pp. 139–42. Leibniz makes many allusions to it in his later writings.

24. See *Specimen Dynamicum* (1695) in *Leibnizens mathematische Schriften*, ed. C. J. Gerhardt (Berlin-Halle: Ascher, Schmidt, 1849–63), 6:241–42 (GM) and letter to de Volder (1699) Ger, 2:170; Loemker, no. 55, pp. 516–17.

25. See, e.g., *"Tentamen Anagogicum"* (ca. 1696), Ger, 7:279, Loemker, no. 50, p. 484; "Critical Thoughts on the General Part of Descartes's *Principles*" (1692), II, *ad art.* 45, Ger, 4:375, Loemker, no. 42, p. 398.

26. Letter to *Journal des savans* (18 June 1697), Ger, 4:464, Wiener, p. 100.

27. (1693) Ger, 4:466, Wiener, p. 102. As Gerd Buchdahl has pointed out, Leibniz fails clearly to distinguish *inertia* (a fundamental concept of Descartes' physics, taken up by Newton and reexpressed in his First Law) from *reaction* (the concept of Newton's Third Law), (*Metaphysics and the Philosophy of Science* [Cambridge, Mass.: MIT Press, 1969] pp. 421–22). However, it does not seem to me that Leibniz's argument against the Cartesian conception of matter depends in any important way on this confusion. In one letter to de Volder, further, Leibniz very explicitly distinguishes a version of the law of inertia ("each thing remains in its state unless there is a reason for change")—which he says is "a principle of metaphysical necessity"—from the law of reaction (24 March/9 April 1699, Ger, 2:170, Loemker, no. 55, p. 516).

28. It is rather interesting, however, to note the contrast between Descartes' *a priori* and Leibniz's *a posteriori* approach to this problem. For an illuminating account of the history of the concept of the essence of matter, see Ivor LeClerc's essay, "Leibniz and the Analysis of Matter and Motion," in his *The Philosophy of Leibniz and the Modern World* (Nashville: Vanderbilt University Press, 1973). Oddly, Leibniz sometimes suggests that the independence of motion from the concept of body proves the necessity of postulating God as the cause of nature (see Loemker, p. 639).

29. Ger, 4:465, Wiener, p. 101.

30. Ibid. See also "Discourse on Metaphysics," pp. xvii–viii, Ger, 4:443–44, trans. Lucas and Grint, pp. 28–32.

31. This point is made by Carolyn Iltis, "Leibniz and the *Vis Viva* Controversy," *Isis* 63 (1970): 26ff. (Iltis provides a very helpful critical analysis of several of Leibniz's dynamical arguments against Cartesianism.) One might suppose that in speaking of "conservation" Leibniz must mean that the force of a body *immediately after* impact is the same as the force *acquired* in free fall, and that this is expressed in the quantity mv^2— not that mv^2 is constant *throughout* the fall and rebound event. Certainly some passages lend themselves to this interpretation: cf. "A Brief Demonstration of a Notable Error of Descartes and Others . . ." (March 1686), GM, 6:117, Loemker, no. 34, p. 296; "Critical Thoughts," Ger, 4:370, Loemker, no. 42, pp. 394f. But R. C. Taliaferro seems to suggest a different view in *The Concept of Matter in Descartes and Leibniz*, Notre Dame Mathematical Lectures, no. 9 (Notre Dame, Ind.: University of Notre Dame Press, 1964), p. 29.

The controversy on this issue between Leibniz and the Cartesians is apt to seem utterly mystifying to laymen—and apparently to many physicists as well. Some of the important things to note are these.

1. The *principle* that Leibniz is particularly concerned to reject is the false principle that mv is conserved as scalar quantity, not the true principle that it (understood as the "momentum" of post-Newtonian physics) is conserved as a vector quantity. In later writings he seems to endorse the latter principle (though his concept of mass may not be identical with that of a contemporary physicist). However, he still maintains that mv^2, not mv, is the "true measure" of force in nature.

2. Whether force should be expressed as proportional to the Cartesian quantity mv, or the Leibnizian quantity mv^2 depends on whether one is concerned with force

acting through time or through distance: a body with twice the velocity of another will (in Mach's words) overcome a given force through double the time, but through four times the distance. Thus Leibniz' talk of the "true measure" of force is not defensible.

3. Kinetic energy (represented today as the quantity $1/2 \ mv^2$) is indeed conserved in perfectly elastic collisions. Leibniz of course was aware of the problem posed by inelastic collisions, and dealt with it by postulating that all collisions involve perfect elasticity on the micro-level.

32. Ger, 2:170, Loemker, no. 55, pp. 516–17.

33. As he says in this letter.

34. "Discourse on Metaphysics," p. xxi, Ger, 4:446, Lucas and Grint, pp. 36–37.

35. "On Nature Itself" (1698), Sec. 3–4, Ger, 4:505–6, Loemker, no. 53, p. 499.

36. *"Tentamen Anagogicum"* (ca. 1696), Ger, 7:279, Loemker, no. 50, p. 484. Taliaferro comments: ". . . The *Tentamen Anagogicum* is written for the sole purpose of showing the necessity for architectonic principles in mechanics and the insufficiency of geometry alone" (*Concept of Matter*, p. 31).

37. "Discourse of Metaphysics'" p. xxi. See also "The Principles of Nature and Grace" (1714) Sec. 11, Ger, 6:603, Loemker, No. 66, pp. 639–40.

38. Ibid. (He adds the qualification, *"pour ceux qui peuvent approfondir ces choses."*)

39. *Ethics*, Part I, Appendix. Spinoza's criticism, though vehement, is somewhat diffuse.

40. In *The Existence of God*, ed. John Hick (New York: Macmillan, 1964), p. 126; excerpt reprinted from *Philosophical Theology* (Cambridge: At the University Press, 1930), vol. II, chap. 4, pp. 79–92.

41. Ibid., p. 127.

42. Nicholas Rescher is therefore quite wrong in stating that, with respect to the Argument from Design, "the only characteristic touch Leibniz adds to the classic pattern of reasoning has to do with the pre-established harmony [among substances]" (*The Philosophy of Leibniz*, [Englewood Cliffs, N.J.: Prentice-Hall, 1967], p. 151).

43. See xviii, Ger, 4:444, Lucas and Grint, p. 32.

44. II, *ad art*. 64, Ger, 4:439, Loemker, no. 42, p. 409.

45. Loemker, no. 32, p. 278. This work was translated by Loemker from an unpublished Latin manuscript.

46. For example, the paradoxes of division; also the argument that since extension involves plurality and repetition, while substance is by definition a "true unity," we must postulate indivisible, unextended entities whose repetition somehow accounts for the well-founded phenomena of extension. Leibniz also has another sort of dynamical argument for force, derived from the relativity of motion: see Bertrand Russell, *A Critical Exposition of the Philosophy of Leibniz* (London: Allen & Unwin, 1900; 2d ed. 1937), chap. 7, esp. Sec. 41. This argument seems so confused that I have ignored it in the text.

47. Ibid., p. 87.

48. *"Tentamen Anagogicum,"* Ger, 7:279, Loemker, p. 484.

49. See n. 42.

50. See n. 38.

51. *"Specimen Dynamicum,"* GM, 6:241–42, Loemker, no. 46, p. 441.

52. See especially "New System of the Nature and Communication of Substances" (1695) Sec. 3, Ger, 4:478, Loemker, no. 47, p. 454.

53. "Possible Worlds in Leibniz," *Studia Leibnitiana* 1 (1969): 161–75.

54. Ibid., 166.

55. See e.g., Fifth Letter to Clarke, Sec. 4, Ger, 7:389, Loemker, no. 71, p. 696; *Theodicy*, "Discourse of the Conformity of Faith and Reason," Sec. 2, Ger, 6:50.

56. See above, p. 275. My interpretation, incidentally, accords with that of Bertrand Russell, who also interprets the remark to de Volder as showing that Leibniz regarded resistance as a contingent feature of bodies (*Critical Exposition*, p. 79). However, for independent metaphysical reasons Leibniz probably *should* have held that the Cartesian physics is impossible (see above, n. 38).

57. For a lucid defense of this claim see A. O. Lovejoy, *The Great Chain of Being* (Cambridge, Mass.: Harvard University Press, 1957), pp. 172ff. I have stated some reservations about Lovejoy's position in "On Leibniz's Explication of 'Necessary Truth'," in Frankfurt, ed. *Leibniz*. See also N. Rescher, "Contingence in the Philosophy of Leibniz," *Philosophical Review* 6 (1952): 26–39; and *The Philosophy of Leibniz*, chaps. 2, 3, and 5. This problem can be derived from the theory of truth, but also arises independently of it if "God chooses the best world" is taken to be a necessary truth.

58. In Note II to Proposition 33 of *Ethics* I, Spinoza does speak of the "perfection" realized by God in the creation of things; elsewhere, however, he explains that perfection is to be understood as the same thing as reality. Understood otherwise, perfection and imperfection are "merely modes of thinking": the judgment that things in nature are "well-ordered" reflects merely the fact that they happen to conform to our imagination. See the Appendix to Part I, and the Preface to Part IV.

59. Some participants in the discussion at Ohio State did object to this claim. To the extent that their objection may have resulted from a feeling that necessitation by final causes is still necessitation, and that is all that really matters, I am not inclined to concede it. (I do not see why this is *all* that really matters, although I agree it is one of the things that really matter.) However, their protest also made me aware of some purely logical difficulties in the conclusion of the paper as originally presented, which I have attempted to correct.

Compossibility and Law

THE NOTION of compossibility performs two related functions in Leibniz's philosophy. It helps to explain why not all possibles (possible substances) are actual: not all possibles are *com*possible, or such that they can exist *together*. And it underlies the partitioning of possibles into different *possible worlds*: a possible world is just a set of compossible possibles (and, it seems, there are infinitely many of these worlds).

But what is the basis of compossibility? Generally Leibniz regards a possible as that the concept of which is free from self-contradiction. To illustrate *im*possibility in a concept Leibniz cites the example of "the most rapid motion": he argues that this description cannot be satisfied because its ascription sustains contradictory conclusions.[1] But the concept of possibility at issue in this case is, more specifically, that of "logical" or "metaphysical" possibility: Leibniz uses the terms 'possibility' and 'impossibility' in other senses as well. For instance, an event may be (merely) "physically" impossible (in a given world) if it simply fails to conform to the general laws of nature in that world.[2] Thus there is room for legitimate doubt about how, precisely, the term 'incompossible' should be understood.

Two alternate interpretations of incompossibility prevail in the recent literature. Most critics think that the notion must, indeed, be understood as implying a logical relation among possible substances, or substance concepts: two such possibles are incompossible just in case the assumption that both are actualized gives rise to self-contradiction.[3] Some, however, have held that Leibniz's concept of compossibility has to do not with logical relations but with orderliness and lawfulness of relations among substances: two substances are compossible if and only if they relate to each other in suitable ways under possible laws of nature. (On this reading the notion of compossibility seems more closely tied to the Leibnizian conception of "physical" possibility.) Ian Hacking is a recent proponent of this interpretation, and Gregory Brown has expressed at least a leaning toward it.[4] They both cite Bertrand Russell as the originator of this understanding of compossibility: thus Brown often alludes to "the Russell-Hacking interpretation."[5] Fred D'Agostino has characterized these respectively as the "analytic" and "synthetic" interpretations of the compossibility relation.[6] I personally would prefer some other characterization of the distinction (such as "logical" vs. "lawful"); but because I want to draw on passages from D'Agostino shortly, it will be convenient to accept his terminology.

The analytic understanding of compossibility is widely regarded—even by some of its proponents—as ascribing to Leibniz a position apparently inconsistent with one or two other tenets of his philosophy. The synthetic interpretation, on the other hand, has been held untenable on the grounds that it deprives incompossibility of an essential part of its role in Leibniz's system. I believe that the negative arguments are in *both* cases inconclusive: my first step in what follows is to explain why (section I).

I go on to argue (section II) that there are simple reasons for regarding the analytic understanding of (in)compossibility as *basically* correct. But, as I explain in section III, there are also some textual grounds for thinking that lawfulness (and hence "synthetic" features) must come into the picture somehow.

I go on to suggest two paths for accommodating the notion of lawfulness within an analytic understanding of (in)compossibility. The first is one that, oddly enough, I derive from Russell. But on my reading of Russell he is not so much rejecting the analytic view as refining it. That is, he introduces the notion of lawfulness into the interpretation of Leibnizian compossibility in such a way that the coinstantiation of incompossibles would still result in logical contradiction. (Thus I deny that there is such a thing as "the Russell-Hacking interpretation.") Russell's reading, however, relies on a notion of what could (logically) count as a "sufficient reason" for God's creative act that may be problematic.

The second approach I will sketch is in some ways simpler than Russell's. It allows us to recognize the relevance of lawfulness in interpreting compossibility, without relying on the potentially awkward restrictions on sufficient reason that Russell's proposal seems to require.

In conclusion (section IV) I acknowledge that my efforts to account for incompossibility in analytic or logical terms are very much bound up with highly idiosyncratic Leibnizian metaphysical assumptions. That is, I do not pretend to offer an intuitively satisfying sense of the notion, but only a viewpoint on certain interpretive issues.

I

A prominent argument *against* the "synthetic" line of interpretation rests on a particular understanding of the role of incompossibility in Leibniz's system. According to this argument, incompossibility must be interpreted logically to serve the purpose of separating Leibniz's system from Spinozistic necessitarianism. Fred D'Agostino, for instance, notes the importance for Leibniz of the view that not all possibles are actual:

> . . . for Leibniz, not all possible individual substances are actually realized in the world. . . . It is important for Leibniz to make this claim, because, without it, his system collapses into Spinozistic necessitarianism of a kind he wished to avoid.[7]

D'Agostino goes on to cite a remark recorded by Leibniz the day after his meeting with Spinoza in 1676:

> If all possibles existed, no reason for existing would be needed, and possibility alone would suffice. Therefore there would be no God except in so far as he is

possible. But such a God as the pious hold to would not be possible if the opinion of those is true who believe that all possibles exist.[8]

D'Agostino thinks this passage implies that Leibniz's opposition to "Spinozistic necessitarianism" hinges on the claim that not all possible substances are compossible.[9] He thus maintains that a viable notion of incompossibility is essential to Leibniz's defense against Spinozism.[10] He then argues that only an analytic notion will really do for this purpose. On a reading that finds the source of compossibility—and hence of partitioning into possible worlds—in lawful relations,

> God's role as Creator logically presupposes his role as Law-Maker. Any argument of this form against necessitarian atheism is thus surely a very weak and nearly circular one. This difficulty seems intrinsic moreover to any synthetic solution to the incompossibility problem, and thus suggests that we must seek an analytic solution.[11]

I take it D'Agostino's point is that if God is brought in as the ground of incompossibility—as the partitioner of possibles into worlds according to laws—then one cannot very well argue from the plurality of incompossible possibles to the need for a divine chooser among them. As the passage indicates, this is his main ground for rejecting the synthetic type of reading. But I think it is not a cogent one, for the following reason.

It is one thing to say that Leibniz needs to postulate unactualized possibles—and the concomitant requirement of "a reason for existing"—to avoid Spinozistic necessitarianism. It is quite another to say that he needs these assumptions to ground an independent "argument" for a wise Creator.[12] Leibniz does, to be sure, regard the "harmony" of the actual world as the basis of an argument for the existence of a wise and beneficent Creator.[13] But *this* argument—and the general opposition to Spinozism—requires only the assumption of (possibly?) unactualized possibles: it does not rely on any particular interpretation of incompossibility. To the question, "Why did God not actualize *all* the possibles?" a sufficient answer would be: "Because not all possibles are compossible in the sense of relating to each other under suitable laws of nature." Thus a God-independent conception of incompossibility is not an essential component of the rejection of Spinozism.[14]

Further, the doctrine of incompossibility—on any interpretation—is not *sufficient* to defeat Spinozism if (as I suppose) this requires establishing a wise Creator. Leibniz does, after all, speak of the incompossible possibles struggling for existence *on their own*: it is an interpretive *problem* to relate this *Dasseinstreben* picture to the conception of a beneficent creative will.[15] In fact, the notion of incompossibility becomes crucial to maintaining a gap between the actual and the possible, just insofar as one *abstracts* from the divine power and beneficence.

Thus, on the one hand, I do not think that D'Agostino succeeds in showing that a logical conception of (in)compossibility is necessary for Leibniz's strategic purposes. But, on the other hand, I agree with his contention that frequently mentioned arguments against the opposite, analytic view are not compelling.

One such argument rests on the claim that logical incompatibility between any two possible entities is hard to conceive—or is even unintelligible—in Leibniz's system. For Leibniz himself rules out logical incompatibility among primitive concepts. The following early passage is often cited:

> It is yet unknown to me what is the reason of the incompossibility of things, or how it is that different essences can be opposed to each other, seeing that all purely positive terms seem to be compatible.[16]

As D'Agostino points out, this passage does seem to show that Leibniz was *thinking of* incompossibility in the logical way when he wrote it—a far from negligible point. But many critics have taken the view expressed in this passage to show that such a notion of incompossibility is, at best, deeply problematic for Leibniz.[17] (They differ on whether or not some form of "analytical" reading can be salvaged.)

To me it seems rather strange that the "positive primitive concept" issue has so readily been taken as weighty, either with respect to the interpretation of Leibniz's notion of incompossibility or with respect to its cogency. The early passage just does not take us that far with respect to understanding Leibniz's mature views about compossibility.[18] Further, the postulation of (logically) incompossible possibles—whatever its difficulties—seems easy and almost obvious in comparison with the doctrine that all concepts are analyzable into primitive positive properties (identical, as Leibniz also says, with the attributes of God).[19] Why should one suppose that the latter element in Leibniz's early thought came to repel the former? Or, if we have to abandon, on Leibniz's behalf, one doctrine or another, why not the primitive positive concepts one? D'Agostino gives fairly detailed reasons for discounting the positive primitive concepts "problem" for the analytic interpretation; I will not take time to retrace them here.

But even if one discounts the primitive positive concepts issue, it seems that there is another, connected reason for doubting that an analytic interpretation of incompossibility is available for Leibniz. For logical incompossibility would require irreducible relations, whereas Leibniz is widely thought to have denied such things (for reasons to some extent distinct from the primitive positive concept theory). Thus D'Agostino (among others) notes that irreducible relational predicates, together with negation, "seem to be necessary and sufficient conditions for solving the incompossibility problem" within a logical framework.[20] He illustrates how incompossibility can be achieved, assuming negation and irreducible relations, by the following example:

> If it is part of the complete individual concept of one substance A that it stands in a certain symmetric relation R to every other substance, *and* if it is part of the complete individual concept of another substance B that it does not stand in the relation R to any other substance, then A and B are clearly incompossible substances.[21]

One can more intuitively (and trivially) illustrate incompossibility, given relational predicates, by drawing on Leibniz's theory that there is for every possible substance a "complete concept" containing all the predicates of that substance, and that all the predicates are essential to the identity of the substance in question.[22] That is, part of the reason our world can have only one of the many "possible Adams" Leibniz discusses in the Arnauld correspondence—and not a whole slew of them—is that there cannot, logically, be two "first men." Because there cannot, logically, be more than one "fastest thrower on the Mets in the late 1980s," "our" Doc Gooden and George Plimpton's Sidd Finch cannot both be on the pitching staff at that time.

D'Agostino (following Rescher and Hintikka) backs up his example by arguing that Leibniz is not, after all, committed to the irreducibility of relational predicates. The latter issue remains, however, a focus of ongoing debate in the Leibniz literature: it is certainly a dauntingly complex as well as a controversial one. I want to avoid committing myself to any view on the subject, as much as possible.[23] For present purposes, I think it is sufficient to make three rather general points. First, the very difficulty in making out just what Leibniz's position on relations is (or positions are) indicates that it may be acceptable to interpret it (or them) in a way consistent with the logical understanding of (in)compossibility, if we have good reasons for wanting to do so. (Once again, there is more than *one* way to resolve any conflict that might arise.) Second, in any case, the synthetic approach to compossibility has to help itself to relational predicates, too: laws themselves, obviously, have to do with relations among entities.[24] Finally, as I shall explain later, even logical incompossibility may not strictly require irreducible relational predicates after all, given certain tenets of Leibniz's metaphysics.

II

Now I want to indicate briefly the simple reasons in *favor* of understanding incompossibility in terms of freedom from contradiction. The first has to do with the context in which the term 'incompossibility' typically occurs. When Leibniz tells us that not all possibles are compossible, we naturally assume that 'possible' means the same following 'com' as it does on its own, in the same sentence—and Leibniz (it seems) never explicitly says anything to forestall this assumption. But in all the contexts I have seen cited, 'possibility' is used in the logical or metaphysical sense.

The second consideration has to do with some (admittedly exiguous) textual evidence. As we saw above, Leibniz's very worry about the primitive positive concept theory in connection with incompossibility suggests that he was thinking of the latter notion analytically. Further, Leibniz at one point actually defines a *compossible* as "what, when taken with another does not imply a contradiction."[25]

Finally, constraints of lawfulness and order of *some* kind are needed to define the "pre-established harmony." Invoking them to account for compossibility as well risks collapsing what seem to be intended as distinct concepts into each other.

III

This cannot be the end of the story, however. For there is, after all, good textual reason to suppose that Leibnizian incompossibility has *something* to do with laws. I am not really persuaded by Hacking's argument to this effect, but I do find Russell's impressive. I will first take a look at Hacking's—a major source in the literature for the "synthetic" interpretation—and then take up Russell's more compelling textual point.

Hacking mentions Leibniz's late discussion of the novel *Astrea*, where Leibniz links compossibility with "connections with the rest of the universe," as indicating that Leibniz understood incompossibility as depending on synthetic laws. In a letter to Louis Bourguet Leibniz remarks:

> I do not agree that "in order to know if the romance of 'Astrea' is possible, it is necessary to know its connections with the rest of the universe." It would indeed be necessary to know this if it is to be *compossible* with the universe, and as a consequence to know if this romance has taken place, is taking place, or will take place in some corner of the world, for surely there would be no place for it without such connections. And it is very true that what is not, never has been, and never will be is not possible, if we take the *possible* in the sense of the *compossible*, as I have just said.[26]

Hacking asks: "Now let us suppose that *Astrea* is pure fiction, and contains no identifying reference to anything historical. Then how could *Astrea* fail to be compossible with the existing universe?" He goes on to propose that *Astrea*'s incompossibility derives from its events not happening to relate in a lawlike way to any spatiotemporal arrangement of the actual world—rather than from any logical inconsistency between entities of the fable and actual beings.

It strikes me, however, that there is more than one way that a proponent of the analytic line of interpretation could reply to Hacking's rhetorical question. One might suggest, for instance, that it is a matter of logical or metaphysical necessity that a series taking place in the world must have a suitably specified spatial and temporal location within the world. Compossibility (with actual substances and events) can be achieved only by satisfying these logical conditions.[27] Or, one could draw on the complete concept account of substance, and the accompanying theory of truth: if both are taken as logically necessary, then, one might argue, *Astrea* is logically incompossible with us substances in the actual world if *our* concepts contain no identifying connection with *it*. (A substance, I assume, is *not in a world*, unless there are "truths" relating it to other substances of that world.)[28] Leibniz's reference to the need for "connections" between a possible entity and actual ones can, in other words, be interpreted in logical terms as easily as in terms of lawfulness.

Russell, though, gives more compelling reason for thinking that Leibniz connected compossibility with (synthetic) lawfulness. He cites the following passage from the Arnauld correspondence:

There were an infinity of possible ways of creating the world, according to the different designs which God might form, and each possible world depends upon certain principal designs or ends of God proper to itself, i.e. certain free primitive decrees (conceived *sub ratione possibilitatis*), or laws of the general order of this possible universe, to which they belong, and whose notion they determine, as well as the notions of all the individual substances which must belong to this same Universe.[29]

Fortunately, one can accommodate such passages as this, incorporating some of the benefits of the synthetic reading, without giving up the analytic or logical understanding of incompossibility. This is the approach I want to attribute to Russell himself. His resolution turns on, as he puts it, "the necessity for *some* sufficient reason of the whole series." He continues,

Although this or that sufficient reason is contingent, there must be some sufficient reason, and the lack of one condemns many series of existents as *metaphysically impossible*. (emphasis added)[30]

He then quotes the passage from the Arnauld correspondence I have given above, and concludes:

This passage proves quite definitely that all possible worlds have general laws, which determine the connection of contingents just as, in the actual world, it is determined by the laws of motion and the law that free spirits pursue what seems best to them. . . .[31] Possibles cease to be compossible only when there is no general law whatever to which both conform. What is called the "reign of law" is, in Leibniz's philosophy, *metaphysically necessary*, although the actual laws are contingent. If this is not realized, compossibility must remain unintelligible. (emphasis added)

Russell's repeated stress on metaphysical necessity in this passage seems to have been overlooked. He is not saying *merely* that A's incompossibility with B is a matter of A's not being linked with B through suitable general laws (as Hacking suggests). He is saying further that the obtaining of such general laws, as a possible sufficient reason for the series' existence, is *metaphysically necessary*. Thus it is *metaphysically* impossible for both A and B to exist. And I take it this means—as it generally does in Leibniz—*absolutely* or *logically* impossible.[32] Russell's point is that the impossibility is not generated by considering A and B *alone*, in abstraction from the metaphysical necessity of a sufficient reason. His reading serves to accommodate the textual indications that "laws" figure in the partitioning of possible worlds, without (ultimately) giving up the "analytic" understanding of (in)compossibility.

There is, however, a problem for this reading that derives from a well-known passage from the *Discourse on Metaphysics* (vi), where Leibniz says that "one cannot even feign" something "absolutely irregular." No matter how apparently chaotic the data one starts with may be—say, a scattering of dots on a page—it will always be possible to subsume them under *some* law of interrelation. (That is, I take it, there will be a formula allowing us to predict the whole set, given one of its members.) He continues:

Thus one can say that in whatever way God had created the world, it would always
have been regular and in a certain general order. But God has chosen the one which
is the most perfect. . . .[33]

So, it seems, *any* putative group of possibilities must conform to some law or
other; the Russellian formulation turns out to be *vacuous* on Leibnizian principles.[34]

This objection can be met, however, if we may suppose that not just any
"law of the general order" qualifies as representing "a design which God might
form," and hence as providing a possible sufficient reason for creating a given
set of possible substances. I admit that this proposal requires a rather strained
reading of the relevant section of the *Discourse*. But, on the other hand, it does
seem consonant with certain passages of the Arnauld correspondence, including
the one on which Russell particularly relies. When Leibniz says that "each
possible world depends upon certain principle designs or ends of God proper to
itself, i.e. certain free decrees . . . or laws of the general order," his language
does not at all suggest the follow-the-dots model of *Discourse* vi. In a similar
vein he writes:

. . . as there exists an infinite number of possible worlds, there exists also an infinite
number of laws, some peculiar to one world, and some to another, and each possible
individual of any one world contains in the concept of him the laws of his world.[35]

So,

for instance, if this world were only possible, the individual concept of a body in
this world, containing certain movements as possibilities, would also contain our
laws of motion . . . but also as mere possibilities.[36]

I take it that Leibniz is here talking about something at least close to laws of
nature in the standard sense. It may be, in other words, that the requirement that
individuals, to be compossible, must conform to possible basic designs and
primitive free decrees of God expresses a *metaphysical* condition that is not
trivially satisfied by *just any* group of possible substances.[37] That is, he may
be assuming that only possible substances linked by fairly simple lawful generalities present a world that God could, logically, have sufficient reason to create.[38]

But maybe the passage just quoted also shows us an *alternative* way of relating
analytic compossibility and law—one that avoids the potential complexities
inherent in Russell's appeal to sufficient reason. For, as I read the passage, it
seems to indicate that each individual substance concept contains in itself a set
of world laws in a quite determinate way. That is, if we think of laws as *facts*
(of a certain kind), then individual substance concepts imply these possible
facts. Then incompossibility can be (partly) explained as follows. Possible substances S and T will be (analytically) *incompossible* if the complete concept of
S contains a fact, F, concerning the laws of nature of any world in which S
might find itself, and the complete concept of T contains a fact that is (directly)

logically inconsistent with F. For example, S's complete concept might contain the "fact" that e $=$ mc^2, while T's complete concept includes the "fact" that e $=$ 2mc. To suppose that S and T are both created is to suppose that, in actuality, e $=$ mc^2 *and* c $=$ 2mc—a *logically* self-contradictory assumption, we may suppose.[39] While lawlike relations of this sort may not be *all* that incompossibility consists in, we may still allow that the incompossibility of substance S and T has *partly* to do with the laws included in the concepts of the two substances respectively.

This way of construing the analytic conception of incompossibility involves an important departure from Russell, in that it requires us to hold that, after all, the incompossibility of two possible substances A and B *can* be established by considering A and B *alone*. But it does preserve the relevance of "laws of a world" to (in)compossibility judgments, while preserving the "analytic" intent of Russell's account (as I understand it).[40]

It also suggests the interesting point, in relation to the notion mentioned above, that incompossibility requires irreducible relational predicates. Once one allows substances to contain propositions, one can provide examples of incompossibility that do not rely on relational predicates—not even on "laws." For instance, if (substance) S is p; and T is q; and T "contains" the proposition 'If anything is p, nothing is q,' S and T are analytically incompossible.[41]

IV

In conclusion, I mention and concede that the views about compossibility I have proposed on Leibniz's behalf are tightly bound up with some pretty esoteric aspects of his metaphysics. For instance, the notion of possible *substances* containing *facts* (lawlike or otherwise) seems to get things more or less the wrong way round from the point of view of much traditional metaphysics. I admit it seems bizarre to me, even if it is (as I think) strongly suggested by certain Leibnizian texts. And ideas about incompossibility based on Leibniz's (supposed) "superessentialism" seem contrary to mainstream conceptions of essence, both traditional and contemporary. Thus, as I pointed out earlier, one seems to get logical incompatibility between possible Adams, within Leibniz's systems, by noting that there cannot, logically, be *two* first men. (While this notion may sound sophomoric, I do suspect it underlies what sense one may have of intuitive understanding of Leibniz's "possible Adams" talk.) But, of course, a more Kripkean notion of individual essences would allow us to say that "our" Adam could very well have existed without being "first." And Dwight Gooden just might have had the Mets' *second* fastest fastball in the late 1980s. If there is any "intuitive" explication of the notion of incompossible entities (and I am not sure there is), it may very well have much more to do with lawfulness than logic.[42]

NOTES

1. "Meditations on Knowledge, Truth, and Ideas," Ger. IV, 424 (L 293).

2. Additionally, an event can be "morally" impossible if it violates the principle that a rational being always chooses the apparent best. But this does not seem to be a notion that even potentially excludes any collections of substances as compossible; and I therefore set aside the notion of moral possibility in what follows. For fuller discussion of Leibniz's distinctions among senses of 'possibility' see my dissertation, *Leibniz's Doctrine of Necessary Truth* (Harvard University, 1965; New York: Garland [Harvard Dissertation Series], 1990).

3. See, for instance, Benson Mates, *The Philosophy of Leibniz: Metaphysics and Language* (New York: Oxford University Press, 1986), p. 75; Nicholas Rescher, *Leibniz's Metaphysics of Nature* (Dordrecht: D. Reidel, 1981), p. 57; Jaakko Hintikka, "Leibniz on Plenitude, Relations, and the 'Reign of Law,'" in *Leibniz: Critical and Interpretive Essays*, ed. Harry G. Frankfurt (Garden City, N.Y.: Doubleday, Anchor, 1971), pp. 158–59.

4. Hacking, "A Leibnizian Theory of Truth," in *Leibniz: Critical and Interpretive Essays*, ed., Michael Hooker (Minneapolis: University of Minnesota Press, 1982); and Brown, "Compossibility, Harmony, and Perfection in Leibniz," *Philosophical Review* 96 (1987): 173–203. Hacking says straightforwardly, "It is not logical inconsistency that prevents compossibility"; and Brown says that he is very strongly inclined to agree with Hacking's interpretation. (In the end, though, it is not entirely clear to me that Brown does agree with Hacking on the principal issue of whether incompossibility is a matter of logical inconsistency.)

5. Fred D'Agostino, who opposes the type of interpretation defended by Hacking, also cites Russell as an exponent of it. See his "Compossibility and Relational Predicates," in *Leibniz: Metaphysics and Philosophy of Science*, ed. R. S. Woolhouse (Oxford: Oxford University Press, 1981), pp. 89–103 (originally published in *Philosophical Quarterly* 26 [1976]).

6. Ibid.

7. Ibid.

8. *Opuscules et fragments inédits de Leibniz*, ed. Louis Couturat (Paris: Alcan, 1903), p. 530 (Loemker 169). In the preceding paragraph of this note, Leibniz claims that the fact that minds *have no volume* rules out their incompossibility or incompatibility "with all other things," or their "imped[ing] the course of things," and thus helps establish their immortality. This crude conception appears to have the implication that all minds are compossible (compatible). Clearly, it is not consistent with a theory of incompossibility within the context of Leibniz's later position, which holds that all possible substances are unextended. (The passage in question is among those cited by Ian Hacking in the essay I briefly discuss below.)

9. Compossibility is, indeed, a topic of the previous paragraph (see note 8).

10. D'Agostino, "Compossibility and Relational Predicates," pp. 90, 92.

11. Ibid., pp. 94–95. See also Rescher, *Leibniz's Metaphysics of Nature*.

12. For present purposes I go along with what I take to be a problematic interpretation of Spinoza's necessitarianism.

13. See, for instance, Bertrand Russell, *A Critical Exposition of the Philosophy of Leibniz* (London: George Allen and Unwin, 1937 [2d ed.; 1st ed. 1900]), pp. 183–85.

14. I think that Brown's paper, while ostensibly focused on the explication of (in)compossibility, is really fundamentally concerned with providing a positive answer to

---

(Full text)

the question whether, under the Principle of Perfection, God could rationally decide to create *less than* the maximum number of possibles.

15. See, for instance, David Blumenfeld, "Leibniz's Theory of the Striving Possibles," in Woolhouse, *Leibniz*, pp. 77–88 (this paper was originally published in 1973).

16. Ger VII, 194.

17. See Louis Couturat, *La Logique de Leibniz* (Hildesheim: Georg Olms, 1961 [2d ed.; 1st ed. 1901]), p. 219; G.H.R. Parkinson, *Logic and Reality in Leibniz's Metaphysics* (Oxford: Clarendon Press, 1965), pp. 83–85; Hide Ishiguro, *Leibniz's Philosophy of Logic and Language* (Ithaca, N.Y.: Cornell University Press, 1972), p. 47; C. D. Broad, *Leibniz: An Introduction* (London: Cambridge University Press, 1975), pp. 161–62; Hacking, "A Leibnizian Theory of Truth," p. 192; Mates, *The Philosophy of Leibniz*, p. 76. See also Russell, *Critical Exposition*, pp. 19–21.

18. As I have already indicated, the same reservation holds with respect to the early passage on the compossibility of (immortal) minds with all other things, also stressed by Hacking.

19. See Brown, "Compossibility, Harmony, and Perfection," pp. 181–83, for references. (Brown mentions a passage as late as 1696 in which Leibniz identifies primitive ideas with the attributes of God.)

20. D'Agostino, "Compossibility and Relational Predicates," p. 97. D'Agostino acknowledges that he is following Hintikka's reasoning in the article cited above. See also Rescher, *Leibniz's Metaphysics of Nature*.

21. D'Agostino, "Compossibility and Relational Predicates," pp. 96–97.

22. I assume for present purposes a "superessentialist" interpretation. (See, for instance, Mates, *The Philosophy of Leibniz*, pp. 75, 92).

23. Note, though, that 'incompossible' is itself a relational term.

24. Brown, noting this, pauses in his exposition of a version of that reading to point out that there is a "growing consensus" that Leibniz did not regard relational predicates as necessarily reducible to nonrelational ones ("Compossibility, Harmony, and Perfection," p. 194).

25. Grua, vol. 1, 325; quoted by Brown, "Compossibility, Harmony, and Perfection," p. 178. Brown cites Grua's dating for this passage of 1683–94; R. C. Sleigh, Jr., however, indicates that more recent scholarship has tentatively resulted in a much earlier date range of 1679–85. See his *Leibniz and Arnauld: A Commentary on Their Correspondence* (New Haven, Conn.: Yale University Press, 1990), pp. 172–73.

26. Ger III, 572 (L 661).

27. In *Leibniz's Metaphysics of Nature*, pp. 86–92, Nicholas Rescher maintains that differences in the "spaces" of different possible worlds *derive from* the analytic incompossibility of their respective substances: "Substances are located in different spaces *because* they contradict one another . . ." (p. 87). Rescher provides considerable support for his reading—though it does seem that in the *Astrea* passage Leibniz is representing compossibility as dependent on spatial connection (rather than the other way around).

28. ". . . it is in the nature of an individual substance to have such a complete concept, whence can be inferred everything that one can attribute to it, and even the whole universe because of the connexions between things" (Leibniz-Arnauld Correspondence, Ger II, 41; LA 44).

29. Ger II 51; Russell, *Critical Exposition*, p. 67.

30. Russell, *Critical Exposition*, p. 67.

31. I have omitted a sentence that reads, "And without the need for *some* general laws, any two possibles would be compossible, since they cannot contradict one an-

other." This sentence derives from Russell's acceptance of (a version of) the primitive concept worry, which I tend to reject. Note, though, that this sentence, too, indicates that Russell *understands* compossibility as a logical relation, just as Leibniz's expression of that worry indicates that *he* does.

32. On the previous page (66) Russell explains a "possible world" as a world "internally free from self-contradiction." I take it his subsequent appeal to Sufficient Reason is a way of maintaining a logical understanding of compossibility, while giving up the notion that it is entirely a question of "internal" factors.

33. Ger IV, 431; Lucas and Grint, p. 10.

34. Gregory Brown, "Compossibility, Harmony, and Perfection," emphasizes this difficulty for Russell's position.

A similar point is sometimes made with respect to Leibniz's concept of "expression." If 'expression' is understood in a broad way, so that *any* "constant and regular relation" is sufficient, any two possible substances will express each other, on Leibniz's principle. If it is understood more narrowly, as requiring *simple* relations, then it seems to collapse into harmony.

35. Ger II, 40; LA, 43.

36. Ibid.

37. Earlier I suggested (section II) that the analytic interpretation has the advantage of preserving a clear-cut distinction between compossibility and harmony. Insofar as one begins to build considerations of *simplicity of laws* into the interpretation, one does tend to lose this advantage.

38. Sleigh, *Leibniz and Arnauld*, pp. 52–53, argues for a sharp distinction between "laws of the general order" and "laws of nature" in Leibniz. I am not sure that the distinction is really as sharp in the texts as he suggests, but certainly his claim deserves fuller consideration than I have been able to give it here.

39. One might seek less anachronistic examples in Leibniz's conception of the laws of impact, and the conservation of "vis viva."

40. I suppose it is debatable how far this reading can accommodate the spirit of the passage from the Arnauld correspondence on which Russell principally relies. It might help, though, to propose that while compossibility with respect to laws is analytic in the way just suggested, the issue of God's choice among worlds raises a separate question about the potential attractiveness to God of the various systems of laws reflected in the substances belonging to the worlds thus partitioned.

No doubt any description of incompossibility that relates the concept to *lawfulness* should take account of Leibniz's distinction between the primitive and the derivative predicates of a possible substance concept. It seems to be generally accepted that laws are what make possible the deduction of the latter from the former. So we must ask whether compossibility enters at the "primitive" level, or only after the laws are "added." Or does a combination of primitives—a collection of not-yet-complete substance concepts—automatically generate its own laws? (Russell does not deal with this issue, and to that extent his treatment of compossibility must be judged incomplete; Brown treats it in detail in "Compossibility, Harmony, and Perfection.") The only observations I want to make on the point here are that, first, I have not claimed that incompossibility has to do *exclusively* with laws; and, second, to the extent that it *does* have to do with laws, it will obviously come in at the level of primitive concepts, just in case they do *determine* laws (as opposed to the laws being "added on").

41. I owe this point (down to the exact phrasing, as far as I can recall) to Robert Sleigh, who raised it in discussion. If Sleigh's suggestion is, as I think, compelling, it

perhaps deserves an essay in itself, given the prominence in the interpretive literature of the contrary assumption—that analytic compossibility requires irreducible relations. (For a similar example, see Nicholas Rescher, *A Theory of Possibility* [Oxford: Blackwell, 1975], pp. 78ff. Rescher, however, does not draw the same conclusion from the example as did Sleigh.)

42. Versions of this chapter were read at the New School for Social Research and at Rutgers University. I am grateful to all the participants in the discussions for their comments; I particularly thank Robert Sleigh, Dorothy Stark, Sarah Stroud, and Martha Bolton. The discussions made me all too aware of more problems and complexities in what I say here than I have been able to address in revision.

History of Philosophy in Philosophy Today; and the Case of the Sensible Qualities

RECENT decades have seen a tremendous outpouring of books and papers on figures and topics in the history of western philosophy. This remarkable scholarly production has accompanied, and has been reinforced by, a wide range of important editorial and translation projects, and the promotion of forums for oral exchange, including ad hoc conferences of every sort and size, and societies devoted to the ongoing study of the philosophies of individuals, periods, or ideological traditions. At one time—not that long ago—English-speaking philosophers interested in historical topics often talked mainly to each other. (Or at least those interested in certain particular periods—notably the early modern—did. I can't speak for work on, say, ancient Greek philosophy; but I suspect the point holds even in this case, if to a lesser degree.) Part of the reason for this isolationism was, simply, linguistic. American scholars, in particular, were often ill-equipped to deal even with original language texts (unless these happened fortunately to be in English), let alone with substantial volumes of secondary literature in French, German, or other continental European languages. Another part of the reason, however, was more ideological: "we" sometimes assumed that our investigations into historical subjects were motivated by "philosophical concerns," whereas "they"—French and German writers in particular, both past and present—were engaged mainly if not entirely in exegetical work. (Or, if "they" did approach historical figures from the perspective of present-day philosophical interests, the interests in question (it was assumed) were likely to be of a nature alien to "us"—or at least to those of "us" trained in analytically oriented graduate philosophy programs.)

To a large extent this isolationism is a thing of the past. It is more and more taken for granted that anyone wanting to make a significant contribution to the study of historical figures simply *must* be able to work with original language texts, and at least *ought* to have some command of important secondary literature in the major European languages.[1]

Although American education doesn't seem to have improved all that much with respect to language instruction in the last thirty years or so, it has become quite common for philosophy professors and graduate students alike to go about equipping ourselves with the linguistic abilities we find we need to come fully to grips with the subjects of our interest. Meanwhile international conferences, and more private academic arrangements, have increasingly fostered interaction among historians of philosophy of many nationalities—not only those from North America, England, Australia, and the Continent, but also Latin Americans, Israelis, Japanese, and others. And—rather curiously—ideological and methodological differences have turned out not to be so very formidable, after all.[2]

Study of the history of western philosophy, then, has become a thriving international "industry." But how much reason is there to think that all this activity is likely to bear *philosophical* fruit? Do historians today normally see themselves as joined in common cause with their nonhistorian colleagues—the cause, that is, of advancing philosophy per se? To what extent is the increasingly professionalized activity in historical studies actually relevant to the concerns of contemporary philosophers? Do contemporary philosophers even *care* about the positions of their (more or less) glorious predecessors—however casually or conscientiously interpreted? And to what extent *should* they care? (Is my colleague Gilbert Harman correct in maintaining, with respect to major figures of philosophy's past, that "their problems are not our problems; there are no perennial problems of philosophy"?[3] And if he is, does it follow, as I take Harman to suppose, that contemporary philosophical work is not likely to benefit from historical study?)[4] Are there perhaps, in the intellectual climate today, common influences affecting how both philosophy and the history of philosophy are "done"? How sharp, anyway, is the division between historians of philosophy and philosophers? (Was Quine right in joking—if he did—that they are the "two sorts of people interested in philosophy"?)[5] Is it desirable, or counterproductive, to conduct historical and philosophical inquiries in tandem?

In the second section of this paper I will document some close interrelations between historical study and philosophical argument with respect to an issue that has been as salient in recent philosophical work as it was historically, in the early modern period: the nature of sensible qualities. I hope to make plain that this example illustrates the possibility—indeed the actuality—of close interconnections between historical and philosophical writing. (My understanding of this distinction is, roughly, as follows: historical work is primarily concerned with interpreting (perhaps to some degree critically) the positions of philosophers of the past; people writing "philosophically" rather than "historically" are primarily concerned with developing and defending positions of their own on philosophical issues.)[6]

One thing I hope to make clear from this discussion is that recent and contemporary philosophers writing about sensible qualities often *do see* their problems as the same, or very nearly the same, as those of much earlier figures such as Descartes, Locke, and Berkeley. In section III I will argue, though, that philosophizing about sensible qualities *ought* to have been altered more than it in fact has been by post-seventeenth-century intellectual developments. I certainly don't draw from this line of reasoning the conclusion that studying the history of philosophy is a waste of time for people whose purpose is to make advances in philosophy per se. Rather, one way in which historical understanding can contribute to philosophy is to help us see how traditional and still influential conceptions of philosophical problems may be bound up with assumptions that require fresh evaluation today.

But before getting down to the concrete case, I would like to comment more directly on some of the questions raised above, with reference to recent work in philosophy and the history of philosophy. It was, in fact, a specific request of the editors of the *Philosophical Review* that I should offer some reflections on such general questions, particularly the question of "how contemporary philosophers view their history." The first observation I want to make, though, is that there is probably no general view about the relation of philosophy and historical study that presently enjoys wide acceptance—and perhaps none that deserves to.[7] One does encounter strong statements on various sides of the question whether historical understanding is essential, or important, or wholly irrelevant to good philosophical work. There are diverse views as well—often strongly held—concerning whether a philosophical agenda—or "philosophical motivation"—tends to contribute positively or negatively to worthwhile historical interpretation. Often these views are tied in with a strongly critical attitude to styles of philosophy or historical writing that are regarded as prevalent, or even towards individuals held to be "representative" of such styles. Understandably, therefore, they may give rise to resentment. It is not clear to me that they have had more desirable effects. Too often they seem to reflect an excessively simplified view of the attitudes, practices, and achievements of others working in philosophy and the history of philosophy. The remarks of the next section, at any rate, are intended to promote a softening of ideological division, rather than to advocate any general thesis, factual or normative, about the relation of philosophy and history.

I

"Analytical" philosophers have come in for criticism, in recent prohistorical writings, for evincing a delusory postpositivist denial of the philosophical relevance of the history of philosophy, and of their own historicity. Their philosophical imagination, and intellectual self-awareness, are said to suffer from this neglect.[8] "Analytical historians" who do attempt to integrate their own properly philosophical inquiries with historical commentary are often faulted for imposing their "own preconceptions" on the texts that interest them, and for neglecting aspects of older thought that do not conform to contemporary notions of live philosophical issues. Often critics seem to imply that *all* significant historical commentators brought up in the "analytic tradition" approach their interpretive tasks under the influence of a contemporary philosophical agenda.[9] Relatively little notice seems to be taken of another striking phenomenon on the current and recent philosophical scene: the fact that many writers *alternate* between producing wholly or largely historical studies (often of extremely high quality) and defending philosophical positions of their own in separate works. (It follows that historians of philosophy *cannot* be, categorically, two sorts of people—unless the very same human being can be two sorts of people at once.) I want to discuss these three points in reverse order. (For reasons of personal limitation, I will stick mainly to examples relating to (philosophically speaking) metaphysics and epistemology and (historically speaking) the early modern period.)

Any informed list of the most interesting and influential books on Descartes's philosophy since the late sixties would surely include Anthony Kenny's *Descartes*,[10] Harry Frankfurt's *Demons, Dreamers, and Madmen*,[11] and Bernard Williams's *Descartes: The Project of Pure Inquiry*.[12] While these works may not have the sheer textual weight of, say, Martial Guéroult's *Descartes selon l'ordre des raisons*,[13] each book combines textual seriousness with philosophically illuminating—even transforming—commentary. (In the case of Kenny's and Williams's books the commentary is not restricted to the *Meditations* and closely related texts, but extends to some less familiar parts of the Cartesian corpus, including some of the scientific work.) These works—especially, perhaps, Frankfurt's—are highly respected not only by English-speaking Descartes specialists, but also by scholars working outside of what we tend to consider the "analytic" tradition, including many of the French.[14]

Examples abound also from the study of other early modern philosophers—including those whose work is in one way or another more remote or difficult than Descartes's. Alan Donagan's recent book on Spinoza is well informed about the scholarly literature, and by no means inattentive to historical context.[15] Robert Merrihew Adams, well known for his work in ethics, philosophical theology, and theory of modality, has written two long papers on complex issues in Leibniz's philosophy that—a decade or two after their composition—are still dazzling in their combination of critical insight and total textual mastery.[16] David Armstrong's early work on Berkeley's theory of vision has only recently been surpassed.[17] George Pitcher's *Berkeley* is as solid and influential a contribution to Berkeley studies as the work of anyone not known, as well, for contributions to philosophy proper.[18] Barry Stroud's *Hume* is widely regarded as a classic.[19] The understanding of Kant's philosophy has been advanced by largely or (almost) strictly historical work by Charles Parsons, Jaakko Hintikka, Wilfrid Sellars, and Michael Friedman, among others known as well for independent philosophical contributions. Strawson's *The Bounds of Sense*,[20] while admittedly closely tied to a personal philosophical agenda, has had a major influence even on Kant scholars not very interested in the metaphysical and metaphilosophical commitments of *Individuals*.

Such examples are sufficient to call into question some of the aspersions that seem to be cast increasingly on "historians of philosophy in the analytic tradition," as found, for instance, in the interesting Prospectus for the *Cambridge History of Seventeenth Century Philosophy*:

> An important purpose of the volume [the editors write] will be to provide material for a reassessment of those canonical seventeenth century texts which have long been familiar . . . to students of philosophy at every level. They appear again and again in the curriculum . . . , from introductory courses to graduate seminars, and our view of philosophy as a discipline has in large part been shaped by a standard

account and critique, in many respects tendentious and oversimplified, of the various philosophical positions for which the great names of the early-modern period are the supposed spokesmen. Commentators in the analytic tradition, in particular, writing very much out of their own philosophical interests and preconceptions, have often lost sight of the complex context in which seventeenth century philosophy was written. In doing so, they have not only distorted its achievements but have denied themselves the tools necessary for the interpretation of the very words and sentences they continue to read and expound.[21]

They propose for their volume "a more strictly historical approach," which, among other things, will take full account of the interrelations between mechanistic or corpuscularian science and the various areas of philosophy. They say that this approach should have a "beneficial" effect, with respect to present-day philosophical interests, noting that "we must certainly understand past philosophies before we can legitimately or helpfully use them, or indeed learn from them."[22]

I would be the last to deny that "reassessment" of the aims and positions of historical figures, in relation to the "complex context" in which they wrote, can be an excellent thing. Like anyone else with a serious interest in the history of philosophy, deeply impressed with the intellectual achievement of philosophers of previous eras, I can easily be exasperated by casual treatment—or, even worse, purported "refutation"—of these philosophers, especially when the discussion seems to be based on erroneous or superficial understanding of what they were up to.[23] But I do regard the implication that this is a widespread failing of "philosophers writing in the analytic tradition" as a fairly bum rap. Apart from the examples I have already cited of outstanding interpretive contributions by such philosophers, I believe "analytic" philosophers have been by no means as broadly oblivious to historical context—and particularly its scientific dimension—as the *Cambridge History* Prospectus would suggest. (I will return to this issue in section II.)

(Critics of "historians in the analytic tradition" do not always offer specific examples in support of their generalizations. When they do get down to specific cases, they tend to focus on writings—not necessarily recent—which offer particularly doctrinaire statements concerning the relation of philosophy and history, such as Russell's 1900 (!) book on Leibniz, A. J. Ayer on Berkeley (from the mid thirties), Jonathan Bennett on several modern figures, John Mackie on Locke.)[24]

But, second, I think we need to avoid accepting as dogma the assumption overtly guiding the *Cambridge History* editors—which at first sight may seem almost tautological—that "we must certainly understand past philosophies before we can legitimately or helpfully use them. . . ." That professional historians may be uncomfortable with what we see as inaccurate or "mythical" use of the history of philosophy doesn't necessarily show that such use is invariably nugatory. As Jonathan Rée remarks (in a not unsympathetic review of the pro-historical collection *Philosophy in History*):

Th[e] desire to correct misconceptions about the past certainly makes a change compared with "conventional history of philosophy" which, as Bruce Kuklick diplomatically remarks [in his essay in this volume], "does rest on a feeble inquisitiveness about the past. . . ." Uncooperative analytic philosophers, however, will be wholly unmoved by these demonstrations. They will merely observe that some of their colleagues seem to be abandoning their vocation and joining history instead; they will not acknowledge that their work is a new turn in philosophy itself. And their position is not unreasonable. Why should historical accuracy be expected to pay philosophical dividends anyway? Intellectual historians may be able to show that the Great Dead did not actually hold the opinions which "conventional history of philosophy" unthinkingly attributes to them. But the actual opinions might well be philosophically impoverished compared with the imagined ones; and in that case, the historical errors might best be left undisturbed.[25]

Rée's position is, of course, provocative; I suppose most would find it at least overstated. An interpretation that to one person seems "philosophically poorer" than a commonly accepted one can well seem more satisfying and illuminating to another, precisely in virtue of providing deeper insight into the actual thought patterns of a strong philosophical intelligence. I only want to agree with him that imaginative distortion of the views of philosophers of our past isn't inevitably all that pernicious. Bennett and Strawson, for example, minimize the scientific realist thrust of Kant's philosophy, portraying him as a more straightforward type of ordinary-experience phenomenalist; and this seems to me to be wrong. But their readings have a power and authority of their own; and have helped many people begin to come to grips with the text of the First *Critique*. (Kant himself is capable of "playing fast and loose with the texts" of such predecessors as Berkeley and Leibniz, not always without philosophical effect.)

Of course there is no inconsistency in holding at once that historical accuracy does, or can, "pay philosophical dividends," and that historical misconceptions in the hands of an imaginative thinker can be used to good purpose. Both points can be supported by reference to recent treatments of the sensible qualities issue, as I will try to establish below.

I want to enter one further reservation concerning efforts to tie the prevalence of historical misconceptions to the personal philosophical commitments and lack of historical seriousness of "philosophers in the analytic tradition." It needs to be remembered that even the most dedicated and distinguished *historical scholars* may well be influenced by distorting "preconceptions" and personal agendas—interpretive, apologetic, or critical.[26] I personally believe, for instance, that Descartes's preoccupation with "answering the skeptic"—and particularly with skeptical concerns derived from later Greek philosophy—has, in the relatively recent past, been greatly overemphasized. (And the reasons for this distorted emphasis are in line with the *Cambridge History* editors' remarks, for they include insufficient attention to Descartes's announced revolutionary scientific and scientific realist objectives, and the philosophical preoccupation with skepticism evident through much of this century.) But any interpretive distortion that may exist is not confined to the work of philosophers pursuing their own overt epistemological programs. It is found as well in the writings—valuable and interesting as they are—of such truly major contemporary historical scholars as Richard Popkin and Edwin Curley.[27]

A. A. Luce's apologetic interpretation of Berkeley as a commonsense realist provides another example. As I. C. Tipton accurately observed in 1974, Luce "has combined the role of being the most important and influential Berkeley scholar of the century with that of chief apologist for the Berkeleyan philosophy" (specifically with respect to the credibility of Berkeley's claims to defend common sense).[28] Tipton goes on to provide a highly effective textual refutation of this central theme of Luce's reading. But what motivated Luce to defend Berkeley's credentials as a commonsense philosopher in the first place? Did he have no philosophical preconceptions of his own? If his scholarly and critical work in fact reflected personal philosophical commitments, were these only coincidentally related to the programs of commonsense philosophers in the decades in which he wrote? Although I cannot answer these specific questions, I think they are legitimate ones. (In section II I will try to show that recent *historical* interpretation of the views of figures such as Locke and Berkeley concerning sensible qualities has changed in ways suggestively parallel to changes in philosophical ideology.)

So far I have argued that views of "philosophers" and "historians" as separate groups of individuals occupying separate—perhaps opposed—intellectual camps today flies in the face of the facts; that prominent characterizations of "analytic historians" are too simplistic; and also that calls for separation of historical inquiries from philosophical preconceptions involve some questionable preconceptions of their own. I now want to point out that attitudes towards the philosophical relevance of the history of philosophy among prominent "analytical" philosophers take a variety of forms, even when "analytic history" is not directly at issue.

That "analytical" philosophers very often detach their writing from historical tradition is undeniable. But we need to consider what this detachment really shows about attitudes towards the history of philosophy. It is really unequivocal evidence of an arrogant sense of superiority in relation to one's predecessors, or at least towards one's more remote predecessors? I think that contemporary philosophers' ahistorical stance can, in many cases, be viewed less ideologically and more charitably, as an acknowledgement of human limitation—or perhaps even defensiveness concerning the standards that a well-meaning philosopher should be expected to meet.

Consider, for instance, the following statement from the preface to David Lewis's *On the Plurality of Worlds*:

It may come as a surprise that this book on possible worlds . . . contains no discussion of the views of Leibniz. Is it that I consider him unworthy of serious attention?—Not at all. But when I read what serious historians of philosophy have to say, I am persuaded that it is no easy matter to know what his views were. It would be nice to have the right sort of talent and training to join in the work of exegesis, but it is very clear to me that I do not. Anything I might say about Leibniz would be amateurish, undeserving of others' attention, and better left unsaid.[29]

There is an interesting change of focus in this passage from the question (roughly) of why Lewis doesn't take account of Leibniz's position to the question of whether Lewis is qualified to contribute to the scholarly exegesis of Leibniz's ideas. Further (the devil might advocate) if Lewis *really* believed that there were any strong possibility that Leibniz was on to something important that he, Lewis, might have overlooked, Lewis would probably have managed to arrive at a reasonably well-informed opinion on the historical matter in a fairly short time. Still, I think, Lewis is right to suspect that *the best contemporary historical writers on Leibniz* have not arrived at sufficiently clear agreement about his position on possible worlds—in relation, say, to the theory of counterfactuals—to provide a nonspecialist with adequate guidance in considering Leibniz's ideas. It may be, indeed, that the very detail and professionalism of much work in the history of philosophy today—of the sort desired for their volume by the *Cambridge History* editors, for instance—can tend to *discourage* "use" of historical figures by contemporary philosophers of a certain conscientiousness, in developing their own positions. Naturally, I'm not holding that this is universally the case. But I do think that the sort of problem Lewis touches on is too much overlooked by those who dwell critically on the "ahistoricity" of "analytic philosophers." One can do only so much.[30]

Able historical writers may cite similar practical and personal reasons—rather than ideological commitments—for restricting themselves to "exegetical," as opposed to "philosophical" objectives (or to "internal," as opposed to "external" criticism). It is interesting to compare with Lewis's explanation the following comment by Robert Sleigh in the introduction to his recent book on the Leibniz-Arnauld correspondence:

> I am not arguing that exegetical history is preferable to philosophical history. I am simply more comfortable with, and I believe, more competent at exegetical history. Even there, I have regard for my considerable limitations. The *via negativa* has always come easier to me. It seems to me extraordinarily difficult to make out just what Leibniz is up to in the texts under study here.[31]

(Since these texts include considerable discussion of "possible worlds," it's clear that Sleigh is in accord with Lewis on the "difficulty.")[32]

On the other hand, just as some writers (with whom Sleigh contrasts himself) do practice "philosophical history," so do not a few contemporary philosophers "in the analytic tradition" develop their own ideas against a historical background. Sticking still to examples from the general area of epistemology and metaphysics, one may cite works as diverse as Saul Kripke's *Naming and Necessity*[33] (in which Kripke defines his issues and position in relation to the views of Kant and J. S. Mill, as well as Russell and other twentieth-century figures); David Armstrong's *Universals and Scientific Realism*[34] (in which Armstrong seeks to define and evaluate a wide range of positions on universals, from Plato on, in the course of defending an *a posteriori* form of realism); and Barry Stroud's *The Significance of Philosophical Scepticism*[35] (substantial portions of which are concerned with examination of the positions of Descartes and Kant).

It is not easy, though, to locate a common "view" about the relevance of historical knowledge to philosophical inquiry, even among those who prominently connect the two. Stroud, for example, opens his study with comments about the value of understanding the traditional "sources of philosophical problems as they now present themselves to us" (x).[36] Armstrong eclectically mixes ancient, medieval, early modern, and recent philosophers as representatives of various contrasting positions on universals. Kripke introduces Mill and Kant as figures whose positions—on the theory of names and the epistemological status of necessary truths, respectively—were still familiar and (in the case of Kant) even dominant at the time of his lectures. The prominence of Aristotle, Hume, Kant, Mill, and other major historical figures in writings on ethics and other areas of contemporary value theory reflects, I suspect, still different motivations.

But if views about the relevance of historical study and reference to philosophy today are as diverse as I have held, this still leaves open the question of whether historical consciousness is in some way contributory—if not essential—to *important* philosophical achievement. Are philosophers who largely repudiate historical interests, for instance, automatically disadvantaged in relation to their more historically inclined contemporaries? Quite frankly, I do not think that a strong case for this suggestion has yet been made; and I think that the history of philosophy itself reveals the dimensions of the difficulty in making it. Rée is not alone among reviewers of *Philosophy in History*—including other historical specialists—in finding less than convincing the case made by its various contributors for the categorical importance of historical consciousness to philosophers; and I have to admit I tend to agree with these critics' reservations.[37] But apart form the theoretical debate, one can site specific examples. It is true that some major philosophers—such as Aquinas, Heidegger, and Peirce—have developed their positions, or substantial parts of their positions, in conscious relation to the views of remote (as well as less remote) predecessors. But others, such as Descartes and Wittgenstein, evince little or no direct concern with defining their positions in relation to the long history of philosophical thought; and the depth of their implicit historical knowledge is at best controversial.[38] The same point can be made with respect to significant philosophers of lesser stature: some do (self-consciously or implicitly exhibit useful results of historical study); some don't.[39] In a certain sense, it is up to individual philosophers to choose our own ancestors (as Richard Rorty has said); or even to choose whether to "have" ancestors.[40]

At least in the present intellectual climate, a parallel position of pluralistic tolerance is appropriate with respect to approaches to historical writing. People with their own philosophical ax to grind shouldn't necessarily (depending on their gifts and results) be treated deprecatingly by dedicated historical scholars.

And others content to be viewed as historical scholars—especially if they are very good at this line of work—shouldn't have to answer to others (for instance, members of departmental hiring committees) for lack of "philosophical motivation."

Many of those attracted to philosophy programs—both undergraduate and graduate—find the study of ideas of the past challenging, rewarding, and fascinating. Some may be looking for "philosophical dividends," in the form of direct contribution to the formulation or solution of contemporary issues. Some may profit in philosophical growth from exposure to comprehensive and systematic philosophical thought—of which the past provides so many powerful examples. Some may be interested in understanding their own, and their peers' and teachers', philosophical concerns in relation to historical dialectic. Some— let's face it—may just enjoy "scholarship," and take their satisfaction from feeling that they can contribute to ongoing interpretive debate. There is room for all these motivations, and more, in the complex crosscurrents between historical and philosophical interests that do exist today.

II

Now I turn to a particular issue on which work of philosophers primarily interested in developing their own positions has often converged, in recent years, with historical interpretation. The historical connections of the issue in question—the status of sensible qualities—trace predominantly to pre-Kantian modern philosophy, particularly Locke and Berkeley, rather than to the strong Kantian influences that—as I obliquely indicated above—are also a prominent feature of the contemporary scene.[41]

While the understanding of "the issue" does vary from writer to writer, some of the main assumptions and questions frequently connected with it can be sketched in a broad way. Nearly everybody among recent philosophers, and most, at least, of the earlier figures, accept that we perceive "by our senses" a world of "physical objects" which "have" various "qualities." Most contemporary writers, in fact, simply accept this assumption uncritically. It received more open-minded, critical, and perhaps more imaginative treatment from several early modern philosophers (such as Descartes, Spinoza, Malebranche, and Leibniz), who did not consider the causal account of perception, and the effort to explain the nature of body, as wholly "commonsensical" enterprises. Nevertheless, the assumption does underlie, in one way or another, most discussions of sensible qualities.

Further, most writers tacitly—or sometimes explicitly—assume that for purposes of the philosophy of perception we can focus on a short list of "basic" or "simple" qualities that are supposed to be proper to physical objects. The lists standardly include color, odor, taste, sound, warmth and cold, size, shape, motion and rest, and position; other qualities, such as "solidity," may be included as well. The central questions of the discussion then turn out to be something like this. Is there reason to regard some of these quality types as in some way mind-dependent or subjective, and the other qualities, by contrast, as genuine, intrinsic, qualities of objects? If so, how exactly should we understand this distinction (commonly known as that between "secondary" and "primary" qualities); and what are the important considerations that support it?[42]

This issue is interesting in a number of ways pertaining to the relation between philosophy and its history, and current views about that relation. A certain amount of avowedly historical or interpretive work has been philosophically critical and even creative, while much of the work that disclaims historical and scholarly concerns has been, to greater or lesser degree, historically informed and illuminating. Indeed, some of the avowed historians appear to be favoring (up to a point) the views of the major historical figures they discuss; and some of the avowed nonhistorians frankly present themselves as championing (up to a point) the views of one or another major early modern figure (usually Locke and/or Berkeley). There seems to be little dispute that this is an area of philosophical doctrine which has, on the one hand, salient historical roots and, on the other hand, continuing significance in something like its historical form.

In one sense, then, discussions of the issue provide quite a strong and exemplary case of the fruitful interaction—almost merger—of historical and original philosophical interests. They show that study of the history of philosophy can be seriously "relevant" to contemporary philosophical concerns, and nicely illustrate how the latter can enliven the former.

In fact I have chosen the case partly *because* it provides an especially good example of how historical and philosophical interests can converge or interact, given the right circumstances. (I don't claim that it is in this respect *typical* of issues currently claiming philosophers', or historians', attention. Many issues in contemporary philosophy of language, metaphysics, and theory of modality, as briefly suggested above, lack at least *readily accessible* historical background. Possibly this situation will eventually be altered through improved understanding of thirteenth- to fifteenth-century philosophy, and a more clear-cut consensus about the nature of Leibniz's contribution, for example.) But I haven't chosen the sensible qualities issue for discussion here merely to exhibit a best-case scenario of historical and philosophical interaction: there are some other points I want to make about recent treatments of this issue, as well.

I will begin by sketching a view—some of it now common wisdom—of changes during the past fifty years or so in the understanding of the primary-secondary quality distinction in early modern philosophy. I will suggest that these developments in the historiography of the sensible qualities issue to some extent parallel a broad change in philosophical outlook, within the "analytic" tradition, including a change in philosophical approaches to this specific issue. Developments in both interpretive work and philosophical theory seem to reflect a changing conception of the relation between philosophy (past or present) and science. At the same time (and perhaps paradoxically) one phase of the recent debate provides a plausible piece of support for Jonathan Rée's notion

that dubious historical interpretations can have philosophically worthwhile results. Finally (in section III) I will present some reasons for thinking that contemporary discussion is *overly* captivated by the seventeenth-century framework. Problems already apparent when the framework was laid down have still
not been adequately addressed; and later conceptual and empirical developments are still being unduly neglected.

Much of the historical literature on the primary-secondary quality distinction
is concerned specifically with Locke's *Essay*—particularly the famous discussion at *Essay* II.viii—and Berkeley's attack in the *Principles of Human Knowledge* and *Three Dialogues Between Hylas and Philonous*. Locke's remarks in
Essay II.viii.19–21, as we shall see, constitute a sort of watershed of historical
interpretation.

In the first of these sections Locke notes that in the dark the colors of proph-
yry "vanish," and he comments:

> Can anyone think any real alterations are made in the *Porphyre*, by the presence or
> absence of Light; and that those *Ideas* of whiteness and redness, are really in *Por-
> phyre* in the light, when 'tis plain *it has no color in the dark*?

He goes on to observe that "both Night and Day" porphyry possesses

> such a Configuration of Particles as are apt by the Rays of Light rebounding from
> some parts of that hard Stone, to produce in us the *Idea* of redness, and from others
> the *Idea* of whiteness: But whiteness and redness are not in it at any time, but such
> a texture, that hath the power to produce such a sensation in us.[43]

Section 20 consists of only one sentence:

> Pound an Almond, and the clear white *Colour* will be altered into a dirty one, and
> the sweet Taste into an oily one. What real Alteration can the beating of the Pestle
> make in any Body, but an Alteration of the *Texture* of it?[44]

In Section 21, which is longer and more complex, Locke begins:

> *Ideas* being thus distinguished and understood, we may be able to give an Account,
> how the same Water, at the same time, may produce the *Idea* of Cold by one Hand,
> and of Heat by the other: Whereas it is impossible, that the same Water, if those
> *Ideas* were really in it, should at the same time be both Hot and Cold.[45]

He goes on to say that the phenomenon can be understood if we assume

> *Warmth*, as it is *in our Hands*, to be *nothing but a certain sort of degree of Motion
> in the minute Particles of our Nerves, or animal Spirits*. . . .

For then the same corpuscular motion in the water can be supposed to *increase*
the corpuscular motion in one hand and *decrease* it in the other, if the antecedent corpuscular motions in one hand are appropriately different from those in
the other (i.e., respectively less and greater than the motions in the water), "and
so cause the different Sensations of Heat and Cold, that depend thereon."[46] In
passing Locke notoriously adds that figure perceptions, by contrast, do not vary

in this way, "that never producing the *Idea* of a Square by one Hand, which has produced the *Idea* of a Globe by another."

A string of well-known commentators on Locke and Berkeley from the late 1920s through the early to middle 1960s describe these sections as presenting "Locke's arguments" for the claim that colors, warmth, etc.—that is, "the ideas of secondary qualities" generally—are not (to quote J. R. Thomson) "really in the things to which we ascribe them."[47] Supposedly, Locke is here arguing that the fact that the perceived color, heat, etc. are relative to the condition or circumstances of the perceiver,[48] establishes that these apparent qualities, as we experience them, are not real, intrinsic qualities of bodies; as they are in the bodies, secondary qualities are "only Powers to produce various Sensations in us by their *primary Qualities, i.e.* by the Bulk, Figure, Texture, and Motion of their insensible parts . . ." (*Essay* II.viii.10; cf. 15). Of course Locke, when he is being careful about his distinction between ideas (sensations in the mind) and qualities, would not want to say that ideas of primary qualities are in the objects, either. But the commentators seem to suppose that Locke takes the alleged constancy of the primary quality ideas produced by a given body to support the notion that qualities *resembling* these ideas do really exist in the body, whereas the ideas of secondary qualities "have no resemblance of them at all" (*Essay* II.viii.15). (Thus the distinction between ideas and qualities isn't as crucial to the discussion of primary qualities as it is in the case of secondary qualities.) Commentators may then go on to discuss Berkeley's objection that (despite what Locke seems to imply in II.viii.21) primary quality perceptions, too, tend to vary with the circumstances of the perceiver, and must no less be denied to reflect perceiver-independent qualities. An occasional commentator endorses Berkeley's view that Locke's position is "confused," partly on the basis of this objection.[49]

A more complex and sophisticated variant of this general approach to Locke was provided by Jonathan Bennett in his 1965 paper "Substance, Reality, and Primary Qualities."[50] (Much of the material from this paper is incorporated in Bennett's book *Locke, Berkeley, Hume: Central Themes*.)[51] I characterize Bennett's reading as a "variant" of the earlier reading, despite its originality, for the following reasons. Like the commentators who construe II.viii.19–21 as presenting Locke's arguments for the primary-secondary quality distinction, based on considerations of perceptual relativity, and unlike commentators to be mentioned shortly, Bennett sees "what Locke wanted to say" about primary and secondary qualities as depending directly on truths about ordinary experience. He insists, that is, that Locke's position "is a philosophical thesis whose support involves no recherché scientific information, no appeals to microscopy or the like, but only to . . . unexciting . . . empirical material. . . ."[52] Further, Bennett seems to view II.viii.19–21, among other passages, as intended by Locke as "arguments" for the distinction, though he considers the arguments bad.[53]

According to Bennett, "the truth after which Locke is fumbling" concerning the difference between primary and secondary qualities,[54] in his passages on the relativity of secondary quality perceptions, is captured by the following observations. Some observable properties of bodies (those on Locke's list of second-ary qualities) have relatively few "obvious, familiar, inescapable connections" with observable facts other than the body's effect on human observers. (This is not to deny that there may be "a tight correlation between," say, "wavelengths of reflected light and the colors seen by most people in sunlight," nor that we normally make associations between the colors of particular kinds of things and their other qualities: red wines do have a characteristic taste.)[55] On the other hand,

> there are countless familiar, exoteric, general facts about the connections between a thing's primary qualities and its way of interacting with other things: a rigid thing cannot be enclosed within a smaller rigid thing; a thing cannot block another thing's fall to the earth without touching it; a cube cannot roll smoothly on a flat sur-face . . . ; and so on, indefinitely.[56]

Thus, Bennett says, it would be reasonable for us to continue, for instance, calling things that look red to us 'red', even if wavelength correlations and more ordinary associations with particular kinds of red things should break down. On the other hand,

> just because of the numerousness and familiarity of the connections between the primary qualities of things and their ways of interacting with each other, no clear sense attaches to the suggestion that something might persistently fail to obey these general connections. If a thing's purported size is belied by enough of its ways of interacting with other things, there is no point in saying that it does have that size.[57]

Conversely, someone "blind" to a primary quality such as shape or size would find his deficiency tipped off by many aspects of things' interactions with each other, while a person unable to discriminate within secondary quality modalities would not.

Bennett holds that these observations "could without absurdity be summed up in the Lockean remark that it is true of secondary qualities, in a way in which it is not of primary, that they are 'merely' the powers which things have to affect us in certain ways." (Or, as he later expresses the point, something's looking square in specified conditions is *not* "more or less definitive of its squareness"; whereas how something looks (or smells, tastes, sounds, feels) in specified circumstances *is* definitive of its possessing the appropriate secondary quality.)[58]

Bennett's treatment of this issue is interesting from several points of view. One, which I have already stressed, lies in his contention that Locke's distinc-tion rests on arguments from certain familiar facts of experience elaborated by Bennett—even if Locke himself perceived these considerations only in a "fum-bling" or "muddled" way. More generally, Bennett holds that it is not to be believed that such a "philosophical" doctrine rests on "esoteric" scientific infor-mation or appeals to microscopy: *even if possibly Locke himself did not see the matter this way.*[59]

Also interesting is the general approach to historical interpretation exemplified by Bennett's indication that "only in the light of what is true about primary and secondary qualities can we understand what Locke wanted to say about them."[60] No doubt Bennett thinks of this as a sort of charitable approach to the interpretation of historical figures: his Locke, after all, ends up on the side of *the truth*, even if Bennett's arguments are admittedly not found in Locke, and he is forced to conclude that Locke saw the truth only "dimly"; and was "struggling to express and defend" it.[61] In a similar vein Bennett finds it necessary to dismiss as "deplorable" Locke's quite insistent and salient denial that colors (and so forth) are "really in the object."[62] It seems that Bennett's treatment of Locke on sensible qualities is a sort of paradigm case of a philosopher attempting to expound historical figures from the standpoint of his "own preconceptions."

Furthermore Bennett's analysis is in its own terms deficient. Bennett claims that the ordinary esoteric considerations he mentions capture Locke's distinction extensionally, but in fact they do not. For example, heat and cold, which are standard examples of secondary quality ideas, and which are the specific example of *Essay* II.viii.21, seem to satisfy admirably Bennett's own criteria of primary qualityhood.[63] A thing's shape or size, on the other hand, do *not* all by themselves connect in numerous observable ways with the thing's observable interactions with other things—as Bennett's mention of "rigidity" in a statement quoted above covertly indicates. As far as ordinary observation of interactions goes, it doesn't make much difference whether we perceive, say, soap bubbles as spherical or ovoid. And so forth.[64]

But—and this is my final point about Bennett—his attempt to explain what Locke was "dimly" pursuing is rather intriguing, for all its deficiencies, historical and philosophical. There seems to be *something* to what he is saying philosophically, whether he himself succeeds in expressing it clearly or only dimly. The proposal that the way things look, smell, sound, etc. to us *constitutes their being* red, fragrant, loud, etc., whereas their appearing square or large doesn't *constitute their being* square, large, etc. still has a following today; and Bennett's suggestion that this fact can be understood in terms of "exoteric connections," though not acceptable as it stands, remains in broad terms a plausible insight.[65] Bennett's views about the primary-secondary quality distinction are at best loosely connected with Locke's; his successors (as I'll explain shortly) have done much better with the interpretive task. But Bennett succeeds in defining an approach to the issue that, reflecting philosophical commitments of his time rather than of Locke's, is still inherently interesting enough to survive the objection of historical irrelevance.

Beginning around the early to mid sixties new commentators began to claim that their predecessors had completely misunderstood Locke on the primary-secondary quality distinction, as a result of being overly influenced by a mistaken interpretation "deriving from Berkeley," according to which (in Maurice Mandelbaum's words) the *Essay* is "an epistemological treatise devoid of a scientific substructure."[66] These commentators deny that Locke thought that the distinction could be made from *within sense experience*, "on the basis of differences between the *ideas* of the various qualities of bodies."[67] They argue that, on the contrary, Locke's distinction "was made on theoretical grounds in relation to possibilities of explanation."[68] Locke's conception of the possibilities of explanation, however, is entirely a function of the atomism that he inherited from Robert Boyle.[69] *Essay* II.viii.19–21, which Berkeley and previous commentators had misunderstood as an attempt to *argue for* the primary-secondary quality distinction from relativity considerations—or considerations of perceptual illusion—must rather be interpreted as providing clarifying examples of the power of corpuscularian explanations, by showing how otherwise perplexing variations in perception can be "explained" in atomistic terms.[70] The principle idea common to the several commentators just cited is that the so-called primary qualities are distinguished from the secondary qualities by virtue of being necessary to, and sufficient for, intelligible mechanistic explanations of phenomena—including our sense perceptions in general, and our "ideas of secondary qualities" in particular. (This view about the appropriate explanation of natural phenomena is, purportedly, as one of the main features that distinguishes the seventeenth-century scientific-philosophical program from the Aristotelian and Scholastic principles that it sought to replace.) A realistic interpretation of the qualities required in the explicans is taken for granted by Locke, who simply follows Boyle in this respect. Locke also follows Boyle in construing "secondary qualities" *as they exist in objects* as powers possessed by the objects to cause or produce the ideas of colors, sounds, warmth, etc. in us: powers grounded in the primary qualities of the objects, together with features of the medium and our own sensory systems, which are also wholly describable in terms of primary qualities.[71]

This account of Locke's distinction seems to require understanding the "explanatory" role of primary qualities in perception on two different levels. On the one hand, the explanation of perception is to be conceived in *corpuscular* terms. At this level the important question is what qualities need to be (or can be) ascribed to the "insensible particles" or corpuscles (including the qualities, such as texture and macroscopic size, possessed by *combinations* of corpuscles).[72] Another level of explanation is invoked, however, with respect to Locke's claim that our ideas of the primary qualities of *macroscopic* objects— ordinary "sensible objects"—"are resemblances of them" (while our ideas of the secondary qualities resemble nothing really "in" the objects).

> The *Ideas of primary Qualities* of Bodies, *are Resemblances* of them, and their Patterns do really exist in the Bodies themselves; but the *Ideas, produced* in us *by* these *Secondary Qualities, have no resemblance* of them at all. (II.viii.15).

In section 18 Locke elaborates:

> A piece of *Manna* of a sensible Bulk, is able to produce in us the *Idea* of a round or square Figure; and, by being removed one place to another, the *Idea* of Motion. This *Idea* of Motion represents it, as it really is in the *Manna* moving: A Circle or Square are the same, whether in *Idea* or Existence; in the Mind, or in the *Manna*.

In these passages (as in the globe/square remark in viii.21) Locke seems to be assuming some sort of resemblance of *determinates*: our idea of the manna's squareness, and the squareness really in the manna. Such remarks really do seem to support the earlier commentators' view that Locke was insensitive to the fact that perceptions of bodies' size and shape are as subject to relativity considerations as those of color and warmth (and therefore vulnerable to Berkeley's observations to the contrary).[73]

"Corpuscularian" interpreters have tried to subsume such passages under their own reading by noting that macroscopic shape, size, motion, and so on play an irreducible role in *scientific* explanation of the production of "ideas of shape" (etc.) (whether of sight or touch). The perceived size and shape of ordinary objects such as manna can be (roughly) identified, that is, with the size and shape of theoretically postulated *large clumps of corpuscles* external to the sensory system. Locke's claims about primary quality ideas "resembling" qualities in bodies should be, they hold, understood in this loose way. Curley, for instance, writes:

> Locke's point, I take it, is this: If we consider the kind of causal account we would give of our (visual) perception of, say, the shape of an object, we will find that it involves descriptions of how rays of light are reflected from the surface of the object and focused by the lens of the eye on the retina. The nerve endings in the retina which are stimulated by the light rays transmit a message to the brain and a perception of a particular shape is produced. We see the object as elliptical, perhaps. It is not essential to the story that the object be elliptical, but it is essential that the object have *some* shape and that that shape be a causal factor, via the laws of perspective and refraction, in determining the pattern of stimulation of nerve endings in the retina.[74]

Similarly, the attribution of *some* situation to an object will enter into the explanation of why the thing is perceived as having situation; and the movement of *something* (body perceived, perceiver's body, or some other body) will enter into the perception of an object as moving.[75]

The trouble with this reading is that it doesn't really accommodate Locke's text very well. Locke *seems* to be saying that the particular or determinate shape of the manna is accurately represented in the idea—not that some shape or other must be postulated "out there" if we are to explain mechanistically how our "perceptions of" a piece of moving manna come about.[76]

(It is not clear whether Curley intends to make a true philosophical point as well as an interpretive one. The fact that his discussion is cast largely in the first person plural, however, tends rather to suggest that he does. ("If we consider the kind of causal account we would give . . . , we will find. . . .") If so, it's worth noting that the "essentiality" thesis is subject to counterexamples—even if one doesn't fuss too much about the meaning of 'essentially' in this context. A person can have "perceptions of motion" when neither he, nor anything macroscopic in his visual field, is moving—for example, through successive or alternating emissions of light in a pattern, or rapid successive projections of images.

In such cases of "apparent motion," explanations of our "perceptions of motion" must be cast in terms of "sequenced flashing of physically stationary objects.")[77]

Another quotation from Curley's paper gives grounds for doubt about the *coherence* of the position he is attributing to Locke. He writes:

> While the causal explanation of our perception of the shape of an object enables us to understand why we perceive it as having a shape (since its having some shape is essential to the explanation) nothing in the causal explanation of our perception of color really makes it intelligible that we should see the object as colored (since only primary qualities are involved in the explanation).[78]

Now in fact (as Curley observes in a footnote to this passage), Locke regards the relation of *all* perceptual experience to material processes as unintelligible. Thus, it seems that the relevant difference between shape perception and color perception can only amount to the fact that the former, but not the latter, involves attributing the quality in question to the cause of the perception of the quality. But if we are really dealing with "explanation" here, shouldn't the explanation of our color perceptions *in terms of primary qualities* at least be expected to make *somehow* "intelligible"—*as* intelligible as explanation of shape perception—why we "see the object as colored" (for, after all, we do)?

I think that it may be difficult to arrive at a completely clear account of Locke's position, simply because Locke does not, *pace* Curley, tie his account of primary qualities to corpuscularian explanation in a way that parallels his account of secondary qualities.[79] Although there is room for criticism of some details of the "corpuscularian" interpreters' reading of Locke on primary and secondary qualities, however, it seems to me that they are absolutely correct on the main points. The view of sensible qualities—particularly secondary qualities—that Locke elaborates in II.viii is patently based on what he conceives as the scientific conception of bodies and their effects on us; and sections 18–21 in particular are not attempts to justify the primary-secondary quality distinction by considerations of perceptual relativity.[80] It is true that there is an appeal to ordinary experience in sections 18–21: "it is plain that" porphyry has no color in the dark; "pound an almond," etc.[81] But we need to remember that seventeenth-century mechanistic science, though in large degree theoretical and technical, was thought to give straightforwardly intelligible explanations of ordinarily observable phenomena, in terms of concepts perfectly accessible to ordinary understanding. We are supposed to just see and agree, for example, that the only intelligible conception of what happens to an almond when it is pounded is that it is broken up into parts, and to conclude accordingly that other sensory changes must be explicable in terms of this change alone (as the corpuscularian theory holds).

Reading Locke from this point of view also takes the mystery out of his claim that objects lack, for example, color (in the dark or otherwise). He means, of course, that ideas of color, and of the other secondary qualities, "have no similitude" with anything attributable to bodies *conceived in terms of mechanis-*

tic science (*Essay* II.viii.13). Of course there are features of bodies that systematically correspond to all the sensible ideas they produce in us: these, strictly, *are* the secondary qualities. But the fact that secondary qualities are "in" the objects does not mean that colors as we experience them are.[82]

It does seem to me, however, that the "corpuscularian" commentators typically give a rather misleading impression of the differences between their own approach to Locke, and that characteristic of "the long tradition" (in Curley's words) that they mean to oppose. Most of their predecessors provide a pretty full acknowledgement of Boyle's influence on Locke; and very few of them, actually, show all that much sympathy with Berkeley.[83] The central difference really does seem to turn on whether or not Locke needs, and intends to provide (particularly in II.viii.19–21), independent "philosophical" arguments for the primary-secondary quality distinction.[84]

There is one further step in the historical understanding of Locke's position that it is important to mention here. The strong recent emphasis on Locke's Boyleanism seems finally to be giving way to a broad awareness that most of the elements of Locke's position on sensible qualities were in fact pervasive in early modern philosophy from Galileo and Descartes on. (Thus the doctrine is neither exclusively "empiricistic" nor even exclusively "atomistic.")[85] It is easy to document at length—though I won't attempt to do so here—antecedents in the writings of Descartes, Hobbes, Malebranche, and others, as well as in Boyle, for many of the claims so prominent in Locke's treatment of the issue: for example, that our experiences of color, odor, taste, and so on do not "resemble" any qualities really in bodies; that our senses deceive us insofar as they seem to "teach us" to the contrary; that the "real" qualities of physical reality include figure, size, and motion or rest; and that these views about the qualities of things are grounded in the explanatory power of mechanistic science, particularly with respect to the explanation of perception.[86] Even idealists such as Leibniz and Kant held a quasi-realist conception of "scientific entities" sufficient to ground a distinction between real physical qualities and powers and mere sensations "produced" by them.[87] As A. D. Smith remarks,

> the distinction between primary and secondary qualities was central to a unified metaphysical and scientific view of the world that dominated the seventeenth century.[88]

(Of course rationalist accounts such as Descartes's, according to which the fundamental aspects of our apprehension of physical reality have a source independent of sense, differ from Locke's in certain ways.) Also common to most of these writers is a tendency to vacillate, just as Locke does, over whether terms like 'color' and 'red' denominate physical structures, or the "powers" that (partly) result from the structures to cause sensations, or (as Locke seems usually to suppose) the sensations themselves.

As an improved and far more extensive understanding of early modern thought on sensible qualities thus unfolds, we are reaching a better understanding also of the nature of Berkeley's attack. Certainly Berkeley does suggest, in both the *Principles* and the *Dialogues*, that the fact that primary as well as secondary quality perceptions vary with the state of the perceiver undercuts "modern philosophers'" defense of the distinction between "qualities really in objects" and mere, "non-resembling" ideas or appearances. As Barry Stroud has argued persuasively, however, even these passages in Berkeley have been misunderstood, insofar as they've been read as implying a purely experiential or epistemological conception of what the "modern philosophers" had in mind.[89] And, I hope, the suggestion of Locke's "corpuscularian" interpreters that Berkeley's attack in general is predicated on native misunderstandings of his predecessors' positions—particularly on a failure to take account of their scientific realist motivations—has become untenable. Berkeley in fact understood very well the fundamental points of his materialist opponents' position: that the ordinary sense-based conception of the properties of bodies is delusive and "deceptive"; that colors and various other sensible qualities can be counted as physically real only in so far as they are *not* identified with the shades, sounds, etc. that we ordinarily take to be presented by the senses; that the size, figure, position, and motion that we take ourselves to perceive in bodies—though inseparably blended in sense perception with the merely "apparent" qualities— have a different sort of claim to physical reality, in that our perceptions of the former directly "resemble" qualities actually in the bodies; and that this whole anti-commonsense picture of the world is supposed to rest on the explanatory power of mechanistic science, particularly its ability to "explain perception." In the *Principles of Human Knowledge* and *Three Dialogues* Berkeley systematically and appositely addresses these points.[90] In the *Principles* and other works (especially *de Motu*) he further sketches strategies for accommodating the explanatory power of modern mechanistic science on his own "immaterialist" terms.[91]

The increasingly widespread recognition of the close dependence of early modern treatments of sensible qualities on assumptions connected with anti-Aristotelian mechanistic science (so much in accord with the program of the *Cambridge History* editors) has broader implications also with respect to the interpretation of classical philosophical works of the period. On a traditional view, inculcated in many of us as philosophy students, and exemplified, for instance, in Richard Rorty's *Philosophy and the Mirror of Nature*,[92] epistemological foundationalist concerns, bound up with skeptical preoccupations, were the dominant concerns of early modern philosophers, particularly Descartes, Locke, and Berkeley. Once the scientific realist preoccupations of the era are given their full due, however, the basic conception of what these philosophers and their contemporaries were trying to accomplish undergoes transformation. Descartes, though indubitably concerned to some extent with "indubitability," uses methodic doubt as a device to help establish mechanistic physics as providing the true view of the nature of body, by freeing us from uncritical "dependence on sense." Locke may be viewed as *taking for granted* much of the "ideas" theory, as well as the accompanying distinction between "resembling" and "nonresembling" ideas. The conception of Locke as a foundationalist gives way to a more accurate appraisal of his epistemological concerns as directed, just as he says, at clarifying the nature and extent (or *limitations*) of human knowledge. And Berkeley can more adequately be read as concerned to repudiate *all* the aspects of materialist scientific realism incompatible with his *esse est percipi aut percipere* principle—not merely as seeking to address and counter the skeptical pitfalls of his predecessors' conception of matter.[93] Further, the comparative lack of concern with the problem of external world skepticism in Leibniz and Spinoza no longer has the tendency to make these great figures seem strangely out of step with their contemporaries.

I noted above that the newer "corpuscularian" interpreters of Locke tend to see their predecessors' readings of *Essay* II.viii.19–21 as reflecting excessive commitment to "Berkeleyan epistemology" (where Berkeley is assumed to be oblivious to the relevance and/or power of the scientific realist program). I also mentioned that sympathy with Berkeleyan philosophy is not, as far as I can see, anywhere near as prominent in the writers whom the "corpuscularian" interpreters seem to have in mind as the latter suggest. Nevertheless, it seems a reasonable conjecture that earlier readings of II.viii.19–21 as arguments from perceptual relativity do in part reflect the preoccupation of many philosophers of the time (particularly the '50s and early '60s) with phenomenalism and sense data theory. Similarly, historical interpretations focusing on issues of skepticism and foundationalism to some extent tie in, chronologically, with strong philosophical focus on these issues. During this period, it seems, many philosophers tended to conceive of philosophy as an autonomous discipline, concerned with *ordinary* language and *ordinary* experience. Possible tie-ins between philosophy of perception and the conceptions of science—whether in the psychophysiology of perception or the physical theory of matter—could be given short shrift. So, for example, D. J. O'Connor could remark concerning the primary-secondary quality distinction (in a peice on Locke published in 1964):

> Clearly all this is a great muddle. The doctrine of primary and secondary qualities is, in truth, nothing but some scientific truths dangerously elevated into a philosophical doctrine.[94]

Rorty's reading of Descartes and Locke as providing the roots of contemporary "epistemologically" oriented philosophy seems in fact to reflect back upon the seventeenth century the philosophical commitments of this later period.

Against O'Connor's remark can be placed the following comments from A. D. Smith's 1990 paper "Of Primary and Secondary Qualities":

> I take it that the majority of philosophers today, at least in the "Analytical Tradition," would endorse a distinction between primary and secondary qualities. (221)

> [M]ost of them . . . do so because they believe that science tells thems so. (231)

Writing chronologically about halfway between O'Connor and Smith, J. L. Mackie observed:

The suggestion that primary qualities are to be distinguished from secondary qualities is one that seems to bring science and philosophy into head-on collision. Primary qualities like shape, size, number, and motion have been treated very differently by physicists, at least since the seventeenth century, from secondary qualities like colours, sounds, and tastes. But philosophers have on the whole accepted arguments that would show either that no such distinction can be drawn at all or at least that none can be drawn in the way in which we are initially tempted to draw it.[95]

Mackie goes on to defend the view that "physical considerations," supplemented by a "philosophical" appeal to Occam's razor, "show that there is no good reason for postulating" in nature "thoroughly objective features which resemble our ideas of secondary qualities."[96]

Moreover, Mackie's view of the close relation between philosophy and science, and the implications he draws concerning the distinction between real physical qualities and mere sensible appearances, were not as out of favor philosophically at the time he was writing as he seems to imply. J. J. C. Smart, for example, wrote in 1963:

In recent years I have been moving away from a roughly neo-Wittgensteinian conception of philosophy towards a more metaphysical one, according to which philosophy is in a much more intimate relation to the sciences.[97]

Smart's endeavor to present a "metaphysical" philosophy leads him into detailed discussion of the primary-secondary quality distinction, with special reference to Locke. (Smart rejects Locke's view because of its postulation of irreducible mental qualia; but he does note its "positive merits.")[98] Wilfrid Sellars's classic account of the distinction between the "scientific" and the "manifest" images—which Sellars elaborates with particular reference to seventeenth-century thought—also dates from the early 1960s.[99]

I have noted above that scholars writing on Locke in the early 1960s and afterwards saw themselves as breaking with past tradition in presenting his treatment of sensible qualities as derivative from scientific assumptions that he accepted from Boyle. What I now want to suggest is that this change in scholarly tradition coincides rather intriguingly with a change in leading philosophers' conceptions of the relationship of their own endeavors to present-day science. The historical relations of early modern philosophy and science seem to receive their full due just as philosophers themselves become more interested in trying to accommodate "what science tells us."[100]

III

It seems, then, that work of recent decades has resulted in a generally clearer and more widely shared understanding of certain fundamental aspects of early modern philosophers' positions on sensible qualities. Of course, significant work remains to be done in this important area of historical interpretation. To mention just one example, the details of Descartes's treatment of visual perception, and their possible relation to his central metaphysical commitments, are just beginning to receive full critical attention. But at least there seems to be broad consensus today concerning the grounding of most early modern treatments of sensible qualities—and particularly the primary-secondary quality distinction—in the widely endorsed program of mechanistic science. Further, I don't see that there can any longer be reasonable doubt that major early modern philosophers—with the exception of Berkeley—saw their commitments to mechanistic science as dictating acceptance of what has come to be called the "error theory" with respect to colors, odors, tastes, sounds, and the like: in seventeenth-century terms, the claim that the senses deceive us in leading us to construe such experienced qualities as resembling real features of external objects.

It is notable, however, that the emerging consensus about historical intepretation has certainly not been accompanied by emerging agreement about the philosophical truth of the matter with respect to sensible qualities—as anyone aware of the huge and contentious recent outpouring of philosophical writing on color, in particular, can attest. To some extent the strong divisions of opinion among contemporary philosophers are doubtless bound up with more exacting standards of rigor than were characteristic of seventeenth-century treatments of qualities. For example, as I indicated above, Descartes, Boyle, Locke and other writers of the earlier period could vacillate rather unselfconsciously among the views of, say, colors as dispositions or powers to cause sensations, as the mechanistic structures in objects that accounted for the "powers," or as the sensations themselves. Present-day philosophers may find it necessary to defend *one or the other* of these (or still different) positions, while conscientiously seeking to demonstrate the untenability of its rivals. But to some extent, also, the striking discord in contemporary debate seems to reflect uneven success in confronting the significance of many relevant changes in both scientific and philosophical viewpoints since the early modern period. We have yet to come fully to terms with the distinction between what philosophers today can legitimately claim to "learn from" older positions, and aspects of these positions which subsequent developments have rendered highly problematic, if not obsolete.[101] I will conclude by mentioning some specific considerations in behalf of this suggestion.

1. The Status of the Concept of "Primary Quality" in View of Developments in the Physical Theory of Matter. Seventeenth-century mechanists largely conceived of the qualities of the insensible entities to which their explanations appealed in terms of qualities "given" in ordinary experience of big, perceivable bodies: especially size, shape, and motion. It is true that the need for concepts of "force" began to pose problems for the geometrical Cartesian viewpoint in the post-Cartesian period, and that certain visionaries (such as Leibniz) saw that any form of mechanistic corpuscularianism might involve too simplistic an approach to understanding nature. Still, there was little awareness that fundamental explanatory concepts in physics might be as remote from those applied in everyday experience—and from "philosophical intuitions" based on ordinary experience—as has in fact proved to be the case. The traditional concept of a primary quality was, it seems to me, very much a product of the assumption of this fairly simple relation between (certain) ordinary sensible qualities of perceivable objects, and the nature of the insensible entities which constituted them, providing the basis for explanation of observable interactions in terms of universal laws. The assumption is entwined with an essentialist conception also characteristic of the period: that there is one small set of qualities which *necessarily characterize* both bodies considered as objects of the senses and the intellectually postulated constituents involved in scientific explanations of the large bodies' behavior.[102] The primary qualities are, as Locke writes, those

> utterly inseparable from the Body, in what estate soever it be; such as in all the alterations and changes it suffers . . . it constantly keeps; and such as Sense constantly finds in every particle of Matter, which has bulk enough to be perceived, and the Mind finds inseparable from every particle of Matter, though less than to make it self singly be perceived by our Senses. (II.viii.9; 134–35)

Various recent philosophers have duly noted that the traditional concept of a "primary quality" is a sort of hybrid notion, relating simultaneously to ordinary phenomenal experience of macroscopic things, and supposed basic explanatory concepts of physics. They have observed that developments in physics have to some extent called into question the possibility of the same set of qualities continuing to play this dual role, but (it seems to me) they have underplayed the difficulty of maintaining a close variant of the traditional conception in the light of these developments.[103] Some assert, for instance, that spatial properties and motion, at least, still play a part in scientific explanation comparable to that envisaged by Boylean science, though solidity does not.[104] But if they mean that such qualities are universally and irreducibly ascribable to physical entities as the "starting points" of scientific explanation, their claim is surely open to challenge.[105] If they mean something else, we need to be told precisely what.[106]

Again, as I have noted above, some contemporary philosophers alternate rather casually between speaking of (macroscopic) primary qualities as "explaining" our perceptions *of them*, and of (microscopic) primary qualities as "explaining" secondary quality perceptions.[107] Yet microphysical explanation is an achievement of empirical science; while (some hold) the distinction between secondary qualities and primary qualities must be arrived at *a priori*: the disposition to produce experiences in us is constitutive of secondary qualityhood; whereas (in Colin McGinn's words) "experience must be as of primary qualities; for if it were not, experience could not be *of* an objective world, since the objective world is precisely *constituted* by objects with primary qualities."[108] This rather protean approach to the status of primary qualities, with respect to sense experience, science, and "explanation" is more or less intelligible in the framework of seventeenth-century epistemological and scientific assumptions. My suggestion, though, is that it no longer holds together: at the very least it rests on assumptions which stand in need of concentrated critical scrutiny.

2. Developments in Scientific Accounts of Color and Color Perception. Certain recent writers have argued convincingly that philosophers speculating on, say, "the nature of color" ignore at their peril advances in the physical and psychophysiological accounts of color perception. As I have said, early modern theorists sometimes think of particular colors as "manifest" (nondispositional) microstructures, correlating in more or less simple ways with "standard" color perceptions; sometimes as consisting in dispositions to cause a specific type of color sensation ("simple idea of sense"); sometimes as (or as pertaining to) the sensation itself. All these views provide ancestry for twentieth-century positions. But both the view of colors as "manifest" (i.e., nondispositional) microstructural qualities, and the dispositional view, have recently come under attack as involving simplistic assumptions incompatible with the discoveries of contemporary color science: such as the tremendous variability of the physical "causes of color," "color constancy," metamerism, and problems with the notion of "standard conditions of observation" (which seems crucial to dispositional theories), among many other factors.[109] Further, contemporary philosophers have been criticized (plausibly, I think) for continuing to adhere to the early modern notion of color "sensations." Quite apart from materialist discomfort with its traditional dualistic connotations, the notion is objectionable because it is involved with an outmoded assumption of radical distinction between what is ineluctably and determinately "given in sense" and the results of cognitive interpretation or "active" intellectual processing.[110]

I don't mean to imply, in invoking these lines of objection, derived from contemporary color science, to recent philosophical accounts of color, that they are all correct or incontrovertible. I do consider them sufficient to sustain my baisc point: that contemporary uses of historical precedent, with respect to the conception of sensible qualities, can run into difficulty and confusion if too many traditional assumptions are allowed to pass uncriticized. Anachronism can work both ways.

3. Philosophical Developments. Seventeenth-century scientific realism was a fairly naive position. Rough agreement concerning the scientific facts tended almost automatically to be translated into broad areas of agreement about the real qualities of physical objects, and about the illusoriness of the ordinary sense-based conception of bodies.[111] As I've just observed, a certain amount of the disagreement in recent discussions of sensible qualities consists in some philosophers charging others with not being up to date concerning established empirical results and current scientific theory. But of course there are other major areas of disagreement as well, concerning properly philosophical and metaphilosophical commitments. This point can be illustrated by certain recent discussions of the "error theory." Someone sympathetic to conceptual relativism, who doesn't necessarily disagree with scientific realist colleagues about "what science tells us" concerning the nature of matter and so forth, may nevertheless resist the scientific realist's inference that "science tells us that" ordinary beliefs about ordinary objects are shot through with illusion and error.[112] Others may draw from Wittgensteinian (or quasi-Wittgensteinian) views about belief ascription and meaning the conclusion that the error thesis is unintelligible.[113] It seems, however, that some writers on sensible qualities continue to write as if the philosophical terrain—as well as the scientific—were not all that much more complicated than their early modern predecessors found it.

4. The Continuing Limits of Our Ability Really to "Explain" Perceptual Experiences, Including Sensible Quality Perceptions, in Physical Terms. My previous remarks focused on areas in which seventeenth-century assumptions relating to the treatment of sensible qualities have been undermined, or rendered more problematic, by subsequent intellectual developments. There is one respect, however, in which the appropriation of early modern ideas appears problematic partly because of a *lack* of developments.

As I noted previously, early modern figures did often explicitly base their notion of physical reality, including the primary-secondary quality distinction, on claims about the explanatory power of mechanistic science. At the same time, they tended to acknowledge that there was something peculiarly unfathomable about the "manner of production" of ideas of sense by any strictly physical process that they could envisage. The result was a tension in their position—one which Berkeley exploited to great advantage.[114]

At the same time, however, the pervasive theological commitments of early modern philosophy provided its practitioners with some resources for accommodating this problem within a generally accepted framework. Descartes, Locke, and others addressed it by appealing to arbitrary divine decrees of principles of correlation between brain events and ideas ("superaddition" in the Lockean terminology).

Some today would argue that "since Hume" there should be no objection to settling for mere correlations between brain states and sensations—even if the latter are conceived as irreducibly "mental." Some who base scientific realist positions on claims of explanatory adequacy seem simply to ignore the issue.[115] Other have argued that, contrary to the Humean view, "explanation" requires something more than brute assertions of correlation, and have agreed with early philosophers that we are facing a genuine, serious problem here: the mind-body problem.[116] Of these, some have proposed various versions of physicalist identity theory, eliminative materialism, functionalism, and the like, while others have rejected such approaches as having no "intrinsic plausibility."[117] At least one of the latter group has gone so far as to suggest, in effect, that the seventeenth century got as far with this problem as it is possible to get: he proposes, that is, to return to the theological option.[118]

My moral, again, is that the seventeenth-century approach to sensible qualities carries with it a formidable difficulty (one that, in this case, philosophers of that period tried to address). Many philosophers today have struggled to deal with it; some have (it seems to me) swept it under the carpet. Whether we are stuck with it forever, or whether scientific and/or philosophical progress will eventually lead to broader agreement and, perhaps, more satisfactory understanding still remains to be seen.

5. Metaphilosophical Issues. Finally, a more general question can be raised about how those philosophizing about sensible qualities in recent times view their enterprise in relation to that of the early modern figures to whose work they so often allude. As I have repeatedly indicated, it is now pretty clear what seventeenth-century writers were basically aiming at in articulating their positions concerning sensible qualities. They were, above all, explaining and advocating a view of the relation between sense experience and physical reality which they saw as rivaling and replacing recently dominant Aristotelian-Scholastic assumptions, a view consistent with a dramatically more successful and fundamentally different science of nature. Now clearly, late-twentieth-century philosophers are not doing *that*. Further, philosophers today seem faced with a problem about distinguishing their own proper activities from those of scientists that is quite remote from the seventeenth-century framework—in which what we now regard as two distinct modes of intellectual activity were often seamlessly combined. The positivist program, and then ordinary-language philosophy, had ways of addressing this problem, but both are generally regarded as failed movements. The confident sharp distinction between "philosophical" and "scientific" claims, exemplified by D. J. O'Connor and others cited above, has been muted in the works of many philosophers who see themselves returning to a form of philosophizing that is in some ways open to "what science tells us." But making philosophy "scientific" does not make it science. If philosophical work, at least in some areas, is no longer supposed to be *independent* of scientific results and theory, then what is its specific and peculiar role in telling us in what, say, the nature of colors consists?[119] My point, again, is that for understandable reasons this was not an acute issue for early modern thinkers; but it is one that, it seems, we need to address more self-consciously today. Certainly we cannot get around it by tying our efforts to a program several centuries old, whose assumptions, objectives, and opportunities are in deep ways no longer ours.

The remarks of this section have not been intended as "antihistorical"—though I'm afraid they might seem so at first. On the contrary, I have meant to suggest that fuller understanding of past philosophy is—or can be—as "philosophically valuable" in helping us grasp the *limitations* of its relevance to currently viable enterprises, as in providing a more mature conception of common ground.[120]

NOTES

1. It would be wrong to think that this observation is at odds with mentioning (as I did above) *translation* projects as contributing to an upsurge of interest in the history of philosophy. For one thing, of course, one may very well *start* with translations as a student, then go on to develop a competence in the original language, as a result of the interest engendered by the translated works. For another, translated editions can be compendious, or valuable for their scholarly apparatus. (The two-volume Cottingham,

Stoothoff, Murdoch edition of *The Philosophical Writings of Descartes* (Cambridge: Cambridge University Press, 1985) is a good example of the former virtue; Edwin Curley's edition of *The Collected Works of Spinoza* (vol. 1, Princeton: Princeton University Press, 1985; vol. 2 in progress) a fine example of the latter.) Also, translation is to some extent a matter of intuition and informed opinion (especially perhaps with respect to ancient languages). Someone baffled by a passage in *The Ethics*, for instance, might well want to find out how the Latin was *translated* by knowledgeable Spinoza scholars such as Curley and Samuel Shirley. And, finally, even scholars competent in a philosopher's original language(s) often find it convenient to work with translations for day-to-day purposes.

2. In their preface to the proceedings of an international conference on Spinoza's philosophy held in Chicago in the fall of 1986 (*Spinoza: Issues and Directions*, ed. Edwin Curley and Pierre-Francois Moreau [Leiden: E. J. Brill, 1990]), the editors mention that a purpose of the conference was "to bring together the two worlds of Spinoza scholarship." They note that a postwar "split between the styles of philosophy popular in the U.S. and on the Continent" has "made communication difficult" between philosophers educated in the two traditions (ix). The conference papers themselves, however, which include many cross-references between the two "worlds," tend to call into question the assumptions of fundamental "difficulties of communication" deriving from differences of philosophical commitments. Certainly in the case of Descartes scholarship—to take the example about which I can speak with most assurance—the greatly increased communication over the last decade or so between Anglo-American and other scholars is largely attributable simply to increased mutual awareness.

3. The comment is abstracted from Harman's introduction to a colloquium on issues in epistemology today, Princeton University, January 31, 1991.

4. As a number of the contributions to the work cited in the next note make clear, the "perennial problem" view is particularly out of favor among some of the strongest advocates of the importance of historical awareness to philosophy.

5. The remark is cited by Alisdair MacIntyre, "The Relationship of Philosophy to Its Past," in *Philosophy in History: Essays on the Historiography of Philosophy*, ed. R. Rorty, J. B. Schneewind, and Q. Skinner (Cambridge: Cambridge University Press, 1984), 39–40. (I don't really mean to question the accuracy of his report—only to acknowledge that I don't have first-hand knowledge of the "joke.")

6. I take it as unproblematic that nearly all philosophers writing today respond to the history of philosophical discourse to the extent of taking directly into account work published in the last few years, and even (depending, to some extent, on the issue) in the early twentieth to late nineteenth century. It is certainly possible to take a primarily historical approach to, say, Russell or Wittgenstein, but the "liveness" of their views doesn't seem to be much in dispute. The acute issue, for present purposes, is the degree to which *much* earlier philosophers' concerns and contributions are relevant to contemporary philosophical endeavor.

7. In their introduction to *Philosophy in History* the editors comment: "it is hopeless to say something general and interesting about the relation between philosophy and history" (p. 9). I'm not quite sure why they make this statement, since it does seem that the basic point of their own and others' contributions to the volume is to try to do just that. However, I'm inclined to see the statement as all too true, at least at the present time.

8. See, for instance, the editors' introduction to *Philosophy in History*, 13–14.

9. Ibid., 11–12.

10. New York: Random House, 1968.

11. New York: Bobbs-Merrill, 1970.

12. Harmondsworth, England: Penguin, 1978.

13. Paris: Montaigne, 1952 (2 vols.); 2d. ed., 1968.

14. I am aware that some deny that the expression "analytic philosophy" has much ideological significance today, and that some have held that the "analytical tradition" is "bankrupt." I have no desire at all to perpetuate the notion that an ideological movement appropriately identified as "analytic philosophy" is alive and well, and proceeding according to a well-understood program. But like it or not, the terms 'analytic philosophy' and 'analytical tradition' are still widely used—and used in particular for identifying purposes by many of the writers I will cite. For this reason, and because any alternative designation I can think of seems unmanageably periphrastic, I will continue to use these expressions in the paper—although I place them in quotes, to remind the reader that their connotations may be in doubt.

15. (Chicago: University of Chicago Press, 1988.) I cite Donagan's book as a primarily historical and scholarly contribution by someone who has also achieved prominence for nonhistorical writing. I should mention, though, that Donagan does offer a sort of philosophical rationale for his work—though to my mind a rather oblique and unusual one. He explains that his "primary object" in writing a book on Spinoza "is to help philosophers who aspire to work out an adequate naturalism to learn from the greatest of their naturalist predecessors" (xiv). But he goes on to note parenthetically that he *himself* accepts "the supernaturalist [philosophy] presupposed by the Jewish and Christian faiths Spinoza repudiated."

16. "Leibniz's Theories of Contingency," *Rice University Studies* 63 (1977): 1–41, reprinted in *Leibniz: Critical and Interpretive Essays*, ed. M. Hooker (Minneapolis: University of Minnesota Press, 1982), 243–83; "Phenomenalism and Corporeal Substance in Leibniz," in *Contemporary Perspectives on the History of Philosophy*, ed. P. A. French, T. E. Uehling, Jr., and H. K. Wettstein, *Midwest Studies in Philosophy* 8 (Minneapolis: University of Minnesota Press, 1983), 217–57.

17. By Margaret Atherton's major study, *Berkeley's Revolution in Vision* (Ithaca, N.Y.: Cornell University Press, 1990). Armstrong's work, *Berkeley's Theory of Vision*, was originally published in 1960 (Parkville: Melbourne University Press), reprinted by Garland (New York and London) in 1988.

18. London: Routledge and Kegan Paul, 1977.

19. (London: Routledge and Kegan Paul, 1977.) In his preface Stroud acknowledges the limitations of his study, with respect to his lack of attention to Hume's views on religion, economics, politics, and history, suggesting that these views are less "fundamental" to Hume's philosophy than the topics he does cover. It is very clear, however, that Stroud does not mean to dismiss the former aspects of Hume's thought as unimportant or not "genuinely philosophical." Therefore I think his approach counts against, rather than in favor of, the portrayal of "analytical historians" offered in the introduction to *Philosophy in History*.

20. London: Methuen, 1966.

21. Daniel Garber and Michael Ayers are the editors of this work from Cambridge University Press (which printed the Prospectus) [The *History* appeared in two volumes in 1998]. Some similar generalizations about "the kind of history of philosophy to which analytic philosophy has given rise" appear in the introduction to *Philosophy in History*, 11–12. The editors of the latter collection also hold that "it has become customary" among historians influenced by analytic philosophy "to take the concerns of contemporary analytic philosophy as the center of attention. . . ." But they go even further than the

Cambridge History editors, insisting (bizarrely, to my mind) that such historians construe their subjects as "people who stumbled upon the 'real' philosophical questions but did not realize what they had discovered." See, also, Jonathan Rée's contribution to *Philosophy and Its Past*, by Rée, Ayers, and Adam Westoby (Hassocks, England: Harvester Press, 1978), 27–28.

22. Prospectus (no page numbers). For closely similar statements see Alan Donagan, *Spinoza*, xi–xiv. Donagan notes the perils in anachronistic analytic readings of Spinoza, but holds that some philosophers in the analytic tradition—notably Pollock and Curley—have "rescue[d] Spinoza for the twentieth century by restoring him to the seventeenth." Donagan continues, "Useful inquiry cannot begin into whether Spinoza's philosophy can be adapted to the thought of our day until it has been reconstructed in its relation to the thought of his" (xiii).

23. In *Descartes* (London: Routledge and Kegan Paul, 1978), I maintain that Descartes's arguments have been misunderstood and wrongly criticized as a result of isolating them from their context and failing to recognize his broad (and intentionally revolutionary) intellectual objectives—especially with respect to dethroning Aristotelian science.

24. See, for instance, Quentin Skinner's discussion of Mackie's *Problems from Locke* (Oxford: Oxford University Press/Clarendon, 1976), which Skinner regards as a "representative" and "particularly clear" example of "the prevailing approach to the history of philosophy" ("The Idea of Negative Liberty," *Philosophy in History*, chap. 9, 200–2). I can't resist mentioning a characterization of Mackie's book that I once saw somewhere, even though I can no longer remember whose it was. The work was described as "a good philosopher getting in the way of a great one." But whatever truth there may be in this slightly cruel description—and I admit that I don't find it wholly unjust—Mackie's work has many merits *as Locke interpretation*—including a strong awareness of the relevance of corpuscularian science to the doctrines of the *Essay*. (See section II, below.)

Jonathan Bennett is, perhaps, an even more popular target for critics of historians of philosophy "writing in the analytical tradition." See, for instance, Michael Ayers's contribution to *Philosophy and Its Past* ("Analytical Philosophy and the History of Philosophy," 54ff.). (Ayers also focuses on Russell's book on Leibniz, Ayers's discussion of Berkeley, and H. H. Price's 1940 study of Hume, though he does cite examples of more recent writing, besides Bennett.) Like Mackie, Bennett makes a point of denying that his concerns are "historical" or "scholarly" (see *Locke, Berkeley, Hume: Central Themes* [Oxford: Oxford University Press, 1971], preface). Unlike Mackie, he quite often adopts a condescending tone towards the historical figures he discusses. The latter trait can certainly be exasperating, but I deny that it is in any way typical of recent writing on historical figures by those with, or without, professed historical concerns.

25. *History and Theory* 25 (1985–86): 207.

26. In fairness I must note that Ayers himself makes this point in passing ("Analytical Philosophy and the History of Philosophy," 49).

27. Popkin, *A History of Skepticism From Erasmus to Descartes* (Assen, The Netherlands: Van Gorcum, 1960; rev. ed., 1964) (among other writings); Curley, *Descartes Against the Skeptics* (Cambridge: Harvard University Press, 1978). See also Myles Burnyeat, "Idealism and Greek Philosophy: What Descartes Saw and Berkeley Missed," *Philosophical Review* 91 (1982): 3–40; reprinted in *Idealism Past and Present*, ed. G. Vesey (Cambridge: Cambridge University Press, 1982). Curley does discuss the relation between Descartes's metaphysics and physics in his first and last chapters, and Burnyeat mentions it in passing, but both place primary emphasis on his relation to classical

skepticism. If, on the other hand, my reading of Descartes (and some of his successors) goes too far in the opposite direction, this is no doubt the result of certain evaluative "preconceptions" of my own.

28. *Berkeley: The Philosophy of Immaterialism* (London: Methuen, 1974; New York: Garland, 1988), 16.

29. (Oxford: Basil Blackwell, 1986), viii.

30. The point is made in a somewhat different way by Robert Solomon in his work on *The Passions* (Garden City: Doubleday, Anchor Books, 1976; Notre Dame: Notre Dame University Press, 1983). Solomon does not disqualify himself from contributing to historical study, and in fact his book contains some historical discussion. But he notes:

> My intention was to begin with an analysis and a critique of traditional philosophical theories of the emotions, especially in Aristotle, the Stoics and St. Augustine, Descartes, Hume, Spinoza, Hobbes, Rousseau, Whitehead and Sartre. I quickly found, however, that such an intention was bound to absorb my entire project, which, after all, was to get clear about "the passions" for myself, and share my thoughts with my readers. (131)

After noting some difficulties about incorporating the views of some of these thinkers, Solomon remarks,

> I found myself caught in academic scholarship and forced to choose between historical inaccuracies and a purely historical book. I chose to do neither.

He decided, rather, "to save these analyses for another publication" (132).

31. *Leibniz and Arnauld: A Commentary on Their Correspondence* (New Haven and London: Yale University Press, 1990), 6. In the immediately preceding pages Sleigh introduces and discusses the distinction between "exegetical" and "philosophical" history. While praising certain examples of the latter enterprise (including work by Bennett and Mackie), Sleigh suggests that efforts at philosophical history often suffer from lack of clear objectives, and fail to measure up to standards of both historical and philosophical rigor.

32. Benson Mates, in *his* introduction to another major study of Leibniz's philosophy, observes that "such criticism as is included will be, for the most part, internal, taking note of contradictions and other unwelcome consequences that seem to follow from [Leibniz's] principles" (*The Philosophy of Leibniz: Metaphysics and Language* [New York and Oxford: Oxford University Press, 1986], 3–4). He continues, "external criticism is rather out of place here, though I shall probably not be able to conceal from the reader that much of Leibniz's doctrine strikes me, as it did Russell, as a certainly interesting and perhaps heuristically useful fairy story" (4). The latter remark seems strangely juxtaposed with Mates's comment, a page earlier, that the "remarkable rebirth [in recent years] of interest in the philosophy of Leibniz" has to do with the relevance of Leibniz's "deeply intuitive" views to current work in logic, philosophical logic, and philosophy of language.

33. Cambridge: Harvard University Press, 1980. (Originally presented as lectures in 1970.)

34. 2 vols. (Cambridge: Cambridge University Press, 1978).

35. Oxford: Oxford University Press/Clarendon, 1984.

36. For a closely similar statement see Charles Taylor, "Philosophy and Its History," in *Philosophy in History*, 17.

37. Other reviewers include Anthony O'Hear (*Inquiry* 28 [1985]: 455–66); Ezra Tal-

mor (*History of European Ideas* 6 [1985]: 355–58); and J. E. K. Secada (*Philosophy* 61 [1986], 409–14).

38. In his contribution to *Philosophy in History*, Charles Taylor offers Descartes as an example of a figure who arrived at his position "by one of those creative redescriptions which I am arguing are of the essence of philosophy" ("Philosophy and Its History," 19). Taylor has just said that "those who have made successful such redescriptions . . . have had recourse to history" (18–19). He does not explain in just what sense he regards Descartes as having had "recourse to history." Perhaps he has in mind Descartes's reintroduction of Augustinian themes, and/or his use of traditional skeptical arguments. But these features of Descartes's thought don't in themselves establish that his (real) attitude to past thought was much different than that ascribed to "most analytical philosophy" by Ayers: that it provides "a useful ragbag of logical insights and confusions" (*Philosophy and Its Past*, 63).

Of course I don't mean to imply by these remarks that Descartes's vehemently ahistorical stance should be accepted at face value: only that we need to be told what to think about it, if generalizations such as Taylor's are to be regarded as credible. Several contributors to *Philosophy in History*—including the editors, in their introduction—mention a sense of the "contingency" of one's philosophical concerns as an advantage deriving from historical consciousness. This, too, seems to me a quite suspect idea, given the strongly absolutist stances of many of the greatest philosophers.

39. In the work previously cited, R. C. Sleigh partly explains his reservations about "philosophical history" as follows:

In my opinion, the effort attendant on philosophical history is often not justified in terms of the purely philosophical product. This outcome is not entirely surprising. If you want to work on the problem of personal identity, it is useful to read John Locke's writings, but it is more important to read Sydney Shoemaker—in part, of course, because Shoemaker has incorporated Locke's insights into his own work. If you are interested in making a contribution to the metaphysics of modality, it does no harm to study Leibniz, but Kripke is really more to the point. Philosophy is not related to its history in the way physics is to its history, but there *is* progress in philosophy, and it is not necessary to study the history of a philosophical problem in order to make a fundamental contribution toward the understanding, perhaps even the solution, of that problem. (*Leibniz and Arnauld*, 2–3)

40. *Philosophy in History*, 67.

41. It is interesting to note that John Passmore, writing in 1984, could observe that "empiricism of the classical British sort is now at a low ebb," having succumbed to the Kantian revival (*Recent Philosophers* [La Salle, Ill.: Open Court, 1985], 19). This claim surely requires modification, in view of much of the work that I will cite below. (Of course philosophical accounts of sensible qualities have roots much further back in history; but my discussion here will be limited to early modern and contemporary views.)

42. It's a familiar view, of course, that the earlier-mentioned qualities are distinguished from the latter by virtue of being "special sensibles," that is, conveyed (in the old terminology) by one sense alone. In general, however, early modern figures did not put much weight on the special/common sensible issue in maintaining that only a subset of the apparent qualities are, as we perceive them, really in the objects (although there are occasional passages to the contrary). The relation between the common/special sensible distinction and the objective/subjective quality distinction is, nevertheless, a complex and interesting one, both historically and philosophically. Berkeley saw the notion of

common sensible as tied up with the concept of mind-independent physical qualities that he wished to oppose, and partly for this reason mounted an attack against the very idea of a common sensible. Recently A. D. Smith (dismissing the attack of "Berkeley and his ilk") has claimed that there is such a thing as common sensibility, and that it does have an important role in determining objectivity ("Of Primary and Secondary Qualities," *Philosophical Review* 99 (1990): 221–39). But because this notion plays only a marginal role in the work of most of the writers I'll be discussing, I will set it aside in what follows.

43. *An Essay Concerning Human Understanding*, ed. Peter H. Nidditch (Oxford: Oxford University Press/Clarendon, 1975), 139.

44. Ibid.

45. Ibid.

46. Note that in this passage Locke seems first to *identify* "warmth as it is in our hands," and even "the sensation of heat and cold" with the degree (or change) of motion in the particles of our nerves, then to revert to his more characteristic talk of heat and cold as sensations that are "caused" by corpuscular motion. I will touch again later on such vacillations in the identification of heat, cold, color, and so on, which are by no means unique to Locke, and which have some interest in relation to more recent views.

47. "Berkeley," in *A Critical History of Western Philosophy*, ed. D. J. O'Connor (London: Collier-MacMillan, 1964), 243. Others include Reginald Jackson, "Locke's Distinction Between Primary and Secondary Qualities" (1928), in *Locke and Berkeley: Critical and Interpretive Essays*, ed. C. B. Martin and D. M. Armstrong (Garden City, N.Y.: Doubleday, Anchor Books, 1968); R. I. Aaron, *John Locke* (Oxford: Oxford University Press, 1937); D. J. O'Connor, *John Locke* (London: Penguin, 1952), 63–72. For additional references, see the first notes of the papers by Edwin Curley (on Locke) and Barry Stroud (on Berkeley) cited below. Stroud mentions Ian Tipton's 1974 study, *Berkeley: the Philosophy of Immaterialism* (37), as exemplifying this reading of *Essay* II.viii.19–21 (which he rejects), but I think this citation depends on a misunderstanding of Tipton. Tipton makes clear (35–37) that he sees Locke as serving as "public relations officer for the scientist," from whom he uncritically adopts the primary-secondary quality distinction, rather than trying to justify the distinction. Tipton's ensuing discussion of II.viii.19–21, which indeed appears at first sight to be construing the sections as presenting relativity arguments, is really meant to be an account of *Berkeley's view* of Locke.

48. Or, as some put it, involve "illusion" or error.

49. See G. J. Warnock, *Berkeley* (New York: Penguin, 1953), 97ff., and O'Connor, *Locke*, 65.

50. *American Philosophical Quarterly* 2 (1965); reprinted in Martin and Armstrong, and in *Berkeley's Principles of Human Knowledge*, ed. G. W. Engle and G. Taylor (Belmont, Calif.: Wadsworth, 1968).

51. (Oxford: Oxford University Press/Clarendon, 1971), chap. 4.

52. This quotation is from *Locke, Berkeley, Hume* (105). Actually, Bennett's discussion in the book seems to take fuller account, though in a rather oblique way, of the connection between some of what Locke says about primary qualities and his scientific commitments. Obviously, though, his view of Locke's distinction as resting on ordinary facts of experience is meant to remain in force. I cannot attempt here to do full justice to the complexities of Bennett's two discussions, let alone some of the subtle differences between them.

53. See, for instance, "Substance, Reality, and Primary Qualities," in Martin and Armstrong, 107–110.

54. *Locke, Berkeley, Hume*, 110.

55. "Substance, Reality, and Primary Qualities," 115.

56. Ibid., 114.

57. Ibid., 115.

58. *Locke, Berkeley, Hume*, 100.

59. In his book Bennett quotes with approval William Kneale's remark that "the distinction between primary and secondary qualities was a philosophical discovery, *and Locke was mistaken when he wrote of it as though it had been established by experiments unfamiliar to plain men*" (ibid., 105; emphasis added).

60. "Substance, Reality, and Primary Qualities," 110.

61. Ibid, 117.

62. *Locke, Berkeley, Hume*, 111. As we will see, other writers have been able to make better sense of this claim.

63. I elaborate this point (and some other philosophical objections to Bennett) in an unpublished paper, "The Primary Secondary Quality Distinction: Against Two Recent Defenses." This (and another of my points) has been explained in print by Edward Wilson Averill in "The Primary Secondary Quality Distinction," *Philosophical Review* 91 (1982): 347–48. See, also, *Essay* II.viii. 10 and 23, where Locke himself mentions various "powers" connected with bodies' heat, beyond that of producing ideas of warmth in us.

64. Averill's article, cited above, provides searching criticism of Bennett's version of the primary-secondary quality distinction on largely philosophical grounds.

65. Bennett's idea has been elaborated by George Pitcher (*A Theory of Perception* [Princeton: Princeton University Press, 1971]) and Colin McGinn (*The Subjective View* [Oxford: Oxford University Press/Clarendon, 1983]).

66. *Philosophy, Science, and Sense Perception* (Baltimore: The Johns Hopkins University Press, 1963), 3.

67. Peter Alexander, "Boyle and Locke on Primary and Secondary Qualities," *Ratio* 16 (1974), 51–67; reprinted in *Locke on Human Understanding*, ed. I. C. Tipton (Oxford: Oxford University Press, 1977). The quotation is from page 70 of the Tipton edition.

68. Alexander, in Tipton, 70.

69. The 'primary-secondary' terminology is used in its modern form by Boyle; it was evidently adapted from Scholastic usage. See M. A. Stewart's introduction to his edition of *Selected Philosophical Papers of Robert Boyle* (Manchester: Manchester University Press, 1979), xiv. I do not know whether Boyle originated the modern usage (Stewart seems to imply the contrary). In *The Assayer* Galileo spoke of the "*primi e reali accidenti*" of a body, in distinction from those supposed qualities that are "mere names" with respect to the bodies themselves (*Il Saggiatore*, ed. F. Flora [Turin: Einaudi, 1977], 224). For some notes on the contrast between the Scholastic-Aristotelian and early modern versions of the primary-secondary quality distinction, see Murray Miles, "Descartes' Mechanism and the Medieval Doctrine of Causes, Qualities, and Forms," *The Modern Schoolman* 65 (1988): 107–8.

70. E. M. Curley writes, with specific reference to II.viii.21:

Locke is not there concerned to argue that, because we may err about temperatures, things do not really have temperatures, or that, because our perceptions of temperature vary with the conditions under which temperatures are perceived, temperatures are not genuine properties of objects. What Locke is concerned with is providing

indirect evidence for a particular mechanical theory about the causation of our perceptions of heat . . . ("Locke, Boyle, and the Distinction Between Primary and
Secondary Qualities," *Philosophical Review*, 81 [1972]: 458)

71. Most commentators note, though, that Locke regarded the corpuscularian assumptions as merely the best explanatory hypothesis we have (or are likely to have)—not as
embodying indubitable, established truths, about the world.

72. See Curley, "Locke, Boyle, and the Distinction," 454: "Locke's characterization
of the primary qualities as 'original' qualities of objects rightly suggests what we would
now put by saying that they are qualities designated by the primitive terms in the scientific theory of perception."

73. Of course, as is by now widely recognized, Berkeley was not the first to stress the
relativity of primary quality perceptions as relevant to the enterprise of undermining
positions such as Locke's. (See my paper "Did Berkeley Completely Misunderstand the
Basis of the Primary-Secondary Quality Distinction in Locke?" in *Berkeley: Critical and
Interpretive Essays*, ed. Colin Turbayne [Minneapolis: University of Minnesota Press,
1982], 108–126 [Chapter 15 of this volume], for discussion and references.)

74. "Locke, Boyle, and the Distinction," 452.

75. Ibid., 454.

76. *Essay* II.viii.23:

The *Qualities* then that are in *Bodies* rightly considered, are of *Three sorts*.

First, the *Bulk*, *Figure*, *Number*, *Situation*, and *Motion*, *or Rest* of their solid Parts;
those are in them, whether we perceive them or no; and when they are of that size,
that we can discover them, we have by these an *Idea* of the thing, as it is in it
self. . . .

What exactly is it that we are supposed to "discover" in the case of macroscopic bodies?
I think the passage is most naturally read as indicating that we discover "the figure"
(etc.) that the body really has. I don't find in this passage, or the manna passage, or for
that matter in the globe/square passage any support at all for Curley's notion that Locke
is making a point about figure (etc.) understood generically being essential to explaining
perceptions of figure.

77. Paul A. Kolers, *Aspects of Motion Perception* (Oxford: Pergamon Press, 1972), 2.
See also Nelson Goodman, *Ways of Worldmaking* (Indianapolis: Hackett, 1978), chap. 5.

78. "Locke, Boyle, and the Distinction," 453.

79. Even today philosophers may speak rather loosely of "explaining" perceptual appearances, particularly with respect to macroscopic primary qualities. Thomas Nagel, for
instance, comments:

I hold the familiar view that secondary qualities describe the world as it appears to
us but primary qualities do not. To be red simply is to be something which would
appear red to us in normal conditions—it is a property whose definition is essentially relative. But to be square is not simply to be such as to appear square even
though what is square does appear square. Here the appearance of squareness is
significantly explained in terms of the effect on us of squareness in objects, which is
not in turn analyzed in terms of the appearance of squareness. (*The View From
Nowhere* [New York and Oxford: Oxford University Press], 101)

Part of Nagel's point is that it is not circular to appeal to the squareness of objects in
explaining the appearance of squareness, since their being square is not just a matter of

their appearing square. But in what sense of 'explain', exactly, does the squareness of something "significantly explain" the "appearance of squareness"? Are we supposed to envisage a complex, empirically based theory involving corpuscles, light rays, and brain motions (or their scientific descendants); or is something more ordinary and "intuitive" at issue? My guess is that Nagel has in mind the latter (whereas Curley tries to interpret Locke in terms of the former). The point, in any case, is that if the primary-secondary quality distinction is to be based on ideas about explanation, one ought to make clear just what sort of "explanation" one has in mind.

80. In fact, as Curley indicates, it is hard to believe today that the earlier commentators, such as O'Connor and Warnock, had actually read these sections very carefully. In "Locke and Pyrrhonism" (*The Skeptical Tradition*, ed. Myles Burnyeat [Berkeley and Los Angeles: University of California Press, 1983], chap. 14) Martha Brandt Bolton makes an ingenious and well-documented case for the claim that a concern with Pyrrhonian arguments, as well as a commitment to Boyleanism, underlies Locke's examples in II.viii. 19–21. I don't deny that awareness of such arguments may have affected Locke's presentation, but I remain unconvinced that Pyrrhonian worries are a main concern of these sections.

81. As Bolton stresses (ibid., 364–65).

82. A lot of the difficulty Bennett has with Locke's denial that colors and so forth are really in the things seems to derive not from "philosophical" considerations that tell against Locke, but from a failure to note that Locke very often uses terms like 'color', 'red', 'taste', 'sweet', etc. to refer to ideas, *and not to secondary qualities*. See Peter Alexander, "The names of secondary qualities," *Proceedings of the Aristotelian Society*, 67 (1977): 203–20. Alexander also discusses this important textual point in his book *Ideas, Qualities and Corpuscles: Locke and Boyle on the External World* (Cambridge: Cambridge University Press, 1985).

83. Section 6 of Bennett's paper, concerned with Berkeley's response to Locke on primary and secondary qualities, is titled "Berkeley's Blunder." Most of the other commentators cited are nearly as dismissive.

84. Reginald Jackson's 1929 essay "Locke's Primary and Secondary Qualities" (reprinted in Armstrong and Martin, 53–77), specifically cited and discussed by Curley, provides a good example for my claim. Although Jackson does, very briefly, endorse the "relativity argument" interpretation of II.viii.19–21, he discourses at some length on Locke's relation to Boyle, and is very hard on Berkeley.

85. Descartes, of course, repudiated "atomism," and even Boyle was uncomfortable with the term. Both wanted to distinguish their positions from the views of Democritus and Leucippus.

86. I don't mean to suggest, of course, that the pervasiveness of these views has gone unremarked until recently; nor do I overlook the strong expositions of it in works such as E. A. Burtt's *The Metaphysical Foundations of Modern Physical Science* (New York: Harcourt Brace, 1932). (Burtt does, however, focus on the notably "scientific" thinkers, to the near exclusion of Locke and Malebranche.) What does seem to be new (in the past decade or so) is the increasingly widespread (though still not universal) recognition of, and emphasis on, the point in historical and philosophical writing, and grasp of its full significance for the interpretation of such "philosophical" works as the *Meditations*. I discuss these points in somewhat greater detail in "Skepticism Without Indubitability," *Journal of Philosophy* 81 (1984): 538ff. (Chapter 1 of this volume). See, also, the paper by A. D. Smith, "Of Primary and Secondary Qualities," cited above.

87. I have defended this claim (which goes against some commonly accepted assump-

tions) in two papers: "The 'Phenomenalisms' of Berkeley and Kant," in *Self and Nature in Kant's Philosophy*, ed. Allen W. Wood (Ithaca, N.Y.: Cornell University Press, 1984), 157–73 (Chapter 20 of this volume); and "The Phenomenalisms of Berkeley and Leibniz," in *Essays on the Philosophy of George Berkeley*, ed. Ernest Sosa (Dordrecht, The Netherlands: D. Reidel, 1987), 3–22. Of course the theory of matter underwent very significant development between the early seventeenth century and the late eighteenth century (as A. D. Smith notes, "Of Primary and Secondary Qualities," 246).

88. Ibid., 221.

89. "Berkeley v. Locke on Primary Qualities," *Philosophy* 55 (1980), 149–66.

90. I don't have space here to document this claim in detail. I discuss aspects of it, however, in the following papers: "Did Berkeley Completely Misunderstand the Basis of the Primary-Secondary Quality Distinction in Locke?" in Turbayne (Chapter 15 of this volume); "Skepticism without Indubitability" (Chapter 1 of this volume); "Berkeley on the Mind-Dependence of Colors," *Pacific Philosophical Quarterly* 68 (1987) (Chapter 16 of this volume); and "The Issue of 'Common Sensibles' in Berkeley's *New Theory of Vision*," this volume, Chapter 18. See, also, John Foster, "Berkeley on the Physical World," in *Essays on Berkeley*, ed. John Foster and Howard Robinson (Oxford: Oxford University Press/Clarendon, 1985), 86; and Kenneth Winkler, *Berkeley: An Interpretation* (Oxford: Oxford University Press/Clarendon, 1989), chap. 8.

91. For recent discussion of Berkeley's philosophy of science, in relation to the views of his materialist opponents, see W. H. Newton-Smith, "Berkeley's Philosophy of Science," in Foster and Robinson, 149–62; and Winkler, *Berkeley*.

92. (Princeton: Princeton University Press, 1979.) Among the oddities of Rorty's version of early modern philosophy is his inability to explain Descartes's *general* emphasis on the "indubitability" of one's own mental states—even those (such as sensations) which evidently have no epistemologically "foundational" role for Descartes.

93. And, one might add, Malebranche can simply be *read*. That is, I suggest, the greatly increased interest in Malebranche in recent years among historians of philosophy writing in English derives in part from his extraordinarily clear presentation of some of the main ideas common to scientific realist philosophers of the period—not merely from a new adventuresomeness with respect to the historical "canon." (See, for instance, M. D. Wilson, "Skepticism without Indubitability" [Chapter 1 in this volume] and A. D. Smith, "Of Primary and Secondary Qualities," as well as Charles J. McCracken, *Malebranche and British Philosophy* (Oxford: Oxford University Press/Clarendon, 1983). McCracken, however, like Luce before him, significantly underestimates the difference between Malebranche and Berkeley, precisely with respect to the latter's rejection of the scientific realist conception of sensible qualities.) Of course, the increased interaction among English-speaking and French scholars, noted in section 1, also has something to do with this development.

94. *A Critical History of Western Philosophy*, 211. O'Connor also characterizes Locke's doctrine as "a rather indigestible mixture of empirical science and *a priori* reasoning" (210–11).

95. *Problems From Locke* (Oxford: Oxford University Press/Clarendon, 1976), 7.

96. Ibid., 18–19. See also Frank Jackson, *Perception* (Cambridge: Cambridge University Press, 1977): "Does Science imply, contrary to what we seem to see, that the pen I am now writing with does not have the property of being blue? I will argue that it does, that Science forces us to acknowledge that physical or material things are not coloured . . ." (120).

Mackie, incidentally, follows Mandelbaum, Alexander, and Bennett in rejecting Berkeley's criticisms of Locke as beside the point (*Problems From Locke*, 24).

97. *Philosophy and Scientific Realism* (London: Routledge and Kegan Paul, 1963), vii.

98. Ibid., 66.

99. "Philosophy and the Scientific Image of Man," in *Science, Perception, and Reality* (London: Routledge and Kegan Paul, 1963).

100. There is some sign also of another parallel, with respect to views about Berkeley. Not only has he begun to receive a fairer hearing from historians than the "corpuscular" interpreters of Locke were able to accord him; but aspects of his antirealist position have even received endorsement. See, for instance, Colin McGinn, *The Subjective View*, chapter 6; and A. C. Grayling, *Berkeley* (Peru, Ill.: Open Court, 1986), especially chapter 4. Grayling thinks the anti-Berkeleyan side of McGinn's position is "unintelligible" for reasons found in Berkeley; he concludes: "There is much to be said . . . on the questions of objectivity, the nature of the deliverances of science, and the fundamental issue of what metaphysical consequences flow from rejecting absolute realism. . . . [W]hat Berkeley had to say on *these* issues . . . is much more pertinent to the question of getting them right than has generally been allowed . . ." (210). Grayling promises to develop this perspective further in later work.

101. I agree with Hilary Putnam's statement that "the task of overcoming the seventeenth century world picture is only begun" (*The Many Faces of Realism* [Peru, Ill.: Open Court, 1987; presented as lectures in 1985], lecture 1, 17).

102. On the notion of a single "essence of matter," in relation to seventeenth-century conceptions of explanation and "primary qualities," see A. D. Smith, "Of Primary and Secondary Qualities," 226 and sections 4–6.

103. See, for instance, Mackie, *Problems From Locke*, 25–27.

104. Ibid., 18.

105. See A. D. Smith, "Of Primary and Secondary Qualities," 248–53. Citing "a certain realist interpretation of probability theory" Smith observes that "spatial and temporal properties now appear as having an almost secondary status: how the objective four-dimensional facts about the world are (mis)conceptualized by our *abgeblendete Bewusstsein*, as Hermann Weyl put it" (253). (See, also, Smart, *Philosophy and Scientific Realism*, 44–45.) Smith ultimately proposes "either simply to ditch the term 'primary quality,' or use the term to advert to the properties deemed fundamental by current science."

Although I consider this a reasonable recommendation, I find it hard to reconcile with a previous phase of Smith's discussion, according to which "perceptible primary qualities" are Aristotelian common sensibles, or "spatio-temporal concepts" which "constitute the necessary structuring of sensory experience in any creature capable of objective perception" (242–43).

106. Mackie appears to have some looser conception in mind on p. 18; but compare his remarks on p. 25 about primary qualities as "starting-points of explanation" and (by implication) "basic" physical features.

107. Cf. McGinn, *The Subjective View*, 12, n. 10; 15; 115.

108. P. 79. Cf. 101: ". . . perceptual experience is necessarily as of an external world of spatially disposed objects, and these objects are objectively characterized by primary qualities. . . ." The necessity in question, he continues, is explained by the fact that it is derived from a general feature of perceptual experience, viz., its outer-directedness. (Similar views are advocated by A. D. Smith in the paper cited.) On p. 114, n. 7, McGinn makes some attempt to relate this view about the *a priori* status of the primary-secondary quality distinction to the empirical basis of scientific explanation.

109. See, for instance, C. L. Hardin, *Colors for Philosophers*, Edward Wilson Averill,

"The Primary-Secondary Quality Distinction," 317–42; "Color and the Anthropocentric Problem," *Journal of Philosophy* 82 (1985): 281–304; and review of McGinn, *The Subjective View*, *Philosophical Review* 94 (1985): 296–99. See, also, the following two papers by Paul A. Boghossian and J. David Velleman: "Colour as a Secondary Quality," *Mind* 98 (1989), 81–103 and "Physicalist Theories of Color," *Philosophical Review* 100 (1991), 67–106.

110. See, for instance, Descartes's account of the distinction between, for example, color and (what came to be called) primary qualities in terms of the sense-intellect distinction in *Sixth Replies* (AT VII, 437–38; CSM II, 295–96). Compare Hardin, *Colors for Philosophers*, 87–88, 96–112. (The latter passage is directed at criticizing Frank Jackson's neo-Lockean endorsement (in *Perception*) of the view that color properties are borne (only) by sense data.) Barry Stroud has also objected to recent philosophizing about secondary qualities (especially color) on the grounds that it tends to depend on an untenable view of color (etc.) "sensations," though he doesn't appeal to scientific developments. He has developed this objection in his John Locke Lectures of 1986, and in an as yet unpublished paper, "The Idea of Reality and the 'Analysis' of Colour." (I've had access only to the manuscript of the paper.)

111. As I mentioned above, even Leibniz's phenomenalism and Kant's transcendental idealism include a wide area of agreement with the simpler forms of scientific realism, including acceptance of the view that "sensations" of color and so on are merely subjective in a way that, say, spatial qualities are not.

112. See P. F. Strawson, "Perception and Its Objects," in *Perception and Identity: Essays Presented to A. J. Ayer*, ed. G. F. Macdonald (Ithaca, N.Y.: Cornell University Press, 1979), 41–60 (especially 53ff.). Strawson, after raising the question whether ordinarily experienced objects can be regarded as identical with configurations of ultimate particles, seems to answer it affirmatively (59). He proposes that we regard common sense and science as providing two (nonconflicting) points of view of the same thing. (Part of Strawson's argument against scientific realism involves a quasi-Berkeleyan denial that its violation of common sense can be mitigated by the notion that *certain* phenomenal qualities [such as shape] can coherently be supposed to resemble "abstract" physical qualities [54].)

Berkeley, of course, had already begun to show another way of reconciling mechanistic science with the inviolability of the manifest image, insofar as he introduced instrumentalist accounts of certain scientific concepts which failed to answer to "ideas of sense" (notably force). However, it seems to be generally agreed that he did not adopt an instrumentalist account of "insensible corpuscles," and it remains controversial whether he had available some other way to accommodate them in his metaphysics—say, by recourse to "God's ideas." (To this extent it remains controversial how much of the contemporary scientific image he could actually accept.)

113. Barry Stroud does, for instance, in the various presentations mentioned above (n. 110).

114. See, especially, *Works* (Luce and Jessop) vol. 2, 308–310 (the reference is to the Second Dialogue). See also M. D. Wilson, "Did Berkeley Completely Misunderstand?" in Turbayne (Chapter 15 of this volume).

115. Jackson, for instance, in *Perception*, and Mackie, *Problems From Locke*, chap. 1. While some scientific realists seem remarkably casual in their claims about the adequacy for explanation of the properties ascribed to the world in contemporary scientific accounts, there are notable exceptions, including, of course, Wilfrid Sellars. For a brief account of his concerns, see Bruce Aune, "Sellars's Two Images of the World," *Journal of Philosophy* 87 (1990): 542–50.

116. See, for instance, Robert M. Adams, "Flavors, Colors, and God," in *The Virtue of Faith* (New York and Oxford: Oxford University Press, 1987), especially 244–45, 251–60.

117. Thomas Nagel, for instance, in *Mortal Questions* (Cambridge: Cambridge University Press, 1979), 194, and more recently Adams, in "Flavors, Colors, and God," 258–60. Scientists frequently acknowledge a continuing "complete mystery" about the explanation of subjective experience in physical terms. See, for instance, James E. Cutting, *Perception With an Eye for Motion* (Cambridge: The MIT Press, Bradford Books, 1986), 249, to pick an example almost at random.

118. Adams, in "Flavors, Colors, and God."

119. As Stroud argues (in the work cited in n. 110), proponents of a "biconditional" account of color (and presumably at least some of their opponents as well) appear to think that they are providing an "analysis" of color that can add something special to our stock of knowledge. But (apart from criticisms that their account cannot stand up to sophisticated work in color science), this assumption seems no longer to claim grounding in a respectable epistemology.

120. I am grateful to Allen Wood for detailed, constructive criticisms of an early draft of section 1, and to James Ross for very helpful, extensive comments on drafts of all three sections. The editors of the *Philosophical Review* provided some incisive criticisms of a draft of section 2. I also want to thank Adam Reffes for valuable research assistance. The article was written while I was on leave, with partial support, from Princeton University.

I dedicate the paper to the memory of Alan Donagan.

Animal Ideas

In December of 1648 Henry More, the Cambridge Platonist, wrote to Descartes:

> . . . There is none of your opinions that my soul, gentle and tender as it is, shrinks from as much as that murderous and cutthroat view you maintain in the *Discourse*, that deprives the brutes of all life and sense. . . .[1]

That the gentle and tender More should resort to such fierce terminology helps to illustrate in somewhat extreme form, the significant interest among seventeenth and eighteenth-century philosophers in the topic of beasts' mentality. Often expressions of this interest are tied in with a traditional catch-phrase, "the difference between men and beasts." Perhaps philosophers of the period didn't accord this topic quite the degree of attention recently documented for ancient and medieval philosophy by Richard Sorabji (in his fascinating study, *Animal Minds and Human Morals*).[2] But they showed, if somewhat fitfully, a keen interest in it. The topic was a live one, philosophically important in a number of respects. And, as More's statement shows, it could engage the kind of passionate concern with which we've recently become reacquainted in debate about the treatment of non-human animals—even about the interpretation of animal behavioral and ethological studies.

Descartes's brash position touched off mainstream philosophical debate of the issue in the early 1640's, and continued to hover in the background of discussion well into the eighteenth century. He famously contended, beginning in the *Discourse on the Method* of 1637, to be able to "prove" that brutes are mere material mechanisms, lacking any form of thought (and hence, by implication, consciousness).[3] We can ascribe to them "ideas" of sense, imagination, and memory; but only in the sense of actual physical traces in the brain, brought about typically by contact with other bodies, and contributing to behavior by physical redirection of the animal spirits. Contrary to More's suggestion, Descartes does not deny brutes "life" (which itself he interprets mechanistically): but More's basic reaction is not misconceived. The clear implication of Descartes's "automaton" analysis—developed in somewhat whimsical detail in a contemporary letter to Reneri[4]—is that there is nothing at all going on in beasts that isn't observable physiologically, objectively, "from the outside": nothing that it's "like" to be, say, a mother bear "trying" to protect her cubs; a sea lion "enjoying" a roll in the surf; or a seriously injured dog (let alone a bat).[5] In late writings, including his response to More, Descartes does weaken his epistemic stance, but he continues to maintain the "probability" of his original claims.

Apart from its more-than-provocative nature, Descartes's treatment is notable among early modern discussions of the issue of animal mentality for the relative clarity and firmness of the reasoning that he puts forward to support it. In his memorable A.P.A. Eastern Division Presidential address of 1972, "Thoughtless Brutes," Norman Malcolm conjectured that the basis of Descartes's position was his supposedly idiosyncratic requirement, implicit in the *Meditations*, that all "thought" must have some kind of propositional structure.[6] But it seems to me that this conjecture, while suggestive, is tangential to the motivation that Descartes himself makes patent in all his writings on the subject from the *Discourse* on (accurately noted by Jonathan Bennett in his more recent address, "Thoughtful Brutes").[7] This is Descartes's contention that all behavioral phenomena can be explained mechanistically, except only those that require the postulation of reason or understanding; and that the behavior of brutes, for reasons soon to be noted, belies the presence of such a "principle." Reason, it seems, is necessary in accounting for some observable human behavior; apart from reason, conscious feeling as a separate explanatory postulate contributes nothing.

Descartes's position was resisted mightily by his immediate critics: More's reaction, as we'll soon see, was far from unique. Later major philosophers of the early modern period, such as Locke, Leibniz, and Hume, also self-consciously opposed Descartes's conception of the difference between men and brutes. Some of the debate concerned moral issues, which I'll unfortunately have to set aside here. Also significant were metaphysical concerns about whether thought (as Descartes held) implies the presence of an immaterial soul, together with related theological issues about immortality. The latter topic also I'll have to neglect, for reasons of time. Concentrating then on issues specifically of cognition and consciousness, the following four questions can be isolated as central:

First, do brutes "reason"; and if so, how does their "reasoning" compare with that of humans?

Second, whether or not they "reason," do they evince still other kinds of mental states, such as non-rational "knowledge" or conscious "sensibility" which are in some ways continuous with those of humans?

Third, are some humans, such as fetuses, idiots, madmen, or (as Locke says) the decrepit elderly, closer than others to the condition of brutes?

Finally, what are the *bases* we have for answering questions about brute mentality in specific ways?

In comparing Descartes's position with the statements of those who rejected it, the last question emerges as particularly interesting. Descartes, as noted, claims to have given compelling "proofs" for his own position in the *Discourse*. (His discussion there takes as background the voluntarily suppressed *Treatise on Man*, which purports to provide detailed mechanical explanations not only of beasts' behavior, but of much human activity as well.) He repeatedly insists that his critics ignore his arguments in favor of dogmatic statements about brutes' "knowledge" and "thought," plus various expressions of incredulity. He attributes their reactions, like other forms of resistance to his mechanical philosophy of nature, to "prejudices" uncritically acquired in youth.

It appears to me that Descartes is largely, and interestingly, right about his critics' failure to produce articulate arguments against him. Further, the various confident assertions about the relation of beasts' and human mentality of later major philosophers of the period are also curiously lacking in coherent support. After sketching some aspects of Descartes's controversies with those who protested his views on the beasts during his lifetime, I'll briefly indicate some contrary views of Locke, Leibniz, and Hume. I'll suggest that in each case these figures' attempts to substitute a less drastic position, interesting as they are in certain ways (and no doubt more sympathetic to most of us than Descartes's "cutthroat opinion"), lack both clarity and cogency. In each case the difficulties seem to tie in with problems in the respective philosophers' accounts of human thought (though, again, I won't have time to develop this suggestion here).

Descartes maintains, in Part V of the *Discourse*, that there are "two certain means" by which we can determine if any of the operations of an entity—machine, beast, or man—come about by virtue of reason or knowledge or mind, as opposed to deriving from purely mechanical structures. The first is the ability to "arrange words differently, so as to respond to the sense of whatever is said in its presence."[8] This true use of speech, he stresses, must not be confused with the ability to "utter words" in response to specific stimuli (a machine could be constructed to do *that*); nor with "the natural movements which evince [*tesmoignent*] the passions, and which can be imitated by machines as well as by animals." No animal besides man, he claims, shows evidence of this ability; while "there are no men so dull-witted or stupid—and this includes even madmen" who do not. This, he concludes,

> shows [*tesmoigne*] not only that the beasts have less reason than men, but that they have none at all. For one sees that only very little reason is needed to be able to speak . . .[9]

The second way of distinguishing entities that possess reason from those that do not has to do with the presence or absence of "the ability to act in all the circumstances of life," such as is found in us. Machines and beasts, to be sure, do better than human beings in certain specific activities. Since "they inevitably fall short in others," however, such limited superiority proves only that they do *not* act from reason or "mind," but only from the mechanical "disposition of their organs"—a particular fixed "disposition" for each particular type of action. For otherwise, he says, "they would have more reason than any of us, and do better in everything."[10] (This emphasis on fixed "dispositions" should not be taken to imply that Descartes regards the behavior of beasts as rigidly instinctual: he elsewhere makes clear that habit or training contributes importantly to the behavior of both beasts and men.)[11] On the other hand, he says, it is "morally impossible" that there could be enough specific dispositions packed into one entity to account for the versatility of human behavior. This can only be explained by the presence of reason, "a universal instrument." Descartes notes, in conclusion of this discussion, that in the *Treatise on Man* he had established that the rational soul alone "cannot be in any way derived from the potentiality of matter, . . . but must be specially created."[12]

It seems to me that both of Descartes's "means" are of enduring significance, though I will not take time to defend this suggestion here. (Bennett, again, provides some defense of the point.) Of course this is not to deny that the *Discourse* discussion is subject to reasonable objections, apart from issues about animal feeling, or feeling for animals. I will mention just two, in passing. First, there appears to be a tension between Descartes's characterization of reason as he delineates it in explaining the two tests. In discussing language, he is at pains to emphasize that there are *degrees* of intellectual competence among human beings. That the beasts "have no reason at all" is supposedly proved by the consideration that "*very little* reason" is required in order to speak. Even the dullest human, even madmen, even children (he says) with defective brains are capable of "arranging various words together and composing from them a discourse by which they make their thoughts understood."[13] Yet surely such intellectually deficient humans "inevitably fall short" in their performance in certain things (as Descartes says of the beasts, in stating the second test for rationality): otherwise they would not be considered intellectually deficient. Indeed *all* of us "fall short" in a considerable range of activities, beyond those that we are disqualified from by obvious bodily limitations.[14] This presents a problem for precisely interpreting the claim, prominent in Descartes's account of the *second* "means," that reason is "a universal instrument." It is just possible that Descartes came to recognize this problem; for in later life he cites the language test alone.

Second, there is the matter of pre-lingual human infants, which Descartes curiously doesn't address at all in the *Discourse* passage. In this case the problem is not that there is tension between his expositions of the two tests. It is rather that the beings in question appear to fail both. Yet Descartes does elsewhere ascribe "thought" to babies and even to fetuses.[15] As it happens, Henry More raised precisely this point to Descartes in a later letter (March 5, 1649).[16] Descartes responded as follows:

> The case [*ratio*] is different between infants and brutes: I should not judge that infants were endowed with minds had I not seen that they were of the same nature as adults; but brutes never develop to the point where any certain sign of thought is found in them.[17]

More should not have been satisfied with this answer. The claim that More meant to support by the example of infants is just that there is no strict correlation between evident linguistic competence, and ascriptions of mentality that Descartes himself would endorse. Descartes's answer does not address this implication.

This objection of More's was one of the most concrete with which Descartes was confronted; but More's attack was by no means the first. A measure of the impact of the *Discourse* account of the human/beast distinction may be found in the fact that the authors of at least four of the six sets of "Objections" originally published with the *Meditations* (in 1641), take this position as a target of criticism—even though the issue of beasts' mentality is not directly broached in the *Meditations*. Among them, Antoine Arnauld, in the Fourth Objections, shows a clear understanding that the question of explanation is central for Descartes; yet he doesn't go beyond a broad claim of implausibility to specific discussion of the "two means." Arnauld simply protests that,

> at first sight it seems incredible that it can come about, without the assistance of any soul, that the light reflected from the body of a wolf onto the eyes of a sheep should move the minute fibres of the optic nerves, and that on reaching the brain this motion should spread the animal spirits throughout the nerves in the manner necessary to precipitate the sheep's flight.[18]

Descartes, in reply, claims that we should not be at all "amazed" by a mechanistic interpretation of the sheep's reaction, given that "our own experience reliably informs us" that many human behaviors, such as thrusting out one's hands when one falls, are performed without the intervention of reason or mind, "just as [they] would be produced in a machine." He then asserts that consideration of the differences between men and beasts, as set forth in the *Discourse*—"the only differences to be found"—makes clear that "all the actions of the brutes resemble only those which occur in us without any assistance from the mind." He goes on to invoke his "prejudice" analysis, maintaining that once we noticed that the mechanical "principle of motion" exists in brutes as it does in us, "we jumped to the conclusion that the other principle, which consists in mind or thought, also exists in them." Beliefs held since childhood, he concludes, cannot easily be eradicated without long and frequent attention to the arguments which prove them false.[19]

Gassendi, in the Fifth Objections, maintains straightforwardly against Descartes though without explanation or argument—that while beasts certainly lack human reason, they do not lack their own form of reason; nor even their own form of speech. "You will say," he suggests, "that they do not exercise reason [*non ratiocinari*]." But,

> . . . although they do not exercise reason as perfectly or about as many subjects as man, they still exercise reason, and the difference seems merely to be one of degree. . . . You will say that [beasts] do not speak. But although they do not produce human speech (naturally: they are not human beings), they still produce their own form of speech, which they use in just the same way as we do ours.[20]

Gassendi contends that it is not "fair" of Descartes to demand human speech of beasts, and not to be prepared "to consider their own." According to Gassendi, beasts "think, or besides the functions of the external senses, are aware of something internal, not only when they are awake, but also when they are dreaming."[21]

In his Reply, Descartes understandably does not deign to address these un-supported claims directly. He remarks that Gassendi simply "strings together objections which the inexperienced generally tend to raise against my conclusions."[22] (And, in fact, Gassendi has notably failed to address Descartes's relatively sophisticated analysis of the difference between human and brute "expression.") Descartes does amplify his earlier remarks in a couple of ways, however. In particular, responding to Gassendi's suggestion that the denial of thought to brutes might lead some to deny thought to humans as well, he observes that we are in a different epistemic state with regard to the attribution of thought to humans and to brutes. The human mind can experience that it thinks "when meditating to itself"; but does not learn in this way "whether the brutes also think or not;" we may only, he says, "investigate this afterwards, a posteriori from their actions."[23]

The authors of the Sixth Objections follow Gassendi in asserting that beasts have thought and knowledge both sleeping and waking: for,

> dogs bark in their sleep as if they were chasing hares or robbers, and when they are awake they know that they are running, just as when dreaming they know that they are barking . . .[24]

They continue somewhat whimsically (and unspeciesistically):

> If you deny that the dog knows that it is running or thinking, then you do not prove what you say; the dog might well make a similar judgement about us, namely that we do not know that we are running or thinking, when we are running or thinking . . .[25]

Descartes is no more able to see the brutes' "internal mode of action" than they are able to inspect his. The Sixth Objectors side with Gassendi in holding that the difference between bestial and human reason is merely one of degree. And they echo Arnauld, in claiming that it is ridiculous to suppose that the operations of beasts can be explained mechanistically, "without sense, life, and soul"; indeed, they are "willing to wager anything you like that this is an impossible and ridiculous claim."[26]

Both Gassendi and the Sixth Objectors have an explicit metaphysical agenda. They use their claims about the continuity between human and brute thought and reason to imply that if dualism is unacceptable in the case of brutes, there is no basis for ascribing an immaterial soul to humans either.

In replying to the Sixth Objections, Descartes sticks to his dualistic principle: if beasts *did* have thought, then it would follow that they, too, have immaterial minds—*not* that human thought is a merely material condition. But, he continues,

> In fact [in the *Discourse*] I did not just say that in brutes there is no thought at all—as my critics here assume—but I proved it by very strong arguments which no one has refuted up to now.[27]

Dogmatic statements about brutes' knowledge and reason, even "wagers," he plausibly indicates, do not count as philosophical counter-arguments.

Despite offering few concessions to the Objectors in 1641, Descartes later on certainly qualified his position on beasts' mentality. (Perhaps he was after all influenced by the "Objections"; though someone has seriously suggested to me that his thinking might have been affected by the simple fact that he got to know a dog well!) The change of attitude is very clearly signalled in his last published work, *The Passions of the Soul* of 1649. In arguing for the physiological basis of habit in human reactions, he notes that the "same thing can be observed in the beasts,":

> for even though they have no reason, nor perhaps even any thought [*ny peut estre aussi aucune pensée*], all the movements of the spirits and the [pineal] gland which excite the passions in us still occur in them, and in them serve to support and fortify, not the passions as in us, but the movements of the nerves and muscles. . . .[28]

"Nor *perhaps* even any thought": no longer, it seems, is Descartes claiming to have *proof* that there is in brutes "no thought at all." This is not an isolated lapse. There is other evidence that by the late 1640's Descartes's conviction has weakened. In a letter of 1646, he maintains that of our external actions only language—the second "means" now seems to be disregarded—demonstrates that "our body is not only a machine . . . , but has in itself also a soul which has thoughts."[29] But he is now willing to accept a consideration other than "external action" as prima facie evidence that there is something not strictly mechanical going on in the beasts:

> The most one can say is that although beasts do not perform any action which shows us that they think, still, since the organs of their bodies are not very different from ours, it may be conjectured that there is attached to these organs some thought such as we experience in ourselves, although theirs would be much less perfect.[30]

Against this suggestion, which he himself introduces, he has "nothing to reply except that if they thought as we do, they too would have an immortal soul."[31] And against *this* conclusion his only argument is that "there is no reason to believe it of some animals without believing it of all; and there are many too imperfect for it to be possible to believe this of them, such as oysters, sponges, etc."

Similar concessions are made to More. Among other challenges, More demands to know how, "without sentiment and reflection," it is possible to explain the "astuteness and sagacity of foxes and dogs?" Or, more colorfully, why,

> when a dog driven by hunger has stolen something, it flee[s] and hide[s] as if it knows that it has done something wrong, and walking with fear and mistrust, does not play up to people passing by, but turning aside from their path, looks for an isolated place with lowered head, drawing on a wise caution, so as not to be punished for its crime?

How explain all this, he demands, "without an interior feeling?"[32]

In reply Descartes again insists that there is no need to attribute to beasts a mental as opposed to a mechanical principle.

> I am not put off [he says] by the astuteness and cunning of dogs and foxes, nor by
> all the other things which brutes do for the sake of food, sex, and fear. For I claim
> that I can easily explain all of them as effected only by the structure of their bodily
> parts.[33]

He again notes that because the beasts lack speech we cannot *prove* that they
have thought within them. On the other hand, he now explicitly concedes that
"I don't think it can be demonstrated that there is none, since the human mind
does not reach into their hearts."[34] (A mysterious phrasing, as Malcolm pointed
out, since it implies that there is some aspect of the beasts that isn't directly
observable to us; and that seems already to concede them subjectivity.)

By the end of his life, then, Descartes has backed off from his earlier position
that the supposed explanatory redundancy of the attribution of reason to beasts
"proves" that they do not think at all, in favor of the far weaker claim that we
cannot prove that they do think. And he has himself enunciated an argument
that he now takes to have some weight on the other side, having to do with the
resemblance of their organs to ours, though he continues to hold that the balance of reasons is on his side. To More's allegation that Descartes's denial of
"interior feeling" to beasts is cruel, Descartes's simply notes that his position
"is not so much cruel to beasts as kind to human beings . . . , since it absolves
them from the suspicion of crime when they eat or kill animals."[35] (One may
wonder, of course, how much *this* consolation would appeal to More's gentle
and tender soul.)[36]

The major issue on which Descartes and More remain in confrontation is
whether or not the behavior of beasts, as exemplified in More's vignette about
the "guilty" dog, warrants the attribution of "interior feeling" to them. More's
compatriot Locke, in his *Essay Concerning Human Understanding*, first published in 1690, implicitly comes out on More's side. Arguing that the Cartesian
claim that "the soul always thinks" is refuted by one's own knowledge that one
passes periods of time in a state of complete unconsciousness, Locke adds,
ironically:

> And they must needs have a penetrating sight, who can certainly see, that I think,
> when I cannot perceive it myself, and when I declare, that I do not; and yet can see,
> that Dogs or Elephants do not think, when they give all the demonstration of it
> imaginable, except only telling us, that they do so.[37]

(Locke does not specify the "demonstrations"; we may assume he has in mind
the sort of things indicated by More.) So much, one might suppose, for the
Cartesian "language test." Yet it will turn out that Locke, too, relies on language to establish his conception of "the difference between man and beast"—
though in a quite different way from Descartes's.

In his endeavor to establish, in the *Essay*, "the Certainty, Evidence, and Extent" of human knowledge, Locke takes as fundamental the concept of an *Idea*,
which he initially explains as "whatsoever is the object of the Understanding
when a man thinks."[38] He identifies having ideas with *perception*. Further, it
seems, perception consists in having ideas "in the understanding":

. . . [W]herever there is Sense, or Perception, there some Idea *is actually produced, and present in the Understanding.*[39]

Perception is "for the most part" passive receipt of ideas; 'thinking', on the other hand, strictly connotes an "active operation of the Mind about its Ideas." For Locke, as for Descartes, thinking is necessarily conscious; I take him to imply that bare perceiving is, too. The term 'sensible' he seems to use as more or less equivalent to 'conscious'.

Despite the anthropocentricity of his initial definition of 'idea', it soon becomes clear that Locke attributes ideas to beasts: indeed (since perception consists in having ideas), to *all* beasts:

This faculty of *Perception*, seems to me to be that, which *puts the distinction betwixt the animal Kingdom, and the inferior parts of Nature.*[40]

If many beasts, such as cockles and oysters, function at a low level of sensibility, so do many humans, such as foetuses and newborn infants, idiots, and the "decrepit" elderly: *their* "intellectual perfections," he says, may not be much above those of the lowest beasts. Degree of sensibility he takes to be partly inferable from the nature and limitations of a creature's sense organs; and also from the state in which nature has placed the creature, to which its organs are "wisely" adapted:

would not quickness of Sensation be an Inconvenience to an Animal, that must lie still, where Chance has once placed it; and there receive the afflux of colder or warmer, clean or foul Water, as happens to come to it?[41]

Apart from the latter considerations, Locke finds it unnecessary to give any reason at all for his view that all beasts are sensible, though in different degrees; nor to confront directly the Cartesian position that beasts' behavior can be explained without recourse to non-mechanical principles. This is the more notable in that he makes clear that, in attributing perception to brutes, he is consciously opposing the Cartesian "mechanist" view (which he does take to provide a satisfactory account of the motions of plants).

While Locke attributes perception to brutes in general, it appears that he may attribute "activity about ideas," or thought, only to some. This seems to emerge as he proceeds to itemize the faculties or operations involved in humans' processing of ideas supplied through perception. In each case he indicates, usually explicitly, the extent to which non-human animals possess the faculty in question.

The first faculty he considers, after perception, is memory or "Retention." Locke implies that some, but not all, beasts possess this faculty:

This faculty of laying up, and retaining the *Ideas*, that are brought into the Mind, several *other Animals* seem to have, to a great degree, as well as Man.

For instance, "Birds learning of Tunes" must have ideas in their memories to use as patterns:

For it seems to me impossible, that they should endeavor to conform their Voices to Notes (as 'tis plain they do) of which they had no *Ideas*.[42]

While birds may be "mechanically" driven away from certain noises, when such flight contributes to preserving their lives, their efforts to imitate past sounds cannot be explained in this way, since such "imitation can be of no use to the Bird's Preservation." (Conceivably, this distinction between activities that "contribute to preservation" and those that do not can be seen as opposed to Descartes's conception of brutes doing things only for the sake of "food, sex, and fear"; and Descartes's conception of brutes' utterances as invariably mere displays of animal passion. But Locke doesn't develop the point.)

Locke is prepared to attribute to beasts in limited degree all but one of the four other basic mental faculties he recognizes. He implies that at least some brutes "discern," or recognize ideas as distinct from each other. With regard to "comparing" ideas, "in respect of Extent, Degrees, Time, Place, or any other Circumstances," thereby creating ideas of relation,[43] he says that it is difficult to tell, "how far Brutes partake in this faculty"; yet (characteristically) he ventures an opinion:

> I imagine they have it not in any great degree. . . . I think, *Beasts compare* not their *Ideas*, farther than some sensible Circumstances annexed to the Objects themselves.[44]

He further supposes that "*Brutes* come far short of Men" in "composition," or "compounding" different simple ideas into one "complex" idea.[45] In fact, it seems, he leans to allowing brutes only the ability to *retain* combinations of simple ideas as presented to them; *not* the ability actively to make combinations. Again, he admits that this position is conjectural. But if there is room for doubt about brutes' power to compound, Locke takes it as sure that brutes cannot form general ideas, or abstract:

> I think, I may be positive . . . that the power of *Abstracting* is not at all in them; and . . . the having of general *Ideas*, is that which puts a perfect distinction betwixt Man and Brutes; and is an Excellency which the Faculties of Brutes do by no means attain to.[46]

This seems to mean that brutes are unable either to isolate repeatable qualities from the particulars of their experience, or to form ideas of sorts of things. Locke's reason for categorically denying them this "faculty" is another kind of language test.

> For it is evident, we observe no foot-steps in them, of making use of general signs for universal *Ideas*; from which we have reason to imagine that they have not the faculty of abstracting, or making general *Ideas*, since they have no use of Words, or any other general Signs.[47]

"'Tis in this," he concludes,

> that the Species of *Brutes* are discriminated from Man; and 'tis that proper difference wherein they are wholly separated, and which at last widens to so vast a distance.

Contrary to the Cartesian claim, *reason* does not provide the fundamental "difference between men and beast":

For if [beasts] have any *Ideas* at all, and are not bare Machines (as some would have them) we cannot deny them to have some Reason. It seems evident to me, that they do some of them in certain Instances reason, as that they have sense; but it is only in particular *Ideas*, just as they receiv'd them from their Senses.[48]

(Locke goes on to discuss idiots and madmen, concluding in an *un*cartesian manner that idiots "make very few or no Propositions, and reason scarce at all.")[49]

So Locke, unlike Descartes, is prepared to grant that non-linguals "reason." But because their lack of general terms seems to him to signal a lack of general or abstract ideas, he concludes that they reason only concerning particulars.

I am very unclear what Locke means in ascribing to beasts just "reason concerning particulars." Further, given Locke's view that the significance of general terms depends on the prior existence of general ideas for the terms to "name," it is hard to figure out why he thinks that beasts' lack of general words implies a lack of general ideas.

Locke does have an entire chapter, late in Book IV, on the subject of reason. Here again he implicitly rejects the view that man is distinguished from beasts by virtue of possessing this "faculty." Nevertheless, he says, it is "evident that [man] much surpasses them" in it.[50] The chapter on "reason" is a long, rambling one, largely concerned with refuting the notion that the syllogism is fundamental to legitimate reasoning. To some extent, Locke associates reason with propositional inference of a more informal kind.[51] But this conception doesn't get us any closer to his notion of the reason of brutes; since he holds that they lack language and general terms; and hence, presumably do not form propositions. Perhaps beasts, like the "countrywoman" Locke mentions at one point, are supposed to "reason" in anticipating, say, a soaking, from such signs of rain as the direction of the wind and the quality of light.[52] We will soon see that Leibniz advances some such conception quite explicitly. Still, I find it hard to guess how even such a process could be understood in a being limited to *non-general* ideas.

It is, then, interesting to notice the extent of Locke's concern with the limits of *brutes'* understanding and ideas. But one must also recognize the conjectural and virtually unsupported nature of much of what he says on this topic.[53]

Leibniz, after an early flirtation with Descartes's position, settled on the view that beasts have immaterial souls (a kind of monads), characterized by "sensation and memory." This places them intermediate between human souls, which possess reason and reflection as well; and the "bare monads," which are wholly unconscious, or in a continuous "stupor."[54] The placing of beasts' souls above the bare monads, and the concomitant attribution to beasts of "heightened" or "distinct" perceptions, might seem clearly to imply that beasts are at least to some degree conscious. But in fact, as Mark Kulstad has shown (in a fine recent monograph), even the late texts are rather ambivalent on this issue.[55] Sometimes, for instance, Leibniz seems to say that it is his recognition, against the

Cartesians, of *unconscious* perceptions that makes it acceptable to attribute immaterial souls to brutes.[56] Nevertheless, I agree with Kulstad's conclusion—for reasons he gives, and others—that Leibniz did come to be committed to some form of consciousness in the brutes; though he sometimes played this down, in order to emphasize the vast superiority of human souls.[57]

Leibniz gives a good deal of attention to beasts' cognition in his commentary on Locke, the *New Essays* (completed in 1704, though first published in 1765), among other writings. He is reluctant to accept Locke's claim that sense distinguishes animals from plants, because of the "great analogy which exists between plants and animals."[58] While accepting Locke's claim that "some dull perception" occurs even in the lowest animals, Leibniz adds that "almost the same could be said about plants." It's hard to know what to make about this nominal disagreement, though, just because 'perception' doesn't connote consciousness for Leibniz, as it appears to do for Locke.

Leibniz agrees with Locke's denial that beasts "abstract," explaining the point as follows. While beasts apparently can, say, "recognize whiteness, and observe it in chalk as in snow,"

> this does not amount to abstraction, which requires attention to the general apart from the particular, and consequently involves knowledge of universal truths, which beasts do not possess.[59]

But he rejects Locke's suggestions that brutes think, understand, and reason, returning to the view that it is, after all, *reason* that places "the difference between man and beast." (Rather startlingly, though, in response to Locke's suggestion that "idiots reason scarce at all," Leibniz decisively alleges that they do not reason, period.)[60]

Leibniz does attribute to brutes what he calls "a shadow of reason," and even "knowledge": the capacity, namely, to anticipate future events to some degree by association of images, based on past experience of repeated conjunction of events. In Leibniz's unpleasant example, a dog that has previously been beaten by a stick will anticipate a beating when it sees its master pick up a stick.[61] Humans, he says, are equally "empirics" in three-quarters of their actions.[62] (He does not indicate whether *such* human inference also proceeds without "abstraction," but I infer that he supposes that it does.) However, humans have in addition true reason: the capacity to grasp the underlying reasons for observed connections, and, reflecting on our own souls, to grasp the innately inscribed "necessary truths" that somehow, in his view, help to provide a secure science of nature. Leibniz writes in the Preface to the *New Essays*:

> . . . only reason is capable of establishing reliable rules, and of supplying what is lacking to those which are not, by allowing exceptions to them; and finally of finding infallible connections in the force of necessary consequences; which often provides a way of foreseeing an event without having to experience the sensible

links between images, as is required for beasts. Thus what establishes inner sources of necessary truths is also what distinguishes man from beast.[63]

Leibniz does not have a sort of basis for attributing immaterial souls to beasts, granted that they have *any* form of "perception": namely his contention, illustrated in the "Monadology" by the famous example of entering a mill, that perception in general cannot be explained by mechanical causes.[64] Still it seems, rather bizarrely, that an important tenet of his mature metaphysics rules out in principle *any behavioral evidence* for the presence of nonmechanical cognitive states. For Leibniz holds quite adamantly that there is no interaction between the mental and the physical: bodily events are to be explained *entirely* by laws proper to matter, laws that are strictly mechanical. As he advises Locke's advocate in the *New Essays*:

> . . . I . . . attribute to mechanism all that occurs in the bodies of plants and animals except their first formation. . . . I don't at all agree that one should have recourse to the soul, when it's a matter of explaining the detail of the phenomena of plants and animals.[65]

In general, states of the soul and of the body occur in "harmony" just by divine arrangement. Thus, it seems, not even in *humans* can any physical manifestation strictly be attributed to a mental cause!

We have seen that Locke, and some of Descartes's contemporary critics, attribute to beasts a reason of their own. Leibniz allowed beasts "the shadow of reason," or empirical inference by association of images, based on past experience of regular conjunction. So (even apart from the long tradition described by Sorabji), Hume is less radical than sometimes supposed in titling chapters in each of his two major epistemological works "Of the Reason of Animals."[66] In fact, a fair amount of Hume's discussion in both these short chapters consist in elaborating the view of beasts' inferences espoused by Leibniz; and already recognized (though as a strictly material-mechanical operation) by Descartes. (Hume, too, features the example of the beaten dog, in both the *Treatise* and the *Inquiry Concerning Human Understanding*.) Given Leibniz's proposition that humans, too, are "empirics" in three-quarters of our actions, Hume is not even breaking much ground, within the early modern tradition, in insisting that the same principle typically governs the inferences of humans, when we "reason" concerning matters of fact. Drawing on a distinction between such custom-based "reasoning," and "abstruse" reasoning or "argumentation," Hume writes in the *Inquiry*:

> Animals . . . are not guided in these inferences by reasoning; neither are children; neither are the generality of mankind in their ordinary actions and conclusions; neither are philosophers themselves, who, in all the active parts of life, are in the main the same with the vulgar, and guided by the same maxims.[67]

What *is* a bit unusual in Hume's presentations—and initially even quite striking—is his contention that a theory of human mental operations will be acceptable just in case it can account for the observed behavior of beasts as well, in those broad areas where their "external actions" "resemble" ours. In the *Treatise* he maintains that it is a "common defect" of his rivals' accounts of "the actions of the mind" that "they suppose such a subtility and refinement of thought, as not only exceeds the capacity of mere animals, but even of children and the common people in our own species."[68] He maintains that *only* his own explanation of the origin of "belief" in "the influence of custom on the imagination" is "equally applicable to beasts as to the human species." "Beasts," he elaborates,

> certainly never perceive any real connexion among objects. 'Tis therefore by experience that they infer one from another. They can never by any arguments form a general conclusion, that those objects, of which they have had no experience, resemble those of which they have. 'Tis therefore by means of custom alone, that experience operates in them. All this was sufficiently evident with respect to man. But with respect to beasts there cannot be the least suspicion of mistake; which must be own'd to be a strong confirmation, or rather an invincible proof of my system.[69]

But it seems to me that there is less here than meets the eye. On the one hand, no philosopher I have discussed—not even Descartes—denies that to some significant extent humans "operate" by the same principles as brutes. On the other hand, if Hume means to take as a starting point the assumption that *no* human belief about matters of fact is influenced by principles not available to beasts, he is, it seems to me, both begging the question against his predecessors; and flying as much in the face of common sense as he takes the Cartesians to do.[70] In fact, in the *Treatise* Hume alludes to "our superior knowledge and understanding"[71]; and in the *Inquiry* he concedes that he may be required to explain "how it happens that men so much surpass animals in reasoning."[72] In the latter passage he goes on to cite nine respects in which some humans surpass others in developing inferences, implying that these considerations can be extrapolated to provide "the reason of the difference between men and animals." Of course, nothing on the list implies insight into "necessary connections in nature"; nor access to a science of nature grounded in "necessary and eternal truths," such as Leibniz seems to suppose is available to humans. But, like the "Rules by which to judge of causes and effects" which Hume proposes in the *Treatise*, the *Inquiry*'s list does seem to suggest strong qualification on the view that animal association is the sole basis for human inferences about nature.[73]

In conclusion, some final observations. It is notable that neither Descartes nor any of his opponents has much to say in detail about the behavior of nonhuman animals. All sides seem to rely on a very few crude examples: often, banal instances of dogs' behavior, and sometimes birds', are taken to suffice. I can't say to what extent this limitation is tied to an actual lack of available observational data, as opposed to lack of curiosity and scholarship. But of course much current knowledge and theory about the behavioral (including "linguisitic") capacities of beasts, from bees to chimpanzees to whales, derives from studies of quite recent date; and issues of interpretation remain highly controversial—sometimes in ways reminiscent of the divergence between Descartes and More.

In a recent *New York Times* review of three books on the mentality of apes, D.H. Chadwick traces back to Descartes's conception of beasts as automata a lack of basic empathy—in contrast to "science-speak"—that he considers to mar the works under review. Of Descartes he says:

> Choosing to ignore intuition and the evidence of his senses, the great reasoner managed to reason himself into a patently chowder-headed position.[74]

Although I'm not sure how one would say 'chowder-headed' in Latin, this sounds a lot like Gassendi. Anyway, whatever Descartes's limitations as an animal behaviorist, relative to our time or even to his own, the fact remains that he does offer *reasoning* in support of his views of beasts. The same, I have suggested, cannot generally be said of his critics and immediate successors— engaging as their claims often are, in various other respects.[75]

NOTES

Presidential Address delivered before the Ninety-First Annual Eastern Division Meeting of The American Philosophical Association in Boston, Massachusetts, December 29, 1994.

1. December 11, 1648; AT, Vol. V, p. 243. René Descartes, *Correspondence avec Arnauld et Morus, Texte latin et traduction*, ed. Geneviève Lewis, Paris, J. Vrin, 1953, p. 104. In general translations in this address are my own responsibility, though I have profited from previous work, especially Lewis' (later known as Rodis-Lewis) French version of the Descartes-More correspondence; and the now standard three-volume English edition of *The Philosophical Writings of Descartes*, translated by John Cottingham, Robert Stoothoff and Dugald Murdoch, Cambridge, Cambridge University Press, 1985–91 (CSM). (CSM drew substantially on Anthony Kenny's previously published English edition of Descartes's correspondence for their Volume III, and Kenny is listed as co-translator of that volume, designated CSM-K.)

2. *Animal Minds and Human Morals: The Origins of the Western Debate*, Ithaca, NY, Cornell University Press, 1993. Although mainly focussed on Ancient and Medieval views, Sorabji's revelatory book touches to a significant degree on "modern," and even contemporary, writings on the mental and moral status of beasts. I have drawn a good deal more from it than is adequately indicated by my explicit mentions. I also want to acknowledge the helpfulness of Stephen Walker's *Animal Thought*, London, Routledge and Kegan Paul, 1983. While Walker's book is not primarily historical, he ably and interestingly discusses views of 17th, 18th, and 19th century philosophers in his first chapter.

3. *Discourse on the Method*, Part V, AT VI, pp. 55–60; CSM I, pp. 139–41.

4. To Reneri for Pallot, April or May, 1638: AT II, pp. 39–41; CSM-K III, pp. 99–100.

5. See Thomas Nagel's famous paper "What is it like to be a bat?", Nagel, *Mortal Questions*, Cambridge, Cambridge University Press, 1979, ch. 12. The paper was originally published in the *Philosophical Review*, Vol. LXXXIII, October, 1974.

6. *Proceedings and Addresses of the American Philosophical Association*, Vol. XLVI, 1972–73, pp. 5–20. See, especially, pp. 7–13.

7. *Proceedings and Addresses of The American Philosophical Association*, Supplement to Vol. 62, #1, September, 1988, pp. 197–210; see pp. 198–99.

8. AT VI, pp. 56–57; CSM I, p. 140.

9. AT VI, p. 58; CSM I, p. 140.

10. AT VI, pp. 57–9; CSM I, pp. 140–41.

11. See *Passions of the Soul*, I.50, AT XI, pp. 368–70; CSM I, p. 348.

12. AT VI, p. 59; CSM I, p. 141.

13. AT VI, pp. 57–58; CSM I, p. 140.

14. I briefly discuss this problem in my *Descartes*, London, Routledge and Kegan Paul, 1978; pp. 183–84.

15. See, for instance, Descartes's *Fifth Replies*, AT VII 356–57; CSM II, pp. 246–47. Gassendi's objection which provoked this response is at AT VII, 264; CSM II, p. 184. On this topic and certain others touched on here—especially with regard to Hume's position—I have profited from Ruth Barcan Marcus' paper, "The Anti-Naturalism of Some Language Centered Accounts of Belief," *Dialectica*, forthcoming (1995).

16. AT V, p. 311; Lewis ed., p. 146.

17. To More, April 15, 1649: AT V, p. 345; CSM-K III, p. 374.

18. AT VII, p. 205; CSM II, p. 144. The translation is CSM's, without change.

19. AT VII, pp. 229–31; CSM II, pp. 161–62.

20. AT VII, p. 271; CSM II, p. 189.

21. AT VII, p. 262; CSM II, p. 183.

22. AT VII, p. 353; CSM II, p. 244.

23. AT VII, p. 358; CSM II, p. 247–48.

24. AT VII, p. 414; CSM II, p. 279.

25. *Ibid.*

26. *Ibid.*

27. AT VII, p. 426; CSM II, pp. 287–88.

28. *PS* I.50, AT XI, pp. 369–70; CSM I, p. 348.

29. To the Marquess of Newcastle, November 23, 1646: AT IV, p. 574; CSM-K III, p. 303. In this letter Descartes does again remark on the fact that beasts may excel—and even "deceive"—us in certain ways. He indicates that such specific superiorities can be understood without postulating thought in beasts; but he does not, as in the *Discourse*, claim that versatility of competent behavior provides a second test (together with language) for the presence of thought.

30. AT IV, p. 576; CSM-K III, p. 304.

31. *Ibid.*

32. December 11, 1648: AT V, p. 244; Lewis edition, p. 107.

33. AT V, p. 276; CSM-K, p. 365.

34. AT V, 276–7; CSM-K, III, p. 365.

35. AT V, pp. 278–9; CSM-K, III, p. 366.

36. For other discussions of Descartes's views about non-human animals, see John Cottingham, "A Brute to the Brutes?: Descartes' Treatment of Animals," *Philosophy* 53 (1978), pp. 551–59; and Peter Harrison, "Descartes on animals," *The Philosophical Quarterly*, Vol. 52 (1992), 219–27. I have also benefited from seeing a manuscript paper

by Stephen Gaugroger, "Cartesian Automata and Perceptual Cognition." I believe I may differ from all these writers in finding a marked *change* in Descartes's position between the earlier *Discourse* and *Replies*, and the later *Passions* and letters to More and Newcastle. I think I am more persuaded than Cottingham or Gaukroger that Descartes's ascriptions of "sensation" and "emotion" to beasts should be viewed as implying only certain kinds of physical (functional) states, unless there is clear evidence presented that the ascriptions have some connotation of conscious feeling. But this is not the right occasion for pursuing fine points of scholarly debate.

37. *Essay* II.i.19; Peter H. Nidditch, editor, Oxford, Clarendon Press, pp. 115–16. All citations of Locke are from this edition.

38. *Essay*, I.i.8, p. 47.

39. *Essay*, II.ix.4, p. 144.

40. *Essay*, II.ix.11, p. 147.

41. *Essay*, II.ix.13, p. 148.

42. *Essay*, II.x.10, pp. 154–55. A related example is mentioned by Gassendi in the *Fifth Objections*: AT VII, p. 270; CSM II, p. 189, though Gassendi's point is a bit different.

43. *Essay*, II.xi.4, p. 157.

44. *Essay*, II.xi.5, pp. 157–58.

45. *Essay*, II.xi.7, p. 158.

46. *Essay*, II.xi.10, p. 159.

47. *Essay*, II.xi.10, pp. 159–60.

48. *Essay*, II.xi.11, p. 160.

49. *Essay*, II.xi.13, pp. 160–61.

50. *Essay*, IV.xvii.1, p. 668.

51. See, e.g., *Essay*, IV.xvii.4, p. 672.

52. *Essay*, IV.xvii.4, p. 672.

53. For additional critical discussion of Locke's claims see Kathleen Squadrito, "Thoughtful Brutes: The Ascription of Mental Predicates to Animals in Locke's *Essay*," *Dialogos*, Vol. 58 (1991), pp. 63–73. Squadrito discusses many of the same passages that I cover here.

54. See, for instance, "Monadology" (1714), secs. 24–29; in Ger VI, p. 611. For an account of Leibniz's early leanings to a Cartesian view of animals as mere machines, see Mark Kulstad, *Leibniz on Apperception, Consciousness, and Reflection*, Munich, Philosophia, 1991, pp. 70–72; also pp. 168–70.

55. See the previous note. Kulstad builds his case gradually, throughout the monograph; but see especially pp. 76–81.

56. See, for instance, "Principles of Nature and of Grace," section 4: Ger VI, p. 600; and Kulstad, p. 159.

57. Kulstad, pp. 160–72.

58. *Nouveaux essais*, II.ix.11, in DA Vol. VI, p. 139. The now-standard English translation follows the DA pagination: G.W. Leibniz, *New Essays on Human Understanding*, translated and edited by Peter Remnant and Jonathan Bennett, Cambridge, Cambridge University Press, 1981.

59. *New Essays*, II.xi.10; DA p. 142.

60. *New Essays*, II.xi.13; DA p. 143.

61. *Loc. cit.*, section 11; cf. Preface, DA p. 51.

62. See, for instance, "Monadology," sec. 28, Ger VI, p. 611.

63. DA p. 51; cf. ch. IV, pp. 475–6, on "connection of truths."

64. "Monadology," sec. 17, Ger VI, p. 609; cf. *New Essays*, DA pp. 65–67.

65. *New Essays*, II.xi.11; DA p. 139.

66. *A Treatise of Human Nature*, Book I, Part III, ch. xvi; *An Inquiry Concerning Human Understanding*, IX. Page citations for the former work are from P.H. Nidditch's revised version of the edition of L.A. Selby-Bigge, Oxford, Clarendon Press, 1978; for the latter, from the edition of Charles W. Hendel, New York, The Liberal Arts Press, 1955.

67. P. 114.

68. P. 177.

69. P. 178; cf. *Inquiry*, p. 112.

70. See *Treatise*, p. 176.

71. P. 126.

72. P. 114, n.

73. Interesting recent discussions of Hume's views on the mentality of non-human animals include a paper by Antony E. Pitson, "The Nature of Humean Animals," *Hume Studies*, Vol. XIX, No. 2, November, 1993, pp. 301–316; and Wayne Waxman, *Hume's Theory of Consciousness*, Cambridge, Cambridge University Press, 1994, *passim*. Pitson focusses on Hume's position about the relation of human beings and beasts with regard to issues about morality and the passions: issues which I've not been able to address here.

74. *NYT Book Review*, December 11, 1994, p. 18.

75. I wish to thank Hamline University for the opportunity to present more extended versions of the material covered here in a two-lecture series (The Hanna Lectures), in November, 1994; and the individuals who participated in the valuable discussions on those occasions. I thank Princeton University for providing a partially supported leave, without which I could hardly have completed the project. I'm also indebted to Shawn Travis for extensive practical assistance; and more friends than I will attempt to name for very helpful suggestions and advice.

S O U R C E S   A N D
A C K N O W L E D G M E N T S

Chapter 1: From *Journal of Philosophy*, October 1984, pp. 537–44. Reprinted with permission of the *Journal of Philosophy*.

Chapter 2: From *Reason, Will, and Sensation: Studies in Cartesian Metaphysics*, edited by John Cottingham. Oxford: Clarendon, 1994, pp. 209–28. Reprinted by permission of Oxford University Press.

Chapter 3: From *Essays on the Philosophy and Science of René Descartes*, edited by Stephen Voss. Oxford: Oxford University Press, 1992, pp. 162–76. Copyright © 1993 by Oxford University Press, Inc. Used by permission of Oxford University Press, Inc.

Chapter 4: From *Philosophical Topics*, vol. 19, No. 1 (Spring 1991), pp. 293–323. Reprinted with permission of *Philosophical Topics*.

Chapter 5: From *Central Themes in Early Modern Philosophy* (Jonathan Bennett Festschrift), edited by M. Kulstad and J. Covel. Indianapolis: Hackett, 1990, pp. 1–22.

Chapter 6: From *Nous*, vol. 10 (Spring 1976), pp. 3–15. Reprinted with permission of *Nous*.

Chapter 7: Previously published in Portuguese (translated by Ethel Menezes Rocha) in *Analytica*, vol. 1 (March 1998). English version published with permission of *Analytica*.

Chapter 8: From *Essays on Descartes' Meditations*, edited by Amélie Oksenberg Rorty. Berkeley: University of California Press, 1986, pp. 339–58. Copyright (c) 1986, The Regents of the University of California. Reprinted with permission of the publisher.

Chapter 9: From *The Philosophy of Baruch Spinoza, Studies in Philosophy and the History Philosophy*, vol. 7, edited by R. Kennington. Washington, D.C.: Catholic University of American Press, 1980, Ch. 7, pp. 103–20. Reprinted with permission of the publisher.

Chapter 10: From *God and Nature: Spinoza's Metaphysics*, edited by Y. Yovel. Leiden: Brill, 1991, pp. 133–60. Reprinted with permission of the publisher.

Chapter 11: From *Midwest Studies in Philosophy*, University of Minnesota Press, 1983, pp. 181–91. Reprinted with permission of the publisher.

Chapter 12: From *New Essays on the Rationalists*, edited by Rocco Gennaro and C. Huenemann. Oxford: Oxford University Press, 1999. Copyright © 1999 by Oxford University Press, Inc. Used by permission of Oxford University Press, Inc.

Chapter 13: From *American Philosophical Quarterly*, Spring 1979, pp. 143–50. Reprinted with permission of the *American Philosophical Quarterly*.

Chapter 14: From *Philosophical Review*, vol. 91, April 1982, pp. 247–52. Copyright © 1982 Cornell University. Reprinted by permission of the publisher.

Chapter 15: From *Berkeley: Critical and Interpretive Essays*, edited by Colin M. Turbayne. Minneapolis: University of Minnesota Press, 1982, pp. 198–23. Copyright © 1982 by the University of Minnesota. Reprinted by permission of the publisher.

Chapter 16: From *Pacific Philosophical Quarterly*, vol. 68, nos. 3 and 4 (1987), pp. 249–64. Reprinted with permission of Blackwell Publishers.

Chapter 17: From *Essays on Berkeley*, edited by John Foster and Howard Robinson.

Oxford: Clarendon Press, 1985, pp. 131–47. Reprinted by permission of Oxford University Press.

Chapter 18: Not previously published.

Chapter 19: From *Journal of the History of Philosophy*, vol. IX (October 1971), pp. 459–75. Reprinted with permission of the *Journal of the History of Philosophy*.

Chapter 20: From *Self and Nature in Kant's Philosophy*, edited by Allen Wood. Ithaca: Cornell University Press, 1984, pp. 157–73. Copyright © 1984 Cornell University. Used by permission of the publisher, Cornell University Press.

Chapter 21: From *Essays on George Berkeley*, edited by Ernest Sosa. Dordrecht: Reidel, 1987, pp. 3–22. Copyright © 1987 by D. Reidel Publishing Company. Reprinted with kind permission from Kluwer Academic Publishers.

Chapter 22: From *Rice University Studies in Philosophy*, Fall 1977, pp. 123–37. Reprinted with permission.

Chapter 23: From *Minds, Ideas and Objects*, edited by Phillip Cummins and Guenter Zoeller (volume 2, North American Kant Society Studies in Philosophy). Atascadero, Ca.: Ridgeview Publishing Co., 1992, pp. 135–50. Reprinted with permission of the North American Kant Society.

Chapter 24: From *Journal of the History of Ideas*, vol. 28 (July 1967), pp. 347–66. Reprinted with permission of the *Journal of the History of Ideas*.

Chapter 25: From *Archiv für Geschichte der Philosophie*, Bd. 58, Heft 4 (Sonderheft for Hans Wagner, 1976), pp. 335–52. Reprinted with permission of the editors, *Archiv für Geschichte der Philosophie*.

Chapter 26: From *Canadian Journal of Philosophy*, vol. 3 (June 1974), pp. 495–513. Reprinted with permission of the *Canadian Journal of Philosophy* and the University of Calgary Press.

Chapter 27: Originally published in *The Review of Metaphysics*, June 1979, pp. 717–33. Reprinted with permission.

Chapter 28: From *Motion and Time, Space and Matter*, edited by R. Turnbull and P. Machamer. Columbus: Ohio State University Press, 1976, pp. 264–89. Reprinted with permission of the publisher.

Chapter 29: From *Causation in Early Modern Philosophy*, edited by Steven Nadler. University Park, Pa.: Pennsylvania State University Press, 1992, pp. 119–33. Copyright © 1992 by the Pennsylvania State University. Reproduced by permission of the Pennsylvania State University Press.

Chapter 30: From *Philosophical Review* Centennial Issue, vol. 101 (January 1992), pp. 191–243. Copyright © 1992 Cornell University. Reprinted by permission of the publisher.

Chapter 31: From *Proceedings of the American Philosophical Association*, November 1995 (1994 Eastern Division Presidential Address), pp. 7–25. Reprinted with permission of the American Philosophical Association.